THE BOLSHEVIKS

THE
BOLSHEVIKS

The Intellectual and Political History

of the Triumph of Communism

in Russia

ADAM B. ULAM

THE MACMILLAN COMPANY · NEW YORK

COLLIER-MACMILLAN LIMITED · LONDON

CONTENTS

PREFACE

The story of the Bolsheviks, the creators of communism, is one of drama and success unparalleled in modern history. From the twenty-odd people who first called themselves by that name in 1903, they grew within fourteen years to a party that seized the government of Russia. Barely more than another generation was to pass before communism would rule over one-third of mankind and aspire to the mastery of the whole world.

Yet the story is not only one of triumph. It contains more than a hint of the great personal tragedies which were to beset the lives of the founders of communism. In the ideological splits and controversies which convulsed the Bolsheviks could be seen the seeds of future totalitarianism and of the present quarrel which has divided the Communist world into two camps.

The history of the Bolsheviks and of the Russian Revolution has to be focused around the life of one man: Vladimir Ulyanov—Lenin. Himself the heir of the long revolutionary tradition, Lenin imparted to Bolshevism and communism not only ideology and tactics but also many of his personal characteristics. The cult of Lenin has always united Communists of the most divergent views. Both Trotsky and Stalin claimed to be his legitimate heirs. Communist China as well as Soviet Russia invoke his authority on behalf of their respective positions. Yet this founder of a world movement was thoroughly Russian. He and the people he gathered around him cannot be understood except in terms of their contemporary Russia and the native revolutionary tradition which goes back at least to 1825. The Decembrists, those aristocratic rebels who rose against autocracy; the great revolutionaries of the century like Bakunin, Chernyshevsky, Herzen and the conspirators of the People's Will who finally tracked down and assassinated Alexander II—they all were in different ways ancestors of the Bolsheviks.

The main part of this book is concerned with the events and personalities of 1900 to 1924. By the time Lenin died the character of the Soviet state was determined. The Bolshevik old guard went on to its annihilation under Stalin, but the state Lenin established bears into our own days the imprint of his paradoxical personality. Even such typical elements of Stalin's Russia as the "cult of personality" and the purges find their partial explanation and source in the events and moods of Lenin's leadership of the Bolshevik movement. The extraordinary events that took place during Lenin's fatal illness may throw some light on the mystery still surrounding Stalin's last days, or even that attending the dismissal of Nikita Khrushchev.

When it comes to telling the story, an author has to be both grateful for the vast evidence at his disposal and anguished at the unsatisfactory character of so much of it. Many Bolsheviks, as well as their rivals in Russia's other Socialist parties, were born historians and gossipmongers (Lenin himself was a notable exception on both counts). Having achieved power, they were eager to tell all (well, *almost* all) about their past exploits and conspiracies, and what they left out is often filled in by the memoirs of their defeated enemies. Soviet historical journals between 1920 and 1925 especially are a rich mine of information.

On the other hand, with Stalin in power the flow of reminiscences and reports of past indiscretions were quickly arrested. Only that which the despot deemed to be in his interest was allowed to be published about the history of the movement or the life of its founder. Lenin's own works were censored, and the memoirs of those close to him, including his wife's, had to be rewritten according to the new formula, emphasizing the dead leader's infallibility, his total lack of the usual human weaknesses, and his boundless trust in and admiration of Stalin. Nineteen fifty-three brought a considerable improvement to this picture. The Soviet archives have yielded documents such as the diary of the secretaries attending Lenin in his illness, released in 1963—presenting new evidence on the struggle for succession between Trotsky and Stalin.

There is still a severe limit to what can be revealed about the past. Nothing is allowed to mar the official image of Lenin and of the origins of communism. But one must be grateful to the Soviet historians and archivists for what, within their limited possibilities, they have been able to achieve within the last ten years.

I have used the fourth edition of Lenin's works. It began to appear in the 1940s, hence in some respects it is less satisfactory than the previous ones. But it contains an occasional document not found in the former editions, and its Stalinist character is corrected by the supplementary volumes published after 1953. All references in this book are in English, and the fact that the given work is in Russian is noted only if it appeared outside the U.S.S.R. For prerevolutionary Russia I have adhered to the calendar then in force, which in the nineteenth century was twelve days and in the twentieth century thirteen days behind the Western one. I have followed the Russian usage in identifying people by their given names and patronymics. Thus, Lev Davidovich Trotsky—Lev, son of David; Maria Ilinichna Ulyanov—Maria, daughter of Ilya.

My gratitude is due to the Russian Research Center at Harvard Uni-

versity, which shelters my researches, and to my many friends and associates there who have been very helpful. My special thanks go to Professor
Richard Pipes, who has drawn my attention to some little-known facts
in the Russian revolutionary history; to my research assistant, Susan
Salser, who has valiantly struggled through mountains of Soviet books
and periodicals; and to my former secretary, Mary Towle, who patiently
lent her hand to this book—the third of mine for her.

ADAM B. ULAM

Harvard University,
January 19, 1965

I

THE FAMILY

Vladimir Ilyich Ulyanov, who took the name Lenin, was always reticent about the origins and background of his family. It is not that there was anything in the history of the Ulyanovs that could have been embarrassing to the leader of world communism. Quite the contrary. Lenin's reticence was simply in line with his usual reserve and feeling for privacy where his personal affairs were concerned. In filling out his Party questionnaire in 1920 Lenin professed not to know the profession of his paternal grandfather.

The vast biographical literature that followed Lenin's death in 1924 and included the reminiscences of his surviving two sisters and brother did little to throw much light on the origins of the Ulyanovs or those of Lenin's mother's family. Such omissions cannot be ascribed simply to the conviction that the story of Lenin's ancestors was of little importance when compared to various incidents of the hero's revolutionary struggle. To the Soviet biographer it has always been a bit embarrassing that Lenin did not come "from the people." But, and this could not be obscured or omitted, in fact his father had been a loyal servant of the Tsarist state and a faithful son of the Orthodox Church, and his mother a daughter of a small landowner. With the cult of Russian nationalism introduced under Stalin it became even more embarrassing and risky to pry further into the family tree and discover the non-Russian ancestors of the founder of the Soviet state. Furthermore, if the relatively high social status of Lenin's father was already a bother to the biographer, then paradoxically the low station in life of the grandfather made the picture worse. If Tsarist Russia was literally "the prison of nationalities" and an oppressive class society, as Lenin himself had taught and Soviet historians have insistently repeated, how can one explain the career of his own father? Ilya Nikolayevich Ulyanov, born of a poor father and an illiterate mother, of a family with at least a strong admixture of non-Russian blood, died a high civil servant entitled to be addressed as "Your Excellency," and a hereditary noble. No wonder many Soviet writers overlooked the shadowy but inconvenient grandfather, or made him into a "petty official" or a "poor *intelligent*," hardly a correct description of the status of a man who was in actuality a tailor.

More scrupulous than most of the Lenin biographers, Soviet novelist

Marietta Shaginyan stumbled upon the data about Lenin's ancestry while working on her novel *The Family of Ulyanovs*.[1] Ilya Nikolayevich Ulyanov was born in 1831 in Astrakhan. The old town in the mouth of the Volga has long been a trade emporium with the East. Waves of Mongol and Turkic invasions and migrations swept through South Russia and left a lasting imprint on the composition of the population. In 1831 the town and the neighboring countryside were a veritable melting pot where the Tartars, Bashkirs, Kalmyks and other nationalities mixed with ethnic Russians. Ilya's mother, Anna, came without a doubt from a Kalmyk family and there is strong circumstantial evidence that his father Nikolay was also of the same racial origin.[2] To be sure, both the names and the membership in the Orthodox Church testify to the russification of the family, but the inheritance is unmistakable in the Mongolian cast of features of Ilya Nikolayevich and the often commented upon "hint of Tartar" in the appearance of his famous son.

Nikolay Ulyanov began the process of social ascent which was to conclude with his grandson the ruler of Russia. Born a serf and indentured to learn a craft in the city, he evidently managed to buy his freedom and to become inscribed as a burgess. The latter is a rather awkward translation of the Russian *meshchanin,* which carried none of the suggestion of opulence of the English term, nor of the (to a Marxist) opprobrious connotation of the French *bourgeois,* but was simply the legal definition of those townsmen who were neither peasants, nobles, nor inscribed in the guilds of merchants. A burgess could be a man on his way to becoming a millionaire entrepreneur or, as in this case, a poor tailor.

That the Ulyanovs were poor, a comforting thought to the Soviet biographer for whom even a tailor could be, God forbid, an "exploiter," that is, an employer of labor rather than a "petty bourgeois" who himself does cutting and sewing, is proved by the circumstances of the family on Nikolay's death. He had married late in life and on his death at the age of seventy-four his son Ilya was only seven years old. Ilya's brother Vasily, who was ten or thirteen years older (there are glaring discrepancies as to the dates and ages in Shaginyan's account) had to become the family's provider. From his teens until his death, Vasily worked in an office. In his later years Ilya would often refer with gratitude to his elder brother who himself would have liked to obtain an education, but who sacrificed his dreams to support his family. It was largely Vasily who enabled his younger brother to go through the high school and the university (he was also helped by his godfather who was an Orthodox clergyman).

It is all the more remarkable that Vasily, who remained a bachelor and did not die until 1878, seems never to have visited his brother's family.

[1] Moscow, 1959. The novel, appearing in 1937, incurred official wrath and was not reissued until after the denunciation of Stalinism in 1957.

[2] Kalmyks, a branch of the Mongol tribe, were settled in the region in the seventeenth century.

On his death a commemorative slab was put up on his tomb by his fellow employees. Ilya's mother and his two sisters hardly engaged the attention of the Soviet chronicler whose main preoccupation is to demonstrate that Lenin's ancestors were always among the "exploited" rather than the "exploiters." Once Lenin's father entered the university, his ties with the city of his childhood grew more and more remote. Was the State Councillor Ilya Ulyanov eventually to become embarrassed about his humble beginnings, especially in view of his wife's origins in a more cultured milieu? This would seem hardly consistent with what we know of the character of the man.

The story of the Ulyanovs serves as a useful corrective to many of the stereotypes of Tsarist Russia. The Astrakhan gymnasium (high school) in which Ilya Nikolayevich began his social ascent in 1843 could, in the variety of subjects and the quality of teaching, vie with similar institutions of contemporary France or Prussia. Here, in a semi-Asiatic city in backward Russia, the son of a one-time serf received a sound preparation for a university and a future pedagogical career. How many American students of today are put through a high school curriculum that demands the study of two modern foreign languages and Latin, and a fairly advanced acquaintance with mathematics and physics, as well as with a wide variety of other subjects? Since the university in Russia was and has remained the place for specialization, it was in the gymnasium that Ilya Nikolayevich had to acquire the foundations of general education that enabled the descendant of simple Kalmyk people to become a typically cultivated Russian gentleman.

On the other side of the ledger, there is the undeniable fact that this cramming of information plus harsh discipline made the gymnasium a somewhat oppressive institution. The Russian pedagogue of the nineteenth century, often a devoted and humane teacher, remained blissfully unaware of the future findings of Doctors Freud and Dewey. A student's failure in a subject, a common occurrence, was followed invariably by the repetition of a grade. No sports or other forms of student group activity were allowed to relax the atmosphere of intensive learning. It is not surprising that many a future Russian revolutionary would feel the first stirrings of radical protest while oppressed by Greek grammar or logarithms.

On Ilya Ulyanov's graduation in 1850 we encounter a more familiar aspect of the Tsarist regime. Having been an excellent student, Ilya was recommended for a scholarship to the university. But scholarships were then reserved for the children of impoverished nobility slated to enter the state service and not for people of his background, and Ilya Nikolayevich had again to enlist the help of his relatives and to give private lessons in order to support himself through the four years of the university.

Kazan, where he pursued his studies, and where his famous son was to follow him one day, was like Astrakhan a former Tartar capital. Its university, while less fashionable than those of Moscow and Petersburg, could boast of a very good scientific faculty. Its former professor, and rector during much of the first half of the nineteenth century, had been Lobachevski, one of the great names in the history of mathematics. Though he felt some attraction to the law, Ilya Ulyanov decided finally to enroll under the faculty of mathematics and physics, from which he duly graduated in 1854 with the degree of candidate (equivalent to our master) of science. One year later, the great Lobachevski, then deputy curator of the Kazan school region, set his name to the nomination of Ilya Nikolayevich Ulyanov as teacher of physics and mathematics in the high school of Penza.

In Penza, a veritable Podunk of nineteenth century Russia, Ilya began his pedagogical and administrative career, which was to take place exclusively in the provinces. Penza, then the Volga towns of Nizhni-Novgorod (now Gorky) and then Simbirsk were to be his residences for the rest of his life. The capitals, Moscow and St. Petersburg, he was to visit only as a participant in a pedagogical congress or when reporting to the ministry of education. A man of Ilya Nikolayevich's eventual status would often take at least one trip abroad to see the "cultured" West. He never did. Lenin's father spent his life in the torpor of nineteenth century provincial Russia, the same Russia for which Lenin was to feel a strange mixture of affection and revulsion.

In 1863 Ilya Nikolayevich married Maria Blank, daughter of a retired doctor. The family of Lenin's mother is treated by the Soviet biographers even more gingerly than that of the father. The original Ulyanovs were at least incontestably poor, however troublesome their other characteristics. Dr. Alexander Blank on the other hand retired from practice, bought an estate, and was inscribed among the landed nobility of the Kazan province. According to the hideous classificatory scheme of Soviet historiography, he thus became an "exploiter." Nor is the ancestry of Lenin's mother entirely satisfactory from the national point of view. Blank is obviously not a common Russian name, and the doctor's wife was German. We should note that Blank moderated his class characteristics by frequently helping the peasants with medical advice, and concerning his personality we have the testimony of Lenin's sister that her grandfather was an "outstanding man . . . strong and self-reliant . . . Careerism of any kind and servility were alien to his nature." He was also evidently something of a domestic tyrant, with every detail of his five daughters' upbringing and behavior (including the proper position while going to sleep!) being subject to very precise rules.

Maria Alexandrovna thus came from a higher and more cultured environment than her husband, and while the marriage was evidently a very happy one, there are hints that she did not find the life of an official's wife in the procession of grim provincial towns entirely to her liking. She was also more independent and less conformist. Ilya Nikolayevich was deeply religious; his wife "did not like to go to church." She must have been a remarkable person. Without approving, she understood her children's revolutionary activity. After her husband's death her oldest son was executed and a young daughter died of typhoid, but the mother continued to bring whatever comfort she could to her remaining four children through their repeated arrests and exiles.

From Penza, where the pedagogical and living conditions were deplorable, the Ulyanovs moved to Nizhni-Novgorod. There for six years Ilya was the senior science teacher in the gymnasium. In 1869 came an advancement to the post of inspector of the public schools in the province of Simbirsk.

The reforms of the 1860s brought new impetus to public education. The newly created organs of provincial and county government had as a primary task the sponsorship of public schools. The period of reaction and disillusionment was not to come until the late seventies; for the time being both the conservative and the liberal saw the future of the country dependent on the rapid spread of literacy and education among the people, and especially among the freshly liberated peasants. The school inspector and the director of schools (the post to which Ilya Nikolayevich advanced in 1874) became the keystone of the whole system. He was the liaison between the ministry of education and the local boards. Upon his shoulders lay the responsibility for the training, assignment, and discipline of the teachers, and for the organization and curricula of the elementary schools. In a province as backward and poor (even by the Russian standards of 1869) as Simbirsk the job was likely to be of back-breaking proportions. It took not only career considerations but real devotion to education on the part of Ulyanov to exchange the more congenial post of the high school teacher and the more pleasant atmosphere of Nizhni, which had at least some appurtenances of a major city, for the task of supervising elementary education in a bleak province of about one million inhabitants. The town of Simbirsk (now Ulyanovsk) was a typical provincial hole like the ones immortalized in the tales of Gogol and of Saltykov (Shchedrin). A nineteenth century versifier writing about the town referred engagingly to its "pastoral" atmosphere, herds of cattle, and rivers of mud in the spring. In Simbirsk Ilya Ulyanov was to spend the remaining fifteen years of his life, and in it in 1870 was born his second son and third child, Vladimir Ilyich.

Lenin lived throughout his childhood and youth in the towns and villages of the Volga region. This period of life spent in the sleepy Central Russian towns and primitive villages was to leave a definite imprint on his personality. To a child the "lack of culture" of Simbirsk or

Samara was more than compensated by the proximity of the countryside, the river, and the closeness of the family or a student group. For a studious young man it offered none of the distractions one encounters in a great city. A great cosmopolitan center subjects all attitudes and values to a corrosive questioning. When Lenin emerged from the provinces at the age of twenty-three his philosophy and vocation were already determined. In his later life he was never to like the great cities. It was not only nostalgia that made him in England long for his native countryside and a boat ride on the Volga, but also a temperamental distaste for the very same forces and institutions of modern European life that he as a Marxist was fighting to bring about in his backward country. This basic ambivalence characteristic of so many of Lenin's feelings and arguments appears in his letters from Austrian Poland, where he settled shortly before World War I. Cracow and its environs were "a veritable backwater and uncivilized." "Here one cannot speak of culture—it is almost [as bad] as in Russia." At the same time Lenin professed himself healthier and more content than in Paris or Geneva. To be in an environment similar to that of his youth was soothing for Lenin's nerves and beneficial for his work.

The life of the Ulyanov family unrolled with Victorian orderliness and decorum. After Vladimir, the future Lenin, were born Olga (1871), Dimitri (1874), and Maria (1878) to join Anna (1864) and Alexander (1866). Of the sons, Vladimir was to grow up closest in appearance to his father, inheriting Ilya Nikolayevich's slanted eyes and high cheekbones, with red hair that he began to lose at a very early age.

Ulyanov's career moved meantime through promotions and decorations. The post of director of the public schools was equivalent in the table of ranks to that of a major general in the army. The order of St. Vladimir bestowed with it hereditary nobility. It is hardly necessary to add that whatever the official designation, Ilya Ulyanov's advancement brought him and his family into what was in Russia the equivalent of the middle class—the intelligentsia—the stratum occupied by the officials, members of the free professions, and the like. Social classifications must always remain imprecise. In the narrower sense of the term, membership in the intelligentsia came to denote a certain political attitude, one which, again inadequately, can be described as progressive or liberal. But in the wider sense intelligentsia stood for what in nineteenth century Russia was, in the absence of the Western-type business class, the middle station in life.[3]

As an official Ilya Ulyanov was quite different from the Tsarist

---

[3] The preceding sentences cry for warnings and qualifications. Was a police official or an army officer a member of the intelligentsia? No, but his son might be, in the broader sense of the word, if he became a lawyer, and in the narrower if he took to reading J. S. Mill and criticizing the autocracy. On the other hand, the Prince Tru-

bureaucrat made familiar to us by Russian satire: servile to his superiors, brutal and unfeeling to inferiors, venal, addicted to drinking and gambling. All the accounts, some of them contemporary, agree that he was an excellent and conscientious civil servant. His work was the harrowing everyday struggle to raise the level of instruction, to secure adequate school premises and textbooks, and to wrest from the ministry and the local authorities additional funds for the miserably paid teachers. Until 1874 he had to perform alone the work of inspection for the whole province of Simbirsk, which meant being on the road a great deal of the time, going mostly not by railway but on horseback on the horrible provincial Russian roads. After 1874 there were assistants, and he could indulge occasionally in his old profession by taking over classes from ailing teachers.

Primary education was the passion of contemporary Russia. Enlightened noblemen such as Leo Tolstoy and Baron Korff ran model schools on their estates. Ilya Ulyanov was attentive to every fresh pedagogical advance and experiment. His own background may account for his special solicitude for the children of the non-Russian inhabitants (a large proportion of the population of the province was composed of the Tartar and Finnish groups), the defense of their learning ability, and the insistence on instruction in their own language as well as in Russian. In his relations with the teachers he was a stern but fair superior. Nothing, in brief, mars the image of a devoted and humane administrator and pedagogue.

Many Russians of Ilya Nikolayevich's generation who like him advanced through education from simple beginnings became involved in the sixties and seventies in the revolutionary and radical movements. But whichever way a Soviet author may try (and many have), it is impossible to connect Ulyanov with any political protest. His daughter Anna remembers her father singing forbidden revolutionary songs. Marietta Shaginyan would tie him to the progressive circles of his student days. Most brazen of all, the *Soviet Encyclopedia* has Ilya Ulyanov employing the pedagogical methods recommended by the revolutionary thinkers Dobrolyubov and Chernyshevsky. But apart from the utter implausibility of this evidence, would a man under the slightest suspicion of disloyalty be appointed director of public schools in 1874, already a time of hunt for subversion? The very same sources feel constrained to testify to his loyalty to the regime and the church. For Ilya Nikolayevich, Alexander II, who emancipated the peasants and who started his country upon belated reforms, remained to the end "Tsar-

betskoy who became a university professor and a leader of the Constitutional Democrats has to be classified as an *intelligent* despite his ancient title and his lands. The reader may come to share, though for different reasons, the sentiments of Nicholas II who wanted to eliminate "intelligentsia" from the Russian language.

Liberator," and his assassination in 1881 by the revolutionaries was a national calamity. A man of Ulyanov's background and temperament found it easy to be a moderate, and to believe that reforms from above and education would suffice to bring Russia out of her torpor and backwardness.

This attitude, which in time his famous son came to hate more than any out-and-out conservatism and reaction, was as a matter of fact shared by a large mass of the Russian intelligentsia in the 1860s and 1870s. Because we view 1917 as the culmination of Russian history, we have come to regard the preceding century as simply the scene of a struggle between reaction and revolution, and we have often come to disregard the numerous Ilya Ulyanovs who, in a less dramatic way, struggled for a third solution.

The years after 1881 must have been extremely trying to a liberal-minded official. The regime now entered upon a course of reaction that became especially pronounced in the field of education. The curriculum of the high schools became more classical, sciences being held to be particularly conducive to arousing subversive thoughts among the youth. The same obscurantist philosophy dictated general doubts about the desirability of widespread elementary education. A minister of education spoke of the folly and harm done by educating the "cooks' sons" beyond their station in life. (It would not have needed much reflection to realize that it had not been the "cooks' sons" who had been in the forefront of the revolutionary movement.) The stress was now on elementary education through the church schools, and the public schools were relatively neglected. The last four years of Ilya Nikolayevich's life were spent in struggling against the current, and in an atmosphere which no longer held the hopes and promise of the seventies. Official worries were accompanied by anxiety for his eldest son. Alexander had been pursuing since 1883 a scientific career at St. Petersburg University. His views and associations were the source of increasing anxiety to his father. Shortly before his death he asked Anna, then also in St. Petersburg, to implore Alexander to take care of himself "if only for our own sake." In January 1886 Ilya Nikolayevich Ulyanov died suddenly of a brain hemorrhage.

Among the remaining photographs of Ilya Nikolayevich, one shows him with his wife and children. The paterfamilias sits heavily amidst his brood, his right hand thrust in his coat, his two eldest sons in their uniforms of high school students. The severity of the father's expression is enhanced by his period beard and the baldness of his egg-shaped head. Another photograph of the director of the public schools, this time with his staff of five school inspectors, has the same pose and the same unsmiling earnestness.

The family life of the Ulyanovs is usually described in terms of cloying sweetness. The parents loved but did not spoil their children. The children in turn loved their parents; each child had a special affection for the brother or sister closest in age, but he also loved the rest. The reader blinks and reaches for his Freud! Is it necessary to add that the Ulyanovs were taught at an early age to be self-reliant and that they helped around the house? In their attempt to present the Ulyanov family as an example for the Russian youth, Soviet authors would deny the conflicts, cares, and disappointments that beset the happiest and most normal lives.

Some legends are pathetic in their ineptitude. Thus the story of how young Lenin broke with religion: his father in his presence complained to a visiting official ("a major bureaucrat from the ministry") that his children were lax in attending church. "Well, they have to be whipped," advised the representative of Tsarist reaction, looking straight at young Vladimir. Enraged, Lenin ran out, tore the cross from his neck and threw it away. From then on he had nothing to do with religion. One does not have to know much about nineteenth century Russian customs to assert that a man of Ilya Nikolayevich's class and manners would not discuss intimate family matters with a casual visitor, or that it would never enter anybody's mind that he could whip his adolescent children. Besides, even the Soviet reader should know that in filling out his Party question-naire Lenin stated that he had retained his religious beliefs until after he was sixteen, that is, for some time after his father's death.

The haze of propaganda and hagiography should not obscure the fact that, insofar as we know, the Ulyanovs were a happy and closely knit family. But the last cannot mean that there was a place in a Russian middle-class household for the frantic togetherness that contemporary Soviet moralists and American "family councillors" prescribe as the ideal. It was in many ways a typical intelligentsia household. Above all, the parents tried to instill in their children the importance and the pleasure of learning, and it is a measure of their success that all of them became excellent students.[4] Summer vacations in the country provided a release from what must have been a somewhat oppressive atmosphere of hard studying and high-minded thoughts. Maria Alexandrovna inherited from her father a *dacha* (villa) and some land in the village of Kokushkino, and there the young Ulyanovs enjoyed games with their less intellectual cousins. One of the latter was to remember how Volodya (diminutive of Vladimir) subjected him to an examination in Russian literature and then scolded him for not having read Turgenev. However bookish, Lenin became and remained all his life enamored of the country and its diversions. Years later he was to say with some exaggeration to a Party associ-

---

[4] In the gymnasium Lenin was graded "excellent" in all but one subject. This circumstance inevitably inspired a grim Soviet hack to an article: Why Lenin Received only "Very Good" in Logic. The obvious answer: the teacher of logic did not believe that anybody should be graded "excellent" in his subject. Also, the textbook in logic was written from "the vulgar idealistic and antimaterialist point of view" and as such was criticized by Lenin.

ate, "I, too, am a squire's child." Understandably Kokushkino became for the children a place of enchantment, the inevitable yardstick of leisure and enjoyment.

Family accounts give Alexander the characteristic attributes of an eldest son and a revolutionary hero. His natural seriousness would at times turn into melancholy. It was difficult to draw him away from his studies, even to eat. If other children, including the older Anna, were inattentive to their parents, he would scold them and demand an apology. To the sister's question as to his ideal of feminine beauty and appearance Alexander answered dutifully "just like mother." He disliked the formal discipline of the gymnasium, and very early conceived that personal involvement in literature that was the indelible mark of the Russian radical of the times. At the age of thirteen, reports Anna, Alexander found unsympathetic the characters of Prince André and Pierre in *War and Peace*, just as the great novel itself must have seemed to him insufficiently concerned with the social question. In contrast he devoured such contemporary radical and revolutionary writers as Pisarev and Chernyshevsky. In his last years in the gymnasium Alexander converted one of the rooms in the Ulyanov house into a chemical and biological laboratory from which he would hardly budge, even though his parents would ask Anna to lure him out for walks or croquet. In brief, a character who could have stepped out of the pages of Turgenev.

Young Lenin was gay and playful where his brother was withdrawn, attracted to history and languages rather than science. He enjoyed teasing overly serious Alexander. That they were very close friends and that Vladimir shared his older brother's political and social preoccupations is obviously a pious fabrication. In adolescence four years looms like a huge difference in age; it means different friends and different interests even between brothers whose temperaments are not as diametrically opposed as the two Ulyanovs. There are excellent grounds for believing that Lenin's radicalism flowered after Alexander's death, and largely as a result of reading his martyred brother's books. Atheism was a normal attitude of a Russian revolutionary. And Lenin remained a believer until after sixteen, when his brother was already away in St. Petersburg studying science and engaged in the political activities that were to bring him to the scaffold.

The death of Ilya Nikolayevich meant among other sorrows that the family's financial position became precarious. Maria Alexandrovna had to petition for a widow's pension and also had to ask, since under the celebrated red tape of Tsarist bureaucracy even the most reasonable petition took a long time, for an immediate grant in aid. It is characteristic of this strong-willed woman that she did not wire Alexander the news of his father's death for fear of upsetting him when he was just preparing for his exams, but asked a niece to announce the news by letter. Equally remarkable, when Anna offered to come home from her studies in the capital to help her mother take care of the smaller children, Maria Alexandrovna, faithful to the Ulyanov belief in the overwhelming importance of education, refused.

In not much more than a year another and a harder blow was to befall this woman who throughout her many remaining years (she died at eighty-one in 1916) was to suffer the arrests, exiles, and deaths of her children. Alexander was in jail on charges of plotting against the life of Emperor Alexander III. A group of revolutionary students, finding every other form of political activity barred to them, turned to the emulation of the terrorists who in 1881 had assassinated the father of Alexander III. This time the preparations for the assassination were quite amateurish, just as the terrorists, in what became known as the affair of March 1, 1887, were an isolated group and not, like their predecessors, representatives of a wider movement. Maria Alexandrovna rushed to the capital but no amount of persuasion could change her son's determination to admit full guilt and to refuse to ask for pardon.

The standard revolutionary behavior in such matters was set by the condemned of 1881: the accused would not deny his responsibility for terror or seek extenuating circumstances. He would use his court appearance for a ringing denunciation of the autocratic regime, and the promise of more terror, should the government persist in its denial of freedom. Alexander was true to form, and his speech is a document of tragic naïveté as well as heroism.

> Terror . . . is the only form of defense by which a minority strong only in its spiritual strength and the consciousness of its righteousness [can combat] the physical power of the majority. . . . Among the Russian people there will always be found many people who are so devoted to their ideas and who feel so bitterly the unhappiness of their country that it will not be a sacrifice for them to offer their lives.

These are not the sentiments of a revolutionary who has thought through his political philosophy, and who claims to act for an oppressed *majority*. But Alexander put his finger on the root cause of the tragedy of the Russian intelligentsia: ". . . We are encouraged to develop [our] intellectual powers, but we are not allowed to use them for the benefit of our country."

Among her great virtues, Maria Alexandrovna had the inability to be melodramatic. Her accounts of the interviews with Alexander are the more moving because of their simplicity. At their first meeting her son cried, and asked his mother for forgiveness, and to remember that she had five other children. After the death sentence had been pronounced, he could not bring himself, despite her pleas seconded by sympathetic officials, to ask for pardon. What would people say if having accepted a major responsibility for the plot he should now plead for mercy? And having planned to take a man's life, is it not natural that his own should be forfeit? If pardon were granted it would mean lifetime incarceration in a fortress "where they let you read only religious books." This would drive him insane. "Would you wish this for me, mother?" He was eventually prevailed upon to ask for pardon, though this fact is almost always omitted from the official Soviet accounts of A. Ulyanov.[5] Alexander's extreme youth (he was in his twenty-first year), the fact that another (and older) organizer of the plot had his sentence commuted to life imprisonment, might have well inspired hope. But even though Alexander III himself found the frankness of his would-be assassin "even engaging," the sentence was allowed to stand and Alexander Ulyanov was hanged on May 8, 1887.

Years later, already under the Soviets and after Lenin's death, both his sisters and Lenin's widow, Krupskaya, were to assess the effect of Alexander's death on seventeen-year-old Vladimir. Since Anna Ulyanova was capable of beginning a memoir of her own brother with "Our leader Vladimir Ilyich Ulyanov was born . . . ," it is not surprising that her main interest in the story of Alexander is to score propaganda points for the benefit of the Soviet public. Though Marxism condemns individual terror as the means of political struggle, Anna depicts Alexander as practically a Marxist who had helped his brother in his first steps toward Bolshevism. That Alexander's own words at the trial demonstrate how far he was from the basic concepts of Marxism does not bother her a bit. Equally revolting, for among other things they are really irreverent to the memory of both brothers, are the attempts made by those closest to them, Krupskaya and Lenin's younger sister, Maria Ilinichna, to represent Bolshevism as having literally leapt out of Lenin's head the minute he heard of his brother's execution. Speaking to the solemn session of the Moscow Soviet held in memory of Lenin on February 7, 1924, Maria gave currency to the most often repeated tale: on hearing of the execution Vladimir said: "No, we shall not take that road [i.e., the one chosen by Alexander], our road must be different." At the time of the alleged declaration Maria Ulyanova was nine. Lenin by his own avowal did not choose the Marxist road until 1889, some two years later.

That the death of his brother was a great blow is self-evident. Whatever their childhood rivalries and quarrels, Vladimir was deeply attached to him, and he had always had a strong family feeling. But it is difficult, not only because of the tendentious accounts but also because of Lenin's reserve, which made him keep his intimate feelings to himself, to determine the exact influence of this personal tragedy upon his convictions and development. Years later and in connection with another act of political terror Lenin was to write: "The utter uselessness of terror is clearly

[5] See *Alexander Ilyich Ulyanov Collection*, Moscow, 1927, p. 346.

shown by the experience of the Russian revolutionary movement." And further: "individual acts of terrorism . . . create only a short-lived sensation, and lead in the long run to an apathy, and the passive awaiting of yet another 'sensation.'" Here the mature Lenin seems to answer his brother's apology for individual terrorism of fifteen years before.

Among Alexander's university acquaintances was the future distinguished Orientalist, Serge Oldenburg, who jotted down an interesting recollection. In 1891 Lenin, then in St. Petersburg, dropped in to talk about Alexander. Lenin's expression and behavior were strained as if he were reliving the past tragedy. What particularly struck Oldenburg was the fact that he did not want to talk about his brother's political activity or personal affairs. All his questions referred to Alexander's studies. He was eager to know that his brother was genuinely interested in science, and to have a confirmation of the value of his biological researches.

There can be many interpretations of this incident. Was Lenin anxious to learn that his brother did not turn to politics as a result of disenchantment with science? Did he seek to know that his brother's life was not wasted despite the futile gesture and the untimely death? Certainly he grew to regard individual terror as a form of neurotic self-indulgence on the part of some members of the intelligentsia, the result of impatience and of the unwillingness to conduct real political work. The fate of his brother stimulated his interest in social questions. It is only from 1887 on that we have reliable accounts of Vladimir devoting himself to the reading of radical literature with the same thoroughness and passion that he had previously lavished on his study of history and languages.

While Alexander was awaiting first the trial and then the execution, Lenin was finishing his eighth and final year in the Simbirsk gymnasium. Graduation from high school was, for a European adolescent, a formidable and often a traumatic experience. It required not only a successful completion of what corresponded to the American senior year of the school, but also in addition a special examination in several subjects. This examination, the so-called "test of maturity," consisted of written and oral questions and exercises prepared not by the local teachers but by the ministry of education or by the professors of the regional university. Nothing was spared to endow the occasion with awe and tension. The strict secrecy about the content of the examination, the barricaded rooms where it took place, the virtual impossibiliy of beginning professional training if one failed a subject, make the most strenuous American and English academic tests appear innocent and relaxing in comparison. Nervous breakdowns were not uncommon among the students, most of whom were, after all, not older than eighteen or nineteen.

With the earlier noted exception of logic, Lenin completed his high school course with the grade of "excellent" in every subject, including religion. The high school certificate included also such categories as "be-

havior in class," "interest in studies," etc. In all these respects his conduct
was adjudged "exemplary." The final written examinations took place
in the week of his brother's execution. Lenin passed them with the highest
distinction, being awarded the gold metal of the Simbirsk gymnasium
(both Alexander and Anna had received the same award) as the first
student in the class.

The story that because of Alexander Vladimir had difficulties in receiving the medal and then in entering the university is another *canard* [6]
of the Soviet biographers, in line with the mentality of Stalinism in such
matters. Even on purely practical grounds the Tsarist government could
not afford the policy of reprisals against the relatives of political offenders,
for such a policy would have barred some of the most distinguished
Russian families from higher education and state employment. Once
Lenin himself got into trouble, his brother's deed was to be held as
corroborating evidence of his political unreliability. But not before.
Simbirsk was a small town and it was in the nature of things that the
cowardly among the local intelligentsia began to shun the family of the
would-be assassin of the Emperor. But to others, even if conservatives, it
was simply an undeserved calamity that befell a Christian and hard-
working family.

Among the charitable was the Simbirsk gymnasium director, Fyodor
Kerensky (he was, ironically enough, the father of the Kerensky whom
Lenin was to dispossess as the head of the Russian state). His characterization of Vladimir Ulyanov at the time of his final examinations is
warm with sympathy for the youth and with compassion for his family.
Lenin was reported as extremely talented; his conduct throughout the
eight years of the gymnasium had not merited a single reproach.[7] Vladimir's virtues, wrote Kerensky, conscious that he was testifying about the
brother of a condemned terrorist, were related to his moral and religious
upbringing. The only possible personality defect in the young man was
the excessive reserve evidenced by the lack of friends among his contemporaries.

The university chosen was that of Kazan. That the road to the capital universities was now barred to a Ulyanov is unlikely. Two years later
sister Olga was pursuing her higher studies at St. Petersburg. But Maria
Alexandrovna wanted to be with her son during his studies (this was
also advised by Kerensky) and Kazan was close to the family property of
Kokushkino. Mother's influence, it was hoped, would keep Vladimir out

---

[6] Anna's arrest, at the same time as Alexander's, in St. Petersburg was on the
charge of complicity in the affair of March 1. In May she was released and returned
to the family.

[7] There is no way of pleasing a Soviet writer. Commenting on this glowing testimony, sister Anna feels constrained to defend young Lenin from the unspoken suspicion of bourgeois priggishness: he *was* capable of being naughty and of ridiculing
some of his comrades and teachers.

of trouble, and the family was eager to leave Simbirsk and its sad memories.

To most Russian students the university represented an intoxicating world of freedom after the repressive regimen of the gymnasium. The contrast was much greater than that which could be felt by the average English or American college freshman. The student for the most part now lived on his own, free from parental or institutional supervision. The strict supervision of deportment and recitations by rote now gave way to free attendance at lectures and independent study. Most important of all, within the autocratic state the university was in relative terms an oasis of free speech and thought. The students soon felt that they were a separate order in society, free from the obscurantism of the officialdom and the superstitions of the masses. As such they claimed freedom and rights not found anywhere else in the autocratic state. The educated classes, in turn, even the moderate elements within them, tolerated and half expected the students to be rebellious. It was widely felt to be somewhat disgraceful that when Alexander III visited Moscow University in 1886 he was greeted by the youth with flowers and cheers.

It is not surprising that the general situation in the universities was viewed by the Tsarist authorities with less than complete satisfaction. Much of the revolutionary ferment of the 1860s and 1870s stemmed in their opinion from this anomalous—in an autocracy—position of the university. It was not within the intentions and really beyond the powers of a nineteenth century authoritarian regime to achieve the regimentation of youth of which modern totalitarianism is capable. Repressive measures when adopted usually tended to accentuate rather than to repress the unquiet spirit of the youth. Thus the law of 1884 sought to curb the "excesses" of university life. Each student was now required to sign a pledge that he would not belong to unauthorized associations. Since the Russian "angry young men" demonstrated, in the immemorial fashion, their scorn for the hypocrisy and conventions of society by dressing shabbily, the university students were now to wear uniforms just like adolescents in high school. The government stressed the role of the student inspector, the official whose functions were a cross between those of a dean of men and a police spy, and who was usually regarded by the students with feelings that do not have to be detailed. The "reform" was greeted by a reactionary journalist with a ringing editorial entitled "Stand Up, Gentlemen, The Government Is Coming Back." Its repercussions were not long in coming and they went beyond flowers and cheers for the Emperor.

Having signed the appropriate pledges, Vladimir Ulyanov enrolled in the fall of 1887 in the juridical faculty of Kazan. The choice of law disappointed his teachers, who expected their prize pupil to pursue his studies in history and languages, but it was an indication that Lenin now contemplated a more active career than that afforded by high school or university teaching. Had he stuck to law there is little doubt that Lenin would have made an excellent lawyer, as he had the requisite qualities of a precise mind and a psychological insight. Some of the habits of his legal studies and of his brief practicing career were to persist. In the midst of the Revolution and the Civil War a speaker proposing a measure of "class justice" would be startled by Lenin's objection: "But that is not legal. You might be sued." Characteristically, though, in later years few professions were to arouse in him greater distaste than that of the law, few concepts were to bring out greater anger and contempt than that of "impartial bourgeois" justice.

An analysis of the student body at Kazan shows that education in the Russia of the 1880s was not an exclusive privilege of the upper classes. It is doubtful, as a matter of fact, that any of the Western universities could show a greater variety of the social origins of its students, or a higher percentage coming from the lower strata of society. Out of 918 students there were 95 children of peasants and Cossacks, 189 of the lower urban classes, 101 of the clergy (the rank-and-file clergyman, who was the only one allowed to have a family, since the higher ecclesiastical officials were recruited from the monasteries, was usually a person of very modest circumstances) and 16 of the common soldiers. Since Russia's population was overwhelmingly peasant, the figures are far from indicating an equality of educational opportunity, but granting the time and the place they are significant.[8] By far the most numerous group were, like Lenin, sons of government officials. Relatively few were descended from the "real" nobility.

The average Kazan student was not likely to be a rich young man. The reforms of the 1880s brought with them an increase in tuition, which tended to add to the agitation of the student body. The university had, from the government's point of view, a bad tradition. It was a Kazan alumnus, Karakozov, who with his shot at the Emperor Alexander II in 1866 began the campaign of political terrorism that was to culminate with that Emperor's assassination in 1881. Subversive propaganda was being found in the students' quarters, and even the local Midwives' Institute was found infected by revolutionary literature. But it is clear that the main reason for the students' disaffection and rioting, in Kazan as elsewhere, was the natural reaction against the authorities' supervision of and interference with their private activities. It did not take much to provoke a major riot that was to end Vladimir Ulyanov's university career.

The origin of the trouble was in Moscow. There, during a public concert, a student slapped the face of the student inspector. The authorities reacted with their usual clumsy harshness. The culprit was, by an

---

[8] The statistics are drawn from a Soviet source.

administrative rescript, condemned to three years' military service in a
penal battalion. There followed a wave of student protests and demonstrations, one of which had to be dispersed by the soldiers. Stories of
police brutality ran through all the academic centers in Russia. Representatives of Moscow (university functions there had been suspended)
arrived in Kazan to arouse their comrades to a supportive protest. It
was drafted strictly in terms of defense against the violation of the
alleged student, and university rights: "Shall we not defend the ancient
rights of our universities? . . . We believe in the Kazan students and
call upon them to protest openly within the walls of the university."

Lenin had been quietly pursuing his chosen subjects, including,
curiously enough, theology. But he was on December 16 in a crowd of
students who gathered to protest the Moscow indignities and to demand
that the government of the Russian Empire change its laws on the universities. Except for a broken door to the university auditorium, the meeting at first progressed in an atmosphere of exaltation rather than violence.
A delegation of the students of the veterinary institute, which hastened
to express their solidarity with the university, was greeted with "brotherly
embraces and kisses." But the appearance of the student inspector transformed the situation. Unmindful of the incident with his corresponding
number in Moscow, this official conceived it to be his duty to appear
before the crowd and to order them to disperse. At the sight of the hated
spy there were shouts, "Hit him!" And, to be sure, the inspector was
roughed up and thrown out. It was now the turn of the professors who
appeared and begged the students to desist: "In this temple of learning
there is no room for such disorders. . . . You are here to study." These
speeches had the usual effect of similar speeches made under similar
circumstances.

Emboldened, the students passed a series of resolutions. Some of them
were reasonable, but others would make an American or Soviet academic
administrator of today wince. The students demanded that the universities should be run by the professorial senate with no interference by the
ministry. They claimed freedom from any supervision of their private
lives, the right to assembly and to petition. Scholarships and fellowships
were to be adjudged and distributed by the students' elected representatives. And "to satisfy our and society's indignation those officials who
intentionally or through negligence allowed . . . brutal excesses to be
committed in regard to our Moscow comrades . . ." should be punished.

The authorities' answer was to arrest the alleged leaders of the disturbances and in due time over one hundred students were either excluded or asked to resign from the university. Lectures and other activities
were suspended for two months.

Lenin was among those detained, spending two days in jail. He was
one of the forty-five students who were expelled outright. In the official

report Vladimir Ulyanov is alleged to have been running along the corridors "shouting and waving his arms" during the demonstration. If so, it
was behavior very untypical of him. Neither in the past nor in the future
was he to be part of a screaming mob. Because of his red hair he was
likely to be conspicuous in a crowd of milling students. Once the demonstration was over the authorities had to make an example and it is notoriously impossible to find the real leaders in that type of situation. But the
name Ulyanov had definite associations, and Lenin found himself for
the first time in jail. Those expelled were made to suffer for what, after
all, was the collective guilt of the student body. (The persons who man-
handled the inspector received special sentences.) Even so, the expulsion
to most of them was not an overwhelming tragedy. After a few months or
a year they would be allowed to come back and work for their degrees.
It would not necessarily be a black mark on their record. Since student
disorders were such a widespread occurrence, most of those who at one
time or another were expelled and even imprisoned would be allowed
to grow up into respectable lawyers, doctors, and, sometimes, high
Tsarist bureaucrats. But to Vladimir Ulyanov the road back to the university would be barred for three years, not because he was more guilty
than the others, but because he was a brother of Alexander.

The liberal society of Kazan, and especially its female component,
greeted the expelled students as true martyrs for freedom. During
their brief imprisonment they were overwhelmed with presents, food
packages, and even cash. When the expellees were told to pack up and
leave Kazan, their departure to the bosom of their families took on the
appearance of another demonstration. The streets were lined up with
sympathizers shouting encouragement to the young heroes, who in their
turn greeted friends and relatives, and even tossed mimeographed proclamations among the cheering public. One of them began "Farewell,
Kazan, farewell university" and complained, "We hoped that here, in this
temple of learning, we would find the knowledge which would enable us
to grow up into fighters for the happiness and welfare of our weary
country. . . . But what did we find? . . . This 'learning for learning's
sake' which was so ill-naturedly defended by some of the professors. . . ."

Lenin's leave-taking was of a more private nature. He left with his
mother for her villa in Kokushkino, a delightful place in the summer, but
hardly so during the Russian winter. Maria Alexandrovna returned to
Kazan to gather her younger children and then rejoined Vladimir, and
Anna, who had before been ordered by the police to reside on her mother's
estate.

Lenin was to confess that never in his life did he read as much or as
passionately as during his forced stay in Kokushkino. Some of the reading
was connected with his studies, as he hoped to be readmitted to the uni-

versity. But in addition he devoured literature, and became really for the first time engrossed in the social and political question. As mentioned, prior to his brother's death he never evidenced any interest in politics. Like many high school students of his generation, he must have read some of the radical and forbidden literature. But Lenin was a young man of systematic habits and something of a "grind," with whom studies came first. Now his enforced idleness enabled him to plunge into the vast literature of Russian liberalism and socialism. In the house library at Kokushkino he would find not only books, but bound copies of such famous literary and social magazines as *The Contemporary* and the *European Messenger*. The winter of 1887–88 in Kokushkino marks Lenin's apprenticeship in revolutionary thought. It is then that he fell under the spell of Chernyshevsky, the spell that was to turn many of Lenin's predecessors and contemporaries onto the revolutionary path, and was to remain with Lenin all his life. "I read every word of Chernyshevsky's magnificent comments about esthetics, art, and literature. . . . I was conquered by Chernyshevsky's encyclopedic knowledge, the clarity of his revolutionary views, and his unyielding polemical talent." [9] It was not the first time that Lenin encountered this fanatical and uncompromising revolutionary, the hater of liberalism. He had read Chernyshevsky's fantastic novel, *What Is To Be Done?*, years before. At that time it made no impression on him. Now upon rereading it he found it a revelation. To Chernyshevsky, as we shall see, Lenin was to be indebted more than to any other thinker with the exception of Marx for his philosophy and his decision to become a revolutionary.

The expulsion from the university was the first tangible personal experience by Lenin of the injustice and harshness of the Russian political system. Granting the egoism of youth it was a shock, perhaps as great in its effect as the execution of his brother. Prior to the expulsion, Lenin whether by inclination or because of regard for his mother avoided politics, and his involvement in the student riot was not greater than that of many if not most of the students. Now he found himself under virtual domestic arrest and under police supervision. While most of the culprits were allowed to resume their studies, he for the next three years encountered repeated refusals to his petition for readmission. One can imagine with what feelings Vladimir Ulyanov would write the following: "To His Excellency the Minister of Education: The Petition of former student of the Imperial Kazan University. I have the honor to ask most humbly of your Excellency . . ."

But his and his mother's importunings were unavailing. To the authorities in Kazan Lenin became firmly identified as the brother of a condemned terrorist. His role in the student troubles was now magnified to the point that he appeared as one of their instigators. A dull-witted

[9] A. I. Ivanski, ed., *Young Years of V. I. Lenin*, Moscow, 1957, p. 285.

police official could write that Vladimir Ulyanov "actively participated, *and maybe even now participates* [10] in the organization of the revolutionary circles among the Kazan youth." Not even the most assiduous and inventive Soviet historian has been able to dig out any "revolutionary circle" in which Vladimir participated prior to his expulsion. But the local police official, like his successors in Stalin's Russia, had to furnish proofs of his "vigilance" and the ability to spot subversives. The university authorities in turn sought to reduce the cause of the student riots to political instigation, thus to absolve themselves of the charge of tactlessness and the inability to deal with the young.

The minister of education refused permission to re-enter the university. The minister of the interior refused permission to go abroad to study. (To a repeated plea to go abroad for health reasons to take waters at Vichy the Ulyanovs were advised that there were excellent health resorts in the Caucasus.) Vladimir Ulyanov's name was now on the list of those who were barred from state employment without a special permission. Circumstances as well as his convictions were pushing Lenin toward one career that remained open, that of a revolutionary.

[10] My italics. In Kokushkino?!

II

THE REVOLUTIONARY
TRADITION

1. The Decembrists

On December 14, 1825, part of the St. Petersburg garrison mutinied against the newly proclaimed Tsar Nicholas I. To be more precise, soldiers of several regiments were deceived by their officers into believing that the new Tsar was a usurper and came out under arms to fight his accession. The plotting officers, who used their soldiers' ignorance and habit of obedience to promote a revolution, passed into history under the name of Decembrists.

The story of the Decembrists is not, properly speaking, part of the Russian revolutionary tradition. Yet at the same time this tradition and much of Russian history in general cannot be understood without the story of this strange group of men who rebelled against the regime under which they were the privileged class. From December 1825 dates the split between Russian society and the government, the split never entirely healed, which provided the basis for the revolutionary strivings and eventually for that day in October 1917 when another armed uprising, this time successful, established Vladimir Lenin as the head of the Soviet regime.

The conspirators of 1825 came without exception from the members of the secret officers' societies that sprang up in Russia at the end of the Napoleonic wars. To the exaltation of national resistance against the French and then the victorious campaigns through Europe there succeeded the boredom and routine of garrison life, and it was natural for the younger and more active of the officers to seek some form of association in which their newly gained ideas and impressions could be exchanged. The victorious war thus, paradoxically, endangered the Tsarist regime, for it showed to a number of young and sensitive men the then incomparably higher and freer culture of the West. (And more than a hundred years later, after another Russian victory, the Soviet government in 1945 took extraordinary measures to curtail the influx of Western ideas and to isolate from the rest of society those Russians who had been particularly exposed to them.) The officers could not help noticing how even in defeat France shone with culture and lively intellectual and social activity. In the most advanced part of the West peasant serfdom, this most characteristic institution of contemporary Russia, had long ago disappeared, and though there was a class system, one seldom encountered personal servility and the lack of individual rights that characterized Russian life from the top to the bottom of the social scale.

Still other circumstances pushed the young men into their secret and dangerous designs. During the war the Emperor, Alexander I, appeared as the embodiment of national resistance to the French and then as the arbiter of the fate of Europe. But very soon afterward he lapsed into reaction and mysticism. The plans of his earlier years to reform the government and society gave way to reaction and the reliance on the military and the police to preserve the *status quo*, that is, Russia's political and social backwardness. The postwar European settlement emphasized facts injurious to Russian national pride. Finland and the part of Poland granted by the Treaty of Vienna to the Emperor were given representative institutions and autonomy. In them he ruled as a constitutional monarch. But in Russia he remained the autocrat and no representative institution or judicial guarantees interposed between the individual and the absolute regime.

The first secret society was set up in 1816. It was based on the pattern of the Masonic lodges, which had been active in Russia for some time; the membership consisted of three grades of initiates, of which only the highest had the direction of the society as a whole. During the remaining nine years before the exposure, the society underwent several transformations and changes of name. It was eventually divided into two branches, the so-called Northern Society, centered in St. Petersburg, and the Southern Society, centered in the garrison seats of the Ukraine. While the general rules of the society had the usual injunctions about the members working for the general welfare and for the benefit of their country, the impulse of the more hot-headed members drove them from the beginning toward thoughts of a *coup d'état*, and even of the assassination of the monarch. The peculiar conditions of Russia in the 1820s, which remained true until 1905, almost inevitably pushed any organization devoted to the discussion of social and political purposes into the path of illegality and eventually of revolution. The regime did not allow any forum for the discussion of even the mildest reform of the *status quo*. It viewed with increasing suspicion purely social clubs and organizations. This in turn had the natural result of turning a chess club or a literary discussion circle into a potential source of subversion. Since the thought of even a mild reform was liable to be held as treason, people of the most moderate political convictions were drawn at times to contemplate revolution and terror as the means of eradicating the most obvious social ills.

To this vicious circle was added another one which, from the Decembrists on, conditioned every political movement in the nineteenth century. The young aristocrats and officers had to temper their constitutional and revolutionary dreams with the realization that they had no support, and indeed no understanding among the people. There was, in the Russia of the 1820s, no middle class in the sense in which it already existed in the West, and no industrial proletariat like the one which was already growing in London or Lyons. The vast mass of the population consisted of the illiterate peasantry, too passive and ignorant to dream of any political action to further their aspirations. Any movement of reform or revolution had to be a conspiracy, and almost by definition had to resort to drastic and desperate means. One had to strike at the very top of the political pyramid.

The imperial house could not inspire much veneration as a national institution. The grandfather of the ruling monarch Alexander I had been deposed and murdered with the complicity of his wife. His own father and predecessor had been murdered with at least the knowledge of Alexander and the elder of his brothers, Constantine. Still, while the conspirators at times discussed another assassination, many reasons kept them from attempting it, or indeed from coming out in revolt, as long as Alexander lived. For one thing, their aim was political change and not merely a palace revolt that would replace the person of the autocrat. For another, almost all of them had served under Alexander during the Napoleonic wars. He himself, while increasingly reactionary and beginning to remind one of his mad father, was still the same man who began his reign as a reformer desirous to curtail the evils of autocracy and serfdom.

But apart from the lingering personal attachment and distaste for a political murder, there was yet another and weightier reason for the Decembrists' dilatoriness. They were very far from being an efficient and coordinated political organization. Members were drawn into their conspiratorial path through a variety of motivations. Some of them could not stand the brutality of everyday military life with its routine of flogging the soldiers for even minor misdemeanors.[1] Many others found themselves in the society out of friendship or simply a sense of adventure. But there was no commonly held ideology, no jointly agreed-upon course of revolutionary action, and no clear notion as to what form of government Russia should have. The Northern Society leaned toward the idea of a constitutional monarchy with a limited franchise and a federal system. More radical ideas prevailed in the Southern Society, whose members were taken by the example of the Jacobins of the French Revolution

---

[1] A regiment of the Guards refused obedience in 1820 after its commander, having spat in the face of a soldier, ordered a whole platoon to follow his example.

rather than by the example of the English constitution. Had the December Revolution succeeded, it is not unlikely that the two camps would have confronted each other in a conflict or even a civil war.

The radical philosophy of the southern group was the outgrowth of the ideas of one man, Colonel Paul Pestel. Of all the Decembrists, Pestel is the only one to resemble the future figures of the Russian revolutionary movement. The *coup d'état* was for him to be the means not only of over-throwing the autocracy but of establishing a drastically different type of society. In his version of Jacobinism, Pestel came as close as one could in the 1820s in Russia (the term and the movement had not yet been invented) to socialism.

There are yet other "modern" touches about this young officer. Both a revolutionary and a bureaucrat by temperament, Pestel is not unlike some of the early Bolshevik leaders. Of them, Lenin was to exclaim "Scratch a Russian Communist and you will find a Russian chauvinist." Pestel, a German by descent and a Lutheran by religion, was an uncompromising Russian nationalist, believer in a strongly centralized state, and for the purposes of nationalism was ready to use the Orthodox Church as the state religion. The non-Russian inhabitants of the Empire were to be assimilated or, if they refused, to be treated as foreigners. The Jews were to be expelled from Russia and Russian Poland. For the latter the young legislator could not quite advocate a complete subordination to Russia; the Decembrists maintained relations with and counted on the support of the Polish revolutionary societies, but it is clear that he wanted Poland to be, to use another modern term, a satellite state.

Pestel elaborated his ideas, with true Germanic pedantry, in a secret treatise called *The Russian Justice,* which was to serve as the constitution for the postrevolutionary regime, and as the author said, "As an announcement to the nation of what it would be liberated from and what it could expect." When after 1905 Pestel's scheme could finally be published in Russia, its editor in the characteristic manner of the Russian intelligentsia (which believed that everything connected with the struggle against the autocracy was praiseworthy and commendable) wrote: "If one had to defend the person of Pestel from calumnies and reproaches then instead of other arguments one could point at the grandeur of this theoretical work accomplished by Pestel." [2] But if the work for its time is indeed imposing from the point of view of the author's inventiveness and the scope of interests, it is much less so in its general spirit and direction. True, Pestel planned to abolish serfdom and the class differences based on birth. True, he attracts the future Socialists by a measure of nationalization of land and the guarantee to every citizen of a lot of land sufficient for the support of a family. But he goes beyond his Jacobin prototypes in

[2] P. Shchegolev, ed., P. I. Pestel, *Russkaya Pravda,* St. Petersburg, 1906, p. vii.

groping, insofar as one could in the 1820s, toward the totalitarian state. One of his chapters is devoted to the need for and a plan of organization of the secret police and espionage.[3] With a certain lack of humor, Pestel rants against secret societies, and would have his state ban any and all private associations. In tedious detail are sketched also the functions of the uniformed police (among them strict censorship) and their number and remuneration (the systematic German in Pestel makes him elaborate why policemen should be paid much more highly than soldiers: let us face it, their duties are not as honorable!).

To be quite fair, an early nineteenth century reformer had not had the opportunity to observe, as we have had in this age, that oppression in the name of high-sounding ideas tends to be more destructive of human freedom than a defense of vested interests, and there are many in the West who have not learned this lesson even now. Pestel may be excused for not realizing, in 1820, the necessary link between freedom and the government of laws. But he also showed unmistakable signs of dictatorial temperament and ambitions. The parliamentary institutions of England and France were for him (and how often this will be echoed by the Russian revolutionaries of the century) but a cover-up for the domination of the upper classes. Before Russia could achieve a real democracy he envisaged a period of dictatorship exercised by the conspirators, and as members of the Northern Society suspected, it was not difficult to divine who would be the dictator. In his views on terror, Pestel again was more systematic than his colleagues: not only the ruling Emperor but all the possible successors to the throne, including female members of the imperial family, were to be liquidated. In the one political thinker and theorist among the Decembrists there is already much of the feverish taste for violence and coercion that will mark the path of the Russian revolutionary movement.

It was an unusual combination of circumstances that triggered off the revolt. In 1825 Emperor Alexander I, not yet fifty years of age, died suddenly. His official heir was his next eldest brother, Grand Duke Constantine. Since the latter, who inherited more than his share of the family's abnormality, had also contracted a morganatic marriage, he had agreed to waive his right to succession in favor of the third brother, Nicholas. The document determining the succession to the throne was allowed to remain secret, and Alexander's death threw the Empire into turmoil. Constantine was in far-away Warsaw where he commanded the Polish army. Nicholas in St. Petersburg waited for his brother's renunciation, while in the meantime, out of an exaggerated sense of delicacy, ordering

[3] After Pestel's apprehension the authorities probably read with high approval passages like this: "Secret inquiry or espionage is not only allowed and legal but also the most useful, if not indeed the only means through which the services of order [the police] can accomplish their aims."

the military personnel to take an oath of allegiance to Constantine. By the time the renunciation arrived and the troops were ordered to take a new oath to Nicholas on December 14, the conspirators were given a unique opportunity to exploit the confusion for their own ends.

The attempted *coup d'état* involved a gross deception. The Decembrists were aware that their political slogans would find no support, indeed no comprehension, among the populace at large. Hence the desperate attempt to exploit the common soldier's ignorance and the habit of duty by persuading him that Constantine had not renounced the throne but that it was being usurped by Nicholas, who had imprisoned his elder brother. Needless to say, under the existing conditions of communication the action could not be synchronized with the other branches of the Society and the main uprising took place in St. Petersburg. The conspirators' indecision and incapacity (the most resolute among them were far away in the southern garrisons) doomed the uprising from its inception. Only a part of the Guards were deluded into coming out to fight "for Constantine," and the revolt was put down with a cannonade.

Though the mutiny lasted but one day and was suppressed with ease, its aftereffects were to dominate the thirty-year reign of Nicholas I. Many of the liberal historians have taken the rather unreasonable view that the Emperor was unduly excited by the whole affair. But had Nicholas been the most democratic of men rather than an autocrat and martinet by nature, he would still have been shocked by the character and extent of the plot. Within days after December 14 it became clear that the revolt involved not only a handful of officers and their sympathizers in St. Petersburg but conspirators and their sympathizers who were to be found all over Russia. Among them were found the noblest names in Russia, beginning with the princely families of Obolensky and Troubetskoy, and the most promising army officers. Since their acquaintances and friends included in turn the very elite of Russian social, official, and intellectual life, the autocracy appeared to be threatened by the same class which was assumed to be its main support. Nicholas' treatment of the Decembrists, which for most historians bears the imprint of the cunning of a cruel and calculating tyrant, shows also an element of hysteria. He himself interviewed many of the prisoners. At times he raged and abused them verbally, at other times he would adopt a friendly and even brotherly tone. The Emperor of all Russia did not disdain to issue instructions in his own hand as to how the prisoners were to be treated, whether they should be chained, allowed visitors, etc. In fact, he acted less like an autocrat after an abortive revolt than a twentieth century police investigator in a totalitarian state.

From his Siberian exile one of the condemned Decembrists wrote a versified answer to his fellow poet Pushkin, who in a poem-messsage of encouragement referred to the "spark of freedom" set off by the revolutionaries. In it was the phrase "and the spark will set off a conflagration." The first Socialist organ to be published by the Russian revolutionaries in the twentieth century, *The Spark*, was to bear this proud prophecy on its masthead, thus emphasizing the thread of the revolutionary continuity linking the party of the proletariat with the noblemen who, three quarters of a century before, rose against the autocracy.

To be sure this continuity is not one of ideology. The political and social ideas of the majority of the Decembrists were of a fragile kind. Under arrest and investigation they confessed copiously, implicating others, and in many cases recanted their revolutionary intentions, throwing themselves upon the benevolence of the monarch. Their recantations (some of them have the emotional tone of those delivered by the accused in Stalin's purge trials in the 1930s) were in most cases not the product of fear and the hope of leniency; as a group they were men of considerable physical courage. But many Decembrists lacked the real revolutionary conviction of the justice of their cause, experienced a sense of guilt for having involved their friends and families, and became while in jail apologists for absolute monarchy.

But it is the fate and the popular image of the Decembrists that became a powerful impetus to the future revolutionaries. However naïve the former were, however confused their motivations and questionable their means, they were people who felt deeply the injustices of Russian life. A wiser regime and a monarch more sure of himself would have shown leniency toward the people who had recanted and whose attempt had been utterly discredited. The penalities, as much because of their character as because of their severity, surrounded the Decembrists with the aura of martyrdom, and branded Tsarism with the infamy of barbarism. It need hardly be said that there was nothing even reminiscent of a public trial. After a secret commission completed its investigation, the accused had no opportunity to appear and plead before the judges, no lawyers, or other help. Five of the Decembrists were sent to the gallows, the Tsar having commuted their sentence from being quartered to death by hanging.[4] But even the horror at this punishment, which in Russia, unlike in the contemporary West, was unusual even for the most opprobrious crimes, was dwarfed by the pity for about 120 other Decembrists, who were condemned to hard labor and exile in distant Siberia. The latter in many cases were sentenced to life. Their wives could follow them only if they forsook their children and at the price of never returning to European Russia. Some of the 120 found themselves in Siberia simply because at one time they had belonged to the secret society, though they had left it before the actual plot. Guilt by association was a valid

---

[4] Curiously enough, in view of the general barbarity of the Russian penal laws, formal death sentence, because of religious reasons, was not then on the statute book. Legend has it that one of the condemned whose rope broke during the ceremony exclaimed: "Poor Russia! They don't even know how to hang properly."

and eminent basis for punishment. The hardier among the exiles managed
to adjust to the conditions of nineteenth century Siberian life, but the
weaker ones went insane or died. Relatively few worked their way back
to Russia (even on the completion of the prison or hard-labor term, a political offender would be prohibited from settling in European Russia). Only
after Nicholas' death in 1855 was a general amnesty for the Decembrists proclaimed, and the aged survivors could rejoin their families. For
more than a generation the story of the Decembrists and of their families
hung over Russian society as a mute commentary on the inhumanity of
the system that continued to enact vengeance on people who no longer
represented any danger.

The real tragedy of the Decembrist revolt is, however, much greater
than its human component. December 14 set its stamp on the whole
reign of Nicholas I. It is most unlikely that even without it he would
have become a believer in constitutionalism or liberalism. But he was a
man of intelligence who saw and deplored, even if only for power reasons, the sources of Russia's backwardness and social weakness. Had the
rebellion not occurred it is probable that he would have tackled by far
the greatest evil—peasant serfdom. But the Decembrists made him and
his circle fearful of any and every change. During the years of the most
intense industrial and social development in the rest of Europe, Russia's
economy and society remained stultified by serfdom. When the reform
did come in the 1860s it could not undo the damage of four lost decades.
The peasant problem remained in Russia the main source of backwardness
and, in an indirect way, of the revolutionary spasms that intermittently
seized society until 1917. Not for the last time an abortive revolution damaged the cause of reform.

The Decembrists and their legend stand at the beginning of the modern era of Russian politics. The last of the myth of eighteenth century
type of enlightened absolutism was dispersed in Russia with the exile of
the Decembrists. For the rest of the nineteenth century reaction and revolution were to face each other, the periods of compromise and reform
appearing as miragelike interludes in their struggle. To the Tsarist regime
the lesson was very clear: society including its highest and privileged
classes could not be trusted. If a segment of the nobility, many of them
with special ties to the throne, could develop as the act of indictment
charged, "the insane lust for change," where could the security for the
autocratic institution be found? The regime's answer was to attempt to
transform Russia, since the classical model of autocracy in which the
loyalty or apathy of the subjects could be taken for granted was no longer
sufficient, into something more approximating the modern police state.
The immediate bureaucratic innovation was the creation of the Third
Section of the Imperial Chancery. This was the lineal ancestor and prototype of the notorious institutions of secret police that have flourished in

Russia, both Tsarist and Soviet, down to our own day. The Okhrana, the Cheka, and today's Committee of State Security have all shared with the Third Section the grandiose and moralistic concept of preservation of the state going far beyond the prosaic functions of the ordinary police. The Third Section was to preserve and enhance the general welfare by rooting out corruption and subversion. Some of the sentimental feeling with which modern totalitarianism surrounds such institutions was already evident in the legend of Nicholas handing the chief of the Third Section, Count Benckendorff, a white handerchief; the secret police was to dry the tears and soothe the troubles of the faithful Russian people.

More prosaically the Third Section was to engage in wide-scale political espionage, it was to investigate denunciations and, as any wise government would, nip subversion in the beginning before it could (as on December 14) flower into unmistakable treason. Since the ordinary organs of administration had shown their ineptness if not indeed criminal negligence, the secret police was to bypass the routine channels of the ministries, and its head was to become a special confidant of the sovereign and one of the highest dignitaries of the empire. The activities of the Third Section were soon enlarged to include such seemingly unrelated fields as the problems of cultural policy, statistics, etc.[5] The Third Section was to pioneer in the development of what later on became a special contribution of the Russian secret police: a special philosophy of treason or subversion. Most states have had a secret police and many of them have used *agents provocateurs*. In Russia, however, first of modern states, random search for traitors and spies has given place to a more philosophical principle of police action: just as evil sits in every man, so potential treason is always somewhere in society; it may be found hiding in a literary criticism, historical work, or an innocent-appearing painting. Hence the function of an enlightened secret police is not merely to prevent or to punish overt acts of subversion, but also to bring into light and punishment latent and nonobvious treason. We shall see later on how the government agents not only infiltrated the secret revolutionary organizations but also how, paradoxically, they not infrequently initiated and abetted revolutionary activities. And in time the revolutionary movement was to develop strong traits of psychological resemblance to its pursuers: an inquisitorial spirit, constant search for "treason" or deviation, and contempt for legal norms and rules.

The seeds of totalitarianism that Nicholas planted in Russian soil were nowhere more evident than in the cultural sphere. Under the old regime prior to 1825 there was a general uneasiness and a rather clumsy persecution of Western political ideas. The French Revolution had put an end

[5] Under Stalin the secret police was to become the custodian of the state archives, which in a sense made its head, next to the dictator himself, the chief historian of the Soviet Union.

to the flirtation of the Russian autocracy with ideas of the Enlightenment. The year 1815 marked a further step in reaction, which was symbolized in the international sphere by the Holy Alliance of which Alexander was the main founder. With the Decembrists' revolt, the government was brought to the realization of the importance and danger of ideas, philosophical as well as political, and of the far-reaching consequences of artistic and journalistic expression. It now assumed a positive and frightening curiosity as to the press and literature. The *leitmotif* of a historical novel, private passion of a poem, all would now be scrutinized by the highest authorities for the hints of a treasonous or unorthodox sentiment. The regime was now eager to buy journalists and litterateurs. The Emperor's personal protection and censorship was extended to Russia's greatest writer. Pushkin, who had been connected by friendship with some of the Decembrists, had to endure the galling and humiliating treatment of a schoolboy, being in turn praised and scolded for his productions.[6] A whole new breed of journalists, paid by the government, the so-called "reptile press" now sprung into being. They were expected to defend the ideas of absolutism, the Orthodox Church, and Russian nationalism, and to scoff at the foreign ideas and innovations. Since the latter task was impossible without communicating what those ideas were about, even the most servile and mercenary writers would occasionally find themselves in jail. Such was also at times the lot of the official censors who could never be sure that the vigilance and zeal of the high officials would not find a hidden meaning in the most innocuous novel or article.

Modern Russian culture was being born in the atmosphere of intellectual espionage and suspicion. In a sense, this attempt at repression made it inevitable that when some of the chains were removed Russian literature was to become passionately involved in the political and social question, and artistic and intellectual criticism became one of the main avenues of revolutionary propaganda. Try as it might, nineteenth century autocracy was simply incapable of regimenting cultural life in the modern totalitarian fashion. Its repression and chicaneries created this split between the educated class and the government, which in time led to the term "intelligentsia" being almost synonymous with the spirit of opposition to the main institutions of the Empire. It was never healed until both the Empire and the intelligentsia perished in the Bolshevik revolution.

Nicholas' policies had another and disastrous effect on Russian social

---

[6] An article of his (ordered by the government) was returned to him by the Emperor, through the Chief of the Third Section, with the following annotation: "Answer him, thanking him for this paper, but point out to him that the principle he advances to the effect that education and genius are everything is a dangerous one for all governments; one which has actually led him to the edge of the abyss. . . ." Quoted from Sidney Monas, *The Third Section, Police and Society in Russia under Nicholas I,* Cambridge, Mass., 1961, p. 207.

thought, and eventually on the revolutionary movement. They increased the already burning sense of inferiority toward the West. The thought of Russia's "unculturedness" was increasingly to haunt the intellectuals. By a very simple process of compensation for this humiliation at their country's backwardness, nowhere more evident than in the political field, the intellectuals were prone to postulate a messianic vision of their country's future: somehow because of this very same backwardness it was Russia's destiny to avoid the vices and shortcomings of Western civilization and to establish a more just and perfect type of society. We have seen how in our own day the realization of backwardness on the part of the emerging nations often finds an expression in chauvinism, in claims of spiritual superiority over the materialistic West. This process worked more subtly among the nineteenth century Russian intelligentsia, but it also had far-reaching and unfortunate effects. It hampered a realistic accounting of their society's strength and weaknesses. Part of the future popularity of socialism among the Russian intellectuals was clearly a reflection of the fact that here was a *Western* ideology critical and destructive of the contemporary European institutions, which chastised backward Russia without extolling the false gods of the West.

The generation of Nicholas I was to see only the beginning of this involved intellectual journey. For the time being, the imperfect repression of Western ideas endowed them only with the added charm of a forbidden fruit. Official persecution often succeeded in turning commonplace thinkers into heroes of liberty, and a day's sensation into a momentous event in Russia's cultural history. Such was the fate of the celebrated *Philosophical Letter* written by a retired officer, Chaadayev, which through some mischance was allowed to appear in print in 1836. The letter (originally written in French and privately circulated) was a somewhat pompous historical essay bewailing Russia's lack of tradition and culture: "Where are our sages, where are our thinkers . . . who thinks for us today?" The author discounted the previous attempt at civilizing the country; Peter the Great had left Russia only the outer covering of civilization. He referred to the tragedy of the Decembrists: ". . . another great prince . . . has led us from one end of Europe to the other; having returned from this triumphant march through the world's most civilized countries we brought back the ideas and aspirations which resulted in a great calamity which set us back half a century." [7] It was the Orthodox Church that the author held responsible for isolating Russia from the main currents of Western thought.

Little in this elegant exercise of French prose could not be heard daily in the more intellectual drawing rooms of St. Petersburg. But the publication of the letter in Russian was treated as an act of subversion. Fright-

[7] M. Gershenzon, *The Works of Chaadayev*, Moscow, 1913, Vol. I, pp. 84–85.

ful irony was mixed with punishment. Chaadayev was proclaimed to be mentally ill and put under joint medical and police supervision. One recalls how Mr. Khrushchev when confronted with a nonobjective painting by a Soviet artist wondered aloud whether the painter was a normal man or a pervert. But it is a significant measure of the dubious progress in political treatment of nonconformity that Chaadayev's punishment was a calculated piece of sadism on the part of Nicholas' government, while the outburst of Russia's recent dictator seems to have been spontaneous.

Chaadayev's letter stated in sensible, unrevolutionary and unoriginal terms the essence of what was later on to become the argument of the Westernizers: only through the adoption of modern European institutions could Russia achieve a measure of civilization and play its rightful role in world history. That much had already been implicit in the plans of the northern group of the Decembrists, and indeed in the schemes of the Tsars from Peter the Great to Alexander I.[8] By castigating the *Philosophical Letter* as the work of a madman the regime really played a joke on itself insofar as the future course of Russian social thought was concerned. Deprived of any middle ground where their ideas could affect the existing institutions, the Russian political thinkers were bound to find refuge in the realms of philosophical and historical fantasy. Unable to touch the earth, to put their ideas to the test of discussion, popular acceptance, and practicability, the would-be reformers were apt to soar into the heights of metaphysics, heated debates of the philosophy of history, coming down only to construct futile schemes of revolution and ending more often than not in the Tsar's prisons or in exile in Siberia or in the West.

It was in the Russia of the 1840s that the idealistic philosophy of Germany was received most enthusiastically and voraciously. Nothing seems more esoteric under the conditions of Russian society of the time than this passionate interest in the ideas and philosophical constructs of Hegel, Fichte, and Schilling. In the country of their origin these ideas were already losing their hold over the minds of the young intellectuals. One of them, Karl Marx, noted that the philosophers have only been interested in various interpretations of the world while the point was how to change it. But in Russia the German philosophy provided both an escape from the depressing reality of Nicholas' times and a guide to action. There was much of the adolescent self-intoxication with the grandiose concepts of the Absolute, the World Spirit, and the like. But the young Russian intellectuals did not heed Hegel's warning that philosophy comes too late to tell the world what it should be (nor for that matter did Hegel). Sooner or later they would find in Hegel or Fichte what they

[8] Chaadayev's only originality lay in his dubious thesis that the main reason for Russia's stagnation had been her adoption of Orthodox rather than Catholic Christianity. He already displayed the intelligentsia's facility for sweeping historical generalities and their nearsightedness. When they said "the West" they saw France and England and seldom Spain or Portugal.

really sought: a criticism of the *status quo* or even a call to revolution. Alexander Herzen, groping his way to revolution, became convinced that "the philosophy of Hegel is the *algebra of revolution;* it frees man to an extraordinary degree and leaves not a stone upon a stone of the whole Christian world, the world of traditions which have outlived themselves." [9] It is doubtful that Professor Hegel, a loyal subject of the Prussian monarchy, would have agreed with this summary of his philosophy. But twenty years later other Russian radicals found no difficulty in deducing from Utilitarianism, the philosophy of the English liberals, a rationale for terrorism. Political oppression is insufferable without the consolation of a religion. To the young angry men of the 1840s the traditional religious concepts of the Orthodox Church no longer held much validity, though the more conservative members of the intelligentsia, the Slavophiles, were soon to attempt to construct, needless to say with the help of Hegel, an intellectualized version of the Orthodoxy. German idealism came close, for a time, to filling up the void, but then it had to give way to a still newer and more enticing faith, socialism.

This search for a new philosophy-religion among Russia's rising intellectual class had a frenzied character and it would often appear, had not the circumstances frequently been so tragic, as somewhat comical. The great literary critic Vissarion Belinsky (1810–1848) in the course of his brief and troubled life went through the stages of fervent attachment to Fichte then to Hegel, then through a violent reaction against Hegel's "acceptance of reality," and eventually reached for the primitive materialistic viewpoint of another German sage, Feuerbach. The latest issue of a French or German periodical would bring with it a revolution in the young men's beliefs and interests. Belinsky, the originator of the thesis that art must have a social message, the thesis which was to have such sad consequences for the Soviet literature, also went through several political transformations. Once a eulogist of the historical role of the Russian Emperor, he then proclaimed himself a Socialist. His nonliterary judgments were arrived at after a hasty and often very fragmentary reading of the authors. Rousseau was contemptuously dismissed for his "asinine" sentimentality. (He had read only his *Confessions.*) His explorations of German philosophy were limited by his inability to read German. (This fact, more than anything else, has embarrassed his admirers who would drag him in as an ancestor of the Marxian viewpoint on art.) This passionate dilettantism and the tendency to seduction by the latest theory were characteristic of the Russian intelligentsia.

Intellectual life could flourish with relative freedom only in the private circles. The universities were under a continuous and meticulous supervision of the government, and the professors were under a strict and

[9] Quoted in Martin Malia, *Alexander Herzen and the Birth of Russian Socialism*, Cambridge, Mass., 1961, p. 228.

humiliating regimen. (It was not unheard of for a *professor* to be fined for being late for his lecture!) Strict censorship choked the newspapers and periodicals and any publisher or writer was automatically under suspicion. (Belinsky, who never published anything that might be interpreted as subversive, was "invited" while on his deathbed to visit the Third Section and his funeral was attended by its agents on the lookout for his friends.) The circles, groups of friends who gathered for discussion and became in fact private social and literary clubs, were the only places where foreign theories and Russia's social problems could be discussed with relative freedom. As it was, even private houses and discussion groups were not free from an intrusion by a secret agent. In the fantastic world of Nicholas I a discussion group could grow insensibly into a plot and private hospitality could assume the proportions of a state crime.

Such was to be the fate of the Petrashevsky circle. Its originator, M. V. Butashevich-Petrashevsky, was one of those contrary and sardonic natures whose temperament would always draw them to rebellion and nonconformity. As a boy he would smoke in the lyceum (a kind of combination high school and college) because it was forbidden, but stopped when he graduated. When Petrashevsky heard that a person who met the Emperor on his walks and did not salute him was being punished, he is reported to have said that if a similar mishap befell him he would tell the authorities that he was nearsighted and that the Emperor should wear a rattle on his head so that his faithful subjects could recognize him from afar.[10] It is not surprising that Petrashevsky was slated for trouble.

The Petrashevsky circle gained most fame by its connection with the great writers Fyodor Dostoevsky and Saltykov (Shchedrin). Actually the circle deserves more attention from historians of the revolutionary movement, for in it we find some of the ideas and psychological traits that were to be so strikingly developed in the future revolutionary enterprises. Petrashevsky's own ideas went beyond the notions of a plot like the Decembrists' and in the direction of propaganda and agitation. In 1844–45 he co-authored an innocently titled *Pocket Dictionary of Foreign Words in the Russian Language.* The most conscientious and fearful censor would yawn and pass (as one did in the first instance) a book of this kind, which as a matter of fact contained the most unheard of "subversive" sentiments in the guise of explanations and definitions. Into the explanations of such terms as "constitution," "oratory," "nationality," the author slipped criticisms of the Tsarist regimes and references to the Socialist movements of the West. Petrashevsky had a sense of humor, a rare trait in a revolutionary. Under "nationality," after referring to Peter the Great, he writes ". . . [his heirs] have brought us close to the ideal of political, social, and human existence . . . [in our state] *there is no*

[10] V. I. Semevsky, *M. V. Butashevich-Petrashevsky,* Moscow, 1922, p. 147.

*longer place for the domination of sheer custom, routine, and uncon-
sciously accepted prejudices, but it is guided by science, knowledge, and
dignity.*" Under the heading "egalitarianism" he appended an indictment
of peasant serfdom: "As the teaching of Christ is equality, slavery should
be erased in the Christian world. . . . All the landowners should turn
their forests and waters to the community at large." And "there is no example of a successful struggle to recover lost rights without bloody
sacrifices and persecutions." This is already the voice of future revolution.

Alongside the written propaganda (to use the term in the narrower
sense employed later by the Bolsheviks: an attempt to indoctrinate the
educated class), we find in Petrashevsky's activity rudimentary efforts
at agitation, i.e., the spread of political dissatisfaction among the lower
class. This sometimes took odd forms. Petrashevsky disliked women; his
mother was a hateful person, and he was wont to assert that most of the
pejorative words in Russian are of the feminine gender. He would romance women, he explained, only to draw them into revolutionary
activity and through them their men acquaintances. Himself a nobleman,
he joined the Townsmen's Dancing Club so as to extend his romantic-
political tactics to the lower classes.

To organize his circle, the young revolutionary began his propaganda
in his early twenties, recruiting acquaintances from his school and from
the Ministry of Foreign Affairs, where he was a minor official. The circle
took the form of weekly receptions, on Fridays, in Petrashevsky's disorderly quarters. He was one of those persons who through their innate
liveliness, humor, and eccentricity attract companions and visitors. They
came to drink tea and to discuss foreign books. Very soon the evenings
took on a more organized form. One of the guests would read a paper on
a book or a problem and the others would join in a heated discussion, the
very model of those verbal orgies of the Russian intelligentsia where the
talk could begin with a topic in biology, shift to the social question, light
on the deplorable condition of the country, and conclude with revolutionary sentiments.

The word "socialism" was then of very recent currency. It referred
mostly to the teaching of the individuals whom Marx was to call the
"Utopian Socialists," Robert Owen, Saint-Simon, and Charles Fourier.
Their ideas soon circulated in Russia, and the Petrashevsky circle became
the first center of extended discussion of socialism, communism, and
the other exciting French and German novelties that seeped through
Nicholas I's censorship. The Utopians were rather far from being revolutionaries (hence the derisive name given them by Marx). They looked
for munificent patrons, if need be absolute monarchs, to enable them to
put their ideas of social organization into effect. In Russia, of course,
their ideas were immediately linked with plans of a revolutionary trans-

formation of society. Petrashevsky and many of his group became enthusiastic Fourierists. Charles Fourier (1772–1837), an amiable madman,
believed himself to be the Newton of the social sciences who had discovered the universal law of harmony and attraction. It is now perhaps
difficult to see how reasonable people could swallow the insanities of
Fourier's writings and consider him the leading genius of the century.
But he collected an amazing number of disciples, not only in his native
country but also in the distant United States and in Russia. To be charitable, Fourier's main attraction was not his vision of progress wherein
mankind will achieve seas of lemonade, antilions (i.e., creatures which
are as useful and benevolent as their present ancestors are predatory
and dangerous) and other pleasing fancies, but his proposal of *phal-
anstères,* the communities of cooperative labor and living. The phalan-
steries would protect their members from unpleasant work and other
deprivations; no man or woman would be tied down to one job any more
than to one spouse; there would be pleasing alternation and variety in
both respects.[11]

Socialist historians of socialism are somewhat haughty with those who
refer to the undoubted insanity of Fourier and the phantasmagoric character of his system. But to many and fairly reasonable people of his time
the phalanstery could appeal as the dream of an island of harmony and
contentment in the turbulent world of rising industrialism. That his fantastic ideas had an ecstatic reception from persons such as Petrashevsky
and others is a reflection not only of their undoubted eccentricity but also
of the fantastic and hopeless reality of Nicholas I's Russia. From what
direction could one expect reform or improvement? The cruel reality
made one seize upon any, even the most impractical and fantastic dream
of reform and salvation.

Petrashevsky's attempt to put Fourier's teaching in practice is a
pathetic example of the problem the Russian revolutionaries had (and
this remained true at least until the Revolution of 1905) in reaching the
masses on whose behalf they were allegedly striving and suffering. He
decided to institute a form of phalanstery on his own estate. As the first
step he undertook to persuade his serfs to abandon their miserable huts
and to move into a communal building, which he was erecting at his own
expense. But his speeches to the peasants about the benefits of communal
living would elicit no reaction. The peasants would simply say, "It is
your will, you know best, we are ignorant folk, as Your Honor will
order, so we shall do." [12] The communal building was almost ready for
occupancy when one night it was burnt down, obviously by the peasants.
Such was one of the first encounters between the Socialist theory and the
reality of the Russian peasants' life.

[11] Who would do the *unpleasant* work, e.g., garbage collection? Fourier had the
insight that children love dirt. Hence for them this would be a labor of love.
[12] Semevsky, *op. cit.,* p. 174.

The experience did not cure the eccentric young revolutionary of his predilection for Fourier. It only strengthened his conviction that Russia was a "savage country" (Lenin was to say, "We live in a half-savage country"). In a fine optimistic spirit, seldom absent in a Russian radical, he concluded that it would take five years to indoctrinate the masses in the virtue and benefits of Fourier's teachings. The word "masses," another link with the future revolutionaries, was quite often on Petrashevsky's lips. He placed no confidence in the possibility of a military coup in the style of the Decembrists. Military life and discipline, he believed, stultified people. Didn't Fourier consider the military as parasites? And the officers are apt to develop peculiar ideas about most things. No, the only hope was in the masses and in a popular insurrection.

As behooves a revolutionary group, the Petrashevsky circle was split by vigorous debates and dissensions. The Fourierist views were countered by other theories and plans of action. There was a group calling themselves Communists who looked for an immediate peasant uprising. For Petrashevsky himself, Fourier's views were not incompatible with private property, and at one time he believed that they could be disseminated among the landlords. Despite his eccentricity and natural rebelliousness, he was as much a would-be reformer as a revolutionary, and he reminds us of those figures in France who after youthful infatuation with the more bizarre aspects of Fourierism and Saint-Simonianism became entrepreneurs, bankers, and technologists.[13] But there was no scope for an amateur reformer in contemporary Russia and Petrashevsky's most innocuous writings (like his quite sensible pamphlet about the enhancement of the value of the landed estates) were to be used as an additional proof of his subversiveness. A member of the circle jotted down a judgment on his era, which unfortunately is relevant not only to Nicholas I's times:

> In Russia everything is a secret or a falsehood, and therefore one cannot have reliable information about anything. . . . The policy of the government is to keep many things secret or to lie about them. . . . Slaves willingly or unwillingly try to anticipate the wishes of their oppressors. Hence the tendency to secretiveness and to lie has become with us a habit.[14]

The writer adds that he talks about the Russian slaves, i.e., his contemporaries and not those Russians "who after the destruction of despotism will amaze mankind by their example of heroism and noble feelings." Alas!

In 1849 the circle, long infiltrated by the police, was broken and its members arrested. Unlike the Decembrists, the accused did not contain

---

[13] How often the followers of an esoteric political cult become, if given a chance, hard-boiled men of affairs! Who, observing the Russian revolutionaries before 1917, could have foretold how many of them would become the eminently practical administrators, diplomats, and industrial managers!

[14] Semevsky, *op. cit.*, p. 207.

this time members of the higher aristocracy. They came for most part from among the ranks of smaller landowners and petty officials. The secret police attempted to blow up this discussion group into a nationwide conspiracy. The punishments, considering the fact that the accused, unlike the Decembrists, talked but did not do very much about revolution, were startling in their brutality and refined cruelty. Twenty-one members of the circle, including Dostoevsky and Petrashevsky, were condemned to death. They were arraigned for the execution, when the announcement was made that the supreme penalty was commuted to hard labor and exile (the delaying of the commutation till the last moment was deliberate).

The fate of the Petrashevsky circle, a generation after the Decembrists, epitomizes the character and the effects of Nicholas I's reign. On the surface, the suppression of radical activity and thought was complete. The revolutionary years of 1830 and 1848, which shook thrones and upset institutions all over Europe, were reflected in Russia only by increased repression. The Polish insurrection of 1830 was put down and Russian Poland stripped of her autonomy. The Russian state appeared as the fortress of autocracy, the mainstay of opposition to liberal ideas and constitutionalism throughout all Europe. But the stability and the power of the regime were bought at the price of neglecting the needed reforms, and of leaving the Russian Empire incomparably farther behind Western Europe at the death of Nicholas I in 1855 than it had been in 1825. Russia's defeats in the Crimean War (1854-56) showed that reforms could not be postponed, and that the solidity of the imperial institutions had been a mirage.

But the longest lasting and the most harmful legacy of the era was the hostility between the government and the educated classes. In the latter it was to breed a fear and loathing of the autocracy that made them see every government, even one bent upon reform, as an uncompromising enemy. Whatever liberalism was to arise in Russia, it was always to be somewhat shamefaced at not being revolutionary radicalism, and always reluctant to acknowledge that there could be a threat to liberty from the left as well as from the right. The very completeness of political oppression of Nicholas' times, the government's ability to control religion, literature, and other seemingly private concerns of its citizens, taught the society the dangerous lesson that everything in the last resort is dependent on politics. Thus the autocracy prepared the ground for socialism.

2. Bakunin and Herzen

Russian socialism was born as a twin revolt against the native autocracy and Western liberalism. Two names stand at its beginning: Michael

Bakunin and Alexander Herzen. They best epitomize its tone: a tortured, often self-contradictory search for a third solution, its alternating moods of despair at the actual chances of revolution, and of a messianic hope that Russia and the Russians might teach the world and might show the road to freedom and social justice. Strictly speaking, neither Bakunin nor Herzen can be counted as Socialists. They defy classifications, and any description—socialism, anarchism, Populism—fails to do justice to the extraordinary variety and complexity of ideas that sprang from the pen of each man, to the succession of moods and political positions they adopted in their lifetimes. But they were reaching for socialism, i.e., writing and acting in the conviction that a purely political reform is not enough, and only a wide social and economic transformation would regenerate Russia. With them Russian radical thought emerges from the drawing rooms of St. Petersburg and Moscow, appears on the European stage, and in turn begins to feed and form the revolutionary strivings at home.

The legacy of Michael Bakunin (1814-1876) belongs principally to Western anarchism. In his own country, Bakunin left few disciples. But he was in his lifetime the embodiment of the radical *ethos*, an example of sheer revolutionary energy that passed into history as a characteristic of the whole movement.

Bakunin was one of those natures that arouse either enthusiasm or reprobation. Any attempt at a "sober" biography is likely to be tinged with hypocrisy: an unfriendly biographer will inevitably imply that his rebellious spirit was a function of his disorderly personality; no conceivable social system, no conceivable occupation save that of a revolutionary could accommodate and appease him. A friendly writer will have to overlook or minimize his negative sides: his racism, xenophobia, and his utter irresponsibility, which made him associate with clearly criminal and demented characters such as Nechaev. But in Bakunin we see, in an exaggerated form, those strengths and weaknesses of the Russian revolutionary movement which go far to explain its history, at once heroic and pathetic, and its final defeat (for that, in a sense, was the meaning of its absorption by Bolshevism) in which there was more pathos than heroism.

Bakunin was born a nobleman and tried his hand at one of the few professions open to his class: the army. After giving up his commission he served an apprenticeship in the Moscow philosophical and literary circles, and soon sought escape to the freer world of the West. In Europe (that is how, consciously or unconsciously, the Russian intellectuals referred to the West in contradistinction to Russia) this student of German philosophy soon plunged into the radical and Socialist movements that put their imprint upon the eighteen forties and fifties. Bakunin became— he was always to remain—what might be called a visiting revolutionary. There was no insurrection, actual or planned—Prague in 1848, Dresden in 1849, Poland in 1863, the numerous attempted revolts in France and Italy—

in which he was not ready to fight, lend his assistance as a drafter of manifestoes, theorist of revolutionary dictatorship, and the like.

The middle period of his adult life was spent in prison and exile. The Austrian government handed him over to its Russian ally in 1851. There is an anecdote that upon being handed over to the Tsarist police, Bakunin, in his way always a Russian patriot, exclaimed how good it was to be on Russian soil even if in chains. (This was, a twentieth century writer might say, a Freudian slip. The actual transfer of Bakunin, who was a fighter for Polish independence, took place on Polish soil, though within the Russian state.) The unsentimental Russian gendarme replied: "It is strictly forbidden to talk."

During Bakunin's incarceration in Russia an incident took place that his biographers have found difficult to explain. Nicholas I had, as we have seen, a truly Soviet passion for hearing or reading recantations of his imprisoned enemies. It was suggested to Bakunin that he should try. The result was his *Confession* (it came to light only after the Bolshevik Revolution), which the Tsar read with a great deal of interest and, on the whole, approval. In it Bakunin flattered and eulogized the Tsar, and denounced the Western liberals and parliamentarians. It will not do to present the *Confession* as a Soviet biographer, Steklov, did as a clever and justifiably mendacious document designed to enable Bakunin to have his sentence softened, or to hedge on this point as does Professor Venturi, who sees it as "a photographic negative of Bakunin's personality," and its purpose ". . . consciously . . . to deceive and enlist the sympathies of his royal gaoler." [15] Bakunin would not have been human had he not sought an alleviation of his prison regimen, which he felt was killing him. (The next generation of the Russian revolutionaries would have scorned such devices. They sought martyrdom, as we shall see in the case of Chernyshevsky.) But parts of the *Confession* have a very genuine and even passionate ring. Some of the explanation must be that the revolutionary often found it easier, and this was to remain sadly true, to talk and to sympathize with the autocrat than with a Western-style liberal and moderate reformer.

Like his gendarme Nicholas was rather unsentimental and Bakunin's *Confession* did not bring him freedom. It is only in the next reign that the imprisonment in the fortress was exchanged for an exile to Siberia, where Bakunin could at least move around and enjoy human company. Continued imprisonment for a man with his temperament would have ended, as it did for many others, in insanity. From Siberia he found it rather easy to escape. In 1861 he was back in London enquiring about the next revolution.

To a superficial observer, Bakunin was a "typical Russian revolutionary" or, worse yet, a "typical Russian": huge, gluttonous, eternally smok-

[15] Franco Venturi, *The Roots of Populism*, New York, 1960, p. 57.

ing and drinking tea (or stronger stuff), always sponging money from his friends, and most disorderly in his habits. This stereotype is as exaggerated as the other one of the Russian intellectual: fastidious and cultured to a fault. But stereotypes are sometimes more influential than reality. Lenin, and this was not unconnected with his revulsion at much of the Russian revolutionary tradition, displayed the utmost bourgeois sobriety and orderliness in his personal life, and nobody could be more unsympathetic to any kind of bohemianism. The same traits in turn became ingrained in the official Soviet man whose conformity, and not only in politics, would make Bakunin and Herzen turn in their graves.

It is almost superfluous to say that Bakunin never worked out a systematic philosophy of revolution or of socialism. His socialism was mostly of a visceral type: the revolt against any kind of oppression and injustice, rejection of any palliatives or halfway measures. At one time he was a follower of a version of Panslavism, the idea of a democratic federation of all the Slav nations. But no major radical philosophy of his time failed for a period to interest him or to hold his allegiance: Marxism, Saint-Simonianism, Proudhonism. It was inevitable, however, that in practical politics he should be a believer in the necessity of revolutionary dictatorships, and in theory in anarchism. The latter made him sensitive to the authoritarian potentialities lurking in the teachings of Karl Marx. Marxism was to him but another way of arriving at the centralized oppressive state, and "he who says state says 'oppression,' and he who says oppression says exploitation." Bakunin would have approved what another though Christian and pacifist anarchist, Leo Tolstoy, said, that he who has not been in jail does not know what the state is. For his period, with its illusions, it was a most perceptive statement: "Those previous workers having just become rulers or representatives of the people will cease being workers; they will look at the workers from their heights, they will represent not the people but themselves. . . . He who doubts it does not know human nature." To Steklov this is a typical "confusion" of Bakunin, which was dissipated by the clear light of Marxism-Leninism, but the Soviet author who died in Stalin's concentration camp probably had time to reconsider his opinion.[16] To be sure, anarchism is excellent as a critique of other political systems, but hardly so as a positive prescription. Like other anarchists before and after him, Bakunin could only repeat: Smash the state, destroy every relationship of domination and inequality. But then what? To that impolite question Bakunin, like other anarchists, could only answer with vague suggestions of purely voluntary cooperation, federalism of communes, and similar notions.

Marx and Marxism became for Bakunin, toward the end of his life, as much an embodiment of evil as the Tsarist regime. The quarrel between the two men and their followers broke up the First International. In the

---

[16] Y. M. Steklov, *Fighters for Socialism*, Moscow, 1923, Vol. I, p. 227.

West and especially in the Latin American countries the historic quarrel marked the real beginning of the hostility between the Marxist and the anarchosyndicalist elements of the workers' movement, the quarrel that flared up into open fighting as recently as during the Spanish Civil War. There was a personal element in Bakunin's hostility toward Marx, with whom at times he was in friendly personal relations and whose *Capital* he was supposed to translate. (Like most similar endeavors of Bakunin this remained unfinished.) He could write: "Himself a Jew, he attracts whether in London or in France, but especially in Germany, a whole heap of Yids, more or less intelligent, intriguers, busybodies and speculators, as the Jews are likely to be, commercial and bank agents, writers . . . correspondents . . . who stand one foot in the world of finance and the other in socialism." [17]

Anti-Semitism has been, more often than Socialist historians have liked to admit, a strong element in the make-up of radical movements. Marx himself was not entirely free from it. But with Bakunin it was a veritable obsession grounded in his temperament and self-delusion. Forgetting his aristocratic background, he fancied himself as a representative of the "masses." "They [the Jews] are always exploiters of other people's labor; they have a basic fear and loathing of the masses, whom whether openly or not they hold in contempt." Anti-Semitism flowed into and reinforced his Germanophobia. There was an element of personal pique in his hatreds: he had an unmistakable feeling of inferiority toward Marx. But mainly both the Jews and the Germans epitomized the qualities that Bakunin loathed, possibly because he felt their lack in himself: assiduity, orderliness, the practical and business sense. The sum total of those attributes was the autocratic state or, equally bad, the wretched bourgeois culture of the West.[18] Socialism in the West was being ruined by the "Jews" (among whom Bakunin included, at times, persons he disliked even when not Jewish by any possible criteria) who were pushing it into the authoritarian path of Marxism. As for Russia, even Bakunin could not make a Jew out of Nicholas I, but then the imperial house was German in its origin and connections, and so were the higher strata of the officialdom. Thus Russian autocracy was "really" German, or as he phrased it at times "Germano-Tartar." The Russian people, i.e., the peasant masses, were democratic by instinct but enslaved and kept backward by an alien oligarchy.

Bakunin's personal phobias ought not to obscure the ideological element behind them. What he was against were essentially the main components of modern society: industrialism, the centralized state, organization, and the like. Here for all his peculiarities he is at one with a powerful

---

[17] *Ibid.*, p. 288.
[18] The study of the national character can produce almost any conclusion. It was fashionable among certain English historians of the nineteenth century to attribute constitutionalism to the "Germanic spirit" and to contrast with it the instinctive penchant toward despotism found among the Latin nations and the Slavs.

tradition of Russian Populism, the tradition dominant among the revolutionaries until Marxism became influential, and which even penetrated Marxism and gave it much of its appeal and revolutionary energy. What complements this rejection of the "West" (and Bakunin simplifies the task by his fiat that undesirable elements of the Russian reality are Western-German) is the faith in the "people." The latter, who in Bakunin's time meant the peasants, became the repository of moral virtue, as contrasted with the corruption of the Western bourgeoisie. Unsullied by the Judeo-Germanic ideas, uncorrupted by Western materialism, the Russian peasant, thank God, has preserved his simplicity and virtue, his inherent democratic instinct, which will make a fit foundation for the future Socialist commonwealth. That this philosophy combined wishful thinking with ignorance of the actual conditions of the Russian peasant's life, that it equated material backwardness with moral virtues, and that finally it concealed xenophobia and injured national pride caused by the dazzling progress of the Western nations can be seen more clearly by us than by a Russian revolutionary in the nineteenth century. And yet today we hear similar voices and arguments from Asia and Africa, and they find sympathetic echoes in the West. But what has escaped many of the critics of Russian Populism who see its view of the peasantry as a combination of revulsion against the West and a sentimental idealization of the common man is its inherently undemocratic condescension. The peasant is seen as the noble savage. He is an apt instrument, if properly led, to wreak terrible vengeance upon the hated government and the exploiting classes, and to show up the contemptible bourgeoisie of the West with their smug satisfaction in their progress and parliaments.

Bakunin's contribution to Russian Populism was mostly through the legend of his own personality and his revolutionary skirmishes. In his last years in Switzerland, he was the object of much interest and some veneration among the young radical intelligentsia who flocked to the West in the 1870s. His writings and teachings were among the influences that stirred the students to go to the people in the same decade and to try to educate the Russian peasant for the revolution. But the leadership of the radical movement and thought had by the sixties passed into other hands. To the new generation Bakunin still epitomized revolutionary energy and intransigeance, but their minds did not follow his exuberant anarchism and his dreams of vast peasant uprisings. In his own country Bakunin left no school. His violent anti-Marxism made him a rather embarrassing ancestor for the future generations of the Socialists. In the long line of the revolutionary figures that begins with the Decembrists and ends with Lenin, Bakunin stands somewhat to the side, ready to take on any and all proponents of oppression and coercive institutions, and strangely attractive despite his huge faults.

Unlike Bakunin the advocate of action and violence (if with a touch of Don Quixote), his contemporary and friend Alexander Herzen represents the intellectual and moral side of the revolutionary appeal. History has been kinder to Herzen. Though to the Russian "angry men" of the 1860s Herzen was something of a phony, advocating revolution from the safety and luxury of his foreign residence, denouncing materialism while living on the income from one million rubles, and assailing them for their bad manners, the later radical thought reclaimed and acknowledged his services. Lenin himself was to enroll Herzen among the great precursors of Bolshevism. The liberals and Marxists were to quarrel over whom the legacy of Herzen should belong to. But apart from the politicians' quarrels he has an undeniable place in the history of Russian literature. His memoirs, *My Past and Thoughts,* is a masterpiece of its kind, one of the most fetching and moving examples of the autobiographic genre in any language. Even his purely political writings have an elegance and charm that elevate them far above the standard Russian radical pamphleteering with its pretentious "people—yes" tone or its heavy sarcasm about the powers that be.

Herzen has always been a favorite among foreign connoisseurs of the Russian revolutionary tradition. This is not unconnected with his quality, both in life and in writings, of a *grand seigneur.* Like Leo Tolstoy, who also pursued his own brand of unorthodoxy in politics and personal behavior, Herzen could not, even if he wished, erase his characteristics of an aristocrat by birth and intellect. Such traits (a Soviet writer comments sourly but unfairly that they come easily with one million rubles) were not without their negative side. Herzen's sensitivity has at times an appearance of snobbery. Most troublesome of all, there is an element of humbug in his frequent declamations against materialism. Two neighboring passages in *My Past and Thoughts* set this in vivid relief. Herzen has just finished a tirade against the West and a scathing indictment of the prosaic materialistic pursuits of the *bourgeoisie.* Not long afterward he returns to his private affairs. The Tsarist government has denied him, a political exile, his patrimony. Herzen runs to his banker, the head of the Paris House of Rothschild. The banker informs the Imperial government that it would encounter difficulties in the international finance market unless the money were promptly turned over. And as Herzen concludes in a very amusing passage, the roles are seemingly reversed: Like a "merchant of the second class" the Tsar obeys humbly the edict of the emperor of bankers. The money is duly turned over to the political criminal. Nor did the enemy of materialism scorn speculation on the stock exchange and in real estate. He was to feel some remorse (mixed, perhaps, with rancor at his bad judgment) that when the Civil War broke out he banked on the victory of the "forces of reaction," i.e., the Confederate States, and sold his American bonds.

It is peevish to expect Socialists to be more consistent in their ideas and private life than the general run of mankind. And Herzen was most generous in helping the revolutionary cause and the exiles. But Herzen's tirades against the West's corrupt materialism were mischievous for another reason. They taught—and Herzen's influence on the Russian intelligentsia was at one time enormous—that political regeneration of his country could be accomplished by an act of will, that sound economic institutions (in fact healthy materialism) are *not* a necessary prerequisite of political freedom. The history of Russian revolutionary thought is the history of an ascending revulsion against the humdrum, unromantic aspect of the everyday life of most ordinary people, the revulsion which finally burns itself out in terrorism, and is then replaced by a very different, very materialistic preaching of Marxism. A French Socialist whom Herzen admired, Proudhon, wrote in a moment of disenchantment that the people are a "quiet beast" interested only in eating, sleeping, and love-making. Few revolutionaries would subscribe to this unflattering description of the common man, but what irks them most is the adjective "quiet."

Herzen was born of a noble and rich family. He was of illegitimate birth, but his social standing and education were unaffected by this fact. His father was an eccentric aristocrat somewhat in the style of a French nobleman of the *ancien régime,* who affected to disregard conventions, and among them legalized marriage. The first political impulse for young Herzen was provided by the drama of the Decembrists. Herzen was a child of December 14, wrote Lenin. The heart and mind of the fourteen-year-old boy were stirred by the aristocratic martyrs of freedom. Not long afterward Herzen and his friend Ogarev swore a solemn oath to sacrifice their lives, like the Decembrists, for the liberty of the Russian people. It was a romantic gesture much in the style of Schiller, who was then being read avidly by the youth, but Herzen and Ogarev, both to grow up as men of talent and wealth without the necessity for politics to fill up a void in their lives, always remained true to their adolescent vow.

Not that, like Bakunin, Herzen was a born rebel or a restless conspirator. In different times and in a different society he might well have become a Whig politician and man of letters. But Nicholas' Russia made it easy for sensitive young men to grow up into revolutionaries. Herzen's first arrest and exile from the capital were earned because he *knew* some young people who were *alleged* to have sung, in private, revolutionary songs. His second exile in Russia was occasioned by the secret police intercepting his letter in which he alluded to the corruption of the police. In 1847 the young nobleman left his oppressed country to find, as he expected, a haven of liberty and civilization in the West.

Herzen's ideas of the West had been fed upon the Romantic literature, German idealistic philosophy, and echoes of the Western (mostly French) theoreticians of socialism. Though he reached Europe in his manhood, it was still with a youthful shock that he realized that political life in the West did not all turn around the noble and invigorating ideas of republicanism and socialism, and that people in France and Germany were preoccupied with practical concerns and materialistic cares. The revolutions of 1848, after some turbulence and social experimentation, seemed only to have weakened the upper and strengthened the middle classes, and to have enthroned the middle-class viewpoint as the guiding principle of politics. How different from Romanticism! This jarring impact of reality brought out in Herzen the unconscious Russian nationalist. Europe was decrepit and old. The *bourgeoisie* had had its day. At the very moment of the beginning of its mastery Herzen, like Karl Marx, was wishfully confident that he was watching the death throes of capitalism. Certainly it was not from the French *bourgeois* or an English liberal that Russia could expect the inspiration for her freedom.

The usual disgruntlements of a foreigner in France accentuated Herzen's ideological distaste. An aristocratic youth in Russia encountered France in the flesh in the person of French tutors and servants, or in writing in the form of eloquent diatribes against tyranny and exploitation by the French *philosophes* and Socialists. The average Frenchman had nothing servile or tyrannicidal about him. He tended to be self-reliant, caustically practical, and possessed of that eternal French cultural chauvinism that made him criticize good-naturedly the French pronunciation of his Russian friends. It is not uncharacteristic that Herzen was to feel much better in Italy. This country was then divided into a number of autocratic principalities. The Italian *bourgeoisie* was much weaker and poorer and the Italian peasant, closer in his misery to the Russian one, had none of the infuriating traits of his French counterpart. In London Herzen was to experience disgust, but at the same time a certain awe at the supreme self-confidence of this bastion of the capitalist spirit. He could not but admire English liberties and individualism. In Paris, Italy, or even Switzerland one was never quite safe from the long reach of the Tsarist secret service, and the local authorities, at times, were unhappy because of the presence of conspiratorial foreigners. To the revolutionaries the British offered the boon of safety, but also the utmost and insulting lack of interest in their affairs.

Herzen's solution for Russia's ills, once he found the Western remedies and institutions wanting, took the form of "Russian" Populist socialism.[19] How consciously this is a rejection of European constitutionalism is indicated by his famous challenge, "Russia will never be Protestant [i.e., moderate and materialistic], Russia will never be *juste-milieu* [i.e., a prosaic middle-class regime and society], Russia will never make a revolution with the aim of getting rid of Tsar Nicholas and of replacing him

[19] This is discussed at length in Martin Malia's excellent *Alexander Herzen and the Birth of Russian Socialism*, Cambridge, Mass., 1960.

with Tsar-representatives, Tsar-judges, Tsar-policemen." [20] What then?

Behind many an unsound theory there is usually some bad history. And in the case of Russia many historical or philosophical hypotheses that lie at the root of "characteristically Russian" political and economic solutions have been fathered by learned Germans. Herzen's learned German was Baron Haxthausen, whose work on the Russian peasant and agriculture was to have a powerful and fateful influence not only on his but on much of other Russian thought, whether conservative or radical in its tendency. Haxthausen was attracted by one feature of Russian peasant life: the communal organization of the Russian village—in Russian, *obschchina*. The commune both before and after the abolition of serfdom (in 1861–63) was the main type of agricultural organization in most of European Russia. The peasants' land was vested in the commune, not in the individual peasant families. In most communes the assembly of the peasants—in Russian, *mir*—would periodically redistribute plots of land among its members, arbitrate the peasants' disputes, and handle similar matters (subject, of course, to the over-all authority of the landlord prior to the abolition of serfdom, and of the government's representatives afterward). Haxthausen saw the commune as an institution of great antiquity, the relic of ancient communism, which at one time characterized the agricultural organization of all primitive peoples. Russia was lucky to have preserved this grass-roots type of peasant democracy and socialism. It could preserve her from the evils of competitive capitalism of the West where the dispossessed peasants and craftsmen were being turned into the slum-dwelling proletariat of the Lyons and Manchesters.

To the Russian conservative, the Slavophile, the theory of Haxthausen provided an important intellectual weapon against the apologists for the Western institutions. Here, and they argued somewhat in the manner of the Southern defenders of slavery before the Civil War, the seemingly backward institution represented actually both the wisdom of the ages and social justice. The people—the peasants—did not need parliaments; they had a superior form of direct democracy. The commune assured its members economic security, it protected them from the uncertainties and degradations that were the lot of the Western industrial proletariat.

Let it be said once and for all, even as an oversimplification, that in fact the commune was an institution of no great antiquity, that the economic security it provided was at best of a very low level, that despite the periodic redistribution of land it did not prevent economic differentiation among the peasants, and that, most important of all, it hampered social mobility, hurt technical improvement in farming, and thus proved a major obstacle, both before and after the freeing of the serfs, to the industrialization and economic improvement in Russia.

We can see that today, and more perceptive thinkers would see it

[20] Quoted in *ibid.*, p. 408.

toward the end of the century. But a Russian radical of the eighteen forties and fifties recoiled before the picture of the industrialized world with its unregulated factory life, its sordid manufacturing towns with their teeming and brutalized proletariat; it was easy for him to wish to spare Russia a similar experience. For the Russian Socialist even more than for his conservative counterpart, Haxthausen's theories strengthened the already existing idealized vision of the *obschchina* and provided a way out of his dilemma: Yes, Russia will advance to civilization, and beyond that to socialism, but without the industrial travail of Europe. It was pleasing to the national pride lurking beneath radicalism. Who would have thought that backward, autocratic Russia contained an institution and a principle within it which could show the rest of the world the correct path to democracy and socialism!

Herzen's socialism contained, then, the plan for a federation of free peasant communes. First of all there would have to be liberation of the serfs; they must be liberated with their land, with little or no compensation for the landlords.[21] Unlike Bakunin, Herzen did not dwell with pleasure on the possibility of vast peasant uprisings like those that stirred seventeenth century Russia. He looked, at times, for reform from above, and he appealed to the conscience and intelligence of his own class, the gentry. Despite his esthetic dislike of the bourgeois West, he was a good European, at least insofar as he prized individualism and rejected the use of violence before all the possibilities of persuasion and peaceful alteration were exhausted.

Herzen's main contribution to the revolutionary tradition lies not wholly in his agrarian socialism; his views of the commune and his idealization of the democratic and inherently communistic Russian peasant are not, after all, much different from Bakunin's or from other contemporary radicals. His contribution lies in his role as teacher and inspirer. It was he who through the example of his personality and his skill as a writer and journalist created the classical *ethos* of the Russian intelligentsia: the attitude of intellectual opposition to the authority of solicitude for "the people" and of consecration to politics as the duty of every thinking and honest man. It was largely Herzen who is responsible for the creation of Russia-in-exile, the state of mind among the political *emigrés* and escapees who felt that they were not merely individuals fleeing from oppression but that they represented their country's moral dignity and that they bore collective responsibility for Russia's political future. And much of the enlightened opinion at home was in the first

[21] Most of the serfs were landholders, unlike the Negro slaves in the South; that is, apart from their duties on the landlords' lands (sometimes commuted by money payment) they had their "own" collectively held land. Unfree tenants rather than "serfs" would be a more technical description of their status. The peasants' folklore emphasized the contrast of personal unfreedom with the conviction that the land—all the land, their masters' as well as the commune's—was legitimately theirs.

instance taught by Herzen to accept the exiles' self-appraisal and to consider them as the ambassadors of its hope and aspirations.

In London in 1857 Herzen began publishing a periodical, *Kolokol* (*The Bell*). Even earlier he had made efforts at publication and a dissemination of his ideas at home, but it is only with *The Bell* that he became a power in Russian intellectual and political life. Nicholas I had died in 1855, the Crimean War had ended in a Russian defeat, and now the autocracy was relaxing its grip. *The Bell,* officially forbidden, found its way to the most influential circles; even Emperor Alexander II was reputed to be reading it. *The Bell* for a while fitted the mood of transition after the death of the old despot. The regime was bent upon reform—the military defeat had shown the cost of the obsolete social and political system, and the new Emperor had none of his father's obsessive fear of political change. Superficially, there are some resemblances to the post-Stalin era, but the Tsarist government had few of the totalitarian regime's devices to contain the liberalization within safe bounds; it had none of its propaganda skill to blame the past evils on a "cult of personality," but only the equal determination to let no reform affect the basis of its political power.

The Bell at times approved the Tsar's reforming tendencies and promises and at times chastised their dilatoriness. Its main fire was directed at the remnants of the old bureaucratic abuses and at the personalities within the bureaucracy who attempted to continue Nicholas' system. Herzen's genius as political writer acquired for him an audience at home among both moderates and radicals. This success and acceptance had to be short-lived. Herzen, unaware, had caught the infection of Western liberalism and had become (to join the two in his case is not a paradox) a liberal revolutionary. For him, any reform had to be but an installment on future and complete freedom and socialism. By the same token he could not understand or sympathize with the new radical breed who viewed reforms with loathing and sarcasm and who wanted the whole social and political system to be smashed at once before a new and Socialist Russia could be reconstructed from the ruins. The conflict was prophetic of the future splits in the revolutionary movement: each successive generation was to view its elders with a mixture of pity and contempt, as men who have grown soft and alien to the revolutionary strivings of the people.

In politics as in his private life Herzen was a true child of Romanticism, subject to intermittent bouts of exultation and depression, ready with an exorbitant tribute or with a scathing indictment. The news that the Tsar contemplated freeing the serfs threw him into transports of gratitude. He hailed the rather commonplace Emperor as the savior of Russia, and addressed to him through the pages of *The Bell* a series of letters containing unsolicited advice on how to overcome the opposition of the bureaucracy and reactionary nobility. This one-sided "correspondence" took at times a ridiculous turn, as when Herzen undertook to advise the imperial family on the upbringing of the heir to the throne.[22] Once the repressive nature of the regime reasserted itself, Herzen's adulation turned to the severest censure. Essentially this proneness to address the Tsar (and Herzen was by no means alone among the revolutionaries in doing so) was not unconnected with his populism. Did not the peasant believe the Tsar to be his benevolent father and did he not blame the evils of the government on the bureaucracy that deceived the Tsar and kept a barrier between him and his people? So ran the stereotype. In a strange and perverse way even the terrorists who later on hunted and killed the Emperor were the victims of the same emotion, the same belief in the omnipotence of one person: they punished an unjust father who deceived and refused freedom to his people. This heady atmosphere of the revolutionary's intimate feeling about the ruler was to be entirely absent from the make-up of the Russian Marxists. To Lenin the Emperor was "idiot Romanov" and was a person of absolutely no consequence.

The early sixties marked the end of *The Bell's* great influence in Russia. The actual form of the peasants' emancipation disappointed Herzen. Most of all, Tsarism horrified him anew by the bloody suppression of the Polish rebellion of 1863. Herzen was among the relatively few Russian intellectuals who have been genuinely and fervently pro-Polish. For all their close ethnic connection (or maybe because of it), and for all their historical links, the relations between the Poles and the Russians have usually been unhappy. In the contemporary Russian public opinion the Poles fitted the stereotypes not too dissimilar from those attached sometimes to the Jews. The radicals saw in their leaders mainly aristocrats and landowners who exploited their (often Russian) peasants. The conservative Russians regarded the Poles as a nation of revolutionaries, vaunting their superior culture and betraying the Slavic race. Herzen's advocacy of Polish independence at the time when the rebellious Poles were killing Russian soldiers rubbed hard against aroused Russian chauvinism.

Among the more radical souls who would have welcomed any rebellion against Tsarism, Herzen was losing influence for another reason. To the "men of the sixties," or the "nihilists" as they were sometimes known, Herzen was clearly behind the times. He was a product of Romanticism; they imagined themselves as being disciples of "scientific" materialism. For their taste, Herzen's socialism was too humanistic, too much grounded in the hope of change by evolution. They were in many cases men of

---

[22] This burst of enthusiasm for Alexander, explicable by the contrast with his hateful father, was not unusual at the time, even among the radicals. Prince Kropotkin, the famous revolutionary and anarchist, recounts in his memoirs how enraptured he was as a young man by his first encounter with the Tsar-Liberator.

humble birth whose ideological disagreement was enhanced by their personal pique at Herzen's nobleman's manner and the elegance of his language. Their feeling of social and intellectual inferiority was covered up, as is often the case, by biting sarcasm at the expense of the "men of the forties" with their well-intentioned but so obsolete and so useless liberal ideas (the word "liberal" was already becoming a term of opprobrium among the radicals). The new men, such as Chernyshevsky, aroused in Herzen a revulsion not as much political as esthetic. He felt in them, as he probably would have felt in the Bolsheviks, a strange preoccupation with revolution as an end in itself, rather than as the means of assuring human freedom. Behind their professed materialism and dedication to science he saw hostility to traditional culture, to everything that might not be "useful," that is, not in line with their political views and ambitions. Appalled by the new radicals, Herzen used a phrase about them that has always been held against him: the young men, he wrote, retained in their mentality the traits of the "servants' room, the theological seminary, and the barracks." This was a direct reference to their plebeian origin, an accusation of vulgarity and of the young men's social envy of the older, more "refined" generation. In another attack, Herzen initiated the technique that since then has become a commonplace in the revolutionary debates, the full elaboration of which we can see today in the exchange between the Russian and Chinese Communists, that of attacking persons who are left of your own politics as being "really" right-wing and serving the interests of reaction. In the article entitled "Very Dangerous" (somewhat affectedly, the title is in English), he proclaimed that the attacks upon him and his position served the interests of the most reactionary part of the Tsarist bureaucracy, and that the young radicals might live to be decorated by the government.

This bitterness reflected Herzen's realization that the minds and hearts of the young generation in Russia were being increasingly won over by his opponents. But it also bespoke the feeling of hopelessness about his own political position. Herzen could not for long remain a moderate or an enemy of any revolutionary striving. He already had the psychological trait, which was to become the curse of the future liberals and moderate Socialists up to the October Revolution: the consciousness of being outdistanced in one's radicalism and of being confronted with a more uncompromising and unscrupulous revolutionary resolve that produced inner doubts and a sense of inferiority. How well was Lenin to understand and to exploit this infirmity of the liberal mind!

Herzen, because of his temperament, had to return to the out-and-out revolutionary fray. Despite his deep resentment about new radicals, despite his lingering hopes in the Emperor, any and every act of official oppression and brutality would provoke afresh his revolutionary fervor. To the students who now in Russia were becoming the vanguard of revolutionary disturbances Herzen wrote: "Glory to you, you begin a new era, you have understood that the time of whispers, of hidden allusions, of [the secret reading of] the forbidden books has passed." Where should they go when the brutal authorities close down the universities? "To the people, to the people . . . show them . . . that from among you will come the fighters of the Russian people." And the arrest of Chernyshevsky, his main antagonist among the radicals, the man who epitomized to Herzen the narrow "mentality of the seminary," evoked from him a generous tribute and imprecations against Tsarism.

The last years of Herzen (he died in 1870) were clouded with personal and political tragedy. E. H. Carr in his *Romantic Exiles* gives a vivid picture of the turbulent personal life of the revolutionary and his circle, the life poisoned first by the infidelity and then the tragic death of his wife, then by his tortured liaison with the wife of his great friend Ogarev, the liaison that was not allowed to interrupt the friends' intimacy and political collaboration, but which inevitably contributed to Ogarev's moral and physical decline.[23] The decline of *The Bell* as well as personal considerations made him shift his residence to the Continent. Places such as Geneva had at least a considerable Russian colony, and what Russian could for long remain content in London with its bleak Victorian atmosphere, the horrors of the English cuisine, and the lack of such amenities as the French-style cafés, which are almost indispensable to a revolutionary movement in exile? To Herzen, London was an "ant-heap." He had no contacts with English intellectual or political life, and the circle of his acquaintances was almost exclusively among the exiles and radicals of several nations.

Of the new tendencies in European socialism Herzen was no more enamored than of the new Russian radicalism. "Scientific" socialism and the emphasis on the industrial worker were alien to him who had been brought up on the generous, if fantastic, dreams of Saint-Simon and Fourier. "The worker of all countries will grow into the bourgeois" was Herzen's most perceptive even if somewhat overoptimistic and, by his lights, unflattering judgment. The Russian Marxists have never quite forgiven Herzen this dismissal of the industrial proletariat. How could one identify the heroic working class with its privations and its revolutionary drive with the mercenary and philistine spirit of the *bourgeoisie?* His fellow Londoner, Karl Marx, Herzen could not stand. Marx was what he called a "bilious" type of politician, an intriguer who could not indulge

---

[23] Mr. Carr's account, colored by irony but also by compassion, was received rather huffily by such Socialist scholars as the late G. D. H. Cole. The latter implied (unfairly) that Mr. Carr with a kind of Anglo-Saxon condescension represents the great revolutionary and his circle as a bunch of mixed-up foreigners, thus provoking in a casual reader doubts as to what kind of people become Socialists. Even if so, the casual reader can become reassured by the stories of the Marx and Lenin households, with their connubial bliss and bourgeois orderliness.

in polemics without heaping abuse and filth upon his opponent. Herzen did not share Bakunin's almost pathological anti-Semitism and Germanophobia (though he was not fond of the Germans). But Marx was for him an embodiment of the German bourgeois spirit: formal, unromantic, and devoid of those elements of humor and compassion which he deemed essential for a real fighter for the people's right. The news that Doctor Marx was to address or even to attend a political gathering or banquet was cause enough for Herzen to send his excuses.

Herzen's faith in revolution as a moral principle was to assume a different and to him an unpleasant form among the people who were both his successors and his opponents in the revolutionary movement. He wrote, referring to the young hotheads of "Young Russia" who were disseminating terroristic manifestoes, that he had long since ceased, whether in war or in politics, to lust for the blood of the enemy. "Whenever anybody's blood is spilled somebody's tears will flow." But the future of the Russian revolutionary movement belonged to the unsqueamish sentiments of Chernyshevsky: "The path of history is not like Nevsky Prospect [one of the main streets in St. Petersburg], it goes at times through dirt, and filth, through swamps and ravines! If you are afraid of being covered with dirt or of soiling your shoes then don't take up politics." [24] This is an unfair criticism of Herzen, who was not afraid of being covered with dirt while carrying on his mission, but simply did not want revolution to soil its hands in unnecessary blood.

His posthumous "good luck" in being claimed as a spiritual ancestor by all branches of Russian revolutionary thought makes Herzen's position all the more pathetic. For he would not have felt at home among the liberals with their admiration of the Western parliamentary institutions, and he certainly would have loathed Bolshevism. The Communists have always been good at posthumous rehabilitation. The dead cannot be forced to recant, but their shortcomings can be ascribed to their class origins, or to the times in which they lived. And so in the Pantheon of the Communist saints—predecessors of Lenin—Herzen is forced to share the uncongenial company of Chernyshevsky, the terrorists of the People's Will, and of Plekhanov (who also would have cried in outrage at this honor). Nothing is more certain than that were he transplanted into the twentieth century Herzen would be found in Paris or in London (in Bloomsbury) stigmatizing Soviet Russia with the same moral fervor that he expended on Nicholas. One can be equally sure that he would couple the lashing of the native tyranny with scorching protests against the capitalist West, its imperialism, its incomprehension that what is going on in Russia, brutal and tyrannous though it is, *may still* contain the seeds of a freer and better society. And one might even suspect that he would have welcomed the coming of communism in China as representing a

[24] Steklov, *op cit.*, p. 159.

purer, agrarian brand of the ideology, and that he would have been thrilled, at first, at the epic of the Cuban revolution. Perhaps in looking at Herzen's enthusiasms and disenchantments we see not only Russia, and not only the past.

3. Chernyshevsky

With Nicholas Gavrilovich Chernyshevsky (1828–1889) we stand at the real source of Bolshevism. At the age of eighteen Lenin wrote an admiring letter to the great radical, then in exile in Saratov after a long imprisonment in Siberia. And in the office of the Chairman of the Council of the People's Commissars in the Kremlin Chernyshevsky's works shared the place of honor with those of Karl Marx. Chernyshevsky helped to mold the form of the revolutionary; Marx provided him with the message. But not only Lenin was inspired by Chernyshevsky. In the memoirs or even in depositions before the police of revolutionaries of various political persuasions one would often find a phrase, "I became a revolutionary at the age of——after reading Chernyshevsky." The work most often mentioned was the novel that gave Lenin the title for his basic political treatise: *What Is To Be Done?*. When it appeared in the early 1860s this novel and its message were read by the young radicals, as one of them put it, "practically on our knees." But even ten or twenty years later, when its cryptic political allusions could no longer be deciphered by another generation, schoolboys would still be entranced and steered into the revolutionary path by *What Is To Be Done?*.

In Chernyshevsky we see the effects of a social environment widely different from that which had brought forth Herzen or Bakunin. He was the son of an Orthodox priest. The rank-and-file clergy was practically a hereditary class. Since they could not aspire to the higher ecclesiastical preferments, the clerics lived under material conditions usually not much superior to those of their congregations (which in nineteenth century Russia meant mostly peasants). At the same time they had to have a modicum of education. This combination of poverty, imposed dogmatism, and education tended to make the clerical households a breeding ground for the radical and revolutionary intelligentsia. Not only Chernyshevsky and his closest collaborator, Dobrolyubov, but many other revolutionaries were to spring up from this clerical environment.[25]

[25] There is a strong temptation to fall into the current sociological slang and to use the magic word "alienation." But the history of the Russian revolutionary movement shows exactly the limitations of this term. Were the Decembrists alienated from their society? But they represented the ideas and emotions, certainly not of the numerical majority, but of a considerable proportion of members of their class. With the later intelligentsia radicals we find the same phenomenon. They were often the more active, more drastic exponents of ideas that were endemic in their society. Perhaps it was the staunch reactionaries and the defenders of the *status quo* in Tsarist Russia who were alienated and "rebels against their own class."

This background and the fact that he himself studied for a time in a theological seminary left a definite imprint upon Chernyshevsky. His Soviet biographer relates with some distaste that even as a radical and unbeliever Chernyshevsky still liked to attend church services and would cross himself when passing a church.[26] But more important, his strict upbringing by his clerical father bred in the boy timidity and awkwardness in society that he never shed. Like that other alumnus of a theological seminary, Stalin, Chernyshevsky retained traces of scholasticism in his thinking and writing.

It is important to dwell somewhat on Chernyshevsky's private life and characteristics, not for the sake of what might be called historical voyeurism, but because his personality contributes much to the tone of the later radical movement, and because both he and his fictional heroes become the models for future revolutionary fighters.

Again one is tempted to commit a huge oversimplification: Chernyshevsky, below the veneer of extensive education and erudition that he acquired, is the typical Russian man of the people. One finds in him a mixture of peasant slyness and of naïveté; of overpowering if at times sardonic humility, combined with arrogant self-confidence. What other author would address the reader as he does in the beginning of *What Is To Be Done?*, "I don't have the shadow of an artistic talent. I even use the language poorly. But that is not important: read on, kind public, you will read this with benefit. Truth is a great thing; it compensates for the deficiencies of the writer who serves it." From the jail, on the eve of his long exile to Siberia, he wrote to his wife: "Our life belongs to history; hundreds of years will pass, and our names will still be dear to the people; they will think of us with gratitude when our contemporaries are long dead." The same man who warned the reader that he had not a shadow of artistic talent proudly told a police official that his name would live in the history of Russian literature along with those of Pushkin, Gogol, and Lermontov.

Chernyshevsky's endurance of suffering was more than heroic; it turned into an obstinacy that borders on masochism. There was in his nature a blend of resignation and defiance that is bred through more than just political persecution. After ten years in Siberia the government let it be known that if Chernyshevsky petitioned for a pardon he would be allowed to rejoin his family in Russia. The official who brought the message to the exile was greeted with neither elation nor anger. Chernyshevsky answered with a kind of puzzlement: "Thank you. But, look, for what can I 'plead' for pardon? . . . It appears to me that I was exiled only because my head is differently constructed from that of the head of the Chief of the Police, and how can I ask pardon for that?" And to the bafflement and anguish of the official he absolutely refused to ask for mercy. When as

[26] Y. M. Steklov, *N. G. Chernyshevsky*, Moscow, 1928, Vol. I, p. 8.

a middle-aged but already physically ruined man he was allowed to return to European Russia, Chernyshevsky quietly continued his literary occupations. To an idiotic question as to how he had felt in Siberia he replied patiently, and again there was more than just irony in the answer, that those had been his happiest years!

A cynic will see in all that a conscious effort to build a political legend out of one's own life. But the same qualities of endurance, timidity, and resolution are found in Chernyshevsky's private life. He fell in love with a girl from a higher social sphere who was in addition lovely and much sought after. Chernyshevsky was overjoyed and incredulous that his beloved reciprocated his feelings. In a paradoxical fashion he set about demonstrating to the girl that he had no right to marry and involve another being with his fate, since he was drawn to politics, and though by nature cowardly, he would have to join a revolutionary movement if one arose in Russia, and was thus likely to end up on the gallows or in prison.[27] Before their marriage Chernyshevsky made a statement most unusual for the nineteenth century, that he would leave his wife entirely free in every sense of the word. More than that, he declared to his fiancée: "I am in your power, do what you will." To his friends, who warned him about his future wife's character, he said incredibly: "It is all the same to me if I have someone else's child; I shall tell her: Should you prefer, my dear, to come back to me, don't be embarrassed." [28] It was not only love that motivated him but his social conviction. Woman has always been oppressed and now her emancipation must begin by her temporary dominance over man. "Every decent man in my opinion is bound to put his wife above himself; this temporary domination is necessary for future equality." His wife's subsequent infidelities and frivolity were borne by him with the same unshakeable patience and contentment with which he endured exile. He never wrote or treated her except in terms of complete affection and devotion. If her behavior, apart from the disloyalty toward her husband, did not meet Chernyshevsky's conception of how an emancipated and politically conscious woman should act or caused him pain, then he successfully concealed it from strangers.[29] After his exile he returned to his Olga, and worked hard at uncongenial work (translations) for the money to satisfy her slightest whim. What most jars the Soviet commentators about Olga Chernyshevsky is that with her husband on his deathbed she tried to reconcile him to the faith of his fathers.

His most important period of activity encompasses the last of Nicho-

---

[27] One may feel that this was a clever courting technique. But it was more than that.

[28] T. A. Bogdanovich: *Loves of the People of the Sixties,* Leningrad, 1929, p. 24.

[29] An unkind relative in her sketch of Olga Chernyshevsky suggests that her husband's sardonic words about having been happy in Siberia were not unconnected with his wife's absence there.

las' and the first few years of Alexander II's reigns. He had, of course, abandoned any thought of a clerical career and found himself in 1846 at St. Petersburg University. After a stint of teaching in the high school, he became a collaborator on the magazine *The Contemporary*, and before long this priest's son, still in his twenties, was Russia's most influential social and literary critic, the intellectual guide of the new intelligentsia. *The Contemporary* had what in terms of Russia in the late fifties and early sixties was a huge circulation—over six thousand—built up through the collaboration of Russia's leading literary lights. Founded by Pushkin shortly before his death, it was to feature Turgenev and young Tolstoy and many others of this halcyon period of Russian literature.

The radical poet Nekrasov, then editor of *The Contemporary*, recruited Chernyshevsky. The latter with his critiques, essays, and articles changed the direction and the significance of the journal. It became the standard-bearer of radicalism. In that respect its influence rivaled and soon surpassed that of Herzen's *Bell*, even though the latter did not have to grapple with censorship.

In his esthetic views and criticisms Chernyshevsky must be considered an ancestor of Soviet Socialist realism, though its full and appalling character cannot be blamed on the critic who believed that the artist should be free to write or paint as he pleases. But even in his doctoral dissertation Chernyshevsky condemned art for art's sake and science for science's sake and declared that both spheres of activity should be judged in terms of their utility for society. In his criticisms this point of view is carried to further lengths. The common-sense and useful technique of taking into account the social meaning and tendency of a given work of art is allowed by Chernyshevsky to affect his esthetic judgment, and at times to push him into absurdities. His friend and fellow editor, Nekrasov, wrote for "the people," Pushkin did not, hence Nekrasov is a far greater poet. What makes it worse is that Chernyshevsky hastens to explain that he looks at poetry "not at all exclusively from the political point of view." How sadly premonitory is Chernyshevsky's trumpeting of the social responsibility of the writer, the admonition that he should not write "just" poetry, his reminder to Nekrasov that "every decent man in Russia counts on you" (presumably to write the poetry of social protest).

Chernyshevsky's observations on the ideal of beauty are not without interest. Why is "the people's ideal" of feminine beauty connected with the image of a hefty peasant wench with rosy cheeks? Because the common people have to work hard and hence they value evidence of health and strength. But take a society beauty! Generations of idleness have weakened the muscles, hence the small delicate limbs. That much-prized pallor in a lady of the upper classes is an eloquent testimony to the sluggish circulation of the blood. No wonder that headache is a fashionable ailment of the aristocracy; it testifies that its sufferer does not have to work and her blood consequently accumulates in the brain. In the same passage Chernyshevsky somewhat inconsistently ascribes the delicacy and fragility that are the attributes of the aristocratic ideal of beauty to the exhaustion from the sensual excesses to which the idle classes resort out of boredom. It is no wonder that such persons as Tolstoy and Turgenev became uneasy about their fellow contributor to *The Contemporary.*

It is fair to observe that Chernyshevsky was by no means the most extreme among his contemporaries in his "social significance" school of literary criticism. It fell to him to defend Tolstoy's *Childhood and Adolescence* from the charge of ignoring the social problem. A novel intended to reproduce the world of a child, he wrote, can hardly dwell on the basic problems of politics or social philosophy. That this defense had to be made, and of such a writer as Tolstoy, and by Chernyshevsky, is an eloquent testimony to the spirit of the times, or, at least to that of the radical intelligentsia.

Chernyshevsky's political and philosophical viewpoint was formed under many influences. In his university days he was drawn to Fourierism (he had a vague connection with the Petrashevsky circle) and the vision of the phalanstery as an ideal form of social organization stayed with him to the end. After the usual apprenticeship in the idealistic German philosophy he fell under the spell of the materialistic views of Feuerbach. This philosopher, unfortunately for his reputation, is now remembered mainly for his celebrated aphorism: "Man is what he eats," and his logical deductions from this principle (like his recommendation to the working classes that they would never conquer their beef-eating aristocracy as long as they fed on potatoes; they should change their diet to beans). Chernyshevsky was very literal in embracing a body of philosophy and it is no accident that the hero of *What Is To Be Done?* builds himself up for revolutionary work by eating huge quantities of beef! It is necessary to repeat that for many a Russian intellectual, and for none more than Chernyshevsky, the acceptance or approval of a philosophical system was not only a matter of intellectual choice, but a passionate act of faith. He grasped greedily Feuerbach's dictum that philosophy should be replaced by the natural sciences. Science, the study of man and nature, should replace the systems of metaphysics and idealistic ethics as an explanation of life and a guide to action. Chernyshevsky was a leader in the intellectual revolution of the 1860s, which made the young intelligentsia turn its back on German idealism with which men of Herzen's generation had been enamored and look for answers in materialism and scientism. Our thinker expressed this addiction in words which again could come only from his pen: "I am a scientist. I am one of those scientists whom they call 'thinkers.' . . . I have been one since my early youth. It has long been my habit and self-imposed duty to consider everything which comes to my mind from the scientific point of view, and I am unable to think of anything otherwise." Chernyshevsky (and he was not alone) having rejected Christianity never lost the need for faith, for absolute certainty. And like the preceding, the following words appear comical in their conceit only at first, but are full of pathos in their implications: "My mistakes have been only in trifling details which do not affect the essence of my thought."

Like their predecessors who found in German idealism the "arithmetic of revolution," so Chernyshevsky and his followers had no trouble in identifying the message of materialism and utilitarianism with an injunction to revolutionary struggle. The philosophical instrument for this transformation was the celebrated theory of "wise selfishness." It was derived by Chernyshevsky from the English Utilitarians, but Bentham and John Stuart Mill would have been surprised to see its ramifications in the hands of their Russian disciple. Man is naturally selfish, said the radicals of the 1860s, with the rapture and vehemence that usually accompanies a new discovery. Neither God nor any higher moral law but only self-interest guides him in his behavior. But what is the most rational form of selfishness? A "decent," "real," or a "new" man (all those adjectives are used interchangeably by Chernyshevsky) finds his highest interest, the most satisfying sensual pleasure in serving the interests of society. Selfishness = service to mankind = (under the conditions of contemporary Russia) revolutionary activity. In *What Is To Be Done?* various characters go to great (and to the reader exhausting) lengths to demonstrate that their heroic actions, such as giving up a beloved woman, sleeping on a bed of nails to harden oneself for revolutionary work, or other torments are not, God forbid, consequences of their altruism or of the love of mankind, but simply of selfishness. Chernyshevsky's elaboration of "wise selfishness" had more serious results. It is easy to see how it could become a rationalization of political terrorism. What if a majority is content or ignorant enough to endure life under political tyranny? Should not a "new man," if his inner needs impel him so, risk his life for the good of the people? We have seen how Alexander Ulyanov in his speech before the court did not even pretend that in attempting to assassinate the Tsar he represented the oppressed masses. No, he avowed that he spoke for a tiny minority. His deed was that of a "wise egoist."

The "new men" become immortalized in Turgenev's *Fathers and Sons*. For their conservative or even liberal contemporaries they became known as "nihilists," raucous enemies of all conformity, culture, and tradition. Chernyshevsky's novel was intended largely as an answer to Turgenev's *Fathers and Sons* which the young generation felt was a slanderous misrepresentation of their ideas. The subtitle of *What Is To Be Done?* is *Tales About New People*. The most remarkable person, the one intended by Chernyshevsky to be the exemplar of the new man's virtues, is Rakhmetov. It is he who eats huge quantities of raw beef and sleeps on nails, thus ac-

quiring enormous strength and hardiness for revolutionary tasks (Chernyshevsky himself was frail and bookish in appearance). Aside from raw beef,
he would not eat food that poor people could not afford. ". . . in St. Petersburg he ate oranges, but refused them in the provinces. Because in St. Petersburg common people eat them, which is not the case in the provinces."
He is brusque and to the point in his conversation, scorning the effusive politeness customary in a Russian gentleman. Five minutes of skimming the
pages was enough to make him see whether a given book was written
in a scientific, materialistic spirit; if not, it was trash and not worth reading. "I read only that which is original, and I read it only insofar as is
necessary in order to know this originality." As a "wise egoist" Rakhmetov
spends his considerable fortune in helping his fellow men. He is obviously
(though this cannot be spelled out because of censorship) a revolutionary.

Russian society of the late fifties and sixties was not, unlike our own,
jaded by and resigned to the appearance of successive waves of angry
young men. The old type of radical à la Herzen was a man of courtly
manners and culture. But, the "new man" would laugh in your face if
you talked of idealistic philosophy, would gobble down food while discussing the social problem, and sneer at everything unconnected with
science or revolution. Worse still, the "new man" was being joined by the
"new woman" who had cropped short her hair, talked back to her parents,
and intended to study anatomy in order to become a doctor and to work
among the people. To the conservatives, all these horrors indicated that
the relaxation that had followed Nicholas' death had gone too far, that the
youth had to be curbed. When within a few years bad manners turned
into political terrorism they had the melancholy satisfaction of reactionaries of all periods: "We told you so." To the older radicals the extravagant mood of the generation whose standard-bearer was Chernyshevsky
was saddening, but they saw in it a delayed effect of the constrictions and
crudities of Nicholas' times. But though they deplored the crudity of
their successors, and could even, as did Herzen in an unguarded moment, attribute it to the low social origins of its leaders, their greatest
apprehension was aroused by the political temper of the new men.

In politics Chernyshevsky was as shrewd and cautious as he was
naïve and preposterous in the artistic field. He was extremely careful not
to be openly identified with any revolutionary organization or appeal.
His radical ideology and the devastating comments on the autocracy
were put forth under the very nose of censorship. Chernyshevsky smuggled
them into his articles in *The Contemporary*, articles allegedly dealing
with such subjects as the events in Austria, ancient Rome, or the French
politics of the year of revolutions, 1848. His allusions were clear not only
to the initiated but to the public at large. Chernyshevsky's was indeed the

model of this "Aesopian language," of which Lenin and his followers were to make good use in their struggle of wits with the censor.

Russian politics of the late eighteen fifties and early sixties presented a fantastic appearance. The most radical people were never very far away from petitioning or eulogizing the Tsar for this or that reform. The most cautious of the liberals were not far from approving a violent revolution if the Tsar would not listen to the pleas for a redress of popular grievances. Chernyshevsky's political activity touched both spheres. In practical politics he was, like most of the radicals and liberals of his day, a follower of Herzen. It was Herzen who in his youth inspired him with the idea of dedicating himself to the cause of the people and of risking an eventual imprisonment or exile. Chernyshevsky's immediate aims for Russia in the 1850s echoed those proclaimed by *The Bell:* emancipation of the peasants with land (which would keep the commune as a basis for future socialism), an end to censorship, and the calling of a national assembly.

But beneath the level of practical politics there was a fervent revolutionary temperament that could not and would not be appeased by any reforms or schemes of representation. The announcement that the Emperor planned to liberate the serfs evoked even from Chernyshevsky an exclamation of admiration and gratitude. Yet, not only the character of the promised reform but also a whole complex of feelings and causes pushed him in the direction of an uncompromising struggle with the regime. Herzen's and the liberal gentry's continuing illusions about the Emperor increasingly excited the sarcasm and wrath of the radical collaborators of *The Contemporary.* Dobrolyubov and Chernyshevsky stigmatized and denounced the moderates and liberals. In hardly veiled allusions they described how the liberals and the middle class abroad, as in France after 1848, have always "sold out" the people, and having secured their own class interests made peace with the oppressive regime. To them well-meaning noblemen and bureaucrats were epitomized by Oblomov, the hero of the famous novel of the same name by Goncharov, a "superfluous man" always dreaming of great deeds but never having enough energy and courage to put them into execution.

The passion of the new generation found its classical expression in the famous letter to *The Bell* printed in 1860 and signed *A Russian.*[30] The author calls upon Herzen to give up his panegyrics to the Emperor and his hopes for a revolution from above. He states the classical "The worse it is, the better for us" position of the true revolutionary. Under Nicholas I everybody came to understand that only force could win human rights

[30] The authorship of the letter has been in dispute, most of the authorities crediting it to Chernyshevsky, others to Dobrolyubov. Nobody questions that it expresses faithfully Chernyshevsky's ideas.

for the Russian people. Now under Alexander the liberals are confusing the people's minds with nonsensical pleas for patience and moderation, ". . . therefore one now regrets Nicholas. Under him the [needed] work would be carried through to the ultimate end." Russia has always been held in slavery because of the idiotic faith in the good intentions of the Tsar-Autocrat. *The Bell* should not burn incense before the Emperor. "Our situation is tragic and insufferable and nothing can help but the axe." And the famous challenge: "Call upon Russia to raise the axe."

The letter marks a new era in the Russian revolutionary movement. Revolution and violence become the only means of cleansing the national life. There is also a more strident voice of class feeling. The Tsarist regime shares the writer's contempt for the "liberal landowners, liberal professors, liberal authors." This paradoxical hatred of the intelligentsia for the class to which he really belongs and on which he still counts most to ignite the revolutionary fire forms the strongest psychological bond between Chernyshevsky and Lenin.

The actual engagement in the revolutionary struggle followed the proclamation of the Emancipation edict in 1861. The long-prayed-for freeing of the serfs was now a fact and as in the case of every great reform initial elation was followed by disillusionment. The edict freed the peasants *with* land, but in many provinces they were given less land than they had cultivated while in bondage. These "cut offs," which went to the landlords, were to remain an important political symbol and issue well into the twentieth century. Most disappointing of all to the radical, the peasants were put under heavy financial obligations, since they were to pay the government (which had compensated the serf owners) in yearly installments for the alleged value of the land. The commune beloved both by the conservative and the radical was retained as the base of the social and economic organization of the Russian village. The "cutoffs" and especially the fact that the peasant had to pay for "his" land aroused the special fury of the radical. As he had always suspected, the Tsar "sold out" the peasant: the emancipation was a hoax, its provisions benefited only the landlords. That the peasants in some places rebelled, claiming that the Tsar intended to give them land free but that the nobles were cheating them (the intricate financial and administrative features of the reform could but with difficulty be explained to the illiterate masses) was another indication that there was a vast revolutionary potential in the countryside. The years 1861 and especially 1862 became the period of clandestine revolutionary manifestoes. Small groups of students and intellectuals organized themselves into revolutionary circles. The most notable of them (it is still difficult to speak of a party) adopted the name of *Zemlya i Volya* (Land and Freedom), but there were others: one proclaimed itself as Young Russia; most of them consisted of a press and a handful of zealots.

Chernyshevsky's attitude toward active struggle was not without ambiguities. He claims to have sent an emissary to London to represent to Herzen, once more an activist, how improper it was for him to sit in the safety of England and to stir up young people in Russia to dangerous activities. His own prudence was so great that though most of the insurrectionary proclamations have been ascribed to him, there is no definite proof that he was the author of any of them. Yet his influence is traceable in practically all the manifestoes. This mild, bookish man becomes in 1861, along with his coadjutor and closest friend Dobrolyubov (who died in the same year), the inspirer and leader of the revolutionary movement.

Strong evidence connects Chernyshevsky with a series of three insurrectionary proclamations. They were addressed respectively to the students, the soldiers, and the peasants. The last one, composed in the simple folk language, is supposed to have come directly from his pen. It began, "To the landlords' serfs [actual emancipation was to take place only in 1863], greetings from their well-wishers." The essence of the alleged emancipation is demonstrated as a fraud and really a perpetuation of serfdom. Who is responsible? Just some bureaucrats and the nobles? But the Tsar himself is a landlord so why should he not have the interests of the landlords exclusively in view? When will real freedom come for the peasant? When the people will rule themselves, when the peasant will not have to pay the tax, and when he will not be torn away from his family and village to serve for decades in the army. How is this to be accomplished? By a revolution. Let the peasants take counsel with each other, let them approach their brothers who serve as soldiers and prepare for the great day. But until then they should not engage in piecemeal, isolated uprisings against the government. Only when the movement becomes nationwide will the revolution succeed.[31]

Characteristically, it is impossible in Chernyshevsky's behavior in 1861–62 to disentangle several skeins of motivation. Did he seek martyrdom consciously, hoping for an early revolution, or was he simply and unreasonably confident that his caution and reputation would protect him from an arrest? Probably a little bit of each. The right-wing elements were in full cry after Chernyshevsky as the spiritual if not the actual father of the revolutionary proclamations. One story has it that the governor-general of St. Petersburg, Prince Suvorov (he had the reputation of a liberal and in some circles was being advanced as the future head of a revolutionary regime—such were the fantastic incongruities of the 1860s)

---

[31] To an ultra-Bolshevik historian, Pokrovsky, the "moderation" and the counsel for patience of the proclamation to the peasants compared unfavorably with the proclamation signed *Young Russia* by a group of student hotheads who advocated a wholesale carnage of the imperial party, abolition of the family, republic, etc. This Bolshevik worthy, whose historical views after his death in 1932 were branded by Stalin as a vulgarization of Marxism, saw in Chernyshevsky's advice a prototype of Menshevism. Steklov, *op. cit.*, Vol. I, p. 294.

sent an emissary to offer Chernyshevsky a passport and advice to go abroad. But political migration in the 1860s meant something quite different from what it was to become in Lenin's day. Then there was a powerful international Socialist movement that sheltered and supported its Russian comrades and the avenues of easy access to the homeland. Even Herzen with his great wealth and cosmopolitan tastes was now leading an unhappy and restless existence abroad, and his influence within Russia, enormous as it had been, was on the wane precisely because he was losing touch with the new generation. And few of the Russian revolutionaries have been as Russian as Chernyshevsky. He stayed.

In the spring of 1862 a series of large-scale fires plagued the capital. The reactionary press blamed them on the "nihilists" (the phraseology of the proclamation by Young Russia would not rule out its authors resorting to arson); the radicals rejoined that they were the work of the *agents provocateurs* of the right, and claimed that in some provincial towns the nobles were setting buildings on fire to discredit the emancipation of the peasants scheduled for the coming year. Whatever the truth—and in view of the multitude of wooden buildings and the wretched safety conditions in the contemporary Russian cities it is not necessary to assume arson—the campaign against the revolutionaries and their known or assumed instigators was intensified. Repressions included the closing down of the public reading rooms, of several schools, and the St. Petersburg Chess Club, all of them reputed to be infected with the virus of nihilism and alleged gathering places for the radical intelligentsia. *The Contemporary* was suspended for eight months. And it was inevitable that Chernyshevsky, long under the surveillance of the Third Section, would be arrested. He spent two years in the Petropavlovsk fortress while his case was being "investigated." Legally no proofs of subversive activity could be brought against him, and this, which would not have inhibited the authorities under the previous reign, was something of an embarrassment under Alexander. Finally, with the help of some manufactured evidence the sentence was pronounced in 1864. Chernyshevsky was condemned to seven years at hard labor, but such formalities seldom prevented the Tsarist police from detaining a state criminal for an indefinite period. Only in 1883, broken in health, was he allowed to return to European Russia.

Before being sent into exile Chernyshevsky was subjected to the "civil execution." This barbarous ceremony took place before the public. The prisoner was exhibited on a scaffold wearing a placard with the inscription "state criminal." His sentence having been read, he was made to kneel and a sword was broken over his head. Then in chains he was driven back to prison. Reactions of the audience have been differently described. Most eyewitness accounts agree that Chernyshevsky was applauded by some members of the intelligentsia present at the ordeal. But one account has it that a group of workers hissed the prisoner. To the

masses Alexander was still the Tsar-Liberator and his enemies representatives of the "gentlemen" who resented his benevolent intentions for the
people.

The story of Chernyshevsky's martyrdom goes far to explain the feeling of inferiority that the Russian liberals always felt vis-à-vis their more
radical compatriots. In the face of so much sacrifice and suffering it
appeared unworthy to denounce the recklessness of the revolutionary's
views, or even to dwell too much on the esthetic shortcomings of his
literary work. This meek and infuriating man scored a moral triumph
not only over the regime he detested but also over the moderates who had
deplored the savage implications of his views. He and his followers and
successors seemingly forced the regime to persist in its barbarous methods, which sapped the meaning of the major political and social reforms
of Alexander's time, and thus barred an evolution toward enlightenment
and constitutionalism that promised Russia's salvation. Hence the tragedy
of Russian liberalism, and a preview of the fate of this doctrine over
much of today's world.

In the Petropavlovsk fortress Chernyshevsky wrote his *What Is To Be
Done?*. Since the novel was to play an important role in the formation of
Russian revolutionaries, and since it reveals so much (more than many
political treatises and manifestoes) of the psychology of political radicalism in the 1860s, it is well to consider it at some length.

Except for pornography, *What Is To Be Done?* has all the major characteristics of a bad novel: utter unrealism of situations and characters,
lack of literary grace and style, sententiousness, and ponderous moralizing. The author repeatedly addresses, harangues, and nudges "the perspicacious reader" in a way that is unbearable for the most patient of the
lot and must owe something to Chernyshevsky's early theological training. So much for the reactions of a reader today, and his amazement at the
éclat created by the novel is increased when one remembers that it was
published at the time of the greatest flowering of Russian prose. This
inept, dull, and puerile work fascinated the young generation, which
could compare it with the art of Tolstoy, Turgenev, Dostoevsky and,
beyond them, with the works of a score of unusually talented and interesting novelists then at the height of their creative powers. That the radicals were constrained to defend feebly the merit of Chernyshevsky's
novel has already been explained. Herzen, who felt some responsibility
for Chernyshevsky's arrest, praised its "good points." The oracle of early
Marxism in Russia, Plekhanov, denounced the critics of *What Is To Be
Done?* as "obscurantists." Some argue, with obviously bad artistic conscience, that it should not be compared with *Anna Karenina* but, say,
with Voltaire's novels. But the comparison with *Candide* is just as devastating, or rather unthinkable, as with Tolstoy's masterpiece. Yet as
Plekhanov wrote, "we all have drawn [from the novel] moral strength
and faith in a better future," and later on, "From the moment when the

printing press was introduced in Russia until now [he wrote at the end of the nineteenth century] no printed work has had such a success as *What Is To Be Done?*." [32]

The novel's *leitmotif* is the story of a "new woman," Vera Pavlovna, daughter of a depraved and meretricious mother and a father weak and servile toward both his employer and his wife. Brought up in the degrading lower middle-class atmosphere, Vera surprisingly develops a social consciousness and independence. Pressed by her mother to marry a worthless upper-class lout, she is saved by that veritable *deus ex machina* of the nineteenth century Russian story, the impecunious university student who earns his sustenance as a private tutor. He, Lopukhov, marries her, thus saving her from her sordid surroundings and marriage to the upper-class swain. Need it be said that Lopukhov is a "new man," a believer in "wise selfishness" and holder of the advanced views on the emancipation-of-women question and marriage? Thus the union of Lopukhov and Vera is a marriage in the eyes of the law only; they have separate bedrooms, each can entertain friends without the other's permission and knowledge, and their social intercourse takes place in the neutral ground of the drawing room when they assemble to drink tea and to hold interminable discussions about the philosophy of life. To be sure, this marital coexistence at times breaks down into a greater intimacy, but the point is well established: their marriage is one of those nominal unions which in the sixties and seventies many an "advanced" girl contracted to escape parental oppression, and in which the "husband" at least in theory made no demands on his "wife." Inevitably Vera falls in love with Lopukhov's best friend, also a "new man," Kirsanov. And so, heroically, in order to leave his wife and his best friend to pursue real marital bliss Lopukhov blows out his brains. But, oh, does he really? First Vera Pavlovna and then the reader is teased into the realization that Lopukhov simulated a suicide and went abroad. The role of the Greek chorus in the book is performed by our friend Rakhmetov. It is he who explains to the disconsolate "widow" her husband's noble ruse, asks her to repair to her real beloved, and scolds her for forgetting in her private grief her social obligations. End of the story? No. For some years later a mysterious "North American," Beaumont, appears on the scene and marries a patient of Kirsanov, now a famous doctor. The young couple settle down to live right next to the Kirsanovs and "they live in harmony and amicably, in a gentle yet active fashion, in a joyous and reasonable fashion." [33] The perspicacious reader does not need telling who this alleged North American really is.

[32] G. V. Plekhanov, *Works*, Moscow, 1924, Vol. V, p. 115.

[33] Quotations from *What Is To Be Done?* are mostly from Vintage Books edition, New York, 1961, translation by Benjamin R. Tucker, revised and abridged by Ludmilla B. Turkevich. The abridgment omits some of the politically most important passages.

This bare résumé cannot of course render the full flavor of the novel. Its secondary characters are perhaps as noteworthy as the main ones. Vera's hateful mother, the only person in the book drawn with some artistry, embodies all the brutal and grasping characteristics of the lower middle class. There is a proverbial courtesan with a golden heart and in the same line, but at a lower social level, a virtuous prostitute. The latter is saved by Kirsanov who persuades her to exchange promiscuous amours for a more stable existence of having five or six steady customers. After this period of probation, he himself condescends to live with her but since he is slated for Vera Pavlovna, the unfortunate victim of bourgeois society has to be killed off by tuberculosis. But having been regenerated by working in a seamstresses' cooperative she dies happy, warmly recommending her erstwhile lover to Vera Pavlovna.

Throughout the book runs a strange undercurrent of violence. The "new men" are all reason and sweetness, but they can take care of themselves. "What kind of a man was Lopukhov? This will show. . . ." and Chernyshevsky recounts his hero's meeting with an upper-class gentleman who marches straight at him.

> Now at that time Lopukhov had made this rule. "I turn aside first for nobody except women". . . . And he marches straight at the gentleman. The individual, half turning back, said, "What is the matter with you, pig? Cattle!" and was about to continue in this tone when Lopukhov quickly turning around seized the individual around the waist and threw him into the gutter with great dexterity; then standing over his adversary he said to him, "Don't move or I will drag you into a muddier place." Two peasants passing saw and applauded; a clerk passing saw, did not applaud and confined himself to a half smile.

A passage that tells us more than a whole series of political essays.

What might be called direct political and social propaganda is veiled with Chernyshevsky's usual caution in *What Is To Be Done?*. Even so, it is hard to understand how the book was passed by the censor, for it is seeded with Socialist hints and revolutionary sentiments. The "new men" are clearly Socialists. Vera Pavlovna organizes the seamstresses' cooperatives, where the girls live and work together and the profits are shared, clearly a version of Fourier's phalanstery. But the main vision of the better world of the future appears in Vera Pavlovna's dreams, which are set as interludes in the novel. In one of them she sees a society in which poverty and oppression have been eliminated, where women have full equality, and where obviously government and coercion have disappeared. The whole country is covered by flowering gardens. (Very few people in this utopia will live in the cities.) In their midst rise the palaces of steel and glass. Here in the Fourierist fashion thousands of people eat and amuse themselves together. Science has made the deserts bloom, and all work light and joyful. "Everybody lives as he wishes."

Evenings are spent in dancing and singing, though if somebody prefers to sit in a library or museum he is welcome to it. Thus Chernyshevsky's utopian socialism obviously is a throwback to his youthful infatuation with Fourier. The Soviet commentators cannot repress a sigh that in his novel's vision of the future Chernyshevsky seems to have forsaken his materialist viewpoint for this utopian if Socialist idyll. But even so, its influence has seeped through to Bolshevism. What are the Soviet Houses of Culture and Rest but the descendants of his glass palaces where the masses spend their time in innocent, cultured, and mirthful occupations?

The epilogue of *What Is To Be Done?* consists of a scene of revelry led by a mysterious Lady-in-Black, in which our two happy couples participate. To the modern reader this scene is quite bewildering, but to its contemporaries it was an allegory of a victorious revolution, which according to the chronological hints was to take place in 1866. When in that year Alexander II was fired upon, there was some talk in police circles of bringing Chernyshevsky back for an investigation, but this absurd project was abandoned. To the initiated the whole book was replete with revolutionary allusions, and this as much as its romantic *motif* and the daring theme assured its enormous success.

But the appeal of the book deserves a closer scrutiny. To the adolescent the book was, of course, a novel of adventure and mystery. This genre was to be enormously popular in Russia and despite the fact that *What Is To Be Done?* is set not among the Red Indians or in Africa but in Russia of the 1850s, it has certain characteristics of the novel of adventure. Did or did not Lopukhov . . . ? And the interminable suspense in clarifying Beaumont's true identity quickens the adolescent's heartbeat with a joyful expectation. The dialogue with the perspicacious reader, its hopeless sentimentality wrapped up in hard-boiled realism, the sad end of the virtuous prostitute, the mysterious political hints, the happy and heroic ending; they all appeal to the overserious yet childish mind in a way in which *Anna Karenina* or *The Brothers Karamazov* obviously cannot.

To the somewhat older generation the appeal lay elsewhere. For them its primary message was one of political and social liberation, and especially of the emancipation of women. The conservative press assailed *What Is To Be Done?* as a shameless brief for free love, and this idiotic accusation of course enhanced the popularity of the novel. Chernyshevsky was an exponent of somber and humorless morality, and like the more frightening prophets he had the virtue of practicing what he preached. He would have been shocked at *Lady Chatterley's Lover* and yet his moral, "Dare to be happy," is not different from D. H. Lawrence's. *Lady Chatterley's Lover* has as its main *motif* the deadening effect of industrialization on life and love (though this is understandably often overlooked), and Chernyshevsky levels the same accusation at contemporary Russia with its oppression, especially of women. But then Lady Chatterley never organized seamstresses' cooperatives.

The novel's characters, fantastic though they are, did have some prototypes in the circle of Chernyshevsky's radical friends.[34] Both Kirsanov and Lopukhov are hugely exaggerated portrayals of his acquaintances. Even the fantastic Rakhmetov is suggested by one Bakhmetev, a rich eccentric who appeared in London, deposited with Herzen a sum of money for the revolutionary cause, and then vanished without a trace, allegedly on his way to establish a socialistic community in some wilderness. Thus Chernyshevsky's fantasies fitted in with the spirit of the radical youth. For all his shortcomings he was a genius at propaganda: the social and political system is condemned not only because it is unjust, not only in the name of a higher philosophical and historical principle, but mainly because it prevents happiness and fulfillment of man's most intimate needs. Such a lesson could hardly be gleaned from Marx's *Capital*, but it is a part and parcel of the eternal appeal of communism to the young.

The perspicacious reader of today, if he will have navigated his way through *What Is To Be Done?*, will be jarred by one note that remained unnoticed in the quarrel over the novel's alleged moral vices or virtues: Chernyshevsky's incredible condescension if not contempt toward the ordinary run of mankind. What makes it worse is that the novel's professed tone is one of democracy and equality. It goes to extraordinary lengths to assert the natural goodness of man. But it is all the more striking how artlessly he reveals an unusual kind of intellectual snobbery. The "new men" really are quite sure that they stand above the vulgar multitude. "We did not see these men six years ago . . . but it matters little what we think of them now; in a few years, in a very few years we shall appeal to them; we shall say 'Save us,' and whatever they say then will be done by all." Kirsanov's virtuous prostitute dies and the lover-reformer's feelings are described as follows: "His old love for her had been no more than a youth's desire to love someone, no matter whom. It is needless to say that Nastenka was never a match for him, for they were not equals in intellectual development. As he matured, he could do no more than pity her. . . ." The common man for him is often but a well-intentioned slob; Vera Pavlovna's mother is derided among other things for her ignorance of French. This intellectual snobbery is not untinged by a social one: Chernyshevsky denounces the degenerate aristocracy of the capital, but he cannot help describing Rakhmetov's ancient and distinguished genealogy. His biases, like many of his characteristics, are both disarming and frightening; they are expressed with a disingenuousness that would almost make one believe he is satirizing

[34] The tracing of the characters of *What Is To Be Done?* is found in T. P. Bogdanovich, *op. cit.*

his own convictions, but they have their source in the frightful intensity
of the revolutionary's hatred of the world of the *bourgeoisie* and
officialdom.

It is almost superfluous to talk of Chernyshevsky's "influence" on
Lenin or on the subsequent development of the Russian revolutionary
movement. The Soviet historians hail him as the Great Predecessor. In
their classificatory passion they try to fit him into one of their tiresome
categories: Was Chernyshevsky a Populist, or was he a revolutionary
democrat with a touch of Utopian socialism? They stress—and not only
out of duty—that for all his lack of the final grace of Marxism, no figure
looms as great in the history of revolution prior to Lenin. The father of
Russian Marxism, Plekhanov, is by comparison a dry *raisonneur*. The
revolutionaries of the People's Will who offered their lives in fighting the
autocracy are the romantic precursors of the men of 1905 and 1917. But
Chernyshevsky represents not only the idea and the resolve of revolution. He mirrors the mentality of the revolutionary: his cunning and
naïveté, the ability to withstand and to inflict suffering, both the crudity
and the elation of his vision of a better world.

4. Populism

With 1861 there opens a period in Russian history without a precedent
in the life of a modern nation. Choose almost any sweeping political
generalization about the years 1861–81 and it will contain a substantial
portion of truth, and yet standing by itself it will give a distorted picture.
It is a period of intense revolutionary activity; the ideas of socialism and
revolution pervade every segment of the educated classes. Not only the
student body and young intelligentsia, but a part of the officialdom and
of the army officer corps catch the fever. The same years bring a revival
of reaction and Russian chauvinism. The savage repression of the Polish
rebellion of 1863 is greeted with applause by an overwhelming majority
of society. The *leitmotifs* of reaction, the condemnation of Western materialism and liberalism, the exaltation of autocracy, orthodoxy, and the
messianic vision of Russian nationality receive their classical expression
in the journalistic activity of Katkov and the prose of Dostoevsky, and a
rapturous reception by that part of the public which is tired of the
domination of intellectual life by the left.

But the period is not simply one of the polarization of feelings between reaction and revolution. We still witness ascending liberal hopes
and aspirations. It is an era of great reforms. The emancipation of peasants is but the most remarkable of the series of great measures that bring
Russian society and economy squarely into the nineteenth century. The
basis is laid for municipal and regional self-government. The reform of
the judiciary goes so far to meet the current Western example that an

antigovernment critic unwittingly paid it a compliment in declaring that in view of the backwardness of the other institutions, the newly promulgated courts and procedures were like a silk hat on the head of a naked savage. The military reforms strip the common soldier's lot of much of its ancient horror. These reforms, the most fundamental in Russia's history since Peter the Great, only whetted the appetite of the liberal and enlightened elements. Repeatedly, and most often from the privileged classes, the local assemblies of nobility, voices are heard and petitions are addressed to the Tsar asking that the process of modernization should be crowned by the institution of a national parliament, that censorship should be ameliorated or abolished, and that the remaining discretionary powers of the officials to impose penalties without a trial should be abrogated. That a decisive step toward constitutionalism was not taken can be attributed not only to the resistance and ignorance of the regime, but also and mainly to the intensity and character of the revolutionary activity. Revolution checkmated reform, and reaction was the main gainer.

The paradoxes of politics are mirrored by those of the social scene. If the preceding suggests a country seized by a frenzy of political debate and conflict, then a closer look will produce an opposite impression. In no other country in Europe at the time, it is safe to say, was the mass of people as apolitical, as convinced of the virtues and benevolence of the existing regime as in Russia. To be sure, in the non-Russian parts of the Empire, notably in Poland, the lower classes also felt the oppression of the foreign ruler. But even there revolutionary propaganda found a response mostly among the intelligentsia and the upper classes. To the vast mass of ethnically Russian peasantry the young radicals who wanted to stir them up were but "gentlemen" who out of their grievance and personal dissatisfaction wanted to turn them against their protector and benefactor, the Tsar.

Nor was this feeling confined to the villages. Mention has already been made of the allegations that members of the city proletariat who were present at Chernyshevsky's "civil execution" were openly hostile to the victim. There is no doubt that at similar ceremonies for other political prisoners the attitude of the masses toward the victim was not only hostile but bordered on violence. It is only toward the end of the period that there is some political activity among the industrial workers. But even so these beginnings are unimpressive. Soviet historians date the start of mass political activity among the proletariat from the famous demonstration in the Square of Our Lady of Kazan in St. Petersburg in 1876. But by the contemporary accounts this demonstration attracted a maximum of 200 to 250 participants, hardly impressive in relation to the size of the capital. It is fair to say that revolutionary and Socialist propaganda found a scant response among the masses of the people.

Was that situation simply the product of the ignorance of the masses and of their preoccupation with a struggle for existence? So we are led to believe by the writers sympathetic to the revolutionary cause. But this explanation is as tendentious and one-sided as the one offered by the reactionaries that the Russian peasant was endowed with an ineradicable love for his Tsar and the Orthodox Church. The years before the edict of 1861 had been filled with peasant unrest. Following the announcement of the Emancipation, the turbulence in the countryside increased rather than subsided, and the reason is obvious: the peasants were confused by the complicated provisions of the law; in many cases it did not meet their expectations and saddled them with new burdens and responsibilities. But this new wave of unrest, which inspired the intelligentsia's radicals with the thrilling conviction that the Russian peasant was a born revolutionary, receded in the 1870s. The peasant was no more an instinctive revolutionary than he was an instinctive conservative.

The experience of the years 1861–81 was to leave an ineradicable imprint on the future of the Russian revolutionary movement, on Lenin's personality, and on the concept and development of Communism up to our own day. Those were the years of revolutionary struggle. The radical of the period is no longer merely an essayist as was Herzen, or like Chernyshevsky, merely a propagator of Socialist ideas. He becomes an active fighter for revolution, an organizer of revolutionary circles, or an agitator among the peasants or (still infrequent) among the workers. The older revolutionary was (and this held true even for Chernyshevsky) still a disappointed reformer who turned toward illegality and advocacy of violence only after he convinced himself that there was no chance of a reform from above, that the Tsar would not grant a national assembly or that he would not give *real* freedom to the peasant. To the new revolutionary the vision of a violent upheaval crowds out more and more any possible reform; it even obscures the outline of a better postrevolutionary society. To him the revolutionary deed, braving personal danger in the service of an idea, becomes a psychological necessity.

When the hopes of a spontaneous peasant uprising subside as "the people" repulse or ignore the apostles of revolution, the latter turn to the idea of a conspiracy or political terrorism (the two, as we shall see, were not synonymous) in order to accomplish their aims. In their depositions before the courts the revolutionaries often affirmed that they turned to conspiracy or terror only because they had no opportunity to propagate their ideas lawfully. No doubt most of them were sincere in this conviction. But it does not require any special psychological insight —some of them were quite frank in stating this—to see that they viewed with panic any possible development that might cheat Russia out of a revolution. Will not the growing industrialization transform the Russian peasant into a money-grubbing farmer of the West and strip him of his wonderful communistic instincts? And if the Tsar grants a system of national representation will not the people think that the battle has been won and rest content, like the English or the French, to be represented by lawyers and speculators?

This absorption with the idea of a violent overthrow takes on an aspect of revolutionary egotism that grows more and more undemocratic in its unconscious philosophy. Theoretically the young radicals work for the people, and they are genuinely convinced that they want to help them, and are more than willing to share the sufferings and deprivations of the peasants and workers. But revolutionary activity has to come first. It was one of the *more moderate* leaders of radicalism, Peter Lavrov, who warned the Russian intelligentsia that *apolitical* work for the people was both fruitless and treasonous. In an article entitled "The Force That Is Lost to Revolution," [35] Lavrov taunts, coaxes, and threatens those persons who want to go among the peasants and just work for them as doctors, teachers, midwives, and the like. "You think that a national revolution is not for our generation; that our task is to build in the people self-reliance, to cultivate among them useful activities. . . ." [36] These rather inoffensive beliefs are branded by Lavrov (who himself was considered by many as a disgusting moderate) as "foolish and hopeless." In the first place, the regime will not leave you in peace; you are in as much danger of being persecuted as the revolutionaries. In the second place, Lavrov warns:

> Those members of the intelligentsia who acknowledge the existing regime and are ready to assist in its "reforms" take their place among the enemies of the people, who have always brought perdition and misery to the people, who cannot bring them anything else even if they would wish to, but by the nature of things they cannot really wish the people's welfare because their very existence is based upon the continuous exploitation of the masses. [37]

Lavrov's logic and syntax are not clear, but what is obvious is his fear that young intellectuals will defect from the revolutionary camp and simply—work for the people. Thus any school teacher, rural doctor, in fact every educated man not engaged in revolutionary work becomes an "enemy of the people," of the same people who as Lavrov confesses in the same article are as yet very far from feeling the need for a revolution. The intelligentsia has one task, ". . . to bring the propaganda of socialism and of radical revolution to the masses." It is only they who can bring it (to the peasants) and who can explain the need for revolution. "But it [the teaching of socialism and of revolution] is so simple that its meaning once explained is immediately translated into the rev-

[35] Literal translation: *The Revolution's Lost Forces.*
[36] Peter L. Lavrov, *Collected Socio-Political Works*, Moscow, 1934, Vol. 3, p. 145.
[37] *Ibid.*, p. 162.

olutionary movement, and the task of a national uprising." A member of the educated classes in Russia, adds Lavrov imperiously, has no freedom of choice. His role is dictated by "the needs of the people [and] the laws of sociological developments." The intelligentsia cannot choose another path "because every other path except this one is closed."

In his own way (he would have been shocked to be told it was condescending) Lavrov believed in the people. Once the intellectuals explain things and ignite a revolt, they bow out; the flame spreads, Russia is eventually transformed into an association of free peasant communes, the landowners, policemen, and their like disappear. It is another, more activist version of the dreams of Chernyshevsky. But the word "people" in the revolutionary's mouth begins to sound as grating as when coming from a St. Petersburg bureaucrat. They both know what the people want: one, that if they could be rid of their religious superstitions and the belief in the Tsar they would rise spontaneously on behalf of agrarian communism; the other, that if one could only eliminate the outside agitation with their pernicious ideas the peasants would live content under the Tsar and the Orthodox Church. This infuriating complacency is accompanied in the revolutionary by a more practical belief: most of the battle is won if you win the intelligentsia, especially young men of education and professional training. If you don't, then all the "sociological laws," all the instinctive socialism of the peasant and worker will not help: Russia will continue to be ruled by "idiots and bureaucrats." In the succeeding chapters we shall see Lenin watching like a hawk for any new intellectual current or interest arising amidst the intelligentsia. Tolstoyan pacifism, a new philosophical creed, an intellectualized Christianity, they all become the object of a prompt and shrill denunciation; they all threaten to lead the young intellectual away from his absorption in politics. And without the intelligentsia (much as he hated it) leading the masses, Lenin could not conceive of an overthrow of the regime.

Revolution in search of the masses, this is perhaps the most succinct characterization of the period. How are the people to be aroused from their age-long apathy and ignorance and shaken into action? Recipes were many and they reflected not only the underlying philosophy but also the temperament of the revolutionary. The name Populism,[38] which is given by historians to the movement as a whole, obscures some of the basic differences in strategy. We can divide the revolutionaries, according to what they considered the most urgent task, into propagandists, conspirators, and terrorists.[39] The name Populists in the *narrower* sense belongs to the first group. They were the people who wanted to live

[38] In Russian, *narodnichestvo*, the followers of which are *Narodniks*.
[39] The elements of the other two were always present in each group but the emphasis was clearly different.

and work among the peasants, to instruct them and help them by their example, but also to explain to the people the necessity of revolution. A classical example of a (theoretical) Populist was the above-mentioned Lavrov. An army officer and teacher of mathematics by profession, he joined the revolutionary cause rather late in life.[40] After his arrest and escape abroad in 1870, Lavrov settled in the West where he began to edit *Forward*, a journal designed to continue in a way the tradition of *The Bell*. An awkward writer and a muddled thinker, Lavrov was ill fitted to continue the tradition of Herzen. But he was effective in pointing out the deficiencies of the rival revolutionary sects:

> The conspirators are quite capable of disregarding the people's aims, the social revolution; they [often] do not know people, they do not associate with them. . . . [The agitators (here he meant revolutionaries, à la Bakunin)] . . . arouse the passions of the people, they do not think about the organization, its strength, about explaining what it can and must do. In order to agitate they do not distinguish between deception and truth. . . .[41]

Lavrov's own Populism was based on a repetition of a slogan proclaimed by Herzen a decade before: "Go to the people." Let the young intelligentsia go among the peasant masses; let them extract and nourish the people's revolutionary aspirations not through political demands of which the peasants had little comprehension, such as a plea for a constitution, but by dwelling on the peasants' real grievances: their demand for more land, and their oppression by the local officials. Once the seeds of discontent and socialism are sown the masses themselves will rise.

It was voices like Lavrov's that spurred the amazing phenomenon, the Pilgrimage to the People that swept the intelligentsia in 1874. From their little discussion and conspiratorial groups, from the halls of universities and academies, hundreds of young radicals swept into the countryside. Many of them went to carry propaganda and agitation for a revolution. But the main psychological incentive was to be with the people, to share their privations and suffering, and to convert the peasants by example and by helping them in their everyday needs and problems. In the history of the Russian revolutionary movement, 1874 was the height of the belief in "the people." Never again after that disastrous summer would the Russian radical retain the same faith in the simple goodness and socialistic instinct of the common man, in his readiness to rise and storm the bastions of autocracy and privilege. The Russian revolutionary of the early 1860s began with disillusionment in the Tsar and his willingness to reform the society, his successor of the late seventies concluded by being disenchanted with the peasants and their alleged revolutionary fervor.

[40] His dates are 1823–1900.
[41] Lavrov, *op. cit.*, Vol. 3, p. 352.

The missionaries were driven by the most divergent ideas as to what they would find. Many of them tried to assume the identity of itinerant peasant craftsmen, or of workers seeking employment in the villages. Since even in the twentieth century a city dweller will not easily pass himself off as a rural Vermonter or Yorkshireman, it can be easily imagined what success these attempts at impersonation had in the Russia of the 1870s. Others, more realistically, wanted to place their skills at the service of the peasants, working as teachers, medical workers, and at similar occupations. Their reception was often cruelly disappointing. The Russian peasant had a natural distrust of a "gentleman," especially of one masquerading as a man of the people. Fear of the police and the hard conditions of his life made him wary of extending hospitality to the stranger. Not infrequently the students were denied shelter or even turned over to the authorities. In retrospect, it is amazing that in such a country as Russia in the period when so many young intellectuals came from the landowning families, or were themselves but one or two generations separated from peasant origins, the psychology and conditions of life of the people should have been alien to the educated classes; but perhaps the young radical was not different from his corresponding number in other countries and at other times.

Even when a relationship of confidence was established between the peasants and the propagandists the ultimate result was to prove almost equally disappointing. The young students were eager not only to go among the people; in a way they were eager to strip themselves of their noble and bourgeois accoutrements, to forget their sinful comforts, and to "become" the people. The peasants could see little sense in that. One of the "pilgrims" abandoned the thought of medical practice to "help the people." He was told curtly by a villager that he would be of greater use to himself and to others if he finished his studies.[42] Though the more sensible agitators avoided a frontal attack against the peasants' beliefs and tried not to speak against religion and the Tsar, they were still astounded by the strength of the ancient prejudices. A clever propaganda story would often bring an unexpected reaction. Thus a horrifying tale of how in other countries the landowners and capitalists were chasing the peasants off the land brought a villager's exclamation: "Our Tsar would never let this happen." Some in their effort to become like the peasant masses reverted to the religious beliefs of their childhood. The author of the story, O. V. Aptekman, had himself baptized in the Ortho-

[42] Since despite his incomplete training the author of the story was dispensing medical advice along with propaganda, the remark was common sense. An incident of this medical practice deserves repetition. Our student was confronted by a couple who after much hemming and hawing confessed that despite their great love a very essential element of married life was absent and as a result they had no children. His medical resources unavailing to cure this defect in the husband, the author advised the wife, to the horror of his "patients," to find herself a vigorous young man!

dox Church. One cannot resist the impression that the peasants' simplicity and firmness of belief often came close to converting the would-be missionary. It was the government which, by its severe punishments of these by-and-large immature people made sure that they would continue in their original path.

That the Russian peasant was a born Socialist had been a cardinal belief of the revolutionary. A closer look at the noble savage was bound to produce some doubts on that account also. To be sure, the peasants needed and wanted more land and resented some provisions of the Emancipation Act. But they were by no means universally filled with the love of their commune and the abhorrence of the principle of private property. Told of a new order where the nobility's lands would be distributed among the masses, a peasant exclaimed enthusiastically that he would take his share, hire two workers, and lead a life of ease! The propaganda, even had the police not intervened, was simply incapable of producing that vast Socialist indoctrination that such persons as Lavrov believed necessary to light up the flame of a revolution.

Some of the propagandists conceived their task from a different and more activist angle. Russian history in the sixteenth and seventeenth centuries had notable incidents of vast peasant uprisings. One of them, as recently as 1773, led by an illiterate Cossack, Emelyan Pugachev, came close to shaking the foundations of the Empire. Now only a century later it should not be difficult not only to educate the masses but to stir them up to a concentrated if local uprising that would then spread to other localities. It is not accidental that the pilgrims concentrated their activities in the regions where the great *jacqueries* of the past had taken place. Often these ideas were a reflection of the teachings of Bakunin, who in his usual lighthearted way ignored the fact that a hundred years had produced such changes as the railway and telegraph, and that a peasant riot was no longer likely to grow into a countrywide uprising.

The failure and the logical consequences of the Pilgrimage to the People are fully illuminated by the so-called Chigirin affair, which took place in 1876, two years after the crest of the movement. A handful of revolutionaries working in the Ukrainian region of Chigirin set about to persuade the peasants that the Tsar was calling upon them to rise against the nobility and bureaucracy who were frustrating his benevolent intentions toward his people. This madcap venture was in the spirit of the ancient uprisings, which were often led by an impostor claiming to be or to act in the name of the Emperor. Such was the case with Pugachev's rebellion, where he represented himself as the long dead Peter III. The same element was present in the Decembrist uprising, but the Decembrists had at least a partial excuse for their deception: their venture had a fair chance of success; they were not exposing simple and trusting people to danger just to test a theory or out of exasperation with other means of propaganda. This time the revolutionaries, whose original aim was to educate and to improve the lot of the peasants, put their hand to a gross deception that could not but end in a disaster that would bring ruin to hundreds of ignorant and innocent people. The plotters printed false imperial proclamations urging the peasants to form armed teams and to prepare for the struggle. It is a testimony both to the incredible ignorance of the masses and to the isolation of the countryside that the fantastic enterprise enlisted upward of a thousand villagers and remained undetected for almost a year. Once uncovered, it had the predictable brutal consequences.

The Chigirin affair, though it was condemned by many Populists, still demonstrated the logical impasse in which the movement as a whole foundered. The original assumption about a vast reservoir of revolutionary and Socialist feeling in the countryside that was waiting to be tapped had been shown to be an illusion. The affair was symptomatic of the antidemocratic feeling imperceptibly beginning to infect more and more the revolutionary intelligentsia. If the people despite their misery and despite the government's brutality would not rise or even abandon their ancient superstitions, then obviously peaceful persuasion, teaching by example, and urgent propaganda were unavailing. The experience of the 1870s, of the years of hope and communion with the people was to leave a bitter legacy of the revolutionary intelligentsia's impatience with the obtuseness of the peasant masses. Populism and the movements that sprang from it never abandoned the idea of propaganda in the villages, but the more reckless amidst its followers turned to the paths of conspiracy and terrorism. And some in their exasperation with the peasant were to seek a more promising revolutionary material in the urban proletariat.

Even as the Populist propagandists were readying to go among the people, the conspirators among the revolutionaries were decrying the possibility of converting a majority to the ideas of socialism. As early as 1862 a handful of students was to proclaim the need for a secret organization to seize power and impose a revolutionary order upon a passive or hostile majority. In the year of manifestoes, 1862, the most violent among them carried the signature *Young Russia*. Behind this grandiloquent name was concealed the identity of nineteen-year-old Peter Zaichnevsky, who wrote the proclamation singlehanded though after consulting with a tiny group of fellow students. Nor will the reader be surprised to learn—it fits in with this fantastic period—that the proclamation was written in prison where Zaichnevsky was then held for subversive activities, and that this bloodcurdling document calling for a wholesale slaughter of the imperial family and defenders of the old order was conveyed to the illegal printing shop by an obliging policeman! The author's exhibitionist personality and lust for danger are epitomized by this incident; being a political prisoner, Zaichnevsky had the right to receive friends, but he chose a policeman as a carrier of a document which if intercepted would have earned him a lifetime at hard labor.

Zaichnevsky appears to have stepped right out of Dostoevsky's *The Possessed*. In his lifetime he was never identified as the author of *Young Russia*, and to be sure, who had a better alibi? He had an irresistible passion for conspiracy and for leading the authorities by the nose. Most of his adult life was spent in administrative exile in Siberian and provincial towns. Wherever he went there was soon a conspiratorial circle, and his revolutionary appeal was especially strong to young women. Considering his activities and the frequent complaints of exasperated fathers that he was leading their teen-age daughters astray, and not only politically, Zaichnevsky appears to have enjoyed an unusual tolerance of the local administrative and police officials (or of their wives?). To the end of his life (he died still under police supervision in 1896) Zaichnevsky retained his militant extremism and contempt for the idea of converting a majority of the people to revolution. His own political position he described as Russian Jacobinism, the name which stuck to the conspiratorial side of Populism. Its essence was expressed by Zaichnevsky in his very early youth: "Any revolution, afraid to go too far, is not really a revolution." It was logical that the few real disciples he had were to end up in the Bolshevik Party.

Young Russia upon its publication aroused something like a panic in many circles, and not the least among the "moderate" revolutionaries. Chernyshevsky himself (then shortly before his arrest) is alleged to have sent an emissary to find the young hotheads and to persuade them of the senselessness of their extremism. For indeed even his own views appeared as the epitome of conservatism when contrasted with the virulence of the manifesto. In any other time *Young Russia* would have aroused amusement as an obvious prank of unbalanced youths, but this was Russia of 1862. Religion and family were proclaimed as immoral, "incapable of withstanding even a superficial criticism," trade and commerce "organized thievery."

The Central Revolutionary Committee (!), the alleged author of the manifesto, announced that the revolution would take place in 1863. The overthrow would be the work of a small conspiracy, which *then* would take care to convert the majority of the people by the following means:

> We are firmly convinced that the revolutionary party, which will become the government, if the attempt will be successful, ought to preserve its present centralization . . . in order to introduce new foundations of economic and social life in the shortest possible time. It should seize dictatorial powers and not refrain from taking any necessary steps. The elections to the National Assembly should take place under the influence of the government, which will make sure that it will not contain the partisans of the old order (should they remain alive). . . .

This is in many ways a succinct preview of the tactics of the Bolsheviks under Lenin in 1917–18, and it is easy to see how many have seen in Bolshevism a continuation of Russian Jacobinism. Like Lenin, Zaichnevsky rejected terror as the *means of seizing power*, but believed in "prophylactic" terror against the counterrevolutionaries, once power was seized. But in the vision of the new order there is a world of difference between Young Russia and Lenin: Zaichnevsky still sticks to rural socialism based upon the peasant commune as the foundation of his society. Though acquainted with Marxism, he could no more than the other Populists accept the tactics of a revolution based predominantly upon the urban proletariat or a vision of a new society based upon industry.

If Zaichnevsky is a Dostoevskian character, then his contemporary Sergey Nechaev is in fact the prototype of one of the main figures of *The Possessed*. Nechaev (1847–1882) deserves to be noted, not because there is any connection between his thought and tactics and those of Lenin, but because his personality and ideas portray, as if in a crooked mirror, the lust for revolution reaching even beyond political fanaticism into lunacy. With Nechaev we are already beyond Lenin, in the psychological atmosphere of conspiracy at once so grotesque and criminal as to forecast the darkest incidents of Stalinism.

At the age of twenty Nechaev, after an unsuccessful try at becoming a schoolmaster, found himself in the feverish atmosphere of the revolutionary youth in St. Petersburg. At once he set out to form a conspiracy and to build a legend around himself as a martyr for political freedom who had suffered imprisonment. Dostoevsky's picture of a criminal psychopath was later on to arouse protests of other revolutionaries, who reclaimed Nechaev as a good-natured and devoted political activist. Yet it is incontestable that even in the earliest period of his activity Nechaev would denounce his rivals among the revolutionaries to the police.[43]

In 1869 he went abroad. There his fictitious prison sentence and the equally fictitious revolutionary organization in Russia of which Nechaev was allegedly the emissary earned him the acclaim of the political exiles. His lies were readily believed by Bakunin who, hypnotized by Nechaev's personality, experienced a rebirth of revolutionary hope. The old anarchist and the demented young fanatic collaborated on the famous *Revolutionary Catechism*. If *Young Russia* was the product of fanaticism and youthful exuberance designed to make society and especially the liberals shake in their boots, then the *Revolutionary Catechism* belongs to what might be called the psychopathology of revolution. From the

---

[43] This is acknowledged rather good-naturedly by Bolshevik historian M. Pokrovsky: ". . . their quarrels, sad fact, but one should not hide it, were sometimes settled before the table of the investigating officer, . . . Natanson later on related that Nechaev in fact had betrayed him to the police. . . ." Pokrovsky's article is in *The Young Guard*, Moscow (February–March, 1924), p. 246.

definition of the revolutionary as a "lost man" who has no morality, no feelings, no interests except those of the revolution, to the practical counsels as to how to murder, blackmail, and coerce various classes of political enemies the document raves in what is at once a childish and nightmarish manner. The *Catechism* is not really a political manifesto; it is much more an expression of misanthropic Machiavellianism of a perverse and criminal youth. It characteristically hailed the robbers and criminals as expressing the true revolutionary impulse of the Russian people. The *Catechism* reflects all the political irresponsibility and childishness of Bakunin, whom his strange collaborator galvanized into co-authoring a document that really ran against his long-range political philosophy.

Nechaev was soon back in Russia carrying a card of membership signed by Bakunin in a fictitious European revolutionary alliance. He set about organizing a secret society according to the prescription of the *Catechism*. This was no more original than the principle of the chain letter: a group of five, each of whom would recruit five more members, and so on, no rank-and-file conspirator knowing more than just the members of his cell. A member of the original group, Ivanov, expressed doubts about the existence of a vast network claimed by Nechaev and otherwise annoyed him. This was enough to settle Ivanov's fate. Told by Nechaev that he was a police agent, the members of his "five" murdered him. Nechaev then fled abroad but his fellow assassins were apprehended. Needless to say, the regime made the most of the discovery of the crime. The celebrated trial of Nechaev's followers, which took place in 1871, illuminated both the murder and the *Revolutionary Catechism;* those materials provided the basis for one of the greatest novels in the Russian language.

During his second stay abroad, Nechaev managed to disillusion Bakunin. But to a large number of the political *émigrés*, though now revealed as a murderer as well as a man who would not disdain the use of blackmail and robbery, he still remained something of a political martyr. The temper of the revolutionaries moved very far from the situation of a few years before, when Herzen and other radicals could be appalled at the mere idea of violence and bloodshed in politics. When Nechaev was apprehended in Switzerland and handed over to the Tsarist police in 1872 there were indignant protests that the right of political asylum was being violated. Nechaev played to the hilt the role of a political martyr during the trial. Sentenced, he who had no use for and derided constitutionalism and assemblies, shouted "Long live the National Assembly!"

He did not break while imprisoned under the severest conditions, and indeed came close to subverting his guards.[44] As late as 1880–81 the terrorists of the People's Will planned to rescue him from his fortress

[44] He had been sentenced to twenty years at hard labor.

imprisonment and the attempt was abandoned, with Nechaev's consent, only because the first priority was given to the assassination of the Emperor Alexander II.

Nechaev died in his prison in 1882. His career, unlike that of other thinkers and fighters for the revolution, has the morbid fascination that may, excusably but erroneously, lead a Western reader to see in Nechaev a "typically" Russian revolutionary, an ancestor of the revolutionary tactics and mentality of the Bolsheviks. But even Dostoevsky, the exponent of extreme Russian conservatism, saw in Nechaev an exception among the revolutionaries, a maverick and psychopathic representative of the species. What gives his story an ominous and prophetic ring is the hypnotic power which at times he exerted over the radicals who were both sane and alien to his criminal temperament. Murder, blackmail, and denunciation were held to be more than offset by the conspirator's revolutionary zeal and self-sacrifice. The Russian liberal has always been hesitant to denounce the violent means advocated by the revolutionaries, because he felt shamed by the latter's suffering for his ideas. In the same manner the revolutionaries of the People's Will, who claimed high moral standards, saw in Nechaev only intrepid courage and dedication, and disregarded common murder and blackmail. In the topsy-turvy world of the Russian revolutionaries, ominously prophetic of the politics of the twentieth century, the liberal could feel a sense of moral inferiority toward a terrorist, and the idealistic revolutionary would not reject the assistance of a criminal psychopath.

Unlike Zaichnevsky, an eternal adolescent, who despite all the efforts of sympathetic commentators cannot be endowed with a political philosophy, Peter Tkachev was the only representative of the conspiratorial tradition who was a thinker of distinction and of an original turn of mind. Tkachev was born in 1844. His life has the full pathos of the search for self-expression, revolution, and self-destruction of the extremists of that turbulent generation. He served his revolutionary apprenticeship and first imprisonment at seventeen. He was to die in foreign exile, in an insane asylum, when barely in his forties. His first imprisonment provoked Tkachev to express the conviction that a regeneration of Russia would require physical liquidation of everybody over twenty-five years of age. His biographer, who presumably never heard of Sigmund Freud, finds this statement "unduly youthful" and adds reassuringly that Tkachev soon gave up this original plan of a rejuvenation of society.[45]

The early years were spent intermittently in imprisonment and in writing on literary and social themes. Tkachev was acquainted with Nechaev and he was one of the accused in the great trial of the alleged followers of the latter in 1871. Despite the gravity of his offense, the

[45] B. Kozmin, *P. N. Tkachev and the Revolutionary Movement of the 1860's*, Moscow, 1922, p. 19.

authorship of a revolutionary manifesto, Tkachev got off with a relatively mild sentence and in 1873 he was permitted to go abroad.

It was there that he was able to develop his really significant and original insight: The passage of time is not working in Russia for the revolution. Quite the contrary; the growth of capitalism and of industrialization brings with it bourgeois contentment and moderation. An admirer and, like all the revolutionaries, pupil of Chernyshevsky, Tkachev did not believe with his master that the future must belong to the "new man." If you let the opportunity slip away the future will belong to the money-grubbing middle class, and the revolutionary fervor of the minority will collapse. Thus the instinctive fear of the zealots that "their" revolution will run away, that their generation will be cheated out of a bloody and cataclysmic upheaval, receives its strongest and most reasoned expression in Tkachev.

What can save Russia from that catastrophe (i.e., a peaceful transition to constitutionalism) and bring a revolution *now?* Only a united and tightly centralized organization of the revolutionaries. Tkachev has no patience with Bakunin's dreams of vast spontaneous popular uprisings. He scorns the anarchic principle. "We acknowledge anarchy . . . but only as the desirable ideal of the far distant future." [46] Only an organized minority can achieve a revolution. "This minority in view of its higher mental and moral development always has and ought to have intellectual and moral power over the majority." The essence of revolution lies in coercion and thus the revolutionary organization requires "centralization, strict discipline, speed, decisiveness and coordination of activities." [47]

Less than thirty years afterward, V. I. Lenin was to use similar words in describing the revolutionary organization needed by the Russian Socialists. An uncompromising insistence on centralization and discipline, contempt for the possibility of any spontaneous uprising by the majority, those are the threads uniting the Russian Jacobin Tkachev to the Socialist Lenin. Implicit in both is an antidemocratic elitist attitude. Like Lenin after him, Tkachev rejected individual terrorism, not out of any sentimental regard for human life, but because terrorism meant a dissipation of revolutionary resources and energies. The emphasis must be on a centralized, conspiratorial organization to strike at the ripe moment and in a *coup d'état* "bury the old world."

The disparagement of terror could not in a conspirator and former associate of Nechaev be as strong as his contempt for the ideas of peaceful persuasion inherent in the Pilgrimage to the People and similar ideas of rousing the masses. Not having much faith in the general run of mankind, Tkachev looked with skepticism at the Russian peasant and his alleged revolutionary impulses. The average man, he repeated insistently,

[46] P. N. Tkachev, *Collected Works,* Moscow, 1933, Vol. 3, p. 223.
[47] *Ibid.,* p. 225.

is a narrow egoist, thinking of his material comforts, and only a small group of dedicated revolutionaries can rise above this unappetizing reality of human nature.

This disparagement of the common man at times turns to hate, a not uncommon occurrence in the revolutionary or the reformer. When Tkachev did play with the idea of issuing a revolutionary appeal to the masses he did so with unparalleled cynicism. Once abroad it was thought that he should issue an appeal to the peasants. Written in the "popular" language, the draft contained the following passage describing the peasant's existence after the revolution has triumphed:

> And the peasant will live a joyful life. Not copper coins but golden rubles will fill his purse. As to cattle and fowl their number will defy counting. His table will be covered . . . with meats of all kinds, cakes and sweet wines. Drink and eat he will as much as his belly will take, but work only as much as he wishes. And nobody will dare in anything to force him: you want, you eat; you want, you lie in bed. A splendid life.[48]

The Russian radicals of all persuasions were not too squeamish when it came to the means of bringing the peasant to their side, but Tkachev's appeal to gluttony and covetousness was generally thought to go beyond the limit. Lavrov denounced him and Tkachev found himself more and more isolated even among the extremists. His remaining years of sanity were devoted to the publication of the organ of Russian Jacobinism, *The Tocsin,* and to an eloquent though ineffectual denunciation of his rivals among the *émigrés.*

Tkachev's "ideology" can be largely summarized by two words: conspiracy and revolution. He called himself a Socialist, but what Russian radical since Herzen called himself anything else? The Soviet writers on Tkachev are fond of pointing out that he read and commented favorably on Karl Marx. To be sure, he was spared that closer acquaintance with the father of "scientific" socialism which in the cases of Herzen and Bakunin led to lifelong antagonisms and mutual excommunications. But what interested Tkachev in Marx was simply that the latter was an extreme revolutionary, and that he emphasized the role of the economic element in politics. Of the philosophic and historic complexities of the Marxian system Tkachev had no comprehension; if he had, he would have deemed them idle philosophizing that interferes with action. When the cofounder of Marxism, Friedrich Engels, felt called upon to give some fatherly advice to the Russian radicals, Tkachev answered him quite rudely. The debate offered a foretaste of the discussion between the Bolsheviks and the Western Socialists between 1903 and 1914: the latter scandalized by their Russian colleagues' overly conspiratorial ways and extremism advised more caution and a broader, more democratic

---

[48] Tkachev, *op. cit.,* Vol. 1, p. 22.

organization. For such advice Tkachev had even less patience than Lenin. But his answer, ill-humored and impudent as it was, still shows an insight into the revolutionary opportunities of Russia, an insight that was to come like a flash into the mind of Lenin during the March days of 1917.

> It is Russia's backwardness which is her great fortune, at least from the revolutionary point of view. In the West the social order is based on a wide support of the middle class. In Russia this class is just coming into existence. What holds things together in our country? Just the state, i.e., the policy and the army. What is needed to make this state fall into fragments? Not much: two or three military defeats . . . some peasant uprisings . . . *open revolt in the capital.*[49]

Not a bad preview of what was to take place in 1917. The "green high school students" (as Engels qualified Tkachev and his fellow hotheads) were to be shown more perceptive and prophetic than the co-inventor of "dialectical materialism" and "scientific" socialism.

A note of caution is required, however, if we are not to ascribe to Tkachev a second sight that enabled him to lay down *exactly* what was needed to produce 1917. For all his acumen, he was beating his head against the wall of Tsarist despotism as ineffectively as his fellow radicals. He could see what were the elements of weakness of the old order. He perceived the type of organization needed to seize power when a historic cataclysm would overtake Russia. But he lacked those two vital insights that brought success to his great successor: first, that the intelligentsia may and must lead a revolution; it cannot quite make it by itself; and second, that pure revolutionary Machiavellianism is not enough; a party that wants to seize and to *hold* power in such a country as Russia must have a more elaborate ideology. Had Lenin with his more mature views been a contemporary of Tkachev, it is unlikely that he would have been more successful. But had Tkachev with his "Let us seize power, then we shall see" philosophy been present in 1917, it is unlikely that he would have furnished more than a footnote to a chronicle of the upheaval. It is not 1917 that illustrates the full measure of Lenin's genius. It is the years that follow the Great Revolution.

What makes a revolutionary? This question has been asked and answered an insufferable number of times, but a consideration of the conspiratorial side of Russian Populism may still offer some illumination. Dostoevsky posed the tragedy of contemporary Russian society as the main theme of *The Possessed*. Like most reactionaries, he saw extremism as the logical fruit of liberalism. It is the older generation of the intelligentsia who lost touch with religion, with tradition, with the people who produced the "men of the sixties," militant atheists, assassins, and con-

---

[49] My italics.

spirators. The character who stands for Nechaev in the novel is made to be the son of a semicomic, semipathetic liberal of the preceding generation. But not untypically the genius of the writer often transcends his ideological hobby horse. Though he harps on the theme that the loss of religious faith is the ultimate cause of the illness of society, there are passages in which a more complete answer is suggested.

Few scenes in literature combine political satire and political perception as brilliantly as the famous meeting of the revolutionary circle in *The Possessed*. The author utilizes it to present his parody of the various species of the "progressive" zoo. Thus the elderly major who in his youth used to circulate *The Bell* and the revolutionary proclamations and is now no longer engaged in such dangerous activities still likes to hang around where extreme political views are discussed. He is tolerated because "he would never inform the police." At the other extreme is the high school student sitting "with the gloomy expression of a youth hurt in his dignity, and visibly suffering because of his eighteen years." The comical high point is a paper by an amateur revolutionary, who though he has not completed his plan of the society of the future (however, it already has ten chapters) has been able to decide that all the preceding philosophers—Plato, Rousseau, Fourier, and the like—were "fools . . . dreamers . . . ignorant of the biological sciences and of the nature of that strange animal which is called man." His own system "beginning with the premise of unlimited freedom concludes in complete despotism. I shall add that apart from my solution of the social question there can be no other." The philosopher's system calls for one tenth of the population to enslave the rest to the point where they lose their individualities and become like cattle. It is only thus that the people can reach the social paradise. Today perhaps this does not sound quite as funny.[50]

There is more than this frightening parody in the speech of the mad "social philosopher." Petulantly he announces that if his system is not to get a hearing then those present would better disperse, "men to follow their jobs in government service, women to their kitchens." And an echo of the same theme is in the remark of Dostoevsky's "Nechaev," who thinks all discussion of social theories a waste of time. "I understand that you are bored in your little town, so you grasp at those paper images." And indeed these digressions hit close to the mark. In the absence of the free intercourse and conflict of ideas that was the rule in the West, all of Russia to an impatient young man must have presented the aspect of the monotony of a "little town." Beyond the very real political and economic evil the Russian intellectual could feel the general grayness and

[50] In what might have been a paraphrase of Tkachev's youthful predilection for a wholesale slaughter one of the participants in this revolutionary *soirée* finds even this new system too conservative. He would take the intractable nine tenths and "blow them up, and leave only the minority of educated people who would then be able to live in a cultured way."

oppressiveness of his society. For most of them "government service" with its frustrations and limitations presented the only avenue of advancement. Nineteenth century Russia for all its cultural greatness could not offer a sufficient scope for the energies and idealism of the educated young men. It is possible to blame this state of affairs, as Dostoevsky would have it, on the godlessness and superficial liberalism of the educated classes. It is also possible to see the root cause in the lack of that free and vigorous industrial and political activity which in the West absorbed the energies of the contemporaries of Nechaev and Tkachev.[51]

The line that separates the terrorists among the Russian Populists from the conspirators must be somewhat superficial. Yet this classificatory pedantry, which must appear bizarre to the modern reader, is a necessary and meaningful one insofar as the period of the sixties and seventies is concerned. The conspirator felt that political assassination, if excusable under certain circumstances, was still inappropriate as the main weapon of the revolutionary struggle. The terrorist came to feel that the conspirator's scheme of seizing political power by a *coup d'état* was a pipe dream, which under the conditions of Russian life had no basis in reality. Propaganda among the peasants had failed. The expectations of a vast revolutionary upheaval, whether à la Bakunin of a spontaneous anarchic character or according to Tkachev directed by a small disciplined order of conspirators, had alike been mocked by the events. What then remained? It was really in a sense of despair that the radicals turned to what they conceived to be the most desperate weapon of revolution—political assassination.

That individual terror can be the decisive political weapon is refuted by the whole history of the Russian revolutionary movement. The murder of Alexander II in 1881 was to bury for a generation all the hopes of both the revolutionaries and the liberals. Those political parties and groups which relied mainly upon terror suffered demoralization and disruption.

The reasons for it, though later on illuminated by the melancholy history of the Socialist Revolutionary Party, might be briefly noted here. They have to do not so much with the moral revulsion that assassination

---

[51] Scratch almost any Russian revolutionary of the period and you will find a frustrated novelist or literary critic. Tkachev was no exception, and he did indulge in criticism of fiction as well as political and economic works. His political views usually got the better of his critical sense. In Chernyshevsky he saw one of the greatest economists of the nineteenth century. Dostoevsky in Tkachev's view lacked the artistic sense and excelled only in the portrayal of psychic derangement. Reviewing *The Possessed*, the book in which he conceivably might have been the prototype for one of the secondary characters (Dostoevsky had known him as a young publicist in St. Petersburg), Tkachev complained that it portrayed mentally sick people who had nothing in common with the real revolutionaries. It is interesting to note that, with the shining exception of Herzen, the revolutionary camp lacked utterly the literary talent which in the period under discussion was characteristic of the liberals or reaction.

arouses in society at large (and in Russia the "enlightened public opinion" in the nineteenth century was at times tolerant of terror) as with the effects of acceptance of terror on its perpetrators. Apart from the mentally deranged, the idea of political assassination attracts the most idealistic and devoted among the revolutionaries. These individuals become lost to the urgent tasks of political propaganda and organization. The Party thus loses its most effective leaders. From an even more cold-blooded point of view, terror works havoc with the resolution and morale of the conspirators. The stereotype view of the Russian political terrorist as a man of iron resolution and ruthlessness is profoundly wrong. The same involved psychological mechanism that will push an otherwise normal man to an act of violence will more often than not make him irresolute and squeamish on questions of political power. A man ready to sacrifice his own and another's life because of a deep conviction will seldom be the man who unblinkingly will sign a warrant of execution for hundreds or thousands of defeated enemies. The Bolsheviks understood that only too well.[52]

The turn toward terrorism was then dictated by the failure of all other avenues of revolutionary activity. In 1875–76 various groups of the Populists coalesced into an illegal party, which took the name *Zemlya i Volya* (Land and Freedom, the Russian *Volya* meaning either freedom or will). This party, which commemorated in its name the revolutionary grouping of the early sixties, was soon split up by quarrels about its attitude toward terror. The professed aim, the continued agitation among the peasants, grew more and more fruitless. Even the most ardent proponents of "pure" Populism were forced to face the uncomfortable facts: whereas peasant riots were plentiful in the sixties in the wake of emancipation (thus illustrating that frequently the immediate effect of a reform is an increase in discontent within the class that eventually benefits by it), they grew scarce in the seventies and petered out almost completely by the end of the decade. The movement "to the people" still continued. Efforts were made to penetrate the urban workers' circles. But the revolutionary movement was still tied too strongly to its illusions about the peasant, and the industrial proletariat, though growing rapidly, was still too insignificant for the Populists to base their

[52] This point is illustrated in the recollections of a Bolshevik veteran. February 1917 found him in exile in Siberia. Among his fellow convicts was a Socialist-Revolutionary, a renowned terrorist. Despite their different political opinions, the two exiles lived in perfect harmony. The February Revolution freed them and they were returning to European Russia. The Bolshevik's first reaction to the joyful events was the opinion that the imperial family should be physically liquidated. No, replied the terrorist; now that Russia was free no more blood was to be spilt, even that of the former oppressors and exploiters. Soon the former terrorist turned humanitarian and the former opponent of terror turned into a proponent of mass liquidation of the "class enemy" found themselves in a violent quarrel, which lasted the rest of their journey.

activity and hopes on the workers. The People's Will began to indulge in terrorism.

"Indulge" is not an inappropriate word. Terrorism stole in upon the revolutionaries with an unexpectedness and rapidity of an addiction. Though the later accounts try to portray the terrorists as men of inflexible will and resolution, it is clear that their growing addiction was to many a cause for shame and severe moral conflict. It is not that they would have hesitated to take the enemies' and to expose their own lives in an uprising, but the sporadic picking off of the government officials was felt to be ineffective and not advancing the revolutionary struggle. Assassination became a form of self-indulgence and expression of impatience, and the sincere revolutionary would not admit but to himself that it marked a drastic departure from his original ideals. That this method of struggle also tended to attract persons who were unbalanced could not be overlooked. The potential or actual assassin was not infrequently the man who would break most easily under questioning, and turn into a police informer or an *agent provocateur*.

The Land and Freedom felt drawn into the morass of terrorism through the usual stages of addiction. At first it was agreed to resort to assassination "a little bit," killing only traitors within the organization and the particularly brutal governors and police officials. This aspect of terrorism was viewed not without sympathy by a huge segment of the educated classes. After Vera Zasulich had shot and wounded a police official who had ordered flogging of a prisoner she was acquitted by a jury, and became a heroine of "enlightened public opinion." But very soon the intended victims included more than the sadists among the officials and terrorism became a regular form of political activity of the Land and Freedom. Many of its activists chafed under this situation. Their objections were directed not only against terror in itself but also against the transformation that the use of terror was working on the political objectives of the party. The work of propaganda among the peasants and workers was being neglected. And most disquieting of all, in one of those fantastic paradoxes that are the rule in the Russian revolutionary movement, the convinced terrorist became more moderate in his politics than his antiterror colleague.

The explanation of this paradox is actually simple. The "executioner" of the Tsarist officials was not to be identified in his own eyes and those of society with a common murderer. He had to accompany his deed with a political demand. The only one that could find support among the majority of the progressive and educated people was the demand for a constitution: Russia along with every other civilized country should now have a parliament to guide the destiny of the nation. The word *constitution* grated upon the ears of many Populists. Theirs was a kind of formless agrarian socialism. Their tactics were often an incongruous mixture of the ideas of Lavrov, Bakunin, and Tkachev. To demand a constitution was in their eyes to raise a "political" rather than a "social" issue, and this confused objection concealed their fear, and a justified one, that any assembly of the representatives of the Russian people would have no use for socialism, agrarian or any other kind. Were the "political" campaign to succeed, the condition of the nation would become worse, repeated the enemies of the terror. But for their part they could present no alternative to the terror and "politics" beyond the work among the peasants and revolutionary propaganda. And this was beating one's head against the wall of the people's apathy and hostility.

The breach within Land and Freedom was consummated in 1879. The proponents and enemies of terror held heated discussions. The latter at one point threatened that they would warn the intended victims. The terrorists replied that they would not hesitate to turn their guns against the informers. Finally, the organization split into two: the terrorists set up *Narodnaya Volya*, The People's Will; their opponents, the enemies of "politics," called their faction The Black Partition. It was to concentrate on agitation for the redistribution of all the land among the peasants. The two "parties," each of them a mere handful of people, set up their printing presses and began their activities among them, spying on each other. Though the Black Partition was soon to disintegrate, from its ranks were to come the founders of Marxian socialism in Russia—among them the father of Russian Marxism and the teacher of Lenin, brilliant and exasperating George Plekhanov.

Less far-reaching but more spectacular was to be the fate of the People's Will. Though in its proclamations it advanced a Socialist program with the inevitable stress on the peasant commune, its main and immediate demand was for a Constituent Assembly elected by a universal and free suffrage. Its chief, in fact only, means of struggle was to be terror, and its main objective the Emperor. To stifle the remaining scruples it was decided to devote two thirds of its resources to the work in the villages and one third to terror, but that was self-deception. The organization simply had no personnel for large-scale propaganda work, and all its active members had to be drawn into the melancholy task of the preparation and execution of the assassination. That the People's Will contained at its crest as many as five hundred members and sympathizers, as claimed by the most sympathetic historians, is probably an exaggeration. The activist hard core, mainly the so-called Executive Committee, was a mere handful, and for two years this body of twenty or thirty persons was to terrorize the vast empire.

The tragic story of the People's Will is ineradicably linked with the names of Andrei Zhelyabov and Sophia Perovskaya. In the revolutionary tradition, their names epitomize Chernyshevsky's "new men" with their readiness to sacrifice everything for their ideals, not as self-proclaimed martyrs, but as persons who find joy in their ideals. Their love and gallantry in the face of death lends a touch of romance to the depressing tale of the assassination of Alexander and the subsequent trial and execution of the assassins. Their life stories are a testimony to the varied impulses that drove Russian society to its tragic destiny.

Even so, the favored place that Zhelyabov is granted by the Soviets among their revolutionary predecessors is less the product of sentiment and admiration than of deliberation and the usefulness of his legend. Lenin singled out Zhelyabov as a great precursor of Bolshevism, though privately he had but little use for the suicidal heroics of the Populists. Against Lenin's public panegyrics must be balanced his impatient reply to a collaborator who in 1906 wanted a commemorative tribute on the anniversary of Zhelyabov and Perovskaya's deed: "They died, so what? Glory and fame to them, but why should we talk about it?" But for public use Zhelyabov presents a more satisfactory revolutionary precursor than most. He was a man of action, not a writer. Hence he left no legacy of "incorrect" theories. There was nothing psychopathic or excessively introvert about his personality. Zhelyabov's was the proverbially Russian "broad nature"; gay and outgoing, lover of song and dance, he does not fail to present a contrast in these respects to many of the revolutionaries. So much so that the more dull-witted of the Soviet chroniclers feel in turn constrained to defend Zhelyabov from the charge of being a ladies' man and unduly prone to raise a glass. As against such inhabitants of the revolutionary Olympus as Bakunin, with his sexual impotence, and Nechaev, Zhelyabov presents a reassuring picture of normality and enjoyment of life.

Beneath the varnish of the official legend Zhelyabov emerges, of course, as a much more complicated figure. He was the son of a serf and his revolutionary passion was not uninfluenced by the memories of the humiliations and injustices of serfdom, even during its last days. The decision to join and to lead the terrorists did not come to him lightly, and he stipulated that after the Tsar's execution he would go back among the peasants and conduct peaceful agitation. For all his outward gaiety and resoluteness, Zhelyabov's behavior both before and after his arrest betrayed an almost suicidal impulse. He was unusually insistent that the assassination should not involve innocent bystanders, and it is probable that unconsciously he dreaded the deed.[53]

Zhelyabov's companion, Sophia Perovskaya, who after his imprisonment directed the last stages of the assassination of March 1, came from a

---

[53] For an experienced conspirator, Zhelyabov walked too easily into a police trap. From the beginning of his imprisonment he insisted on his responsibility for all the terroristic attempts on the life of the Tsar, thus predetermining his fate.

very different social sphere. Her father had been governor of St. Petersburg, member of a family which furnished ministers, governors, and generals to the state. His own brutality and dissipation were clearly responsible for the young girl's decision to leave home and begin a revolutionary activity. Once she joined the People's Will her commitment to terror was much more straightforward and uncompromising than that of Zhelyabov. This young woman of twenty-six was not interested in the political demands of the organization, but most anxious that the Emperor should be made to pay the ultimate penalty for the tyranny of his regime.

For a year and a half the revolutionaries conducted a veritable chase after the Tsar. There were several elaborate attempts to blow up the imperial train. Another effort that misfired consisted in blowing up the dining room in the Winter Palace; the Emperor had just stepped out and the casualties were limited to the palace servants and soldiers.

It is one of the proverbial ironies of history that while the tyrannical Nicholas I died in his bed, his son the "Tsar-Liberator" was to be the objective of this unremitting chase. He had begun his reign in an atmosphere of enthusiasm. After the announcement of the great reforms, such revolutionaries as Herzen, and even briefly Chernyshevsky, loaded him with praise and declarations of loyalty. In those days he had moved among the people without any security precautions. In 1866 when the first attempt was made on his life, the Tsar's words when the would-be assassin was brought before him were: "You cannot be a Russian" (he believed that only a Pole would raise his hand against the Emperor), and was abashed by the reply: "I am a Russian nobleman." To the growing wave of terrorism during his last years the government's response was a mixture of repressions and of conciliatory moves. The prospect of a fundamental reform was caught in a vicious circle: the introduction of parliamentary institutions in a country as unripe politically as Russia frightened not only the conservatives, but no other step could hope to affect the grim reality.

On March 1, 1881, the Tsar finally yielded to the urgings of his more liberal ministers and signed the law that would bring elected representatives into the state's highest organs. Since these organs were to be of a consultative character, the law was still far from bestowing a parliamentary government on Russia. Yet it would have been the necessary first step, and Russia would have started her experiment in constitutionalism twenty-five years earlier than in fact she did, and with incalculable consequences on her history. But the same day the People's Will cornered its quarry. A bomb was thrown at the Tsar's carriage as he was passing along a street of St. Petersburg. This bomb wounded one of the convoy and a bystander, but left Alexander unhurt. His fearlessness cannot be questioned. Almost any other man in his place would have thought only of gaining the security of his palace, but the Emperor stopped his carriage, got out, and insisted on looking at the wounded.[54] It was then that another terrorist threw his bomb, mortally wounding both the Emperor and himself.

In his youth (he was born in 1850), Zhelyabov is reported to have expressed the wish to "give history a push." The "deed of March 1," of which he was the main organizer, was certainly such a push. As in 1825 after the Decembrists' revolt, the evolution of Russia was pushed backward, and a new period of rigid reaction followed the half-hearted liberalism of the previous reign. The new Emperor, Alexander III, acceded to the reactionary influences of his environment and refused to promulgate the legislative reforms that his father signed on the day of his death. The executioners and planners of the assassination, practically the whole leadership of the People's Will, were soon apprehended, and within two years the organization was in effect annihilated. The deed was supposed to force the regime to grant a constitution, and on the morrow of the assassination a proclamation of the People's Will repeated the demand for a Constituent Assembly. But it had not required much perspicacity to see that the effect would be a triumph of reaction. The new Emperor lacked his father's intelligence and sporadic reforming zeal. In the more conservative circles Alexander II had been viewed as a dangerous liberal, and his death must have been the source of secret satisfaction not only to the revolutionaries.

In society at large the death aroused shock. To a large number of the progressive intelligentsia, such persons as Lenin's father, Alexander II had remained the Tsar-Liberator, and his murder could not but weaken their sympathy toward the radicals and revolutionaries. Among the staunch monarchists the event led to a formation of a counterrevolutionary terrorist organization, the Sacred Band; it did not last long but provided a preview of the much more active right-wing terrorism in the twentieth century. And the people at large reacted with a mixture of horror and confusion. Among the peasants there were stories that the Emperor was done to death by the landlords who hated him for his benevolence toward the simple people.

Much of the revulsion of the educated classes was abated as a consequence of the heroic conduct of the main defendants before the court. Zhelyabov, especially, delivered an impassioned but cogent speech defending the ideals of the People's Will and pointing out how peaceful political activity was barred to him and his generation. His indomitable posture set up the pattern and example of the revolutionary, unmindful of his life, defying the autocracy before the wider tribunal of public opin-

[54] Some accounts friendly to the revolutionaries suggest ungallantly that Alexander simply "lost his head," but he had had considerable experience with attempts on his life, and the possibility of another attempt could not have been absent from his mind.

ion. At times his defiance was excessive: when the prosecutor in the course of his speech delivered a florid eulogy of the late Emperor the accused chortled. "When people weep the Zhelyabovs laugh," said the prosecutor, and even a Soviet historian is forced to admit that he scored a point.[55] Some of the effect of the dignity and defiance by Zhelyabov and Perovskaya was spoiled by the repentance and breakdown of the first bomb thrower, Rysakov. This unfortunate boy (he was in his nineteenth year) begged for forgiveness and offered his services to the police. It is still incredible that he was shunned up to the scaffold by his fellow accused, and that the historians have nothing but harsh things to say about the youth who had been drawn into the conspiracy by Zhelyabov's personal magnetism, and who could not be expected to possess the inflexibility of a mature revolutionary. The result of the trial was foreseeable. The five accused were condemned to death, and the Tsar, despite appeals to show Christian mercy (among them one from Leo Tolstoy), and the lack of precedent for the public hanging of women, sanctioned their execution.[56]

The trial was to have a fateful influence on the future of the revolutionary movement in Russia. Six years later Alexander Ulyanov, with Zhelyabov's example in mind, was also to take the full responsibility upon his shoulders and only the extreme pleas of his mother made him petition, ineffectively, for pardon, something still shamefacedly omitted in most biographies of Lenin's brother. But the mournful legacy of revolutionary heroism was to have an unexpected and sinister effect on the Bolsheviks. In prerevolutionary Russia the accused in the political trial often became the *accuser* and was accepted as such by a large part of society. Hence the Soviet insistence, which to one ignorant of the genealogy of the revolutionary movement appears pathological, that the accused should fully confess and admit the criminality of his real or fictitious deeds. There must be no Zhelyabovs or Alexander Ulyanovs under Soviet justice.

This last cold-blooded deduction from history is characteristic of many lessons that Lenin and his movement learned from their predecessors. He revolted, as we shall see, not only against the Tsarist government and the social system, but against many of the aims and methods of the whole nineteenth century revolutionary movement, and, in a sense, that revolt was the more fundamental one. How revolution can grow out of a small measure of toleration, how fast literary and artistic criticism can be transformed into a social weapon, how the educated young men, unless constantly watched and regimented, will give a political expression to their frustrations and aggressiveness; all those lessons were to be learned

---

[55] A. Voronsky, *Zhelyabov*, Moscow, 1934, p. 331.

[56] The sixth accused, Gesia Gelfman, was discovered to be pregnant and her sentence was commuted.

more thoroughly by the Bolsheviks than by the most reactionary of the Tsar's ministers. But this takes us beyond 1917.

It is tempting to pass a variety of apocalyptic judgments on Russian radicalism. It is more relevant to repeat and conclude that most of the striking characteristics of the Russian revolutionary movements were derived from their numerical weakness. It is a platitude, and most often a correct one, that revolutions are made by militant minorities. Even so, they must find their base and support in *conscious* aspirations of a large segment of the society. Such was not the case, despite all the appearances and self-delusions, with any revolutionary group in Russia between 1825 and 1881. And this lesson could not be lost upon the young man who in the late 1880s was seeking his road to revolution.

III

APPRENTICESHIP

1. Samara

We left young Lenin in the library in Kokushkino in the winter of 1887–88. It was there that the panorama of Russia's revolutionary thought and struggles was first studied by him in the old issues of such progressive magazines as *The Contemporary* and *The Fatherland Notes*. The period of enforced idleness and of intensive radical self-indoctrination continued for almost a year. Not until October 1888 was Lenin allowed to return to Kazan, and there the gates of the university were still closed to the alleged leader of the student disorders. For any normal youth of eighteen or twenty lack of a clearly defined goal or occupation must be depressing and demoralizing, and young Ulyanov was endowed with a surfeit of energy. The petty chicanery of the authorities was bound to produce, possibly more than real imprisonment or exile, an ineradicable hatred of the regime. His voracious reading and the contacts with various radical circles, first in Kazan and then in Samara, could not fill up the void. A more active participation in radical activities was not possible for Lenin even if he had felt so inclined at the time, which is doubtful.

The local police were not taking their eyes off the Ulyanov family, and what probably weighed most heavily on Lenin's mind was the consideration that his mother, having been so recently and so cruelly bereaved, should not be exposed to another blow. She could not help noticing the direction in which her son's inclinations and readings were driving him. Her attempt to interest him in becoming a gentleman farmer failed; throughout his life Lenin was to remain a lover of the countryside and an amateur hunter, but to imagine him as a farmer is clearly incongruous. Even more unthinkable was a career in business. Russia of the time was going through a prodigious industrial and commercial expansion, and a new class of millionaire entrepreneurs was springing up. Still a career in business was thought possible only for a Jew or a member of the lower classes. The only occupations open to a gentleman and an *intelligent* were those in the civil service, the free professions, and . . . the revolutionary.

All these cares and considerations are reflected in the petition that for the *n*th time Maria Alexandrovna addressed to the minister in May

1890. "It is a sheer torment to look at my son, and to see how fruitlessly pass those years of his life which are most suitable for a higher education." The penalty inflicted upon Vladimir does not allow him "since he belongs exclusively to the *intellectual profession* . . . to find even a partial occupation, thus precluding him from devoting his energies to any task." And with the utmost anguish the unfortunate woman states that this type of aimless existence cannot but have a fatal moral influence on the young man: "Almost inevitably it must push him even to thoughts of suicide."

The last passage embarrasses the Soviet compilers. Lenin is always required to exhibit the "joy of living" and revolutionary optimism, and the picture of a bored, morose youth is hardly compatible with the official legend. But though Maria Alexandrovna may have exaggerated in order to soften the minister's heart, her words still convey young Lenin's undoubted despair at his predicament. A university diploma was a sheer necessity for entrance into a profession. And without the latter, political activity was hardly possible for somebody of his status. For one reason, even a revolutionary had to earn his living (those were the days before organized parties, which could subsidize their leading members). For another, a lawyer's diploma and practice were an ideal cover-up for radical activity. Even if arrested, a lawyer was bound to be treated by the authorities with greater respect and leniency than an expelled and unemployed student. And within revolutionary circles social and professional status enhanced one's authority.

Whether those were the main considerations in Lenin's mind or not, it was most urgent that the ministry's prohibition be lifted. Maria Alexandrovna traveled to St. Petersburg to deliver her petition in person. In Tsarist Russia officialdom's rigid and frequently brutal behavior was occasionally relieved by compassion. Somebody in the Ministry of Education must have seen in Maria Ulyanov not the mother of an executed state criminal, and of two other children who had gotten into political trouble, but a sorely tried widow of a distinguished civil servant. This time the petition was granted. Vladimir Ilyich was allowed to take his examination for the degree of candidate for juridical science. In less than a year, studying by himself, he was able to make up three and a half years of missed university studies. He took the examination in two series, spring and fall of 1891, before the juridical faculty of St. Petersburg University. Each of the long series of subjects was passed by Lenin with the highest possible grade: "completely satisfactory." As in practically every examination he took, he was first in his group and received the diploma with high distinction; the road to the bar was open.

But before Lenin became a licensed lawyer he was already a convinced revolutionary and Marxist. It is important to retrace our steps and to examine what we know about his conversion.

In the beginning there was the enormous shock of his brother's execution. This, as we have seen, was followed by curiosity. What could have prompted a young man, seemingly all engrossed in his scientific studies, to choose the path of conspiracy and assassination that was to lead him to the scaffold? Chernyshevsky's *What Is To Be Done?*, which Lenin had read some years before and had found not particularly interesting, now assumed a different meaning: it was not only a work of fiction. The "new men" really existed and Alexander Ulyanov had been one of them. A simple motive of revenge and veneration of his brother would have urged Lenin into the same path, that of a revolutionary and terrorist: Populism. But in fact no sooner was his period of study of revolutionary movements and literature over than the eighteen-year-old Lenin chose a different road to revolution: Marxian socialism.

He chose a political philosophy as yet little known and less popular among the Russian radicals. Its main tenets and prophecies ran against the grain of the most deeply held traditions of the revolutionary movement. Instead of the vision of free Russia unpolluted by capitalism and based on the federation of free peasant communes, it foresaw a period of capitalism and the demise of the *mir* as an obsolete economic and social institution. Instead of heroic acts of terrorism or missionary activity among the peasants, the logic of Marxism enjoined patient propaganda work among the industrial workers, and held the peasants to be but of secondary importance in the future Socialist transformation. No heroics by a minority, no instinctive socialism of the peasant could decisively affect Russia's future: it was bound to develop according to the scientific laws uncovered by Marx and Engels, laws ordaining that Russia was destined to go through the same phases as the "rotten West." [1]

For a young revolutionary to espouse such views as Lenin did in 1889 was still unusual. To be sure the People's Will was finished as a party, and Populism in general was in decline. But the memory of its deeds and attachment to its ideas still constituted the strongest binding sentiment of the radical intelligentsia. In the main industrial cities there were already small Marxist circles. But to proclaim in a provincial town within a radical circle that the peasant commune was doomed and rightly so, and that before socialism could come one must endure the rule of the *bourgeoisie,* was as shocking as to assert that Alexander III was a benevolent and intelligent ruler. [2]

What led Vladimir Ilyich to Marxism? His conversion, he said with

---

[1] I leave for later the discussion of Marx's occasional and quite un-Marxist utterances on Russia.

[2] Maxim Gorky recollects the scene in a revolutionary circle he attended when one of those present started to expound Marxism and to condemn Populism and terrorism: "Suddenly and unexpectedly somebody interrupted the reader and immediately the room was filled with indignant shouts: 'Renegade' . . . 'he spits at the blood spilled by the heroes' . . . 'and that after the execution of Generalov and Ulyanov' . . ." M. Gorky, *Works,* Moscow, 1951, Vol. 13, p. 565.

unusual precision, took place in January 1889, and the books that swayed him were Marx's *Capital*, Volume I, and George Plekhanov's *Our Disagreements*, a brilliant polemical explanation by a Populist-turned-Marxist. For Plekhanov *as a philosopher* Lenin retained reverence to the end though he came to despise him as a politician. Toward Marx his worship remained unabated. Once, and only once, he allowed himself a criticism of his idol. He worshipped not only Karl Marx the revolutionary but also, as the last years of his life were to show, Marx the prophet and apologist for industrial civilization and the centralized state. Thus his espousal of Marxism was not simply a choice of a revolutionary philosophy, but a complete immersion in the grandiose system.

The Soviet legend that attributes to Vladimir upon hearing of his brother's execution the words, "We shall take another road," sins against the historical facts. But it may well hint at the psychological truth. A certain basic contrariness and ambivalence were to characterize his thought and action to the very end. Few persons he dealt with met with either his complete approval or complete rejection. On no political issue, toward no social class was his attitude one of straightforward enthusiasm or straightforward detestation. Admiration of Alexander blended with an element of emulation. His brother's sacrifice provided both an impulse to enter the struggle himself and a warning against the movement and philosophy requiring such catastrophic and fruitless heroics. The tense and agitated Lenin who in 1891 was still enquiring about the value of his late brother's scientific investigations relived, apart from his relationship to Alexander, his own inner struggle about the meaning and value of the revolutionary path.

Within the context of such doubts and of the mixed attraction and revulsion felt by him toward the previous generation of the revolutionaries, Marxism must have appeared as an ideal answer and solution. Within Marxian socialism are found the elements of ambivalence and yet of orderliness characteristic of Lenin's own mind. The emotions and the language of Marxism breathe violence and defiance of all the nineteenth century conventions, and yet its conclusions are coldly rational and practical. Revolution is presented not only as an act of will but of scientific necessity. There is a pleasing vision of the final holocaust of capitalism, of "the expropriation of the expropriators," but no utopian and lyrical evocation of the Socialist world of the future: the entrance to the world of freedom is through an increased productivity and better organization of labor. After the intense emotionalism of Populism, its infatuation with the mythical peasant, its denial of the reality of the all-too-visible and growing "Europeanization" and industrialization of Russia, Marxism must have represented a model of sobriety and realism. By following it one did not cut oneself off from the revolutionary tradition, only from its illusions.

To be sure, by January 1889 Lenin could not yet be a full-fledged

Marxist. His full grounding in the doctrine and an extensive acquaintance with its already vast literature had to take several years more. Not until he left for St. Petersburg in 1893 did he enter upon his lifelong mission, that of a propagandist for Marxian socialism. In Kazan, where he resided until the spring of 1889, and in Samara, where the Ulyanovs lived until 1893, Socialist literature and foreign periodicals were as yet scarce. What political activity there was took the form of little discussion groups, attended by university and older gymasium students. There, in some secrecy, the smuggled writings of the political *émigrés* would be read (often there was only one copy of the precious contraband) and discussed. The young men would then launch into one of those inexhaustible *subjects of polemic* of the Russian intelligentsia: is the peasant commune growing stronger or weaker; is Russia slated to go through all the phases of industrialization like the West, and the like. All that is very innocent by our lights, and for the time and place what alternative forms of diversion were there for earnest and inquisitive young men? But in the eyes of the Tsarist authorities this was a highly subversive activity, and by their spying and persecutions they lent an air of excitement and danger to these highbrow discussions.

After the solitude of Kokushkino, and with his newly formed viewpoint, young Vladimir was naturally enough eager for discussion and for crossing swords with the dominant Populist tendency. Maria Alexandrovna's house became—probably not without some anguish on her part—a place of assembly and political discussion. One surviving participant of those evenings was to remember many years later young Lenin admonishing his Populist comrades: ". . . one should understand the reasons for inequality. And in order to understand, one must above all read and read. . . . We still haven't done enough [reading]. A revolution cannot be achieved by robberies and murders." Particularly interesting in view of Alexander's attempt is the use of the word "murders" for political assassination. If any recollection of exact phraseology after many years must always be somewhat suspicious, then another detail of the memoir is trustworthy. To the disappointment of his comrades who would prolong their bull sessions all night, Lenin, in a very un-Russian fashion, would chase them home. The eye of the police was on the Ulyanov family and he wanted to get back to the university. As it was, though nothing concrete could be brought against him during his second stay in Kazan, the police reports spoke vaguely of Vladimir Ulyanov's associations with suspicious characters.[3] At eighteen he was already far from being a revolutionary hothead.

This caution was not excessive. There was at the time in Kazan another convinced Marxist and the tragic story of his life offers some

---

* The classical Tsarist police term for political suspects is practically untranslatable: ill-intentioned or undependable persons.

instructive parallels and contrasts to that of young Lenin. He was Nicolai
Fedoseyev. Born in 1871, he had already at sixteen been expelled from
the gymnasium for reading subversive literature. Abandoning the thought
of any other profession, he gave himself fully to that of a revolutionary.
In Kazan this boy organized a series of "circles" where he attempted to
propagate Socialist views. Going even further, Fedoseyev acquired a
printing plant, issued Marxist tracts, and drew workers into his organization. His group was uncovered in July 1889. Actually the total number
of the directly accused was thirty-six, many of whom were "guilty" of
spending an evening in a discussion group. For the eighteen-year-old
youth this was the beginning of arrests and exiles that were to last till
his tragic end. Even under those circumstances he continued to write
and to correspond on political themes. Finally in Siberia some of his
fellow exiles reproached him for giving himself aristocratic airs, and (undoubtedly falsely) of misappropriating some money from the common
fund. Overwrought and in ill health, Fedoseyev committed suicide. He
was twenty-seven years old.

It is characteristic that in his Kazan days Lenin never sought
Fedoseyev, though of course he knew of him and attended some of
the circles initiated by his fellow Marxist (the only other one in town).
Some years later they corresponded, but were never slated to meet.
Himself in Siberia when the news of the suicide reached him, Lenin was
shocked. But both in his reaction and in his later reminiscences of the
man who much more than he had been the apostle of Marxism in the
Volga region, there is an undertone of coldness and censure. A revolutionary cannot afford to be sensitive; he must ignore slander and above
all must have strong nerves.

Had he stayed in Kazan until the Fedoseyev affair burst open, recounts Lenin, perhaps a bit guiltily, he too would have been arrested.
But by the summer of 1889 he was out of harm's way, in the village of
Alakayevka in the province of Samara. It was in the spring of 1889 that
Maria Alexandrovna decided to put an end to her son's idleness and
dangerous connections by turning him into a farmer. The money for the
farm was realized by the sale of her Simbirsk house. Vladimir was to
be a gentleman farmer and the family was to spend the winters in the
city of Samara (today Kuibyshev) which, not having a university, was
presumably less infested by the dangerous "circles." Destiny, however,
had foreordained that each step the Ulyanov family made was to sink
them deeper and deeper in the revolutionary world. Thus the seemingly
innocent purchase of the farm, far from lessening, was actually to increase the suspicions of the police. For its previous owner was himself
an ill-intentioned character, one Konstantin Sibiryakov. One-time mag-
nate, who had made his fortune in gold mining in Siberia, Sibiryakov
was a generous contributor to various radical and liberal causes. Having

purchased a lot of farming land, he indulged in various dangerous and possibly subversive experimentations and innovations. Part of the land was given to a group of followers of Leo Tolstoy, who attempted despite the incomprehension and hostility of the neighboring peasants to practice Christian agrarian communism preached by the great writer. On his own estates Sibiryakov attempted to introduce advanced methods of cultivation, importing such—for Russia—unheard-of implements as the steam plow. The end result was a financial ruin that compelled Sibiryakov to sell his land. Its purchasers were viewed with interest by the police, who were not to be easily persuaded that it was a sheer coincidence that the "suspected" Ulyanovs were buying a plot from another "suspect."

As to Maria Alexandrovna's original plan, it was soon shown to be an unqualified failure. A Russian intellectual of Lenin's generation and temper could be counted upon to know in detail the history of the peasant commune, was able to discourse at length about land tenure in France or medieval England, but was completely incapable of and unwilling to undertake the prosaic occupations that constitute commercial farming. Lenin's references to the brief period of his life when he was an active landowner, i.e., "exploiter," were to be very brief and enigmatic. He gave up, he told his wife, because his relations with the peasants were becoming "abnormal." Alakayevka became another Kokushkino, a place for summer vacations. Instead of doing uncongenial work he spent his time in intensive reading, physical exercises, and occasional chats with the peasants.

Equally fallacious was the assumption that Samara would be a safe refuge free from the dangerous "circles." The very remoteness of the town and its lack of a university made it one of those places that the Tsarist government designed for political offenders, who, released from prison in Siberia, were still not allowed to settle in the major and university cities of European Russia.[4] As a consequence the local intelligentsia was seeded with "ill-intentioned" persons. By 1889 the revolutionary potential of the Ulyanov family was also increased by Anna's marriage to Mark Elizarov, son of a well-to-do peasant. Elizarov had finished his engineering studies in St. Petersburg where, almost superfluous to say, he had gotten into political trouble. Both he and Anna were now living with the rest of the family, and under discreet police supervision. Thus Maria Alexandrovna gained not only a son-in-law but a new radical in her family.

Samara though a town of one hundred thousand inhabitants was a somber Russian provincial hole with few attractions or cultural amenities.

---

[4] As in post-, so in prerevolutionary Russia a citizen had to carry his passport specifying his identity, status, and possible restrictions on his freedom of movement. If a revolutionary decided to disregard the latter, e.g., settle in the capital, he would have to, as the phrase had it, "go illegal" and forge his identity papers.

The local newspaper gives a pathetic expression to this standard self-accusation of lack of culture of provincial Russia of the nineteenth century. Exclaims the masochistic editor:

> Take a walk through Samara in the evening . . . look in the citizens' windows and testify with your hand on your heart, whether you can see many people bending over a book. . . . Here they are playing cards; there the ritual of tea drinking is taking place accompanied by such pathetic yawning that one would think that the whole family is singing some ferocious ballad. Here the head of the family is pacing restlessly; there the lady of the house is playing the piano while her husband in his anguish is grimacing as if seized by a violent toothache.

If only nineteenth century Russia had had television!

In its absence, whatever there was in Samara of "society" tended to prize the local radicals, even those who were there under police supervision. They were mostly of the intelligentsia, and their talk would enliven the salon of a merchant millionaire's wife. Some of the younger radicals grumbled at the bourgeois splendor customary upon such occasions and would act in an offensive manner, but they attended them nevertheless. Lenin would amaze his friends by the combination of his revolutionary principles with social poise. He would not, as some of them did, become terrorized by the sight of a white tablecloth, and the profusion of silver, plates, cups, etc., accompanying tea in a bourgeois home.[5] He also displayed some other gentrylike characteristics: on greeting and saying good-bye to his mother he would kiss her hand. Was this reactionary behavior or not? On the whole and in view of his undoubted radical fervor his friends forgave him.

The political activity Lenin evidenced in Samara was again limited to his participation in various discussion groups. Thus unlike Fedoseyev he did not try as yet to propagandize workers or to reprint banned political tracts. That there was a specific Marxist circle led by Lenin in Samara, as is sometimes asserted in Soviet literature, is again an obvious invention. A more trustworthy memoir recalls Lenin simply as one of three young men interested in Marxism who would meet regularly, drink beer or tea, and discuss Socialist literature. Marxism in the Volga region was still in the nature of an esoteric sect, the members of which would travel long distances to bring to a coreligionist the latest book or tract smuggled from abroad. Karl Marx's basic writings, especially Volume I of *Capital* translated into Russian in 1872, were on the other hand

---

[5] Including his own. A radical contemporary recalls this barbarous behavior: "Each of us in his own way reacted to the snow-white tablecloth in the Ulyanovs' house: Sklyarenko hated it, I was afraid of it, and Yasneva, at every opportunity and good naturedly [*sic!*] would spill jam on the cloth, to the obvious anguish of Maria Alexandrovna." A. Belyakov, *Youth of the Leader, Memoirs of a Contemporary*, Moscow, 1960, p. 65.

well known. Much of Marxian literature could be printed and discussed quite legally. In the eyes of the censor those were abstruse economic and political writings, unlikely to stir up conspiracies and assassinations. While Marxism as a movement in Russia was still in its infancy, knowledge of and interest in its theories were growing even in Samara. They would be discussed and usually attacked in young discussion circles of the intelligentsia.

It was as an exponent and able defendant of Marxism that Vladimir Ulyanov first made his mark in radical circles. It was a task that required considerable self-confidence, if not indeed certain insolence, on the part of a twenty-year-old youth to appear within a circle of people most of whom were considerably older, and to defy the still reigning dogmas of Populism. Yet as testified to even by an opponent, he more than held his own.

> Vladimir Ilyich gave the impression of a well-educated man. His knowledge of political economy and history was strikingly solid and many-sided, especially for a man of his age. He could read freely in German, French and English, knew well even then *Capital* and the extensive German literature of Marxism, and gave the impression of a man who has arrived at a definite political conviction. He proclaimed himself a convinced Marxist. . . . He had a presumption that there can be no serious arguments against Marxism.

It would be, of course, an exaggeration to accept Lenin of 1890–91 as a "finished" Marxist, or to credit him with that mastery of foreign languages and materials which he was to achieve only within the next several years. But this sketch conveys the impression he created in Samara, and the fact that he was already felt to be a formidable and authoritative polemicist. One may uncharitably add that it was relatively easy to combat Populism. As a political movement it was in ruins. As a theory, expounded by the so-called legal Populists, it was holding on to a denial of the ever-growing reality: that large-scale capitalism and the development of the *bourgeoisie* and the industrial proletariat were impossible in Russia. One must admit that Lenin's initial successes as a polemicist and social critic were scored in the absence of first-rate opposition.

To be sure, there was one exception. In May 1892 Samara had the honor of being visited by Nicolai Konstantinovich Mikhailovsky. Who was Mikhailovsky? To a Russian intellectual of the period this question would have appeared sacrilegious. He was the intellectual and spiritual head of Russian Populism. His writings are now read only by the most devoted specialists, but in the eighties and nineties each of his articles, sociological treatises, and critiques was greeted by the radical intelligentsia as an intellectual event. Always excessive in their raptures and antipathies, the educated class of that persuasion viewed Mikhailovsky not only as a talented publicist, which he was, but as a sort of Russian combination of Darwin, Karl Marx, and Walter Lippmann, an infallible oracle and the occupant of the throne once held by Herzen and Chernyshevsky. He now condescended to visit a disciple of his in Samara, and the latter issued invitations to the local intelligentsia to view and listen to the great man. Lenin was included and the prospect of an encounter between the divinity of Populism and the brash young Marxist titillated the local circles.

The great day finally came. We must reach across time to the long-vanished atmosphere of the political evening when sharp ideological differences did not preclude the effusive Russian hospitality and social amenities, where the contestants interlarded their arguments and statistics with personal bows to the "highly esteemed" and "dear" opponent. Such terms of political debate as were soon to become standard with the Bolsheviks—"scoundrel," "Philistine," "renegade"—were as yet unthinkable in reference to a radical or liberal opponent. Vulgar abuse and name-calling were thought to be the prerogative of reactionaries and police officials. Gentlemen, i.e., the intelligentsia, could disagree without departing from good manners. It has already been observed that within the Samara circles young Lenin chafed under those civilized rules of the political game, and that his argument tended at times to turn into a personal and venomous attack. Did not Chernyshevsky's Rakhmetov scorn the polite forms of address and discussion as a waste of time and an upper-class residue unworthy of a dedicated revolutionary? But it was still some time before Lenin was to make bad manners an important appurtenance of the class struggle.

The subject of the discussion, as the reader has guessed, was the future of the peasant commune, and whether or not capitalism was bound to triumph in Russia before socialism was to take over. The old champion employed an experienced debater's trick, that of minimizing the differences and attempting to assimilate his opponent's view to his own. Mikhailovsky was himself a Socialist and in a way a Marxist, for did not Karl Marx admit that the peasant commune might enable Russia to skip the capitalist phase, and land in socialism directly after the overthrow of autocracy? But this socialism had to be rural in character. There were as yet not many industrial workers but seventy million peasants. Thus Russia was not bound to follow the Western pattern, and so on. The orator with his feints, thrusts, erudite references to such unquestioned authorities as Chernyshevsky, Herzen, and Marx could not but renew the admiration of his fellow believers.

It was the turn of the challenger. One feels sympathy with Lenin's impatience in pointing out that Chernyshevsky, Marx, and others had all had their say about the peasant commune some time before, that capitalism was growing in Russia by leaps and bounds. The idealized commune existed in the *Narodniks'* imagination and the actual peasant commune was in the process of economic disintegration, for even in the villages capitalism was making headway. His arguments—he was soon to repeat them in writing—were incisive and buttressed by statistics. Tea drinking and other speeches and arguments followed late into the night. When the participants dispersed to sleep in the neighboring *dachas* (the debate was held in the environs of the city), most of them were still overwhelmed by the eloquence and philosophical depth of Mikhailovsky. But the Marxist position had not been annihilated. The "master of thought" of the intelligentsia soon departed, forgetting a silk cap, which was seized and cut into small strips treasured by his disciples in the memory of Samara's great day. He also left behind a generous acknowledgment of young Ulyanov's intellect and debating powers.

With the Samara period of Lenin's life is connected an episode even more significant than his uncompromising defense of Marxism within the midst of the Populist intelligentsia. In the fall and winter of 1891–92 a great famine hit many regions of Russia. Among the causes were the drought of the preceding summer, the prodigious growth in the population, and the inefficient organization of both Russian agriculture and the transportation system. The government compounded the calamity by its policy of exporting grain and by the lack of precaution against a national disaster. Samara was in the center of the most critically stricken area. The actual appearance of the famine shocked the authorities out of their slumber. In addition, for this occasion the most divergent elements in society joined the government in attempting to save the peasants from actual starvation and from the epidemics that followed in the wake of the famine. Leo Tolstoy abandoned for a time his preaching of Christian anarchism to organize the committees of help. The Populists joined with the government officials to set up public works, feeding points, and medical services. In Samara most of the members of the radical circles, whether former political prisoners and exiles or not, joined with the officials in the humanitarian work. One of the few exceptions was Vladimir Ulyanov.

Among the political exiles confined to Samara was Maria Yasneva,[6] who subsequently married one Golubev. We have already met Yasneva as the hideous woman who would, as a gesture of class protest, spill tea and jam on Maria Alexandrovna Ulyanov's white tablecloth. It will come as no surprise to learn that she was a Russian Jacobin, a pupil of Zaichnevsky of *Young Russia* fame. Later on Yasneva-Golubeva became a Bolshevik. She survived Lenin, and as an old witch (one feels somehow confident in this characterization) she would often recall with pride in the Soviet press how of all the young radicals in Samara only she and Vladimir Ulyanov did not believe in working with the govern-

[6] Her maiden name is also given sometimes as Yaseneva.

ment officials in alleviating the effects of the famine. That Lenin opposed such help on principle is confirmed both by Bolshevik and anti-Bolshevik sources. Why?

One of the most trustworthy of the writers of memoirs about Lenin, Nicolai Valentinov (we shall meet him later) gives as his opinion that Yasneva had a definite influence on the formation of young Lenin's viewpoint. She was older by nine years, and was at the time a definite proponent of a life-and-death struggle with the existing social and political system. In her own memoir written in 1924 Golubeva herself implies her influence: "Recalling my talks with Vladimir Ilyich, I conclude now, even more than before, that he had already conceived of the dictatorship of the proletariat . . . [he] often dwelt on the problem of the seizure of power (one of the points of our Jacobin program). . . ." And about the efforts of the government and the "society" to help the starving: "Among all the politically advanced in Samara, only Vladimir Ilyich and I did not participate in these efforts . . . it was not an unwillingness to help the starving that motivated this youth . . . so sensitive to others' suffering. [But] obviously he thought that the revolutionary should take another path." [7]

But there is no reason to attribute this fateful influence to an otherwise insignificant woman. Lenin probably sought her company and ignored her boorishness because he was intrigued by the extreme radicalism of *Young Russia*, with which she constituted a living link. But even at twenty-one, he was a "formed" person politically and unlikely to be swayed by an acquaintance. His refusal to collaborate with the authorities to help the starving cannot even be attributed to his following the slogan of extreme Russian radicalism: "The worse it is, the better" (for the revolutionary cause). Nobody thought that the famished peasants were capable of a revolt. In Lenin's behavior we find for the first time a concrete demonstration of the two characteristics that he was to display throughout his life. First, his general contrariness, which was to make him repeatedly attack and split any movement and cause not initiated or directed by himself. Second, we see here a manifestation of his paradoxical hatred of the intelligentsia and its whole world of ideas, of philanthropy, of the unctuous concern for the poor and underprivileged. This was the class and the mentality from which he himself had derived and he never attempted to masquerade as coming from the proletariat. Many of the local officials who were trying to do something for the poor and starving were no more simple minions of autocracy than Ilya Ulyanov had been, and Lenin always revered the memory of his father. But here, as on many occasions to come, the contemplation of the liberal intelligentsia and of the liberal officials was to arouse in

[7] M. Golubeva in *The Young Guard*, Moscow 1924, No. 2–3, p. 30.

Lenin a paroxysm of opposition and rage, which was often to clash with and to frustrate his political designs.

Young Ulyanov's position could not have made him very popular. Yet such was the tolerance shown by even the most moderate of the intelligentsia toward the radicals that he was not in the slightest boycotted or shunned but continued to be received in the cultivated circles of Samara. He was by this time (1891–92) a licensed lawyer. Upon the completion of his examination he entered practice in the office of a well-known Samara lawyer, Andrei Khardin. The latter knew, of course, of his assistant's advanced views and that his interests now lay elsewhere than at the bar. In a year and a half of his practice Lenin argued only thirteen rather minor cases and does not appear to have exerted himself in any of them. Khardin himself, though a member of the two species hated by Lenin, lawyer and liberal, retained the latter's warm personal regard.

The indulgent counselor and his young assistant shared one great passion. Insofar as Lenin had any obsession apart from politics it was chess. Granted the fact that chess has always been more popular in Russia than in any other country, and that this is one field where the greatest Russophobe will not deny the Russians' claim to pre-eminence, Lenin must be described as a fair country player. Of Khardin, however, great Chigorin himself, contestant for world championship, granted that he was good. The connection through chess antedated (and was probably instrumental in leading to) the two men's professional association. They played by mail when Lenin was still in Kazan, and now in Samara their matches were frequent. Khardin, of course, had to give his opponent a handicap, first a rook and then as Lenin improved, a pawn. The Soviet sources, in their at once schoolmasterish and senseless way, attempt to minimize Lenin's addiction to chess, as if it were a form of intellectual debauchery unworthy of the leader of the revolution. It is clear, however, that he was a most serious and passionate player. He would not let an opponent take back a move. He would sit for hours over chess problems, and would attempt to involve the most uninterested of his friends in the noble game. At times he felt that chess was taking too much out of him, and after the Revolution he stopped playing. To his old friends he gave the excuse of lack of time for such diversions. It is unlikely that this was the whole reason, for even then the Chairman of the Council of the People's Commissars would find time for trips and hunting in the country. But those were precisely diversions while chess had been an addiction and a strain on his nerves.

It is still necessary to recall that Lenin was in his early twenties. Politics, chess, and law could not fill his entire life in Samara. The Soviet sources that insist on Vladimir Ilyich's ever-present "joy of living" do not go into details that would be entirely convincing in the case of a twenty-

or twenty-two-year-old youth. It is granted that he did some beer drinking in restaurants looking out on the river, but those occasions were combined with political discussions. There is a story of a lengthy boat trip on the Volga with picnics and vodka drinking on the shore, but even this has social significance, for in the course of a several days' trip young Vladimir meets some peasants, weans them away from the platitudes of Populism, and confirms his thesis of the growth of capitalism in the countryside. To be sure, Lenin was a very serious young man even for a young generation where earnestness and seriousness were the expected standard, but this picture cannot be complete. Nothing, however, remains or is ever in the future likely to be revealed of the lighter and more intimate side of his youth. In St. Petersburg his circle bestowed upon Lenin the nickname *starik* (old man), a tribute not only to the extent of his Marxist indoctrination but also to the seriousness of his appearance and behavior.

Within its limitations, life in Samara could not have been unpleasant. The not too exacting legal practice, the trips on the river in the spring, and stimulating ideological discussions, all those must have possessed certain if very provincial charm. Summers were spent in Alakayevka where all thought of commercial exploitation had been given up. Here in the garden Vladimir constructed a sort of "office," a table and a bench, and every morning he would plunge into reading and writing. The heavy intellectual labor would end at noon. In his systematic way he allocated the afternoon to physical exercises, and to lighter fiction reading. In the evening there was singing, chess playing with brother Dimitri, and other forms of relaxation. The stress on physical exercise, especially callisthenics, again brings to one's mind Chernyshevsky's Rakhmetov, who believed that the revolutionary should "keep in shape." Lenin would have been scandalized to learn that in his regimen he was following the injunction of an eighteenth century aristocrat. Lord Chesterfield had advised that "morning is for work, afternoon for games, and evening for sociability." But the kind of "sociability" that his lordship had in mind was different from this chaste singing to the accompaniment of Anna or Maria Ulyanova.

Quite apart from politics, the nineteenth century *intelligent* had an unquenchable passion to get to one of the two capitals. "When are we going to get to Moscow?" one of Chekhov's *Three Sisters* keeps asking throughout the play. If one were to write a play about Vladimir Ilyich's life in Samara it could be called very appropriately *Three Marxists* and the same plaintive cry often must have echoed through his mind. In St. Petersburg and Moscow there were already real Marxist circles active among the workers; there were libraries where one could find the latest Socialist literature. Here in Samara within the radical circles the Populist dogmas still held sway and even most of those few who were groping their way toward Marxism were awed and discouraged by the formidable theoretical and statistical apparatus of Volume I of *Capital*. Books could be borrowed if one had a friend who was a member of the Merchants' Club, which possessed the only semidecent library in town. Any more active revolutionary career was practically impossible. Quite apart from the fact that it could not have remained undetected in a place of Samara's size, witness Fedoseyev's fate in Kazan, there was nobody among whom to agitate. There were no industrial workers in the strict sense of the word. As for indoctrinating the peasants in the involved principles of scientific socialism, this was a task that Vladimir Ilyich wisely did not even attempt. Against the tales of his spreading the gospel on his river trips there is the evidence of Anna that Vladimir was eager to hear the peasants talk of their life and grievances but did not express his opinions to them.

Why did Lenin under those circumstances prolong his stay? The family sources attribute his decision, credibly enough, to his concern for his mother. Coincident with his passing the law exams, a new blow befell the Ulyanovs. Sister Olga, closest in age to Vladimir, and a student in St. Petersburg, fell ill and died of typhoid. For another year and a half he had to endure Samara. But finally a feeling of provincial claustrophobia overcame him. Whether it was the proximity of his family, which through its very affection and understanding inhibited his wider activity, or the town itself, or both, he had to get out. To Anna he confessed that the provincial atmosphere was choking him. The liberation came in late summer of 1893. The Ulyanovs wound up their Samara affairs. The rest of the family moved to Moscow but Vladimir Ilyich set forth for St. Petersburg.

2. St. Petersburg

The road to St. Petersburg led through Nizhni-Novgorod, whose Soviet name, Gorky, commemorates the Socialist writer who became Lenin's friend, tried to moderate his intemperate hatred of the intelligentsia, and was to meet his end under mysterious and sordid circumstances in Stalin's Russia. Nizhni boasted a prominent Marxist who wrote learnedly of the peasant question and a few study circles where Marx and Plekhanov were discussed. Lenin was interested mostly in addresses and introductions to similar circles in St. Petersburg. The handful of Marxists in Russia in 1893 reminds one of an American fraternity. You needed recommendations to get into a group; various local circles were in touch or aware of similar circles elsewhere. There was a natural air of conspiracy about them, though as we have seen the purely intellectual dabbling in socialism was looked upon indulgently by the police. Here there were no bomb throwers and instigators of riots but harmless pedants and theoreticians discussing incomprehensible theories. But soon the Tsarist police had an occasion to change its mind.

In St. Petersburg Lenin joined the office of a well-known lawyer, Volkenstein. Like Khardin he was a liberal, and also was to show himself a most indulgent and generous boss to the young revolutionary. By now there was not even a pretense that Lenin was interested in law. The few cases in which he appeared were mostly of a criminal nature and he served usually as a public defender, i.e., without remuneration. He would put on the tails inherited from his father and make a perfunctory appearance in court. The reasons for his hatred of lawyers can certainly not be found in any abuse or indignity at the hands of a member of the profession. Quite the contrary. If there was one civic body in Tsarist Russia that stood out by its liberalism and independence toward the regime it was the bar. Thus when Ulyanov transferred his "practice" the St. Petersburg legal association was discreetly informed by the authorities that the newcomer was not quite dependable from the political point of view. (Presumably the police were not happy that he should be active in the capital and near a university.) Their sense of professional freedom and dignity outraged, the lawyers' association decided to ignore the notice, and indeed it probably served Lenin as a recommendation.[8]

After the parochialism of Kazan or Samara, St. Petersburg loomed as a wide, exciting, cosmopolitan world. It was a city of elegance and culture, the seat of the government, and the center of Russian intellectual life. Moscow then represented Russia's past, the link to the feudal and patriarchal traditions of the Middle Ages. St. Petersburg in contrast, erected by Peter the Great as the window to the West, stood for the modern bureaucratized and entrepreneurial Russia—the combined New York and Washington of the country. But what attracted Vladimir Ulyanov more than all the historical and cultural associations of the place was the fact that the city was an industrial metropolis—there were more than a hundred thousand industrial workers in the grim suburbs of St. Petersburg—and the most active center of intellectual Marxism in the Empire. Of his private life in the capital, where he was to spend just about two years as a free man, we know relatively little. But even then his private life had begun to merge almost completely with his political one. Even his courtship of the woman who was to become his wife took place within the context of a Socialist circle, the courtship interlaced, let us hope, among the discussions of other things, by an exchange of views about Marxism, the condition of St. Petersburg workers, and the like.

This wholesale absorption in politics was facilitated for Lenin by

[8] *The Red Chronicle*, Moscow, 1924, n. 9, p. 13.

the fact that he did not have to earn his livelihood. He soon discovered that the little he made out of his legal work was barely sufficient to cover the cost of the necessary books and documents. But then as always he was a man of very temperate and inexpensive habits, and Maria Alexandrovna out of her modest pension was capable of providing enough for her son's needs so as to free him for his revolutionary vocation. Almost immediately upon his arrival in the capital in September 1893 Lenin visited a person indicated by a Nizhni-Novgorod contact. His host, a nineteen-year-old student at St. Petersburg Technological Institute and a leader of a Marxist circle, saw before him a short but robust man, already bald with a fringe of reddish hair, and a small beard. The first impression produced by Lenin, Michael Silvin was to write thirty years later, was not entirely favorable. The newcomer wanted to be put in touch with fellow Socialists, in the first instance with his, Silvin's circle. This was a request usually not granted immediately and not without a period of probation. A contemporary revolutionary recounts how for a period of time, despite his impeccable credentials, he had been refused entrance into a similar circle. He had graduated from the high school with a gold medal, thus earning the reputation of a "careerist," and he used to run after girls, a symptom of frivolity unbecoming a devoted revolutionary. Then there was a matter of simple caution and, one might add, of certain youthful exclusiveness befitting a fraternity. After all, a lot of young students were craving entrance into the enticing and forbidden circles. But Lenin's references were very good and he was a brother of a revolutionary martyr. And so he found himself a member of a Socialist club of ten or twelve young men, most of them students at the Technological Institute.

Within two years the previously little-known "Marxist from Samara" became one of the leaders, if not *the* leader of the small but already significant Socialist movement in St. Petersburg. The period September 1893 to December 1895 was in fact the foundation of the whole subsequent political career of Lenin. The latter date marked his imprisonment, then the exile in Siberia and abroad. When he was to return to Russia briefly after the Revolution of 1905 it was as the leader of Bolshevism.

Two years mark the beginning of those personal connections that were to grow into lifelong friendships and antagonisms that are part of the history of Russia and of socialism. Among the young intellectuals and students playing at revolution in their little circles there were future commissars of the Soviet Union and veterans of Bolshevism, but there were also persons who were soon to cross swords with Lenin, and to become leaders of "deviations" and heresies that mark luxuriantly the history of the Communist Party of the Soviet Union. Gleb Krzhizhanovsky belongs to the first category. An engineer by profession, he became probably the closest friend of Lenin during his St. Petersburg days and in Siberia. Though he left the Bolsheviks after 1906, he returned to Lenin and the Party after the Revolution, bringing into its ranks his then very rare and desperately needed professional qualifications. His was to be an unusual Bolshevik success story. Head of the electrification plan and then of the Planning Commission, Krzhizhanovsky was to survive the wholesale slaughter of the Old Bolsheviks by Stalin and to die in extreme old age in 1959, the last veteran of those exciting days when Vladimir Ilyich was laying the foundations of the Party that now rules one third of mankind. Leonid Krasin, who had been a member of the same circle though not in St. Petersburg when Lenin joined it, had a somewhat similar career. He also parted from Lenin for a time to become an industrial manager but rejoined him after November 1917. A highly capable Commissar of Trade and then an urbane ambassador to London, Krasin as early as the 1920s tried to convince the Bolsheviks that entrepreneurial ability was more important to socialism than the gift of making stirring speeches, but that point of view, now a commonplace in the Soviet Union, was then hooted down and cost him his influence in the Party.

And there were those who from close comrades working in the common cause were to become "philistines," "renegades," and "scoundrels," some of the descriptions that Lenin was wont to bestow upon those who were to part from socialism or were to oppose his concept of it. The first one to earn those epithets was Peter Struve. In the 1890s he was the shining intellect of Russian Marxism and next to Plekhanov the author of its most influential theoretical tracts. Throughout the period he rendered Lenin many services, arranging for the publication of his works, finding for him literary work while he was in Siberia, and the like. But soon Struve was to become an exponent of the heresy of "economism," then even more heinous, a liberal, and the two men were to become the bitterest of enemies. Almost forty years after their first meeting Struve was to record the impressions of the man who had been successively his protégé, friend, and enemy, and the passage of time served only to harden the initial rancor and rivalry into hatred and loathing.

There were those who remained Socialists but became anti-Bolsheviks. The most prominent among them was a mild intellectual-looking Jew, Julius Martov. His collaboration and then conflict with Lenin constitutes a major part of the story of Russian socialism prior to 1917. Such was the attraction of his personality that Lenin retained toward him traces of affection even after their political breach. Personal friendship for Lenin could not exist apart from politics.[9] But even during his last

[9] As another close associate of those early days recalled, "I began to be separated from the movement and thus completely ceased to exist for Vladimir Ilyich." Michael Silvin in *The Proletarian Revolution*, Moscow, July, 1924, p. 81.

illness he was anxiously enquiring about Martov whom the triumph of socialism once more made an exile from his native land and who was dying.

What made people of such divergent personalities, if not backgrounds, into revolutionaries, and enter upon a career which few of them could doubt would bring them imprisonment and exile? Adhering to socialism, they could not, like the preceding generation of revolutionaries, be attracted by the heroics of terrorism. Their doctrine taught them that the road to revolution was long and laborious, that it lay through patient indoctrination and organization and not through a sudden gust of a popular insurrection.

Julius Martov's autobiographical account casts some light on the variety of motivations that propelled the young men of the 1890s into their troublesome path. He came from a well-to-do and russified Jewish family. Though his origin must have played an undeniable part in his revolutionary resolve, anti-Jewish [10] discrimination was a definite and law-ensconced part of everyday life; his memoir is a record of typical impulses of a rebellious young Russian intellectual of the period.

Of course the first stirrings of social protest came while still on the gymnasium bench; in his first year in the university young Martov was already eager to plunge into the exciting life of an illegal circle. One feels in reading Martov's frank memoirs that dull and stuffy middle-class Russian life made politics one of the few avenues of excitement open to an impatient young man and that the Imperial government in its turn obliged by treating a discussion circle devoted to political philosophy and to reading books (some of them forbidden) as a form of state crime. The serious young men repulsed a would-be participant who wanted to vary the circle's activity with musical performances and social events involving girls. They would have no such careerist and philistine elements in the midst of a group devoted to the welfare of the people. When the almost inevitable happened and the police arrived to search Martov's house for incriminating evidence and to carry him off, he experienced, he tells us, a sense of accomplishment. His titillation was tempered by a certain feeling of surprise. The reading of such indictments of the Russian police state as George Kennan's book on Siberia and the exile system[11] had led him to believe that he would be snatched away by the gendarmes in the middle of the night and conveyed to some secret location. Instead, the arrest was performed by two rather polite policemen who signed a protocol, and conveyed him not to farthest Siberia but to the St. Petersburg house of detention where he could be visited by his family. But this eagerly looked for and unexpectedly mild

---

[10] It is more correct to label it thus than "anti-Semitism" since the legal disabilities were based on religion rather than origin.

[11] Written by the great-uncle of the American diplomat, and then extremely popular among the Russian radicals.

martyrdom was to have tragic consequences. One of the fellow members of the circle, also arrested, when importuned by his mother made a full confession to the police. Once he and Martov were released, he told Martov of his weakness and was told to leave St. Petersburg and to shun politics. He came back some time later and sought readmission to the circle of his friends. But he was shunned and rejected by them and the unfortunate youth committed suicide. Martov had been his closest friend, and writing about the tragedy many years later he feels constrained to add that another personal drama probably also led to the frightful decision.[12]

Initiation into revolution most often took place within the context of the drama of adolescence, and in a sense the Russian revolutionary movement retained some of the emotional air of adolescence: strong personal attachments that would suddenly give way to feelings of betrayal and slight; youthful idealism and ruthlessness that would not allow an acknowledgment of human weaknesses or compromise. But in other respects prison and hardships aged the revolutionaries very fast. When after some months of investigation Martov was released on parole to await his sentence he devoted himself to a serious study of his craft, abandoned an indiscriminate search for revolutionary adventures, and became a Marxist. The road back to the university and to a mundane career was not necessarily closed. His family, the Tsederbaums (Martov was a Party name he chose) had official connections, and the minister of education himself expressed a desire to see the young man, undoubtedly to give him an indulgent fatherly lecture. But Martov would have nothing to do with the hateful Tsarist bureaucrat. So back he went to jail and then, banished for two years from the capital, he chose the Polish-Lithuanian city of Vilno as his residence. In Vilno he again of course plunged into illegal Socialist work, but he was now at twenty an experienced conspirator who knew how to avoid police notice. As we shall see, his experiences in Vilno where, unlike St. Petersburg of 1893, Socialist propaganda was making considerable inroads not only among the intelligentsia but among the workers, were to have momentous consequences for the history of Marxism in Russia.

Such were some of the persons among whom Lenin moved and with whom he worked in St. Petersburg. Their impressions of him were usually recorded many years later, and through the prism of his subsequent greatness and their own disappointments or insignificance. Still we are afforded a glimpse of Lenin during the first period of his political activity.

That the first impressions were mixed was due not only to Vladimir Ilyich's unprepossessing appearance. Lenin's conversation when dealing

---

[12] Julius Martov, *Notes of a Social Democrat*, Berlin-St. Petersburg-Moscow, 1922, p. 128.

with intellectuals had already at that time the hint of irony and brusqueness that were to become a characteristic part of his behavior. He displayed neither the proverbial Russian conviviality, "the wide open nature," nor the fulsome and unctuous politeness of the intelligentsia's discourse. We are again reminded of Chernyshevsky's hero who did not waste his time in polite amenities but was always brusque and to the point.

But Lenin had compensating virtues that became evident upon a closer acquaintance: practicality and the ability and willingness to work hard. His comrades, even if they were not drawn toward him, were soon made to appreciate his talents as a thinker and conspirator. Struve claims to have detected early in young Ulyanov "abstract social hatred," "cold political cruelty," "real asceticism," and "indomitable love of power." But at the time he recorded his impressions Struve was also certain, on unknown grounds, that Lenin died of the effects of syphilis! Equally colored by the subsequent events is the recollection of another future enemy, Alexander Potresov, who saw in young Ulyanov the ability to exert "hynotic power" over people. But such accounts may be more valuable in appraising their authors than the serious young man who had arrived from the provinces and was eager for an entrée into the revolutionary world. Martov is more reliable in differentiating young Ulyanov from future Lenin when he notes that at the time he was still more eager to learn rather than to instruct and that he was not yet endowed with the morbid intolerance and suspicion toward people (let us add, mostly intellectuals) that were to characterize him later on.

Within a short time Lenin achieved the position (again quoting Martov) of the "first among equals" within the Socialist circles of St. Petersburg. It is unnecessary to credit this achievement to an alleged hypnotic power (not even during the Revolution did Lenin display the characteristics of what has become known as charismatic leadership). Nor was it a tribute simply to his intellectual eminence, for in Struve the Socialist groups had his equal in Marxian erudition and theoretical ability. But amidst the young intellectuals with their sensitivities and hesitations, Lenin already stood out and perhaps his very unceremoniousness and brusqueness were contributing factors, marking him as a man of action and determination.

Lenin's circle was to pass into history as the "circle of the old Social Democrats," or simply the "old ones" (the average age could not have been more than twenty-two, but the name separated them from a subsequently formed circle of the "young ones"). It was one of the interlocking groups of Socialist-minded young men engaged in political and economic discussion and in as yet very limited propaganda among the workers. They met to discuss the works of Marx, Engels, and Lasalle and to read their own papers dealing with various aspects of the social problems in Russia. Much of the literature discussed was illegal, but in 1894 Potresov and Struve made the brilliant discovery that a Marxist tract if given an esoteric title had a fair chance of being passed by the censor. Thus Potresov, who was a man of means, succeeded in publishing at his own expense Plekhanov's *The Problem of the Development of the Monistic View of History* and a book by Struve with an equally involved title. The latter was the subject of a critique by Lenin, which later became his essay on Marxism in bourgeois literature. Though not entirely unfavorable, it criticized Struve for his departure from orthodox Marxism.

This type of literary-political activity was but a continuation, to be sure, on a much larger scale and before a bigger audience, of the work begun in Samara where he had already started his first treatise, long, pedantic, and filled with statistics, on the Populist notions of Russia's economic development and the fallacies thereof. But he had craved St. Petersburg not only to write and criticize and discuss. And participation in the St. Petersburg circle finally brought him the consummation of his long-held desire: contact with and activity among the real industrial workers.

The intellectual labors going on in the Socialist circles were designed, of course, as but the preparatory stage for the work among the proletariat. Marxism, after all, was designed as a philosophy of revolution for the working class, and the most erudite theories of Russia's economic future or of the dialectical view of history were not advancing the movement one bit as long as those truths were known and discussed only by the intellectuals. The circles thus reached out to the more advanced and intellectually curious workers. There had been for some time small workers' groups interested in self-improvement and in discussion of their professional grievances, and it is with some of those that the "old ones" established contact.[13] This contact was facilitated by the fact that many of the young Marxists were engineers or engineering students who would encounter the workers in the course of their training. Thus gradually each of the "old ones" acquired "his" workers to whom he would expound either singly or in a group the verities of Marxism and the evils of Russia's autocracy.

How modest were the beginnings of this propaganda and indoctrination that in not too many years were to shake the foundations of a mighty empire can be gleaned from some of the recollections. A worker and future Bolshevik, Ivan Yakovlev, was to remember Lenin under his conspiratorial name of Fedor Petrovich. Every Sunday in the fall of 1894 Yakovlev would set forth from the environs of the city, where the fac-

[13] The intricate interplay of the workers' and intelligentsia's circles is most ably discussed in Richard Pipes' *Social Democracy and the St. Petersburg Labor Movement 1885–1897*, Cambridge, Mass., 1963.

tories and workers' settlements were, for a long ride to its center and the apartment of his then mysterious instructor. There from ten to twelve o'clock Lenin would read from *Capital*, which somewhat irritated his listener ("I could read myself"), but his irritation would disappear when Lenin began to explain the book and to relate it to the reality of Russian life.[14] In return he was most eager to learn from his visitor the condition of the workers' existence. One Sunday his pupil failed to show up, and at a subsequent meeting he explained to his annoyed teacher that he had had an altercation with a policeman and had to spend three days in jail. Disarmed, Lenin announced that he was a lawyer, and had he known he would have defended his "student." The sentence, he added good-naturedly, would have been the same, but they would have had the pleasure of verbally abusing "those scoundrels."

The workers' groups and individual lessons were not the only avenues of reaching the proletariat with Socialist propaganda. Though the average Russian capitalist was not endowed with an excessive social consciousness there were honorable exceptions. Some manufacturers set up Sunday schools and libraries for the workers. Those were often run by girls from the intelligentsia with progressive views. It was inevitable that the young Marxists and the young girls working among "the people" would get together, and the schools set up through the capitalists' philanthropy became regular channels for smuggling in propaganda for the destruction of capitalism. There were other consequences. Political association led frequently to romantic attachments and it is under these circumstances that Lenin met his future wife, Nadezhda Krupskaya. She was a very serious young lady one year older than her future husband, who was attracted to Lenin even before meeting him, so she tells us in her *Memoirs*, by the renown of his erudition in Marxian economics. Beginning with a discussion of the problem of consumers' markets in Russia, their courtship blossomed into what in the radical circles was known as "companionship," and was to remain a lifelong attachment, a source of comfort and strength to Lenin.

For all the propaganda and romantic successes of the circle work, it remained true that the young Socialists' main aim, that of converting the working class to Marxism, appeared as hopeless as their predecessors' attempt to stir up the Russian peasants to revolution. The conditions of the average worker's life did not give him the time or the inclination to pursue political activity, not to mention the elaborate course of study needed to comprehend the doctrine. Even those exceptional workers who took lessons in Marxism or organized their own circles were separated by a wide gulf from their young intellectual friends. The latter would, for instance, disperse during summer vacations, some to their parents' estates, others to seek employment to enable them to finance

[14] *The Historical Archive*, Moscow, 1959, n. 6.

their studies. The workers were then left to themselves, observing sar-
castically that the "Revolution was taking a vacation." Quite apart from
the difficulty of engaging in political work for a man who was working
twelve or more hours per day, the mass of workers were but one step
removed from the villages, and no more intellectual or revolutionary
than the peasants were. This fact was often impressed upon the young
idealists. One of them recalls once passing a church in the workers'
quarters. As behooved a man of advanced views, he did not remove his
hat, a gesture that came instinctively to a Russian of his generation,
whatever his class or views. The workers who observed his ostentatious
impiety set upon him with shouts, forced him to take off his hat, and
the young free thinker was lucky to get away with only a few bruises.
Had they realized he was an *intelligent,* observes the victim, unaware
that all the intolerance and rudeness was not on the mob's side, he
would have fared worse. Such people were not likely to be weaned from
their faith in God and the Tsar by learning the theory of surplus value
and similar Marxian subtleties. Like the Populists before them, the Marxists seemed to be destined to reach but a tiny fraction of the "masses"
whom they desired to save from oppression and superstition.

This bleak situation was transformed by a new discovery and tactic
that within a few years made socialism the militant faith of a sizable
portion of the Russian proletariat. From a fad Marxism became a social
force; all its successes in gaining popular support up to the Revolution
of 1917 can be traced to an idea born in 1893 in the Jewish quarter of
Vilno. Like many ideas that transformed history, the new notion was
simple, commonplace yet brilliant, original though something toward
which many people at the time were instinctively reaching.

The idea had been brought by Martov from Vilno where he had
been exiled for two years in 1893, but its real authorship belonged to
Alexander Kremer. The latter was a Socialist working among the Jewish
proletariat of this run-down metropolis. The usual propaganda tactics of
the Russian Marxists were even less applicable in Vilno than in St.
Petersburg. For one thing, many of the Jewish workers knew Russian
poorly if at all and most of the revolutionary and Marxian classics were
unavailable in Yiddish. To reach the masses Kremer proposed that the
Socialists should forget for the moment about the writings of Marx,
Lasalle, Chernyshevsky, and their like, and instead concentrate on helping the worker to win legal and economic concessions from the employer. One has to be reminded that labor unions were at this time
illegal and that the Russian worker was almost totally unprotected by
law. Kremer dug out an ancient statute of Catherine the Great providing
that the working day for apprentices should consist of 12 hours with a
two-hour break for lunch. This archaic law, never repealed, was now put
forth as the basis of agitation for shorter working hours for the indus-

trial workers. Very soon the wage earners were being taught not to fight for the "end of exploitation," or to "overthrow the autocracy," but to secure better working conditions and higher wages. To the worker the intellectual-Socialist was no longer the dispenser of eloquent but meaningless appeals and theories, but a valuable ally in the everyday struggle for a better life.

Kremer's discovery was embodied in a pamphlet, *On Agitation*, edited by Martov. It sought to reassure the Marxian purists by pointing out sensibly enough that class consciousness does not come to the worker from the air or from books, but from the experience of fighting for better conditions, and from encountering the alliance of the state and the capitalists. It may appear strange that an idea so full of common sense should have been greeted on the one hand as a "geniuslike" discovery and on the other should have aroused violent objections. But Marxism as an ideology has a built-in distaste to catering to the workers' "petty needs," as the phrase goes, rather than to their alleged interest in overthrowing capitalism as a whole. At the time, even in the West, the pursuit of those "lower" aims was largely left to the trade unions, the Socialists as *politicians* devoting themselves to loftier tasks.

When the Vilno discovery was brought up for discussion in the St. Petersburg circles, it led to violent disagreements. As neophytes, the Russian Marxists were much more devoted to the letter of the doctrine than their Western comrades. Fears were expressed on two counts: one, that the new strategy would not succeed, the other that it would succeed too well. Does not Marxism proclaim that the worker's lot *cannot* be substantially improved as long as capitalism lingers on? If on the other hand strikes, legal gambits on behalf of the worker, and similar undertakings should prove to be successful, won't the proletariat conclude that it does not need revolution and an overthrow of autocracy and capitalism to win a better life? Among those most violently opposed to the agitational strategy were some of the worker members of the Socialist circles. The new plan would clearly diminish the importance of their laboriously achieved mastery of the doctrine, would put a premium on the agitational rather than theoretical ability within the movement, and at the same time it smacked of certain condescension toward the rank-and-file worker. The latter would not be initiated into the full mysteries of Marxism; he would be guided imperceptibly to develop spontaneous hostility toward the state and its capitalist bosses.

But the obvious advantages of agitation soon prevailed over the original doubts in Lenin's mind when Martov, his banishment concluded, returned from Vilno in the spring of 1895. A close personal and ideological connection was soon established between the two men and they led the Socialists of St. Petersburg into the new and fateful path. The shift from propaganda to agitation as the main weapon of the class struggle was to serve the Russian Socialists well.[15] To be sure, in the wake of the great successes were to come new dangers and disagreements. The agitational technique not only attracted attention and sympathy of thousands of workers, but was also to sprout the heresies of "economism" and "tailism" soon to divide the Russian Social Democrats. But we are anticipating our story.

For the St. Petersburg Socialists, then, 1895 was an eventful year. From the study groups their efforts were turned to spreading leaflets and proclamations in the factories, taking advantage of any conflicts between the management and the workers. The leaflets were written in simple language and devoted exclusively to the problems of pay and working conditions, but drawing the inevitable moral: the collusion between the government and the owners and the need for the workers to act in unison to secure their rights. Lenin lent his hand in the preparation of the pamphlets, and with his usual thoroughness he plunged into a study of factory conditions and legislation on which he was soon an expert. On a more elevated literary scale the year marked his debut as an author in a legally printed symposium of Socialist essays. Though subsequently the collection of essays was confiscated by the authorities and burnt, several copies of it were saved, and thus for the first time he saw his words in "real" print, rather than in illegally hectographed or mimeographed pamphlets.

The year was to see great changes also in his personal life. For some time he had not been in good health, suffering from stomach disorders, and in the early spring he developed pneumonia. The extent of his mother's alarm—St. Petersburg had already claimed two of her children's lives—can be gauged from the fact that she hurried from Moscow, bringing with her a friend, professor of medicine. But Vladimir was already in competent professional hands, and the crisis passed.

His health gave him an excellent reason to request a passport to go abroad to "take the waters." His request was granted though the police could have but little doubt about the real purpose of his trip. They were soon able to establish, for they had their agents everywhere, that young Ulyanov's tour did not take in the watering places as much as those locations where the most prominent political exiles could be found. For a young Russian in the nineteenth century his first trip abroad was usually an event of major significance. He was leaving behind his "Asiatic" country with its residence permits, passports, and other restrictions and entering the alleged realm of freedom and civilization. The kind of activities that Ulyanov and his friends were pursuing in St. Petersburg, in

---

[15] The famous distinction between the two terms was formulated by Plekhanov and endorsed by Lenin: The propagandist explains many and involved ideas to a few persons, the agitator attempts to infuse many with a few ideas. The implications of this distinction constitute the history of Bolshevism.

daily expectation of an arrest, could in practically every European country of the period be practiced in the open and without risk. But if Lenin felt any exhilaration at his new experiences, or what was the second standard reaction of a young radical abroad, the disappointment at the West's "soullessness" and materialism, he gives no indication of it in his letters home. Those to his mother naturally enough express affection and request money. He was not traveling for pleasure but on business.

Its main goal was to establish a link with the leaders of Russian socialism in exile. For the first time, and with reverence, Lenin encountered the two founders of Russian Marxism: Plekhanov and Axelrod. At thirty-nine and forty-five respectively, they had seemed from Russia to be the veritable patriarchs and almost mythical heroes of the revolutionary movement and thought—especially Plekhanov. A veteran of the People's Will, he had begun almost singlehanded a new tradition in Russian radicalism, and had become a trusted associate of such demigods of international Marxism as Engels and Liebknecht. Every Marxist in Russia was in a sense his pupil and in traveling to Geneva where the master then resided, Lenin was traveling to the source of his faith.

The encounter took place in the spring of 1895 and it produced a favorable impression on both men. Lenin was still full of reverence and becoming modesty toward the older man and Plekhanov was overjoyed at the evidence of the growth of Marxism in his country. He predicted for his young pupil a great future as a working-class leader. Lenin displayed the product of homegrown Marxism, the collection of essays of the St. Petersburg group in which was included his own critical essay on Struve's critique of Russia's economy. Plekhanov tactfully praised this work, though to his friends he was later to confess that young Ulyanov for all his Marxist erudition and correctness could not really write. If he had any reservations about his visitor's views, and here was a small inkling of the future tempestuous quarrels, it was on account of his intemperate language toward the *bourgeoisie* and the liberals. The current Marxist orthodoxy claimed, of course, that the Socialists should work with the liberals in overthrowing autocracy. Theoretically Lenin agreed, but already bitterness toward his own class made him break into abuse whenever he had to deal with the categories of *"bourgeoisie,"* "liberals," or the "intelligentsia." Plekhanov is reported to have observed, "We want to turn our faces to the liberals while you turn your back." But in general the meeting passed in harmony and nothing seemed to augur that the triumph of socialism in Russia would see the pupil the dictator, while the master was dying in privation and in danger of arrest and assassination.

In September Lenin was back in St. Petersburg. The tempo of agitational work quickened in the fall of 1895. The conditions of the Russian workers, especially of those employed in light industry, were reminiscent of those in the beginning of Western capitalism about fifty or sixty years before: the pay was extremely low and no legal regulation or unions could protect them from the exactions of their employers, who were free to cut their wages, lengthen their hours of work, and the like. In November strikes, brought about by really insufferable conditions, broke out in some textile and cigarette factories. (The textile strike was brought about by an arbitrary and mendaciously explained lowering of wages.) The Socialists plunged in with leaflets encouraging the workers and making explicit their demands. Lenin prepared the proclamation to the textile workers. It was written in the style of and as if coming from a rank-and-file worker, though most of the strikers realized that it issued from friendly intellectuals. The strikes failed but they laid the precedent for the future and really mass strikes of 1896 and 1897, which were to win concessions and mark an era in the history of the Russian labor movement.

Another and more immediate effect was a wholesale arrest of the St. Petersburg Marxists. For a long time the police were excellently informed of their activities. For all the conspiratorial precautions employed by the "old ones" and the other circles, their agitational activity was bound to betray them. An *intelligent* appearing in the workers' quarters was bound to attract a policeman's attention: his dress and bearing would give him away and his attempts at disguise often made him obvious. Then there were informers within the Socialist groups. The police, for instance, knew that as early as in 1894 Lenin had participated in illegal workers' activity, that he smuggled into Russia forbidden political tracts, and that he was now setting up a clandestine newspaper to be called *The Workers' Deed.* Early in December the conspirators relaxed from their labors by giving a party. Among the Socialist revelers was one Mikhailov, a prominent member of the group known as "the young ones." Many people frowned upon Mikhailov. He was a dentist, a profession not enjoying much prestige among the revolutionaries, and he seemed unusually inquisitive. This suspicion was amply justified. Mikhailov was a police spy, and he was to pursue his *agent-provocateur* career until murdered ten years later. The day after the party the police hauled in the Socialists, Lenin included. The catch was eventually to amount to 57 persons, thus almost destroying the active Socialist groups in the capital.

For the first time Lenin found himself in "real" jail. The previous arrest in Kazan did not count, for to spend a few days in prison as a result of student disturbances was as common and unsensational in Russia as to be fined for a traffic offense in the United States. To contemplate his imprisonment is again to be reminded of the tragicomic paradoxes of Tsarist Russia. On the one hand there was no nonsense about *habeas corpus,* being represented by a lawyer, or other amenities of the legal procedure. For fifteen months Lenin was imprisoned while his case was being "investigated." (There was really nothing to investigate; the police from the beginning knew everything.) On the other hand, a man is presumably arrested to stop him from continuing his criminal activity. Not so in Russia. Lenin's stay as the guest of the Tsarist government was filled with most intensive political activity. He wrote propaganda and agitation pamphlets, kept in constant touch with the few members of his organization still at large, and deepened his knowledge of Marxist literature. In addition, he told his sister, he enjoyed a great advantage over the vast majority of his fellow citizens: he could not be arrested.

This situation had several causes. In the first place, political prisoners—provided they were not assassins—enjoyed at the time privileged treatment. This was due not to any liberalism on the part of the government, but to the fact that political prisoners were likely to be "gentlemen" and often relatives of influential persons. Then the Socialists were viewed as a lesser evil among the political subversives. "Such a small group," said the indulgent police official in charge of the investigation, "in fifty years something might come out of it." As it was, Vladimir Ilyich received visitors regularly. With relatively little trouble he could smuggle out messages and articles by writing them in milk and lemon juice between the lines of the books he received and then passed back to his sister or other relatives and to Krupskaya who for the purpose of secret communications now accepted the bourgeois status of his fiancée. His future mortal enemy, Struve, was particularly helpful in furnishing him with the latest economic and political books.

Lenin's situation was thus not of the kind described in the famous Russian prisoners' song: "The sun sets, the sun rises, but in my cell there is always night." His passion for physical exercise did not abandon him in jail, and he was very careful to adhere to a regular schedule of calisthenics. Some time later when his brother Dimitri followed the inevitable path of all the Ulyanovs and found himself imprisoned, Vladimir offered him the product of his experiences: it is most important to be careful in one's diet, and to have a regular and varied plan of exercises: pushups, bends, and so on. Insofar as diet was concerned, Lenin gained a special concession of having his prison fare supplemented by meals and milk sent from the outside. Sister Anna is the authority for the surprising comment that in one respect imprisonment seems to have benefited his health: the stomach pains that had pestered him disappeared. His buoyant spirit actually annoyed Anna. He kept her continuously busy running from one end of St. Petersburg to another with political messages and pamphlets so she did not have a moment to spare, and the hard-pressed woman could not conceal her irritation when her brother would ask her how she was spending her time.[16]

Tsarist Russia was an autocracy tempered not only, as the saying

[16] Anna Elizarova, "Lenin in Jail," in *The Proletarian Revolution*, Moscow, 1924, No. 3.

goes, by assassination and corruption but also by "pull." No sooner was Vladimir in jail but his mother and friends exerted themselves through their connections to have him released. The president of the bar association wrote to the minister pleading for a parole for his young colleague, and declaring that attorney Volkenstein, Lenin's indulgent boss, offered to stand guarantee for his good behavior. Such efforts might well have been successful, had not Lenin obstinately refused to admit the evidence against him. No, he had never come near Plekhanov during his trip abroad. He had never engaged in an illegal activity among the workers, but was just dispensing legal advice. This behavior was not yet demanded by the revolutionary code; provided one did not betray secrets or comrades one was allowed to admit facts of which the authorities had undisputable evidence. But Lenin stuck to his refusal, as did most of his accomplices. Not all of them could match Lenin's hardiness and good spirits under a prolonged imprisonment. Some developed nervous troubles, which in one case at least was to lead to permanent insanity. Others suffered physically. But the trials and worries of imprisonment did not diminish the ideological fervor of the young intellectuals or their disputatiousness. Martov relates how a violent dispute divided the political prisoners: the Greek inhabitants of Crete had just rebelled against their Turkish governors. Should a Socialist support the Greeks? To be sure, all good Socialists are for the right of oppressed nationalities to seek freedom. And yet . . . the Tsarist government was instigating the Balkan nationalities against Turkey, and wasn't one in seemingly supporting the Greeks *really* supporting the imperialist designs of the autocracy? Such were the tortuous arguments and concerns of young men who faced long imprisonment and exile.

When the sentences had been handed down in February 1897 they were greeted with relief. What had been most feared was imprisonment in a fortress which, unlike a detention house, could break the strongest nature, or hard labor in Siberia. Actually the severest punishment was one of five years' exile. Lenin and several others were condemned to three years' "free" exile, i.e., they were to be confined to the given locations in Siberia but otherwise not inhibited in their movements. Again Maria Alexandrovna's exertions and connections served to soften the sentence. For "health reasons" he was permitted to choose the Minusinsk region of southern Siberia, which had a tolerable climate and the reputation of being a "choice spot" if one had to be exiled. A rich and influential radical sympathizer, Mme Kalmykova, put Lenin in touch with a member of the Siberian administration who in turn enabled him to choose the exact spot where he would reside. Characteristically and with great wisdom Vladimir Ilyich chose not the larger center of Minusinsk where there were a number of political detainees, but a village, Shushenskoye. He would thus be free from daily contact with unfree men, which invariably led to frayed nerves, violent conflicts, and occasionally, as we have seen in the case of Fedoseyev, to tragedy. At the same time he was to be within traveling distance of other exiles, and thus capable of communication and joint political work.

Some mendacious accounts have Lenin traveling to his destination under armed guard. In fact he was allowed to travel on his own. This was a bit embarrassing since Martov, Krzhizhanovsky, and others *were* being conveyed under police guard. But after some hesitation Lenin saw no reason to incur the unnecessary privations and discomfort and his comrades did not begrudge him his privilege. Mme Kalmykova offered to pay his way, but Maria Alexandrovna pointed out that she could finance the trip, and that the other sentenced Socialists were in greater need.

The same indulgent police official who thought that socialism in Russia might amount to something "in fifty years" allowed the sentenced prisoners an unusual boon: they were granted three days of freedom to arrange their affairs before setting off for Siberia. Lenin managed to stretch his leave for several days by pleading the need to spend some more time with his ailing mother in Moscow. It goes without saying that the "affairs" that the paroled prisoners were hastily arranging during their moments of freedom were concerned mostly with politics.

The fifteen months of Lenin's incarceration were a period of great activity of the St. Petersburg Socialists. A few days after his imprisonment in December 1895 his group adopted the resounding name, Union of Struggle for the Emancipation of the Working Class. The incarceration of most of its leaders did not put an end to its agitation: quite the contrary. The few members left in freedom managed to keep up the salvos of leaflets and proclamations whenever a strike or labor disturbance took place. The great strikes of 1896 and 1897 enabled the St. Petersburg Socialists to attract international attention. Though the strikes represented a spontaneous explosion of the workers' grievances, the Union of Struggle provided a printed expression and explanation of their demands.

Thus while in no sense leading the strike action, as was later to be claimed in the Soviet histories, the Socialists for the first time became known and trusted by the mass of workers as their allies in the struggle for a better life. Abroad, through their contacts in the international labor movement, the Russian Socialists gained expressions of support and even financial assistance for the St. Petersburg strikers.[17] Thus Russian Marxism was gaining international recognition at the same time that it was coming of age at home.[18]

[17] The strikes had the belated result of forcing the government in 1897 to promulgate the law setting the maximum working hours at 11½.
[18] Pipes, *op. cit.*, p. 107.

Compared with the small "circle" beginnings of only a few years before, this was a dazzling success. The time was approaching for widening the scope of the movement. Socialist groups in other Russian industrial centers were adopting the name of the St. Petersburg body, Union of Struggle . . . , and imitating its tactics. From his prison cell Lenin smuggled out a draft program for the proposed united Socialist party. But the very successes brought with them new problems and dissonances and it is to those that the briefly released leaders had to address themselves in February 1897.

The Socialist movement was attracting real workers. High time! But was socialism to be absorbed entirely in the workers' movement? Were its aims and propaganda to be sidelined completely in favor of everyday needs of the working masses? Were the workers to swamp the intellectuals in the leadership of the movement as a whole? In brief, was the Union of Struggle . . . , to function more and more as a clandestine labor union and less and less as a political conspiracy? There could be no question as to Lenin's position; ever since 1889 he had one aim before him—revolution, and everything else including agitation for the workers' rights was but the means toward that end. And his temperamental dislike of the intelligentsia was matched paradoxically by his conviction that no other class could provide the necessary determination and ability for the leadership of the revolutionary movement. His arguments carried the day with most members of "the old ones." Before dispersing to travel to their distant destinations seven Socialists posed for a group photograph. With their very proper bourgeois dress and against the background of some hideous Victorian furniture, the young men hardly suggested the dangerous revolutionaries who in a few years transformed Russian socialism from a discussion club into a movement.

3. Siberia

Though Maria Alexandrovna's pride made her reject the offer of financial help for her son's journey, it is clear that her widow's pension was strained by the expense. It is difficult to account, otherwise, for her petition of February 18 that her son be allowed to join the exiles' party in Moscow and travel at the government's expense for most of the way. (How strange that the mother should continuously petition on behalf of a man in his middle twenties and a lawyer!) But if he were to go at the government's expense, it would have to be like the others, as a prisoner. And so, after another and fruitless effort to postpone his departure, Lenin alone set forth from Moscow in a third-class carriage on February 22. During the first stage of his journey he was accompanied by his mother, two sisters, and brother-in-law.

It was fitting that the St. Petersburg Socialists, who unlike their Populist predecessors believed that capitalism was coming to Russia, should have been among the first exiles to profit by its enterprise. They were to travel on the newly constructed Trans-Siberian Railway. The previous generation of political offenders had to make this trip by slow and painful stages, sometimes on foot and sometimes in chains. If Vladimir Ilyich was conscious of this vast progress it did not diminish his irritability, natural under the circumstances. A fellow passenger during an early part of the trip remembers him reviling the conductor for the overcrowded condition of the train. In Samara, where the train made a lengthy stop, Lenin summoned the stationmaster and in a lordly manner, with a crowd of passengers looking on, demanded attachment of an additional passenger car. Unlike in our democratic and unionized society, a loud and self-assured abuse of a minor official in Tsarist Russia often produced results. "Hitch on another car," ordered the victimized stationmaster, and the political criminal on his way to exile bent to his will the minions of capitalism and the state.

The fellow passenger who was observing with admiration this display of forcefulness on the part of the short young man was none else than the Siberian official whose intercession on Lenin's behalf had been procured by Mme Kalmykova. He recognized Lenin and followed him into the station dining room. The latter was still seething. "You, a police spy?" he greeted the stranger. After introduction and explanations, the two men decided to share a compartment in the freshly procured car for the rest of the long trip. It turned out that Krutovsky, the official, had Populist sympathies. This led to another explosion when he incautiously laughed at Lenin's criticism of the Populist deity Mikhailovsky. But somehow the two men settled down to an amicable discussion and tea drinking and thus they spent the long 3,000-mile trip.[19]

The last railway stop was Krasnoyarsk, the center of the vast Yenisei province of Eastern Siberia. Though it was the size of several Western European states the province contained only about 40,000 urban inhabitants. In Krasnoyarsk Lenin had to wait two months until water on the river Yenisei was high enough to enable him to travel to his ultimate destination. Despite their ideological disagreements, the obliging Krutovsky procured for him not only assignment to a relatively desirable place of exile, but also an introduction to a rich sympathizer of the revolutionary cause in whose house Lenin obtained free room and board. This local angel of radicalism was Claudia Gavrilovna Popova, who for years had helped the political exiles, gave them shelter and money, and whose house was the intellectual center of Krasnoyarsk. Here Lenin stayed between March and May 1897. The only drawback was the fact that occasionally the house would become crowded and Vladimir Ilyich

[19] Vl. Krutovsky, "In the Same Car With Lenin," in The Proletarian Revolution, Moscow, 1929, No. 1.

would have to share his room with other "politicals" passing through the town. They were for the most part Populists, and the close quarters and ideological dissonances would at times lead to violent and loud quarrels, which dismayed the hostess. Lenin was hardly popular with the older exiles. They made acid comments about this new type of revolutionary who traveled to Siberia by rail and at his own expense. Above all, when it came to a political discussion he tended to be aggressive and intentionally rude. When he was bidding farewell to Mme Popova she told him pointedly that she preferred the older (that is, the Populist) generation of the revolutionaries to the new one. Abashed, Lenin thanked her warmly for her hospitality.

Many years were to pass. Socialism had triumphed. In 1921 famine struck large parts of Russia. Mme Popova was now in her seventies, destitute and ailing. There were still people around Krasnoyarsk who remembered her great generosity to the victims of political oppression under Tsarism and they petitioned the local Soviet to grant her special food rations. But to the local commissars she was a "class enemy." And the woman who had helped countless revolutionaries, among them the current Chairman of the Council of the People's Commissars, was allowed literally to starve to death.[20]

Political quarrels did not occupy most of Lenin's time. He was working on the economic treatise begun in the St. Petersburg jail. One would naturally ask where in this Siberian wilderness he could collect materials and statistics relating to industrial development and economic history. But Russian life was full of surprises. Krasnoyarsk, this equivalent of nineteenth century Dodge City, had one of the most remarkable private libraries in the Empire. Its owner was equally remarkable. He was one Yudin, son of a peasant who, having begun by cashing in a lucky lottery ticket, grew to be a rich merchant. Though quite uneducated, he was a fanatical bibliophile who built up a library of 100,000 volumes, full of priceless first editions and manuscripts. A self-made man, Yudin did not like political exiles and, true to his type, he was fearful of having strangers touch his treasures. But in Lenin he evidently recognized a fellow bibliophile, so that it was in this library that Lenin sat practically every day from morning till night. He was already a fanatical lover of books, the same man who as the ruler of Russia would threaten to have officials imprisoned for publishing books sloppily or without an index, and he took delight in the precious collections.[21]

As noted earlier, Lenin's "pull" enabled him to receive a relatively favorable residence in exile. The Minusinsk region was some 280 miles south of Krasnoyarsk and its climate was dry and healthy. Not all the

[20] Mark Gorbunov, "Lenin in Krasnoyarsk," in The Past, Leningrad, 1924, No. 25.
[21] Most of Yudin's library was sold before World War I to the Library of Congress in Washington, becoming part of its Slavonic Collection.

fellow exiles were equally fortunate. Martov and another St. Petersburg Socialist, Vaneev, were assigned to the northern part of the Yenisei province.[22] On the last day of April Lenin set forth toward his destination, traveling by boat and then with horses. It took seven days to reach the town of Minusinsk and then there were about 35 miles to his final destination, the village of Shushenskoye.

This was a peaceful place of 1300 inhabitants, boasting of one church and three large taverns. Its isolation lessened the chance of strict police supervision, and protected Lenin from the continuous squabbles that were the order of the day in such larger places as Minusinsk, with sizable groups of political exiles. In Shushenskoye there were only two others, but they were simple workmen and Lenin got along with them famously. The local constable was an old retired noncommissioned officer. He soon grew fond of Ulyanov and they used to hunt together. Thus one could receive forbidden books and engage in political correspondence without the fear of continuous searches. Vladimir Ilyich proposed to do a lot of writing and reading, and providing the mails arrived fairly regularly he could not have chosen a better spot. He rented quarters in one of the peasant houses, a typical Siberian one-story wooden cottage. It was a simple room with a bed, writing table, and four chairs, but beyond these Lenin required only some bookshelves, which were constructed by his host. Soon he lapsed into the daily routine of his exile, in fact not too dissimilar from his usual occupations: reading and writing most of the day and late into the night. There were regular walks, even when the Siberian winter was at its coldest. Other diversions were equally simple: skating on the frozen river, and in the fall and spring hunting. It might seem that for a young man, who in Samara, a city of 100,000, had suffered from a feeling of claustrophobia, this was an unbelievably lonely and monotonous existence, but by now Lenin had found his vocation and life's work and he was amazingly self-contained. These characteristics are well brought out in his letters. To his mother he writes with real if at times impatient affection. He soothes her apprehensions: Shushenskoye has a splendid and healthful location, he is well, dresses warmly, in fact has gained weight, and sleeps better than ever before (evidently all quite true). There are frequent requests for "finances" as Lenin jocularly calls it.[23] But at times he becomes, if not heartless, then certainly thoughtless of his mother's many worries, not financial only. It is thus odd to find Vladimir inquiring from the relatives about the possibility of purchasing for him in Moscow a hunting dog (sic) or a

---

[22] Lenin's continual preferential treatment cannot perhaps be fully explained by the intercession of Krutovsky, a relatively minor medical official. One suspects that Maria Alexandrovna had a more influential acquaintance in the higher ranks of the bureaucracy.

[23] The government allotted about eight rubles per single exile per month, and since living was very cheap this sufficed for food and quarters, but not much else.

revolver, as if they were unavailable in Siberia. At the very same time Maria Alexandrovna was suffering over another arrest, that of Dimitri, and her finances were further strained by the necessity of sending daughter Maria on a European trip. Eventually Lenin bought a dog himself, and to his mother he dispatched a cheering letter prescribing a schedule of physical exercises and diet to be followed by Dimitri in his prison cell (Maria Alexandrovna never forgot how one of Lenin's fellow prisoners in St. Petersburg went mad and it preyed on her mind).

Much more extensive are letters to sister Anna. She was his main political and literary agent, an intermediary with Struve (who was indefatigable) in procuring for Lenin literary work and publication for his essays, and with the Russian Socialists abroad, such as Axelrod. Upon Anna fell the main burden of assuaging Lenin's inordinate hunger for books, newspapers, and political news. It was she who had to dig up obscure statistical and economic journals and books and dispatch them to the distant Siberian village. (The Russian libraries of the period must have had very liberal lending rules.) The news of publication of a Socialist or economic treatise would send Lenin into a frenzy of impatience and Anna had to endure scolding. In Yakutia (in easternmost Siberia) they already have the latest book by Bernstein, and how is it that he, only 15 days from Moscow, still has not received it! The same avid and impatient interest was aroused by the scraps of news about doings in the Socialist movement. What is the latest about the heresy of revisionism in the German Social Democratic Party? Is Struve really falling away from Marxian orthodoxy? The poor woman had in addition to edit Lenin's works, check his references, go abroad to contact Plekhanov and Axelrod! Anna had a husband and her own profession, and it is no wonder that in her worshipful memories of her great brother one can occasionally detect a note of irritation.[24]

Maria (Maniasha) was evidently Lenin's favorite, and he did not treat her as merely a research assistant and secretary. His letters to Maria are full of an elder brother's sage advice, concern, and teasing. Why does not Maniasha want to go abroad, but prefers to sit in the oppressive atmosphere of Moscow? The young girl's (born 1878) health and nerves suffered obviously because of the family's abnormal situation and she could not do her academic work. Vladimir's advice finally prevailed and she did take a trip with her mother. To her he also wrote in a more relaxed manner and did not conceal the negative sides of Shushenskoye. But even Maniasha is occasionally reprimanded for her dilatoriness in procuring and sending *The Judicial Courier* or Semenov's

[24] Even his mother must have warned Vladimir against overburdening Anna, for he writes: "I fully understand (what you write) that Anna while living in the country will not be able to fulfill my requests about books. But please relent if she should happen to stop in Berlin or Leipzig on her trip back to Russia." Lenin, *Letters to Relatives*, Moscow, 1934, p. 59.

The Historical Account of Russian Foreign Trade and Industry from the Middle of the 17th Century until 1858.

The whole family was harnessed to the needs and activity of the exile. Even brother-in-law Mark Elizarov, to whom Vladimir did not feel particularly close (he addresses him continually with the formal "vi" rather then with the familiar "ti," "thou") served not only as Lenin's political correspondent but also as the source of information about the news in the chess world, and as a business agent in collecting fees for Lenin's articles. There are practically no letters to brother Dimitri, but he was first in jail and then under close police supervision.

Much as Lenin felt himself a man with a mission, and felt no compunction in imposing upon his close ones sacrifices and inconveniences, it would be unfair to see in him a complete egotist. Occasionally, his letters breathe concern about the fellow exiles. Will Anna send children's books for the family of a fellow Socialist? Or musical scores for Krzhizhanovsky, who was very fond of singing and poetry? The constant pathos and the occasional tragedies of Siberian life are mirrored in the correspondence. Martov, sent to a northern region and unable to get along with his companions, implores his father to do everything possible to have him transferred (he never got his wish and suffered greatly). Another of the old St. Petersburg comrades is rapidly dying of tuberculosis. Of his own troubles, rather minor in comparison, Lenin writes somewhat philosophically. He could not get permission in time to go to Krasnoyarsk to have his teeth attended to, and so he had a wrong tooth pulled out!

After one year of solitary exile a great change took place in his life. His companion of St. Petersburg days, Nadezhda Konstantinovna Krupskaya, was in due time arrested and then condemned to three years' exile in the city of Ufa (in the Urals). She petitioned to join Lenin in Siberia. The authorities were understanding but prudish. Yes, she would be allowed to join him, but on condition they get married forthwith. Otherwise it is back to Ufa for her. If we are to believe Krupskaya's and Soviet accounts, this condition was deeply troublesome to the young people. In the revolutionary circles there was the hallowed tradition of "companionship": man and woman living together and working for the cause in the manner of Sophia Perovskaya and Zhelyabov, but formal marriage was a philistine, bourgeois institution. Furthermore, and this is so painful that few Soviet accounts can really go into the subject, there was no civil marriage; you had to be married in the church. Had Vladimir Ilyich ever had an illicit relationship with a grand duchess, it could not be referred to with a greater embarrassment and circumlocution than this lawful wedding of two persons who were evidently deeply in love. As a mitigating factor we are told that Vladimir and Nadezhda on July 10, 1898, arrived at the church by different streets, and having been pronounced man and wife, sneaked back to their house also separately (*sic*) "so as not to attract attention." [25] How this secrecy was possible in a village of 1300 people is something the good author does not tell us. No bourgeois-type reception followed the ceremonial, but only tea drinking with a few of the friendly local peasants. One would like to think that his account is exaggerated. Certainly in Lenin's contemporary letters to his family one finds great satisfaction at the approaching marriage, mixed with comic indignation at its required and religious character. There is also a pleasant and, quite uncharacteristic for Lenin, expression of Russian "wide open nature." Will his family come for the wedding? It is only 3800 miles and not too uncomfortable if one travels second class. But, of course, this proved impossible. However, there was some family present. With Nadya came her mother Elizaveta Vasilievna, and she was a member of the Lenins' household (we use this name though Nadezhda was also after her marriage invariably referred to as Krupskaya) until her death during World War I, helping her daughter with domestic chores. She was the widow of a minor official, and seems to have acquiesced in her daughter's and son-in-law's rather unusual existence.

In Nadezhda Krupskaya Lenin found an ideal wife. She shared his ideas and tastes and was an excellent secretary. We are not allowed a glimpse of their personal life, but the marriage was a happy one, and Lenin's letters to her, even after many years, breathe warmth and great solicitude. But for the biographer of Lenin the marriage was a disaster. Nadezhda Konstantinovna was a person of a narrow and platitudinously fanatical mind. She did her revolutionary work the way other women go about cooking and sewing. The fact that she was married to one of the most important figures of modern times did not imbue her with any feeling of historical responsibility in the sense of preserving for the world a record of her husband's thoughts and actions. From the earliest days she was interested in pedagogical work and her so-called "Memoirs" about Lenin are really an edifying tale for the use of the members of the Young Communist League. Thus, for instance, she records that Lenin was a man of simple needs and tastes (quite true), but this fact, in itself, might lead one to suspect that he was, God forbid, an ascetic, a gloomy introvert in the style of a Populist terrorist. So Nadezhda Konstantinovna cannot refer to the modest circumstances of their existence without intoning: "But we enjoyed life. Ah, yes, Vladimir Ilyich knew how to enjoy life."

It was not altogether the kindness of fortune that made her survive her great husband by fifteen years. She found herself at first in the anti-Stalinist camp, and within two years of Lenin's death his widow was the object of boos and a hostile demonstration at a Party Congress. Later on, silenced and occasionally paraded out for ceremonial purposes, Krup-

[25] S. Belyaevsky, *Lenin in Shushenskoye*, Krasnoyarsk, 1960, p. 19.

skaya had to watch helplessly as her husband's closest collaborators and her intimate friends were vilified and then slaughtered by Stalin. Nor could she interfere with the falsification of Lenin's own career and ideas perpetrated by the tyrant and his henchmen.[26]

Lenin's bachelor quarters were now inadequate to shelter the family. They rented (for four rubles) half a peasant house with a little garden, and it was here that the remaining year and a half of the exile were spent. The chroniclers who shy away at the mention of the church wedding have no compunction in recording that the Ulyanov family became "exploiters," i.e., they hired a peasant girl to help around the house, and for a while she had to sleep on the floor. The everyday activities are now recorded in greater detail, for Nadya now takes the pen to report to her mother- and sisters-in-law Vladimir's doings, and she has a better feeling for what the other women would like to hear.

There is some social life. The other exiles are spread throughout the Minusinsk region. Relations are not close with the Populists among them and very soon they are broken off completely. But there still remain some comrades from St. Petersburg and there are occasional visits and get-togethers. In theory one has to get an official permission for traveling, and Lenin, for all his excellent health, petitions suspiciously often to visit a doctor in Minusinsk or Krasnoyarsk. Occasionally he skips Shushenskoye without permission but it is not safe to do it often. Most of the reunions mix sociability with politics, but there are purely social occasions such as the New Year's celebration where among other things a toast is drunk to mothers and mothers-in-law of the revolutionaries.

Among the "neighbors" the closest to Lenin and the best companion was Krzhizhanovsky. He too lived *en famille* with his mother, sister, and brother-in-law. Krzhizhanovsky, whose name denoted his Polish descent, translated in exile the lyrics of some Polish revolutionary hymns, such as the famous *Varshavianka,* which became the most stirring songs of the Russian proletariat. He was also an excellent skater and always welcome in Shushenskoye, where he taught the niceties of the art to Vladimir Ilyich. There were, alas, no really good chess players among the fellow exiles, so Lenin won with monotonous regularity. He was still a passionate player who in his sleep would shout out moves and combinations.

The scant recollections of those who knew Lenin in exile are colored, of course, by subsequent history. It is, however, quite clear that he played a leading role among the Socialists in the area. As to the exiles of other political persuasions, it was Lenin who was mostly instrumental in persuading the Socialists to break with them, thus destroying the

[26] Z. I. Lilina, wife of Zinoviev, died in 1929. She was probably Krupskaya's closest friend from the days before World War I. Though Zinoviev was then "merely" in disgrace and seven years were to pass before his trial and execution, the obituary in a Party journal did not even mention that the deceased had been his wife. It was signed "an old comrade," quite likely Krupskaya herself.

traditional comradeship that had united the exiles of all beliefs. The rupture reached such proportions that the fellow sufferers and victims of Tsarism would sometimes pass each other without greeting. Amidst Lenin's usual cheerfulness there are echoes of his constant animosity: "Better not wish me here in Shushenskoye a companion from among the intelligentsia," he writes to Anna. To a fellow Socialist he stated that when the Marxists win in Russia they should behave the way the Jacobins did toward their opponents.[27] Yet he would not and he never could shake off his class identity. The same source, a worker who subsequently became a Bolshevik and who writes of Lenin with veneration, still testifies that his behavior was dry and reserved, unlike that of the members of the Populist intelligentsia, who tended to be friendly and effusive.

The Siberian period was, then, one of constant activity. In addition to politics and recreation, Lenin broadened his acquaintance with social and political literature and studied languages. Struve procured him the job of translating Sidney and Beatrice Webb's *The Theory and Practice of Trade Unionism*, which was to earn him about 1000 rubles that came in very handy. Appropriately enough, this work of the famous English Socialist husband and wife team was translated with great assistance from Krupskaya. Their English was not very advanced, but with the help of a dictionary and the German edition they did a creditable job, though as Struve recalls venomously, he had to spend some time straightening out the stylistic and literary side of the translation. More to Lenin's taste, since it was a work of a real Marxist and not of reformist Socialists, was the translation of Kautsky's *The Agrarian Problem*. How lucky, to repeat, was Lenin to be in a fairly accessible locality where mail came regularly twice a week and where conditions of work were reasonably good. Martov, in contrast, languished within the Arctic Circle, with mail reaching him at most eight or nine times *a year*.

It is characteristic that neither in his letters nor anywhere else does Lenin give an exhaustive description of his environment. At most his letters are brief communiques of his everyday activity, but the local color and surrounding atmosphere are entirely missing. He was to be the same when it came to describing his life in Paris, Geneva, or London. One looks in vain for the broad sympathy or even interest in the exotic surroundings that appear in recollections and correspondence of many exiles. Martov, for instance, left a vivid memoir of his life in the wild and inaccessible Turukhansk, which for all its appalling realism is not devoid of humor.[28] For all the changing surroundings, whether in prison, exile,

[27] Alexander Shapovalov, "Lenin in Exile," in *The Red Chronicle*, Leningrad, 1924, No. 1.
[28] The high point of the year was the arrival of the very considerable supplies of vodka, which were to last the 400 inhabitants through the long Arctic winter. (Turukhansk, Martov was certain, had the highest consumption per capita in the Empire.) On its arrival the boat with its blessed cargo was met by a thanksgiving procession headed by the Orthodox priest carrying the cross.

or abroad, Lenin was isolated from the world by his work and its pre-occupations.

As the prescribed term of his exile was drawing to its end Lenin's nervousness was returning. Three years had produced vast changes in international Marxism and in the revolutionary situation in Russia. He was eager to regain freedom in order to realize his dream of creating a Socialist newspaper, which from abroad would reach and unite the Russian revolutionaries. There was always the possibility that the authorities would arbitrarily prolong his sentence. The police were well aware of the fact that "Tulin" or "Ilin," under whose signatures Marxist tracts and articles appeared in St. Petersburg, and the exile Vladimir Ulyanov were the same person. It was only a fortunate accident that a sudden search in the Ulyanovs' quarters in Shushenskoye failed to turn up compromising evidence. But the worst did not happen. In January 1900 Lenin was allowed to return to European Russia. As usual in such cases the main industrial and university cities were forbidden to him. He chose Pskov in Western Russia, close to the frontier; one way or another he had to get abroad. Krupskaya, who had another year of exile to serve, went back to Ufa.

The trip back was hurried. Even in Ufa, where he delivered his wife, Lenin was already plunged in politics and conferring with the local Marxists. One of them recalls that he was unusually security-conscious and conspiratorial. He would not attend the regular radicals' get-together because it was held in the house of a Populist sympathizer. But under the circumstances his caution was quite understandable.

Then Moscow, and a reunion with his family. Maria Alexandrovna's first words were of course "how thin you look," and indeed, as Anna notes, he looked emaciated and unhealthy. It was the suspense and anxiety of the last few weeks that made him lose weight. But he was not allowed to stay in Moscow, and so at the end of February he reached his destination, Pskov.

Lenin's activity between February and July 1900 when he left for abroad partakes of an element of mystery. Frequently he would go to places forbidden to him, Moscow, St. Petersburg, Nizhni-Novgorod, Riga, and other cities, to take counsel with fellow Socialists and to collect funds for revolutionary activities. In Pskov he conferred with Struve, Martov (now also released) and Potresov. The police were excellently informed of all those goings-on. It had occasioned some surprise when earlier they had allowed Struve to publish a Marxist journal, but the surprise was really in store for the Socialists, for its associate editor was a police agent who furnished them with detailed information. It is thus at least curious that Lenin was issued in May 1900, by the governor's office in Pskov, a passport to go abroad "for six months." There could not be the slightest doubt in the dullest police official's mind as to the purpose for which Vladimir Ulyanov sought permission to leave Russia.

The clue to the mystery may be found in the circumstances of Lenin's life in Pskov. Here he was befriended by local radicals, including two rich landowners, Nicholas Lopatin and Prince V. A. Obolensky. The two were representatives of the type Lenin hated fervently most of his life; they were drawing-room Socialists. But they were influential and willing to contribute generously to the cause. It would not be surprising if some official of the governor's chancery found himself richer as a consequence of the former "state criminal" Ulyanov receiving a passport so he could legally go abroad and advocate the overthrow of the government.

The same suspicion is forcibly brought to one's mind by the following curious episode. Toward the end of May Lenin's luck failed and he was arrested during one of his forbidden trips to St. Petersburg. What made it worse was that Martov was arrested there at the same time and that both of them had considerable amounts of cash on their persons. Lenin carried 1400 rubles, the equivalent of a sizable yearly salary. Under questioning he told a surprisingly transparent lie, that the money was a fee for his literary work for Struve (actually he had received and spent the honorarium one year before and the money was from Lopatin). Again the police showed themselves unusually indulgent. The money was returned to him and after several days he was released and sent under police escort to his alleged destination, his mother's residence near Moscow. Here there was a harrowing incident that might have changed the course of history. The policeman released him but proposed to keep his passport. Lenin's status as a gentleman and lawyer stood him in good stead. He shouted at the constable, threatened him with a complaint to the authorities, and left banging the door. The terrified cop ran after him, handing back the precious document. Such, at least, is the official version, but possibly it was another case of despotism being tempered by corruption.

For all the *agents provocateurs,* its excellent (for the times) technique and liaison, and its full dossier on Lenin, the police did not interfere any more. Thus in July he left Russia perfectly legally, but he was to stay abroad considerably longer than six months.

In leaving, Lenin was bidding farewell to the period of his revolutionary apprenticeship. He had gone to Siberia as one of the leaders of the burgeoning Socialist movement in St. Petersburg. He was now ready to take his place on an immeasurably wider stage as a claimant for the leadership of *Russian* socialism. In the Siberian exile he still felt himself to be and acted as a humble follower of the fathers of Russian Marxism, Plekhanov and Axelrod. To the latter, hearing that he had praised his writings for the workers and had expressed the hope that Ulyanov should write more in the same vein, Lenin wrote in the tone of a flattered pupil

"I wish and dream of nothing else but to be able to write for the workers." Toward the end of the exile he was ready to criticize Axelrod. His self-confidence and authority had grown. He was no longer content to rail against the Populists and to expose (but how easy it was!) their theory that the development of capitalism in Russia is an optical illusion. He now emerges as the defender of Marxian orthodoxy, ready to take on those who, in Russia or abroad, would revise or falsify the doctrine of the master. It is this struggle which, strangely enough, would engage his energies even more than the fight against autocracy and capitalism until the Revolution.

In Siberia Lenin was possessed by an idea that led to his journey abroad. This was to build a united Marxian party based upon a journal published abroad and smuggled into Russia. It is easy to recognize the source of this idea. Some forty years earlier, Herzen's *Bell* had achieved a dominant role in Russian radicalism. Before Lenin's eyes there was always the panorama and the lessons of the Russian revolutionary tradition. The People's Will, a mere handful of revolutionaries acting upon wrong premises, still managed to paralyze for two years the government of an empire and to affect decisively the course of Russian history. If only the resolution and discipline of the People's Will could be combined this time with a correct social and political theory, Marxism! . . . The pursuit of this ideal explained the interminable ideological squabbles of the coming years, those wars over the choice of a word in the Party program, those friendships and associations of a lifetime severed because of a minor tactical disagreement. As in a religious allegory, the hero's path takes him from the morass of Populism to the heights of Marxism, where the evil of opportunism awaits him masquerading as Economism. The enemy is overcome only to reappear in the successive installments under the guise of Menshevism, Ultimatism, Liquidationism, and their like. The Marxist is a man who has conquered religious superstition, for whom the struggles of the Antinomians, Nominalists, and Realists are fantastic tales from the age of darkness. But his own path is a narrow and difficult one between the chasms of Revisionism and Dogmatism.

4. Marxism

During his first trip abroad in 1895 Lenin met a noted French Socialist, Paul Lafargue. And what were the Russian Socialists doing, he inquired. When told that they were expounding Marxism to the workers Lafargue, with his innate cultural chauvinism, was politely skeptical. The *French* workers had had Marxism drummed into their heads for over twenty years, yet they could not understand it. How could the Russians? That this involved ideology should have taken root in this "semi-Asiatic" country never ceased to amaze the French or German intellectuals. And the late Lord Keynes expressed typical Anglo-Saxon incredulity: How can a doctrine "so dull and illogical" exert such a potent influence in the world? The great economist was being both a bit unfair and unrealistic. Marxism certainly is not dull. As to being illogical, it is hardly at a disadvantage when we compare it with many other doctrines that have swayed the history of the world.

That fashionable term of modern psychology, "ambivalence," could be inscribed over the whole vast structure of thought of Karl Marx and Friedrich Engels. For looked at closely, Marxism is not a collection of simple prescriptions of unreserved enthusiasms and detestations. Few things in Marxism appear as clear-cut as its call for the overthrow of capitalism, few of its descriptions as moving as its indictment of the capitalist as the exploiter, the man who lives upon and grows rich from the toil and suffering of the vast majority of the population. Yet, in the *Communist Manifesto* and *Capital* there are passages of almost lyrical character in praise of capitalism. Modern capitalism has in the space of a few decades, writes Marx, contributed more to the welfare of mankind than all the preceding social and economic systems. It has bound nations together not only through trade, but also through an intercourse of ideas. Capitalism-industrialization has exposed the foolishness of nationalism and has weakened the hold of religious superstitions (here Marx is at one with the overoptimistic liberal of the mid-nineteenth century). In brief, it has meant civilization and progress. Of that progress the capitalist is the main agent: his innate compulsion to save and to invest is the necessary condition of material and spiritual improvement of mankind.

What is intended as the solution to the paradox is Marx's conviction presented as a scientific inevitability that now (a flexible "now," whether that of 1848, the year of appearance of the *Communist Manifesto,* or 1867, that of Volume I of *Capital*) the progressive and benevolent role of capitalism has come to an end, at least insofar as Western Europe is concerned. Its further existence must produce grinding and *increasing* poverty of the masses. The laws of economics prohibit the capitalist, no matter what his intentions are, from paying the worker more than what he needs for his barest subsistence. (To be sure this again is an elastic term; "barest subsistence" for an English worker has a meaning quite different from its meaning for a Russian worker, is different at different times, and so on.) The same laws of economics ordain that the workings of the industrial machine compel the capitalist to exploit his worker more and more, that unemployment and general poverty must grow, and that finally the capitalist system must dissolve in a series of crises and revolutions. The proletariat economically exploited and politically oppressed (for the *bourgeoisie* and capitalists own the state) grows *spontaneously* more class conscious and organized and finally overthrows its oppressor. (When the "expropriators are expropriated") socialism takes over. Public ownership of the means of production assures a harmonious balance between the forces of production and consumption. The inherent contradictions of capitalism will have disappeared and the further technological changes will lead to greater and greater abundance of worldly goods for everybody. Eventually the coercive institutions, the state included, which are necessitated only by economic inequality will wither away and socialism will give way to communism with its motto: "From each according to his ability, to each according to his need."

The sheer intellectual brilliance of the Marxian system has always attracted to it individuals who live by and for intellectual pursuits. In comparison other Socialist systems appear, as indeed Marx condescendingly characterized them, as moralizing or utopian dreams. In a very science-conscious age, when economics and politics were thought susceptible of being analyzed by rigid laws, Marxism was bound to shine with theoretical profundity and elegance. But not only for the intellectuals. Underneath the mass of statistics and mathematical formulas, and yet plainly visible, there is this stern moral judgment and doom pronounced upon the rich and powerful of this world, all the more satisfying, for it cannot be avoided or softened. It is no wonder that for all its materialistic and free-thinking base Marxism has always held a secret attraction for some religious-minded: it promises, and considerably sooner than in the next world, certain chastisement for those who have succumbed to the false idols of worldly success.

The fortunes of Marxism as a movement were, however, to be bound up not with the intellectuals or the envious esthetes, but with the working class. Its father proclaimed that the emancipation of the working class was to be achieved by the workers themselves. And indeed, quite apart from its theoretical apparatus inherited from German idealistic philosophy and the English liberal economists, Marxism expressed the sentiment and aspirations of the English or French workingman of the 1840s and 1850s. Totally unprotected by the state, buffeted by the anarchic forces of the market, the reflective workingman might well have felt that the Industrial Revolution was only enriching the manufacturers, while making him poorer and less secure, and that politics in which he had no voice was the means through which the *bourgeoisie* kept him in still more complete subjection. It is seldom in the history of mankind that a great technological change or material improvement has not been bewailed as a clear premonition of disaster. So it is with automation in our time, so it was with the steam engine and power loom in the early decades of the last century. To many a worker those mechanical wonders were but the devices through which the rich had destroyed him as an independent craftsman or a small landholder, and forced him into the ranks of the urban proletariat. Their further improvement and adoption threatened him with the loss of even that tenuous and sordid livelihood: he would have to take a cut in pay, work longer hours, or join the army of the unemployed. Those were the feelings and facts upon which Marxism fed and which it translated into a theory and program of political action.

As the years passed, it became clear that what Marx and Engels took for the death throes of capitalism were but its birth pangs. The Western European worker of the 1870s and 1880s no longer felt the hopeless grievance against capitalism and industrialization that had come so naturally to his grandfather thirty or forty years before. His standard of living *had* risen. The state had begun to intervene on his behalf, regulating the hours of work and factory conditions, and laying the modest foundations of what we know today as social security. And in almost every Western state the worker now could vote in the elections, form his own parties and, the bane of revolutionary Marxism, form trade unions, which would remove from the worker this feeling of helplessness in the face of the capitalist. But as the Industrial Revolution moved east its worst side effects, now a thing of the past in England or France, were being reproduced in Russia. As we have seen, only at the end of the century the Russian worker was beginning to gain what his Western counterpart had enjoyed for a generation or two.

The fathers of Marxism were thus confronted with an ebb of that revolutionary feeling which had been such an obvious fact of industrial life before 1850. Class feeling and antagonism to the capitalist system were still rampant among the Western workers, but they were taking on a less urgent and revolutionary expression. In the successive reissues of the *Communist Manifesto* Marx and Engels had to moderate and explain away their predictions of Socialist revolution and an imminent fall of capitalism.

The basic structure of his theory was never changed by Marx. Thus on his death in 1883 the canon of Marxism, much of it a product of theories and conditions no longer relevant in *Western* Europe, stood the same. But as a politician and the spiritual leader of an international movement, the great Socialist had to adjust to the times. Thus, if one looks for the first revisionist, the first man to tamper with Marxian orthodoxy, he is none else than Karl Marx. Confronted with the very unrevolutionary atmosphere of the 1870s, Marx allowed that in some countries, England, the Netherlands, perhaps the United States, the change to socialism might come through peaceful parliamentary means. Compared to the apocalyptic tones of the *Manifesto* and parts of *Capital*, this was an enormous concession and change of tone. In France and especially in Germany the extension of franchise allowed Socialist parties to be organized and to grow in electoral strength if not in militancy. England, the most thoroughly industrialized country in the world, where revolutionary socialism should have triumphed first, mocked the father of scientific socialism by the complete insignificance of its Marxian movement. He blamed it, as Lenin did after him, on the Englishman's stupidly pragmatic turn of mind and the inability to understand social theories.[29]

The same allegation could not be made about the Russian intelligentsia. In the generally bad (i.e., quiet) condition of Europe after the Franco-Prussian War Russia remained a hopeful exception, with its profusion of revolutionary movements and stirrings. Marx could not but be touched by the interest in his works shown by the Russian radicals. The first translation of Volume I of *Capital* appeared in Russian in 1872. As capitalism in Europe was growing stronger and the worker less militant Russia looked more and more promising from the point of view of revolutionary socialism.

The earlier generation of Russian radicals had looked at Marxism skeptically. Marx was honored as a revolutionary but not as a system maker. In their preoccupation with the peasant and their rejection of the Western pattern of economic development the Russian revolutionaries could not accept the philosophy that proclaimed capitalism as the inevitable if passing fate of their country, extolled the industrial worker, and prophesied the end to the "idiocy of rural life." "The worker is the future bourgeois," said Herzen not hopefully but with a shudder. To Bakunin, with his merciless critical instinct, Marxism proposed to replace the capitalist with the bureaucrat, and Marxian socialism would be but capitalism exercised and centralized by the state, more oppressive than ever before.

In one of those utterances that have always fascinated and exasperated the Marxian scholars, the old man went far to meet the objections of his Russian sympathizers. In a famous letter to a Russian revolutionary he indicated that Russia still had a chance to skip the capitalist phase. The peasant commune, Marx wrote, knowing that he would gladden the hearts of his Populist readers, offered Russia the unique chance to jump from the precapitalist phase into socialism. This assertion, Marx must have known, ran against the grain of his whole system. If the possibility of a peaceful evolution to socialism from capitalism already departed from the Marx of the *Manifesto* and Volume I of *Capital,* then allowing Russia to skip capitalism entirely and to pass from an entirely rural economy through a violent revolution and the peasant commune to socialism was simply and drastically un-Marxist. The commune was a relic of the past; it had nothing Socialist about it, it was an almost insurmountable

[29] The first would-be popularizer of Marxism in English, Hyndman, neglected to mention Marx in his exposition. He explained (but this did not improve his case) to the infuriated Socialist patriarch that the English did not take kindly to theories authored by foreigners!

obstacle to rapid industrialization and modernization, and without them, of course, socialism as Marx and Engels understood it was unthinkable.

The Marxian scholars have expended much ink and ingenuity in trying to fit this apparent aberration of the Master into his general scheme. (One of the most exasperating characteristics of the Marxists of whatever persuasion is their insistence that Marxism, i.e., *their* version of Marxism, is consistent and unassailable throughout.) What is most often ignored is the obvious and very human explanation. The great revolutionary was holding on to the one concrete chance of a real revolution the European scene of the late seventies and early eighties seemed to promise. All over Europe even the most devoted Marxists were settling down to prosaic political and labor-union activities. Only in Russia the heroes of the People's Will were acting out a revolutionary drama. Hence his moment of weakness and the apparent readiness to discard the central point of his philosophy if he could claim the Russian Populists for his camp. Certainly Marx was very much taken with the terrorists who assassinated Alexander II and thought that they represented the wave of the future insofar as Russia and revolution were concerned.

This attitude among the Western Socialists survived both the death of Marx and the collapse of the People's Will. Engels, who inherited the Master's mantle, reproached the founders of Russian Marxism for their quarrels with the Populists and thus for their dividing the revolutionary movement. From the perspective of the international Socialist movement this attitude was understandable if somewhat condescending to the Russian comrades. Tsarist Russia was a bulwark of European reaction and of the old order. If this edifice were to come crashing down the course of revolution everywhere would benefit. And the most promising revolutionary movement in that strange country stemmed from the Populist camp. Hence let the Populists, for all their quaint notions, their ignorance of historical materialism, and other failings get on with the job. The handful of the Russian Marxists could wait. This point of view, clothed, to be sure, in a theoretical and lofty language, was bound to chagrin the Russian disciples of Marx. They were in a position not dissimilar from the African or Asian Communists of today when they are told by Moscow to restrain their ideological impatience and to ride the wave of nationalism and anti-imperialism. In a sense, Engels and others shared the opinion of the St. Petersburg police official when he allowed that "in fifty years something might come out" of the homegrown Marxists. But by the end of the century both international Socialists and the Tsarist government were ready to change their minds; something might come out of Russian Marxism much sooner than that.

The attraction of Marxism for the young radicals of Lenin's generation does not need much of an explanation. For many of them Populism was a spent force: it had exhausted itself in its hopeless wooing of the peasant and the catastrophic interludes of terrorism. Where was the theory of socialism and revolution to come from? The ideas of Fourier, Saint Simon, and Bakunin had all had their day and had been found wanting. Proudhon, that other great name of European socialism, enjoyed for a time a vogue in the radical circles. But in a moment fatal for his Russian reputation Proudhon wrote a pamphlet attempting to prove woman's innate inferiority to man. This pamphlet and its assertion that woman belonged either in the kitchen or on the streets could never be forgiven by the Russian radicals for whom the full emancipation of women was, next to the overthrow of autocracy, the most sacred cause. Proudhon was seen for what he indeed very much was, a French *petit bourgeois* whose socialism was a protest against every authority except that of the father of the family.

But Marx shone not only by contrast to his European rivals. Not even the greatest opponent of Marxism can deny the soundness of his views on many problems of economic development, his prediction of the coming of the age of big business, his realizing the significance of science and technology. This common-sense character of much of Marxism must have been especially striking in Russia of the 1890s. Here were the Populists still mumbling about the peasant commune and saving Russia from capitalism, while all over the country factories, railways, and banks were springing up. The growth of capitalism was impinging upon the countryside. The more enterprising peasant who may have saved some money chafed under the restriction of the peasant commune, where the *mir,* its assembly, in many cases periodically redistributed the land, decided how many members of a household would be allowed to go to town, and otherwise restricted individual initiative and the drive to improve agriculture. At the same time the growth of peasant population led to the overcrowding of the villages; this could be solved only by a speedier industrialization and colonizing of the virgin land in Siberia and elsewhere. Thus, the *obschchina* (commune) itself was slowly succumbing to the new economic forces.

If to the economist Marxism made a lot of sense against the background of Russia of the end of the century, then also, to repeat, it could provide a potent appeal to the working class. The Russian proletarian enjoyed none of the benefits won by his Western European brother. On top of his poverty and insecurity he lived within an autocratic system, and there was no reason for him to question Marx's assertion that the state was the executive committee of the exploiting class. In Russia therefore this seeming paradox of Marxian socialism was exhibited for the first time. Here was a doctrine whose author assumed that it would be particularly acceptable and logical in an advanced industrial society. Yet history has shown again and again that Marxism has a peculiar capacity to stir up men's minds and emotions in a society *just entering* the path of modernization and industrialization or, as the current social-science jargon has it, in an underdeveloped society.

Lenin's debut as a political polemicist showed him as a mature and erudite Marxian scholar for whom, as for many, Marxism was not only a convenient cover-up for revolutionary sentiments, but an integral part of the faith. As early as 1893 in a work bristling with statistics he assailed the Populists for refusing to see what was happening before their eyes. With the coming of machinery to the countryside one begins to have class differentiation of the peasants. No use lamenting the passing over of the old primitive peasant economy, of the substitution of machines for handicraft. Those were the facts, and benevolent facts at that. The progress of capitalism in Russia made the peasants live "more cleanly" [30] than before. Thus early Lenin showed himself adept at Marxian circumlocution: you cannot quite say that capitalism has raised the standard of living of the peasant, hence "more cleanly."

The polemic against the Populists occupies Lenin's first full-fledged work, *Who Are the "Friends of the People" and How They Fight the Social Democrats.* Here he took on, among others, the leading star of Populism, Mikhailovsky, and rejected with indignation the Populist claim to a share of Marxian inheritance. This work of a twenty-four-year-old youth had the mark of the mature Lenin, theoretical agility combined with venomous invective: "Scratch a 'friend of the people' and you will find a *bourgeois*" (the word *burzhui* in Russian has a far greater emotional intensity as an invective than its French equivalent). The Populists—"The Friends of the People"—claimed to be heirs of Marxism and yet they understood nothing about it. The teaching of Karl Marx was not another parlor game, not another social utopia, it was a *scientific* presentation of the structure and tendencies of capitalism. Though possible to snatch a stray statement of Marx and to twist it out of context (the famous statement about the peasant commune, a veritable thorn in the side of Russian Marxism), it was impossible to deny the logic of his system, which proclaims that Russia must go through the same stages of economic and social development as Western Europe.

Lenin's early writings provide a clue to his growing authority in the radical movement. He is a very convincing writer who impresses by logic and hard-boiled practicality and not by any rhetorical effusion. Who can quarrel with him when he states that for all the worship of the peasant, the unrealistic claims made on his behalf, the Populists have done nothing to elevate the standard of living of the peasant masses? Where are the model farms, where is a popular agronomic literature? [31] Beyond the

[30] Lenin, *Works,* 4th edition, Moscow, 1941, Vol. 1, p. 90.
[31] *Ibid.,* p. 237.

young revolutionary we are beginning to glimpse the future ruler, the apostle of technology and efficiency, whose religion is production. And this is all very much in the spirit of Marxism.

But such glimpses are as yet infrequent. When Struve, still a friend and collaborator, made his famous statement that the Russians must acknowledge their lack of culture and must be willing to learn from (Western) capitalism, Lenin's feelings were divided. The Marxist in him could but applaud, but the revolutionary as heir of the People's Will had to shudder. Will Russia have to go through *exactly* the same stages of Western development? Will it shake off Tsarist autocracy only to endure a lengthy purgatory of the rule of the capitalists and mercenary parliamentarians before socialism can be reached? The logic of Marxism answered that there was no other choice, but the emotion of the revolutionary whispered that one must be found. This dilemma was to be with Lenin until April 1917. In Siberia he noted the role of capitalism, paradoxical for a Marxist. In his *Development of Capitalism in Russia* he noted that the producers (that is, workers) "suffer both from capitalism and from the insufficient development of capitalism." [32] A very clever statement, but where does it lead?

For all of Lenin's theoretical work he never could be and never was a *pure* theorist. The noted Soviet historian Pokrovsky put it very revealingly, and perhaps from the Communist viewpoint said too much, when he wrote: "You will not find in Lenin a single purely theoretical work; each has a propaganda aspect." [33] And in Siberia he could not indulge in the luxury of purely academic work. He was working above all to transform the Russian Marxist movement into a party, and this was the primary aim of the rather dull and statistic-laden work on economics. But at the same time that Lenin was working to prepare a firm theoretical basis for his dreamed-of revolutionary party, a serious crisis was brewing within Russian and international Marxism.

The many-sided nature of Marxism gained for it converts among people of vastly different temperaments. Some saw in it order and pleasing rationality: mankind is saved through technology, progress, and increased production. Others saw in it mainly the call to revolution, to overcoming each and every conformity. At times the movement would contain both the artist and the intellectual scornful of the bourgeois society that paid them little heed, the bureaucratic-minded who saw capitalism as wasteful because it does not fully control and plan, and the humanitarian who resented social injustice. But the very same diversity of appeal that brought into the movement such incompatible natures was also responsible for its schisms and splits.

Thus, from its beginning Russian socialism had been affected by dis-

[32] Lenin, *Works*, Moscow, 1946, Vol. 3, p. 527.
[33] *The Young Guard*, February–March 1924, p. 248.

sension. One of its first manifestations was the quarrel about *agitation.* It turned, as we saw, on the most expedient way of leading the masses to socialism. The Marxists would embrace the worker's everyday problems and needs, and would, as it were, smuggle in their doctrine amidst the agitation to improve the worker's lot. It is undeniable that this technique involved a degree of condescension toward (some would say deception of) the rank-and-file worker. Why, if the workers through organization and joint action can improve their conditions, do they need the ballast of Marxism? And if on the contrary nothing under capitalism can alter fundamentally their pitiful life, are you not through agitation trading on human ignorance and misery? Aren't you following the sad example of some Populists who tried to deceive the peasants into a revolt by persuading them that the Tsar wanted them to rise against the landlords and officials?

An outgrowth of this debate was the rise of feeling that the leadership of the workers' organization should be vested in workers themselves and not in the middle-class intellectuals. Thus in 1897 an illegal St. Petersburg journal, *The Workers' Thought,* began to proclaim the "workers for themselves" gospel. The main business of the workers is to unite and build a strike fund so that they can win better pay and conditions of work from the capitalists. To be sure, *The Workers' Thought* asserted, the proletarians are full of sympathy toward the radical intelligentsia and its political aims. But please let the workers run their own organizations, their own strike funds, newspapers, and other affairs.

Under the conditions of 1897 in Russia clearly the argument of *The Workers' Thought* was more of a rhetorical flourish than a concrete possibility. How could the average worker find the time, knowledge, and means to lead in the task of organization? The journal referred to Marx's statement that the emancipation of the working class must be the deed of the working class itself. But if so, one might ask, what was Karl Marx doing talking about it? And who were the writers of those anti-intelligentsia strictures? Why, mostly middle-class intellectuals themselves! Had they chosen as their slogan that the destruction of the middle class must be the deed of the middle class itself, they would have come closer to the tragic sense of the Russian revolutionary tradition.

For all its tragicomic undertones, the argument of *The Workers' Thought* was a symptom of an extremely important emotion within Russian socialism. Just as the predecessors of the Marxists, the Populist intelligentsia, idealized the Russian peasant, so the Socialists saw in the worker their own version of the noble savage. Unspoilt by materialism, inherently brave and ready for self-sacrifice, the worker was thought of as almost a different species from the craven and mercenary bourgeois. Let us observe that in the "original" Marxism there was absolutely no warrant for such a romantic idealization of the proletarian. To Marx social classes were defined according to their relationship to the means of production and nothing else. A Rothschild who owns a bank is a capitalist and exploiter, but the same Rothschild without his bank and wealth becomes a proletarian. But to the Russian Marxists class differentiations represented almost biological categories, something which for all the discoveries of modern psychology is still astounding, for many of them came from the upper and middle classes. The use of such terms as "guilt feelings" and "self-hatred" cannot fully explain this indoctrination of the workers that *they* by virtue of their deprivations were somehow purer and worthier and more trustworthy than the most self-sacrificing and revolutionary specimen of another class.

This proletarian mystique assumed at times fantastic proportions. An early working-class Marxist recounts in his memoirs how he inquired of Lenin's friend Krzhizhanovsky (himself an engineer) whether he (Shapovalov) should take a high school examination that would open for him the road to education and professions. Krzhizhanovsky advised him against it; it would separate him from his class. Shapovalov professes that he always remained grateful for this advice. He remained a rank-and-file worker, and that kept him always on the straightforward path of revolutionary socialism, while at times many of the Socialist intelligentsia (including Krzhizhanovsky) abandoned the cause. The same sense of duty as a class-conscious proletarian, Shapovalov assures us, kept him from drinking, smoking, and even courting (though we are finally relieved to learn that he does succumb to a romance with a fellow revolutionary).[34] Thus religious mysticism was grafted upon a doctrine that professes enlightenment and healthy materialism.

Lenin, of course, was himself deeply affected by this mystique of the working class and an almost pathological dislike of his own. In Soviet Russia this doctrine was to receive a legislative sanction, the sins of the fathers (i.e., their class origin) were visited upon their children and for many years a descendant of the "exploiters" found better jobs and entrance to the Party closed to him. But there was in Lenin's nature a strikingly practical side. The bourgeois intelligentsia were hateful, cowardly, and otherwise condemned; the worker was pure, courageous, and otherwise praiseworthy. But when it came to the concrete problems of revolutionary organization in the year 1897 it was ridiculous to think that one could dispense with the intellectuals. Where would a workers' party led solely by workers lead them? Why, toward that specter haunting revolutionary Marxism, trade unionism. For all his venom toward his own class Lenin was capable of brutal common sense. Karl Marx and Friedrich Engels, he wrote, came themselves from the middle class. A revolutionary party needed the intelligentsia, needed converts from every class.

[34] A. I. Shapovalov, *In the Struggle for Socialism, Memoirs of an Old Bolshevik Underground Fighter*, Moscow, 1934.

From this spectacle of two sets of intellectuals quarreling over the question whether the intellectuals can be reliable revolutionaries we are drawn to larger issues. In 1898 Lenin was overjoyed to hear that an all-Russian Socialist Party was finally founded. To be sure, this event so momentous in the history of the world (for here was the formal beginning of the movement that in nineteen years would seize Russia, and in fifty control one third of the world) looked picayune in its immediate circumstances. Here were nine (!) Socialists who met secretly in the bedraggled provincial city of Minsk and proclaimed themselves the First Congress of the Russian Social Democratic Workers Party. Quite a distance, and not only in years, from the First Congress to those more recent congresses attended by thousands of delegates of the Communist Party of the U.S.S.R. in the presence of the representatives of the Communists from every country in the world, the congresses followed with attention and apprehension by the whole world! It was not even clear whether the nine persons who met in 1898 represented many beyond themselves. Three of them came from the Jewish Bund, four represented major Marxist centers in Russia, and two an illegal Socialist paper, but the rank-and-file workers in some of those centers had no idea that they were being "represented" at this momentous event.

The Congress issued a declaration of principles in the standard Marxian phraseology. The immediate goals of the alleged party called for a constitution, the freedoms of speech and press, and a parliament elected by universal franchise. The ultimate goal was to be Socialist ownership of the means of production, including land.

Those in attendance were secondary figures. The fathers of Russian Marxism, Plekhanov and Axelrod, were in the West, such rising leaders as Lenin and Martov in exile. Though not present, Struve was the author of the Party's *Manifesto,* a resounding declaration of principles that contained the famous statement: "The farther East in Europe, the weaker is the political sense, the more cowardly and meaner become the *bourgeoisie.*" Hence it is the worker who will have to win political freedom for Russia.

At the time of the writing of this withering characterization of his own class Struve was already beginning to diverge from orthodox Marxism. In a few years he was to become, to employ Lenin's vocabulary, an "opportunist," then a "renegade," i.e., he was to abandon Marxism and become a Liberal. Why, the reader will ask, was he so hard on the *bourgeoisie?* There was in Russia at the time no middle class in the Western sense of the word, only relatively few large-scale entrepreneurs and merchants. What was in fact the Russian middle class was the intelligentsia, the large body of people in free professions, and similar occupations. It is almost superfluous to repeat that probably no comparable body in any other society ever contained such a high proportion of civic-minded individuals, of radical thinkers and sensitive people ready to stand up against the government and full of sympathy for the needs and aspirations of the lower classes. Was the average member of this much-maligned body "more cowardly" or "meaner" than the typical French *rentier* or the German *Bürger?* Struve's rhetorical flourish was in fact a form of suicidal self-contempt, an augury of the dreadful fate that was to overtake the intelligentsia.

Having returned from Minsk, the founders of the Party were almost to a man arrested—the police had had excellent knowledge of the proceedings of the Congress. However, it was not that the arrested were very important, but rather that another crisis threatened the newly born Party with an immediate demise.

The genealogy of political ideas is not always a reliable guide to their content. Thus the new trend, Economism, was a direct descendant of the philosophy which proclaimed that the workers should run their own affairs and revolutions because, if you please, the intellectuals are not reliable, i.e., not stalwart and militant enough when it comes to a real struggle. But lo and behold, this ultraleft point of view begets Economism, which is very much to the right of official Marxism. The Economists, as those heretics were known, wanted the Russian Socialists to devote themselves to pressing for the economic interests of the workers, to enable them to receive better pay and shorter working hours. When it came to politics, the Socialists should merely second the efforts of the liberals to secure a constitution and Western institutions for Russia.

This startling proposal was jotted down by a young woman, Katherine Kuskova. It was not intended for publication and it simply reflected the impressions of many radical Russian students abroad. They could see that in Europe the greatest gains for the workers were being won by steady nonrevolutionary labor-union activity, at the same time that under the pressure of society as a whole practically every government was being forced to move in the direction of parliamentary democracy. To be sure, Russia was not Western Europe, labor-union activity was forbidden, and you had no parliament, but in due course and rather soon it was clear that those things would come to the Empire.

When Kuskova's declaration ("Credo," as it became known) reached Lenin in Siberia it provoked a quick and violent reaction. He had embraced Marxism as the surest, most scientific and expedient road to revolution. Here Russian Socialism was being emasculated, stripped of its revolutionay meaning, and transformed into a typical "do-goodism" of the intelligentsia. Kuskova appeared to mock all his and his comrades' labor and sacrifices of the last ten years. "Russian Marxism until now," she wrote, "presents a mournful spectacle."

Immediately, Lenin mobilized the small army of the Socialist exiles. Since one of them was in the last stages of tuberculosis the meeting took place in the quarters of the dying man.[35] Seventeen of the exiles were present and they all subscribed to Lenin's violent attack upon Economism, though some of them could not understand why private opinions not intended for publication should be treated as a declaration of war and betrayal. Lenin's answer was entitled *A Protest of the Russian Social Democrats.* Copies were dispatched into distant parts of Siberia to secure the adherence of those Marxists who could not attend. Here already was the Lenin of the next quarter of a century. A private opinion in a philosophical article would reveal to him the seeds of a horrendous heresy, threatening the unity of the revolutionary forces. And he responded by whipping his more easy-going collaborators into a loud and public denunciation.

The *Protest* was a thorough demolition of poor Kuskova's argument. Her assertions were incorrect, her history false, and her intention nothing else but to emasculate Russian socialism of its most vital element, the class struggle. The tone of vituperation employed by Lenin transcended anything that had transpired between, say, Herzen and Chernyshevsky.

For his own stance Lenin chose to reassert the recent *Manifesto* of the Russian Social Democratic Party. Socialism must remain a movement of the working class but it cannot dispense with *revolutionary* Marxism. Its immediate aim is the destruction of absolutism. It must follow in the footsteps of the famous fighters of the People's Will, who despite the unscientific nature of their socialism and their wrong method showed energy and resoluteness worthy of emulating.

The violence of the expression was the product not only of Lenin's fiery nature but also of his cold calculation, which was to serve him well in the future and interminable intraparty squabbles and fights. His opponent would have the choice of humbly expostulating that he was not a betrayer of socialism or an enemy of the people, or simply shrugging his shoulders and leaving the field of battle to Lenin. For a Russian *intelligent*, despite all his radicalism and contentiousness, the style of political polemic indulged in by Lenin was a novelty and a shock, and very few were capable of trading blow for blow. Most often, and this was to be the case of Kuskova and her fellow Economists, they fled the party whose leader indulged in such unrestrained abuse and this was exactly what Lenin wanted. And today, as a glimpse at almost any Soviet diplomatic note will testify, the same polemic technique is employed by the government of the U.S.S.R. and also not without success.

But Economism was just a fragment of the major crisis of Marxism of the late nineties. If Economism was a local outbreak then Revisionism was an epidemic. It threatened to destroy the unity of the mainstay of the international Marxist movement, German Social Democracy.

[35] The meeting took place in September 1899.

The latter was the pride and joy of world socialism. Here, appropriately enough in the country of Marx and Engels, the Socialist Party was unmistakably a major political force. A decade of illegality and persecution by Bismarck had only solidified and toughened the German Socialists. Now every successive election to parliament was bringing them more votes and seats. It was easy to foresee that in due course of time the Social Democrats would become the most numerous party in the Reichstag, and the government of the most powerful country, which was having the most rapid industrial development on the Continent, would be at their mercy. The strength of the party was matched by the excellence of its organization, ampleness of its funds, and richness of its intellectual resources. Its theoretical guides, Kautsky and Bernstein, loomed as the true heirs of the patriarchs Marx and Engels. Dozens of theoretical journals brought the German academic genius to shine on the most minute problems of Marxism. Nothing was forgotten or overlooked in the thoroughness of its organization, which included Marxist choral societies. One hundred thousand workers raised their voices in a harmonious exposition of the beauties of proletarian solidarity, or in a passionate indictment of the inequities of capitalism.

To the Russian Marxists, German Social Democracy was an example and an ideal which, they barely dared to hope, would be realized some day in their country. The German Socialists were not hunted men at the head of a handful of partisans; they sat in the Reichstag and publicly taunted and threatened their Junker rulers, and even the egomaniac Emperor, Wilhelm II, was powerless to do anything about it. To the German Socialists the Marxists everywhere looked for guidance and support. Lenin in his exile would go into a frenzy of impatience at the news of the appearance of a book by Kautsky. At the meetings of the Second International, the Russians, embarrassed to represent the country of despotism and backwardness, where the gospel of Marx was as yet little followed, would go into raptures if Kautsky or Bebel, the political leaders of the Germans, would address a few encouraging words in their direction. Germany was culture and progress and in it Social Democracy clearly represented the wave of the future.

But to the more observant foreigner it had been clear for some time that not everything was right with their German comrades. Political and material prosperity had been accompanied by a visible weakening of the revolutionary spirit. Officially, the Social Democrats proudly maintained the fundamental Marxian program, with its blood-and-thunder vision of revolution and the "expropriation of the expropriators." But its program was not matched by its everyday activity. The German worker under capitalism was steadily winning a higher standard of living. Socialism represented to him a protest against the class society under which he was living and the means of winning political and economic concessions from the capitalists. But apart from the tempestuous oratory on such occasions as the First of May, when dire threats were uttered against the *bourgeoisie* and the monarchy, he was content to lead his peaceful, and horrible to say, increasingly bourgeois existence. The same phenomenon was even more pronounced among its leaders. The Russian exiles passing through Germany could not but be astonished at the comfort and even luxury in which those parliamentary deputies, professors, and journalists often lived. Most of them did not look like the people who would lead the masses onto the barricades. Socialism in Germany was growing, but the prospects of a revolution seemed to be receding.

Many of the German Socialists were also uneasy about the situation in their party, but for different reasons. Its growth did not appear to contribute to any perceptible democratization of German life. For all its parliaments and its rule of law, the executive power of the Empire was in the irresponsible hands of the Kaiser. Despite all the impressive advances in the economy and in social welfare, Germany was the country where militarism and social distinctions were rampant. To overcome them, to turn Germany into a truly constitutional and more democratic society, the Socialists needed allies from the liberal and middle-class elements. But the latter were not forthcoming. The middle-class German was understandably frightened of the party whose program featured the confiscation of private property, the overthrow of monarchy, and more than hinted at the possibility of violence in achieving these aims.

It is under those conditions that the serpent of Revisionism crept into the Socialist paradise. Eduard Bernstein was one of the most revered Socialist leaders. He had been a close friend and literary executor of Friedrich Engels. A man of sterling intellectual honesty and of moral courage that he was to demonstrate several times throughout his long life, he was the least likely person to betray the movement or to succumb to bourgeois corruption. But Bernstein was impressed by the contrast between the outward successes of Social Democracy and its real ineffectiveness. This in turn led him to re-examine some of the fundamental tenets of Marxism. In 1898 he began his celebrated series of articles questioning the orthodoxy. The next year he set forth his views in a book whose English title was, appropriately, *Evolutionary Socialism*, and the scandal was out! From all over the world hundreds of articles and speeches flowed, attacking or supporting Bernstein. In distant Siberian villages the incredulous exiles heard that one of the leaders of world socialism was betraying Marxism, turning into an "opportunist," abandoning that main truth and device of the doctrine, class struggle.

Part of Bernstein's remarks were addressed to concrete problems. He was irritated, reasonably enough, by the petulant behavior of the German Socialists, which did nothing but harm to their cause. Thus to demonstrate their proletarian militancy they refused to stand up when the

Kaiser visited the Reichstag, shouted gross abuse at their opponents, and indulged in other gestures combining Marxian vituperation and a Germanic lack of grace, gestures which beyond causing bad blood between themselves and their Junker enemies had no effect. The Socialists, in view of their numbers, were entitled to one of the vice-presidencies of the Reichstag, which would facilitate their work. But how could a Socialist enter into such a compromising accommodation with the class enemy? To accept a vice-presidency meant putting on a top hat, formal morning dress, and calling upon the Emperor. Rather than suffer this indignity the job was being declined and the parliamentary interests of the Social Democratic faction were allowed to suffer.

But beyond such relative trifles Bernstein hit hard at the heart of the problem: the need to revive or to abandon many of Marx's main tenets and predictions. The most horrendous of all, because it was completely irrefutable, was the assertion that Marx's argument, the key to his system, that under capitalism the lot of the proletariat must progressively grow ✓ worse, was palpably false and must be abandoned.

This was a bombshell. For years now every intelligent Marxist had lived with this guilty secret, but most of them hardly dared admit to themselves that the Master was wrong, and on such a fundamental question. Yet no man in possession of his senses could deny that the Western European worker of 1890 lived infinitely better than his grandfather in 1850, that the rights of organized labor were being expanded all over the West, and that the state, this alleged tool of the exploiting classes, was becoming more democratic and was now introducing social legislation for the benefit of its underprivileged citizens. Some Marxian theorists attempted to skate around the problem by ingenious sophistry or fabrications: Marx had not predicted an *absolute* worsening of the worker's lot, only a *relative* one. But this tortuous reasoning often lacked conviction. The "catastrophic" argument of Marx caused difficulties even to Lenin. In writing about economics he was forced to resort to euphemisms. The Russian peasants under capitalism were beginning to live more "cleanly." He could not bring himself to say "better." ✓

Having committed this monumental indiscretion, Bernstein pressed forward with his heresy. Why not abandon the whole deterministic pseudo-scientific side of Marxism? Why not give up the blood-curdling visions of vast crises and violent revolutions? They do not have any basis in fact, but they serve only to scare off the middle-class would-be allies of socialism. The task before the Social Democrats was to press on with social reform and a democratic reorganization of society. The final goal, wrote Bernstein, i.e., a violent revolution and communism, meant for him nothing but the "movement," that is, a steady improvement of living conditions and the flowering of democracy should mean everything. Marxism, then, should be purified of its class struggle and violent ele-

ments. What remained of it was still a great deal: socialism was preferable to capitalism on humanitarian and rationalistic grounds.

Bernstein's friends wrote to him imploring that he give up his disastrous views. "Dear Eddie" (personally he was very much liked in the
Socialist circles) was admonished that a political movement needed a
dogma and an apocalyptic vision. And to be sure, stripped of its emotional
undertones, of its arrogant self-assurance of inevitability, where would
Marxism, where would German Social Democracy end up? It would end
up as a left wing of liberalism. For men whose whole lives had been
bound up with the bracing appeal of Marxism, for whom it was not only
a political creed but a religion and a way of life, such a result was
unthinkable.

The leader of the Russian Marxists, Plekhanov, epitomized the dilemma into which Revisionism plunged them. Years earlier he had
abandoned his Populism for this surer road to revolution, which Marxism promised and pointed out as inevitable. For its sake he had endured
exile, privations, and a painful separation from his erstwhile friends
and comrades. Finally, after years of isolation during which Russian
Marxism had consisted of just Plekhanov and a handful of disciples
abroad, the movement had begun to grow in Russia, to attract young
intellectuals and workers, and to triumph over the obsolete mumblings
of the Populists. And now, ironically, after fifteen years of labor and
sacrifices, revolution was to be snatched away from socialism and certainly from the dogma. Revisionism would turn the Russian Marxists
into "do-gooders" hardly distinguishable from those liberal capitalists
and noblemen petitioning the Tsar for a constitution and parliament. If
among the German Socialists living under constitutional, civilized conditions Revisionism could be treated with certain tolerance, then for the
Russians it was treason. It was a call to betray the glorious traditions of
the Decembrists, of the First of March 1881, a call to sit down and negotiate with the very same people who were imprisoning the revolutionaries
and keeping the Russian people in slavery and darkness.

From the depths of his bitterness Plekhanov cried out that either
Bernstein would bury Social Democracy or socialism would bury Bernstein. He could not understand why the Revisionists were not being
purged from the German party, how Bernstein could still publish in the
Socialist journals, or that such a pillar of orthodoxy as Kautsky continued to treat the wretch as a comrade. If only Marx and Engels were
still alive! Or, on second thought, they were lucky to be spared this shame
and desecration of their once glorious movement. He bombarded the
leaders of the German Social Democrats with protests, denunciations, and
articles designed to refute the noxious heresy, which could not always
be printed because of their excessive length and intemperate language.
The German Socialists were beginning to shake their heads over the

strange behavior of their Russian comrades, something they were to have an increasing occasion to do over the succeeding years. Their prize pupils were suddenly not behaving in a civilized, European manner. Bernstein's doctrines were rejected by the majority of the German Socialists, but there was no question of excluding him or his followers from the party.

The sounds of battle were not long in reaching Siberia. Like Plekhanov, Lenin was a fervent admirer of German Social Democracy, and for all his increasing doubts about the German comrades' militancy he was to remain one until 1914. The news filled him with dismay and rage. But his reaction was not as hysterical as Plekhanov's. It was always clear to him that "they" (the category including at times intellectuals, middle-class Socialists, and parlor radicals) were always ready to betray the cause, to turn into "opportunists" prepared to abandon the revolutionary struggle and to negotiate with the class enemy. Plekhanov's uncompromising rejection of Revisionism filled him with admiration. Here was a fine uncompromising revolutionary leader, a true heir of Chernyshevsky and Zhelyabov. Alas, a closer contact with the father of Russian Marxism was soon to show him that this idol also had clay feet.

The Grand Inquisitor himself could not have awaited a heretical tract with greater impatience and masochistic voluptuousness than Lenin did the arrival of Bernstein's book. The relatives were scolded for the delays in sending the scandalous document. And finally it arrived in Shushenskoye. After reading but a few pages, Lenin was sure, as he writes to sister Maria on September 1, 1899, that its author was not only an opportunist but a plagiarist as well. The book was weak, it repeated the ideas of the moderate English Socialists, it expressed the cowardly philistinism of the author and his ilk. Did he also think its argument unconvincing? Never in his career was Lenin ready to concede anything to an ideological enemy. Yet the term "fanatic" is well-suited to his case. Two years later, when he was writing *What Is To Be Done?*, Lenin admitted tacitly that Marxism, that product of the thought and conditions of the 1840s and 1850s, needed a thorough revision. But *his* revisionism Lenin was to proclaim as orthodoxy.

Since he had just finished working on the translation of the Webbs' book, he recognized that the sources of the Revisionist infection lay in England, where indeed Bernstein had spent a long time, and with whose liberal political traditions he was enchanted. To an orthodox Marxist England in contrast was a mournful spectacle. Here was the country that had given the world the Industrial Revolution and whose working class some fifty years earlier seemed on the point of rising and fulfilling the Master's prediction. But now the English proletarian was a melancholy spectacle. His only struggle was to receive a few more shillings and pence from his employer, and he was stupidly content to vote for his betters for Parliament. The blame lay, the Marxists agreed, in English trade unionism, with its unheroic slogan of "a fair day's wages for a fair day's work." This posture of the British workers was also, as we have seen, attributed to the revoltingly pragmatic temperament of the British race and the British inability (how unlike the Germans!) to appreciate the beauty and importance of theoretical questions.

But how could one, then, explain the spread of Revisionism in Germany and its echoes in Russia? For Lenin, then in the last year of the Siberian exile, the question became increasingly connected with the problem of the correct organizational expression for Marxism. *The Communist Manifesto* was written when a European revolution appeared imminent. Marx wrote at the period of the greatest and most excessive rationalistic optimism. Discover the correct social theory, announce to the workers where their real interests lie, and they will do the rest themselves. They will have no difficulty in understanding that social legislation, higher pay, parliaments, and the like could not improve their lives. The very conditions of their existence will teach them to organize themselves and to rise to "expropriate the expropriators." But fifty years of history had shown, at least to Lenin, that while Marx's theory was not to be touched, his predictions were overoptimistic; the workers would need help. And this help could come only from a tightly organized, centralized Socialist party which, unshaken in its orthodoxy, would still be able to be nimble and flexible in its tactics.

The full flowering of his ideas on the structure of the Party belongs to the period abroad. But even in Siberia he put his hand to a draft of a Socialist program. Here the Leninist-Bolshevik gift of having one's cake and eating it too is fully visible. The Party is to retain all the fundamental assertions of Marx as a matter of faith, yet its immediate program is to be flexible enough to disarm the liberals and to lure the peasants. The thesis that capitalism *inevitably* leads to the worsening of the worker's standard of living is to be retained. Despite all the claims of the Revisionists this statement is true, and it makes *excellent material for agitation among the workers.*[36] Scathing things are noted about parliamentarism, but the Party's aims are to be a universal suffrage, unlimited freedom of speech, press, and conscience. Above all, a doctrinaire approach is to be avoided in approaching the peasant question. The peasants are to be promised concrete economic concessions: more land and a relief from payments to the state. (Forty years after their emancipation the peasants were still paying installments for the land that was "given" to them with their freedom.) Nothing in the agitation is to tell the peasant what Marxism must eventually have in store for him: the abolition of private property in land and assimilating his lot to that of an industrial worker.

[36] Lenin, *Works*, Vol. 4, p. 214.

And elsewhere he wrote: "The seizure of power was never set by the [Russian] Social Democrats as the most immediate task of the Russian workers. The Socialists have always said that only under [conditions of] political freedom with broad and mass effort will the working class be able to organize for the final victory of socialism." [37] Here is an impeccably democratic Lenin: with an overthrow of autocracy and with universal suffrage the Socialists would openly and legally strive to achieve power and to convert the nation to their philosophy. If so, why rave about the Economists, why demand the ejection of the Revisionists from the international movement?

But this paradox, liberal and democratic phraseology veiling a deeply intolerant temperament, a doctrinaire capable of the utmost tactical flexibility, is characteristic of all Lenin's activity and of that of the party he was to create. It is certainly in 1900 both naïve and unjust to judge him insincere. The Marxist in him taught him to be patient, to let Russian history develop through the foreordained economic and political phases; the revolutionary in him was already impatient and contemptuous of the liberal and democratic claptrap. The same amalgam appears in his writings about the Revisionists. How unjust, he complains, in a respite from a bitter invective, to accuse us of attempting to turn the Socialist Party into an order of "right believers" who want to persecute "heretics" for their departure from the dogma.[38] For "us" Marxism is not a dogma, not a religious belief, but a social and economic scheme that warrants a different course of action under different circumstances in different countries. Like many men of action he had the blessed gift of a complete lack of introspection.

The party that was to inherit this characteristic was already in Lenin's mind before his departure in 1900. So busy was he in arranging the organizational details and financial help for his enterprise that he forsook during his last months in Russia his usual contentiousness. We have seen him counseling amicably with Struve, already tainted with Revisionism. Perhaps it was his immense practicality which made him realize that an internal quarrel at this time would alienate the rich well-wishers of the movement, and without their support he would never be able to put out a journal. And talented writers such as Struve might still be useful for an article or two. Equally practical was the realization that the journal had to be published abroad, and that that was where he, Lenin, belonged. This decision aroused some dismay among his associates. Wouldn't he lose his touch with conditions in Russia and become like Plekhanov and company, a professional émigré? But heroic posturings were quite alien to his nature. It was one thing for a rank-and-file revolutionary worker to live in constant dread of arrest; it was quite another

[37] Ibid., p. 243.
[38] Ibid., p. 191.

and senseless thing for a revolutionary *leader* to run this risk. To an apprehensive comrade he said frankly, "To allow oneself to be sent into [Siberian] exile once is permissible, to do so for a second time would be stupid." [39] In years to come he was often exposed to the reproach that while sending others on dangerous missions he stuck to the security of Geneva or London. But such taunts never disturbed Lenin.

Nor was he embarrassed by the somewhat self-proclaimed nature of his leadership of the working masses. Mme Kalmykova, from whom Lenin expected and did get a lot of money for his journal, was present at a private gathering in Pskov, where he tried out his ideas. He sketched out an editorial in which he spoke repeatedly "on behalf of the working class." For all her admiration Mme Kalmykova was understandably skeptical. Where was this united Russian working class and how could Lenin presume to speak in its behalf? In reply the old lady heard: "It [the working class] *will* become infused with the conviction that it already exists and that those are its sentiments and demands." [40] One feels that the young Rockefeller or Carnegie could not have exhibited more convincing self-assurance when first seeking financial backing for his enterprise.

The long-dreamed-of journal appeared at the end of 1900. Its title, *Iskra* (*The Spark*), commemorated the pledge of a Decembrist poet that appeared on its masthead: "Out of this spark will come a conflagration." The first issue published in Germany saw the light of day almost exactly seventy-five years after the Decembrist plot. The journal not only claimed to represent the rising Socialist movement, but also to be the heir of this long-drawn-out and painful struggle of the Russian people for freedom. Lenin's editorial made clear that the movement and the paper would not be merely passive representatives of the interests of the working class. Any Socialist party worthy of its name must lead the masses and must instruct them as to where their real interests lie. The masses may want to slacken in their march toward the revolution, to content themselves with economic concessions; the party must urge them on. Political as well as economic struggle must be the constant aim of Russian socialism.

[39] M. A. Silvin, *Lenin During the Period of the Birth of the Party, Memoirs*, Leningrad, 1958, p. 219.
[40] *Ibid.*, p. 237.

IV

THE LEADER

1. The Iskra Period

In Europe of 1900 a Russian revolutionary was no longer a lonely, shunned figure like his predecessor of thirty or forty years before who, unless he was a man of means, like Herzen, could consort only with small uninfluential groups of fanatics or anarchists in France or Switzerland. Now, especially if he was a Socialist, he could expect that in every major European center he would find co-believers ready to help, if need be, to provide him with shelter and funds, and to protect him from the long reach of the Tsarist police. Were he to be molested by its agents questions would be asked in Parliament, articles printed in the local papers, and in brief, any European government that would try to oblige the Tsar's would find itself in more trouble than it was worth. The Second Socialist International was then in its heyday. It united Socialists of all varieties from the very revolutionary ultra-Marxist to some very temperate believers in gradual evolution toward socialism. Practically all of them, including those Lenin was to brand intermittently as "opportunists," "philistines," and "traitors," were ready to help the victims of Tsarist oppression, much as at times they were astounded by the unseemly squabbles and intemperate language of their Russian guests. France was by now an ally of Russia and close dynastic ties still prevailed between the German imperial house and the Romanovs. But neither the French republic nor even Wilhelm II, with his ingrained belief in the divine origin of royal power, would dare to interfere seriously with the right of political asylum for the people who were quite evidently plotting the downfall of an ally and a fellow monarch.

Mme Kalmykova had been dispatched abroad before Lenin's departure to explore Germany for the most suitable location for the publication of *Iskra*.[1] The German Socialists undertook to set up the type for the

[1] Since this lady has already made an appearance in these pages she deserves a few words. Alexandra Mikhailovna Kalmykova was a well-to-do widow who owned a bookshop and patronized radical causes. She was especially close to Struve. In her recollections she calls Struve her "'adopted son," but the relationship in fact was quite different, even though Mme Kalmykova was more than twenty years older. She helped Lenin and *Iskra* generously, but then their relations cooled off after the split among the Russian Socialists. After 1917 the old woman was rebuffed in her attempt to renew the acquaintance with Lenin and his wife. To quote Krupskaya: "In 1922 Vladimir Ilyich had written Alexandra Mikhailovna a few lines of fervent greeting, such as only he could write." N. Krupskaya, *Memories of Lenin*, New York, n.d., p. 14.

paper, and advised that it would be more diplomatic to transact the business of the paper away from Berlin. It was thus in Munich that Lenin supervised the first issue. But before that historic event the whole enterprise had almost collapsed.

The difficulty turned on the personality of Plekhanov, who was to be one of the editors of *Iskra*. The patriarch of Russian socialism [2] resided in Geneva, where Lenin had repaired directly from Russia. It soon became apparent that Plekhanov was one of those men with whom it was practically impossible to collaborate in any collegial capacity.

"Georges," as Plekhanov was known a quarter of a century earlier among the revolutionaries of the Land and Freedom, was then a favorite of his colleagues. He stood out by his daring, energy, and wit. It was a major blow to the People's Will that he did not choose to join their ranks, but followed his own path, which in the 1880s was to bring him to Marxism. We have seen how in the course of his struggle he had to overcome the doubts of Marx and Engels themselves, the taunts of the Populists, and for years, virtual isolation from the majority of the Russian exiles in the West. But there was in addition a long period of poverty and privation, and the illness, tuberculosis, which was to be with him till the end of his days. He became a prolific author, today still held in high esteem among the connoisseurs of Marxian literature. To be sure, much of his writing, especially his polemics against the Populists, is incisive and brilliant. But like any writer who has to struggle against the current, Plekhanov at times tends to become doctrinaire and repetitive, and, at his worst, a frightful bore who fills his pages with interminable citations and references, especially to *the* authority. At times a casual glimpse at a page of Plekhanov's will not be sufficient to tell whether it is written in Russian or in German. With his increasingly assumed role as the high priest of Marxian orthodoxy, he became intolerant of the slightest deviation from the doctrine and more impatient with the younger men who did not "understand" or "vulgarized" Marx. This intellectual intolerance was matched by a certain personal aloofness which conveyed, often unjustly, a feeling of arrogance and superiority. Essentially a kind-hearted and noble-minded man, Plekhanov could not refrain from pointing out at times that his young protagonist was not yet born when *he* walked in the shadow of the gallows. Or when his opponent was both orthodox and respectful, Plekhanov would find something wrong with his literary style! He was very conscious of being the heir of Herzen and Dobrolyubov as the representative of revolution in the republic of letters. His first reservations about Lenin come from his objections to Lenin's admittedly pedestrian style.

[2] It is almost impossible to avoid the terms of most of the revolutionaries who, being very young themselves, ignored the distinction between middle and old age. Plekhanov actually was forty-four. Mme Kalmykova, referred to above as an old woman, was then fifty-one.

To worship such a man from afar was one thing, to work with him another. Lenin tells us himself that he had been "in love" with Plekhanov, but that had been during his Siberian exile. Now they were sitting and quarreling in Geneva and he was discovering what many a Russian Marxist had already discovered: it was impossible to work with Georgi Valentinovich on any basis of equality. What made it worse was that Plekhanov's dictatorial temperament, unlike Lenin's, was not accompanied by a sense of practicality or an organizational ability. A popular saying about the Russian intelligentsia was that "they knew about everything but could do nothing," and Georgi Valentinovich appeared to be a prime example.

That the clash was patched up and somehow the two men managed to work together for the next few years was largely due to the intercessions of others. Plekhanov had two collaborators, or rather satellites, like himself veterans of the Populist struggles of the 1870s—Axelrod, whom we have already met, and Vera Zasulich, who, as a young woman, electrified all Russia when in 1878 she shot a Tsarist official who had ordered the flogging of a political prisoner. She was acquitted by a jury and escaped abroad before the police could correct this unexpected misdeed of the judiciary. The young terrorist had grown into a Socialist old maid; kindly and sentimental, she assuaged the terrible temper of "Georges," to whom she was slavishly attached. It was through her efforts and through the pleadings with Lenin of another veteran, Lev Deutsch, that *The Spark* was not extinguished. The agreement about the direction of *Iskra* embodied several compromises. As planned earlier, the editorial board was to consist of six persons: three "oldsters"—Plekhanov, Axelrod, and Zasulich—and the three recent *émigrés* from Russia—Lenin and his friends Martov and Potresov. In theory Plekhanov was to be "more equal" than the other editors, for he was given an additional deciding vote if the board split three to three. In fact Lenin became the managing editor, for the paper was to be published in Germany by him and his friends. Thus, in addition to other difficulties *Iskra* was to be published by a board split among three countries, for Plekhanov continued to live in Geneva, Axelrod in Zurich, and Vera Ivanovna was to return to London. Though this arrangement was most inconvenient—editorial matters had to be settled by mail—the agreement promised to spare the editors' nervous systems.

A vain hope! On May 14 we find Lenin writing to his irascible master: "A fine idea you have about tact when it comes to dealing with your colleagues on the editorial board. . . . As concerns [our] personal relations . . . they are thoroughly ruined by your action, or to be more precise, you have brought them to an end." [3] Yet despite this and other

[3] *Works*, Vol. 34, p. 82.

explosions the collaboration between these two men was to endure for three years. Lenin knew how to be diplomatic when he needed to, and at times he shamelessly appealed to the vanity of the older man by assuming the tone of a humble and reverential pupil. Plekhanov for all his growing distaste for Lenin saw in him something he himself lacked: unflagging energy and organizational ability. Without Lenin he would revert to the role of a Socialist *philosopher* with a small retinue of elderly and semiretired revolutionaries. With this unpleasant young man doing the bulk of administrative work, he, Plekhanov, was the *leader* of a revolutionary party, and every Marxist was conscious that theoretical and literary leadership was of infinitely greater importance than the ability to tend to the petty organizational details.

But apart from such calculations and miscalculations, the two men were united by a real bond: their conviction of the imperative necessity of preserving Marxian orthodoxy and their devotion to the revolutionary cause. For all their growing animosity and a brilliant perception of each other's personal defects, Plekhanov would for long feel drawn to Lenin because of his revolutionary energy, and the latter in turn never stopped admiring the older man's intellectual intolerance and his refusal to yield an inch in an ideological struggle. Lenin's abusive pen was not to spare his closest friends and collaborators, not to speak of his enemies. Martov, for whom we are told he felt a special affection, still became at times "scoundrel" and "rascal." His future great companion in the Revolution could not for a long time be mentioned by Lenin without such characterizations as "Trotsky, the empty chatterbox" or "hypocrite." It is only when it comes to Plekhanov that Lenin observes a shade of restraint in the midst of a most violent polemic. In his case this means a great deal.

The two men were united in their detestation of anything that smacked of Revisionism or Economism. Neither of these varieties of heresy was to be admitted into the orthodox Marxist paradise of *Iskra*. But this again even before the first issue had appeared posed a painful organizational problem. What to do with Struve? He was by now unmistakably tainted with Revisionism. At first Plekhanov would not hear of collaborating with the renegade. But as we have seen, Lenin who already in 1899 had decided that Struve was "ceasing to be a comrade," had some very practical reasons for wanting to string him along. Struve had the golden touch. Under his influence society ladies and liberal noblemen would give generously to the revolutionary cause. The first short-lived arrangement was perhaps the first attempt at "peaceful coexistence." Struve and his ideological companions would contribute to *Iskra*, but its editors reserved the right to denounce Revisionism and to warn the readers against the influence of Struve and his ilk. Not surprisingly this arrangement soon collapsed. *Iskra* developed alternative sources of support. By January 1901 Lenin began to refer to his erstwhile

colleague and financial and intellectual sponsor as Judas Struve. He in
turn ended his long flirtation with socialism to become a pillar of Russian
liberalism. As such, he became much less hateful, at least politically, to
the revolutionary leaders. If a man declares himself openly your class
enemy you know where he stands. You may want, if an occasion arises,
to arrange with him a temporary alliance against another enemy. But
to have a man like that right in your camp, putting forth his poisonous
doctrines as a variety of Marxism, confusing and destroying class vigilance of simple, unsophisticated party members— Never!

In his recollections of the period Struve still labored from a sense of
guilt and indignation that he, like so many liberal and democratic Russians, was made an accomplice in building and preserving the movement that was to deal a death blow to their ideals and expectations.
More than thirty years had not stilled his wounded pride at being used
and then discarded by Plekhanov and Lenin. Not only did they fail to
"show the consideration which I could claim as a political and intellectual personality," but they showed their contempt for a whole class,
for as Struve claims, he was "a genuine representative of a social milieu
which could be neither ignored nor rebuffed." [4] But how pathetic these
words of an *émigré* sound against the background of Stalin's Russia!

And thus after the quarrels and difficulties of which the preceding
was but a part, there began what is known in the Soviet histories as the
Iskra period. The paper did live up to its proud slogan: it started a conflagration to which, as we write more than sixty years later, there still
seems to be no end.

To be sure this great historical achievement is hardly understandable
if we look at the issues of the paper. Amongst its editors there was one,
Plekhanov, who was a gifted and eloquent essayist. Both Lenin and
Martov had a flair for political and polemical journalism. But the paper's
main function was presumably to make converts among the rank-and-
file workers in Russia and for that its tone and content were quite un-
suitable. Its collaborators could not, even if they wanted to, speak the
worker's language and enter into his everyday problems and worries.
The whole concept of agitation required close physical contact with the
proletariat, and that could not be achieved by an organ published in
Munich or Geneva. The readers of *Iskra* were fed a steady fare of attacks
against Economism, appraisals of liberalism and of the chances of wresting
a constitution from the Tsar, and so on. Characteristically, visitors from
Russia pleaded insistently that the editors publish another paper, which
would be more accessible to the working masses. More than once Lenin
had to justify the whole idea of publishing a revolutionary organ abroad.
To publish in Russia, he wrote with his usual common sense, would
endanger a lot of people, and would require great sums of money, which
now we have put to a better use by smuggling *Iskra* into the country.

---

[4] *The Slavonic Review*, Vol. XIII, 1933–34, p. 81.

He was, of course, right, though smuggling and spreading the paper within Russia did endanger a lot of people, but those were common soldiers of the revolution and not its generals. The historic role of *Iskra* lay exactly in the fact that it gave a sense of mission and unity to the isolated groups of intellectuals and advanced workers who constituted Russian Social Democracy of the period. The "Iskrists," as they became known, were hardened in the way of conspiracy. It was a source of comfort to know that though this or that agent of the paper might be arrested the leaders of the movement were safe, that the work of the party, unlike that of the People's Will, could not be completely liquidated by the police. It was, to use a modern parallel, a form of political guerrilla activity against the Tsarist regime, and like all such successful activity it drew its strength from its leadership and sources of supply being beyond the reach of the enemy. Nothing destroys the morale of a revolutionary group like the sense of isolation, the witnessing of a progressive attrition of the revolutionary strength, and the feeling that there is nobody to carry on the work of the fallen. Thirty or forty years later people would be amazed at how the Communists in some distant country would carry on their hopeless struggle, reassured rather than repelled by the knowledge that their leaders enjoyed security and comfort in the Soviet Union. It is during the *Iskra* period that this paradoxical element of the revolutionary's psychology became evident.

From Irkutsk to Odessa the Marxist groups could feel themselves part of a unified movement led by the most prestigious heroes of the revolutionary movement. The Socialist in Russia could not know of the constant dissension and the growing conflict on the board of *Iskra*. All he knew was that it was a harmonious group perfectly balanced between such revered veterans as Plekhanov and Zasulich and the rising leaders fresh from the struggles and exiles within Russia. The influence of Economism, once in ascendancy among Socialist circles and groups, visibly waned in 1901 and 1902. *Iskra* could not expect to sway the mass of workers, and as for the peasant, he remained totally immune to the doctrine of Marx. But to an elite of revolutionary-minded intelligentsia and workers it spoke with a growing authority and conviction. And to Lenin it was already the professional revolutionary rather then the "masses" who held the key to the victory of socialism.

Those grandiose plans and conceptions were being formulated against the background of incessant work and petty annoyances of *émigré* existence. Lenin and his collaborators were living in Munich under false names and passports, partly as a precaution against the Tsarist authorities learning their identities and protesting to the Imperial German and Bavarian governments.[5] But another and perhaps more important reason

---

[5] Needless to say, this masquerade was in vain. The Tsarist police through their foreign agents were soon informed as to the identity of editors of *Iskra*, where it was being published, and so on.

for this deception was the hope, also vain, of escaping another professional hazard of the revolutionary's existence: the famous Russian sociability.

Most Russians abroad felt that any compatriot was a fair prey for a lengthy discussion. Munich, it had been thought, was relatively free from Russians, but like every major European cultural center of the time, it did have a Russian student colony. It was laughable to think that Lenin could maintain the identity of a "Herr Meyer," or that Martov or Potresov, whatever names they chose, could be taken for anything but what they were: members of the intelligentsia and revolutionaries. They all soon became objects of interest and of importunities for the local Russian colony.

Vladimir Ilyich felt that *Iskra,* at this crucial point where the whole enterprise was being set on its feet, required his constant attention and work. As usual, he had but little time and less inclination for the social amenities so beloved by his compatriots. A collaborator from this early period remembers Lenin working from nine in the morning until late at night. At times he could be dragged to a neighboring café for a glass of beer, but this brief relaxation was likely to have a most un-Russian ending: after a half hour he would begin to squirm and was liable to pull out his watch and announce "Two more minutes, finish your glass." Very rarely would he heed pleadings to go to the café patronized by the local Russians. One might, one was sure, in fact, to arrive in the middle of an argument among the *émigrés.* It was inconceivable even to Lenin that one could leave with the argument (whether it was about politics, literature, or anything else) unsettled. This in turn meant staying until the closing hours, and even then one was not safe. For how could one avoid inviting one of the disputants or being invited by them to an apartment where the discussion would rage on? They were liable to be young people of inexhaustible energy and lust for debate, with their voices toughened from singing rousing revolutionary songs, and the neighbors would curse those quarrelsome and loud foreigners. This was the Russia that Boris Pasternak had in mind when he wrote in *Doctor Zhivago:* "They talked in the way only Russians can talk." This infinite running off at the mouth of the Russian *intelligent* was deeply distasteful to Lenin, but most important, he usually had some work to do, and what free time there was could be spent more profitably in reading or physical exercise. But Martov, who was unmarried and felt lonely, soon succumbed to the lure of café life.

Lenin's self-sufficiency was buttressed by the constant presence of his family. Sister Anna visited him in Munich and very soon he was rejoined by his wife. Again it is noteworthy that Krupskaya, upon the expiration of her administrative exile, encountered no difficulty in procuring a passport and leaving Russia. She was, the authorities knew, going to join her husband who had overstayed his permitted stay abroad and was pursuing the career of the revolutionary. With her arrival in April 1901 Vladimir Ilyich's existence became less harried. They moved to a modest house in the suburbs where Nadezhda Konstantinovna could cook and run a regular household, thus freeing Lenin from dependence upon the hated cafés and restaurants. It also put some distance between him and his collaborators and made it less likely that Martov would drop in daily for his five- or six-hour talk. Lenin still loved him dearly, but he was frantic for time as he was then working on what was to become the bible of Bolshevism: *What Is To Be Done?*. But distance and Nadya's hints would not have sufficed to keep Martov away, except for a fortunate coincidence. Another revolutionary friend, Dan, arrived and settled *en famille* in Munich. For an inveterate bachelor Dan's household had a vast advantage over the Ulyanovs': they had children, and Martov, of course, practically moved in with them.

But Krupskaya's function was not only to guard Lenin's privacy. She became a secretary to *Iskra* and assumed increasingly the burden of expediting the paper to Russia and of communicating with *Iskra*'s agents within the country. For Lenin the contact with the homeland was of supreme importance; after all the paper's main function was to build the skeleton of a party organization, and he was eager to win and retain the loyalty of the men who were carrying on this dangerous work. There was always the danger when abroad of losing touch with men and conditions in Russia, and of becoming just like some of his colleagues on the editorial board, just a name to those in active revolutionary struggle. Hence his readiness to attend to the tedious and time-consuming work of administration.

There was the constant trouble and worry of getting *Iskra* into the Empire. Trusted persons returning legally were provided with double-bottomed trunks like those in which Lenin himself had carried forbidden literature on his return from the West in 1895. Or there was an outright smuggling through the frontier posts in Austrian Galicia or Prussia. At times, through connections in the international labor movement, a ship docking in Odessa or other Black Sea ports would also carry a consignment of the revolutionary journal. There could never be a certainty that the given shipment had in fact been delivered or, if delivered, that it was being distributed.

By the end of 1901 there had appeared thirteen issues, but their circulation within Russia was beset by enormous difficulties. The small network of *Iskra*'s agents had the combined functions of receiving the shipments, distributing them, acting as correspondents, and sometimes even collecting funds. This, of course, tended to multiply the usual hazards of revolutionary and conspiratorial existence. The archives of the Tsarist police make it clear that they were very well informed as to the identity of many agents and the main distributing points of the contraband. Frequent arrests disrupted the network. Copies of Lenin's and Krupskaya's letters would find their way to the police, and they were not usually thrown off the scent by the rather amateurish code or the "invisible" ink. Once delivered, *Iskra* was to be distributed in the factories, or its copies were to rain down from the gallery during a play. Many agents shied away from such dangerous activities, and in fact some shipments even if delivered would remain undistributed. Lenin's letters reflect this nagging uncertainty, whether this product of so much effort and labor was making any impact at all. Some correspondents were scolded for their "passivity." Are you just distributing *Iskra* or organizing the workers as well, he writes to one. Another trusted agent turned out to be a scoundrel. He collected money for *Iskra,* but then used it to print his own illegal journal with an Economist inclination. He had to be told to hand over the money.[6] There were hundreds of details to be attended to. Should *Iskra* people be allowed to collaborate with the Economists against the common enemy? Could the paper be reproduced within Russia? Why was there not more news sent out about the recent series of peasant disorders?

The strain and the constant harassment of the *Iskra* period (1901–3) and most of all the underlying uncertainty whether all this effort was producing results was to have telling effects on Lenin's psychology. The biographies of Lenin and the recollections of his contemporaries tend to blunt the impression, which nevertheless emerges from some episodes, that this was the period of great inner turmoil and transformation. As a revolutionary in Russia he lived under conditions where the uniting bond of danger and a clear sense of mission and direction obscured the personal defects of his co-workers, and acted as a brake on his own intolerance and imperiousness. Now as the leader he was made all too conscious of his closest friends' shortcomings, or of their incomprehensible blindness in not seeing problems the way he did. Plekhanov, the idol of his youth, now appeared at times as a pompous and thin-skinned *intelligent.* Renowned revolutionary heroes once abroad turned into chatterboxes. Even in Russia comrades unless nagged constantly were settling into professional and family lives. Persons such as Krzhizhanovsky and Lepeshinsky, closest to him in the Siberian exile, were now apathetic in pushing the affairs of *Iskra.* With his own energy and temperament Lenin could not admit or tolerate the fact that revolutionary enthusiasm and readiness for self-sacrifice were largely a function of youth and that his friends were growing into middle age. There was also only so much that some of them could endure in the way of exiles, arrests, and conspiratorial existence.

Apart from his intolerance of human weakness, he was growing in-

[6] Lenin, *Works,* Vol. 34, p. 71.

tolerant of intellectual disagreement. Years before he had adopted Marxism because it promised the clear, rational path to revolution. Yet it was now obvious that you could not construct a Marxian party without the whole structure next day threatening to fall like a house of cards. United, the Russian Marxists had braved and exposed the fallacies of Populism. But very soon after gaining intellectual ascendance within the revolutionary camp the Socialists themselves split into warring factions. Hardly had *Iskra* confronted the heresies of Economism than within its body there began to develop a split. Was there to be no end of this fragmentation and division of revolutionary socialism? And what was the use of Marxism as a philosophy if everybody was free to interpret it according to his own lights? The Russian Marxists instead of being a united army marching to overthrow first autocracy and then capitalism, seemed like a formless horde of intelligentsia arguing over each step, some hanging back, others impatient to run too fast.

Attempts to reassemble the pieces and to put together the Russian Social Democratic Party had been having but scant success (any unity or organization created by the Minsk Congress of 1898 had, of course, proved ephemeral). In 1902 most of the Russian Socialists abroad were still Economists and even within the country their influence was far from extinguished. In 1902 delegates from various places were to assemble in Bialystok in Russian Poland, where it was to be hoped the second, but really the founding, congress of the party was to take place. Had the congress in fact materialized, the party would have found itself in the hands of anti-*Iskra* people, for the majority in Bialystok was composed of Economists and other opponents of the Plekhanov-Lenin line. But the intrigues of the *Iskra* delegate, plus the fact that the authorities had obligingly arrested many of the delegates, led those present at the meeting to declare themselves but a "conference" without the competence of a full congress, and to elect but an organizing committee. At any rate most of the latter were soon also arrested. It was clear that it was impossible to hold a founding congress within Russia.

Even before the Bialystok congress Lenin's ideas on the future party organization began to diverge from those of his colleagues on the editorial board of *Iskra*. In their discussions Lenin often remained silent. In her recollections V. Kozhevnikova mentions such a meeting, which took place in her apartment in Munich. Vladimir Ilyich acted bored and he welcomed the diversion provided by the appearance of her two small children. But the other assembled potentates exploded. Was she out of her mind to allow children to interrupt such weighty discussions? The poor woman fled in tears to the kitchen, probably to assuage the wrath of the leaders with tea and *zakuski*, the Russian hors d'oeuvres. Lenin soon followed her to moderate her grief and to assure her that nothing would come out of this idle chatter anyway. He was already in the habit of conferring with the emissaries to Russia on his own and behind the backs of his colleagues.[7]

Whether the German Socialists were tired of their Russian colleagues or whether they were really, as they told them, afraid of complications with their government, they managed in any case to persuade the editors of *Iskra* to shift their operations out of Germany. To keep away from the baleful presence of Plekhanov, Lenin insisted on moving to England, and in the spring of 1902 he and Krupskaya arrived in London.

The disconcerting elements of life in this Babylon of world capitalism soon made themselves obvious. For one thing, though they translated (with the help of a dictionary) English economic works, Lenin and Krupskaya were completely at sea when it came to spoken English. For another, they had to struggle with the philistinism of the English bourgeois habits. Their landlady was suspicious: they claimed to be married but they did not wear wedding rings and why would they not put curtains on their windows? But not only the middle classes were disgustingly philistine. Krupskaya, who was a revolutionary snob, was appalled to hear an English Socialist declare that he would be in despair if his wife were put in prison. She was also irritated—and one sympathizes with her—by the incongruous element of evangelism that character-ized the English Socialists of the period and with their psalm-singing propensity.

Russian revolutionaries abroad often lived in "communes," i.e., joint households, but Lenin again insisted on the privacy of a separate apart-ment. This was infinitely more important in London than in Munich. A Russian Socialist was likely to have some knowledge of German but none of English. London was bound to bring out their most intense loneliness and frantic search for a fellow Russian soul. Persons who with-stood the brutal Siberian winter would be laid low by the peculiar com-bination of the British climate and the heating arrangements. One such martyr recalls his surprise at the discovery that on a winter day it was often warmer on the outside than within a "heated" English flat. The doughty revolutionary accustomed to finding his way in a strange town would be lost within the maze of this huge city with its politely in-different and incomprehensible natives. In Munich or Paris one had, at least, cafés which somehow protected one's home from a direct as-sault, but in London it was assumed that every Russian who had more than one bed ran a hotel where his countrymen might stop for a night or a month.

Lenin begged the local *Iskra* agent to keep the visitors, except those with the most urgent business, away from his apartment, but how could one do this? One comrade proved such a continuous nuisance that

[7] V. Kozhevnikova, "The Years of the Old *Iskra*," in *The Proletarian Revolution*, Moscow, 1925, No. 2 (25).

Vladimir Ilyich would explode, "Does he think that we are having receptions every day?" It is only some time later that Lenin perfected a technique of defense that did not make his wife very popular. Confronted by an intruder, Nadezhda Konstantinovna would station herself in front of the door with a "they shall not pass" expression and would intone "Vladimir Ilyich is not at home," or "V.I. is working." But even that technique did not stop the most determined.

Still a private apartment provided a minimum of protection and not least for the digestive system. (When it comes to the English cuisine Krupskaya ceases to be a revolutionary and party worker and utters the anguished cry of the Russian housewife.) Martov, Vera Zasulich, and another comrade decided to live in a "commune," which consisted of five rooms in a lower-class district and was equipped with a gas stove. Imagination staggers at the thought of what this household must have been like. Even among the most bohemian revolutionaries Vera Zasulich was famous for her untidiness. Her reputation in this respect, however, paled beside that of Martov's. His guests very often refrained from partaking of that staple of Russian hospitality, tea, because sugar was as likely as not mixed with pipe tobacco. Even amidst the "lower depths" of London the commune with its constant traffic of loud foreigners was more than the neighbors could endure. As a result of their importunities the landlord finally gave notice and the commune was dispersed.

Apart from the losing struggle with visitors, Lenin was not displeased with London. It had two things that he valued most in a city: splendid libraries and parks. If anything could reconcile him to this bastion of plutocracy it was the British Museum. Here one could work as in one's own study, and he never ceased to be astounded that the administration of the great library considered themselves to be servants of the readers. Lenin delighted in exhibiting "one-upmanship" over his fellow émigrés when it came to practical matters. Even before his arrival he had studied the plan of London and now he evoked the admiration of even the long-time residents by his skill in navigating through the confusing maze of streets, courts, and squares. Unlike Zasulich, who for all her years in England did not know a word of the language, he set out to learn conversational English. His advertisement proposing an exchange of lessons in English and Russian contained an element of misrepresentation untypical for Lenin though very minor. He advertised himself as a "doctor of laws," whereas in fact his Russian degree of "candidate" was equivalent to that of master.

Beyond the three persons with whom he exchanged language lessons, Vladimir Ilyich does not appear to have become acquainted with any Englishmen during his year's stay in London. The local Socialists belonged to various reformist or evolutionary tendencies of radicalism for which he had no patience. One is, however, again astounded by this

intense parochialism of a mind otherwise so energetic and full of curiosity. There is no record of a visit to Parliament, no testimony of any
striking aspect of British affairs or society. As always abroad he lived
within the self-imposed intellectual ghetto of Russian *émigré* politics.
Such observations on English life as one finds in his letters or in Krupskaya's accounts are confined to the Socialist platitudes about the gap
separating the rich and the poor, the contrast between the luxurious
town houses and the proletarian quarters in London, and the like. There
is on the other hand a declaration of a heartfelt longing for a boat
trip on the Volga now that spring is here and reminiscence of a concert he
attended with praise of Tchaikovsky's Sixth Symphony. England to be
sure was the seat of the enemy, the bulwark of the world capitalist
system. It was the country where Karl Marx had lived completely ignored by the natives during the latter half of his life, and whose working
class had belied his predictions by turning away from revolution to
tame reformism and trade unionism. But beyond that Vladimir Ilyich's
almost complete insulation from foreign life and customs is a testimony
to something else. He was, and he would have been shocked to realize
this, a passionate Russian nationalist.

The London year was filled with hectic political work. Events in
Russia were moving at an unexpectedly rapid pace, and the *Iskra* organization had to be spruced up if it were to hold its own within the
revolutionary movement. For one, Populism, which a few years before
seemed to be expiring as a political movement, now experienced a rebirth. In 1901 the party of the Socialist Revolutionaries was formed.
Claiming the heritage of the People's Will, the new party offered a confused amalgam of Populist and Marxist principles but it was oriented
toward the peasant rather than the worker. Its link with the past was
most pronounced by the renewal of one of its segments, the Fighting
Organization, of political terror. The lesson of the 1880s, that terror de-
moralizes and then destroys the revolutionary body that resorts to it,
was temporarily forgotten. To the new and impatient generation of radicals the Socialist Revolutionaries were at least *doing* something: they
were terrorizing the government and assassinating its most reactionary
members. In contrast, their Socialist opponents appeared to be ceaselessly
arguing among themselves, and their activities consisted in distributing
theoretical tracts.

At the very same time the progressive elements among the professional classes and the gentry were coalescing into what eventually was
to become the Constitutional Democratic Party, the body of liberals
bent upon wresting a constitution from the Tsar and ending the shame
of Russia being the only European country (except for Turkey) under
an autocratic government. Thus the Social Democrats were being threatened both from left and right. The revolutionary component in their

ideology tended to alienate those who thought Russia's destiny was following that of Western Europe with its parliamentarism and constitutions. The young worker or *intelligent,* on the other hand, who wanted action would grow impatient of *Iskra's* strictures against terror and its "Socialist revolution, but not yet" teaching. To an outside observer the Social Democrats had an excellent chance of falling between two stools; they were destined to remain a small sect composed of the more pedantic among the revolutionaries and of the more audacious of the moderates.

To the older members of the *Iskra* board this state of affairs did not appear alarming or require any basic transformation of the Party. They had been waiting for a long time, since 1883 as a matter of fact, when Plekhanov created the Emancipation of Labor group, and they were, to be sure unconsciously, prepared to wait longer, confident that they had the infallible key to Russia's future: Marxism. Compared with the possession of this precious doctrine, of what value was the growing popularity of the Socialist Revolutionaries among the students and young radicals, or the increasing enlistment of the "respectable" elements of society in what was to become the Constitutional Democratic camp? History in due course was going to vindicate the Russian Marxists after the phantoms of both liberalism and terrorism had disappeared. Such complacency was entirely alien to Lenin's nature. Temperamentally he was closer to Zhelyabov, who wanted to give history a push, than to a theoretical type of Marxist waiting patiently for one of the numerous inevitabilities that the doctrine promises to the faithful.

The Lenin of 1902 was still not the man he was to be in 1917. He was not ready to burn his bridges behind him without a careful assessment of the terrain. The situation called for careful probing, investigation and the recruitment of new forces. It was a cautious Party strategist who in June 1901 wanted to mollify those impatient for direct action. There was always a chance, he wrote, that the Tsarist regime would collapse suddenly under unforeseen circumstances, but it was foolish to count on such an occurrence soon. In principle the Russian Socialists did not unconditionally condemn terror, but at that moment terror was inappropriate and demoralized the Party using it rather than the government.[8] Temperamentally averse to anything that smacked of liberalism, venomous toward the liberal as a species, Lenin still realized that the Socialists might have to endure a lengthy peaceful coexistence with the liberals in their common struggle to overthrow autocracy. When Professor Miliukov, the leader of the liberals, passed through London Lenin conferred with him. The good professor was not free from the vice of the intelligentsia: an indulgent view of violence if it was directed against autocracy. *Iskra,* he thought, overdid its campaign against terror.

[8] *Works,* Vol. 5, pp. 7–8.

One or two more political assassinations and the government would be forced to grant a constitution.[9]

In 1902 yet another encounter with liberal Russian professors took place. Some of them organized in Paris the school of Higher Social Studies. One of the lecturers invited was "the well known Marxist author V. Ilin," author of *The Development of Capitalism in Russia*. He duly made his appearance; then it was discovered that Ilin and the already notorious revolutionary Lenin were one and the same person.[10] The professors were perplexed: they had their jobs back in Russia to think of. It was one thing to invite a theoretical Marxist whose work had been legally published in Russia and another to invite the editor of *Iskra*. Lenin, who probably enjoyed their panic, went on to deliver four scholarly lectures. The professors were not made to suffer any consequences. There would have been very few people left to teach in Russian universities had the government punished every professor who was ever involved in similar incidents.

But the main burden of work was on keeping up contact with the *Iskra* organization within Russia. Every fresh arrival bearing news from home was eagerly seized upon by Lenin, and the usual defenses against persistent visitors were for a time discarded. Thus, much fuss was made over Ivan Babushkin. He was a genuine worker, still a rarity among the political *émigrés*, and a veteran of the St. Petersburg Union of Struggle for the Emancipation of the Working Class. Babushkin was eager to return to the revolutionary struggle at home, but Lenin persuaded him to sketch his recollections as a proletarian revolutionary. It was of supreme importance to display to everybody the fact that self-taught workers were enjoying an important role within the *Iskra* organization, and that Marxism was accessible and appealing to the "real" proletarian. Babushkin performed another major work; he cleaned up the Martov-Zasulich commune. His explanatory statement, which obviously enraptured Lenin, is preserved for history by Krupskaya: "The Russian intellectual is always dirty. He needs a servant, as he is himself incapable of tidying up."

But an even more momentous encounter was to take place during the London period. A violent knocking aroused the Ulyanovs early one October morning. Krupskaya ran down to open the door before the landlord could create a scene and in burst Lev Bronstein—Trotsky. He was already renowned among the Social Democrats in Russia and had just escaped from Siberia. Soon Lenin, still in bed, and the man whose name, like his own, is indelibly linked with the Revolution, were in an agitated conversation. They were agreed on the inadmissability of vari-

[9] N. A. Alexeyev, "V. I. Lenin in London," in *The Proletarian Revolution*, No. 3, 1925, p. 152.

[10] Prior to 1901–2 Lenin had used a variety of pseudonyms: Ilin, Tulin, and others, but now he invariably used the name that was to pass into history.

ous Socialist groups in Russia having their own clandestine newspapers rather than supporting and distributing *Iskra.*

Trotsky was then twenty-three and already the dashing and somewhat theatrical revolutionary figure. At that time Lenin, sorely tried by his coeditors, could see only his energy and brilliance. It was important to gain the brilliant youth for his plans and enterprises. Quite apart from any element of deliberation in his wooing of Trotsky, Lenin was always, in a somewhat adolescent fashion, ready to have a "crush" on a new collaborator, just as almost invariably a prolonged acquaintance would lead him to discern elements of weakness and corruption in a person. As his widow notes ruefully: "Vladimir Ilyich was always having these periods of enthusiasm for people." But seldom for very long.

Trotsky became a valuable contributor to *Iskra.* In March 1903 Lenin proposed to coopt him to the editorial board. But Plekhanov would not agree. Trotsky was brash, and in his case it was literally true that he had not even been born when he, Plekhanov, was already . . . And Trotsky's flowery and indeed at times florid style did not meet the standard of restrained elegance in which the heir of Herzen believed the organ of revolution should speak to the Russian people. Vera Zasulich seconded Lenin's effort on behalf of Trotsky but she could not sway Plekhanov. It was enough for "Georges" to fold his arms and give her a withering look, and the woman who had shot a general and then had surrendered calmly to the police would quiver and become flustered. Trotsky was not promoted and Lenin had another reason to be dissatisfied with the conditions that prevailed on the editorial board.

A year's stay in London was all that some of the revolutionaries could stand. Martov fled to Paris. Potresov became seriously ill. Apart from the incompatibility of England with the Russian way of life, the majority on the editorial board felt the natural urge to move to a larger center of Russian political migration. There was a sizable colony of Russian Jews in Whitechapel, but they would be absorbed into the business life of the vast metropolis and become lost to politics. Paris, Geneva, or Zurich with their little Russias of *émigrés* and students exerted, in contrast, a fatal attraction on those people starved for companionship and Russian talk. In the spring of 1903, with only Lenin dissenting, it was decided to transfer *Iskra* to Geneva.

The Ulyanovs had become acclimatized in London. Its vast distances offered some measure of protection against the importunate visitors. The city had the best library in Europe, and the English countryside was for Lenin an adequate compensation for its grayness and foreignness. Geneva, within an area not greater than one of London's boroughs, contained a high concentration of the Russian *émigrés* and promised constant interruption in one's work. Also, he would have to live in close proximity to Plekhanov. Krupskaya reports that overwork and the necessity of moving led Vladimir Ilyich to develop a nervous ailment, which from her description sounds like shingles. On his arrival in Switzerland in April 1903 Lenin broke down completely and had to spend two weeks in bed. But this breakdown was succeeded by a new surge of energy and determination. He was ready to make his bid for a drastic reorganization of the party, and from one of the leaders of the Russian Socialists he was to become *the* leader of Bolshevism.

2. *What Is To Be Done?*

The celebrated pamphlet which bears this name was published in March 1902. Considered by Lenin the crowning work of his theoretical and organizational activity, it was distributed among the *Iskra* agents in Russia. Five months later we find him writing anxiously to his Moscow contacts "Do you have enough copies of *What Is To Be Done?* Have the workers read it and what is their opinion?" He was eager for the people in the country to express their agreement with his ideas. Let them put it in the form of an official letter and then *Iskra* would publish it.[11] This anxiety was understandable. Lenin staked everything on the interpretation of Marxism and revolutionary activity contained in the pamphlet. It was to guide him through the intra-Party struggle that began in 1903 and lasted through the Revolution of 1917. His increasing nervousness and strain throughout 1902-3 are easily understandable. He was either going to remake the Socialist Party in the image of *What Is To Be Done?*, and for that he was ready to break up friendships and ties of long standing, or he was going to remain an isolated figure, another in the gallery of pathetic failures of the revolutionary movement. Were he to succeed, on the other hand, in creating a Socialist Party in his image, it would remain immune to periods of crises and reaction, it would always carry the seed of revolution within it, and one day usher in the era of socialism.

The title (in Russian it sounds much crisper: *Chto Delat'*) is, of course, taken from Chernyshevsky's famous novel. How seemingly paradoxical to call this dry theoretical and organizational tract after the effusive, sentimental, and fantasy-filled work of fiction! But for Lenin this paradox does not exist. Through Chernyshevsky's pages there move men of action and devotion to the cause. How different is Rakhmetov from typical Socialist windbags by whom Lenin was now surrounded! How "scientific" and businesslike are the heroes of the book in their revolutionary activity: they see that at a certain point all idle talk is to be curtailed, personal vanities and sentiments are to be discarded, and action is to begin. And not for a moment are they downcast because there are so few of them. They know that inevitably the time will come when the masses will turn to them for guidance for what must be done. To a generation that has not yet forgot-

[11] Lenin, *Works*, Vol. 6, p. 186.

ten Chernyshevsky, though his star had paled in Russia in the last ten years, Lenin argues that the scientific doctrine of Marxism must be supplemented by a revolutionary faith and that the Social Democratic Party must also become like a military order. At one time his firsthand acquaintance with Populism led to a disenchantment. As against its terroristic heroics and belief that individual action can affect the course of history, Lenin sought the orderly world of Marx with its historical laws, with the masses responding rationally and automatically to changed economic and political conditions. Now he was again disenchanted, not with Marxism, to be sure, but with its adherents, whom he had seen at close quarters. And it is characteristic of the man that he seeks to infuse the Marxists with the revolutionary fire and conspiratorial discipline that had belonged to the heroes of Populism.

On its face, *What Is To Be Done?* is a long polemic against Economists. What, the reader may ask in his understandable impatience, were the heinous crimes of that much-maligned group of Russian Socialists? We have heard already that they believed in the economic struggle of the worker. But so did Lenin, for whom strikes and other manifestations of class war between the employer and the worker were a necessary part of Socialist activity. Were the Economists (and such is the hypnotic effect of repetition by the Soviet writers that the Western historians have come to half-believe it themselves) lukewarm in their opposition to autocracy and neglectful of the struggle for civil and political rights of the people? Nothing of the kind. They were uncompromising in their struggle against the Tsar and the bureaucracy. They worked under conditions of illegality and were exposed, as much as the *Iskra* people, to arrests, exiles, and the like. They did believe that much of the fight for a constitution and parliament for Russia had to be carried on by the middle classes and the liberals. But so did Lenin. Was there then a disagreement over the Economists' insistence that the intelligentsia should not interfere too much in the workers' organizations? To be sure. But even here the quarrel was more over appearances than substance. Lenin was frantic to have workers at all levels of his organization. For all their supposed anti-intelligentsia attitude and mannerisms, his opponents could not get away from the fact that *any* political organization, formulation of programs, editing of journals, or similar work must be guided by educated persons who had some leisure, that is —pardon the word—intelligentsia. What then?

"We differ only on organizational matters," said Lenin to a visiting Economist, "but they are all-important." But if so, *What Is To Be Done?* does not support this analysis. The Economists are "opportunists." They have deviated from Marxism and fallen into the hideous heresy of Revisionism. Why, their main tracts are allowed in Russia and some of them are even passed by the police chiefs! Certainly a disagreement over "organizational matters" would not justify this violence of expression.

Let it be said right away that the argument touches on democracy. Few Russian revolutionaries from Herzen on can be classified as democrats in the literal sense of the word. Practically all of them would have been shocked at the suggestion that revolution is just and legitimate only when more than fifty per cent of the people desire it or conversely that revolutionary activity is immoral because (and most of them would have granted it) a great majority of the Russian nation believed in the Holy Orthodox Church and the Tsar. But they were certainly democrats in their belief, or self-deception, that they spoke for the "real" interests of the masses, the ones which, if the people could overcome their superstitions and poverty, they would readily and insistently express.

But is that formula sufficient for Lenin? Is the worker's enlightened self-interest, that is, his realization that he must struggle against his employer in order to live better, much of an improvement on his unenlightened acquiescence in the benevolence of the Tsar and the capitalists? Certainly not! "Socialist consciousness cannot exist among the workers. This can be introduced only from without. The history of all countries shows that by its unaided efforts the working class can only develop a trade-union consciousness, that is to say, a conviction of the necessity to form trade unions, struggle with the employers, obtain from the government this or that law required by the workers, and so on. . . ." [12] Socialism, to paraphrase the witticism of Clemenceau, is too important to be left to workers. Once having joined in an attack Lenin loved to shock his opponents. They would be left breathless by the audacity and impudence of his formulations, often too scandalized to think of an answer. And in *What Is To Be Done?* Lenin calmly says that socialism has but little to do with the workers. Marx and Engels were middle-class intellectuals. In Russia Socialist ideas have come always from upper- and middle-class intellectuals.

There were some timid objections, and not only from the Economists, that this was not Marxism. Certainly, by any objective standard Lenin revised the doctrine of the Master as much as Bernstein did. To Marx, class consciousness of the workers, that is, their striving for socialism, was a *spontaneous* product of the economic condition under which they lived. Now his Russian disciple asserted that the worker wants to be paid more, and that socialism has to be beaten into his head by the outsiders, the intelligentsia. But Bernstein had frankly avowed that he *was* revising the doctrine, pruning it of its illogical and obsolete parts. Lenin, with the sure instinct of a theologian, was proclaiming *his* revisionism to be Marxian orthodoxy.

What Is To Be Done? is, then, a theory and a panegyric in praise of *the Party*, something then a novelty in political literature. The past political theorists and prophets extolled and claimed political power on behalf of a king, church, class, or leader. As yet this party existed only in Lenin's

[12] *Works*, Vol. 5, p. 347.

mind. It was to be composed of professional revolutionaries, but it was not a mere conspiracy. It was to enlist intellectuals, indeed from among them were to be sought its leaders, but it was to avoid the intellectuals' vices of continuous doctrinal dispute, indecision, humanitarian scruples, and the like. It was to rely upon workers, but certainly the Party's aims transcended the petty interests of the working class in securing a better livelihood and conditions of work.

Lenin thought of himself and wrote as a humble disciple of Karl Marx. His orderly and prosaic mind would have rebelled at the idea that his vision of the Party was closer to that of a collective superhuman Nietzschean hero or some medieval order of chivalry than to that of a humdrum political association, which the Social Democratic Party was supposed to be. Years were to pass before a French poet was to sing of "my beautiful Communist Party." Admission to it in Russia for long depended on purity of (that is, proletarian) descent and is still preceded by a period of probation. Individuals are being chastised for "anti-Party activity," and weaknesses of the flesh are deemed "unworthy of a Party member." This language and ritual would make that nineteenth century rationalist Karl Marx cringe, and much of it would disgust Lenin himself. But the source of it all is in *What Is To Be Done?*.

What is this collective hero to do? The Party is to fight "spontaneity" and "opportunism." Again the parallel with the medieval table of vices is irresistible. Spontaneity stands for our old friend: Sloth. In their historical march the working classes tend to acquiesce in petty material gains, lose all too easily their class and militant drive. The Party is to prod them, to explain their revolutionary tasks, and to endure until the victory is won. Opportunism is closely related to greed. How easy it is for the Socialist leaders to acquiesce in small victories and in concessions by the *bourgeoisie*, and to become tempted by parliamentary and ministerial positions, pushing the idea of a decisive assault upon capitalism farther and farther away from their minds. Again the Party knows how to accept, but never to rest content with concessions, just as it is capable of suffering a temporary defeat and then regrouping for a renewed assault. The Socialist (the temptation is great to write here anachronistically Bolshevik or Communist) should know how to avoid self-indulgence. And in the latter is found the source of terrorism. Overwrought intellectuals are incapable of patient and long-range revolutionary action. It is easier to commit an individual act of violence, but does not the whole history of the revolutionary movement show the futility of such acts?

The last point recalls us to a constant characteristic of Lenin's designs. No sooner is one tempted to feel condescending toward the theological, or, depending on taste, adolescent quality of his thinking, than one is sobered by his immense practicality and common sense. How childish and unrealistic at first glance is this concept of a Socialist Party as a body of revolutionary palladins, directed by the true faith of Marxism, unswerving in their devotion and uncorruptible. But, on the other hand, granted the premises of revolutionary socialism, what other model of a party can one construct for Russia in 1902? The weaknesses of his opponents' position are dissected most convincingly. The Socialist Revolutionaries and their penchant for terror have already been dealt with. The Economists talk and write as if Russia were a Western European state which grudgingly allows economic struggle by the workers. But in fact the Tsarist government will not allow free trade-union activity. The only unions it tolerates are those controlled by the police agents. There are those who complain about *Iskra*'s (i.e., Lenin's) dictatorial and centralistic tendencies. But again Russia is not the West. You cannot have Kiev Socialists deliberating whether they will agree with their Odessa comrades or not. You dare not have each national group in the Empire have its own independent Socialist organization, the Jewish, Armenian, and other workers all pulling in different directions. There must be one centrally controlled Socialist Party speaking with one voice, composed not of well-intentioned people interested in political freedom and related ideas, but of active, professional revolutionaries.

What Is To Be Done? is not written in exaltation. It is not a messianic vision of a better world. On its face it is a laboriously, awkwardly written polemical pamphlet. Its flashes of insight, its hints of inspired revolutionary audacity are all but lost within the context of pedantic, organizational strictures and attacks upon groups and personalities, now only of historical interest. The ostensible targets of the tract, the Economists and their journal, *Rabocheye Delo* (*The Workers' Cause*), have long reposed, to use Trotsky's famous phrase, on "the rubbish heap of history." The people against whom Lenin exerted his fine Marxian vituperation, Krichevski, Struve, Bulgakov, Martynov, are now familiar only to the specialist in the period. Certainly to a contemporary Socialist they loomed as important as Lenin. Had Russia followed a constitutional and parliamentary path, as she seemed to promise between 1906 and 1914, it is their names which would enjoy the place of honor and importance in her history, while that of Vladimir Ulyanov-Lenin would now be known only to a historian. Though he could hardly have realized it, Lenin was writing a primer of politics for the twentieth century, a model for the movements—not only the Marxist ones—that have increasingly displaced liberalism and democracy.

And because this impression emanates, however dimly, from the pages of the pamphlet, *What Is To Be Done?* marks the beginning of the real split within Russian Social Democracy. It is no longer the question of the Economists. By 1902–3 most of them went their own separate ways. But within the *Iskra* group Lenin's ideas led to as yet ill-defined uneasiness. On the surface he was but a defender of orthodoxy and of political action by the

Socialists, something that Martov and Plekhanov can but applaud. Who can object to the guiding motto of *What Is To Be Done?*: "without a revolutionary theory there cannot be a revolutionary movement"? But most of Lenin's colleagues began to sense that there was something new in his Marxism.

To the less perceptive the pamphlet was but an organizational handbook. To listen to Krupskaya: "It put forward a complete organizational plan in which everybody could find a place, could become a cog in the revolutionary machine. . . . [It] called for plodding, tireless work to build that foundation so necessary for the Party in the conditions then prevailing, if it was to exist not in words but in deeds." Indeed, the literal mind of Krupskaya hit the nail on the head; one of the troubles was that *everybody* was being invited to become a cog in the machine. Who was going to run it? It was somewhat difficult for such persons as Martov and Trotsky to think of themselves as mere "cogs" in a perfectly functioning machine.

References to Plekhanov in *What Is To Be Done?* were still those of a pupil to a master. There is no doubt that this played a part in Plekhanov's determination to stick with Lenin during the subsequent split among the Socialists. Thus Lenin took over Plekhanov's famous definition of the roles of the agitator and the propagandist. The former propagates a few simple ideas to the masses, while the propagandist expounds elaborate theoretical schemes to a more limited audience. This distinction, which always remained important for Lenin, shows clearly his elitist cast of mind. The Socialist leaders, he writes, belong clearly either to the propagandist or the agitator type. It is not unfair to surmise that he considered himself an exception, combining both crafts.

The organizational scheme propounded in *What Is To Be Done?* would vest the control of the Party within the central organ (that is, the editorial board of *Iskra*) published abroad. The Central Committee residing within Russia would in contrast have mostly administrative functions. This is, then, a strictly hierarchical organization, and indeed the Party is likened to an army sending its detachments in all directions. Under the network of the local committees controlled by the central organs Lenin envisages a body of professional revolutionaries. One cannot be a part-time revolutionary, working ten or eleven hours in a factory and carrying on the struggle in one's "spare" time. Hence his vision of a great number of activists, living illegally, that is, with forged papers, and devoting all their time to the task. No police in the world, he wrote rather overoptimistically, could handle a party based on such principles.

Has not Lenin forgotten something? The Party is to be like an army, but an army needs a general. Who is to decide which cogs are to fit various parts of the machinery? Unconsciously Lenin has sketched a blueprint for a dictatorship. That it was unconscious, at least at this juncture, we need not doubt. In reflecting many years later on his successful rival, Martov insists that he never saw in him personal vanity or power-seeking. But the whole logic of *What Is To Be Done?* cries out not only for leaders but also for *the leader*, and that, in Russian revolutionary thought and tradition, was a vast novelty. The Decembrists had appointed a "dictator," but only for the purposes of the uprising. Within the revolutionary Populist organizations leadership was always collegiate. Zhelyabov might through his ability and moral authority dominate his colleagues, but nobody thought of him as *the* leader or as the only man entitled to give directions. If in the Socialist organizations there was a tradition of leadership it was always associated with intellectual pre-eminence and guidance. It meant that, say, Plekhanov, because of his seniority and his theoretical work, was listened to with more respect than his less prestigious colleagues. But that a decision could be reached without a discussion, that people could be simply commandeered to do this or that job, that the Party cells were expected to report to and obey the center, all those things presaged a vast and new development. In twenty years an official with the humdrum title of Secretary General would appear and he would cap the structure.

But such grandiose and ominous perspectives were still hidden in 1902–3, though soon after the Second Party Congress the charges of sheltering dictatorial ambitions were to be addressed against Lenin. And indeed how could even the most sanguine Socialist, Lenin included, foresee the moment when his party alone would rule Russia? *What Is To Be Done?* was taken not as blueprint for seizing power, but for saving and strengthening what was left in the way of the Social Democratic Party. The Russian Socialists were being threatened from all directions. The trouble as usual was with the flighty intelligentsia. The young students flocked to the Socialist Revolutionary camp. Their elders, the professional classes, were enlisting under the banner of liberalism with Economism often acting as a sort of ideological decompression chamber between Marxism and liberalism. Worst of all, the workers were being organized for the first time on a large scale, but by whom? Why, by the police.

This ingenious scheme, a direct precedent for the various labor fronts and the like of the fascist regimes, originated in the agile mind of a Moscow police official, S. V. Zubatov. An erstwhile radical, Zubatov persuaded his superiors that the revolutionaries could be beaten at their own game. He was far from being a mere cynical manipulator. On the contrary, Zubatov believed in what might be called a Populist version of autocracy. The Tsar could be brought close to his people, and the workers could be shown that they did not need the noxious intellectuals who stirred them up for their own purposes. He organized unions and pressured employers for concessions to their men. Since, this being Russia, even police unionism could not entirely dispense with the intellectuals, Zubatov procured the collaboration of some professors and journalists, who gave lectures to his unionists. The tenor of this instruction was, to use another anachronistic expression, national-socialistic. The Tsar was one with his people, and the employers in exploiting the workers acted against his desires. Since many of the industrial enterprises were foreign-owned, it could also be added that many of the exploiters were not Russian anyway.

Zubatov's successes panicked the Socialists. At one point he was able to muster about 50,000 workers at a ceremoney of laying wreaths at the monument of Alexander II. He managed to create a police-sponsored union even among the most class-conscious proletarians, the Jewish workers in the Ukraine. But Lenin remained relatively unperturbed. He forecast accurately that the Zubatovs come and go, but that the workers will have learned the lesson of organizing and of pressing their demands. And so it was; the ingenious servant of autocracy was clearly in advance of his time. He soon became the object of professional jealousy and complaints. The industrialists besieged the Ministry of Finance. Was this a way to promote Russia's industrial growth, by stirring up their workers against them? The French ambassador remonstrated with the Ministry of Foreign Affairs; certainly the government of an allied power was duty-bound to protect the French capitalists rather than to attack them. The right-wing press for some reason began to picture Zubatov as a "servant of the Jews." These attacks plus an inopportune "success" of his movement—a wave of strikes conducted by the police unions broke out in the summer of 1903—led to Zubatov's dismissal. In a manner befitting a real revolutionary the inventive policeman was sent into administrative exile. For all its "ingratitude" he remained a fervent believer in autocracy, confident, like many others, that had *his* advice been taken it would have saved Russia. And in 1917 upon hearing of the abdication of Nicholas II Zubatov ended his life with a bullet.

But in the spring of 1903 this "police socialism" was still deemed a danger. From Lenin's point of view it had, however, the advantage of further compromising the Economists' position. Weren't Zubatov's unions a vivid demonstration of what happens when you yield to the workers' "spontaneous" drive just to receive better conditions of work and pay? This was but flogging a dead horse, for Economism was now collapsing, and new heresies and struggles loomed over the horizon. Geneva that spring was providing a prelude to another historical milestone in the life of Russian socialism: the delegates were assembling for the Second Congress of the Russian Socialist Party, which was to take place in the summer.

"Accursed Geneva" was the way Lenin referred at times to this charming Swiss city. His irritation at the time was well grounded, for no sooner was he recovered from his ailment than his energies had to be expended in constant consultations, "lobbying," and the like, with the comrades who were already there or arriving from Russia. Superficially, his living conditions were vastly preferable to London. The Ulyanovs occupied a small but comfortable house. The domestic chores were handled by Krupskaya's mother, who had arrived some time before and now relieved her daughter of the household drudgery. In that respect Nadezhda felt like any other middle-class housewife. She did not mind working around the house, she said, but she did not like domestic chores to occupy her mind. In other words, she needed servants. Lenin and his wife lived rather more comfortably than most of the Russian refugees, many of whom were compelled to earn a living as waiters, porters, and in like occupations. Lenin paid himself a modest salary out of the *Iskra* funds, and all the "extras" had to come from the family in Russia. It was thus a rapturous event when a collection at home enabled Vladimir Ilyich and Nadya to purchase elegant bicycles. With childish pride Lenin exhibited the machines to his comrades, extolling the generosity of his mother and brother-in-law. The gift was all the more precious to him as a token of Maria Alexandrovna's love and consideration.

To a visiting Russian radical Geneva was now a sort of revolutionary Olympus. Walking along the lake one might run into legendary figures of revolutionary history such as Lev Deutsch or Vera Zasulich. Deutsch more than a quarter of a century earlier was one of the heroes of the Chigirin affair, when the Populists with forged manifestoes persuaded the peasants that the Tsar wanted them to rise against the nobles and the bureaucracy. Since then he had been involved in innumerable exiles, imprisonments, and escapes. And Vera Zasulich! In addition to her renown for shooting Trepov, she was the very same person who in 1881 received the famous letter from Karl Marx, in which the Master allowed that Russia might pursue her own path to socialism. Or Paul Axelrod, the man who was probably the first Russian Marxist.

But even their fame paled beside that of Plekhanov. His reputation transcended the Russian revolutionary camp, and his name was renowned among all the European Socialists. It would not have amused Vladimir Ilyich to learn that when *What Is To Be Done?* appeared the Bulgarian Socialists concluded that the author of this tract could be none else than Plekhanov masquerading under the pseudonym of Lenin! [13] Every newcomer from Russia was eager to meet Georgi Valentinovich, which by now was not easy since the great man was rather chary of granting audiences. But one could repair to the reading room of the public library, and if lucky catch a glimpse of Plekhanov, his noble brow bent over some theoretical treatise.

Those who were vouchsafed a closer acquaintance were to record mixed impressions. Even his future enemies, who were to hold him at a disadvantage when compared with Lenin, are constrained to admit that Plekhanov was a fascinating thinker and conversationalist. When the dis-

---

[13] G. Bakalov, "How the Bulgarian Communists Made the Acquaintance of Lenin," in *The Proletarian Revolution*, Moscow, 1929, No. 10, p. 109.

cussion did not touch any of his numerous sensitive points he sparkled with wit and anecdotes. He was a man of deep culture and erudition and a favored visitor was likely to be dragged to a concert or a picture gallery where Plekhanov would provide artistic and technical explanations.

The complaints that echo across the years about him and his ways are a testimony not so much to his weaknesses but to the partisan fervor and to the at times appalling narrowness of mind of those Bolsheviks who recorded them. Thus he is pictured as excessively "European" and reserved in his personal relationships. With Lenin, so runs a standard reminiscence, one felt, on the contrary, being with "one's own," a real Russian. Leaving apart the accuracy of this description of Lenin, the diarist simply ignores the fact that Plekhanov was not only a much older person, but also that he was chronically ill. He had to husband his strength and time, and was simply incapable of engaging in effusive Russian sociability with people half his age. But the comment is instructive because it shows that as early as 1903-4 the thing was true that Lenin himself was to deplore in 1919: "Scratch a Russian Communist and you will find a Great Russian chauvinist." Equally petty and intolerable were the complaints that Plekhanov's daughters spoke French better than Russian (how could they help it, never having lived in Russia!), that he was always elegantly dressed and had his shoes shined, and so on. It was begrudged this sufferer from tuberculosis that after years of grinding poverty he was finally able, because of his wife's earnings as a doctor, to live in comfort. The Russian Socialists (and this was true not only of the future Bolsheviks and the rulers of Soviet Russia) were a peculiar lot. Their idealism and their prowess for uncritical enthusiasm were not matched by a capacity for compassion and understanding.

Perhaps the main reason was the streak of adolescent feeling that figures strongly in the make-up of the revolutionary. These men who had braved arrests and exiles "ran after" their celebrated leaders almost in the fashion of today's teenagers pestering the celebrities of the stage and screen. Youthful enthusiasm was likely to be followed by the full bitterness of youthful disenchantment. One remembers Lenin's experience with Plekhanov. Now in Geneva the comrades, if they had their way, would not leave a moment's peace to their hard-working idols. Their authority had to be invoked or their counsel taken on the most improbable subjects. Is it legitimate for a class-conscious Socialist to take pleasure in flowers? This question, a contemporary tells us, was discussed in Lenin's presence.[14] Why, said a zealot, you begin by liking flowers and soon you long to be a Russian landlord resting in a hammock with a French novel in hand while servants busy themselves around your garden! It aroused astonishment of those present, followed by a rapturous amazement at the

---

[14] N. Valentinov, *Meetings with Lenin* (in Russian), New York, 1953, p. 157. An invaluable description of Lenin's life in Geneva c. 1904.

breadth of his views and his tolerance when Lenin adjudged that a revolutionary not only could but should admire the beauties of nature. A Caucasian Socialist recalls his visit of some years later to Lenin. Subsequently he and his companion almost came to blows while quarreling over which of them Vladimir Ilyich had been paying more attention!

This childishness, helped by the Russian "wide-open nature," very often led to contentiousness and constant quarreling. If the problem of flowers threatened for an instant an ideological split, one can imagine the intensity of feelings generated by the Party program, the future constitution of Russia, and the like. At one Party Congress, one delegate recalls, he got so mad at a "betrayal" by a fellow delegate that he decided to beat him up. It took an hour's long talk by Lenin to dissuade the overwrought youth, who wrote that at the end he broke down and cried like a child.[15] The Party gatherings, discussions of the most solemn problems, were constantly interrupted by some member demanding angrily that the speaker "take back" something he said, or jumping up feverishly and exclaiming that the protocol should make special note of this or that accusation or epithet. The quarrel between Martov and Lenin that was soon to enliven the life of Russian Social Democracy turned largely on the dispute about "who started it," and who tried to trick whom. Friends of long standing, men who had braved danger in the service of a common ideal, would turn on each other and exhibit their coldness and mutual scorn with the ridiculous theatricality of two estranged high school boys.

But those were dangerous and fateful games, for in the 1930s, in Stalin's Russia, the demand to "take back" one's word would grow into the frightful ritual of recantation. At the purge trials old Bolsheviks were called upon to take back and revile their whole past and to find treasonous motivations for their thoughts and actions. The childish impulse to be noticed, to hurt, and to bend another's will to one's own flowered into the weird ceremonies of purging and "brain washing." Today, when we see the Communist parties of two great countries hurling epithets at each other, demanding apologies, admissions of guilt, each strutting in its preposterous pose of self-righteousness, how strange it is to reflect that it all began with some very young men arguing in a Swiss café.

Himself part and parcel of this disputatious and quarrelsome tradition of Russian radicalism, Lenin was at the same time its severest critic. We have seen him enough not to be surprised at this seeming paradox. A member of the intelligentsia and yet unequaled in hatred for it, a fervent believer in the dictatorship of the proletariat but thoroughly skeptical of the ability of the rank-and-file worker to run anything, Lenin exhibits some of the contradictions in his nature and beliefs. In the spring and summer of 1903 before the Second Party Congress, Lenin believed that

[15] A. Shotman, "On the Second Party Congress," in The Proletarian Revolution, Moscow, June–July 1928, p. 63.

there was a middle way between this natural and perhaps desirable (for it testified to their enthusiasm and energy) quarrelsomeness of the comrades and the need for a disciplined party. Let people quarrel and trick each other to their heart's content at the conferences and congresses, but once a decision is made, let the Party march as a united army. An admirable compromise, which neglected only one eventuality: what if the decision was wrong, that is, if the majority voted against Lenin?

To avoid this possibility Lenin spent the spring of 1903 in careful preparatory work. For once he was open and accessible to all the Russian visitors to Geneva, much as this endless politicking and discussion detracted from his literary work. In addition he mended his relations with Plekhanov, whose support was indispensable if he were to reshape Russian socialism. Participation in the social-political life of the *émigré* colony in Geneva involved appearance at meetings where discussions often grew disorderly and at times threatened to turn into a fight. Some were to recall an occasion when a group of drunken anarchists interrupted a Socialist meeting, and with uplifted stools and chairs were ready to settle Russia's future path right then and there. Lenin and Plekhanov, though physically threatened, kept calm, and the anarchists, overawed by the sturdy young comrades, retreated in some confusion.

When the Second Party Congress finally assembled in Brussels on July 30 Lenin could have every confidence that his work had not been in vain. The *Iskra* forces were going to the meeting as a united force. *What Is To Be Done?* was, it had been agreed, to become the basis of the Party's program and activity. Unlike the First, the Second Congress could lay a real claim to being representative of the feelings of Russian Socialists; most delegates from home managed to cross the frontier and to arrive in Brussels, and a great majority were *Iskra* partisans. To be sure, how fairly the Russian Socialists at home and abroad were represented was another question. Thus out of 51 mandates at the Congress only five represented the Bund, the organization of the Jewish proletariat, though undoubtedly there were then more Socialists among the Jewish workers than among the ethnic Russians. Such other important centers of Marxist influence in the Empire as Russian Poland and Latvia were virtually unrepresented. But one could not expect perfection under the current conditions of revolutionary and conspiratorial work. In contrast to 1898, when nine Socialists who represented themselves had proclaimed their gathering a Congress, this was an enormous progress, a sure harbinger that Russian socialism would overcome its difficulties and become a "real" party.

The picturesque circumstances of this founding of the force that was to crush not only empires but also most of the individuals who assembled in a Brussels warehouse on a July afternoon have often been related.[16]

[16] Nowhere better than in Mr. Bertram Wolfe's *Three Who Made a Revolution,* New York, 1948.

The place was infested by fleas. Within a few days the chicanery of the Belgian police forced the Congress to shift to London, and there it continued to meet until August 23, 1903. When it adjourned not one but two parties had been born.

Why this happened had been the subject of both angry recriminations and learned analyses. In retrospect it is tempting to see Lenin as already a would-be dictator, and his opponents as defenders of democracy finally rising to the realization of his inordinate lust for power. But that would be a huge oversimplification.

Essentially, and this was a revelation and a lesson to Lenin, any *free* congress of Russian Socialists was almost bound to lead to a split, and bitter antagonism. The very same energy, ambition, and idealism that drove those men to their dangerous careers made them utterly incapable of settling their disagreements in a parliamentary way, acknowledging defeat, and submitting to the leadership of a former opponent. Even in Soviet Russia, Party congresses, until Stalin's iron hand made them a parody of their past, were to witness continued and frantic intrigues, explosions of pent-up personal hatreds, and irreparable fissures in the "monolithic unity" of Bolshevism. Now in 1903 the Russian revolutionaries could work together like brothers when facing danger at home. They quarreled furiously but usually parted as friends when within the intimacy of a small circle. But the presence of a forum, the clash of opinions, were to act upon them like an energizing drug, unleashing the violence that had made them what they were, and had been contained only by a common task and the hatred of a common enemy.

Thus for a while the Congress acted according to the prepared script, with Lenin performing his agreed-upon role as the manager of the majority. Then the emotional tempo quickened. Personal epithets were tossed around. Delegates walked out in indignation and with threats. Hurried consultations and the shifting of sides took up time between the sessions. And toward the end this group of 50 to 55 individuals could scarcely conduct any business at all. It was an achievement of no small order that the Congress did adjourn with some decorum and some very artificial assurances of unity.

In purely human terms Lenin did not show at a disadvantage when compared with other leading personalities. Plekhanov, for whom this meeting was the consummation of hopes and labors of twenty years, made a painful impression. He was, of course, acclaimed the president of the Congress, and yet failed to be a force for moderation or conciliation. Instead, the father of Russian Marxism displayed rather heavy humor: "If Lenin really disagrees with Engels he should be hanged"; awkward examples of his erudition: "Napoleon had a passion for making his marshals divorce their wives"; and revolutionary name-dropping: "I remember Engels saying that when you deal with a professor you should prepare for the worst." [17] Trotsky, in his irrepressible way, was jumping up and speaking on every point, here assuming the role of a spokesman of the Jewish proletariat, there referring condescendingly to another speaker as a "young comrade" (the man was actually older than Trotsky). He was already demonstrating the combination of brilliance and arrogance destined to secure him a dazzling career, but which also helped to push him toward final pathetic defeat. Even Martov, for all the saintly reputation that attaches to his name, cannot escape the reproach that when the moment came for a showdown he displayed—this became a characteristic of the party he was to lead—an excessive sensitivity combined with insufficient tactical ability or the readiness to fight it out.

It is difficult on the other hand to fault Lenin for his behavior at the Congress. With *What Is To Be Done?* he had laid his cards on the table, and thus how could anyone be surprised that he sought a strongly centralized party composed of professional revolutionaries? As for his bid for power, it was premature, we repeat, to see Lenin in 1903 consciously striving to be a dictator. Any person within any party has the right to seek leadership, to try to sway votes, to maneuver and to cajole, and the like. Legend has compensated his numerous enemies for their defeat by representing them as defenders of democracy. Not many of them in fact deserve this reputation.

In the beginning the sessions went off better than Lenin could have expected. His initial fears that Economism would again raise its head were dissipated. There were but two or three delegates willing to defend that point of view and they were faced by a solid bloc of 41 mandates supporting *Iskra*.[18] Another and related fear that there would be a widespread demand for additional Socialist papers, which would be more accessible to the rank-and-file worker, and thus would challenge *Iskra*'s monopoly of agitation and guidance, also vanished. In fact his version of the Party program was receiving an enthusiastic support of the majority of the delegates.

But even within this initial atmosphere of agreement and self-congratulation there was heard a voice of dissent and warning. It fell to one Akimov, an obscure figure before and after the Congress, to play the combined roles of an *enfant terrible* and a Greek chorus. Akimov amused rather than irritated the delegates by his tactless questions and observations. But the future was to show them endowed with a prophetic sense. He saw that the proposed Party program followed *What Is To Be Done?*. And does not Lenin's pamphlet treat the workers as a passive means to be driven and controlled by an elite Party? Is not the proletariat's struggle for

---

[17] *The Second Congress of the Russian Social Democratic Party. Protocols,* Moscow, 1959, p. 271.

[18] There were in the beginning 43 delegates empowered to vote, but nine of them disposed of two votes each.

better living conditions presented as something in which the Socialists are not really interested? What does Lenin mean by saying that the central organs should control the Party publications? Are *we* going to have a censorship? And turning to the revered teacher of Social Democracy, Akimov expressed incredulity that such undemocratic and un-Marxist sentiments could have the support of Plekhanov.

But the latter was in one of his periods of revolutionary euphoria and renewed admiration for Lenin. He was not going to be "divorced from Lenin" (it was here that appeared the "joke" about Napoleon, his marshals, and their wives). Plekhanov was constrained to add, to show that he was a revolutionary first and a democrat second, that all the constitutional and democratic rights must cede to the needs of the revolution. If the people elect a parliament with a Socialist majority, well and good. If on the other hand the ignorant populace should elect a parliament inconvenient for the Socialists, then the "revolution" should chase it out. This was still strong medicine and there were some boos. But there is no doubt that Plekhanov captured the mood of revolutionary violence of the majority. Later on, when it was proposed to include in the program the demand for abolition of the death penalty, it was rejected by a large majority with shouts, "And what about Nicholas II?" Practically all those present were beneficiaries of the fact that political crimes as such were not punished by death, even by the government of Nicholas II.

The same *Iskra*-led majority still held firm when it came to the question of the inner constitution of the Party. The delegates of the Bund were determined to win for their organization an autonomous position within the broader Russian Social Democratic Party and the exclusive claim to represent the Jewish workers that to Lenin and his group was quite unacceptable. Concede to one nationality the right for an almost independent Socialist party and the others will demand the same: the Poles, Letts, Georgians, all the others. What would become of your centralized disciplined organization? All they were willing to concede to the Bund was a very subordinate position of conducting agitation and propaganda in Yiddish, of being just a transmission belt to those Jewish workers who were totally unassimilated and almost ignorant of the Russian language.

Some years before, to his sister Anna Lenin confided a high appreciation of the Jews. Our Russians, he said, are too easy-going, too readily tired of the revolutionary struggle. The Jews, on the other hand, with their stubbornness and fanaticism make excellent revolutionaries. This made him all the more unwilling to abandon direct control over the Jewish revolutionaries to a semi-independent organization. The drama that unfolded over the Bund demands was again prophetic in its implications. About half the delegates were of Jewish origin. But to the handful of the Bund emissaries the Russified Jews had no right to speak for the Jewish proletariat. They viewed the rejection of their pleas with multiple bitterness. The

Bund had been instrumental in creating the Russian Socialist Party in the first place. It was grossly underrepresented at the Congress. And toward such persons as Martov and Trotsky their speeches exuded (how strange among fellow Socialists!) real class antagonism. Trotsky and his like, for all the accident of their birth, were for them typical gentlemen from the Russian intelligentsia. How long since they had soiled their hands (if ever) working among the oppressed Jewish workers? The discussion inevitably ran into the mutual, barely veiled insinuations of Jewish chauvinism on the one side and anti-Semitism on the other.

The Bund delegates were eventually to stalk out of the Congress proclaiming the secession of their organization. But the legacy of bitterness was not only theirs. The debate had been one of many in which the question posed concerned not only the Party but the integrity of many of the individuals present: were they or were they not Socialists, democrats, Jews? As their inner conflicts grew so did the tension until it had to find a release in an explosion.

A preliminary clash took place over the wording of Article One of the Party Statute. Lenin's formulation defined the Party member, among other qualifications, as one who actually participates in one of its organizations. Martov's alternative draft was almost identical, but it diluted the "activist" element: a member is required to support the Party "by personal assistance under the direction of one of the Party organizations." One is reminded of Gibbon's description of how the difference of one word in a theological formula divided Eastern from Western Christianity. Here the dispute possessed some substance insofar as it expressed the growing resentment against *What Is To Be Done?*, with its concept of the professional revolutionary being taken as the basis for the Party statute and philosophy. This up to then had been Lenin's Congress. He had dominated its decisions, he had captivated Plekhanov, and that, quite apart from theoretical and organizational questions, explains Martov's need for self-assertion against his closest friend. On this issue the majority was for Martov, 28 to 23, and the "softer" version prevailed.

Krupskaya was to write in her simple-minded way that Vladimir Ilyich believed that "At the Party Congress all personalities should be discarded, nothing be concealed, and everything should be said openly." These excellent sentiments notwithstanding, Lenin for some time had been organizing his own faction among the *Iskra* partisans. He managed to rescue a solid phalanx of 24 votes, and that became the majority when the five Bundists and two Economists stalked out of the Congress. And now the stage was set for the Great Split. · · · ·

It would take several volumes of this size to review all the evidence, all the charges and countercharges, as to who "started it," who "betrayed whom," who "broke his word," and so on. In the simplest terms Lenin wanted to secure a majority on the central organs of the Party. Most im-

mediately he desired to reduce the editorial board of *Iskra* to three instead
of six. It was to consist of Plekhanov, Martov, and himself; Axelrod,
Zasulich, and Potresov were to be dropped. Upon this announcement
pandemonium broke out among the delegates. On the face of it the proposal was quite sensible. The three proposed candidates had carried most
of the paper's work anyway. It was desirable to have a smaller number of
editors to cut down the endless debates and prolonged correspondence
that had hampered the work of the old board. But many delegates who
had unsentimentally cast out the Bund with its thousands of Socialists, who
unblinkingly and delightedly faced the prospect of executing the "enemies
of the people," could not bear the thought of two venerable veterans,
Axelrod and Zasulich, being dropped back into the ranks (nobody cared
very much about Potresov). Why, this was a shameful vote of non-
confidence against those two revolutionaries with their glorious past. The
minutes of the meeting now bear annotations of "universal disorder,"
"threatening shouts," "cries of 'lies,' 'shame.'" Friendships of a lifetime were
abruptly broken. Vera Zasulich, suffering from laryngitis, was screaming
in a croaking voice at her erstwhile idol, Plekhanov, who was in agreement
with Lenin. The latter claimed that Martov had previously endorsed the
new board. Martov, for his part, implied that Lenin was lying.

The issue was elaborated later on into one of principle. Lenin, said his
opponents, wanted to dominate the editorial board, which in turn could
dictate to the other Party leading organs: the Central Committee (composed of three members and resident in Russia), and the Party Council. At
this early date at the Congress Martov said, in a transparent allusion, that
the Party did not need a *leader,* it only wanted to have *representatives* in
its central bodies. But if so it was late in the game to express democratic
scruples. And it was improbable that Lenin's plan was motivated by a
conscious desire to seize control of the Party. He would be one of three
editors. To be sure, he had for the moment the support of Plekhanov, but
the latter was notoriously changeable, and was as likely to side with
Martov as with him. In brief, the notion of a Machiavellian design behind
the plot to drop the revered but incompetent collaborators is hardly ten-
able.

But there is no doubt that the Congress marks the end of a profound
evolution in Lenin's psychology. In *What Is To Be Done?* he had sketched
unconsciously the blueprint of the Party as consisting of the Leader and
the "cogs," his followers. When charged with dictatorial manners he now
proudly accepted the challenge and scorned any excuses: "Yes, Comrade
Martov is perfectly right. . . . Against the undependable and wavering
elements [in our midst] we not only may, we must proclaim a state of
siege. . . ." This again sounds like childish petulance: if *they* want to
make a dictator out of him he is going to be one and he is going to show
them. But the consequences were to be far from childish.

And thus Russian socialism, which like some primitive organism seemed to multiply incessantly by fission, split again. On the slim foundation that toward the end of the Congress Lenin's followers could muster 24 or 25 votes against Martov's 20 or 19 they were christened Bolsheviks (the "Majoritarians"), and their opponents Mensheviks (the "Minoritarians"). At first these names were employed in mutual derision and in quotation marks, but later on they stuck and the inverted commas disappeared. Why a political organization should cling to a name which commemorates the fact that it was once in a minority, but naturally conveys the impression that it is predestined to be so, is one of those impenetrable mysteries of the Russian soul. Despite the thin veneer of unity under which the gathering adjourned it was clear that irreparable damage had been done. Martov said flatly that he would not serve on the new board with Lenin and Plekhanov. The Bolsheviks thus monopolized the central bodies of the Party. Some of the Mensheviks hinted darkly that their opponents would not be provided with funds for a return to Russia. But all the returning delegates, Mensheviks and Bolsheviks, faced the same perturbing problem: how to explain to the Socialists at home the madhouse that went under the name of the Second (Founding) Congress of the Russian Social Democratic Party?

3. From the Rift to the Revolution of 1905

The only side which could fully congratulate itself on the results of the Second Party Congress was the Tsarist police whose agents, of course, were well informed about what went on there. It had been an inspired case of inefficiency to have allowed most of the delegates to get abroad and attend the Congress, for the Party was now rent in two. As the delegates skulked their way home they were met by expectant Socialists eager to hear how their Party was finally put upon a solid and unified basis. One can well imagine the amazement, dismay, and the angry recriminations that now took place in Socialist circles all over Russia as the incredible story was being pieced together. The Bolsheviks were under the heaviest barrage of reproaches. Why did they humiliate Vera Zasulich, the very same woman who in 1878 shot Trepov, who received the famous letter from the hand of Karl Marx, whose name was indelibly cast in the annals of revolution? And old Axelrod?! A fine reward for more than thirty years of working for socialism. But the Mensheviks were not spared. What kind of behavior was it for Martov to declare that because he was defeated he was not going to serve in the post to which the Congress delegated him?

The Party's committees in Russia became preoccupied with the struggle between the two factions. To the rank-and-file Party member, as a matter of fact, to anybody who had not witnessed the Congress, the split was incomprehensible. It had been assumed that the *Iskra* editors had been working like a band of brothers. Now they were ranged against each other. Inevitably the split had to be reproduced within the Party committees in Russia. And thus those persons continually dodging the police, struggling against the rising wave of the popularity of the Socialist Revolutionaries, had in addition to expend precious time and energy in resolving a domestic quarrel the causes of which could hardly be explained. And the rich sympathizers at home and abroad were growing unwilling to contribute to a movement that seemed destined to lapse into warring sections and insignificance.

Before he could encounter the consequences Lenin had to face a personal crisis. The notion that there had been any conscious Machiavellianism on his part in provoking the split is sufficiently disproved by the fact that once again he was prostrated by a nervous ailment. Already sick in London, he had to spend some time in bed after his return to Geneva. In time his health returned. He repaired with his wife for one of his beloved long trips into the mountains. Refreshed by a few days of solitude, he was ready to return to the fray.

But the aftereffects of the breach never left him. It meant more than separation from the closest friend of his youth, Martov; it meant in a sense the end of his youth. From then on Lenin shirked friendship and intimacy. He would have no more friends, only collaborators. Whereas before he addressed Martov as "thou," now, if he had to communicate with him at all, he began drily with "esteemed comrade." In general his outlook on people, his view on life hardened. The Congress marks a dividing line between a young revolutionary whose ruthlessness was still tempered by occasional toleration of human weaknesses and the Lenin who derives pleasure in reflecting that after the Revolution those who were not with him "will be stood up against the wall and shot." It marks a further step in his obsessive hatred of the intelligentsia. The Congress, after all, demonstrated what happens when a group of Russian intellectuals (there were only four "real workers" among the fifty-odd delegates) is called upon to agree on a joint course of action. Martov showed himself a typical envious and hysterical intellectual. The others, Deutsch, Zasulich, and very soon Plekhanov, also exhibited the overweening vanity, the self-centered sensitivity characteristic of the species.

In the immediate wake of the Congress it was still difficult for Lenin to face the full consequences of the split. To Potresov, who had once been close to Lenin, and whose demotion had occasioned least heat, he wrote: "Why should we, I ask myself, part for all life as enemies?" He realizes, he writes, that at times he had acted in an overwrought way, in a frenzy, but this had been provoked by the atmosphere of the debates. Lenin tried to reconstruct his own tactics at the Congress and confessed that his defeat over the phrasing of Article One of the Party Statute (about membership) made him all the more insistent to elect his slate of candidates for the editorial board and the Central Committee.[19] It was sad to go against Martov, but he was wrong and had to be defeated.

Yet the very same day Lenin wrote to Krzhizhanovsky in Russia. He had been his only other intimate friend addressed "thou," and had to be appraised of the betrayal: "Don't look at Martov in the old way. The friendship has ended. Down with any softness." According to Krupskaya this letter was never sent. But her testimony, this time given for a very laudable reason, cannot be trusted.[20] To Krzhizhanovsky Lenin wrote repeatedly at this period, not only about Party matters—Krzhizhanovsky being one of the three members of the Central Committee—but also because he had the need to communicate with his one remaining close friend. These letters bear witness to the rapid deterioration of his mood. At the Congress and immediately afterward, he preserved his composure, though it cost him a great deal. Now he grows almost hysterical, intermittently exultant and almost despondent. The Mensheviks are scheming and trying to undo the decisions of the majority at the Congress. "They think that they will turn the trick." But they will fail. But what is this news that the Mensheviks have captured the Party committees in Kharkov, the Don region, and elsewhere? He implores Krzhizhanovsky "for God's sake" to throw his weight against the vile intrigues. One can hardly imagine the baseness of the "Martovists," the full extent of the lies and villainies employed every day against him. Why, the other day Axelrod accused him, Lenin, of being a would-be dictator, and the Bolsheviks of having degenerated from revolutionaries into bureaucrats. "For Heaven's sake come here."

It often happens that a movement or cause defeated by history gains the reputation for moral probity and democratic scruples. Such has been the case, and in the main justly so, with the Mensheviks. But in 1903 they were still capable of some very energetic intrigues of their own. And Lenin's frantic tone was not unjustified. Had he remembered his addiction to chess he could not but have admired the cleverness of the moves with which the Mensheviks set out to wrest the Party and the precious *Iskra* from his grasp. In the first place, Martov and his partisans resolutely declined any compromise that would have left Lenin substantially in control of the Party's central organs. These negotiations were conducted by Maxim Litvinov. It was the debut in diplomacy for the future enormously skillful Commissar for Foreign Affairs and Ambassador to Washington. But this time the man who was to convince the world that Stalin's Russia desired collective security and peace failed. He was recognized as a tool

---

[19] *Works*, Vol. 34, p. 137.

[20] When she wrote her memoirs Stalin was already beginning his pitiless purges of the Party. The only way left for the old woman to indicate her disapproval and to hint at the need for moderation was to emphasize how tolerant Vladimir Ilyich had been and how much it cost him to part with those comrades who had erred. Hence she makes a great point of, and in the process probably exaggerates, Lenin's scruples over breaking with Martov.

of Lenin and not a genuine conciliator. "He should be chased out with a kick," wrote Martov, who with evident delight was plotting counterstrategy against his old friend. "Now," he continued, "our spirit is not broken by all those grotesque theatricalities [of Lenin], everything points to the fact that serious Socialists are with us and if we fight resolutely we shall win." [21]

The vulnerable point in Lenin's "control" of the Party and the logical target of the Mensheviks' attack was, of course, Plekhanov. It was unrealistic to assume that he would indefinitely remain "married" to Lenin, or that the admiration for the younger man would for long prevail over a nostalgic regret at parting with Axelrod and Zasulich. The meeting of the Emigré League of the Russian Socialists took place in October. This, according to the decision of the Second Party Congress, was the only legitimate representative of Russian Social Democracy abroad. But the Leninists expected the worst. Most of the Russian Socialists in Europe were bourgeois intellectuals likely to fall for the wiles of Mensheviks and incapable of appreciating the "hard" line sponsored by Lenin. And to be sure the majority of the League ranged themselves behind Martov. Lenin had, he thought, a card up his sleeve, in the presence of "his" man, a member of the Central Committee. The latter somewhat in a manner of the Tsarist police chief now declared the meeting illegal, and its decisions void. But even before that a decisive event took place. Martov and Lenin in their speeches reached new heights of bitterness and mutual recriminations. The former told all present that while arguing for the three-man editorial board Lenin had confided that the two of them could always outvote Plekhanov. That did it. Though Plekhanov listened to the charges with a forced smile and continued voting with Lenin, he now decided to shift his position.

"Overnight Plekhanov betrayed us," wrote Lenin. "Plekhanov came to us with a white flag," exulted Martov. In more prosaic terms the changeable patriarch demanded a reconstitution of the former editorial board of six persons, otherwise he would resign. Lenin rejected the ultimatum and himself resigned. Thereupon Plekhanov, as the sole remaining editor, coopted Martov and the three remaining old editors. Thus the decision of the Second Party Congress was within three months completely reversed. Lenin had split the Party to gain control of *Iskra* and now it was snatched, "stolen" from his hands. The joy of his opponents was great and Plekhanov's latest aphorism was much quoted: "Robespierre has fallen." But it was not only in deeper historical terms that the satisfaction and self-congratulation of the Mensheviks were premature. It was still impossible to have harmonious relations on the editorial board. To have Plekhanov as an ally was almost as time-consuming and irksome as to face his hostility.

[21] *The Letters of P. B. Axelrod and J. Martov* (in Russian), B. Nikolayevsky, Berlin, 1924, p. 92.

Soon he was talking of resigning again if this young insolent Trotsky were allowed to remain a contributor. Old Axelrod, the one man among the Socialists who enjoyed the friendship of Plekhanov and a kind of veneration from Trotsky, was finally able to smooth over their quarrel. But the latter was now also disenchanted with the Mensheviks and his brilliant articles appeared but rarely in *Iskra*.

This last incident is characteristic of a fatal weakness of the Mensheviks. Lenin's concept of party organization led logically to the emergence of one supreme leader. But the Mensheviks in rejecting this notion were incapable of producing a unified and disciplined party of their own. Eventually their group was bound to dissolve into a chorus of quarreling prima donnas. Their ideology, not to mince words, was, like that of the Bolsheviks, authoritarian: militant, revolutionary Marxism, which claims it has all the answers. In the struggle for political power it is fatal to combine an authoritarian ideology with democratic and humanitarian scruples. And in time under revolutionary conditions Lenin was bound to regain partisans in Russia. The revolutionary fever was rising, 1905 was approaching. And in a situation that called for action many of the reservations, scruples, and sentimental regard for the venerable veterans, which appeared to constitute the essence of Menshevism, were clearly irrelevant. Lenin's reputation in contrast was bound to grow. He was resolute, he was "hard," and he stood alone against those leaders who would talk socialism into its grave.

But at the end of 1903 those comforting signs were but dimly visible. For the moment Lenin had to settle down to save as much of his influence within the Party as was possible. Beaten within the Socialist circles in the West, could he not recoup his influence by working on the Socialists at home? With the help of the Central Committee within Russia he managed to procure a number of resolutions, written in suspiciously identical language, condemning the Mensheviks and demanding that they submit to the majority. The technique was both exasperatingly laborious and transparent. He would in effect draft the resolutions himself and then his agents in Russia would bully, hector, and cajole various "local" committees into sending them out west where he could display them triumphantly as a proof that the "masses" were behind the Bolsheviks. But the Central Committee, though now enlarged and of solid Leninist orientation, was growing weary of the Party dissension. Almost everybody at home wished for a reconciliation, could not understand why, with the moment of revolutionary struggle approaching, the Party could not present a solid front. Thus in the fantastic garden of Marxian heresies a new evil weed appeared. It was "Conciliationism" and against it Lenin was to inveigh throughout 1904 with a violence that led some of his strongest partisans in Russia to suspect that he was losing his mind. And within a few months "his" Central Committee had gone the way of "his" *Iskra*. In December

1904 his letter to the Caucasian comrades had blood-curdling references to new treacheries: "You are far from knowing in full the reptilian vileness of the Party Council and the Central Committee." Elsewhere he was willing to lift the curtain of mystery from the "reptilian vileness": "they" had systematically lied to the Party members at home, "they" had coopted new members to the Central Committee (which they had a perfect right to do—Lenin did not complain when he had been coopted in November 1903), "they" had exposed Lenin's part in splitting the Party to foreign Socialists. Intermittent with the denunciations were insistent pleas to the very same Central Committee to call another Party congress. This was to go unheeded until the Revolution of 1905. A Party congress meant a lot of expense, trouble, and danger. And the experience of the Second Congress was hardly of a nature to inspire great hopes in a new assembly. At times Lenin would turn upon the handful of his faithful followers. Nine tenths of them, he said, in February 1905, were "formalists," and he would gladly make Martov a present of them. But by then the revolution was in full swing and Lenin never had the chance to elaborate "formalism" into a fully grown heresy.

The two years between the Second Congress and Lenin's return to Russia provide one of the best-documented periods of his life. His base was again Geneva, and there amidst the divided and quarrelsome Russian colony he pursued his political and literary labors.

The relations between the Mensheviks and Bolsheviks in Geneva, still officially members of one Party, offer an early example of what the Soviet statesmen were to define as "peaceful coexistence." On occasion they could act in unison provided there was a joint enemy, like the resident Socialist Revolutionaries or anarchists. There were also, at times, social contacts and joint meetings though the latter were likely to turn into brawls. But in general each camp kept to itself and excessive fraternization was frowned upon by the leaders. It was not, for instance, considered permissible for a rank-and-file Bolshevik to socialize with, say, Martov without a special dispensation from Lenin, and whenever such unauthorized behavior was brought to his attention he would grow suspicious and the culprit would suffer a period of disgrace. For those people away from home, and united after all by their common hatred of Tsarism, politics still presented an almost insuperable barrier, even for a friendly chat. Thus one time Lenin forgot himself to the point of discussing intra-Party affairs with a Socialist Revolutionary. But soon, though the man in question was a veteran of the Land and Freedom movement, "Vladimir Ilyich became angry with himself that he had come to talk of Social Democratic affairs with someone who was a stranger to the Party."

But a "peaceful coexistence" within the Party involved incidents grimly reminiscent of intra-Party feuds in Soviet Russia. In Lenin's defense it must be pointed out that he was taunted almost beyond endurance. "Don't be too hard on Lenin," wrote Plekhanov in a letter that became public, "I think that much of his strange behavior can be simply explained by the fact that he totally lacks a sense of humor." Martov was plainly insulting; Lenin had realized how powerless he was; in resigning from *Iskra* he had run away crying "foul." He, however, gave back more than he received. An enthusiastic follower informed Lenin that he had known Plekhanov's brother in Russia. And what do you suppose he was? A police official! [22] There was nothing unusual, not to say disgraceful, about it. What revolutionary from the intelligentsia did not have a relative in the Tsar's service? But this was too good an opportunity to let pass. The young Bolshevik was appropriately instructed. At a public meeting and in the presence of the victim he shouted out his secret: the founder of Russian Marxism had a brother who was a police chief in a small town! Plekhanov sat staring without a word at his tormentor. For Valentinov the passage of fifty years did not erase a feeling of burning shame at the memory of his disgraceful performance. Another Bolshevik with a talent for drawing celebrated the discovery with a caricature. The scene: a Russian police station. The chief, Plekhanov, sits surrounded by police agents and constables with unmistakable features of the leading Mensheviks. Lenin was delighted.

There was this difference in the attitude of both sides toward their feud: the Mensheviks attacked, but in an almost playful spirit, expecting that some time everybody would shake hands and be friends again. Lenin reacted with a growing conviction that there was no room in *his* party for such personalities as Martov, Plekhanov, Trotsky, and the others. They were "anarchistic individualists." Martov's polemical blast, *The Struggle with the "State of Siege" in the Party*, is written with some levity. Lenin is needled on account of his "bonapartism" and bureaucratic tendencies, but there is no air of solemn excommunication. In Vladimir Ilyich's *One Step Forward, Two Steps Back or The Crisis in Our Party* it is not an injured individual who speaks and argues. It is as if the voice of history, of the working class, was addressing the Mensheviks warning them to mend their ways before it was too late. The phrasing of Article One, the problems of organization, those are not light matters, their resolution is not a game depending on a shifting majority or a clever speech. On one side is the "correct," the only way of settling those matters; on the other side, apostasy and a "betrayal" of the working class. Temperamentally Lenin was already eager to break definitely with the Mensheviks but imperative practical reasons kept him back. The leaders of international socialism would not tolerate it, the people back home would not understand.

Bolshevism as a state of mind was born, then, during those two years in Geneva. Lenin's relative isolation, his repeated defeats, would have been

[22] Valentinov, *op. cit.*, pp. 275–78.

unendurable without the growing conviction of his own infallibility on doctrinal and organizational matters. That conviction in turn led to an almost pathological suspiciousness about the motivations of the people who could not see the plain truth as expounded in *What Is To Be Done?* or in his latest article. Was it because they had studied under a renegade from Marxism? Did they fall under the spell of some strange reactionary philosophy? Or were they simply unable to cast off the habits and vices of the intelligentsia? Gradually this suspiciousness and intolerance of disagreement were to reach into spheres of thought and activity having nothing to do with politics.

Who were the people who were able to "take it," who clung to Lenin at this period? Many attempts have been made to generalize as to the distinctive traits of the Mensheviks or the Bolsheviks. The Mensheviks were, it has been observed, to a much larger extent of Jewish origin. Bolshevism, it is asserted, tended more to attract the ethnic Russians. Such generalizations may have some slight statistical justification, though like most political conclusions based upon race or religion they are exaggerated. The vital differences lie elsewhere. Organizations that emphasize firm leadership appeal often to the young, the activist, and the unreflective. They enlist doers rather than thinkers. Among Lenin's companions during his years in the wilderness, 1903–5, few had any independent moral or intellectual stature, as he himself was to recognize after 1917 when most of the survivors of the small band were relegated to very minor Soviet positions. One side of Lenin's nature exulted at the readiness of flighty intellectuals to flock under the Menshevik banner. On the other hand, since one *had* to have some intellectuals, was it not better to have the first-rate ones rather than second-rate? He viewed with mixed feelings also the brawling type of the revolutionary who, in compensation, was more attracted to the Bolsheviks than to their opponents. Many moral transgressions could be excused if the man was a resolute proletarian fighter but he did not always display a great sense of responsibility. One specimen, having been furnished with a passport and funds for a mission to Russia, got no farther than the nearest brothel, where his money vanished. And, despite all his instinctive liking for men of the people vs. intellectuals, Lenin could not shake off his distaste for their philosophical crudity. Many a Bolshevik was surprised to be told to have a brush-up session with Plekhanov, whom for all their intermittent warfare Lenin valued as a master of theoretical Marxism.

But it would be a mistake to forget Lenin's personal appeal. Valentinov's memoirs sketch its main ingredients very well. There was about Lenin, as there often is around a leader, a certain air of mystery. Valentinov, who after all was not a schoolboy (he was going on thirty) recounts his hanging around his leader trying to find out what made this man tick. Other luminaries in Geneva conformed to the revolutionary stereotypes: Plekhanov—the thinker; Martov—the polemicist; Trotsky—

the man of action. In Lenin there appeared to be something else, a peculiar gift both to attract and to repel people. What could account for those abrupt shifts of mood from immense reasonableness to frantic irritability, from comradely joviality to abusive rage? Was there some incident in Lenin's past, a secret wound, a love affair perhaps, to explain this puzzling personality? There was a noticeable feeling of distance between Lenin and the others in his camp. One did not really have conversations with him, one reported or listened to instructions and aphorisms. This ability to convey a sense of superiority while living in such close quarters with a small band of followers, and at a time when his political fortunes were low, goes far to explain Lenin's future domination of his colleagues in Soviet Russia, and his ability to carry the day even over those who, like Trotsky, were intellectually his superiors.

This feeling of distance did not at the same time suggest, as in the case of Plekhanov, a sense of professional or *grand seigneur* aloofness. His manners were simple and direct. He would join in singing and joking with his enchanted disciples. He took a childish delight in physical exercise and in hiking through the Alps. Lenin captured Valentinov's heart forever, it seemed, that afternoon when he helped him carry a very heavy trunk across Geneva (Valentinov was earning his livelihood as a porter and was performing this service for a more affluent Socialist). Certainly nobody could have ever expected Herzen, Bakunin, or Plekhanov to help a humble follower on an errand of this kind! But in Lenin's gesture there was neither a pose nor a hint of fraternization. It was the kind of simplicity and good nature that could only rivet more firmly the affection and reverence of an impressionable young man. And there were other incidents of this kind.

The other side of the coin was Lenin's air of self-assurance and the ability to mesmerize an opponent in a dispute through sheer intensity and repetition. The protagonist would emerge shaken, either coerced into accepting the revolutionary gospel according to Lenin, or utterly revolted by the strange power that emanated from the man. Lenin argued not with the polite and condescending witticisms and quotations of Plekhanov, he argued as if exorcising his opponent of the demons of opportunism, Martovism, all others. The Russian revolutionary tended to be either a vacillating soul or, on the contrary, given to despondency when the desired aim was not immediately in sight. Lenin impressed both by his iron will and his evident ability to wait out the periods of defeat and disorganization. He was sure, he told Valentinov, that he would live to see the triumph of socialism in Russia. Another follower in 1907, when the triumph seemed further away than ever, was questioning what would happen when the revolution came. Lenin, the account continues, answered jocularly that people would be asked whether they were for or against the revolution. If against they would be stood up against a wall and shot, if for it they would be invited to work with the Bolsheviks. This simple formula aroused a humanitarian objection of his wife, the only recorded instance of Nadezhda disagreeing with Vladimir Ilyich: you would be penalizing people for having the courage of their convictions, and encouraging hypocrites. There was a great deal in this objection, notes the author, but he adds, when the Revolution did come Lenin's "joke" turned out "more or less" a correct interpretation of the events. How could it be otherwise, he asks philosophically.[23] This ability to portray with conviction the future moments of triumph and retribution was another source of his appeal to the wavering and uncertain, seeking assurance that their toils and sacrifices were not in vain. In the more sensitive such "jokes" produced a feeling of revulsion, combined at times with an impression that their author was not to be taken seriously. But the appeal of violence was inherent in the revolutionary's make-up. That Lenin made no bones about it was another asset in his struggle against his rivals. They, for all their blood-and-thunder oratory (witness Plekhanov at the Second Congress) were suspected, rightly, as the events were to show, of being incapable of truly decisive measures in dealing with the class enemy. In 1904 while his competitors had merely adherents, Lenin had followers.

It was a small group of them that gathered in August to renew the struggle.[24] Their number was not imposing: only twenty-two including Lenin and his wife. The manifesto of the twenty-two repeated the indictment of the Mensheviks at which he had been hammering with a wearying insistence: they were "intelligentsia elements" incapable of submitting to the Party discipline. They were "anarchistic." On behalf of the now clearly fictitious majority was invoked the equally fictitious voice of the masses of proletarians in Russia demanding the calling of the Third Party Congress. The Menshevik leaders were characterized as "the old literary colleagues who have lost the confidence of the Party." It was a splendid defiance of the logic of events, though largely fraudulent insofar as its assertions were concerned. A lesser man confronted with the lack of funds and desertion of partisans would have capitulated. Lenin persisted and fought.

His strength of will was not superhuman. After the conference he had to take a month's rest from politics. On his return his spirits were buoyed up by the Bolsheviks' ability to produce some funds for the production of their own paper. Their source remains obscure, though the Mensheviks claimed that they came from the misappropriated general Party funds. From December 1904 *Vperyod* (*Forward*) gave Lenin a platform for blasting the Mensheviks and for commenting on fast-changing conditions

[23] V. I. Adoratsky, "Meetings with Lenin," *The Proletarian Revolution,* Moscow, 1924–26, No. 3, p. 97.

[24] One participant claims it took place actually in September but for conspiratorial reasons (?) it was called the August Conference. M. Lyadov, *From the Life of the Party 1903–1907,* Moscow, 1956, p. 61.

in Russia. Once he could write, thunder, and denounce, his good spirits returned. His group now daringly and grandiosely declared itself the Bureau of the Committees of the Majority and its agents pursued its aims within Russia. In view of Lenin's denunciations of the "anarchistic intellectuals," it is noteworthy that his two main lieutenants of the time could well serve as the classical examples of the species. They were A. A. Bogdanov, much given to obtuse philosophical speculations, and A. V. Lunacharsky, a second-rate dramatic author and *bon vivant*, the future Soviet Commissar of Education. That he found himself in such uncongenial company was a reflection of the fact he often bewailed in private: the Bolsheviks lacked people with literary talents, and he had to cling to what was available.

And so the wrangling went on while in Russia the revolutionary game was beginning to be played in earnest. Ever since February 1904 the Empire had been at war with Japan. The disappointments, then the defeats of the war heightened the revolutionary fever of the society. On Sunday, January 9 (22 in the West), 1905, the St. Petersburg police fired on an unarmed crowd of workers marching on the Winter Palace to submit a petition to the Tsar. The January massacre (according to the authorities casualties ran into the hundreds, according to others into the thousands) marks the beginning of the revolution, a general rehearsal for the greater one. All the main ingredients of 1917 were already present: riots and barricades in the main cities of the Empire, widespread peasant disorders and seizures of land, military and naval mutinies, all against the background of a military defeat.

One would have expected that at the news of the January massacre all the quarreling Socialist potentates would have composed their differences and immediately rushed back to Russia. This was after all the moment for which they had lived, worked, and prayed ever since their youth. Nothing of the kind! At home the Mensheviks and the Bolsheviks joined in the uprisings. The squabbles about Article One, about the old versus the new editorial board of *Iskra* were shoved aside in view of the more important and immediate tasks. But in Geneva or Paris the exiled leaders were not in an undue hurry to return and give direction to their followers. Tactical advice and appraisals of the revolutionary situation flowed freely in the columns of both *Iskra* and *Vperyod*, but so did mutual recriminations and rival political programs. Not until November, ten months after the beginning of the revolution, when the crest of the revolutionary feeling had been reached, did Lenin return to guide his followers in Russia.

Uncharitable commentators have attributed his dilatoriness to nothing more complicated than fear for his person. To be sure, in both 1905 and 1917 he was most unwilling to expose his person to danger. By November an amnesty had been proclaimed and it was relatively safe to return. As early as 1900 Lenin expressed his conviction that it would not do for *a leader* to expose his person needlessly to arrests and imprisonment. This common-sense viewpoint was subsequently elevated by the Soviet histori- ans into another attribute of his conspiratorial genius. "He had a remark- able sense of knowing when to flee," wrote their luminary Pokrovsky. The Mensheviks ran at the last moment, Lenin always well in advance of the police.[25] But even this prudence, if unheroic, was not the main reason for his delay in 1905. He simply could not bring himself to believe that a So- cialist revolution *then* had any chance of succeeding.

   This must seem as the most outrageous paradox of all. How could Lenin, who from the beginning urged armed action by the Socialists, de- nounced moderation, upbraided the Mensheviks for their alleged lack of militant spirit, be accused of faintheartedness about the masses seizing power? He who was fully confident of seeing socialism triumph in his life- time! But there is really no paradox, no contradiction between those atti- tudes. What revolutionary leader in 1905, for all the readiness with which the words "masses" and "revolution" came to their lips, could believe in the imminence of a *Socialist* victory? The whole history of the Russian revolutionary movement had testified how virtually impossible it was to stir up the people at large on behalf of a Socialist ideal. The most success- ful exploit of Land and Freedom consisted of persuading the peasants of a small region that the *Tsar* wanted them to rise against the landowners and bureaucrats. Lately socialism had been growing among the workers, but it was still a small minority of a class that was itself a small segment of the population that could be counted upon to follow revolutionary Marx- ism. The very spontaneity and violence of 1905 came as a surprise not only to the Tsar and his advisers but also to such persons as Lenin. And even then, for all his bitter invectives against the liberals and constitu- tionalists he believed that a period of a bourgeois democratic republic must intervene before a real Marxian revolution would take place. It was the obliging democratic bourgeois regime that by granting political freedom would enable the Socialists to organize the *whole* working class and to lead it in the decisive combat. Thus there was no hurry to return to Russia.

   We must not superimpose the Lenin of 1917 upon the Lenin of 1905. Then he was ready to echo Tkachev's insistent cry: "To prepare a revolu- tion is not up to the revolutionary. It is being prepared all the time by the exploiters, capitalists, landowners. . . . The revolutionary does not *pre- pare* but *makes* the revolution. Then make it. Do it right away. It is crimi- nal to be indecisive, to delay. . . ." In 1905 he was still preparing the revolution. The very militancy and violence, he counseled the workers, was in order to push the cowardly middle class to greater decisiveness, to an overthrow of autocracy.

   How unsure of themselves the Socialists really were is well illuminated by the events that took place a few weeks after the Bloody Sunday of Jan-

[25] *The Young Guard*, Moscow, 1924, No. 2–3, p. 248.

uary 9. To Geneva came Father Gapon, the Orthodox priest who had led
the masses in their march to the Winter Palace. There could be no doubt
about Gapon's background. He had, with the encouragement and subsidies
of the police, organized a workers' union, thus continuing the work of
Zubatov. The union had scrupulously excluded Socialists and Jews. For a
while the police could congratulate themselves on their enterprise. Gapon
seemed to be a born leader inculcating in the growing mass of his followers loyalty to the Tsar and faith and obedience to the Holy Orthodox
Church. What finally led this obedient tool of the authorities to lead the
strike and the procession that triggered off the revolution is still uncertain.
His head was obviously turned by his success, his sympathies clearly
aroused by the misery of his men. There is every likelihood that, like many
who found themselves at once in the revolutionary movement and within
the world of the police, he became mentally deranged. The march was to
be peaceful, he told the workers; they were going to lay at the feet of the
Tsar a humble supplication to relieve the misery of his people and to grant
them freedom. Yet he also talked wildly about a revolution if the Tsar was
to scorn their pleas. Some argue that Gapon had the fantastic vision of the
Emperor summoning him to his side to be his minister and to rule Russia.
After the catastrophe Gapon hid and then fled the country, leaving behind
a manifesto cursing Nicholas II as the hangman of his people and urging a
revolution.

It was this man who now appeared in the West dressed in the aura of a
people's leader and mortal foe of the autocracy. George Gapon was lion-
ized and fussed over by the Socialist and progressive circles in Germany
and France, besieged by pleas for articles, memoirs, and the like. The Russians had every reason to know better: Gapon had certain peasant cunning, but was politically illiterate, and his personal tastes were rather
inappropriate for either a revolutionary or a priest: he was unusually fond
of gambling and drinking. Yet he became an object of a spirited competition among various branches of the radical movement. At first this
priceless asset was seized by the Socialist Revolutionaries. Their agent
Rutenberg, with him ever since the St. Petersburg days, was charged with
protecting him from the wiles of the Social Democrats and others. But
Gapon now envisaged himself as the leader of the whole revolutionary
movement, and would grant audiences, and preside over conferences.

Lenin was not backward in this sordid competition to capture and use
the man who was mentally unhinged and had all the mannerisms of a con
man. The reason was obvious: Gapon had obviously a special gift to capture popular imagination and to lead the masses. He had spoken to, inspired, and led thousands of workers. Lenin had once addressed fifteen
Russian workers, he recalled ruefully in 1904. In the wake of the
Bloody Sunday he wondered whether the "little father" [26] was despite his
shady past a genuine Christian Socialist, a representative of the young and

[26] An actual form of address to the parish priest.

more progressive clergy (Gapon was Lenin's age). Soon he became more affirmative: "Facts have decided in favor of Gapon." And in a tribute to Gapon's movement, he asks, and this has an eloquence of its own: "Can the Social Democrats seize this spontaneous movement?" [27]

But it proved to be impossible to ensnare Gapon. He started by playing the role of the leader of *all* the revolutionary parties. When that proved impractical he announced his conversion to Social Democracy and held a series of conferences with Lenin. To his credit, Plekhanov viewed the whole plot with distaste and skepticism. When the "little father" announced his conversion and repaired to Plekhanov, the still acknowledged pope of the Russian Marxists, the latter told him not to speak nonsense but to read some books and find out what Marxism was about. Some days later he met Gapon on the street. Asked how his education was progressing the "little father" announced his return to the Socialist Revolutionaries; there, he explained, one did not have to read dull books; the Socialist Revolutionaries instructed him in such interesting occupations as shooting, riding, making bombs, and the like. Plekhanov, for once living up to his reputation as a wit, informed Gapon that the perfidious Socialist Revolutionaries were withholding from him their greatest secret. Like most of his kind Gapon was inordinately suspicious and he begged to be let in on the secret. Why, how to fly in a balloon, said Plekhanov with a straight face. The "little father" glared and there was no more question of his accession to the Social Democrats. The circumstances of Gapon's death do not reflect credit on the revolutionary movement. He soon returned to Russia, but it proved impossible for him to resume his previous role. He entered into negotiations with the police. Informed about this by his guardian angel Rutenberg, the Central Committee of the Socialist Revolutionaries passed a sentence of death on the man who had deceived their hopes. Even by the strict revolutionary code there was scant justification for this decision: Gapon had not as yet betrayed any revolutionaries and a public warning rather than an execution was in order. Rutenberg, who had grown fond of this strange man, had to arrange the assassination of his friend. After the deed the Central Committee compounded its unsavory role by issuing a public denial of its complicity in the murder. All in all, the Social Democrats could congratulate themselves on their failure to win Gapon to their cause.[28]

But the whole episode underlines the frantic search of the Social Democrats, Lenin included, for some means, some person, to enable them to

---

[27] *Works*, Vol. 8, p. 93.

[28] The Socialist Revolutionaries' denial placed the unfortunate Rutenberg in an impossible position within the revolutionary circles. He bitterly fought for years for a vindication. Some years afterward it became clear that the leading spirit of the Socialist Revolutionaries at the time of Gapon's execution in 1906, Yevno Azev, was a police agent himself and probably had personal reasons for wishing him out of the way.

grasp control of the masses gripped by the revolution. For a century the Russian radicals had despaired of seeing the masses in actual revolt against the Tsar. They would grasp at every straw to persuade themselves that the people could rise. The brigands and impostors of the seventeenth and eighthteenth centuries were elevated to the stature of revolutionary heroes because they could sway masses of ignorant Cossacks and peasants and turn them against the government. Some members of the People's Will were encouraged by the anti-Jewish pogroms, not because they were anti-Semitic, but because they saw in them a proof that the people's wrath could be turned against law and order. But by and large both the terrorism of the Socialist Revolutionaries and the Marxism of the Social Democrats had reflected their disbelief in the possibility of enlisting the people behind their course: individual acts of violence and economic changes respectively were to bring about an overthrow of autocracy. Now the revolution was teaching them to be more optimistic but hardly more democratic. The people *could* be stirred up to revolutionary violence, but not behind any concrete political aims. Hence if one wanted to capture the masses one had if necessary to deceive them, ride the crest of their grievances and aspirations, even if the latter had nothing to do with or even ran against the principles of Marxism.

To Lenin the violent events of 1905 were a special revelation and lesson. He had thought of a revolution in terms of propaganda, agitation, and a party well organized and disciplined but of necessity small. Now another and vital element was added, the manipulation of the aroused masses. His still lingering doubts about the possibility of a *Socialist* revolution, combined with his growing faith in the possibility of *exploiting* a general disorder and anarchy, are well expressed in the proclamation of his Bureau of the Committees of the Majority printed in *Vperyod* on March 8 and distributed in Russia. On one hand it warns: ". . . One should not forget that the revolution is strong morally but not physically. The basis of that [moral] strength is the sympathy and support of all the classes save a handful of reactionaries. Consequently . . . one should not forget the interests and the psychology of those classes. . . . One should protect private property from *aimless* damage and looting. . . ." On the other hand: ". . . To be sure there can be no unconditional restraints on the defense of the revolution . . . under certain conditions all means become allowable . . . arson . . . terrorist acts. . . . *As a general rule such means should be avoided.*" [29]

This is already a considerable step in the direction of Lenin's tactics of 1917. But as yet there was a considerable diffidence and caution, and an utter disbelief that the Socialists, not to mention the Bolsheviks, could seize power in Russia.

[29] Italics in the original. Quoted from *The Third Congress of the Russian Social Democratic Party, Documents and Materials*, Moscow, 1955, pp. 63–64.

Thus 1905 closes another period in Lenin's life and in his development as a political leader. Had the revolution not come (and the same would be true of the war of 1914) it is likely that Bolshevism would have remained an isolated and not very potent element in Russian politics. The revolution was to raise his hopes and then to disappoint them cruelly. But from it, as from most adversities in his political life, he was to draw lessons that served him well in the hour of triumph. He liked to quote the peasant proberb: "He who has been whipped is worth two who have not."

At this mid-point Lenin was still something of an enigma to his followers as well as to his enemies. His appearance was quite ordinary: a bit shorter than the average (five feet six), though there are inexplicably some references to him as "tiny." He was now bald with a fringe of reddish hair and beard. Nearsighted in one eye, Lenin was wont to squint. Some of his contemporaries remembered Lenin's appearance as either "striking" or "repulsive." A Soviet hagiographer presents it as that of a "wise peasant," but those are later emendations. With his large head and Kalmyk features he looked not untypical of a Russian from the Volga region. His dress and demeanor again were characteristic in a Russian of his class.

If it were possible for a moment to forget about his politics, Lenin appears as the very embodiment of the middle-class intelligentsia virtues. He was a devoted son and husband and a solicitous brother. The very avidity with which the biographers seize upon an isolated incident such as his quarrel as a boy with Alexander, or talking back to his parents, is a proof of his irreproachably normal family affections. Few persons, let alone revolutionaries, could have endured as good-naturedly the presence, in cramped quarters, of the mother-in-law who was constantly with the Ulyanovs until her death in the beginning of the War. The inability to have children was to Lenin a source of profound regret. At every step in his career Lenin sought and found help within his family, from Anna editing his literary works to Maria's care during his last and fatal illness. Even brother Dimitri, not particularly close to Lenin and evidently not held by him in high esteem, was enlisted for advice (he was a doctor) when Krupskaya fell ill. In brief, a thoroughly harmonious and unsensational setting offering no handle for Freudian speculations and conclusions. His sole addictions were chess and books.

As in the case of Queen Victoria, confronted with so much virtue the modern writer gropes for some evidence of the weaknesses of the flesh. He has every right to be exasperated and even suspicious, for not content with letting well enough alone, the Soviet authorities have censored or embellished the available evidence to the point where Lenin appears not human at all. Still, the pickings are very slim. Mr. Bertram Wolfe has devoted considerable effort to tracing Lenin's relations with Inessa Armand, a fellow Bolshevik whom we shall meet in the next chapter.[30] But all that

[30] See *Encounter*, January, 1964.

can be established is that Lenin at one period of his life was very much attached to the woman who in addition to sharing his political beliefs was obviously livelier and more intelligent than Krupskaya, and that he addressed her by the familiar "thou." Even if there was a more passionate connection it was evidently managed with discretion and was not allowed to interfere either with his marriage or with his vocation. And so our historical voyeurism must remain unsatisfied.

Indeed the bohemianism and dissipation not absent in many revolutionaries' lives were alien to Lenin's nature, though his distaste for them never degenerated into an obsession. He viewed philosophically but with evident disapproval the loosening of family and moral bonds, an inevitable side effect of the Revolution and the Civil War. He would not try to impose, as Stalin was to attempt in the 1930s, a code of middle-class moral values on Russia. All this talk and practice of free love, of the abolition of the family, and so on, was for him yet another "infantile disease" of Communism, a necessary if regrettable symptom of the transition from bourgeois to Socialist society. And in the latter one would achieve a genuine basis for conjugal relations and parental authority. A sensible middle-class attitude, especially when constrasted with the nervousness of the current Soviet authorities when it comes to sex or youthful exuberance, not to mention the hideous puritanism of the Chinese Communists.

The same balanced view characterized Lenin on the subject of the arts and literature. "Shameful not to know Turgenev," he used to say, though his favorite author was the very embodiment of "rotten liberalism" in politics. He appreciated even that arch reactionary Dostoevsky, and like almost every Russian, though fearful of Tolstoy's moral and political influence, he paid homage to his genius. Modern art, modern poetry were a closed book. "What do they teach them now," he sighed when the Communist youths proclaimed that they no longer studied Pushkin, a "bourgeois" poet, but were enraptured by the "proletarian" poetry of Mayakovsky. But that too shall pass; and there was nothing in his disapproval of that obsessive rage with which his successors greeted the new, the experimental, and nonconformist in the arts.

In brief, he was a typical cultured Russian gentlemen of his generation, with a touch, much as he would have resented the knowledge of it, of bourgeois sentimentality in his tastes. He could listen, he declared, for hours to Tchaikovsky or Beethoven, but at times classical music instead of soothing his nerves excited him. It evoked languor and contentment, and yet there were urgent political tasks calling for concentration and ruthlessness! He seldom could sit through a concert. In contrast there were the stirring popular and revolutionary songs, conducive to alertness rather than lachrymose contemplation.

The words "culture" and "cultured" had long been used by the Russian radicals in a special sense, and so they were by Lenin. Russia was "uncultured" because of her autocracy, because of the peasant, and because of the grossness of her social relations. But in addition to anguish there was an unconscious element of national sensitivity and defiance in this oft-repeated declaration. Just because of her backwardness Russia was going to "show" the world some day. And how really "cultured" was the West with its vast disparities of wealth and its bourgeois hypocrisy? Outwardly, as behooved a Marxist, Lenin was a Westernizer with none of the Populist's guilty passion for the primitiveness of the peasant or other aspects of the Russian scene. But his deeply felt nationalism became evident during his long years in exile. He moved through Paris, London, Cracow, and other cities almost oblivious of his surroundings (except for libraries and parks) as long as they had nothing to do with politics. In his two years in Austrian Poland he failed to learn Polish, even to the point of getting the gist of a newspaper article. Yet the proximity of the two Slavic languages is so great that it is almost incredible for a Russian to spend two years in a Polish-speaking environment without learning it. He was horrified to discover that Kautsky did not know who Nekrasov was, though there was no obvious reason for a German Socialist to know the not very distinguished Russian poet. To be a Russian chauvinist was for Lenin "uncultured," to adhere to the bullying ways of Tsarism. But his very parochialism made him leave an imprint of nationalism on Bolshevism, and thus set the stage for Stalin.

Martov, who had no reason to be tender toward his victorious enemy and knew him better then most, thought Lenin personally modest and devoid of vanity. Hard as it is to endorse this judgment, the fact is that Lenin never tried to create a mystique around himself, strove to exact homage, or posed as a great thinker. A hardened egotist would hardly worship (as he did at times) Plekhanov or the German Social Democracy, or feel so deeply their subsequent betrayal or weakness. There is, with one huge exception to be noted below, no trace of fanaticism about Lenin, no irrational drive or ambition. He was a passionate but prudent politician, always capable of accounting for the possibility of defeat or delay, gauging realistically the strengths and capabilities of his opponents. We do not find in Lenin the sadism and personal vindictiveness characteristic of Stalin. But as the aftermath of the Revolution was to show, he was equally incapable of true generosity toward a defeated enemy, or of gestures of humanitarianism where no political gain was evident.

One must turn now to one great exception to what has been said, one great passion of Lenin's life that cannot be accounted for by politics, which as a matter of fact often clashed with his political judgment and undid or threatened to undo his rational designs. This was his hatred of the intelligentsia. It runs like a thread through his personal and public life, and provides much if not most of the emotional intensity behind the revolutionary strivings. Phrases such as "the intelligentsia scum," "the scoundrelly intellectuals," "that riffraff," run continually through his writings.

Nor is it easy to account for this feeling by the currently fashionable view of a man's frequent dislike for his own class, nation, or race. The concept of the Russian intelligentsia was so amorphous, the world of its beliefs and habits so widespread and unstable, ranging from liberalism to terrorism, that it appears to be a bizarre target for so much genuine hate. The revolutionary has often exalted the simple people and denigrated the intellectual, but never with the same intensity as is the case with Lenin. Even the staunchest reactionary who blamed all of Russia's troubles on the Jews and the intellectuals seldom approached Lenin's violence. His fury was aroused by any concept, any postulate, any phenomenon that in some circuitous way could reflect the mentality of the intelligentsia: liberalism, independence of the judiciary, parliamentarism. Very often while arguing for the very same postulate, say for an alliance between the liberals and the Socialists, Lenin still broke out with the most intemperate abuse of the people he wanted as allies.

In January 1905 Lenin addressed a letter to be smuggled to some Bolsheviks awaiting a public trial in St. Petersburg. In itself the gist of the letter is not without interest and some unconscious humor. His main concern was that the accused should cast good figures in court. The Socialist Revolutionaries, when tried, scorned to plead extenuating circumstances and in the manner of Zhelyabov proudly advertised their beliefs and accused the regime. Now it was important that in the eyes of the revolutionary youth the Social Democrats should also appear as heroic figures braving danger and scorning leniency. That there was something incongruous in giving this instruction from the safe haven of Geneva did not even occur to Lenin. The defendants not surprisingly were abashed at this authorization to become martyrs.

But the most revealing part of the letter is Lenin's almost insane eruption of hatred toward a leading segment of the intelligentsia, lawyers. Their advocates, he helpfully advises the defendants, are to be treated roughly and to be put in an exposed position! Those scoundrels of the intelligentsia are apt to create trouble. The people who are faced with the threat of years at hard labor in Siberia are to instruct their lawyers as follows: "If you son of a bitch will allow yourself the slightest indecency or political opportunism (like talking about the political immaturity of the defendants, the errors of socialism . . . repudiation by the Social Democrats of force, the peaceful nature of their teaching, etc.) then I the accused will give you hell publicly, will denounce you as a scoundrel, and renounce you as my counsel." [31] That the letter was written by a man possessed can be seen by its very incoherence. The defendants are to say all those things to their lawyers not crudely but "softly and cleverly." Lawyers are not to be believed, *especially* if they declare that they are Socialists themselves. They are to be told: "You little liberal clown cannot

[31] *Works*, Vol. 8, p. 51.

understand my convictions." And thus Lenin about his own profession. If there was one institution in Russia that stood up to the Tsarist regime and many of whose members exemplified civic courage, it was the bar. Lenin himself had been a beneficiary of this progressive and civic-minded spirit of the legal profession. But as we shall see repeatedly, personal favors dispensed from the hands of the intelligentsia and liberals only hardened his contempt and hatred of the class.

That there was something elemental and inexplicable in his passion against the intelligentsia was seen and deplored even by those closest to him. Krupskaya tried to account for it by an edifying tale: on brother Alexander's arrest the liberal society of Simbirsk shunned the Ulyanovs. Nobody would accompany the mother of the would-be assassin of the Tsar on her journey to the nearest railway point, which the poor woman had to make alone and on horseback. But that, as we saw, was hardly the whole story. There were people, such as the director of Vladimir's gymnasium, who were most helpful to the stricken family. And the very regime that martyred his brother was never hated by Vladimir Ulyanov with the same passion he expended on his own class.

Perhaps a clue may be found in Lenin's awareness of how much he himself belonged to that class and his apparent inability to shake off many of its mannerisms and characteristics. His attempts in that direction often involved him in semicomical dilemmas. The Russian radical could hardly indulge in any activity without gravely considering its "class character." Lenin was extremely fastidious. He cleaned his desk every day, sewed on his buttons, while Krupskaya was busy decoding letters from Russia or at similar work. But while this was a mark of distinction from a *revolutionary intelligent* with his notorious disorderliness, was it not really the kind of behavior appropriate to a bourgeois intellectual? The same with sports. He liked to hunt and to hike in the mountains, at the time rather unusual amusements for an average middle-class person. But weren't those the avocations more befitting a nobleman than a revolutionary? But, as he explained precisely, the revolutionary had to keep in shape, for he might have to overpower or to outrun a policeman.

The same dilemma with manners. By upbringing he was a cultured gentleman. A Russian equivalent of a four-letter word did not come to his tongue as naturally and spontaneously as it does to Mr. Khrushchev's. Yet by design he could be vulgarly abusive, both in speech and in writing. This was the product of a philosophy enunciated to Valentinov: "You are obviously shocked that in the Party we do not use language appropriate in a girls' finishing school. . . . If the Social Democrats in their politics, propaganda, and polemics would employ nothing but tame and nonprovocative language they would be worse than those melancholy Protestant ministers. . . ." [32] And he invoked the highest authority: how vulgar and abusive Marx was when dealing with a political opponent.

[32] Valentinov, *op. cit.*, p. 333.

There is a pathetic footnote to this contrived philosophy of bad manners. Lenin was lying paralyzed during his last illness. He learned from his wife that Stalin was rude to her. There is no reason to put any sinister interpretation upon this incident, as many have. Krupskaya naturally wanted to preserve the invalid from agitation. But at this slight to his wife Lenin, in the manner of a typical *barin,* a gentleman of the old regime, dictated a note to Stalin breaking off personal relations. And he wrote a note urging Stalin's removal as the General Secretary because of his *rudeness.* He was still aware how incongruous it was for him to allege bad manners as the grounds for a political decision. Rudeness and bad manners, he wrote with a sick man's defensiveness, are for us Communists "trifles," but "such trifles may sometime assume a decisive character."

Lenin's pathological hatred of the intelligentsia and the middle class was combined, the greatest paradox of all, with a very distinctive intellectual snobbery. He did not believe that either the revolution or the Socialist state could dispense with the leadership of educated and technically qualified people. This never-resolved conflict between his emotions and his practicality will be best illustrated during the Soviet period. There we shall see Lenin intermittently exulting in the sufferings inflicted upon the intelligentsia and pitifully bewailing the lack of educated, "cultured" people to run the institutions of the Socialist state. For the "common man's" ability to run a revolution or a state he had nothing but contempt.[33] But it was not that the realities of power sobered him, for throughout his political life Lenin never forgot that the hated intelligentsia were still the key to the success of the revolutionary or of any political movement in Russia. Lose its sympathy or allegiance and your vaunted masses would be like so many sheep. Any philosophical or religious fad that might turn the interests of the middle class away from politics, Tolstoy's Christian anarchism, the neo-idealist philosophy, became for him an enemy dwarfing even the Mensheviks or autocracy.

Was there one institution of the bourgeois intellectual world that Lenin regarded with awe and the rules of which he was unquestioningly ready to respect? Yes, there was: libraries and library regulations. A fervent book lover, Lenin judged the degree of culture of a given locality according to its library resources. If anything could reconcile him to London, that bastion of plutocracy and imperialism, it was the wonders of the library of the British Museum. In 1920 the Chairman of the Council of the Commissars and virtual dictator of Russia wrote this humble letter to the Rumyantsev Public Library in Moscow: He understands that books are not lent out, but might he have just overnight two Greek dictionaries, and he promises to return them first thing in the morning? And practically on his deathbed he addressed an urgent note to Anna: a book lent out to him, again in the way of an exception, has disappeared and it is evidently her

---

[33] We shall consider the apparent rebuttal to this contained in his *State and Revolution.*

adopted son who took it. If so will he return it as soon as possible, for Lenin will be blamed! [34] If the Guild of Librarians, that much-suffering segment of the intelligentsia, needs a patron saint, surely it ought to be Vladimir Ilyich Lenin.

Generations of the Russian radicals have had a love affair with "the people." But by 1900 this love affair had cooled off. Certainly for a Marxist the peasant could not be the object of the naïve worship of the Land and Freedom radicals: the exemplar of moral virtues, an instinctive Socialist, the pillar of future Communist society. In fact he was something of a savage whose ferocity if properly exploited could be turned to use in overthrowing the old regime, but who, by the same token, was going to make trouble when it came to establishing a rational, "cultured" Socialist society. Many Marxists simply disregarded this inconvenient feature of the social scene. But for Lenin the peasants still constituted an overwhelming majority of Russia's population. One could not simply consign them to the category of petty bourgeois, sigh over their invulnerability to Marxism, and let it go at that. The Revolution of 1905 opened the eyes of the Socialists to the still crucial position of the *moujik*. This strange creature at times would show revolutionary zeal: the peasants would seize the gentry's lands, burn their residences, and attack the police. But then they would subside into their age-long lethargy. The peasant soldier would show no compunction when ordered to fire on his fellow peasants.

Lenin viewed the peasant without any sentimentality. For him as to his successors up to this very day, he was the clod standing in the way of progress, his psychology primitive and narrowly materialistic and incompatible with the requirements of socialism. But he saw that one could not approach him, at least in Russia, from the doctrinaire Marxian point of view. A revolution could not be achieved without winning over or at least neutralizing a large segment of the peasantry, if need be by forgetting Marxism and catering to its aspirations. The heirs of the Populists, the Socialist Revolutionaries, were proving to be influential in the countryside. The Marxian Socialists had to compete with them and outbid them for the peasants' affections.

Thus 1905 marks the beginning of the concentrated effort to woo the peasant. From the beginning this effort was marked by insincerity and irritation, for the peasant could not be told what was his final destiny in the Marxist commonwealth: "the idiocy of rural life," as Marx puts it, liquidated, and the villagers assimilated to the status and condition of the industrial workers. No, the peasant has to be promised the satisfaction of his craving: land, more land. Had Lenin's allegiance to Marxism been superficial this need for political maneuvering would not have been felt so hard. But since he took his ideology seriously, this obstinate preference of the peasant to live poorly and primitively on *his own* plot rather than to be a

---

[34] *Works*, Vol. 38, p. 459.

workman in a large scientifically run state farm was felt to be an aberration, a sin against enlightenment and progress. In struggling with the peasant mentality, the Bolsheviks were already beginning to feel that they were struggling against the kingdom of darkness. Here were the seeds of the fury with which the Party under Stalin was to fall upon the countryside to beat and to coerce the peasants into collectivizing, to pay them back for all the temporizing measures and concessions it had granted for a quarter of a century.

For the Socialists the peasant's role of the *noble* savage was assumed by the worker. For Lenin the faith in the natural goodness of the proletarian was the reverse side of his loathing of the intelligentsia. But like the latter it often gave way to practical and political considerations. The workers are heroic and pure but alas, few of them are capable of leadership or of administering the Socialist state. If in their ignorance they should stray from the path of socialism, they have to be dealt with severely. After power was in his hands but a few days Lenin was not squeamish in calling for the suppression of those labor unions that opposed the Bolsheviks. He was to shed no tears over the ruthless massacre of the Kronstadt sailors and proletarians. We shall not be far wrong in attributing to Lenin the sentiments toward the workers that the European officers in the imperial days had toward their native troops: affection, not unmixed with condescension.

That there was real affection and an element of envy, one might almost say, of the proletarian's simple mentality, untormented by the intellectual's doubts and scruples, there can be no doubt. Toward the end, appalled by the dissension within the Party, Lenin was to feel that it could be cured by the addition to the Party's central organs of fifty-one hundred rank-and-file workers. Somehow the presence of those simple and righteous people would shame Trotsky, Stalin, Bukharin out of their squabbles and intrigues, and would make them pursue the path of Communist virtue.

This engaging faith in the common man led Lenin not infrequently into serious lapses of judgment. Part of his initial enthusiasm for Gapon was due no doubt to the fact that the "little father" was of simple peasant antecedents. If the masses occasionally produced a man of ability he was to be more trusted than his opposite number from the intelligentsia. Thus for a long time Lenin was to trust and favor Roman Malinovsky though there were insistent rumors, which turned out to be true, that he was an *agent provocateur* who kept the police informed about the Bolsheviks. But Malinovsky, even though he also had a criminal record, was a "real" worker, a man of the people, and it was difficult for Lenin to conceive that such a man could turn traitor. And it is not unlikely that his preference of Stalin, which caused headshaking among the Party's intellectuals, also had source in this reverse snobbery. The "wonderful Caucasian" was the son of a shoemaker, and how solid and uncomplicated he appeared compared with the vain and excitable intellectuals! With his bourgeois probity Lenin had no sympathy with the view once held by some Populists that crime (when committed by the lower classes, to be sure) was a primitive form of social protest. But his weakness often made him lenient toward perpetrators of hooliganism or brigandage, when those had their source in an excess of proletarian zeal. The law-abiding, orderly Lenin struggled, not always successfully, with his pleasure at the discomfitures of the middle class; could gloat over how those stuffy and pompous lawyers, professors, and their like, with all their chatter about personal inviolability, legality, and so on were being shoved around by his proletarian "boys."

Such was Lenin in 1905. The subsequent years were to modify his views and affect his tactics, they were not to change the man.

V

REVOLUTION
AND REACTION

1. *The Revolution of 1905*

It was the great rehearsal: so Lenin was to write of the Revolution of 1905. Most of the elements of 1917 were already present: defeat in war, hostility toward the monarchy by the educated classes, peasant unrest, and the workers demonstrating in the streets with red flags. But even before the Bloody Sunday of January 9 lowered the floodgates of violence and anarchy it had been obvious that Russia was approaching a fateful period. Respect for law and order had been eroded, and this among the very classes that had most to lose by violence and lawlessness. Assassinations of Tsarist officials and ministers were greeted by society indifferently if not with approval. When Pleve, Minister of the Interior, was murdered in 1904 by a Socialist Revolutionary the news was greeted with joy! A prominent lawyer recalls being in company of Prince Troubetskoy, a leading nobleman and landowner, when the news was brought in. The Prince made a sign of the cross, was obviously going to say "Thank God," but seeing the shocked face of his companion contented himself with "Heaven have mercy." [1] An escaped political convict would often seek the nearest doctor or lawyer, confident that he would not be turned over to the police but provided with shelter and funds.

The striving for political freedom had become universal. Russian autocracy was felt not only to be an anachronism and a national shame as in the previous generation, but the source of all evils beginning with her backwardness and ending with her defeat at the hands of a petty Asiatic state. Throughout 1904 there had been an epidemic of political meetings, most often taking the form of banquets of professional associations at which were voiced the most insistent demands for a constitution and parliament. At his accession to the throne young Nicholas II had characterized such pleas as "senseless and vain dreams." Now society was rapidly coming around to the conclusion that only violence could nudge the Tsar and his reactionary advisers into granting what in every civilized state was

---

[1] To be sure, Pleve had the reputation of a scoundrel and a mainstay of reaction. His "execution" gladdened even Plekhanov, a lifelong enemy of terror.

the normal political system. Subversive sentiments were voiced by the elements that traditionally stood around the throne. Assemblies of nobility competed with lawyers', doctors', and other associations in passing constitutional resolutions. At the banquet of the engineers' union, where the most severe criticisms of the regime were heard, there were present the leading industrial managers and fifteen army generals.

With Bloody Sunday events moved beyond resolutions and petitions. At the news that government troops had fired on unarmed workers marching peacefully to petition their Emperor, barricades were thrown up in the main cities and workers throughout Russia responded with strikes and violence. The first wave of unrest soon subsided, but the idea of a violent revolt had now taken root.

In March 1905 a leading St. Petersburg Bolshevik was invited to a conspiratorial meeting. It was held in a private room of one of the city's most luxurious restaurants. The table groaned under bottles of vodka and liqueurs, he recalls. Lunch was accompanied by champagne. "For reasons of conspiracy ladies were present." But the business of the meeting was serious: how to overthrow the regime, if need be by seizing the Tsar. His fellow conspirators represented the Socialist Revolutionaries, the liberals, and . . . the revolutionary organization of the Guards' officers.[2]

Thus within the very elite corps of the army there was—and how reminiscent of 1825 it was—an organization devoted to the overthrow of autocracy. Its representatives wanted to know how many workers the revolutionaries could produce at the moment of the uprising. The Socialist Revolutionaries promised ten thousand: the Social Democrats could vouch for only a few hundred. For reasons that are but hazily recalled by the narrator (not surprising, considering the setting) the discussion ended in a disagreement and nothing came out of the meeting. But the story is certainly instructive as to the state of mind of Russian society in the year 1905.

But to us the most interesting sidelight of this bizarre incident is the frank avowal of the Bolshevik that his group could mobilize but a few hundred workers. This slip (for at the time of the memoir the Soviet historians already were representing the Bolsheviks as leading the masses in 1905) illuminates Lenin's caution in the beginning of the dramatic events of the year. The Socialists, both the Mensheviks and the Bolsheviks, were weak. They were distrusted by the mass of the workers in St. Petersburg. Those of them who had tried to join Gapon's organization and to turn it in the Socialist direction had been chased out as disloyal to the Father-Tsar. To be sure, a firsthand experience with the Tsar's benevolence soon persuaded the workers to turn to the revolutionary organizations. Before long the Socialists would be capable of riding the crest of the wave, to in-

[2] S. Gusev in *1905 Materials and Documents—the Fighting Section of the Socialist Party*, Moscow, 1927, pp. 19–21.

struct and to persuade the workers their ranks would grow, likewise their influence. But then Lenin's restless mind would see another danger. The revolutionary wave threatened to engulf not only the Tsarist regime but the leadership of the Bolsheviks and the Mensheviks. Their doctrinal and organizational squabbles now appeared to the people in Russia as not only petty, but ridiculous and irrelevant. With Tsarism tottering and Russia seized by a revolutionary fever, the events at home were uncovering new Socialist leaders and new heroes who could not care less about the old vs. the new *Iskra,* and other debates and amusements of their titular leaders in Geneva or Paris.

To Lenin's tidy mind, for which every situation had to be approached with a preconceived plan and an organizational chart, this situation was fraught with danger, and not only to his personal fortunes. He always distrusted "spontaneity"; witness *What Is To Be Done?.* The revolution filled him not only with elation but also with fear that an undirected, spontaneous revolutionary zeal of the working masses would lead them to a disaster. In its course he was to display hesitation, doubt, and even defeatism. It is a measure of his greatness that he learned a lesson, and when the second installment was to come in 1917 he was to appear sure of himself and decisive, in command of events and not tossed to and fro by them. But in 1905 he needed a firm organizational basis under his feet before he would venture into the fray. And thus while the revolution was ripening in Russia Lenin called a meeting in April of his supporters in London.

It was proclaimed grandiloquently, though the Mensheviks were absent (they were holding their own meeting in Geneva), the Third Congress of the Social Democratic Workers Party. That it was clearly illegal by the Party Statute was coolly confessed by Lenin himself: "The Congress is perfectly legal. To be sure, according to the *strict letter* of the Statute it can be considered illegal; but we should be guilty of a grotesque formalism if we should interpret the Statute that way." [3] This was typical Leninist logic. But even though the Congress was composed of firm Leninists and entirely free of the hateful "Martovists," the delegates from Russia would not hear of a definite break with the Mensheviks, which was desired by their leader. Even to the most loyal of the Bolsheviks Lenin's insensitivity to the conditions of Party life and struggle at home was incomprehensible. [4] The spurious Congress voted to work for a reunification of the Party and elected a purely Bolshevik Central Committee. This committee (that is, Lenin) then had the gall to announce to the International Socialist Bureau that the Russian Social Democrats now recalled

[3] *Protocols of the Third Congress,* Moscow, 1959, p. 46.
[4] In a letter almost as fantastic as the one quoted in the previous chapter Lenin in February 1905 upbraided his agents in St. Petersburg for not getting enough subscribers for his journal *Vperyod.* Subscribers to this clandestine journal need not be afraid of arrest. The police, he says reassuringly, will be lucky if they catch as many as one third of them! *Works,* Vol. 8, p. 124.

Plekhanov as their representative in the Bureau and delegated instead Comrade Ulyanov. This action by a fraudulent Congress defies for the purposes of description the resources of the English language, but there is a Russian word for it, *khamstvo*, which conveys the qualities of presumption, vulgarity, and boorishness. When the astounded Bureau referred this letter to Plekhanov he answered with amazing restraint that the Bolsheviks represented, at most, one half of the Party. Lenin's brazenness had the usual paralyzing effect on his opponents. Instead of shouting to high heaven that he was stealing the Party and retaliating in kind, the Mensheviks meekly called their own gathering a *conference* rather than congress, and acquiesced in the Bolshevik Central Committee. Plekhanov's nerves gave way at this ungentlemanly wrangling: He announced that he stood apart from both factions.

In his attitude toward the revolution Lenin failed to display the same decisiveness that he showed in intra-Party intrigues. The Communist legend has since proclaimed that in 1905 only the Bolsheviks were ready to go all the way. The Mensheviks skulked behind, and the liberals betrayed the revolution. Yet at this very Congress in April Lenin confessed the impossibility of achieving a *Socialist* revolution. "If we were now to promise to the Russian proletariat that we can seize full power we would be repeating the error of the Socialist Revolutionaries." [5] If we strip the resolutions of the Congress and his speeches of the emotional and agitational phraseology, it is clear that the most he expected out of the situation was a bourgeois-liberal regime in Russia. *Later* he was to cry out that the Mensheviks were cowardly, ready to follow in the footsteps of the "rotten" liberals. But at the Congress he criticized Plekhanov and the Mensheviks precisely for their radicalism and ultraleft views. The Bolsheviks were willing, he made clear, to participate in a liberal-led bourgeois government, should such be established in Russia. The Mensheviks' argument that it was inconceivable that the Socialists should share ministerial portfolios with bankers and landowners was refuted by copious quotations from Marx and Engels, often a sign in Lenin that he was arguing in favor of something he found emotionally distasteful.

In fact, his whole behavior at the Congress exuded lack of confidence in the possibility of a Socialist victory and lack of belief in Socialist influence upon the masses. He grasped at every straw. Thus to the obvious displeasure of some of the assembled he referred to "Comrade Gapon" (there were shouts, "How come he is a comrade, when did he join the Party?"). He let the assembled in on the secret that Gapon "told me that he shares the viewpoint of the Social Democrats, but because of certain reasons cannot reveal it openly." Even more incredibly, for this had to be a lie, he announced that Gapon gave him the impression "of a man fully devoted to the revolution, clever and full of enterprise." [6] He was

[5] *Works,* Vol. 8, p. 353.
[6] *The Third Congress,* p. 370.

fighting desperately on two fronts: first to retain his hold on the Bolsheviks within Russia, who he thought would be impressed by his capture from the Socialist Revolutionaries of an asset as valuable as the "little father," and second to persuade the world and perhaps himself that the Bolsheviks were in the forefront of the revolutionary struggle, when the facts told quite a different story. It says a great deal for Lenin's power to dominate people that despite his transparent insincerity and their obvious rancor at some of his decisions, the thirty-odd delegates reaffirmed their loyalty and then many of them went back to Russia to risk their heads in the struggle he still did not care to join. The decisions of the Congress enjoined them to expose to the workers the untrustworthiness and cowardice of the liberals, but also to work with them if such a collaboration should prove practical. The Bolsheviks were to organize military units to fight the army and the police, but were to avoid foolhardy acts of premature insurrectionism. The Congress welcomed the deepening social anarchy but warned against seizures of private property. Under the circumstances this was sensible double talk, an attempt to insure against all eventualities. But where is the Lenin of the legend, whether of his enemies or his admirers, always decisive, farseeing, and uncompromising in his aims?

That he exhibited none of those characteristics is simply a testimony to the fact that he was not superhuman, as the Bolsheviks would have it, nor, as his enemies have held, a fanatical doctrinaire. The events of 1905 had puzzled and disorganized everybody: the Tsar and his advisers, the liberal reformers, and the revolutionaries. To have held stubbornly to the same position throughout the year would have been unreasonable.

Having held his little band together, Lenin relapsed into the role of an observer and critic of events. By the summer there was an intensification of the revolutionary atmosphere. Russia's defeat by Japan was now complete. It was a humiliation much greater than that suffered in the Crimean War, when the Empire after all was confronted by a coalition of the leading European powers. Society greeted this defeat with indifference, the liberals and revolutionaries with exultation. It had been widely believed that the regime had embarked upon its aggressive policies in the Far East in order to offset internal pressure. "What we need is a splendid little war," the late unlamented Pleve was quoted as saying. And the Emperor had been wont to refer to the Japanese as the "little monkeys." Now his fleets were sunk, the armies defeated and on the brink of mutiny, and the treasury bankrupt. Russia sued for peace. The Emperor turned to one Russian statesman who enjoyed a European reputation, Serge Witte, to bring him peace with honor.

With Witte's personality we encounter a Russia different from that of the intelligentsia and the revolutionaries. It is the Russia of the reformers and administrators, who despite all the glaring defects and social evils managed to keep their country going, make it a great military and industrial power, and *almost* to save it from the revolution. His career presents a useful antidote to the stereotype view of the intelligentsia. He belonged to it by his upbringing and occupation, having received higher education in mathematics, then serving as an industrial manager and civil servant. But we will not find in Witte the temperamental or intellectual traits of the *intelligent*. No self-questioning, no search for an ideology. His prose is crude and at times ungrammatical, unembellished, unlike every educated Russian's who put his pen to paper, by literary quotations and allusions. He was, in fact, a rough-hewn manager-bureaucrat type, almost of the quality of his Soviet successors. Had he been younger by some two decades (he was born in 1849) and survived into the Stalinist era it would not be incongruous to see him as the Chairman of the Planning Commission or Commissar of Finance. Devotion to people who fostered his career and to loyal subordinates, hatred and intrigues against his rivals constituted the mainsprings of his politics. But as an administrator interested in efficiency and in the success of his enterprise, whether it was a railway line or the economy of the country, Witte could often see farther and better than others who viewed Russia through the prism of Marx, Chernyshevsky, the idealized peasant commune, Slavic solidarity, and the like.

By temperament he had to be a believer in absolutism. He idolized Alexander III, who brought him up from the obscurity of being a railway manager to the position first of Minister of Communications, then of Finance and being the virtual Prime Minister.[7] But he perceived it beyond the personal resources of Nicholas II to continue autocracy. Anyway, it was not practical in the twentieth century to rule Russia according to the old ways. And so, for purely pragmatic reasons, Witte leaned toward reforms. "The one and perhaps the main cause of our revolution," he noted in his memoirs, "has been lateness in developing the spirit of individuality, and in acknowledging the need for the civic spirit and political freedom."[8]

But his horizons were broader than those of a purely political reform. Russia's main evil, he memorialized the young Tsar, was the degrading status of the peasants. Three quarters of the population lived unfree as wards of various authorities. The peasant's spirit of enterprise, his longing for private property, were suppressed by the commune. It was imperative

---

[7] The circumstances of his advancement throw some light on the mores of nineteenth century Russia. Witte served as the manager of the railway company owned by a rich Jew. In that capacity he would not allow the Imperial train to exceed the regulatory speed, explaining before the horrified courtiers that he would not have the Emperor break his neck on "his" railway. Alexander, who on that occasion had exclaimed that he always could go as fast as he wanted except on "this Jewish line" did in fact have an accident later on another railway, remembered fondly the outspoken manager, and this was the beginning of Witte's official career. When Witte married a lady with a shady reputation (he bought her from her previous husband for 30,000 rubles, claimed his rivals) the Emperor continued receiving him and his wife at court, thus sealing Witte's admiration for this very unexceptional monarch.

[8] He died in the beginning of World War I and refers to the Revolution of 1905 and to the revolutionary feeling in general.

both for the preservation of the monarchy and in Russia's national interest to give the peasant full civic rights, to free him from the shackles of an obsolete institution, and to build up a vigorous rural middle class, which would have a stake in political and economic stability. In his shame at Russia's backwardness Witte was one with all the thinking men of his times. The Russians drink less than other nations, but there is more drunkenness among them. They work less productively than the Westerners, but nowhere is labor harder, more oppressive, and less rewarding than in Russia, he wrote bitterly. As Minister of Finance Witte sponsored industrial development and the flow of foreign capital into the country, but he professed his inability to change the picture unless basic reforms were tackled. His warnings fell on deaf ears, partly because of bureaucratic inertia and partly because of the Emperor's limited intelligence. Nicholas was too engrossed with plans of Imperial expansion in China and the Balkans. Witte's opposition to them led to his dismissal from the post of Minister of Finance in 1903. He was kicked upstairs to an honorific position that gave him no power to arrest the drift toward war and revolution.

It is to this man that Nicholas II entrusted negotiations with the Japanese, to be held in America at President Roosevelt's invitation. Witte was hated by the circles close to the Emperor. The reactionaries spread rumors that this willful man, who barely concealed his contempt for the Tsar, aimed to become the first president of the Russian republic. And his personal ambition combined with his unpolished demeanor did not gain him many friends among the liberals. But it was universally agreed that he was the only man capable of negotiating a tolerable peace and, equally important, of securing a large loan from the European bankers. His reputation stood high with the foreign capitalists and only his return to power could dissipate their understandable apprehensions about investing in Russia's future in the middle of the spreading anarchy.

From the summer of 1905 until the embers of the revolution were to die down in 1907 the regime pursued the policy of intermittent reforms and repressions. The Tsar announced his intention of instituting a legislative assembly. But it was to have only an advisory function, and the time for such half-measures had long passed. The announcement only whetted the appetites of the radicals. The government granted a large measure of autonomy to the universities. This led to an intensification of revolutionary disturbances among the students. The halls of the institutions of higher learning became the privileged sites for holding mass political meetings where the most subversive sentiments and demands were voiced while the police looked helplessly on. Even the approaching peace with Japan held the promise not only of relaxation of terror, but also of new dangers. In what mood would the soldiers of the defeated armies return from the Far East, where they witnessed the catastrophic inefficiency and corruption of the Imperial administration? The imbecility and panic of many in the government is best pictured in the advice of one of the ministers: soldiers should not be returned to European Russia but settled on virgin lands in Siberia. The worthy administrator did not pause to consider how most of the warriors eager to return to their homes and families would take to their forcible transformation into colonizers of the wilderness.

In reports of the Minister of the Interior "most humbly submitted for the most august perusal" the Emperor could read daily about new disturbances in various regions of his vast Empire: strikes in Kiev, nationalist demonstrations in Warsaw, the report almost monotonous in its repetitiveness about a political meeting held at —— University, where the representatives of most diverse political opinions ranging from moderate liberals (often titled or former officers and civil servants) to the anarchists approved a resolution calling for an end to autocracy and a *real* parliament and civil freedom. But the most ominous note of all began to creep in with the summer: reports of unrest in various regiments and garrisons, of the soldiers' refusal to fire upon demonstrators, or even of courts-martial of army officers apprehended for participation in revolutionary activities.

In June one of the most dramatic incidents of the revolutionary year took place: the mutiny on the battleship *Potemkin* in the Black Sea. The story immortalized in Eisenstein's famous film is still for the Western cinema-goer the most convincing depiction of the elemental character of the revolution. Revolutionary agitation often found more fertile soil among the sailors than in the army. The latter was mostly peasant in its composition. The sailors came predominantly from among the urban workers and craftsmen. It was all the more striking that the most famous uprising exploded on the *Potemkin,* whose crew was judged backward by the radical agitators since, uncharacteristically, it was recruited from among the peasants. But infected by the revolutionary epidemic and provoked by the inhuman conduct of the ship's command, the sailors rose, shot and imprisoned their officers, and raised the red flag over the most powerful man-of-war of the Black Sea fleet. It seemed for a while that the rest of the squadron would follow the *Potemkin's* example. Sailors on other ships refused to fire on the mutinous vessel, and in some cases overpowered their own officers. Uprisings and disturbances seized the naval base of Sevastopol and the great port of Odessa. To the few Socialists (alas! Mensheviks) who gained access to the *Potemkin* to "educate" the crew and to turn the mutiny in the revolutionary direction, it seemed that soon all southern Russia would follow their example, and then the rest of the country. But as the Soviet historians are constrained to admit, the revolt was too disorganized, the sailors were too ignorant politically, to achieve more than a local and temporary success. Not until 1917 would the sailors be in the vanguard of the revolutionary movement, and then for a time would provide the most reliable armed force at the disposal of the Bolshevik leaders. In 1905 it was anarchy and not yet the Socialist revolution that was seizing hold of Russia.

It was this very anarchy that some in the government tried to exploit to forestall a revolution. Latent among the masses of eastern and southern cities of the Empire was a violent anti-Semitic feeling, and it was not too difficult to bring it to the surface. Many officials regarded with indifference, some actively encouraged, the anti-Jewish pogroms. This exploitation of lawlessness and hooliganism lurking in the masses was not limited to racial hatreds. In a perverse variant of Socialist propaganda the reactionaries tried, often with success, to turn the ignorant populace against the "traitors"—the intelligentsia and the liberal gentlemen who had risen against the Father-Tsar and the Holy Orthodox Church. The Black Hundreds, as those groups of hooligans became known, indulged in beatings and terrorism directed against the university youth and members of free professions. It was not only the revolution that was a beneficiary of the deepening breakdown of law and order that began with the summer of 1905.

Lenin's activities throughout this period reflect a growing excitement at the prospect of a great upheaval, combined with the still great wariness at plunging into the revolutionary caldron or committing himself and his Party prematurely. The correspondence with the Bolshevik committees at home, carried on mostly by indefatigable Krupskaya, bears but little relation to the events that were convulsing Russia and attracting the attention of the whole world. Much of it is a monotonous repetition of the complaint that the people at home were not selling enough copies of Lenin's journal *The Proletarian*,[9] and that not enough money was being sent out of Russia to the Bolshevik central organs. That was accompanied by equally monotonous complaints about the Mensheviks' misdeeds: they refused to submit to the decisions of the Third Congress, they seized Party funds, and so on. What becomes obvious also from the correspondence is the Bolsheviks' weakness or disorganization at the main points of the revolutionary upheavals. At the time of the *Potemkin* mutiny, when the rebellious battleship anchored off Odessa and threatened to set off a city-wide uprising, the local Bolshevik committee was in a state of complete collapse. As to the very center of mutinous feeling in the Black Sea fleet, the great base at Sevastopol, Krupskaya had to confess that she did not know whether there were any Bolsheviks there at all. Yes, she knew of one Bolshevik in the Ukrainian city of Melitopol. It is understandable that many, even the most loyal Bolsheviks at home, felt that there were more urgent tasks than a subscription campaign on behalf of *The Proletarian*. They were also in-

[9] It was *Vperyod* (*Forward*) continued under another name. The Third Congress with a typical and transparent insolence declared that *Iskra* (long in the Mensheviks' hands) was no longer the organ of the Social Democratic Party, and that on their part the Bolsheviks generously agreed to wind up *Vperyod* and to collaborate on the new all-Russian journal, *The Proletarian!*

creasingly prone to join with the Mensheviks and even the Socialist Revolutionaries, and to disregard warnings and rebukes that their leader still addressed from distant Geneva. Lenin also found himself under increasing pressure from the international Socialist circles to compose his quarrels with the Mensheviks now that the hour of opportunity had struck for socialism and democracy in Russia. His personal vendetta against Plekhanov especially chagrined and shocked the German Social Democrats, for whom the latter had been a comrade and trusted friend of twenty years' standing. And as late as July Lenin had the indecency to refer to his old teacher, in a letter to the International Socialist Bureau, as "citizen" rather than "comrade" Plekhanov.

To the Mensheviks the idea of a reunion was much more acceptable than to their opponent. It was silly, they felt, in the face of events, to continue this division in the ranks of Social Democracy. But their leaders, though not angels themselves, felt with justification that every gesture for a reunification would be exploited and distorted by Lenin. His utter lack of scruples in intra-Party struggles was already becoming legendary. He no longer was the same man who had been so mortified at the split and the end of personal friendships in 1903. Brazenly he attempted to steal the Party's name and organization. Lenin himself openly and somewhat naïvely advertised his lack of political scruples. "In politics there is only one principle and one truth: what profits my opponent hurts me and vice versa," he said to a partisan shocked by the behavior of one of his lieutenants.[10] Rumors were circulating among the Mensheviks that this cynicism extended beyond the intra-Party dissensions. The Bolsheviks were alleged to be in contact with agents of the Japanese government, which of course was not unwilling to subsidize the revolutionary movement within its enemy's territory.[11]

Why not a fresh beginning, wondered some Mensheviks, notably old Axelrod. Forsaking the old *émigré* dissensions and intrigues, a new workers' party should be organized in Russia. The revolutionary impetus should be exploited by the workers' setting up their own representative organs, culminating in a workers' congress. This organization would absorb all the existing factions, would speak for the class as a whole, and should affect decisively the fortunes of the revolution. Here was the seed of the idea which within a few months was to create the workers' soviets (councils) all over Russia. But in the summer of 1905 this concept of Axelrod was viewed without enthusiasm by many Mensheviks and with positive horror

[10] P. A. Garvi, *Memoirs of a Social Democrat* (in Russian), New York, 1946, p. 423.

[11] The Bolsheviks admitted that they kept in touch with the Russian prisoners of war in Japan, but only through their connections with the Japanese Socialists. Some revolutionary Socialist organizations in Russia, such as the Finnish, and the Polish Socialist Party did have connections with the Japanese agents. See I. Volkovicher, "The Party and the Russo-Japanese War," in *The Proletarian Revolution*, December, 1925.

by Lenin. Where and when in Russia's history had the workers been capable of organizing by themselves without the tutelage of the intelligentsia or the police? And after years of sacrifices, of tedious and painstaking building of the organizational network, both factions were being invited to commit hara-kiri at the altar of proletarian solidarity, their leaders to be pushed aside by some new Gapon or an equally unlettered common worker!

And so for a time Lenin continued what in view of the events was rapidly becoming political daydreaming. Here in his writings were the Bolsheviks solemnly laying down the conditions for collaboration with the liberals in a provisional government. Elsewhere, he proclaimed that one should not be afraid of a full victory of the Socialists in Russia. It would start a European revolution. The news of increasing violence and chaos at home made his tone more militant, but still did not produce a coherent program of action. "We" stand for the confiscation of landed estates. But to whom shall this land be turned over? Here, Lenin declares that "we" shall never tie our hands.[12] "We" shall also organize revolutionary committees, which will include not only workers but also peasants, soldiers, paupers, and prostitutes.

The majestic pronoun, the unconvincing pose and pretense of the Bolsheviks leading the revolution, gave way at times to a peevish criticism of events and admissions of the weakness and unpreparedness of his faction. Why were the September strikes and riots in Moscow so badly prepared? No military units joined the workers' demonstrations and no bombs were used against the police. And on the eve of the great events in the capital he chides the St. Petersburg organization: "Good God, how sad! We have talked about bombs for more than six months and not a single one has been manufactured." *Now* he is for direct action: "For Christ's sake spit on formalities and elaborate schemes." His reservations about terror now give way to a frantic espousal of violence. Form small units of three or ten fighters. Arm them with guns, knives, or kerosene. Let them learn by attacking police stations, expropriating banks, etc. Much can be learned even by shooting single policemen!

This surge of militancy was bound up with the crescendo of the revolution. Conclusion of peace with Japan in August only intensified the general unrest. In September and October it turned into open revolts and general strikes in the major cities and on the railways, which the government no longer seemed able to control or to bring to an end. In St. Petersburg the strike paralyzed all public utilities, including the railroad line between the capital and the Tsar's country residence and factories. The workers' elected representative—the soviet (council) of the workers' deputies—soon became transformed from a mere coordinating committee for the strike into the virtual government of the city. To the economic de-

[12] *Works*, Vol. 9, p. 213.

mands of the strikers was joined a political program: a constituent assembly and civil liberties. The capital's example was followed all over Russia, where the whole country appeared to become one vast public meeting. Railways and communications were not functioning. The city councils abdicated their functions to the local soviets. The regime resorted to isolated acts of repression but was powerless to stop the general strike and did not dare for more than a month to touch the St. Petersburg soviet, which more and more began to remind one of a revolutionary government.

In the Tsar's entourage the most reactionary courtiers begged him to grant a constitution and political freedom, as an alternative to an overthrow of the dynasty and a flight abroad. With Witte called upon to become the first constitutional Prime Minister, the Autocrat of All Russias issued the famous Manifesto of October 17. Even in the midst of a revolution the announcement was hardly credible: Russia was to have a real parliament, and laws were going to be formulated guaranteeing political freedom and personal inviolability. What followed the initial amazement and incredulity was of course an intensification of the revolutionary movement. The soviet demanded as the first installment a full political amnesty, evacuation of the city by the army detachments, and creation of a people's militia. In some cities crowds attacked jails, bent upon liberating the political prisoners. In the capital Witte, who now had the thankless task not of preventing the revolution but of conquering it and of restoring some semblance of order, was negotiating with the soviet, while his sovereign was hiding in his country residence protected by elite detachments of the army. He addressed an appeal to the strikers, calling upon "brothers" to put an end to anarchy and to return to work. The soviet retorted that the proletarians did not feel that they were in any degree related to Count Witte. But despite such rebuffs, and to the obvious anguish of the Socialists within the soviet, Witte impressed many of its members both because of his liberal reputation and by his simple "essentially Russian" manner. In the presence of its delegates he put in a telephone call to the Emperor's sanctuary and then turned to the workers: "Well! Thank God. I can congratulate you gentlemen. The Tsar has just signed an amnesty." The delegates could not fail to be impressed: who could have thought this was the way the government was going to be run?

The news of the amnesty and the apparent triumph of the revolution finally stirred up most of the Socialist potentates to return home. Trotsky had already been there and was covering himself with glory as a leader of the St. Petersburg soviet. Vera Zasulich, always unhappy abroad, had to be restrained several times from bolting to Russia, even before the amnesty. Plekhanov, again sick, never got back. Others, including Lenin, were returning eagerly, but not without serious misgivings. There was the natural worry about their personal safety; for all the regime's promises the possibility of an arrest and a long-term imprisonment had always to be considered. But most of all there was the fear that the fast-moving events would make them obsolete and unacceptable as political leaders. A new generation of revolutionary heroes was already visible. The chairman of the St. Petersburg soviet was a previously obscure young lawyer, Khrustalev-Nosar. Its vice-president, the author of its manifestoes, editor of its paper, the rising star of the revolution, was none other than Trotsky. The new times called for new skills: first of all, public oratory. Lenin had previously never addressed a crowd. Now there were continuous mass meetings with thousands participating, and the obnoxious young Trotsky (as he appeared at the time both to Lenin and to the Menshevik leaders) was already established as an unrivaled orator. Political journals could be published legally. This was a tremendous boon, but also the source of possible embarrassment. The wide reading public could not be expected to appreciate the style of political polemic in which Martov and Lenin excelled: their private jokes and sarcasm at each other's expense, their strictures about the alleged betrayal in the summer of 1903 in London, or in the winter of 1904 in Geneva; the Bolsheviks' caricatures of the Mensheviks, the Mensheviks' gloating at Lenin's discomfiture on being left in the lurch by Plekhanov, and so on. Street fighting and armed insurrections were the order of the day. Here again for all their cheering from the sidelines the old leaders could contribute but little. They were out of touch with the conditions at home, engrossed in their obsolete quarrels. They barely visualized the kind of arguments and the technique of agitation that could bring the army and navy units to the side of the revolution. In brief, the ultimate defeat of this revolution not only was to give the Tsarist regime a brief lease on life; it is not too much to say that it saved Menshevism and Bolshevism as political movements.

Confronted by this bewildering combination of opportunities and dangers, Lenin once again was transformed from a raving and incoherent polemicist into a practical and shrewd politician. Even before setting homeward he was taking pains to bind the old wounds and to prepare a feasible basis for political work at home. The Bolsheviks were ready to start a journal within Russia and he needed authoritative contributors. The paper, *New Life*, was already assured of distinguished literary contributors, but Lenin needed something more: a man whose name and writings still had an unequaled prestige among the Socialists and radicals of all persuasions. Hence to Plekhanov, the very same man whom a few weeks before he had refused to acknowledge as a comrade, he addressed in October a letter cloying in its reverence and sweetness. It went without saying, he informed "highly esteemed Georgi Valentinovich," that "We Bolsheviks want fervently to work with you." Will he condescend to become a member of the editorial board of *New Life?* The Bolsheviks, as they have always, want Plekhanov's "leading, close and direct" participation in the Socialist movement. Their past disagreements? Why, mostly misunderstandings. He, Lenin, "never wanted to bind any Social Democrats by his own views." [13]

Calls for help went also to other Socialist luminaries. Sybaritic Lunacharsky had just settled down in Florence to pursue leisurely literary activity when he was summoned in November to St. Petersburg to join in the work on the paper. And in the same month after long and incomprehensible delays Vladimir Ilyich himself, traveling through Sweden and Finland, finally reached the capital.

For all the previous intimations, the atmosphere was intoxicating: so Martov wrote of his first impressions of Russia. Only five years before, he and Lenin left the country where Socialist propaganda was confined to small clandestine circles, and where any public political activity was unimaginable. Now vast crowds listened to inflammatory speeches, while the police stood helplessly by. In the municipal and university auditoriums spokesmen for rival radical parties advertised their respective wares. It appeared inevitable that the revolution would continue. The announcement of the regime conceding a constitution and parliament only whetted the appetite of the extremists, but paralyzed the authorities even further. One day after the Manifesto, on October 18, a noted Moscow lawyer attended a public meeting. The subject of discussion was whether the Mauser or the Browning was a more suitable gun for street fighting.[14]

Socialism as a movement was flourishing, but of the thousands now eager to enlist under its banners few cared about the distinction between the Mensheviks and the Bolsheviks. Money was pouring in, much of it from rich manufacturers, for the Socialist newspapers and pamphlets. The papers, New Life and the Mensheviks' Beginning, each reached a circulation of around fifty thousand.

In view of this literally frightening success, Vladimir Ilyich attempted first to secure some foothold in the situation. There was, first of all, the problem of the Bolsheviks' attitude toward the soviets. Their emergence, and particularly that of the one in St. Petersburg, was greeted by them with hostility, which then turned to an embarrassed collaboration and awkward attempts to seize control of this new form of proletarian organization. Their leader had, after all, taught them to distrust "spontaneity." The St. Petersburg Bolshevik committee, which represented at most a few hundred workers, had demanded that the soviet, uniting representatives of tens of thousands, should be subordinate to it. Lenin soon saw that such claims were childish, but he still did not

[13] Works, Vol. 34, p. 315.
[14] V. A. Maklakov, The Government and Society—Memoirs of a Contemporary (in Russian), Paris, 1937, Vol. 3, p. 406.

know what to do with this "unexpected child of the revolution." At one time he leaned to the acceptance of the soviet as a possible provisional government of the revolution. In 1917, upon his arrival in Russia, he was to utter unhesitatingly the slogan, "All power to the soviets." But in November 1905, once in St. Petersburg he was to use this ambiguous formula: "The soviet is not a parliament and not an organ of proletarian government but a fighting organization for specific purposes."

Seldom in his political life did Lenin cast such an insignificant figure against the background of momentous events as in November and December 1905. He, a self-proclaimed leader of the proletariat, was practically a passive observer of events while in the very same city the council of the workers' deputies was legislating on its own, negotiating with the Tsar's ministers, and—for once this phrase does not sound fraudulent—leading the masses. To cover up this humiliating fact Soviet historians resort to outright lies: in fact Lenin *was* directing the policies of the soviet; or somewhat less brazenly, in its solicitude for the safety of their leader the Bolshevik committee forbade him to participate in the work of the soviet. But in truth Lenin's realism in the face of a political setback is a much surer sign of his greatness. To faithful Lunacharsky he freely confessed the temporary impotence of the Bolsheviks. And to the leading spirit of the soviet, the man who more than anyone else had denounced and abused him for the past two years, Lenin did not fail to pay a grudging tribute. He said with a sigh, recalls Lunacharsky, "Trotsky has earned this place by relentless hard work." [15]

In the face of the hard realities of political life, so infuriatingly combined with the dazzling opportunities for the revolution, Lenin exhibited an amazing suppleness and ability to adjust. Much of his time was spent in writing and editing New Life, the legal Bolshevik newspaper. Its great popularity was due largely to the distinguished literary talent that the Bolsheviks' friend and financial angel Maxim Gorky enlisted as contributors. Gorky himself was at the height of his fame as a proletarian writer and for this enterprise he secured such stars of the contemporary artistic and literary firmament as Balmont, Leonid Andreyev, and Chirikov. The official publisher was Gorky's "companion," as the phrase went in the progressive circles, the famous actress Maria Andreyeva. It was a strange crowd for Lenin to be associated with: esthetes and bohemians, the kind of people his successors were to castigate as "literary innovators" (very bad!) and "rootless cosmopolitans." But he was tactful and friendly in his relations with them. For Gorky, who for all his radicalism hobnobbed with millionaires and grand dukes, Lenin always retained strong affection that survived future political dis-

[15] Lunacharsky penned his recollections when Trotsky's career in Soviet Russia was already in an eclipse. See *The Proletarian Revolution*, No. 11, 1925, p. 56.

agreements. Gorky was his liaison with society; he subsidized the Bolsheviks both out of his own pocket and that of the revolutionary-minded capitalists.[16]

"Let us be done with the choking atmosphere of *émigré* intrigues," wrote Lenin in his first article in *New Life* on November 10. He had now reassessed the situation and become a fervent advocate of intra-Party unity. References to the soviet and to the Mensheviks became more and more cordial. Equally sudden and unexpected was his conversion to "spontaneity," the warm welcome extended to thousands of workers who now declared themselves Socialists. On behalf of the Party apparatus, of the old *émigré* leaders, Lenin now professed humility and the willingness to learn from the rank-and-file proletarians. What did the leaders have to contribute to the revolution, he ruminated publicly, but bookish theories? The masses were bringing life.

There is no reason to see insincerity in these words or to attribute them merely to a desperate attempt to recoup some of the old position and influence the Bolsheviks had held. Lenin was learning that in a revolution all the preconceived schemes and theories had to be discarded and that one had to move with its momentum or be crushed by it. The Mensheviks had been willing from the first to join and guide the soviets, the Bolsheviks had held back. It was time to acknowledge this mistake and to work for an intra-Party reunification that alone could restore to the veterans from abroad some influence over events.

But in this recognition there was no capitulation. There was going to be a united, mass Social Democratic Party, but he was not ready to give up a smaller conspiratorial nucleus. The majority of the Mensheviks were tired of conspiratorial ways and habits. It was not, as the Bolsheviks were to allege, a symptom of faintheartedness and defeatism. They were willing and eager to confront the regime in open insurrection in street fighting, and in the soviets. But they were tired, as they phrased it, of the "accursed illegal existence" of faked passports, secret meetings, and other paraphernalia of the past. Either an open revolt or, if the regime grants genuine political freedom, open struggle as a political and parliamentary party. This far Lenin was completely unwilling to go. The need for conspiracy was for him not only a matter of political conviction, it was an obsession. Much of his energy was expended in those months in continuous change of his living quarters, in frantic worry that the police were on his track. In November and December such precautions were both unnecessary and ludicrous. The police, he must have

---

[16] Not such a rarity in contemporary Russia. If one feature of the nineteenth century was the "guilt-stricken" nobleman who in his anguish at serfdom turned to liberal or radical activity, then in the twentieth century one often encountered a "guilt-stricken" manufacturer. One of them, Sava Morozov, before shooting himself, thoughtfully bequeathed a considerable sum for the Bolsheviks. Another one in the days of the insurrection in Moscow armed his own workers and fought the police.

realized from experience, knew perfectly well of his whereabouts. And the government that hesitated to arrest the leaders of the soviet was not likely to alienate society by holding him or other Socialists for past offenses that were covered by amnesty. But to live openly under his own name and with his wife, as he did for a while as a matter of fact, was not so much dangerous as a concession to bourgeois customs and legality. And thus the continuous hysterical and purposeless change of address and identity papers.

To such a man the idea of discarding illegal apparatus and of abandoning the conspiratorial game was inconceivable. Were Russia to become the freest country in the world, he would still not give up his own organization, would not resign himself to playing at parliaments and elections. Hence, along with a united legal Marxist party, Lenin postulated the absolute necessity of preserving a secret network. It was not only a matter of political design and of a (reasonable) lack of faith in the government's promises and concessions; conspiracy had become with him a passion and part of nature.

Yet one cannot help wondering what would have happened had Russia emerged from the revolution with a *genuine* constitutional and parliamentary regime rather than a very lame one. Conspiracy would have become obsolete. Lenin's hold over his followers was not what it was to be twelve years later. Would he have become a tame parliamentary leader of a Socialist party? For all his passions and obsessions Lenin was essentially a very practical man.

Events were to spare him the agonizing dilemma. Fortunes of the revolution were bound up most of all with the St. Petersburg soviet, and by December it was clear that most of the hopes and fears centered on this institution were going to be dissipated. The soviet could not by its very nature become a revolutionary government, nor could it become the coordinating organ of a national uprising. It was an unstable body of several hundred members ever changing in personnel, most of them politically unsophisticated and of widely divergent opinions. Under the inspired guidance of Trotsky the soviet was capable of imaginative acts of defiance. Thus it proclaimed that no papers would be published unless they dispensed with government censorship. For several weeks, and for the first time in its history, Russia had "American-type freedom of the press," as Trotsky said.[17] Conservative editors bewailed that they were being coerced and deprived of their freedom to submit their copy to the Tsarist censor. Some of them were spared this cruel dilemma by the soviet refusing to authorize publications of the most reactionary hue. But the mass of the workers, on whose endurance the soviet depended, was

[17] Needless to say, during the Soviet period this phrase had to be explained away: true, in comparison with Tsarist Russia, the American press was relatively free; nothing, however, like the true freedom of the Soviet press.

growing weary. The general strike was suspended. To keep the workers' interest through measures directly affecting their welfare the soviet now decreed an eight-hour working day. This time the manufacturers, who in many cases had in their terror continued paying the wages of their striking workers, became emboldened to the point of instituting a lockout. There was another proclamation of a general strike, but by this time the prestige of the soviet was visibly declining. Witte, infuriated by the joke that Russia had two governments, his and the soviet, had been biding his time for countermeasures. Now, encouraged by the growing apathy of the workers and by the lack of response to revolutionary appeals by the troops, he moved in to arrest its chairman, and when that did not lead to any grave consequences soon the whole soviet of 190 members, including Trotsky, found itself under lock and key. After fifty days, on December 3, the Tsar had repossessed his capitol.

The revolution had lost its first and major battle but it was far from being over. In many provincial cities conditions were more chaotic or, depending on one's view, more promising than in St. Petersburg. In some the local authorities capitulated completely to the soviets. In one case at least, the governor issued arms to the revolutionary organizations, begging them to prevent looting and hooliganism. Government officials in order to travel had to seek authorization from the strike committees of the railway workers. Not a few localities became, for all purposes, independent "republics" with the soviets in full power and the workers' militia patrolling the streets, while the titular rulers and the troops kept tactfully out of the way. No detail of this fantastic situation embittered the government as much as the news that the governor general of Moscow would appear on the balcony of his residence during revolutionary manifestations and remove his hat at the passing of the red flag.[18]

Even more ominous, in view of the composition of the army, was the wave of peasant disorders and land seizures that convulsed the Russian countryside. Often the peasants would appear at the landlords' residences and declare that while they did not have anything against them personally, they were going to take over their land one way or another. Outright violence, killing of the gentry, and burning of their residences was also rife. Unrest among the peasants was all the more frightening because it bore an even more elemental character than the uprising in the cities, and it was based on the indisputable fact of the peasant's misery and lack of land. The growth of population in European Russia and the inefficiency of farming under the commune system led to a fantastic pressure on the available land.[19] That the troubles in the countryside

---

[18] S. Witte, *Memoirs,* Moscow, 1960, Vol. 3, p. 170. The poor man had every reason to be broadminded. His predecessor had been blown to bits by a bomb thrown by a Socialist Revolutionary.

[19] The commune hampered mobility of the peasants. In many cases land was still redistributed periodically among its members, which of course had a telling effect on the quality of cultivation.

had their root not only in revolutionary agitation but in the inescapable facts of economics was recognized even by the generals who were being dispatched with troops into various provinces to restore the panic-stricken landlords. Their reports declared that without a basic reform, which would assure the peasant of more land, no end could be foreseen to the anarchy in which the countryside had been plunged. Repression was not enough.

That indeed was the sentiment of Witte himself, who with but little support from his Imperial master pressed on his combined policy of pacification by force and of reform. The latter was aquiesced in rather than supported wholeheartedly by the court circles. But the ungrateful task of countering violence with repression was not shirked either by the Prime Minister. Punitive expeditions were dispatched along the Trans-Siberian line to break down the strike of the railway workers and to restore to government control the major communication points held by the revolutionary soviets. Allowing for the inevitable violence of the virtual civil war, the terror applied by the punitive expeditions still must be described as savage and unrestricted. Strikers were often shot without the formality even of a court-martial. But the greatest ferocity of all was displayed in putting down revolutionary disturbances in Poland and Latvia. Detachments of the army and the Cossacks would shoot up, burn, and plunder the countryside they were ordered to "protect." It was not an accident that twelve years later the regiments recruited in Latvia would provide the mainstay of the revolutionary army and become the elite guards of the Bolsheviks.

The height of the revolutionary violence, insofar as the Socialist movement was concerned, was the Moscow uprising of December 1905. In emulation of St. Petersburg, the ancient capital of Russia had had its soviet since October. Its first meeting comprised 180 delegates representing 80,000 workers. The news of the suppression of the St. Petersburg soviet led the corresponding body in Moscow to proclaim a general strike and then to prepare an armed uprising. This was the last attempt of the radicals to decide the issue by force of arms and to counteract the demoralizing effect of the news from St. Petersburg. The Bolsheviks for a change played an important role in the Moscow soviet, though subsequent attempts to represent them as guiding the strike and the insurrection are sufficiently refuted by Lunacharsky's admission: "In Moscow . . . we also were not the leading force." The insurrection itself was a desperate and suicidal attempt to regain the initiative for the revolution. A few thousand people armed with revolvers and rifles could not be a match for the regular troops equipped with artillery. Hopes of a sympathetic response among the soldiers were deceived when the government, not trusting the Moscow garrison, brought for support the Semenov Guard Regiment from St. Petersburg. The one-sided slaughter that resulted, in which not only workers but high school and university students perished, was viewed by many, including Plekhanov, as a needless sacrifice of human lives that did not benefit the revolution. It could not but be contrasted with St. Petersburg, where Trotsky's skillful leadership saved the proletariat from such desperate and useless sacrifices. But the Bolsheviks viewed the Moscow slaughter as a beneficial lesson, and were, much later, to be sure, to reproach Trotsky for his alleged faintheartedness. A thousand or so killed, the atrocities committed by the army and the police against unarmed civilians and prisoners, were to Lenin a small price for the lesson in street fighting and for the deepening chasm between the regime and the workers. "The one who has been whipped is worth two who have not" was still his favorite proverb. An unsuccessful strike, a savagely repressed rebellion, did not in his mind represent a total loss. They instilled militancy and the thirst for vengeance among the proletariat and made social reconciliation and successful constitutionalism all the more difficult to achieve.

He was constrained to realize after Moscow that large-scale insurrections were for the time impossible. All over Russia the soviets, impressed by the show of strength by the government, were giving up; the little "republics" were abdicating to the Tsarist authorities. In his search for the means of preserving the newly acquired militancy of the Bolsheviks Lenin hit upon the expedient of partisan warfare. He was still an enemy of individual terrorism as practiced by the Socialist Revolutionaries. But he came dangerously close to it. In Poland one branch of the Socialist movement, the Polish Socialist Party (the P.P.S.) was engaging in large-scale attacks upon government offices, banks, and the like, partly to paralyze and to destroy the morale of the Russian bureaucracy and partly to collect funds. Lenin did not care for the P.P.S.; they combined Socialism with strong Polish nationalism, and were never close to the Bolsheviks. But he now advised his followers to follow the same technique of hit-and-run attacks and of "expropriations" of state and private funds for Party purposes. This was to be accomplished by teams of three to five persons specializing in such activities. Lunacharsky tells us that this decision heartened many Bolsheviks. To be sure, many of them were depressed by the sudden turn of events, and were looking for a new direction in which to expand their frustrated militancy. But there were obvious dangers in this new course of action. It ran against the whole tradition of Social Democracy. A very indistinct line separated expropriation from sheer brigandage, and it tended to draw into the Party undesirable, sometimes criminal elements. Even from Lenin's own viewpoint the partisan activities involved a great risk, as events were to show. They instilled not only militancy but also the lust for armed action for action's sake. They tended to detract from the vital tasks of propaganda and agitation. Lenin's association with this campaign, which could only with great difficulty be distinguished from terrorism, was to become a constant theme of accusations against him by the Mensheviks and in foreign Socialist circles. It was, one is tempted to conclude, an act of self-indulgence on his part. The Bolsheviks were drawn late into the revolutionary struggle; they now tended to compensate for this fact by excessive militancy when it no longer served any useful purpose. Even from the financial point of view, what the expropriations brought in was probably more than balanced in the negative sense by loss of support from rich sympathizers. As in the case of terror after 1918, Lenin could not resist the temptation to show himself "hard," scornful of the amenities and traditions of both bourgeois liberalism and Social Democracy, to give vent to a pent-up fury and violence that made him at times appear a disciple of Nechaev or Tkachev rather than Karl Marx.

With the suppression of Moscow the revolution changed its character. Mass demonstrations and the soviets were now on the decline, but violence still remained endemic. Not all of it by any means was the product of terror by the left or of repression by the government. For with the Manifesto of October 17 another and ominous element appeared on the Russian political scene, a movement of reaction: the Union of the Russian People. In an unorganized form the elements that came to coalesce into the Union had, of course, existed for a long time. They had found their support in those members of the officialdom and the Orthodox clergy for whom the prospect of a constitutional Russia was as distasteful as revolution, if not more so. Russia and autocracy were in their minds indissolubly bound together. Constitutionalism was a foreign and subversive invention. All Russia's evils were blamed on the intelligentsia and especially on the Jews. To the Union of the Russian People, Witte, who was trying desperately to save the monarchy and to restore order, was an agent of the foreign capitalists and, needless to say, of the Jews, and the promised constitution itself a device by the Jewish bankers to separate the Russian people from their Tsar.[20] The reaction of many local authorities to the first wave of revolutionary disturbances was to tolerate and in some cases to encourage the anti-Jewish pogroms. With the publication of the Manifesto of October 17 this took a more systematic character. Mobs carrying ikons and portraits of the Emperor paraded to the tune of "God Save the Tsar," and the slightest incident or provocation would unloose a wave of looting and violence directed against the intelligentsia and the local Jewish population. "I cannot do anything," the commandant of Odessa said to the Jewish delegation that begged him to

[20] How strange to find a similar anti-Semitic taunt coming from Trotsky, who writes repulsively: ". . . Mendelsson and Rothschild were for the Constitution: both the laws of Moses and those of the Stock Exchange forbid the use of fresh blood." L. Trotsky, *Works*, Vol. 2, p. 2, Moscow, 1927, p. 41. Witte's appointment was to be sure largely motivated by his ties with foreign capitalists, and the expectation he fulfilled of securing a large loan. But neither the Rothschilds nor the Berlin banking house of Mendelsson participated in the loan, their reluctance being based, among other things, on the persistence of the anti-Jewish laws.

protect them during one of the most violent pogroms. ". . . There you have your Jewish freedom." The more decent officials, Witte included, were largely powerless to curtail the outrages, in view of the well-known sympathy of Nicholas and some in his entourage for the Union of the Russian People. A derelict governor or city commandant who collaborated with the Black Hundreds would often be fired, only to have the Emperor reassign his faithful servant to a different post. It is difficult to conceive how Nicholas could show lack of intelligence, not to mention moral deficiency, to the point where he received the leaders of the Union and thanked them for their good work in supporting the throne. With the Duma (parliament) already in existence, the Emperor addressed the scoundrel who was the head of this organization, one Dubrovin, in a public telegram as follows: "May the Union of the Russian People be My trusty support, serving for all and in everything as an example of lawfulness and [a force for] civic order." [21] The last injunction was followed by those pioneers of fascism not only in organizing the pogroms but also in attempts at assassination of the radical and liberal politicians. One attempt was organized against Witte, some time after he had been discharged by his gracious sovereign.

It was under those unpromising auspices that Russia was to venture on an experiment in constitutionalism. Extremism from the left and the right did not pre-empt the political spectrum of the year of the revolution. Indeed, to contemporary observers the most prominent and hopeful part of the political scene was occupied by the Constitutional Democrats, known from the initials as Kadets. Poor Kadets! They have passed into history as a movement almost synonymous with political pusillanimity and ineffectiveness. Their very name has an ironic tinge. The Kadets had nothing of the military and little of youth about them. It was a party of substantial intelligentsia: professors, doctors, engineers, reinforced by a considerable element of the liberal aristocracy and gentry. Few political movements in history have had behind them such a high proportion of their society's brains as the Kadets, who within the Russian context appeared to combine some of the characteristics of the Americans for Democratic Action and the nineteenth century English Whigs. Few parties have had as ephemeral a success and as tragic an ultimate fate. Government was thrust into their shaky hands in 1917, but instead of presiding over a rebirth of Russia they were destined to watch helplessly the anarchy engulfing the country and then Bolshevism sweeping aside both them and the other liberal and Socialist parties. In migration and exile their former leaders were for decades to quarrel bitterly over the chances and tactics of the bygone years: had they been too yielding, too naïve in dealing with the extremists? Or on the contrary, had their mistake lain in not pushing the struggle against autocracy resolutely

[21] D. Izgoyev, *P. A. Stolypin*, Moscow, 1912, p. 64.

enough, forgetting their constitutional and law-abiding scruples? Those are the questions that have been asked in the past fifty years not only by the ex-Kadets: their fate epitomizes that of liberalism and moderation over much of the world as we know it.

But sadistic derision that the historian is often tempted to exhibit toward those movements which had their chance and failed is scarcely justified when it comes to the Kadets. They were the first to tread the ground between irrational conservatism bent upon self-destruction and the obsessive and unscrupulous forces of the revolution, which considered political freedom an opportunity rather than a goal. In 1906 the Kadets became the leading force on the Russian political scene. Elections to the first Duma were to bring them a brilliant victory: they were its most numerous party. More than once did the Tsarist regime open negotiations with the distinguished lawyers and professors who led the party to induce them to join the ministry. But they hesitated and passed up several chances. For one, the habit of opposition to Tsarism and a distrust of its agents was too deeply ingrained in the Russian liberal. Ever since the 1860s he labored under a feeling of inferiority toward the outright revolutionary. At the height of the revolutionary depredations in 1905 the Kadets could not bring themselves emphatically to condemn violence and illegal seizures of land, though many of them were substantial landowners. And precisely this was the reason: were they going to put their economic interest above that of the people's "freedom"? It is easy to second-guess them, but difficult to fault them. Russia had the institutions of constitutionalism, but was far from being a genuinely constitutional state. The *Almanach de Gotha,* that directory of monarchs and nobility, put it with unconscious facetiousness: Russia was a "constitutional monarchy with an autocratic Emperor." The first time the Kadets were asked to join Witte's cabinet they were supposed to serve with the Minister of the Interior, one P. N. Durnovo, an old bureaucrat and reactionary. It was common knowledge that the late Emperor Alexander III, following some usual administrative scandal, had given the following instructions about Durnovo: "Let this swine be fired within twenty-four hours." This was the man the fastidious professors and barristers were to admit as a colleague. Both Witte and his successors were not prime ministers in the usual sense of the word. Large areas of decision-making found themselves under more or less direct control by the court camarilla. Within the Ministry of the Interior was the department of the police, almost a state within a state, the center of fantastic intrigues, its agencies enmeshing the revolutionary parties, often acting independently of their nominal superiors: a worthy predecessor, though on a less ambitious scale, of the future Soviet secret police. How could those who looked upon themselves as Russian disciples of John Stuart Mill and other luminaries of European liberalism agree to become partners or adjuncts of this police state? Lenin was fond of saying that one cannot expect the realm of revolution to be a drawing room with a polished floor, which one enters in white gloves. The same is true perhaps of politics in general. But this was still the pre-World War I world, where the liberals were squeamish about their liberal virtue. And thus the opportunity for Russian liberalism vanished to reappear temptingly but illusorily in 1917.

To Lenin the Kadets' hesitations and scruples were a comforting confirmation of what he had always felt about the liberals and the intelligentsia. But at the same time there was an air of discovery in his comments about the ill-fated party. To Marx the middle class was a blood-sucking monster, a power-greedy organism, which once having seized a chance to rule was not going to pass it by. How different was the reality! The Kadets, wrote Lenin perspicaciously, are not really a party; they are a symptom of the times. Their very composition makes them ineffectual: the *cowardly* intelligentsia and the reactionary landlords find themselves within the same movement. Political weakness and indecision was for Lenin the gravest of sins. And thus of the Kadets: they really didn't want to rule.

At the time he wrote this, in April of 1906, Lenin did not have a much higher opinion of the workers' soviets, which a few months before he had hailed as organs of revolutionary power and (perhaps) as the revolutionary government. "Even the soviets were better than the Kadets," he says grudgingly. His old pique against Trotsky returns in the statement, quite contrary to the facts, that the St. Petersburg soviet was the weakest of them all! Surveying the Russian scene Lenin saw hope only where there was most violence. His great expectations were now founded on the continuing revolutionary ferment among the peasants. That the Social Democrats including the Bolsheviks were almost without any influence among the peasantry was of lesser consequence. More and more his mind turned to the countryside with its explosive potentialities. The Mensheviks, of course, were still the butt for reproaches: it was they who extolled the soviets, saw in them organs of revolutionary self-government. We, writes Lenin shamelessly, always saw the soviets as relatively powerless.

His bilious tone was clearly a reflection of irritation at the turn events were taking, especially at the growing pressure for a reunification of the Party. At the Tammerfors [22] conference of the Bolsheviks it was decided to call a new Party Congress, this time comprising both factions, which would arrange for a reunification. It would have been much simpler, so it would seem, to prepare a reunion by negotiations between the leaders

---

[22] Party meetings and discussions were often arranged in Finland because it was safer. Finland still had rudiments of autonomy from Russia, and the Finnish officials and police were not too eager to facilitate their Russian colleagues' life.

of both factions. The revolution was still under full steam. How absurd to occupy the energies of the Party members and to expose them to the police by having a series of electoral meetings where the Mensheviks and Bolsheviks would extol their respective platforms and plead for votes! But Lenin thought that through this method he could snatch a majority at the Congress. Thus the incongruous spectacle of the first months of 1906: the workers and other Party members gathered in great numbers, chaperoned no doubt by police agents, to listen to the endless discussions of the virtues of the Bolsheviks' vs. the Mensheviks' position on the peasants, the Duma, the Party organization, and the like. Lenin for "conspiratorial reasons" affected a bourgeois disguise, wearing a derby and sometimes glasses. He spoke often, but would never preside at the meetings of his partisans. As to the approaching "unification" Congress, he had very specific ideas of its possible outcome. He said to Lunacharsky, "with a smile," the latter recalls: "If we [the Bolsheviks] achieve a majority on the Central Committee . . . we shall insist on the strictest Party discipline." [23] He was confident that the Mensheviks would not be able to stand it and would march out of the Party, branded as traitors to proletarian unity. Lunacharsky queried, rather unnecessarily, what would happen if indeed, as it came to pass, the Bolsheviks would find themselves in a minority. Lenin replied that the Bolsheviks would never allow themselves to put their heads into a noose.

Such was the small world of intra-Party affairs as against the great events taking place all around it. Seldom had Lenin's self-control and his statesmanlike instincts been subject to such pressures of his embittered disposition and spite as in this year of 1906. His closest collaborators of the time were persons whom he really despised and with whom he was soon going to break: Bogdanov and Lunacharsky, both already professing rather odd philosophical views incompatible with Marxism, and Leonid Krasin, an industrial manager by profession and a leader of revolutionary partisan activity by avocation. All three of them represented the type that Lenin cordially disliked: the intellectuals who join revolutionary action largely out of a thirst for excitement, and who, once the movement de-emphasizes the conspiratorial side, are unable to endure prosaic political work. It was under such depressing circumstances that Lenin approached the foredoomed attempt to restore the unity of the Russian Social Democrats.

2. The Ebb

To Stockholm in April 1906 came about one hundred fifty Russian Social Democrats [24] to participate in what is almost derisively called

[23] *The Proletarian Revolution*, February–March 1930, p. 89.
[24] Including representatives of the Social Democratic Party of Poland and Lithuania, Latvia, the Bund, and a few other national organizations within the Empire.

the Fourth (Unity) Congress. The number of delegates reflected the growth of organized socialism in Russia. At the First Congress only nine persons participated; God knows whom they represented beyond themselves. The Second and Third congresses were still small affairs. The Fourth was a full-fledged Congress worthy of a movement which, if we count all the factions and national affiliates, could boast over one hundred thousand members.[25]

But the difference was not only in members nor in the total membership, swollen by the Revolution of 1905, which nobody yet thought was entering a decline. The previous congresses were in the nature of intimate reunions of close friends and comrades. The Brussels-London meeting bore all the traces of a family gathering, a family to be sure that soon broke out into dissensions, almost came to blows, but a family nevertheless. Now, at Stockholm, those ties and the unbearable emotional pressures were no more. Nobody at the Congress would, as a delegate did in 1903, break into hysterical sobbing in anguish over disunity. The Bolsheviks and Mensheviks eyed each other coldly and warily. If they came together it would be a business merger and not a family reconciliation.

But come together they had to. Their followers at home would not hear any more of reasons, real or pretended, for perpetuating the division that robbed the party of its unity and made Russian Marxism impotent at this fateful period. This impatience was well expressed in the speech of the Polish Socialist: ". . . everything which happens here concerns all of us—the Jews, Poles, Letts, as well as the Russians . . ." and a warning: "the Poles want to join the Russian Party but not if the Mensheviks and the Bolsheviks continue fighting and butcher each other off."[26] The same note was sounded by the rank-and-file delegates: For heaven's sake be done with the factions and get to business!

Almost six decades separate us from the Congress, but there are at the time this is being written at least two prominent links with the historic event. One is Klimenti Voroshilov, then a delegate from the Donetz Bolshevik organization. What would have been more difficult to predict in April 1906 than that this obscure delegate would rise to the position of the head of the Soviet armed forces, become at one time second only to Stalin in the Communist hierarchy, and after the latter's death the titular head of the Soviet Union? Or that as an old man of eighty he would be publicly denounced and disgraced by Khrushchev for his alleged scheming against the new dictator, have a humble apology read on his behalf, and be physically ejected from the space reserved for the Soviet dignitaries on the top of the Lenin monument?

[25] At the time one source gives the number of Bolsheviks as 13,000; of the Mensheviks as 18,000. *The Proletarian Revolution*, No. 5, 1922, p. 75.

[26] *The Fourth (Unity) Congress of the Russian Social Democratic Party. Protocols*, Moscow, 1959, pp. 27 and 29.

Less exalted but undoubtedly happier has been the fate of Stanislaw Strumilin. Today this man of eighty-seven, the dean of Russian statisticians and planners, is still active in scholarly work, still listened to when it comes to his country's economic problems. Years have not dimmed his recollections of the Stockholm gathering. He, along with some other delegates, set out there from Finland in a small steamship. Hardly had the Russian Socialists fallen to discussing the agrarian program of their Party when their boat struck some submerged rocks. The Finnish sailors began to run about frantically, trying to prevent the boat from sinking. And the Russians? Why, they went on discussing what should be the attitude of Marxism toward the peasant and the land problem. As the discussion grew more heated it had to be transferred to the upper deck, as the lower cabins were filling with water. "Strange people, those Russian revolutionaries," said a Finnish sailor. Fortunately for the Stockholm conference and for the future of Soviet statistics, the delegates, still arguing, were transferred to another boat, and reached Sweden without harm. There the young economist was to meet the men who made the history of the next half century, among them Lenin, Plekhanov, Stalin, and the future chief of the Soviet secret police, Felix Dzerzhinsky.[27]

All the luminaries, as a matter of fact, were in Stockholm except for Martov and for Trotsky, still in jail awaiting trial for his activities in the St. Petersburg soviet. This insured that sparks would be flying. The Bolsheviks were in a minority: out of 112 delegates with voting rights Lenin could count on about 46; his opponents could muster 62. Yet paradoxically the names stuck: the Bolsheviks, in a minority, continued to refer to themselves and be referred to as "Majoritarians." The Mensheviks made no move to reverse the Party labels. Perhaps everyone realized that things were confused enough as they were. Lenin when in a minority was a formidable defender of minority rights. Witness an early session: Lenin: "The proposal . . . is a gross mockery and abuse by the majority of minority's rights." The chairman interrupts him. Lenin: "I repeat, this is a gross mockery of the rights of the minority, an attempt to destroy its rights which are guaranteed by the Statute." [28] And he had his way on that issue.

He was a very different man from the Lenin who had held those emotion-tinged debates with Martov in 1903. His behavior was now measured and stern. His opponents could not figure him out. At times he was all business: he presided over some of the sessions with decorum and impartiality. At other times something would be struck within him and he would be transformed into a raving zealot. "I was having a talk with comrade Lenin . . . ," said one of the Menshevik speakers, on the

[27] S. G. Strumilin, *From My Past*, Moscow, 1957, p. 211.
[28] *The Fourth Congress*, p. 14.

floor of the Congress, ". . . when out of the hall where the deliberations were held Lunacharsky ran out, screaming excitedly 'they do not
want to insert the word *revolutionary.*' Immediately he and Lenin ran
back to the hall and raised their hands voting to insert *revolutionary,*
though Lenin did not even know what it was all about and where it was
proposed to insert the word." [29] Yet this zeal had a magnetic effect, not
only on the Bolsheviks, but on their antagonists as well. They were all
revolutionaries, and a man who wanted to include "revolutionary" in
every conceivable statement could not be read out of the Party of militant
Marxism. Thus, though he did not have a prescribed number of votes
(received by Plekhanov and Menshevik F. Dan), Lenin through the
courtesy of his adversaries was included as the third member of the
Presidium. As one reads the proceedings one is struck by the impression
that Lenin, though in a minority, was the dominant figure. How to refute him or to cajole him or to expose his views as non-Marxist was the
main preoccupation of the hostile leaders. And this fact, naturally, filled
the Bolsheviks with defiant pride. Plekhanov, said one of them, evidently reduced his argument to the following: "Comrades, on all issues
vote against Lenin." Indeed, for the first time he dwarfed the other figures: the venerable veterans Plekhanov and Axelrod, Mensheviks Dan
and Martov, were but secondary figures in the drama. What a comeback
—through sheer strength of will—for a man who had appeared so discredited and insignificant when the great events were taking place in St.
Petersburg.

And thus the Congress went, in an atmosphere of petulant discussion,
quarrels, and protests. Almost every session witnessed one or more incidents: here the chairman interrupted the speaker for an unseemly reference to a fellow delegate, there somebody protested against being mis-
quoted. A Menshevik jumped up to draw attention to the Bolsheviks'
intrigues: "I must reveal that Comrade Lenin and others are collecting
agitational materials against the decisions of this Congress, hamper and
delay its labors, which is most undesirable because time is so short." The
Bolsheviks objected to their rights being violated. Plekhanov, as usual,
was droll and erudite, but not always felicitously so: "Already the
Pythagoreans stated that three is superior to two." How incredible that
some of those men would, before long, seize the government of a vast
country and that they would build the most disciplined and one of the
most efficient ruling classes that the world has seen!

There was an undoubted symbolism in the delegates' ship almost
sinking while they were arguing vigorously as to what policy their Party
should pursue toward the peasant. For the problem of land and its
cultivator more than any other engaged the attention of the Fourth

[29] *Ibid.,* p. 199.

Congress, led to the most fundamental disputes, and was to prove decisive in determining the future of the Russian Socialists and of their country.

From their master the Marxists could not draw much enlightenment as to what to do with the peasant, for in Karl Marx's system the peasant would not be around when a country was ripe for socialism. He would have disappeared, along with the craftsman, the small manufacturer, and their like, replaced by vast scientifically run farms, which the Socialist state would confiscate as easily and with as little fuss as the heavy industry and banking. This is what was happening in his lifetime in England: the vast estates of the nobility were replacing the small landed proprietor. Capitalism transforms the small farmer into a hired hand, or sends him to the city to become a proletarian.

Fine for Marx, and how fortunate for the English Marxists that they did not have to think of the millions of small peasant holders, but when the revolution came would have to contend with a relatively few dukes and city magnates who had accumulated all the real estate in Great Britain. But what are the Russian Socialists to do? Wait decades or centuries until capitalism has produced the English situation in their countryside? Or tell the peasant, the Russian peasant who craved land, *his own land* and more of it, and whose whole existence and all aspirations were tied to this postulate, that should they win they would transform him into a hired hand on a state-run farm? In the latter case one also might forget about the revolution and socialism for Russia. The peasant— and let us repeat, the vast majority of the Tsar's soldiers were peasants— would fight to the death against anybody who threatened to take his plot away, and who would make him a hired hand.

Thus the peasant program of all the Russian Marxists had to be tinged with doubt and insincerity. They all longed to exploit the peasant grievances and to enlist this huge multitude in revolutionary striving. But by the same token they could not tell the Russian peasant frankly what was in store for him once Marxism triumphed.

This dilemma had been with Lenin for a long time. As early as 1896 or 1897 he formulated an ingenious recipe for enlisting the peasants' support. At the time of the Emancipation in 1861 some land was actually taken away from the peasant plots and turned over to the landlords. In addition, the latter retained much of the pasture land, commons, and woods that they had held earlier. These cut offs, as they were called, were a source of grievance to the peasant, and an element of his continued dependence upon the landlord. To have grazing rights or to supplement his meager earnings from his diminished plot, he would often have to hire himself to the neighboring potentate. Lenin wanted the Social Democrats to promise the peasant the return of the cut offs and to make it the central point of the Party's agricultural program.

This was an idea fertile with mischief and impracticability. Who, if you please, in 1900 was going to find out about or restore what was or was not cut off in 1862 or 1863? In some cases towns and factories had spread over what had been both the peasant's and landlord's forty years before. Lenin could not have meant it seriously, but it was an agitational slogan with great potentialities.

The events of 1905 and 1906 made this mischief-breeding proposal anachronistic. The peasant, through his spontaneous revolts and land seizures, showed clearly that he wanted more land, whether it belonged to the state, church, or landlord, and not just the little piece that Count X reclaimed from his grandfather when the latter was emancipated. The city disorders and the soviets had subsided, but the countryside still stayed ominously restive, and there was the next great chance for the revolution.

Hence in Stockholm the Social Democrats faced the unpleasant task of promising the peasant what none of them really believed should be promised him, more land for his private enjoyment. But both sides (the Mensheviks and the Bolsheviks) faced the dilemma: how to square up their wooing of the peasant with their Marxist conscience. Or, to put it differently, how to convince the *moujik* that the revolution would give more land without, God forbid, committing themselves to perpetuating millions of independent peasant households waxing ever stronger, an indomitable barrier to ever socializing Russia and abolishing private property? And the latter is what Marxism is supposed to be about. Hence there was little support at the Congress for what would have been, to a non-Marxist, the simplest way to the peasant's heart: the promise that in the revolution the Socialists would confiscate the landlord's, the church's, and other lands and turn them over to the peasant communes and households. Both sides, it is fair to say, strove after a formula to convince the peasant that this was what was going to happen, while concealing from him what in the longer run was the Socialist design for land ownership. The subtleties of the Mensheviks' and Lenin's plans are only equaled by the subtlety of the mutual critiques of the respective plans, and finally by the subtlety of the Russian peasant, who found no use for either and continued to distrust the Marxists of all shades, until the events of 1917 delivered him into their hands.

Lenin's formula was nationalization: the right to *all* land vested in the state (in the nation, says Lenin, to becloud the formula). The peasants will take it, argued Lenin, and rightly so (for how long he does not say), that their rights in their land will be undisturbed and that only the magnates and their like would have their holdings confiscated. Why, shouted the Mensheviks, this is in the first place un-Marxist, and in the second place would only alienate the peasant. Un-Marxist, because "we" know that the state after the next revolution will not yet be in the hands

The Ulyanov family. 1879. Standing, from left to right: Olga, Alexander, and Anna. Seated: Maria Alexandrovna with Maria Ilinichna, Dimitri Ilyich, Ilya Nikolayevich, and nine-year-old Vladimir.

Lenin and other members of the St. Petersburg Union of Struggle for the Liberation of the Working Class, assembled on the eve of their dispersal to serve out their sentences. Sitting on Lenin's right hand, Krzhizhanovsky; on his left, Julius Martov. February 1897.

Vladimir Ilyich Lenin: Al'bom Fotografi, мoscow, 196

The editorial board of Iskra. *1900–1903. From left to right, Upper: P. Axelrod, Lenin, Vera Zasulich. Lower: Julius Martov, George Plekhanov, Alexander Potresov and N. Krupskaya (secretary of the board).*

Lenin, followed by sister Maria, on their way to the Fifth Congress of Soviets. Moscow. July 1918.

Lenin: MOSCOW, 1961

Lenin: MOSCOW, 1961

Lenin in 1910.

Lenin Al'bom: MOSCOW-LENINGRAD, 1927

Group of delegates to the Second Congress of the Comintern. July 1920, Petrograd. Directly behind Lenin stands Maxim Gorky, on whose left is Zinoviev.

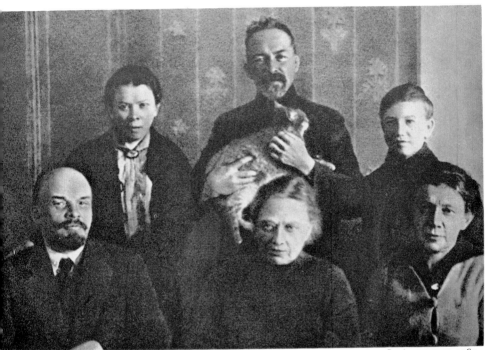

*Lenin in the Kremlin in the autumn of 1920 in a family circle.
Sitting: Lenin, Krupskaya, Anna Ilinichna. Standing: Maria, Dimitri
Ilyich, and Anna's adopted son.*

Lenin Al'bom: MOSCOW-LENINGRAD, 1927

LEFT. *Lenin and Trotsky amidst the group of delegates to the Tenth Party Congress, who have returned from the suppression of the Kronstadt Rebellion. At the lower right hand corner, Anastas Mikoyan. Standing directly behind Lenin, Klimenti Voroshilov.*

BELOW. *The very same picture as it now appears in Soviet photographic compilations. One person is missing.*

Lenin: MOSCOW, 1961

Lenin: MOSCOW, 1961

Back at work. Moscow. 1922.

LEFT. *Lenin convalescing in Gorky, with Krupskaya, in 1922.*

On the bier in Gorky.

Lenin Al'bom: MOSCOW-LENINGRAD, 192

of the Socialists; it will be in the hands of the liberal *bourgeoisie*. And *they* will use land nationalization to strengthen private property. Why would it alienate the peasant? Because (this argument is in plain contradiction of the preceding one, but logic plays little part in such disputes) the peasants will understand that nationalization threatens their property too! Now comrade Lenin wants to nationalize the peasants' own lands. A fine way to make them trust the Social Democrats.

The Mensheviks, for their part, came up with the formula of "municipalization," that is, the right to land is vested not in the state but in the institutions of local government which would administer it, and presumably also spare the peasants' land while expropriating all the rest. It was the turn of the Bolsheviks to jeer: "The peasants will not buy that." Who will control those institutions of local self-government? The *bourgeoisie*. Will they be interested in undercutting the development of a rural middle class hostile to socialism? Of course not. Thus for both political and ideological reasons the Mensheviks' "municipalization" is wrong.

The reader will be spared the variants and the countervariants on both schemes that developed in the interminable discussion of the problem. But one more voice must be quoted on the peasant issue. A delegate from the Caucasus delivered a remarkably common-sense opinion: the peasants want neither municipalization nor nationalization; they want land. If the Socialists desire an alliance with the revolutionary peasantry let them declare for simple confiscation of the estates and their distribution to the land-hungry peasants with no "buts" and "ifs." This was young Stalin, and he was already demonstrating his impatience with ideological objections to what is sound politics. But then to many he must have seemed, as befitted a Caucasian, an ignoramus when it came to the finer points of Marxian dialectics.[30]

The agrarian debate derived its importance and emotional intensity from another and closely related problem. What was going to be the future of revolution in Russia? What was going to be its character? Here again the scriptures of Karl Marx warned as well as exhilarated his followers. Only a thoroughly industrialized country where the majority of the population was composed of the urban population was ripe for a *Socialist* revolution. This presented an unbearable dilemma to the Russian Marxists. Emotionally they all craved for a revolution tomorrow, for socialism the day after tomorrow. But the doctrine was stern and unyielding. Russia of 1906 was no more ready for socialism than any other previously peasant country, barely more so than, say, Guatemala

---

[30] To many of the Russian Socialists their Caucasian brethren appeared as little better than barbarians. At one time Dan observed that Zhordania, being a Georgian, probably did not understand correctly a Russian phrase. The urbane future president of the Georgian Menshevik republic retorted that he did not need lessons in Russian.

REVOLUTION AND REACTION

or China. If one wanted to follow the doctrine of the Master to its inexorable letter one would have to settle for a long wait for socialism. First a long purgatory of a bourgeois capitalist state, something like contemporary France or Germany. Then the social conflict sharpens, the working class grows, and only after many decades would Russia be ready for Socialist revolution.

Had the Russian Marxists been able to acquiesce in the full implications of their doctrine, it is safe to say that none of them would have entered the arduous path of the revolutionary. They were not sacrificing their lives, suffering imprisonments, exiles, and other hardships just so that their country would become merely another constitutional monarchy or bourgeois republic, which they loathed scarcely less than their native absolutism and bureaucracy. Democracy and parliamentarism were for them but the means to an end: a speedier coming of socialism. In their separate ways they all, like the Populist Zhelyabov, wanted to "give history a push," to see a Socialist revolution in their own lifetimes, to live and to die for it, and not just to prepare it for future generations.

Why could not Russian history skip a phase of the Marxist scheme? It was young Trotsky who was beginning to ask this question in 1905. In partnership with a Russo-German Socialist, Parvus, Trotsky was sketching out his famous theory of "permanent revolution." [31] Though the theory was his own and that of "Fatty" (as he was fondly known among the fellow Social Democrats) Parvus, it expressed, it is not too much to say, the secret wish and hope of other Marxists. Its gist: the middle class in Russia is too weak and cowardly to effect a bourgeois-democratic revolution. As events of 1905 were showing, the Russian proletariat, though not strong numerically, was still infused with so much revolutionary spirit and hardness that it would conquer democratic liberties and the constitution. But having conquered it, would the working class be willing to endure decades of capitalist exploitation, of parliamentary games, of the fruits of its heroism being enjoyed by the plutocracy and the *bourgeoisie?* Certainly not! Insensibly the democratic revolution would be followed by and merge with the class struggle from which socialism would come out victorious.

Trotsky's theory was much derided and attacked by the others, Bolsheviks and Mensheviks alike. Here was a presumptuous young man who thought he could improve upon Marx. Such was the strength of the dogma, such was the weight of all that Marx had written about the revolutions of 1789, of 1848, that nobody would rally openly to Trotsky's side. Only in 1917 would the Bolsheviks re-enact their own version of permanent revolution, and worry afterward about the Marxian stages of development.

[31] See the discussion of its genesis in I. Deutscher, *The Prophet Armed, Trotsky 1879–1921*, New York, 1954. Chapters IV–VI, pp. 98–174.

But there is no doubt that in spirit Lenin in 1906 lusted for a full, final revolution. Behind his scriptural references to Marx, obeisances paid to the historical precedents, there is his impatient vision of events crowding each other, rushing forth toward cataclysmic struggles and the glorious revolutionary conclusion. He is for a democratic republic in the first instance. But that would only accentuate the class struggle: "After a full victory of democratic revolution, the petty proprietor will inevitably turn against the proletarian, and he will do so the sooner their common enemies are overthrown: i.e. the capitalists, landowners, the financial *bourgeoisie*, etc." [32] Here is this terrible impatience, the utter inability to conceive of a breathing spell, the almost irrational enjoyment of the vista of continuing struggles and violence that Russia is to endure. This is one of those moments when the term "Marxism," with its stages, cautions, and democratic phraseology, fits him badly. There are no historical stages, he seems to be saying, only enemies who are to be liquidated one after another: first autocracy, then the capitalist, then the very person he now wants to enlist in the struggle against the others, the small peasant proprietor.

But this is not Marxism, cried Plekhanov and the Mensheviks. Lenin is reviving the plan of seizure of the state by a conspiratorial minority, the very idea for which he and other Social Democrats had condemned the fanatical dreams of Nechaev and Tkachev! "The revolution must be carried through to the end," Lenin keeps repeating obsessively and almost incoherently. What this end is can be seen in 1906 but dimly. How can he, the leader of a minority within a Party which itself plays a secondary role in Russia's political life, confess either to himself or to others that the "end" should be full power for the Bolsheviks? But this is an important psychological step on the road to 1917, to the realization of what the ultimate end of the revolution must be.

In 1906 Lenin masked his uncertainty under the assertion that a "democratic republic in Russia" (again this obfuscation: he wants to say Russia conquered by the Socialists) would find a ready ally in the Western European Socialists and working class. This is the germ of the idea which in 1917 would drive the Bolsheviks to seize power: let the Marxists in Russia conquer their backward, unprepared country, for a few weeks, for a moment. They may, and they probably would, collapse under the blows of domestic reaction, but the flame of revolution having been lit in the East will sweep the industrialized and civilized West and in due time will return to the country of its origin. But in 1906 this vision was far from complete.

The voice of his opponents was the voice of Marxist orthodoxy, a stern reminder of what the science of history teaches. Russia was now ripe for capitalism, not yet for socialism. "What is this democratic repub-

[32] *The Fourth Congress*, p. 127.

lic for which we are now striving?" asked Plekhanov. "It would be a bourgeois republic." Lenin's revolutionary thinking is utopian, his dreams of the seizure of the state, whether through a peasant revolt or with the help of the foreign Socialists, unworthy of a Marxist. How can a believer in scientific socialism hold to the view that the Socialists can or even should attempt to seize power in a primitive, mainly peasant society? And thus they wrangled and for the hundredth time a stray observer could have sworn that he had stumbled upon a meeting of medieval schoolmen rather than that of revolutionary politicians. Would the people who were so much a prey to emotions and to bookish formulas ever be able to sway the destinies of their country?

But this impression of impracticality and of fanaticism (a much overworked word when it comes to the Russian Socialists and especially Lenin) is never allowed to linger too long. The assembly turned its attention to the two interrelated problems: what should be the attitude of the Social Democrats toward the parliamentary elections, then reaching their last phase in Russia,[33] and what if any preparations should the Party undertake toward a renewal of an armed uprising against the Tsarist regime?

The crux of both questions was the problem of legality. Does it behoove the revolutionary Marxists to vote, to be elected to and to participate in, the work of an *Imperial* legislature? And contrariwise, should they await, hope for, and prepare for a decision not at the polls but in renewed fighting in the cities and the countryside? Let us observe immediately Lenin's excellent revolutionary pragmatism. If we cut through the doubts, phrases, and contortions, his answer was "Yes," to both questions. Let us prepare for the eventuality of a new armed uprising, but let us do so in a professional way. Let us exploit the opportunities for agitation afforded by this constitution granted by the Tsar, though it is but a sham and a cover-up for the continuation of autocracy.

This is a blurred preview of Communist tactics many years after. In democratic countries they would be indefatigable parliamentarians, scrupulous defenders of civil rights when in a minority, but would in no case abandon striving for power by nonparliamentary and conspiratorial means. But this was still far away in the future and Lenin's recipe for eating one's cake and for having it too was far from having been finally worked out. And furthermore, though he dominated his followers, he still could not command them. He could infect them with his revolutionary zeal, but he could not impart to them his practicality. If you preach and breathe revolution and call for partisan warfare, how can you turn around and demand patient electoral work and participation in this fraudulent parliament where voting is weighted in favor of the possessing classes? Ever since the elections to the Duma were announced some

[33] Elections to the state Duma were staggered through several phases, and some were still to be run while the Congress deliberated in April 1906.

months before, Lenin had been under a strong temptation to use this constitutional device for Bolshevik purposes. But how could he? His closest collaborators were persons who saw in Bolshevism the promise of immediate exciting action, not of parliamentary harangues. "For us [Bolsheviks] a new uprising is a question of months," shouted one of them. Men such as Krasin and Lunacharsky lived for the excitement of organized violence. If they were to be told that revolution required a more peaceful and pedestrian activity they would soon turn, as they were to do in the coming years, to the quiet and security of industrial management and philosophical and literary activity. Thus until Stockholm Lenin supported boycott of the Duma elections. Now he turned around and agreed with the Mensheviks that the Social Democrats could participate in the voting that remained, and if elected should form their own faction in the parliament. But relatively few of the Bolsheviks followed him in this concession and the only Socialists in the First Duma were to be Mensheviks.

We must not imagine that the eagerness of the latter to participate in the elections was based on any belief in parliamentarism. The Socialists were to sit in the Duma to expose the sham of constitutionalism, to push the cowardly liberals (the Kadets) toward more provocative acts against the regime, in brief to create as much trouble as possible for everybody concerned. Was there no voice pleading for genuine democracy amidst this meeting of people who called themselves Social *Democrats?* Yes, one. We met him earlier at the Second Congress, where he shocked the assembled by inquiring whether the Socialists were not really more eager for power than the interests of the working class, and upbraided Plekhanov for his antidemocratic statements. Now Akimov, this Cassandra of Russian Socialism, had the audacity to state that the summoning of the Duma was a promising and progressive phenomenon. If the parliamentary institutions should guarantee freedom of speech, assembly, and political activity, the Party had no right to call for an armed uprising, and should collaborate with the liberal and progressive forces in the country for their further democratization. An armed revolt should be the last regrettable resort in the case of a return to an unbridled despotism.

The delegates listened to him more with amusement than with hostility. What could one expect from a former Economist, a man who was barely admitted to the Congress as a guest? Some Mensheviks may have been embarrassed, for secretly they shared Akimov's sentiments, but how could true revolutionaries condemn emphatically and publicly the armed uprising, and expect anything good out of parliamentary institutions? The Bolshevik spokesman ironically congratulated Akimov on his courage [34] for openly saying what the Mensheviks had in mind. Indeed, Lenin had been for allowing him to participate in the Congress, savoring in

[34] *The Fourth Congress,* p. 365.

advance this intrepid man's indiscretions. Better to have an open "opportunist" such as Akimov than the Mensheviks, with their double-meaning phrases about an armed uprising (but no technical preparation, please!) and other infamies.[35]

The reunion achieved at Stockholm could persist only in form. The Mensheviks' resolutions carried on the most important issues, and they secured a majority of the Central Committee. The Bolsheviks promised submission to the Party's will but they criticized the decisions of the Congress and they were obviously not going to give up their own tactics. The Russians bade goodbye to their amiable hosts, the Swedish Socialists, and dispersed back home or to the West. The Fourth Congress does not have the historic significance of the Second, where the initial split had taken place. But it was a significant step toward and a preview of October 1917. The Mensheviks were already increasingly caught in doubts, scruples, and fears of all kinds that would deprive their party of an effective policy in the greater Russian revolution, and would cast it, as Trotsky has mercilessly put it, on "the rubbish heap of history," while Lenin was seeing his way toward that tactical flexibility and revolutionary audacity that would carry the day.

For the time being, he returned to a conspiratorial existence in St. Petersburg. This meant a resumption of the hide-and-seek game with the police, living under forged passports, and frequent change of address. Increasingly, he switched his temporary quarters to nearby Finland, and from the beginning of 1907 he lived there almost permanently until his second migration to the West. His ability to avoid arrest requires some comment, though it must remain in the nature of a puzzle. Finland was a privileged territory insofar as the Russian revolutionaries were concerned. The Finnish officials, profiting by the semiautonomous status of their country, were not too eager to facilitate the work of their Russian colleagues. Still, the authority of the government reached into Finland. Lenin made trips to Russia even after January 1907, and the police could not have been totally unaware of his whereabouts. He was now known as the leader of a sizable revolutionary group. He lived in Finland in a villa known as the shelter for the revolutionaries. Why wasn't he seized?

The answer must depend on a number of conjectures and the swiftly changing circumstances of the political situation. Prior to the middle of 1906 the government did not feel strong enough to challenge public opinion by arresting political leaders unless they were clearly connected with an act of violence. Even after that date the energies of the police

---

[35] ". . . We have proposed to the Congress to invite the most typical opportunist, Akimov, who would not be afraid to spell out his thoughts. The Mensheviks did not believe in the revolution . . . but were afraid to say so openly. Let them now openly repudiate Akimov." M. Lyadov, *From the Life of the Party in 1903–1907*, Moscow, 1956, p. 165.

were more directed to discrediting the Kadets and chasing the Socialist Revolutionaries and other out-and-out terrorists, rather than the pursuit of the Social Democrats still held to be a more distant danger. When they turned in that direction Lenin was in Finland; when they sought him in earnest he bolted abroad, exemplifying his famous skill to be one jump ahead of the police. The inner workings of the Okhrana—the Tsarist secret police—was a multiple web of intrigue and mystery. This super-Machiavellianism often resulted in imbecility. The policemen thought that they could control and keep in check the revolutionary organizations through their *agents provocateurs,* planted in practically all of them. The disastrous experience with Gapon could not disabuse them of the idea that they knew how to handle "their" revolutionaries, knew which were dangerous, and which when left at large would only cause trouble to their own cause. Lenin was known as the source of contention and division within his party. With him away the Mensheviks and the Bolsheviks might well be able to coalesce harmoniously. Why, they might even throw their support to the Kadets without any compunctions and help establish a real constitutional regime in Russia! And where would the secret police be then? It lived on only because of revolutionary activities and terror. Such considerations may well have stayed the hand of the authorities from seizing Lenin when they had a chance. When such doubts weakened, he was gone.[36]

At no period in Lenin's career does his nervous energy appear as astounding as during the year and a half separating Stockholm and his flight West. At the height of preparations for the coup of 1917, or even during the darkest periods of the Civil War that followed, the course was set and there could be only victory or defeat. But in 1906 and 1907 while dodging the police he was fighting on several fronts: against the Mensheviks, to wrest from them the control of the Party; he directed the "partisan" activities of his followers, the Bolshevik preparation for an armed uprising that never came off; he struggled against the "constitutional illusions" of the Duma, and he fought to have the Bolsheviks abandon their fruitless boycott of the Parliament. He wrote feverishly throughout. He, who had never spoken before a large non-Party audience, now for the first time addressed crowds.[37] In the midst of all that

[36] This thesis is strongly supported by the excerpts from the Okhrana's archives published by the Bolsheviks after the Revolution. They show that throughout 1906–7 the police had the knowledge of his whereabouts, that they intercepted his and Krupskaya's correspondence, and that they knew where Lenin's pamphlets were being printed and sold. Some information was sloppy: Lenin in 1907 is described as being 42–44 years old, which does not speak well of the police filing system. But when he was hiding in "great secrecy" in Finland the Okhrana was able to ascertain the exact whereabouts of his hideout. *The Red Archive,* Moscow, 1934, Vol. 1, pp. 174–208.

[37] On May 9, 1906, Lenin made his debut before a public meeting. He spoke under the name Karpov and carried his audience with him in an attack upon the Duma and the "constitutional illusion." Krupskaya recalls her husband as being terribly

he found time and strength to attend yet another Party Congress and an International Socialist meeting.

Truly an amazing performance. But what is most amazing is that much of the time he was virtually alone in his politics. His closest collaborators could not anticipate his sudden shifts, his frequent and complete reversals of his previous position, and continually had to be whipped into the new line. In the Revolution he would be surrounded by supremely talented lieutenants infinitely devoted to "Ilyich," seldom for long daring to challenge his commands. Now he knew that Krasin and Lunacharsky were with him when it came to armed action and expropriations, but that they would sulk and revolt when orders went to the Bolsheviks to campaign in the elections, or for other less dramatic political work. There was yet no Trotsky or Sverdlov to relieve him of administrative detail or to support his policies. For the moment Bolshevism, with its confusing variety of instincts and policies, was embodied in this one man.

What was the source of this frantic energy, and what is the explanation for Lenin's shifts and reversals, which have not ceased to astound his friends, enemies, and biographers? The root cause was the same that made him write *What Is To Be Done?* in 1902 and minimize the importance of the soviets in 1905: the growing doubt about the possibility of a Socialist revolution. For the Marxists, the coming of revolution and socialism was as certain as the promise of future life for a pious Christian. They might be cheated temporarily out of a propitious moment for action; the Socialist paradise might recede farther into the future, but the laws of history foreordained that it must come. Lenin would have thought it sacrilegious to question this dogma even to himself. But his activities in 1906 and 1907 indicate that he felt that revolutions are made by men and circumstances, and are not the inevitable consequence of the laws of history. On the contrary, if you let a favorable moment escape, you may never get another chance. Here was Russia in 1906: the high point of the revolutionary struggle had passed. Constitutionalism, if successful, might lead to a social reconciliation and to acquiescence in parliamentarism. Others could view such a prospect with equanimity. A constitutional monarchy or a bourgeois republic was at worst a purgatory through which the working class would pass until it was strong enough and militant enough to seize power by itself. Lenin did not believe in the spontaneous striving of the proletarian for socialism. The "passing phase" of constitutionalism might become permanent, the worker would attend to his material interests, the peasant could be conciliated by a land reform, and the intelligentsia would be absorbed in its profes-

excited: "For a minute he stood silent, terribly pale." No wonder. He had been diffident of his ability to sway a non-Marxist audience, and had been envious of those who addressed large crowds.

sional and intellectual pursuits. This was a vision of hell. Had it come to pass, Lenin, such was his superhuman endurance, would still have found a role to play and would not have abandoned his strivings. In moments of discouragement after 1907 he doubted that he would live to see a repetition of the great events and opportunities, but this did not mean settling down as a lawyer or a journalist. If need be, he would plunge into the miniscule affairs of the Swiss Socialist Party and attempt to turn it to the revolutionary path.

But *now* there would still be time to head off the dangers of moderation and constitutionalism and to keep the revolutionary caldron boiling. The hectic, seemingly inconsistent tactics always had this purpose. If revolutionary activities were receding among the proletariat, then it was time to turn more to the still promising situation in the countryside. Attacks upon the Mensheviks were designed not only to seize the Party for his faction, but also to shame them into a more revolutionary and irreconcilable posture. And even the hated liberals—the Kadets—could be, through verbal abuse and the exposure of their alleged love for freedom, terrorized out of any compromise with Tsarism, out of any policy that would bring political pacification in Russia. The future ability of the Communists to hypnotize their Socialist and liberal opponents into a sense of guilt over their inadequate radicalism found its lesson in Lenin's campaign in those years. And when the inevitable has happened in our own days and the international movement has split, one part of it, the Chinese Communists, have been pursuing similar harassing and scurrilous tactics against their now more sedate Russian colleagues.

Such reflections come easily today, but within the context of the times Lenin's course of action could not be easily explained. The long-awaited moment of the assembly of the first Russian parliament in modern times took place in April 1906. Constitutionalism was not being born under the most hopeful signs. The meeting was *preceded* by the proclamation of the Fundamental Laws of the Empire, which left all executive power in the hands of the Emperor, and put considerable limitations and restraints even upon the Duma's legislative authority. This body itself had been elected through a cumbersome indirect and weighted voting system. Needless to say, every Russian liberal felt that his country was ready for the most democratic franchise possible, and both the character of the assembly and its powers were viewed with dissatisfaction. Lenin dwelt gleefully on the defects of the Duma and the predicaments of the liberals—the Kadets—who emerged as its most numerous party. Why was the Duma there in the first place? What true democrat could have submitted to that parody of the electoral process? Almost in the same sentence Lenin called upon this assembly, mainly of liberal cowards and turncoats, to assert themselves as republican heroes, and to seize power from the Tsar and his ministers. That the latter would happen in the form of the Tsar entrusting the government to the Kadets and other parliamentary moderates was in fact one of Lenin's worst nightmares. But he put on a brave appearance in the face of this horrendous possibility: the working class would only profit by those lawyers and professors accepting ministerial posts from the blood-stained hands of the Tsar. Why? The Kadets would only "exhaust" themselves, and above all, they would be "unmasked" [38] before the working class. He had forgotten that he had been unmasking them ever since their party was created.

His fears and the others' hopes had but little chance of becoming a reality. The reactionary circles, having recovered from their fright, were now begrudging even the timid venture into constitutionalism represented by the Duma. Even before it assembled the Tsar had dismissed Witte: he had stemmed the biggest wave of the revolution, secured a huge loan from the French bankers, so there was now no further use for him. His replacement was a bureaucratic nonentity. On its part, the Duma was in no mood to collaborate with the government, even on a limited basis. For many Kadets its platform was but another stage of the battle for a fuller democratization of Russia. Many of the other deputies were peasants: the franchise law had been fairly generous to the peasants in the optimistic belief that for all their recent misconduct the mass of the peasantry was faithful to the Tsar and order.[39] The largest peasant group, the so-called Trudovik (Labor) faction, ranged themselves left of the Kadets; many of them were close to the Socialist Revolutionaries in spirit (officially the Socialist Revolutionaries also boycotted the election) and demanded free distribution of the landlords' and state lands to their constituents. There was simply no middle ground between the autocracy and this multiparty, most radical parliament. Habits of accommodation, of mutual concessions by the left and the government could not take root in Russian soil. Lenin fretted needlessly, conjuring up the specter of a government responsible to Parliament, of Russian politics assuming the peaceful and disgusting characteristics of the West. In little more than two months the Duma was dissolved. How poorly the rules of the parliamentary game were understood in Russia is well underlined by the sequel: two hundred Duma members traveled to Finland and there issued a manifesto branding this act as illegal and calling upon the nation to refuse payment of taxes, recruits for the army, and the like. This was a call to rebellion in answer to government action that was perfectly constitutional. The Vyborg manifesto was signed by many Kadets, the party that contained the most eminent lawyers and constitutional historians of the day.

Lenin's reaction was predictable: the manifesto was grossly inade-

[38] *Works*, Vol. 10, p. 455.

[39] Thus the Imperial bureaucracy had shared in the universal delusion of practically every Russian political group: they knew "their" peasants and what they wanted.

quate. What was needed was an armed uprising, 1905 on a much larger scale. For a while it seemed that this was going to happen. There were mutinies in the fleet, calls for a general strike, and a wave of terror and assassinations that persisted through the summer of 1906. But the country had been exhausted by a year and a half of revolutionary strivings. Violence continued, but the revolution receded. Lenin continued his appeals for mass action. In August he wrote: "The Social Democracy should acknowledge and accept mass terror in its tactics." The news of naval mutinies at the bases of Kronstadt and Sveaborg threw him into a rapture. He demanded the proclamation of a general strike in their support. For some time now he had been pressing for the organization of special fighting squads. This work and general attention to partisan activities in which the Bolsheviks participated occupied his attention throughout the remainder of 1906. Beginning with the end of the summer he spent more and more time in Finland. It became more risky for the revolutionaries to spend much time within Russia proper. There was a new spirit and new determination in the government.

". . . All those [revolutionary attacks and propaganda] can be reduced to the following ultimatum addressed to the authorities: 'hands up.' In answer, gentlemen, the government with complete calmness [and] in the conviction of its righteousness, can only answer: 'You will not frighten us.'" The words are those of the new Prime Minister and Minister of the Interior Peter Arkadievich Stolypin. For all his talent in choosing nonentities, Nicholas II in the summer of 1906 nominated one man who combined unfeigned loyalty to the throne and determination to crush the revolution with a statesmanlike plan of curing Russia's ills. With all Witte's ingenuity when it came to social engineering, Stolypin lacked the former's sense of social inferiority and envious careerism. The post he accepted and the policies he was going to follow meant a possibility, indeed a probability, of assassination. His fervent patriotism made him accept this eventuality with Christian resignation: ". . . [Every] evening, when I return to my bedroom, I tell myself that I should thank God for an additional day of life bestowed upon me. This is the only consequence of my constant awareness of the nearness of death as the price for my convictions." This stoicism was incongruously combined with readiness to use very questionable means to crush the revolution and to preserve the throne. But his ideas went beyond repression and chicanery toward the vision of social reconciliation and a firm basis for Russia's place and prosperity.

But pacification had to come first. Another Duma was to be elected, for Stolypin believed in parliamentarism provided it could be reconciled with the Tsar's authority. But he was going to use the interval before Parliament met both to put down violence and to introduce the most urgent reforms. Almost simultaneously the government proclaimed the institution of courts-martial to deal with revolutionary disturbances and a comprehensive program of peasant and land reforms. Repression on one hand and reform on the other, this was Stolypin's formula. He tolerated and defended the murky and unsavory doings of the Okhrana, but extended an offer to the representatives of the moderate constitutional parties to enter his cabinet. It was his tragedy and Russia's that to the liberals Stolypin had to appear as a ruthless executioner, and to the reactionaries even this thoroughly conservative and fervently nationalistic man took on the appearance of a dangerous reformer.

In Kuokkala, an hour and a half from St. Petersburg, Lenin contemplated the new turn of events. In years to come he was to pay a grudging tribute to Stolypin's policies. He never denied strength and determination in his enemies when it was there. The Kadets, the Mensheviks, the ordinary Tsarist bureaucrats attracted his contempt largely because of their weaknesses and vacillations. When the enemy stood his ground as did Stolypin or as the German military machine was to do in 1917, he was spoken of with respect. At the end of 1906 and the beginning of the next year it was still too early to say with assurance that the revolutionary opportunity had passed, not to reappear for another ten years. Stolypin's courts-martial were functioning with a severity not exceeded even by the punitive expeditions of the year before. Then government repressions were unsystematic, savage in some regions, half-hearted in other places. Now in the first six months of their existence the courts passed 1042 death sentences.[40] The hangman's noose became known as "Stolypin's necktie." The Socialist Revolutionaries' terror and the Bolsheviks' own variant of it, the "partisan activities," and expropriations, continued. It was becoming clear, however, that the government had the upper hand insofar as the use of violence was concerned. In 1905 the revolution had fed upon the unprecedented strike movement. In 1906, while the strikes were still numerous, participation in them amounted only to 40 per cent of the previous year's figure. The revolution was being beaten down, though not yet extinguished.

Villa Vaza in Kuokkala was the nerve center of the Bolshevik conspiracy. Here Lenin conferred with his closest lieutenants, Krasin and Bogdanov, and here emissaries from the Bolshevik organizations all over Russia would arrive with their reports and for instructions. The conspiracy was twofold: first against the government and then against the Mensheviks. The Bolshevik center flagrantly ignored the Stockholm decision against factional activities. It worked indefatigably for a new Party Congress, where Lenin was confident he would recapture the majority and control over the central organs. Clashes with the Mensheviks continued: over the policy to pursue in the coming elections to the new Duma, over the armed robberies in which the Bolsheviks indulged de-

[40] *The Red Chronicle*, Moscow, No. 2, 1925, p. 139.

spite the prohibition of the Stockholm Congress, over the Party finances, and the like. A particular scandal erupted at the conference of the St. Petersburg Social Democratic organization in January 1907. There were mutual accusations of forged mandates and finally the 31 Menshevik delegates walked out in a huff. Lenin was delighted. He broadcast the Mensheviks' alleged sins and intended treacheries in a wild pamphlet, *Elections in St. Petersburg and the Hypocrisy of 31 Mensheviks*. For this contribution to working-class unity he was brought before the Party court of honor. Half childishly, half with his usual deliberation, he advertised openly his Machiavellian tactics. Yes, it was his duty to confuse and blacken the reputation of the Mensheviks. Only that way could the workers be prevented from being made the dupes of the Kadets, whom the Mensheviks wanted to support in the elections. It was crystal clear that no Party court was going to contain this man who mocked at Party discipline unless it was of his own making.

Lenin was now for participation in the elections, to the growing disgust of his more militant followers. His mind grasped at various most complicated schemes of coalition in the voting with various parties of the left, most notably the Socialist Revolutionaries and the Trudovik (Labor) Party. As usual, the appeals for such combinations were joined with a violent vituperation of the proposed allies. No Bolshevik was to imagine that they were genuine revolutionary parties. Why, even the Socialist Revolutionaries were essentially the representatives of the *petite bourgeoisie*. It was only after many years that Lenin discovered a felicitous phrase that represented his feelings about the nature of an alliance between the Bolsheviks and other political bodies. Writing after World War I to the British Communists to make them realize the necessity of entering the Labor Party, he advises them to support the British Socialist leaders in the way that the noose supports a hanged man. The idea of political alliances has always been one of the most fertile sources of that paranoia which crops up in Communist behavior. You join forces with party X in order to defeat a greater enemy, party Y. But you do it also to expose and unmask X, to show its insufficient courage and pusillanimous leaders. But then a horrible thought: What if the "masses," deceived by this alliance, begin to think of X as a genuinely proletarian party? What if your own people get really chummy with the Socialist Revolutionaries and forget their petty bourgeois character? What if *they* use you, instead of vice versa? What if . . . ? This frantic tossing to and fro in one continuous political nightmare is probably the reason that the Communist oligarchy appears to be the unhappiest of history's succession of the ruling classes. Even the capitalist with his ulcer and a weary eye on the tax man has his moments of relaxation and enjoys life more.

The originator of this unhappy tradition showed but little the effect of this fantastic profusion of anxieties and rages. True, the visitors to Villa Vaza in Kuokkala often wondered whether he got any sleep at all. Days were spent in conferences with the Party emissaries, and at night he wrote those vitriolic pamphlets that would fall like bombshells upon the Mensheviks or his own followers. But externally Vladimir Ilyich preserved his composure and strict adherence to the traditional Russian hospitality. Even for the humblest visitor he would busy himself to prepare tea and a meal, would make his bed if he was spending the night. This simplicity and the ability to be considerate and genuinely friendly even with persons who were illiterate in Marxism and the political problems of the day stood Lenin in good stead when it came to retaining the faith of his rank-and-file followers. They could never believe that this simple and unpretentious man could be guilty of all the intrigues and villainies charged to his account. There was in Lenin no prickly sensitivity, no self-imposed aura of the leader, as was the case with many revolutionary notables.

Seldom did he live so much for his work as during the year in Finland. His wife either commuted to St. Petersburg every day or stayed there for longer periods, always busy with the Party correspondence and administration. Vladimir Ilyich's capacity for being surrounded by his family even under the most conspiratorial conditions was still amazing. Thus in Kuokkala he enjoyed at times the company of sister Maria and of his mother-in-law. It is unclear how seriously he believed that the police were unaware of his hideout. Certainly Villa Vaza had a history of revolutionary associations. As Krupskaya records: "The people living there formerly were the Socialist Revolutionaries who manufactured bombs." Any real secrecy in Finland, where the revolutionaries felt emboldened, was really impossible. They were still compulsive "droppers-in." One day Nadezhda Konstantinovna arrived home after considerable detours to shake off the police, only to find seventeen Bolsheviks demanding food and drink. In far-away Berlin the Bolsheviks' agent was one Doctor Jacob Zhitomirsky. He also worked for the police and repeatedly drew their attention to the Ulyanovs' hiding place in Kuokkala. But as said previously, the Okhrana authorities were often too sophisticated to arrest the revolutionary leaders. Some of its agents may have savored the situation where those damned radicals schemed, conspired, and hid while they had a perfect knowledge of it. At other times the threat of arrest grew. As Krupskaya rather quaintly put it, "The police were getting more and more impudent." Some time later on (Lenin was already in the West) Stolypin got tired of the revolutionaries vacationing in the bracing Finnish air, and annexed to Russia proper the districts of Finland closest to St. Petersburg.

A new Social Democratic congress—the third in three years! From the Caucasus, Siberia, Finland, Poland, to London in May 1907 flowed hundreds of the leading Bolsheviks and Mensheviks, the Bundists, and others to renew their wrangles. They left behind their partisan activities, bomb manufacturing, agitation among the workers, to plunge once more into interminable debates. They could not agree earlier, and there was no earthly chance of their agreeing now. It was not so much various "issues" and points of the Social Democratic doctrine that divided them as the will of one man. Whatever Lenin's position was at the moment, and it changed as we have seen almost constantly, there, he insisted, was the only path to the revolution, the only Marxian orthodoxy. Everything right of it was "opportunism," everything left of it "adventurism" and "anarchism."

The unfortunate Mensheviks. As the non-Communist historian watches them marching to "the rubbish heap of history" there is an almost irresistible temptation to nudge them, to whisper a warning and advice. Why did they not eject Lenin and his phalanx in Stockholm where they had a majority? Why did they not break cleanly with the Bolsheviks in London in May 1907, where it was clear to the most obtuse that Lenin had not kept to his Stockholm commitment and would never agree to Party unity except on his own terms? In both cases the Bolsheviks would have suffered in membership and influence at home and would have been definitely disgraced in the eyes of international socialism.

But to the Mensheviks Lenin was now a combination of their hair shirt, God's visitation, and the naughty boy who sticks out his tongue when your back is turned. The hatred of Lenin served to unify the Menshevik leaders. Thus in a sense he was almost necessary to them, and the denunciations of the common enemy and troublemaker were the main platform on which people with as diverse views and personalities as Plekhanov, Trotsky, and Martov could find a temporary agreement.

The fury with which Lenin was viewed found its expression in the Menshevik spokesman's indictment: "You [the Bolsheviks] cannot even speak clearly, because straightforward language would reveal fully the contradictions in your thought and your positions. Language, grammar, logic—they fall sacrifice to the confusion which dominates your views. . . . You were against the participation in the Duma, now your representatives sit in it." [41] But though there was no Lenin among the Mensheviks, their own confusion was hardly less apparent. Were *they* for a peaceful, parliamentary path to Russia's freedom? Not quite. The same speaker (Dan) characterizes the idea that a social regeneration can be achieved through parliamentary means as "parliamentary idiocy." There was one species of courage that the most reasonable of the Russian Socialists lacked: the courage to be moderate, to bury once and for all the

[41] *The Fifth (London) Congress of the Russian Democratic Party. Protocols,* Moscow, 1963, pp. 566 and 567.

dreams of bloody convulsions as the main means of political salvation. Akimov had come closest to that position in Stockholm, but his name was now a synonym for faintheartedness. The Mensheviks had now fallen to the level of Akimov, said a Bolshevik.

The London Congress was an organizational feat. It is still hardly credible that a conspiratorial, illegal party could summon and transport to a foreign capital upward of three hundred delegates. Represented were not only the warring factions of Russian Marxism, but also this time as full-fledged participants and not merely as guests as at Stockholm, the Polish Social Democracy, the Jewish Bund, and the Latvian Socialists. The Party membership represented by the gathering was claimed at 150,000, probably an exaggeration.[42] This, on the surface, most impressive demonstration of the strength of the Marxist movement in the Tsar's realms was summoned at Bolshevik insistence. Lenin had hoped to reverse the verdict of Stockholm and to achieve a majority. His superior resources, the product of expropriations and manipulation with the Party funds, enabled him to obtain a slight edge over the Mensheviks. He wooed successfully some of the non-Russian Socialists. But effective majority escaped him. Five years were to pass before he finally concluded that he could not seize the Russian Social Democracy as a whole, and had to build upon his own people, the Bolsheviks.

The most convincing proof came in the Congress' overwhelming vote in condemnation of partisan activities and expropriation. It was hardly a secret; an abundant testimony rested in Lenin's writings that the Bolsheviks encouraged, prepared, and drew profit from such activities. Even when it came to the assassination of individuals—something Lenin never approved—as distinguished from mass terror,[43] the Bolsheviks' hands were not clean. Some of the bombs used in the Socialist Revolutionaries' terror campaign against the government officials, notably in the attempt on Stolypin's life in August 1906, were produced in Krasin's laboratories. That the Mensheviks did not at the time make more of the compromising evidence was due to their fear of its effect on public opinion abroad. Would not the Russian Social Democracy as a whole be compromised in the eyes of foreign Socialists and sympathizers if it became common knowledge that a group within it sanctioned robberies and murders? But the resolution carried by an overwhelming majority condemned partisan activities and expropriations and ordered the dissolution of the special fighting detachments of the Party, which in fact had been under the control of the Bolsheviks. The resolution recognized,

[42] The Latvian Socialists claimed a membership of 13,000 to 14,000, which would have made Latvia, with its population of 1½ to 2 million, the most Socialist area of the Empire.

[43] It seems like a silly hair-splitting distinction, but in view of Lenin's background and his attitude toward the Socialist Revolutionaries, it is important to keep it in mind.

though in a halting language, that such acts brought suffering to innocent people, demoralized and alienated the mass of the people, and in
brief, were detrimental to the cause of socialism. The Party members
guilty of persisting in those activities were to be ejected from its ranks.
The latter sanction, said a delegate naïvely, could mean the ejection of
"many leading members" (who could he have been thinking of?).
Lamely, Martov, the mover of the resolution, explained that the sanction was not going to apply to acts committed in the past. Hoping
against hope, the Mensheviks still clung to the notion that Lenin,
Krasin, and others would behave on this count and be shamed out of
their un-Marxist and anarchistic policies.

Lenin and thirty-four others voted against the resolution, even after
this conciliatory statement of Martov. There were many Bolsheviks
who resented their leader's venturing into terror and who did not appreciate subtle distinctions between its "mass" and individual expressions. But out of the sense of loyalty they refrained from voting.[44] The
issue was far from having been buried. The most notorious Bolshevik
expropriation took place in June 1907. In years to come the subject
would return to haunt Lenin and to become, as we shall see, one of the
most scandalous and troublesome memories besetting Bolshevism between 1908 and World War I.

At the time of his vote against the resolution, Lenin, however, was
already convinced that armed action on a large scale was becoming inappropriate. It was not the silly scruples of the Mensheviks that carried
weight with him, but objective facts. If the moment for an armed overthrow of Tsarism had passed, then the continuing partisan struggle was
losing most of its justification. It meant now the frittering away of the
Bolsheviks' human resources, concentrating on them the attention of the
police, and most important, the weakening of their ability to work patiently on the long-term tasks of agitation and organization.

From London Lenin returned to Finland determined to force his
followers to turn their attention to parliamentary struggle. This change
of tactics was not sudden; it corresponded not only to changed circumstances but also to some very basic traits of his character.

For all his occasional lusting for violence, for all his visions of dramatic revolutionary cataclysms, Lenin had very little of the military
leader in his make-up. In the years of the Civil War after the Revolution he would not dream, though he had every opportunity to do so, of
assuming the office or the pose of the generalissimo. He would not, unlike Trotsky or Stalin, affect the military uniform or intrude his judgment in technical military affairs. He was very much a civilian, a man
accustomed to fight with his pen and speech, an advocate (in the broad

[44] The vote on the resolution condemning expropriations and partisan warfare was
170 in favor, 35 against, and 52 abstaining.

sense of the word) and journalist by temperament. Though he detested parliamentarism, he loved an argument and delighted in the clash of viewpoints and an opportunity to display his oratorical powers and his incisive logic.

Thus when the Second Duma assembled in February 1907 Lenin became increasingly involved and interested in its proceedings. This Duma was more against the government and to the left than even the first one. The number of Kadet deputies was halved, but there were now sixty-five Social Democrats sitting in the Parliament, and determined not only to expose and arraign the government, but also to unmask and to push further to the left the hapless liberals and moderates. Eighteen of them were Bolsheviks. In the fashion that was to become standard with the Communists, the Bolsheviks did not consider themselves representatives of their constituents, but rather agents and subordinates of the highest Party authority, in theory the joint Central Committee, but in fact Lenin. He, for his part, became increasingly entranced by his vicarious parliamentarism. He would write speeches to be delivered by the Duma Bolsheviks, dictate their parliamentary tactics, write increasingly about the debates and issues before the Parliament. The weapon of parliamentary struggle was more and more to his liking. Why print clandestine Bolshevik tracts at a great expense and difficulty, when the same propaganda could be freely delivered from the platform of the Duma and become immediately known and discussed all over Russia?

For one of his deputies Lenin wrote a speech to be delivered on the subject of the agrarian problem, a cogent, sarcastic, and effective criticism of the government's land reforms that Lenin viewed with a growing alarm. Stolypin wanted to allay the peasant unrest by promoting migration to the virgin lands in the North and in Siberia. Why should the peasants go there? Let the landlords go to the inhospitable North and the wilderness of Siberia. The only solution is the confiscation of the gentry's estates and their free distribution to the land-hungry peasants. His penchant for statistics made him go into elaborate figures to "prove" that only such measures would appease the land hunger.[45] It is all very simple: if *all* the landlords' and state domains are turned over to the peasants, each household will get forty additional acres! [46] That much of the land he proposes to give to the peasant is composed of forests and otherwise unfit for cultivation, that his statistics are questionable in the first place, matters less than the wonderful opportunity for the Bolsheviks to appeal to the countryside. He noted greedily similar points made by the peasants' own spokesmen. Even the Orthodox priests on the peasant benches indulged in praiseworthy talk about the confiscation of the

[45] "Give me but leave to use statistics and I shall prove anything," said an English parliamentarian.
[46] *Works*, Vol. 12, pp. 241 and ff.

large estates. The Kadets' measly compromise: let the landlords be bought out, aroused his fury. He would quote approvingly the *moujik's* reaction: "Why should we buy out land? Are we foreigners?"

In June 1907, Stolypin tired of the Second Duma. Its dissolution was followed by the government revising the electoral law in such a way as to ensure more docile parliaments in the future. Members of the Social Democratic group were arraigned on the charges of inciting to an armed rebellion.[47] Their arrest failed to disturb Lenin. Most of them were Mensheviks (thirty-six to eighteen Bolsheviks) and anyway the parliamentary deputies were by definition expendable. Both before and after he had urged the Duma deputies to deliver seditious speeches. Their apprehensions that for all their parliamentary immunity they might be arrested failed to move Lenin. "Why, it would be a fine thing!" The workers would realize how their representatives are treated and the constitutional illusions would be further revealed as a fraud.

But the more serious element in the situation was the practical certainty that the Third Duma would be a docile tool of the government. The new law made it certain that the ranks of the left and of dissatisfied national groups would be depleted. What should be the reaction of the Socialists to this willful autocratic act of the regime? A strict boycott of the new phony elections? A general strike? An armed uprising?

Here Lenin performed a breath-taking about-face that threatened to lose him the most loyal followers. He who had stood for a boycott of the elections to the First Duma, grumbled about participating in the Second, was now insisting that the Bolsheviks should participate in the election to the Third, though it was going to be but a mockery of a representative assembly. To his own mind his reasons were excellent and consistent with his previous position; the others might be excused for thinking them perverse: a bad, reactionary parliament is obviously a much better thing than a good progressive one. No danger of constitutional illusions, of, God forbid, liberals joining the government and giving it respectability. It would remain a pleasing group of reactionaries and bureaucrats. As to the fact that only a few Socialists could hope to get to the Duma under the new franchise, this was clearly of little consequence. The revolution was never going to be accomplished by getting a parliamentary majority, and two or three Bolsheviks could shout propaganda from the parliamentary rostrum as well as ten or twenty.

On July 8 in the Finnish haven of Terioki a Social Democratic conference of the St. Petersburg region took place. Here Lenin had the somewhat novel experience of being attacked by a number of Bolsheviks led by young Lev Kamenev,[48] his future close collaborator. Further meetings produced more dissensions. The Bolshevik center began to dis-

[47] See details in Alfred Levin, *The Second Duma*, New Haven, 1940.
[48] *The Red Archive*, Moscow, 1934, No. 62, p. 209.

integrate, for two of its members, Krasin and Bogdanov, could not see
eye to eye with Lenin on his latest shift. To them it was incongruous that
the Bolsheviks should expect their followers one moment to attack police
stations, banks, and similar establishments, and the next to troop obediently to the polls and vote for the Imperial Duma. Lenin was unyielding: the propitious moment for an armed uprising had passed, and other
means had to be used to further the revolutionary cause. Within a year
he was to find himself more isolated than at any time since late 1903.

In August 1907 Lenin took a working vacation. He left Finland to
participate in the International Socialist Congress in Stuttgart. If the
fortunes of the revolution and the conditions in the Bolshevik group depressed him, then he could hardly be cheered by the state of affairs in
international socialism. The Socialist International was far from his ideal
of a militant Marxist organization. It included Socialists of all descriptions and policies from the "renegades" and opportunists to the (alas!
few) uncompromising revolutionaries like himself. Take, for instance,
the British Labour Party. Its leaders believed in peaceful reform, were
monarchists, and instead of manufacturing bombs attended garden parties at Buckingham Palace. A demoralizing spirit of toleration prevailed
in this cosmopolitan congregation. The fiery Rosa Luxemburg, who injected revolutionary pyrotechnics into German, Russian, and Polish socialism was ideologically fairly close to Lenin. But Rosa's militancy did
not prevent her from respecting and befriending Jean Jaurès, the great
French leader, who in Lenin's eyes was a disgusting moderate.

Even to the Mensheviks the world of the Second International appeared strange and unsocialist. One might have thought one was attending a convention of the Kadets, the emphasis being so much on reconciling
opposite points of view, on peacefulness, on parliamentary procedures and courtesies. The Russians must have blinked when they saw
Eduard Bernstein, the unrepentant heretic, author of scandalous Revisionism, rubbing shoulders with and not in the least snubbed by the
orthodox Marxists. But even the latter succumbed to the enervating
amiability and the cosmopolitan spirit of the occasion. There was much
embracing and fraternizing between the French and German Socialist
leaders, accompanied by mutual promises that never again would their
working classes be allowed to fight each other. The uncompromising pacifism of the majority of the delegates disturbed Lenin. Their main concern was to avoid a European war by threatening a general strike. A true
Marxist should think of war as an opportunity to further the cause of
revolution and socialism.

On their part, the foreign Socialists were anguished and uncompre-
hending about the savage quarrels agitating their Russian colleagues.
"But you are children," said venerable August Bebel, the leader of the
German proletariat, to Maxim Litvinov when the latter was attempting

to initiate him into the Bolshevik viewpoint. In time, Bebel concluded, the Russians' "childishness" would pass, and they would behave, like the Germans, in a mature, civilized way.[49]

For all the trials and tribulations of such an uncongenial association, Lenin had to endure it as well as the patronizing way of the Germans. A condemnation or ejection from the Second International would have meant the end of foreign support and sympathy, an utter isolation on the international scene. Where could the Party hold its congresses, who would protect the political exiles from being sent back to Russian prisons, if the Bolsheviks broke away from the international movement? But apart from the practical reason, he still treasured the tie with the German Social Democracy, the direct heir of Marx and Engels, and still stood in awe of its organization and of its erudite theorists. Whatever remained in Lenin of the Social *Democrat* was due to the lingering veneration of his German masters and teachers. When that veneration disappeared and in 1914 was replaced by hatred and contempt of the German party, Bolshevism lost its last democratic scruples.

Back in Finland, Lenin resumed his political generalship, now directed increasingly at holding the Bolsheviks together. When the Third Duma assembled in November 1907 he as well as Stolypin could breathe more freely. It had a pleasingly reactionary complexion, the largest bloc of seats going to the far right. There was now no chance of a Duma ministry, no prospect of a real conciliation between the progressive elements of society and the Tsarist regime. The eighteen Social Democrats included five Bolsheviks and this was enough. His interest in the proceedings of the assembly continued unabated. It was hopeful that the peasant deputies, while declaring their loyalty to the Tsar, still attacked the gentry's land holdings, and demanded their confiscation for the benefit of the poor and landless. The future of the revolution lay in the exploitation of the peasant grievances. A European war or a new wave of revolutionary unrest might yet interrupt the formation of that formidable barrier against socialism, the peasant middle class.

But for the time being there was little point in remaining within the Empire. The Bolshevik organization lay shattered and the task of rebuilding could be best begun in the safety of the West. It was a situation almost analogous to 1900, when Lenin had gone abroad for his first long stay for the task of building the Party then required. That preliminary theoretical and literary work could not be done in Russia. Now, again his pen had to become the revolutionary's weapon, for Lenin longed to unleash a series of literary thunderbolts against the recent deviations: against those Bolsheviks who were creeping away from the Party and finding their solace in weird philosophical cults, against the Mensheviks,

[49] A. Martynov, "Recollections of a Revolutionary," in *The Proletarian Revolution,* No. 11, November, 1925, p. 281.

who allegedly abandoned conspiratorial work and engaged in safe and legal trade-union activity, against the intelligentsia, who now as always were cowardly and treacherous, and so on. All this could not be done while continually dodging the police in Finland. And now that the struggle was over he probably longed for those splendid libraries of London and Geneva, where there were abundant materials with which he could support his arguments and confound those of his enemies. In December 1907 Lenin began his second and final migration.

VI

THE YEARS OF WAITING:

1908-1917

1. *Splits and Scandals*

The Russian revolutionaries, who two to three years before had set out for their country with such high hopes, came back in 1908 to Geneva to nurse their wounds and to escape the police now hunting for them in earnest. Lenin was in the van of this return migration, arriving in January with his wife and soon followed by his mother-in-law and his new chief lieutenant, young Gregory Zinoviev. Then came the others, the Mensheviks, the Socialist Revolutionaries, the Anarchists. Again the cafés and meeting rooms resounded to angry arguments, turning mostly on the reason for the collapse of the revolution. What went wrong? Who betrayed?

Lenin's reaction was as usual a sober evaluation of the situation combined with an intemperate attack upon his own class. The Tsarist government was now much stronger than before the revolution because for once it was pursuing intelligent policies. About yet another elegy of the peasant commune he wrote: "Wake up, professor. Shake off the dust of beggarly Populism." Stolypin was winning because he had understood the need for economic development, for building a Russian middle class. Hence he was destroying the peasant commune, the tears of the Populists and the conservatives notwithstanding. His social engineering, Lenin thought, would immunize Russia against revolution for a long time to come.

That the same reasoning led many radicals to abandon their conspiratorial activities and to settle down to their professional lives was, however, unpardonable. The intelligentsia, he wrote to Gorky, was running away from the Party. Let them go! The riffraff, scoundrels! His correspondent, who had some reason to suspect that he himself was not excluded from that polite characterization, wrote Lenin a reproachful letter and invited him to his villa in Capri. Lenin in a somewhat repentant mood replied that he did not mean to chase the intelligentsia out of the Party. But the latter would only grow stronger, as it was becoming more proletarian in membership.[1]

This assertion was based upon a fiction. The ranks of both the Men-

---

[1] *Works*, Vol. 34, p. 335.

sheviks and Bolsheviks dwindled throughout 1907 and 1908, and the defections were most pronounced among the workers. The Russian worker
had been exhausted by struggles and sacrifices of the revolution. Statistics
of the number of strikers tell the story: in 1907 they were but 26 per cent
of the figure for *the* year of the revolution, 1905; in 1908, 6 per cent; 1910, 2
per cent.[2]

What could be done in view of this depressing situation? One had to
start anew, ponder the lessons of the defeat, build a new organization, and
wait out the reaction.

The years 1908-1917, especially the prewar period, were for Lenin the
supreme test of endurance. To many he appeared at times a pathetic, discredited figure. The scandals connected with his expropriations and with
his methods of raising money for the Bolsheviks were to haunt him for a
long time. His closest collaborators of the revolutionary period either
turned against him or left political activity. In 1910 it was widely said
among the Mensheviks that Lenin was finished. In 1914 he was about to
be censored by the international Socialist movement. Against the background of the generally declining fortunes of Russian Marxism, Lenin's
personal position appeared the most vulnerable: assailed from both left
and right, widely blamed as the main agent of its disunity, he was a man
with no political future.

Or so it seemed. In retrospect, his very isolation in those years and
the virulence of attacks upon him were to become the main reasons for
his greatness in 1917. There was then nobody to share with him the leadership of the extremist course. The legendary trouble-maker and dogma-
tist became the only man to suit the violent and impatient mood of the last
stage of the Revolution. His opponents and denigrators of the past years
came back happy to serve under his command or tried helplessly to bring
up the disreputable past. For all his trials and personal dreams, the years
of the second exile provided him with the final complement of that supreme self-assurance that enabled Lenin to dominate morally and intellectually that group of willful and brilliant men who assembled around him in
the hour of triumph.

Such dazzling perspectives were hidden in 1908. The first order of
business was to resume the publication of *The Proletarian,* and the tedious
business of smuggling it to Russia; then the never-ending tissue of intra-
Party disputes on questions of philosophy, organization, and finance. The
defeat had not led to unity in the retreating ranks of the Russian Social
Democracy. On the contrary, deep fissures had now appeared within each
of its subgroups.

Not much time had passed since the Bolshevik meetings in Russia argued over the relative virtues of various makes of guns and revolvers for
street fighting and how far the Marxists should emulate the Socialist Revo-

[2] S. G. Strumilin, *op. cit.,* p. 213.

lutionaries in the use of terror. What did the Bolsheviks argue about in this year 1908 and what, at least ostensibly, led to a split in their ranks? Mach and Avenarius. Oh no, perspicacious reader, as Chernyshevsky would say, these are not the leaders of the Jewish Bund, nor those German Marxists who popped up simultaneously and confusingly in the ranks of the German, Russian, and Polish Social Democratic parties. A hurried look into the encyclopedia will reveal that Richard Avenarius (1843-1896) was a German philosopher, Ernst Mach (1838-1916) an Austrian physicist and philosopher, and that their philosophy centered around the problem of the theory of knowledge. One reads on: phenomenalism, empiriocriticism. All of which seems many light years removed from concerns of the Bolsheviks and the Russian revolutionaries in these fateful years.

But only on the surface. As happens often in Marxism and most insistently in communism, philosophical problems cannot be detached from politics. The grandiose and exasperating system does not leave many areas of intellectual autonomy. And so poor Mach and Avenarius became entangled in the political questions dividing the Bolsheviks immediately after the defeat of the revolution. From empiriocriticism and the theories of perception runs a tangled line to such brutally pragmatic questions as to whether the Bolsheviks should participate in the elections to and work in the Duma or abjure any and all legal activity in Russia.

As early as 1904 Lenin was aware that his allies, Bogdanov and Lunacharsky, were dabbling in some very suspicious philosophy. He himself had no need or inclination for such occupations. Marx's simple and straightforward materialism, its equally straightforward interpretations by Engels and Plekhanov were sufficient for Lenin. Only enemies of Marxism, he felt, would go whoring after strange philosophies, seek esoteric religions, and abandon the wholesome and necessary materialism of the Master. Valentinov recounts in his recollections how he tried to interest Lenin in new philosophical trends and discoveries. Nothing doing! He received such intelligence with growing irritation, refusing to read books containing such dangerous novelties. The true Marxist's instinct, he told his pupil, warns him off any philosophy that departs from materialism. If one sees a pile of manure, one does not need to rummage in it to find out what it is. So why waste time on some philosophical nonsense?

To many such as Valentinov and Bogdanov, the new trends were on the contrary alluring. The same youthful curiosity and excitement that drove them to revolutionary activity made them seek new philosophies and new explanations of the world and knowledge. Materialism and rationalism in the form professed by Marx as well as by many other philosophers of the nineteenth century were, after all, old hat. The end of the nineteenth century and the beginning of the twentieth saw a prodigious growth of the new schools of philosophy and psychology. There was Dr. Freud in Vienna, William James, and Henri Bergson. And Mach and

Avenarius. But Lenin would not hear of them. Except insofar as he himself revised Marx everything in the gospel was to remain intact. He chased Valentinov out of the Bolshevik group for his heresy. Why did he then tolerate Bogdanov and Lunacharsky with their more active espousal of the heretical theories? It was a case of sheer political necessity. Between 1904 and 1906 Bogdanov was second only to Lenin in his prestige among the Bolsheviks, Lunacharsky an invaluable propagandist and writer. Thus Lenin controlled his irritation, unlike Plekhanov, who would not even hear of writing in the same journal with Lunacharsky. He, Plekhanov, was the official philosopher of Marxism, and how dare an upstart challenge *his* philosophy, which had been blessed by Friedrich Engels himself?

By 1907-8 Lenin had concluded that his tolerance had been a mistake. Bogdanov and Lunacharsky had shown their true colors. They were for the policies to which Lenin now prescribed an end—fruitless armed action —and against concentration on tasks of propaganda, the Duma elections, and the like. Was it an accident that people who were showing themselves adventurists, who sulked because the new times required new methods of Party work, were often the very same who had professed the strange un-Marxist philosophical views? Of course not! Abandon the safe ground of orthodoxy in one respect, indulge your whims for novelty, and before long you will revert to being a capricious intellectual rather than a disciplined Party member.

Hence cautiously at first, but then with growing passion, Lenin began his philosophical campaign. Initial caution was required, as this was hardly the moment to split the thinning ranks of the Bolsheviks still farther. The strange new currents attracted many people with whom Lenin was fearful to break. Maxim Gorky was one of the proponents of the new philosophies. He had rendered Bolshevism and Lenin particularly invaluable services by providing funds, contacts with rich benefactors,[3] and giving the Party the prestige of his name. And, besides, he liked Gorky, and thought a deviation in a writer less heinous than in a real Bolshevik. His letters to Gorky at this period are cautious feelers as to how far the writer has plunged into heresy, and diplomatic attempts to detach him from its baneful influence. Yes, he is eager to have Gorky write for *The Proletarian*, but please, not about philosophy. Is Gorky's "companion" (actress Maria Andreyeva) also attracted to the new trends? No, it is absolutely not true that he had abused Gorky for his views. He, Lenin, believes that an *artist* has the right to use any philosophy he chooses, but when it comes to Party affairs the situation is quite different.

In April Lenin visited the proletarian writer, who was living in some splendor on the island of Capri. He enjoyed the fabulous surroundings and the rest from Party affairs. For all Lenin's diplomacy he could not

[3] At the London Congress in 1907 the delegates ran out of money to return to Russia, and it was Gorky and Plekhanov who induced a rich Englishman to help.

detach Gorky from his dangerous associations. His letters for the next two years abound in cordial expressions toward the writer and Andreyeva, but there is an obvious strain and apprehension beneath this cordiality. It was hard for Lenin to be tolerant and to preserve friendly relations with a man who, he felt, was for all his virtues and services helping to lead the Bolsheviks astray.

But with his former lieutenants Lenin had but little patience. When Bogdanov was to deliver a philosophical lecture he was to be confronted during the ensuing discussion by a list of questions designed to "unmask" him. They were cleverly prepared by Lenin to apply the method of police interrogation to philosophical problems. Thus Bogdanov was to be asked whether he "confesses" that dialectical materialism is the only philosophy compatible with Marxism. Will he deny that Ernst Mach has nothing in common with Bolshevism? Was not Lenin always an enemy of Mach's philosophy? Is it not true that some Mensheviks are the most fervent followers of Mach and Avenarius? [4]

It must be said that when the modern reader begins to scrutinize the views of Lunacharsky and Bogdanov he is bound to have a sneaking sympathy with Lenin's impatience, if not with his methods of polemic. From Mach and Avenarius the heretics proceeded to some muddled philosophy of their own, variously described as "God seeking" or "God building." The proletariat was to have a secular religion of its own. Wrote Lunacharsky: "You seek God? God is mankind. Build up God and mankind by joining with the leading elements [in society]." Such sophomoric mumblings should not obscure the fact that the "God seekers" were really searching for something more inspiring and emotional than the historical categories and laws of Marx which, they probably felt, were too fatalistic to endow the proletariat with hope and endurance in this hour of defeat. They were not the only ones at the time to reject the arid and naïve materialism of the preceding century, and to grope for a religion.

The seriousness of the threat inclined Lenin to do what he had refused to do four years before: to rummage in what he considered philosophical nonsense and obscurantism, and to unmask the trend as a whole. Hence the most lamentable of his literary productions, *Materialism and Empirio-Criticism*. He worked on it furiously throughout most of 1908. In May he abandoned pressing Party work and rushed to London to the British Museum to collect materials or, speaking more properly, the incriminating evidence.

For the book is one long indictment of philosophers past and present who diverged from simple, straightforward materialism à la Marx. Someone who reads the book unaware of the history of philosophy might well conclude that beginning with the eighteenth century the nonmaterialist philosophers and scientists had been engaged in a vast continuous plot to

[4] *Works*, Vol. 14, pp. 3-4.

split the ranks of the Russian Marxists in the twentieth century. It is a denunciation before the Marxist gods of history of the luminaries of philosophy both dead and alive, a search for damaging quotations in the works of persons as different from each other as Hume, Berkeley, the great French mathematician Henri Poincaré, and many others. It is a style of vituperation with which we have become unhappily familiar in the Soviet polemics against the unorthodox or currently unfashionable historical and philosophical views, vituperation that does not refrain from blackening the opponent's reputation even independently of his views. Ernst Mach? A plagiarizer, says Lenin. Even into spheres where he does not have the slightest competence Lenin advances boldly, armed with his Marx and Engels. What nonsense is it to write of a great number of dimensions! Everybody knows that there are just three. Those scientists who want to persuade us that there are more are really theologians in a scientific disguise. Relativism leads to idealism and where the latter leads everybody knows. And thus for three hundred pages. Even Lenin's sister Anna, who edited the work and arranged for its publication in Moscow in 1909, was scandalized by its personal attacks and managed to soften some of the most scurrilous passages.

The philosophical struggle now merged with an open split in the Bolshevik ranks. The "God seekers," known from the name of their paper as the *Forward* group, continued their attacks and counterattacks on the political as well as the philosophical fronts. They deplored the Bolsheviks' participation in the parliamentary elections, Lenin's willingness to use the Duma for the purposes of propaganda. Not a single but a twin heresy now put forth its shoots. Some of the Forward people were Recallers, that is, they wanted the Bolshevik deputies to give up their mandates and to denounce the whole farce of parliamentarism. Others, to plague the student of the Party history, would not go that far but contented themselves by being Ultimatists. They wanted their parliamentary representatives to subject themselves to strict Party discipline, to pledge to work illegally, in fact to make their parliamentary work impossible, and an expulsion from the Duma and arrest inevitable.

For once Lenin's mastery of himself appeared to give way. He was being assailed from left and right. The Bolshevik delegation in the Duma was his main political card, the main avenue through which he could spread political propaganda in Russia, keep some hold on the remaining working-class Bolsheviks, most of whom were happily unaware of the tangled skein of intrigue and scandals dividing their leaders. To give it up meant conceding all the legal opportunities for Party work in Russia to the Mensheviks, meant beating one's head against the wall in reverting to armed action that had no chance of success. Where to turn, whom to enlist in his struggle against the rebels who were taunting him with his own extremist slogans of two years before, who were withholding Party funds from him just as he had withheld them from the Mensheviks, who were taking the fight into the Bolshevik organizations in Russia? At one time he turned to Trotsky. The editorial board of *The Proletarian* invited Trotsky to participate in the journal. (Lenin recounted to Gorky that he would not write Trotsky himself because of all the unpleasant things they had said about each other in 1903–5.) His future war minister did not deign to answer in person. Somebody on his behalf answered that Comrade Trotsky refused. This haughty behavior reawakened Lenin's hostility. Isn't Trotsky a *poseur!* [5] In 1909 and 1910 he began to seek solace and support from Plekhanov, an invariable sign that Lenin was desperate.

The competing factions felt that they had the need for trained propagandists of their respective viewpoints. This led to competing Party schools, where the cadres were to be organized, indoctrinated, and then sent back to Russia to carry on the good work. The initiative belonged with the Forward people. Profiting by Gorky's hospitality, the enchanting island of Capri became the incongruous setting where thirteen Party members from Russia (including the inevitable police agent) were to be instructed in revolutionary activity, Marxian dialectic mixed with a dash of "God seeking," and so on. The organizers, Bogdanov and Gorky, invited Lenin to be one of the lecturers. This was indeed an insult added to injury. He was to play second fiddle to Lunacharsky and his ilk, and be isolated amidst the Recallers, Ultimatists, and "God seekers." No, he wrote to the "students," he could not come to Capri, he had no money to travel. But would they not come to Paris on their way home? There he could lecture to them to their heart's content, and he could also promise to produce some other real Marxist speakers and instructors. The curriculum of the school, he wrote, filled him with dismay. How about the "course" entitled "The Philosophy of the Proletarian Struggle." What nonsense. Come to Paris for the real stuff.[6] Pulled to and fro by competing celebrities, the students split themselves into the Leninist and the Forward groups, and the former left for the rival Mecca of Paris.

Undaunted by this failure and by the arrests that greeted those who had patiently completed the course when they got back to Russia, the Forward group organized another school the next year, in Bologna. The participants were elected by various workers' committees in Russia. The four students from the Urals had an additional reason to seek the sunny skies of Italy: they had been engaged recently in expropriations, or, to use a less polite expression, armed robberies, the fruit of which they were bringing as, so to speak, their tuition.

The organizers again taunted Lenin with their infuriating tolerance. Would he not come and speak? Also invited were various Mensheviks and Trotsky. This was really too much: hardly containing himself, Lenin re-

[5] *Works,* Vol. 34, p. 335.
[6] *Works,* Vol. 15, p. 437.

ferred indelicately to how the "school" was being financed partly by robberies and partly by the money that Bogdanov had illegally withheld from
the "real" Bolsheviks.

The city of Bologna was then as now one of the centers of radicalism in
Italy and its Socialist administrators welcomed their Russian brothers. The
school organized itself into an exemplary Russian commune—the students
and the faculty living together, though the latter were given more space.
Mme Bogdanov ruled over the kitchen, just as her husband presided over
the school. The curriculum was varied: Trotsky lectured on Tolstoy,
Lunacharsky on philosophy. The future head of the Soviet secret police,
V. Menzhinsky, instructed in the rather unexpected subject, the Russian
legal system. But there were more practical courses: how to organize a
conspiracy, how to use a code, how to combat the arguments of the Socialist Revolutionaries, anarchists, and the like. That the Mensheviks participated in this school financed by the proceeds of a robbery has always
amused the Soviet historians.[7]

But the tolerance of the organizers was mostly on the surface. It was
soon discovered that some of the students corresponded on their own
with Lenin. Scandal! Threats by the school directorate and counterac-
cusations by Lenin's correspondents that their letters were being intercepted. A Lenin partisan had accepted an invitation to lecture in Bologna,
only to disrupt the school and again to woo the students to come to Paris,
where they would be purged of "God seeking," "proletarian culture," and
the like.

Fights and alarums with the band of the God-seeking Ultimatists and
Recallers filled the years 1908–1910. The group was never very impressive
in terms of its support among the workers at home, but it contained the
leading intellectual lights of Bolshevism. What was most irritating was
that they copied Lenin's tactics against the Mensheviks: they claimed to
be a "literary group" and their main aim was but to restore the unity of
Bolshevism. At the same time they complained about their erstwhile leader's dictatorial manners. Lunacharsky bombarded the German Socialists
with complaints about Lenin misappropriating the Party funds and violat-
ing comradely comity. They clamored for a Congress but Lenin's passion
for such gatherings was temporarily in abeyance. He would cast a sorry
figure leading the disgruntled and divided remnants of Bolshevism. And
he would have to endure, and before a large audience, the Mensheviks'
taunts about his advocacy of violence and robberies between 1905 and
1907, and the unspeakable Ultimatists' accusations about his lack of militancy in the subsequent period.

In late 1908 one of the Bolsheviks still in Lenin's confidence, Zhitomirsky, advised him to move to Paris. He would, so the argument ran, be less

[7] See S. Livshitz, "The Party School in Bologna," in *The Proletarian Revolution,*
No. 3, 1926.

likely to be followed by the Okhrana agents in a big city than in Geneva. Since Zhitomirsky was still working for the police, the real reason for the advice was the exact opposite. The Mensheviks and the Socialist Revolutionaries had already transferred their headquarters, papers, and quarrels to Paris, where appropriately enough resided also the main foreign agency of the Tsar's secret police, faithful Zhitomirsky, one of its most useful informers. But it is very likely that Geneva irritated Lenin by the memories of 1903-4. Here he began his creation of Bolshevism, and here after four years and a revolution he was exactly where he had started. Maybe Paris with its exhilarating and militant proletariat would bring better luck. But he really could not endure great foreign cities. Krupskaya's satisfaction at leaving the "small, quiet, petty-bourgeois town of Geneva" soon gave way to apprehension. Her husband liked even less to live in the large, exciting center of the European *bourgeoisie*. Paris was a monument to the civilization and the class he detested, and its triumphant wealth and elegance appeared to mock and dwarf the picayune quarrels of the exiles.

It is an open question to what extent his dislike of the great European cities was based on a positive abhorrence of what they represented and how much it was based, on the contrary, on the fear that their beguilements might soften the stern resolve of the revolutionary. At times, Lenin was carried away by the all too visible contrasts to his own "half-savage" country. He wondered aloud to a group of delegates to the London Congress whether they would ever have in Russia something like Hyde Park Corner, where anybody, whatever his political persuasion, might get up and harangue the crowds. And the French café—there Anarchists, Socialists, and the like would loudly discuss their politics, not troubling in the least about the police. Those were, however, temptations of the devil, the bourgeois civilized devil, but devil nevertheless. And to compensate for such guilty sentiments, Krupskaya listed gleefully the glaring defects of the vaunted "European" civilization: the London slums, the venality of French politics, and the poverty of the Parisian worker. At least in Russia one did not have to contend with all that hypocrisy; there was no veneer of civilization and phony democracy covering the stark facts of exploitation and the class struggle. Whenever the reader of Nadezhda Konstantinovna's memoirs begins to suspect that the Ulyanovs enjoyed themselves in the bourgeois Babylon he is given a nudge reminding him of their stern revolutionary virtue. In the summer of 1910 they had a delightful seacoast vacation in Brittany. Lenin swam, praised the lobsters provided by his landlord, a coast guard functionary. A carefree relaxation, unaccompanied by revolutionary vigilance? Not quite. The landlord and his wife turn out to be violently anticlerical, not bereft of the proper class feeling. "And this is why Ilyich praised the lobsters so highly" says this implacable woman.

But Party affairs did not allow too many holidays. Lenin was waging his struggle on two fronts. In 1909 the Recallers and Ultimatists were thrust out from Bolshevism, though as seen in the Capri and Bolgna episodes some very guarded negotiations and relations persisted between them and Lenin. At the same time the Mensheviks, or most of them, were being branded by him as Liquidators, those who would dissolve the whole illegal network of the Social Democratic organizations in Russia and content themselves with the meager opportunities for legal political action allowed by the Tsarist regime.

The charge was absurd and inconsistent. From the point of view of such of his former allies as Krasin and Bogdanov, Lenin himself was something of a Liquidator, only *they* did not have his talent for inventing opprobrious epithets that stick to the pages of history. The Mensheviks believed in working in the Duma and so did Lenin. They believed in taking advantage of every legal opportunity for propagandizing and agitating among the workers; so did he. Lenin no less than Martov came to the conclusion by the end of 1907 that armed action against the regime was no longer feasible, thus breaking with the left-wing Bolsheviks. Where was the difference? The Mensheviks could not, even if they wanted to, dispense entirely with illegality and conspiracy: conditions in Russia simply did not allow the kind of free activity for a Socialist party that was possible in Germany or France. Throughout the period in question the Mensheviks as well as the Bolsheviks were being arrested and persecuted by the police. Yet Lenin fell upon the Mensheviks with his full vituperative violence, convinced Plekhanov and many future historians that indeed they were capitulating to the Kadets, why, to Stolypin himself! (In his least restrained moments he called the Mensheviks "Stolypin's Labor Party.") Since he needed one person upon whom to concentrate his attack, he vented his fullest wrath upon his old comrade of the early 1900s, Potresov. He was the arch Liquidator, "petty-bourgeois democrat," and an "opportunist." [8]

To some extent Lenin's campaign against the Liquidators follows his usual polemical tactics: you attack your opponent for his unmanly and unrevolutionary behavior, which under Russian conditions puts him on the defensive, compromises him in the eyes of the radical intelligentsia and the workers. In this particular instance it was a form of counterattack. For years the Bolsheviks had been denounced for their toleration during the Revolution of banditry under the name of expropriations, and for their

[8] There was an excellent tactical reason for thus singling out Potresov. The latter had offended Plekhanov by some sins of commission or omission while writing on the history of the Russian Socialist Movement in the great compendium being prepared by the Mensheviks under the title *The Social Movement in Russia in the Beginning of the 19th Century*. Plekhanov, who felt his historic role was being slighted, wrote to Martov refusing to contribute himself because "you will see for yourself the muddy opportunism in which Potresov is sinking." *The Social-Democratic Movement in Russia*, eds. A. N. Potresov and B. I. Nikolayevsky, Moscow, 1928, p. 188. Thus, in singling out Potresov as the prime target, Lenin was indirectly courting Plekhanov, whose support at the time was very important for him.

other scandalous methods of obtaining funds for their purposes. In crying Liquidator against the Mensheviks, Lenin hoped to stifle their charges that the Bolsheviks had indulged in anarchistic terror and armed robbery.

Here it is necessary to go back. The Bolsheviks, as we have seen, had plunged into the revolutionary struggles of 1905 late and behind the other Socialist and radical groups. To compensate for his initial doubts about the success of the Revolution and for the Bolsheviks being in the rear of the movement, Lenin soon shifted to extreme militancy and authorized the so-called partisan activities, attacks upon the police stations, banks, post offices, and the like. It is quite possible that those activities did go farther than he originally had intended. They were under the direction of Leonid Krasin and this urbane engineer and industrial manager was by temperament a terrorist. It was he and another Bolshevik, Professor Tikhvinsky, who manufactured the bombs used by the extreme Socialist Revolutionaries in their attempt to blow up Stolypin in his villa in August 1906. Even after he had broken with Lenin and abandoned active participation in Party affairs Krasin kept up with connections with the expropriators. In 1912 he planned the hold-up of state mail and by that time he had been read out of the Party.

But there is no doubt that Lenin was directly implicated in the most notorious expropriation, which took place in Tiflis on June 13, 1907. The London Congress had just banned partisan activities and expropriations and ordered ejection from the Party of those who would continue them. But on this date Semyon Ter-Petrosyan, the famous Kamo of the Caucasian terrorist exploits, directed the bombing and hold-up of an armed convoy transferring 250,000 rubles to the state bank.[9] Proceeds of the robbery, the Bolshevik source states unequivocally, were conveyed to Lenin in Kuokkala. The smaller denominations were left there; some five-hundred-ruble notes of which the police had the serial numbers were sewn by Krupskaya, among others, in the vest of a Bolshevik courier who conveyed them abroad.[10] Other high denominations were carried to Berlin by Kamo himself. The attempt to exchange them, directed by Krasin, who then lived in Berlin, led to the arrests of the Bolsheviks all over Europe.

The resulting scandal might well have led the Mensheviks to break definitely with Lenin, but once again they showed their fatal weakness and vacillation. All Russian Social Democracy would be discredited if too much fuss were made over the expropriations, Lenin was obviously on the point of breaking with his most terroristically-minded associates, and so on. But the scandal grew. When Kamo himself was arrested by the German police it became obvious that he had been planning an expropriation, this time in Berlin, that the Bolsheviks were preparing a wholesale counterfeiting of the Russian banknotes, and similar undertakings.

Kamo went through a long period of simulating a mental illness both

[9] *Kamo*, by B. Bibineshvili, Moscow, 1934, pp. 118-39.
[10] *Ibid.*, p. 130.

in Germany and in Russia, to which he was extradited, despite the protest of "the liberal public opinion." He managed to flee from a Tiflis jail, thus escaping a death penalty. In 1911 he visited the Ulyanovs in Paris. Reading between the lines of Krupskaya's memoirs, one gathers that he was now a source of considerable embarrassment to Lenin, who made no effort to keep him from going back to Russia and certain apprehension. Kamo's first loyalty was still to Krasin, and at his command he planned another armed robbery, was caught, and by some miracle escaped the death penalty. The Revolution in 1917 released him from jail. In Soviet Russia he was like a fish out of water, tried ineffectually to learn some civilian skill, and it was possibly a kindly fate that made him die in 1922 in an accident. It is very difficult to see in him, as some have, a dedicated revolutionary, or even an idealist terrorist of the Zhelyabov kind. Even his official Bolshevik biography, which extolls him especially, since his direct boss at one time was none else than Stalin, makes it clear that Kamo was politically illiterate, and that his primary passion was killing (he expressed his regret on hearing that Stolypin had been assassinated; he wanted to get the Prime Minister himself). After the Revolution many people of his temperament found their way to the *Cheka*, the Soviet secret police. But Kamo was evidently thought to be too unbalanced even for that occupation and so he was relegated to the Tiflis customs office.

The Tiflis scandal merged with another one: the affair of the Schmidt money. Schmidt was the young man who in the Moscow uprising armed the workers of his factory and fought with them in the December uprising. Captured by the police, Schmidt, according to different versions, either committed suicide or died of wounds in prison. He intended to leave his estate to the Bolsheviks, but it came into the possession of his two sisters. The profession of the revolutionary gigolo was not unknown in Russian annals. Zaichnevsky, of *Young Russia* fame, had boasted of his combining seduction with political agitation. A Bolshevik emissary, one Taratuta, seduced one sister and blackmailed the other into turning the bulk of her inheritance over to his group. The money thus secured was very handy to Lenin. Testifies Krupskaya: "This is why Ilyich was so certain that *The Proletarian* would pay for articles, and that delegates would get money for their traveling expenses." [11] The Mensheviks can be excused for a jaundiced view of the transaction.[12]

Those were some of the reasons that explain Lenin's distracting shouts of "Liquidator!" The attacks upon him from many directions go very far to explain the fact that never was his pen as scurrilous, as unrestrained, as during 1908-1910. It is par for him to call Lunacharsky, his future Commissar of Education, "scoundrel," and to use similar expressions about Martov, but he goes beyond it when he compares Potresov to Azev, the

[11] *Memories of Lenin*, Vol. 2, n.d., New York, pp. 25-26.
[12] See also Bertram Wolfe, *op. cit.*, pp. 380-82.

notorious terrorist-police agent who had just been unmasked,[13] or when his obituary notices of the deceased Kadet and radical leaders exude unrestrained hatred and abuse. January 1910 marks the lowest point of his political fortunes. Even within his closest circle he was finding little support for his furious fights on many fronts. Thus he was constrained to get together with the Liquidator-Mensheviks, and to agree to yet another illusory and short-lasting compromise. The meeting of the Central Committee once again tried to abolish factions and condemned the extremists of both persuasions. Most of the money acquired by the Bolsheviks through such indelicate means was to be handed over to three German Socialist trustees.[14]

It required incredible naïveté to believe that Lenin would abide by the agreement. The year was not over when he denounced it, demanded the money back, and declared that the Bolsheviks were returning to their previous position.[15] For several years the unfortunate German trustees found themselves under constant fire for refusing to hand over the funds. In the winter of 1912 Lenin himself went to Berlin to squeeze the money out of Kautsky, one of its three guardians. The German Socialists, whose patience with their Russian colleagues had been truly Christian, were by this time heartily sick of Lenin. The latter wanted his Berlin agent, Adoratsky, to initiate legal action against the trustees for the return of the funds. It would have been an interesting case: a suit for the recovery of money obtained by robbery and blackmail. Adoratsky objected that he did not have enough to hire a counsel. Again Lenin's ingenuity shone: he knew that the German newspapers in their struggle for circulation guaranteed free legal services for their regular subscribers. Let Adoratsky subscribe to a paper and then get after Kautsky and his colleagues. Unfortunately, nothing came of it and Lenin had to turn to other sources.[16]

Life in Paris continued with its minor splendors and major miseries of the political exile's existence. Among the first were the usual celebrations of the revolutionary anniversaries, which momentarily united the leaders of the warring factions and provided an opportunity for stirring oratory. At the anniversary commemoration of Herzen's death Lenin found himself in the presidium of the meeting together with Plekhanov and Martov, though his personal relations with the latter were now completely severed. Occasionally he injected a political note into his commemoration of the past. The Paris Commune, he declared at a festive meeting in its memory, failed to display enough resolution in dealing with its enemies, and thus allowed them to recover and crush it.

The inevitable quarrels and brawls of the exiles now affected him

[13] *Works*, Vol. 16, p. 222.
[14] Leonard Schapiro, *The Communist Party of the Soviet Union*, New York, 1959, pp. 116-17.
[15] *Works*, Vol. 16, p. 304.
[16] *The Proletarian Revolution*, 1924-26, No. 3, p. 101.

much more than similar incidents in the past. Krupskaya recalls one unpleasant scene: the Bolsheviks used to gather in a café on Avenue d'Or-
léans. One day a group of the Forward dissenters broke into their meeting
intent on a fight. They were led by the former Bolshevik Duma deputy
Alexinsky, who in 1917 was to accuse Lenin of being in the Germans' pay.
After some struggling, Alexinsky was ejected, and the *patron* turned out
the lights, thus extinguishing for the time being the struggle of orthodox
Bolshevism and Recallism. But the interesting point is Lenin's reaction to
this silly incident, which would not have perturbed him in the old Geneva
days. Krupskaya writes that he roamed the streets for most of the night
and could not sleep till the morning. He was now forty. After years of
the revolutionary struggle the Tsarist regime still stood and he, Lenin,
barely avoided being beaten up in a French café. He might have reflected
also on what had made him welcome to the Party brawlers and hooligans of the type of Alexinsky. Perhaps this was one night when Lenin
came close to being a Liquidator himself.

In 1911 there was a slight upturn in his political and personal fortunes.
The Bolsheviks now organized their own Party school in Longjumeau,
near Paris. This was Lenin's attempt to rebuild the nucleus of his Party in
Russia and to counteract the effect of the two anti-Leninist schools in
Capri and Bologna. It would have been simpler to hold the lessons in
Paris, but as usual, Lenin had the senseless idea that he could shake off the
agents of the Okhrana with which Paris was teeming. He and his wife
and the Zinovievs lived in Longjumeau during the spring and summer.
Those who commuted from Paris had to come on bicycles, watchful that
they were not being followed by a spy. As usual, such precautions were
useless; there was a police agent among the students, and the *Okhrana*
received detailed reports about the school and its activities.

Lenin's closest collaborators and co-lecturers were two men whose
names were to become almost inseparable until twenty-five years later
they were to meet a common fate before a Soviet firing squad: Zinoviev
and Kamenev. Another person giving seminars at the school and acting, so
to speak, as the stewardess of the establishment was Inessa Armand, who
was to play an enigmatic role in Lenin's life during the next few years.

The school was the first step in what was clearly Lenin's new design to
break definitely with the Mensheviks, and to build upon what was left of
the pure Bolshevik faction. This decision was based upon a sober appraisal
of the situation at home: there was no prospect of an early repetition of
1905, when the masses would press for a unity of the Social Democrats or
simply choose their own leaders. If the revolution was to be indefinitely
postponed and would, as he already began to believe, come under circumstances quite different from those of the past, it was better to end the
troublesome coexistence with the Mensheviks, Ultimatists, and other
such groups, and to build a true Leninist Party. It would be small; he

might be read out of the international Socialist movement, but he would be spared the constant sniping and intrigues resulting from the nominal unity of the Social Democratic Party. He finally capped his organizational philosophy, which was to have such a fateful effect on communism; purges and constant denunciation of the leaders were an excellent thing for the Party. Very likely it was a consequence of his retrospective condemnation of his own "liberalism" in admitting "alien" elements into its ranks, of his past collaboration with the Menshevik chatterboxes, of the welcome extended to the terrorists and hooligans, and the like. There was an element of resignation, but also of defiance and the ultimate faith in that decision to build a *Bolshevik* Party.

Needless to say, there were, in the preparations for the final split, the usual tactical feints and intrigues designed to throw the responsibility for it on the Mensheviks. The Bolsheviks were leaving but they were trying to take the Party label with them. Hence a confused story of the alleged meetings of the Central Committee of the whole Party, actually packed by Lenin's supporters, of the Bolshevik seizures of the Party funds and records. The secretary of the foreign bureau of the Russian Social Democratic Party was a Bolshevik, Dr. Semashko. On Lenin's orders, Semashko (one day he would become the Soviet Commissar of Health) abandoned the bureau but not the funds and records, which he brought to Lenin. The news of the scandal reached Russia, but was spoiled by exaggeration. "The Jews" Lenin and Semashko, wrote a reactionary journal, stole their comrades' money and escaped to America.[17]

But Lenin's destination and the use to which he was going to put the money obtained in this new variant on expropriations were different. The alumni of Longjumeau were busy in Russia rounding up credentials real or fictitious for the new Party conference, which was going to consecrate the division that had existed in fact since 1903. Where to hold the conference? London, Paris, Geneva were all full of the Russian *émigrés* ready to descend on it and to denounce it as a sham. Vienna was currently full of Trotskyites. And so, after some discreet inquiries from the Czech comrades, quiet, charming Prague, almost entirely free of the quarrelsome Russians, was selected.

The Conference that met in January 1912 usurped the rights of an all-Party Congress. In fact it was a gathering of twenty persons (among whom were fourteen voting delegates). It represented almost entirely the Leninist faction. For appearance's sake Trotsky, the *Forward* group, and Plekhanov had been invited, though Lenin must have known that Trotsky, whom he at this time regularly called "little Judas Trotsky" and the equally maligned Forward group would not attend. As for Plekhanov, for all his current rapprochement with Lenin he would not lend his name to this usurpation of the Party's name, the most shameful yet. Two of his followers did attend, but they were merely helpless, sometimes protesting, witnesses of the usurpation.[18] The Central Committee elected was entirely Leninist; it included Zinoviev, Kamenev, the then rising star of Bolshevism and police agent Roman Malinovsky, and "Sergo" Ordzhonikidze, who was to play an eminent role in Stalin's Russia, but was eventually (if we are to believe Khrushchev at the Twenty-second Party Congress) to die by his own hand. Stalin himself was shortly afterward coopted into the Central Committee. Thus except for Lenin himself, the Central Committee contained none of the great names of the Russian Social Democracy, none of the great intellects and revolutionary leaders of the past decades. They were all (except Malinovsky) faithful servitors of their leader, as yet almost unknown to the Socialists at home and abroad.

Soon after this coup Lenin moved his residence to Cracow in Austrian Poland. It was more than a symbolic detachment from the great centers of the Russian political migration. He was now going to live in a small, entirely Bolshevik entourage close to the borders of the Russian Empire. It was thus to be a double exile: not only from Russia, but from Russia-in-exile. He was going to wait.

With the Paris period is connected what some have professed to see as the great romance of Lenin's life: his association with Inessa Armand.[19] We met Inessa as Vladimir Ilyich's faithful collaborator in Longjumeau. Though born in France, and married to a man of French extraction, she had been brought up in Russia. After a spell of family life (and five children) she abandoned her manufacturer husband, and plunged into revolutionary work. From 1910 on she was frequently in Lenin's entourage, returning home with him in 1917. In 1920 she died of cholera, in the Caucasus.[20] Such are the bare biographical facts, and even about them there is some contention: her birth date is variously given as 1874, 1875, and 1879. Though an early memoir makes her die of cholera, elsewhere the cause of death is stated as typhus.

It is safe to say that *had* there been evidence of a love affair it would have been suppressed by the Soviet authorities. If Chekhov's correspondence with his *wife* has been censored of quite innocent passages referring to conjugal love, it is not to be thought that the Soviets would ever authorize the publication of letters or papers revealing the guilty passions of Lenin toward Inessa or toward anybody else. At the same time, the non-Soviet biographer has an almost irresistible temptation to catch Lenin in love. The very name, Inessa Armand, so unusual among the crowd of Veras and Nadyas grimly doing their work for the Party, is redolent of Paris and romance; his natural grudge against Lenin's wife and her prig-

---

[18] *The Prague Conference of the Russian Social Democratic Workers' Party of 1912*, Moscow, 1937, p. xxxiii.

[19] The facts and theories concerning this relationship are presented in Valentinov, *op. cit.*, and especially in Bertram Wolfe's "Lenin and Inessa Armand," in the *Slavic Review*, March 1963, pp. 96–114.

[20] *The Proletarian Revolution*, 1921, No. 2, p. 119.

gishness, all these and other reasons push the biographer into the supposition that Vladimir Ilyich did for once yield to the temptations of the flesh. But the evidence is, alas, skimpy. It rests entirely on what some ancient Communist ladies remembered of their younger days, and on (this much more substantial) the fact that in some of the letters the Institute of Party History saw fit to publish Lenin addressed Inessa by "thou"; and there were very few persons aside from his family, and no woman, whom he ever thus addressed in his correspondence. The evidence of the old ladies can be safely discounted, since it contains scraps of gossip palpably untrue, such as Lenin siring a daughter by Inessa, dying eventually of a broken heart, and the like. One of them, Alexandra Kollontay, had been a proponent of free love, challenged Lenin on politics during the Soviet period and was exiled by him to a diplomatic post, all of which makes her recollections (which we have secondhand after her death in her seventies) very suspicious indeed.

The available correspondence can but testify to a very close friendship between Vladimir Ilyich and Inessa. He entrusted her with important Party missions, commented upon her literary work and readings, alluded to his own state of mind. That he was very much taken with this attractive woman who combined revolutionary passion with broad culture is clear. That he had a fleeting romance is possible. But that he had a long-drawn-out liaison with Inessa (an American magazine greedily concluded, "She was his mistress for ten years") is most unlikely. In view of both his own and the general Russian revolutionary mores, it would have been inconceivable for him to conceal such a liaison, to go on living with his wife (and mother-in-law) while sleeping with another woman. The moral standards of the revolutionary intelligentsia (and as concerns them Lenin was the strictest conformist) required in such a case an open and public break. Nadezhda Konstantinovna would undoubtedly have gone on handling the Party correspondence and other chores, but Lenin would have moved in with Inessa. This also would have been kindlier than a long-drawn-out deception of his wife, of whom he always remained very fond.

All in all, we remain thwarted when we try to penetrate the more intimate side of Lenin's nature. And here there are questions of really greater importance than his relationship to Inessa, What was the source of his savage passion against his own class? What were his inner feelings at the lowest ebb of his political fortunes between 1910 and 1912? Whatever the crises and doubts he mastered them, to persist in the now apparently hopeless path of the revolutionary.

2. On the World Stage 1912–1917

In 1909 there appeared in Moscow a remarkable collection of essays entitled *Vekhi* (Russian for "landmarks" or "signposts"). Among its authors were some of the most notable contemporary philosophers, essayists, and literary critics, including N. Berdayev, S. Bulgakov, our old friend Struve, and M. Gershenzon. The essays created a sensation: they went through several reprints in the very same year, and for a long time continued to be the subject of vital interest and debate among the intelligentsia, to whose assessment the symposium was devoted.

In Paris Lenin greeted the appearance of *The Landmarks* with a fury that cannot be explained only by the fact that one of its authors was the "arch renegade" Struve. For once he was not alone in his vituperation. Other Socialists and the Kadets joined in the attack. The essays were immoral, they slandered the famous tradition of Russian radicalism, they sought to libel the noble ghosts of Belinsky, Chernyshevsky, and so on. The element of piquancy was provided by the fact that most of the authors at one time or another had found themselves in the camp of radicalism or even of Marxism. Now they preached moderation, a return to religion, reassessed as destructive the whole trend toward novelty and irreverence toward tradition among the educated classes. How disgusting!

"The greatest evil of our society is the spiritual rule by children." [21] This is perhaps the central theme of this contrition for the sins of the intelligentsia. We have grown accustomed in this day to dramatic repudiations by the ex-radicals of their previous extreme political positions. The breast-beating ex-Communist who has often passed through the decompression chamber of Trotskyism is a familiar figure in Western intellectual life. He has become disillusioned; the scales have fallen from his eyes after the Soviet-Nazi pact, after Korea, after Hungary in 1956. Hence much of *The Landmarks* sounds surprisingly modern. But its scope is broader than that of a mere recantation; for it searches for the reasons of the intellectual's dissatisfaction with the world around him, his constant pursuit of political and social panacea. The word "alienation" had not yet come into fashion, but even had it been in use in its psychological sense the authors would have been hard pressed to specify what they were accusing the intelligentsia of being alienated from. The Tsarist regime, which even they had to hold as backward and a source of national shame? The Orthodox Church, which in its then current state could not inspire much respect?

But if weak in alternatives, they put their finger on the source of evil: spiritual rule by children. In its irrationality, quarrelsomeness, and lust for heroics Russian radicalism did perpetuate traits of adolescence. The learned authors did not realize that this was not only its deficiency but also the source of its enormous attraction. To be a revolutionary was to stay young no matter what one's years, to remain adventurous in spite of the boredom of one's professional career. What could the authors offer in exchange for that life of adventure, enthusiasm, and righteous indignation? We need to give up fruitless anticultural moralism and adopt a creative

[21] *The Landmarks, Collection of Essays About the Russian Intelligentsia,* Moscow, 1909; 4th printing, p. 43.

religious humanism, wrote one of the contributors. And indeed some of them were to return to the faith of their fathers.

But to a revolutionary the appearance of *The Landmarks* was a danger sign. The most fertile spring of the Russian revolutionary fervor was drying up. For all his feigned satisfaction that "the intelligentsia scoundrels and riffraff" were leaving the cause, Lenin realized the indispensability of this despised class for the revolution. Years later he still wrote, "This shamefully notorious book, *The Landmarks,* is having a great success among the liberal bourgeois society which is imbued with renegade sentiments. It has evoked but an unsatisfactory reply and insufficiently deep analysis from the camp of democracy." [22]

The Landmarks pinpointed another danger signal for the revolutionary: the growth of hedonism and sexual license among the youth. A Kinsey-like poll taken among students (really how infuriatingly contemporary the Russia of 1909 sounds) indicated that most of them had had sexual intercourse by the time they entered the university, and that many of them had sexual initiation in their early teens. The authors coupled this behavior with the young men's revolt against society, but Lenin knew better. How sternly moralistic was his own generation in its youth, with sex and romance subordinated, at least in theory, to the cause of freedom. Sexual license was really a symptom of growing individualism among the young. Next they would dissipate their energy in sports (and not merely as a healthful and allowable relaxation from revolutionary activity), or, worst of all, devote themselves to making money and careers. Who nowadays read Chernyshevsky? Most of the literature produced now in Russia, Lenin gloomily concluded, was pornography. Even the cult of Tolstoy that flared up at the great writer's death in 1910 had its dangers. Genius though he was, Tolstoy professed Christian anarchism and taught nonresistance to evil. In the universal mourning for the great man that enveloped all Russia from the Tsar to the revolutionaries, Lenin detected something of a plot. Aren't the liberals, by hypocritically praising Tolstoy, trying yet another gambit to wean the Russian youth from the revolution and violence?

The situation was bleak not only among the intelligentsia and students. In 1906 (it now seemed ages ago) Lenin's great hope was the revolutionary uprising among the peasants. He observed with satisfaction in 1905–6 more than two thousand landlords' residences were burnt by the aroused *moujiks*. Now he had more distressing statistics to ponder. Stolypin had abolished most of the civil disabilities of the peasant, giving him the right to feel that the last remnants of serfdom had been cast off. Most important of all, the hunger for land was being appeased through a vigorous colonizing policy. This movement in its scope and intensity reminds one of the settlement of the American West. Between 1906 and 1910, Lenin

[22] *Works,* Vol. 18, p. 285.

acknowledges, 2.5 million peasants moved to Siberia. By allowing the individual peasant to opt out of the commune and to consolidate his holdings, the Tsarist statesman was building a rival middle class. Ten, twenty years more of this policy and the Russian peasant, imbued with the sense of private property, would stand as an unbreakable barrier to socialism and the revolution. What appeal could the old slogan of seizing the gentry's land have when the peasants with the state's help were already in a fair way of buying out the gentry's estates?

From the intelligentsia to the peasant, everywhere, signs of unwelcome pacification and social reconciliation: in 1907 the combined Social Democratic membership in the Empire was about 150,000. Now who knew how many were left, perhaps 30 to 50,000, he wrote despairingly. At times it would appear that the violent revolutionary in Lenin died a little, and the Marxist believer in the *evolutionary* process grew stronger. Stolypin brings capitalism to the countryside? Well, on second thought it was not really too bad. The faster the growth of capitalism, the sooner, teaches Marxism, socialism must triumph. There are delusive flashes of tolerance in his writings: no reason why priests cannot be accepted in the Party. The next phase of Russia's development must be a bourgeois republic. "The more democratic the system in Russia becomes, the faster, stronger, and wider capitalism will develop." [23] And it would be a good thing. Is Lenin mellowing with age and defeat? Then a violent diatribe against the Mensheviks or a scurrilous epigram about the liberals makes us abandon such suspicions.

Bleak though they were, the prospects for a revolution in Russia were not hopeless. Stolypin's social engineering as yet lacked a solid foundation. It was the work of an enlightened bureaucrat, it could be interrupted or frustrated by less intelligent successors or by war. The Prime Minister saw that it would be an irretrievable catastrophe if Russia, its social system still not fully modernized, were to enter a European conflict. But his authority did not extend to foreign relations. Even in domestic affairs Stolypin was hampered by the narrowness of views of his sovereign. As earlier with Witte, so with Stolypin, the court circles begrudged his authority and insinuated to Nicholas II that this man was interposing himself between the Tsar and his people. In his attempt to remove the grosser injustices and to dam the sources of revolutionary sentiment Stolypin proposed to relieve the civil disabilities that were the lot of the religious minorities. He carried through a legislation that improved the position of the Old Believers and of other Christian sects and denominations that had split from the Orthodox Church. But when it came to the Jews, whose status in Russia was a world scandal, and who suffered from humiliating and uncivilized legal disabilities, the Emperor balked at relief. His "conscience," he wrote

[23] An editorial in *Northern Pravda* (a legal Bolshevik journal published in St. Petersburg), September, 1913.

Stolypin, would not allow him to grant the Jews first-class citizenship.

The attempt to transform Russia into a civilized, even a semiconstitutional monarchy had to be conditioned by the personality of the Tsar himself. And by temperament and upbringing Nicholas II was totally unsuited to be a constitutional monarch, just as he was unable to be a reforming autocrat. His very private virtues added up to a public disaster. A model husband and family man, he was under the influence of his wife, a neurotic German woman who, though a granddaughter of Queen Victoria, abominated constitutionalism and was bound to intrigue against any minister who because of ability and reforming zeal appeared in her imagination to threaten her husband's prerogatives. Had the Emperor been devoted to pleasure and less tied down by what he conceived to be his duty, he might have welcomed a relief from his enormous and, by twentieth century standards, obsolete responsibilities and power. As it was, he was constantly worried that by having agreed even to this very limited constitutionalism he had betrayed his heritage and robbed his successors. The world of modern ideas was for him an enigma and an abomination. In personal habits he was, like every contemporary nobleman, a fervent Anglophile, but in politics he detested Britain and the British. England, even more than France, was the source of the dangerous ideas of constitutionalism and an asylum for the revolutionaries from his country. The English press daily berated Russia for its uncivilized autocratic ways. "The English are just like the Yids," the Autocrat of All the Russias used to say elegantly to the appalled Witte.

Apart from the personality of its holder, the crown as an institution could not maintain its prestige. The Empress' worry about her hemophiliac son made her seek help in a succession of faith healers, the last and most notorious of whom was Rasputin. The charlatan's influence within the court camarilla, his interference in the affairs of the state and church, became a public secret and scandal. To an enlightened conservative, even if, like Witte, he despised the Tsar, prestige of the monarchy was an essential element of social cohesion and national unity and this prestige was rapidly disappearing even among the classes traditionally loyal to the throne. In contrast to the regime of Alexander II, the crown became associated with reaction and religious obscurantism and could not serve as a stabilizing factor in Russia's attempted passage from autocracy to the modern age.

The revolutionary's violent detestation of the monarchy and its holder was based not only on its history but also on the realization of its lingering role as a symbol of national unity and its alleged hold on the masses of the peasantry. In its terroristic campaign the Fighting Organization of the Socialist Revolutionaries deliberately refrained for long from attempts against the Tsar's life. Memories of public reaction to the assassination of March 1, 1881, were still vivid. When a Kadet leader on his visit to London in 1909 stated that as long as Russia had a parliament the liberals would remain "His Majesty's Opposition and not an opposition to His Majesty," Lenin was beside himself with fury.[24] A revival of the prestige of the crown and its transformation into a constitutional symbol of national unity was one of the revolutionaries' worst nightmares. But such fears were needless.

Nor could the reforms claim a firm basis and support within the ranks of the bureaucracy. The traditional hostility of the educated classes in Russia to authority had its basis also in the not unreasonable feeling that the agents of the state, whether ministers or policemen, were not servants of society but an independent and oppressive order. To instill the rule of law and order in a country that had recently known but revolution and repression, one had to restore trust in the public authorities. That had also proved beyond the resources and in some cases beyond the intentions of Stolypin. In his speeches to the Duma he emphasized that he was master of his own house and that he would "tolerate no dark forces" within the bureaucracy impervious to public scrutiny.[25] No provincial governors or police chiefs were going to instigate pogroms; the secret police was not to be allowed to pursue its machinations independently of the minister.

Such assurances were soon exposed as hollow. In 1909 the Azev scandal broke out. It was revealed that the man whom the *Okhrana* considered its most reliable informer had been the instigator and organizer of the assassinations of the highest state officials, and that the same man trusted by the Socialist Revolutionary Party and head of its Fighting Organization delivered many of the revolutionaries to the police.[26] The blow was severe to both sides. Granted, as Stolypin claimed, that any government in its struggle with subversion must resort to informers and "planted" agents. It was still revealed that there were "dark forces" behind and at times independent of the ministers. If the revolutionary organizations were shot through with *agents provocateurs* then by the same token the police department, the alleged defender of order and legality, was shown as being filled with deranged and criminal elements often pursuing their own game and uncurbed by any scruples. Stolypin attempted to put a brave and untrue interpretation upon the facts: Azev had been a loyal police collaborator and he had not been involved in the murder of Pleve and Grand Duke Serge! In September 1911 another double agent, anarchist

---

[24] *Works,* Vol. 15, p. 428.

[25] Lande (pseudonym for A. Izgoev), *P. A. Stolypin,* Moscow, 1912, p. 29.

[26] Yevno Azev had been a police agent and . . . a revolutionary since 1893. The surviving photographs of Azev make one wonder how a man with his repulsive appearance could have been entrusted with the secrets of a revolutionary party and the lives of hundreds of its fighters. Indeed, in retrospect many of his contemporaries were to testify to the revulsion his behavior and appearance had produced in them, and to wonder at their own naïveté. But the unhappy fact was that the revolutionaries taught themselves "to rise above prejudice" and to welcome in their midst a resolute fighter no matter how obnoxious his personality.

by conviction and police informer by profession, resolved his inner conflict by shooting and mortally wounding the Prime Minister. Thus Stolypin was not given the chance to keep Russia out of war and to consolidate his reforms, which in the opinion of many might have prevented the events of 1917.[27]

Thus behind the impressive façade of the post-1906 reforms there still remained the basic weakness of the Tsarist edifice. The year 1912 marks a resurgence of industrial strikes on a wide scale.[28] The strike action was to grow until the war. Still, a repetition of 1905 seemed most unlikely, but was the regime strong enough to withstand an external emergency?

It is important to note that beginning with 1911–12 Lenin's attention turned more and more to the international scene. Prior to that period his gaze was riveted almost exclusively on Russia. Member of an international movement, he did write occasional articles and pieces about problems of socialism in foreign lands. But now almost instinctively he wrote and speculated about the wider world stage. It is as if his mind were already groping for a more circuitous path to the revolution in Russia: the disheartening trend of events could be interrupted by an international conflict and war. After 1910 there were increasing signs that the great powers were set on a collision course. If a localized war in the Far East triggered off one revolution wouldn't a general European war bring a much greater one? The symptoms of social unrest in Europe, the nationalist stirrings in Asia, were now carefully noticed. Of Chinese revolutionaries and especially of Sun Yat-sen he wrote: "They are all subjectively socialists because they are against the exploitation and oppression of the masses,"[29] one of the first inklings of the tactics that would serve communism well. He began to perceive that the European state system, this seemingly invulnerable

[27] The whole subject of the *agents provocateurs* is an important part of the pathology of the revolutionary movement. Every radical group was shot through with them. At the Prague Conference of 1912, out of twenty persons present two were police agents. It is likely that some of them have never been unmasked though the revolutionary movement had its own counterespionage agency, headed by Vladimir Burtsev, who tracked down Azev, and who in his Paris journal, *Byloe* (*The Past*), published regularly the names of the double agents he was able to discover. Lenin viewed the problem philosophically: the *agent provocateur* was mainly a danger to groups like the Socialist Revolutionaries, who relied upon terror (he overlooked how close he came to their tactics in 1905–7). He could do but limited damage to the Social Democrats, whose main weapon was the education and indoctrination of the mass of workers, and who employed legal as well as illegal means. Still, the havoc wrought by somebody such as Roman Malinovsky was very considerable. The prevalence of double agents explains why, during the purges in Stalin's Russia, many of the condemned had tacked on the charges of having worked for the Tsarist police, the British Intelligence, or other agencies. To those who had grown up in the underground in Tsarist Russia there was nothing improbable in the charges, absurd as they were.

[28] In 1912 troops fired on the striking workers of the Lena goldfields in Siberia. This aroused a wave of protests throughout Russia. In connection with the Lena events the country first heard the name of young attorney Alexander Kerensky.

[29] *Works*, Vol. 18, p. 146.

mainstay of the capitalist civilization, had an Achilles heel in its imperial possessions. To the smug exploiting classes of France, Britain, and Germany the colonial problem was a double threat, bringing them into conflict with each other and confronting them with the growing resentment and movement for independence among their Asiatic subjects (no one yet thought of Africa in this connection). "The Awakening of Asia" is the title of one of his articles. Just as his eye had scanned all classes and social problems in Russia in search of a promising revolutionary opening, so he began to look for hopeful signs on the international scene. A lot of time had passed since Dr. Marx had taken the pulse of Western capitalism and pronounced it on its deathbed. It had been the source of fury and secret inner doubts of his followers that in sixty years since that diagnosis the patient, far from dying, had prospered on a scale unparalleled in history and that the institutions and mores of the *bourgeoisie* had marched triumphantly all over the world. Only now there appeared signs of the weakness of the whole structure.

Connected with this new dimension of the revolutionary problem was Lenin's enhanced interest in the nationality question. It had been in the back of his mind for some time: what Russian revolutionary could be unaware that his cause was a beneficiary of the Tsarist oppression of national minorities and dominion over non-Russian peoples? For the revolutionary organization Lenin had always demanded unity and centralization transcending national distinctions. For revolutionary propaganda he always extolled the slogan of national self-determination. His pragmatism was outraged by the tedious scruples of those Marxists who insisted on spelling out the consequences of every propaganda position. How can true Marxists, they cried, be for *unconditional* national self-determination? Would it not mean turning Poland over to the Polish landowners and the *bourgeoisie*, the Turkic-speaking regions of the Empire to the feudal Moslem chiefs and religious leaders, etc.? The most insistent of such voices was that of Rosa Luxemburg, who though in Germany kept a hold on the Polish Social Democratic Party, which condemned the idea of Polish independence as a gentry-bourgeois design to enslave the Polish workers. Lenin in general liked Rosa for her fine revolutionary fervor, and for the fire with which she castigated the opportunists and Revisionists of the German Social Democracy. But when she crossed him on the nationality question or the intrigues he was currently stirring up within the Polish Social Democratic Party, she became "pompous Rosa" and a senseless fanatic. It was difficult to look around the world in 1912 and not to see the overwhelming appeal of nationalism. The strongest force for socialism among the Poles in the three empires was not Rosa Luxemburg's group but the Polish Socialist Party, openly and strongly nationalistic. The constitutional system of Great Britain was being threatened because of the Irish problem. Was militant Marxism going to discard this ready-made weapon because of some very hypothetical dangers?

Lenin was blissfully unaware that he was a Russian nationalist. Denunciations of "Great Russian chauvinism" came to him easily both before and after he seized power. Yet he never possessed the liking and tolerance for other nations and cultures that must be the basis of genuine internationalism. There was nothing cynical or hypocritical in his belief in political centralization on the one hand and his loud denunciation of chauvinism on the other. He bridled at any manifestation of gross, bullying Russian nationalism. He delighted in exposing intolerance in assimilated non-Russians who, naturally enough, were often more chauvinistic than Russians by descent.[30] He reprimanded a Caucasian Bolshevik, Shaumyan, for his opposition to language autonomy. And to another Caucasian, Stalin, he entrusted the writing of an article spelling out the Marxian (that is, Lenin's) position on the nationality problem.

Stalin's article was an elaboration of Lenin's own views. As in everything, there was a striking ambivalence about them. Every national group inhabiting a contiguous territory had the right to its own language. Lenin for this purpose praised "civilized" Switzerland for tolerating many languages, contrasting it with barbarous Russia trying to suppress Polish, Ukrainian, Armenian, and other tongues. The right of every nation for self-determination was again loudly proclaimed. But . . . decentralization and federalism were condemned as unsuited for the modern industrial state, just as they were incompatible with the organization of a revolutionary party. What is granted in the cultural domain is withdrawn when it comes to politics. To a Pole or an Armenian living within the Russian Empire and suffering national persecution, Lenin's program opened a dazzling vista of free national development. But what was in fact the small print in this generous acknowledgement of the right of national independence foreshadowed the future Communist policy: to insist on this right in a *Socialist* state or even to demand meaningful autonomy is to be against the revolution and guilty of treason to the working class. The *promises* of Lenin's nationality policy served the Bolsheviks well in their struggle for power, were to save them in the Civil War, while upon its almost hidden *premise* was to be built the centralized, politically monolithic edifice of the Union of Soviet Socialist Republics.

It is curious how the problems of the future crowded upon Lenin in this prewar period. To the contemporaries, whether the Mensheviks, Trotsky, or the Tsarist police, he was still the arch intriguer, the man who kept the Russian Socialists from reuniting and leading the working class. But in some ways he already looked beyond the Mensheviks and even beyond the revolution. He had for long had a great if somewhat dilettantish interest in problems of productivity and industrial organization. From

---

[30] "It is well known," wrote that other Russian nationalist, Witte, ". . . that there can be no greater enemy of a nation or a religion than a renegade. No greater Judophobe than a Jew converted to Orthodoxy. No greater enemy of the Poles than a Pole who has entered the Orthodox Church as well as the Russian Secret Police." *Memoirs*, Vol. 3, Moscow, 1960, p. 468.

Siberia he used to write asking for the latest books on new mechanical inventions, especially those distant ancestors of today's mechanical and electronic computers. Now his interest quickened in such devices and techniques apparently far removed from a revolutionary's immediate concerns. The speed-up system devised by Taylor, he wrote, was obviously a capitalist's device to exploit the worker. But the Socialist state would be able to put Taylor's system to its own use to increase the productivity of labor. The news of Sir William Ramsay's technique of extracting gas from coal made Lenin forget for a moment Martov, Trotsky, and the others. This invention opened splendid perspectives for socialism. With it and with similar scientific devices, they should be able to reduce the working day from eight to seven hours.[31] Nothing refutes more fully the thesis that Lenin is another Nechaev or Tkachev, merely a man obsessed with the revolution, than this very practical, very Marxist concern with labor-saving devices, with productivity and applied science. *His* Russia would not be like Chernyshevsky's, one vast choral society dedicated to healthful and innocent amusements. It would be, first of all a country of hard work, of strict industrial discipline and organization, where socalism would turn into a cult of production unmatched by the most exacting capitalism.

There scarcely could be a more incongruous setting for such technocratic visions than Cracow, the charming Galician city still filled with the monuments and memories of the Middle Ages when it was the capital of the great Polish-Lithuanian state. He lived here from June 1912, very close to the borders of the Russian Empire, very far from the Russian migration. St. Petersburg papers took but three days to reach Cracow. Couriers to and from Russia could cross the frontier with little difficulty. Government officials in Galicia were mostly Polish and they were almost solicitous in facilitating the work of a Russian revolutionary. To a Pole living under an indulgent rule of the Hapsburgs, Tsarism was the main enemy and its enemies his natural allies. Shortly after his arrival Lenin was visited by a police official. Was Mr. Ulyanov quite sure about a recent arrival from Russia who frequented his apartment? The gentleman in question acted quite suspiciously; he might be, God forbid, an agent of the Russian secret police. Lenin was able to reassure the obliging policeman.[32] For their part, the Imperial authorities in Vienna looked through their fingers at Austrian territory being a base for subversive activities directed against Russia. The Polish Socialists were practically openly, with the connivance of the Austrian General Staff, organizing military units for the approaching war between the two empires. The Russians were retaliating by fomenting anti-Austrian and anti-Polish feelings among the Ukrainians of Eastern Galicia. Such were the little games played by the European powers in preparation for the big one.

[31] *Works*, Vol. 19, p. 42.
[32] S. Bagocki, *Meetings with Lenin in Poland and Switzerland,* Moscow, 1958, p. 7.

The two years spent by Lenin among the Poles in Galicia furnish valuable evidence of his deep if unconscious Russian nationalism. As mentioned earlier, he managed the feat, almost incredible in view of the similarity of the two languages, of not learning Polish (though he at times proudly delivered himself of a phrase or two). Cracow, for all its provincial airs, was a center of vigorous artistic and cultural activity and the seat of an ancient university. Insofar as Lenin was concerned, it all might have been taking place in China. "Volodya . . ." wrote Krupskaya jocularly but expressing a great truth to her mother-in-law, "is a passionate nationalist." He would not go to any Polish artists' exhibitions, but a mere catalogue of a Moscow museum would send him into a nostalgic rapture. Cracow, he wrote very unfairly, was "backwater and uncivilized . . . almost like Russia." [33] Such was his contrariness that this lack of culture was at once soothing and infuriating. Except for those Poles who were within the Bolshevik circle, his social contacts were nonexistent. With the leaders of Polish socialism, though he availed himself freely of their hospitality and services, his relations were distant. They were Poles first, Socialists second: in brief, by his lights a "petty bourgeois" party much worse even than the Mensheviks. His main relaxations were walking and bicycling. Now and then he would allow himself to be dragged to a concert, but music frequently made him nervous and melancholy.

The pleasing-infuriating resemblance to Russia appeared to be especially strong in the countryside. Here, one must admit, he was on a more solid ground. The Galician village was poor. Seeing its barefoot women and bemused children one might imagine oneself in the vicinity of Samara or Simbirsk. Nadezhda's bad health and recurring thyroid condition (she suffered from goiter) made the Ulyanovs move for the summer to Poronin in the Tatra mountains. The current medical opinion held mountain air good for her ailment. To live in Poronin, she wrote, was almost like being again in their Siberian exile, only the mail arrived faster.

Actually, though her condition did not improve, Vladimir Ilyich enjoyed the mountains. He reverted to mountain climbing and hiking, which he had prized highly in Switzerland. As usual, sport and physical exercise transformed him into a different man. He was relaxed and jocular, and his energy would wear out his younger companions. One of them recalls him arriving for an expedition dressed in a suit and with an umbrella, while the others wore the proper mountaineer's garb. He endured their taunts good-naturedly and even walked apart from them in order not to compromise the climbers by his city dweller's appearance. Lenin's revenge came when a sudden rainstorm made the others envy the protection of his umbrella. Lenin sat proudly apart, chuckling and enjoying their discomfort, until a gust of wind tore the precious object from his hand, and he joined in the universal laughter.

But naturally the mountain air could not cure Krupskaya's affliction.

[33] *Works*, Vol. 38, p. 434.

Her disease gave her spells of dizziness, irregular heartbeat, and excessive fatigue. Like most persons passionately devoted to their work, she had a fear of doctors, who would prescribe a rest or a time-consuming treatment. For a long time she tried to deceive her husband into believing that she was feeling better, and was capable of handling the usual chores. To send her to a doctor Vladimir Ilyich had to resort to such tricks as dispatching her on an alleged social call on a person who turned out to be a medical specialist. Nadezhda Konstantinovna persisted in the fanatical creed of her youth: one had no right to take time out for one's own ailments and problems while there was Party work to be done. Some years later, after the Revolution, Lenin was to be pushed to desperate contrivances in order to assure his wife rest and recuperation, unobtainable in a Russia torn by the Civil War: a friend of his going on a mission to Switzerland was practically to kidnap Krupskaya and force her to spend a few weeks away from the scene of strife and epidemics. Now it was only the utmost exertion on his part and that of her aged mother that made her agree to an operation. Wisely, he did not trust the local surgeons: the thyroid operation was still in the nature of a novelty. In June 1913 the Ulyanovs went to Berne, where the celebrated Dr. Kocher performed the surgery. Krupskaya spent some time in the hospital, but would not hear of a prolonged convalescence in Switzerland; urgent Party matters were recalling them to Cracow.

The daily routine was resumed. By nine or ten in the morning Lenin was at work writing for the Bolshevik press, composing instructions for the handful of his followers in the Duma, and corresponding with the Party agents at home and in the West. The high point of the day was the reception of the mail from Russia. There was seldom any good news; for all the upturn in strike actions, reaction still held sway. Lenin was now the undisputed leader of the Bolsheviks at home. Still it was difficult from afar to imbue them with his full fury against the Mensheviks, to keep them from a dangerous flirtation with the alleged Liquidators. There was an almost automatic tendency for the Socialists in Russia to draw together in the face of common problems and dangers, and it took Lenin's daily bombardments to stymie such actions.

There were other worries and grievances compounded by the distance between the choleric leader and his befuddled followers. Those running the Bolshevik organ at home could not always follow the tortuous workings of his mind and sometimes misconstrued his instructions. The reaction was usually swift and terrifying: "I received a stupid and insolent letter from the editorial board," he blurts out. The secretary of the *Pravda* editorial board to which these epithets were applied was a young engineering student, Scriabin, better known as Molotov. In dealing with Vladimir Ilyich he was receiving lessons in humility and submission that were to be useful during his long service for Stalin. The people in St. Petersburg did not send Lenin the newspapers he required. Almost more important:

he had not got the honorarium for his articles. How did they imagine he could live in Cracow without any money?

There was a steady stream of visitors from Russia. Members of the Bolshevik Central Committee and the Duma group would meet in Cracow or Poronin and discuss the strategy for the difficult and tedious undertaking of rebuilding a mass party. "For God's sake give us connections," wrote Lenin to a Party committee. So much had to be done: with the Lunacharskys, Bogdanovs, and Krasins gone one had to build up the Party intelligentsia from what one had at hand. Thus he tried his hand at converting a rough and ready Caucasian revolutionary into a theorist. Stalin was dispatched to Vienna for a few weeks' brushing up on the Austrian Socialists' literature and the national question, and then with Lenin's guidance he produced his tract. The teacher was satisfied and referred to his eventual successor as "a wonderful Georgian." All this proved that one did not need bourgeois and intelligentsia turncoats and scoundrels for intellectual work. With a few weeks' briefing the son of a Georgian cobbler would produce a perfectly satisfactory treatise.

His immediate entourage consisted first of all of Zinoviev and his wife. As a Menshevik paper wrote venomously, "the seat of all Marxist wisdom for Russia is evidently wherever Lenin sits with his lieutenant 'Grishka' Zinoviev." The latter was to be his inseparable companion until the Revolution. Lev Kamenev spent a considerable time in Cracow. So did Inessa, unaware that her presence would scandalize the future biographers.

The intra-Party struggle still absorbed most of Lenin's energies. Or rather it was a struggle against pressures from home to reunite and to confound the Bolsheviks once more within the motley crowd of the Social Democrats. In the election to the Duma in 1912 the two main factions collaborated, and in the new Parliament the six Bolsheviks sat peacefully together with seven Mensheviks. The united Social Democratic faction infuriated Lenin still further by coopting a Polish Socialist who, he repeated tediously, was not a Socialist at all. This redoubtable defender of minority rights was full of indignation when the Mensheviks used their majority of one (or two, counting the contentious Polish Socialist) to make their views prevail within the parliamentary fraction. He bombarded people at home and the German Socialists with some very peculiar statistics of his own, "proving" that the Mensheviks were in fact in a minority among the workers and that their electoral successes were due to the votes of the *bourgeoisie*. In 1913 he finally compelled his parliamentary followers to break with the Liquidators and to establish a group of their own.

The Bolsheviks in the Duma were drawn from the rank and file of the Party. This was understandable since their main task was to read provocative propaganda declarations, written as often as not by Lenin himself. As in many parliaments, the Duma regulations prohibited reading of the speeches and that led to countless quarrels between the presiding officer and the Bolshevik deputies, who were simply not cast for the role of orators and felt lost without a script. One exception was their chairman, Roman Malinovsky, the rising Bolshevik star of these years. Being of "true proletarian" origin, he soon gained Lenin's confidence, despite his very uncertain past and very recent (1911) conversion to Bolshevism. He had had in fact a criminal record and was an agent of the police who facilitated his election to the Duma. One cannot accuse the *Okhrana* of a disregard for parliamentary institutions: upon his election Malinovsky's police salary was duly raised.[34]

From the beginning Malinovsky's behavior was suspicious. Lenin's emissaries recently in contact with him, such as Stalin, would be arrested. There would be mysterious departures from the script in his Duma speeches. But Lenin treated all such rumors as evil gossip inspired by the Mensheviks. Malinovsky was a welcome guest of the Ulyanovs in Cracow and in Poronin. When in the beginning of 1914 Lenin went on Party business to Paris, he took his favorite with him. Relating to a Party gathering the iniquities perpetrated upon the Duma Bolsheviks by their Liquidator colleagues, Malinovsky burst into tears. How could such a man be an *agent provocateur?* Lenin's trust withstood the final blow. Malinovsky's new police boss decided in the spring of 1914 that his continued presence in the Parliament would lead to a scandal. He was ordered to lay down his mandate, which he did, and then fled to Lenin's protection in Cracow. The cry that he was a spy was now universal. On the face of it, his action was a violation of the Party discipline; he had laid down his mandate without its authorization. But Lenin still stuck with his "proletarian." It was a Menshevik slander that brought Malinovsky close to a nervous breakdown and pushed him into his undisciplined but forgivable action. Weren't the Mensheviks ashamed of themselves? This faithful son of the working class, this man who had enjoyed its confidence, was pushed by them to such extremities. Lenin persisted in his defense until after the Revolution when police files and testimony made clear Malinovsky's role. Even then he held that despite all his betrayals the *agent provocateur* by his Duma activity had rendered services to the Revolution. Somehow it was still the Mensheviks' fault! Malinovsky himself, it is obvious, was not simply a cold-blooded police agent, but a man divided in his loyalties. With his role unmasked he returned to Russia in 1918, counting, perhaps, on Lenin's protection, but was tried and shot. Some would make Lenin aware of his double role but that is most unlikely. When a man was useful to him he would close his eyes and ears to any complaints or insinuations. And Malinovsky was not an *intelligent,* so prone to betrayal. He was a real proletarian!

The disunity of the Social Democrats was now all the more paradoxical because Leninists as well as their opponents were taking advantage of all

[34] A. Badaev, *The Bolsheviks in the Duma*, Moscow, 1957, p. 282.

opportunities for legal work within Russia. They published their paper *Pravda* (*Truth*) in competition with the Mensheviks' *Ray;* they ran in the elections to the workers' insurance councils, and were otherwise active.[35] How much better could the Socialists have exploited those opportunities, and profited from the growing class consciousness of the workers if they had been united! Attempts at a unity *without* Lenin were occasionally undertaken, but there was nobody in the opposing camp who could match his endurance and energy, outshout him in agitation and propaganda, or anticipate and frustrate his divisive moves. In 1912 Trotsky tried his hand at regrouping and uniting the anti-Lenin forces. A conference in Vienna in August brought together the Mensheviks with the remnants of the Ultimatists and the Recallers. But this August bloc, as it became known, had too many incompatibilities in its composition to endure. It gave rise to some of Lenin's choice epithets: Trotsky now pre-empted the position once held by Struve and then by Martov of being the arch enemy. "A friendly Trotsky is more dangerous than a hostile one," he wrote of the man with whom in four years he would be fighting shoulder to shoulder.

Like kindly, well-meaning schoolmasters eager to appease their children's quarrels, the leaders of the Second International never ceased their attempts to arbitrate and to reunite the Russians. One of them even traveled to Russia to find out on the spot what the truth was about all the allegations and counterallegations flowing continuously from the Mensheviks and Bolsheviks. It was July 1914, the shots of Sarajevo had already been fired, but the International Socialist Bureau summoned a conference on the Russian problem in Brussels; all the various groups and subgroups of the Social Democracy in the Tsar's dominions were represented. Lenin did not go himself. He probably did not care to experience the embarrassment of being attacked by practically all the remaining factions. There was no prospect of his agreeing, as he had done in 1907, to a reunion under any conditions. Some years earlier, Plekhanov had observed that when Lenin wanted to merge with another group he did so in a manner of a hungry man desiring to "merge" with a piece of bread. But now even that type of merger was unthinkable: granted, which was most unlikely, their complete submission, the Mensheviks and the others would prove indigestible. The copious instructions prepared for his delegation at Brussels testify to his irreconcilability.

It was to Inessa Armand that he entrusted the presentation of the Bolshevik position. It is possible to see in this designation another proof of his infatuation, but it is likely that he felt that he could count on Inessa, while another more prominent Bolshevik could not be entirely immune to the siren call for unity coming from his old comrades. The conditions laid

[35] The fact that *Pravda* would be periodically closed down by the authorities did not faze the Bolsheviks; it would reappear as *Workers' Truth, Northern Truth,* or under some other name.

down by the Bolsheviks for a reunion were clearly absurd and unacceptable. The other splinter groups were called upon to recant their principles, to subscribe to the slander about "liquidationism," and so on. The Mensheviks were to submit to the Bolshevik Central Committee, the Polish Social Democrats (present at the conference) were to be branded as "bourgeois democrats." "They" were going to take back their slander about the Bolsheviks, tainted money, and Roman Malinovsky. In his private instructions for Inessa, Lenin underlined the fact that the Bolsheviks were not going to pay the slightest heed to any majority against them. Nor would they agree under any circumstances to an all-Party Congress where, most likely, they would be isolated and in a minority.[36]

With the Bolsheviks in a minority the Brussels Conference voted to work for unity among the Russian Social Democrats. A progress report on this work was to be furnished to the Congress of the Second International, due to meet in Vienna in August. Had the Congress met, it is very likely that Lenin and his group would have been severely reprimanded, and possibly expelled by the international Socialist movement. But the war intervened.

Its outbreak found Lenin in Poronin. The fact that he was on vacation and away from Cracow proves that to him as to a vast majority of his contemporaries it had been incredible that the European crisis brewing since the assassination of Archduke Franz Ferdinand would actually turn into a world conflagration. For some years now Europe had passed from one international crisis to another. Everybody who followed world events half expected and half dreaded the coming catastrophe, but few expected it to happen in this beautiful summer of 1914. Successive crises breed false complacency (we ought to remember it today): the Great Powers would not allow a "real" war to occur; the working class of Europe would frustrate the designs of their masters to turn them into cannon fodder for their profits. Such were the delusions that clashed with the ever more ominous facts.

For some years the inevitability of a world conflict figured in Lenin's calculations, but even in his mind it clashed with sober reason. Would Tsarist Russia with her social and political wounds still unhealed plunge into a conflict which would dwarf the one that had led to the Revolution of 1905? He was also sure that given an occasion, the Western Socialists would betray the working class, and that all the talk about stopping the war through a general strike was typical opportunist window dressing. Still, when it did occur it came as a shock. On August 5 Krupskaya deciphered from the Polish newspapers that the German Social Democrats had joined the other parties in the Reichstag in voting for the war credits. Lenin would not believe it. He never expected anything better from most of them, but there were in the group such militant Marxists as Karl

[36] *Works*, Vol. 20, p. 495.

Liebknecht, who could not have associated themselves with such a dastardly act.[37] He turned to a Polish-speaking member of his entourage; Nadya must have misunderstood. But a more expert translation confirmed the fact: the parliamentary representatives of the party of Marx and Engels, leaders of world Social Democracy, voted *unanimously* to support their government in its imperialistic war.

The immediate practical concern did not allow Lenin to give vent to the mixture of fury and exultation soon to characterize his reaction to the war. He was a Russian national in a country at war with Russia. There was a natural spy mania, even among those simple mountain people who could not quite understand what it was all about. An obliging peasant informed the police that the mysterious Russian gentleman in Poronin would often sit on a hill, undoubtedly making sketches of strategic objectives. A police search in the peasant hut rented by the Ulyanovs turned up a paper full of figures, undoubtedly a ciphered message for the invading Cossacks (it was actually a manuscript on the agrarian problem, full of statistics). Even so, the police were lackadaisical in the typical manner of Hapsburg official-dom. The "spy" was told to turn himself in next day to the police in the nearest town. There he would presumably be questioned and interned by people who knew more about such things than a simple village con-stable.

The prospect of spending the war as an internee did not enchant Lenin. He called for assistance from Jacob Fuerstenberg-Hanecki, a Polish-born member of his Bolshevik entourage, then, fortunately, in Poronin. We shall meet Hanecki again. He was to be the Bolshevik wartime representative in Sweden and played a key role in the mysterious financial dealings between the Germans and the Bolsheviks. In Soviet Russia he occupied posts in the Commissariat for Foreign Affairs, and then was to meet the usual fate of the Old Bolsheviks under Stalin. Now he mobilized his acquaintances among the Polish Socialists in Galicia to intervene on Vladimir Ilyich's behalf. On August 8 the latter turned himself in to the authorities in the town of Novy Targ, where he was lodged in jail.

Despite his predicament he was in excellent spirits. It was obvious that his imprisonment would not be long; influential voices were being raised on his behalf.[38] Hanecki contacted the leaders of the Polish Socialist Party, Daszynski and Marek. In Lenin's eyes they represented the most degenerate and chauvinist type of socialism. In 1920 Daszynski would be the vice-premier of the Polish government whose armies routed the Bol-

---

[37] In fact, there were 14 Social Democrats who were against the credits, but bound by the Party discipline they had to vote with the majority.

[38] His fellow prisoners hailed him as *"byczy chlop,"* which Krupskaya, always eager for a class angle, translates as "sturdy peasant." Actually in colloquial Polish it means simply "a stout fellow" and is entirely devoid of any social connotation.

sheviks on the approaches to Warsaw. But their ideological differences did not keep the Poles from intervening vigorously on Lenin's behalf. They pointed out the full absurdity of accusing this inveterate revolutionary of being a spy for the Tsar. Krupskaya wired to the Austrian Socialist Victor Adler to plead with the Imperial authorities in Vienna, one of the relatively rare documents signed with her married name, Ulyanova. Much later on, Hanecki was to write unimaginable nonsense as to what arguments were used to procure Lenin's release: the Austrian authorities were fearful of holding a man who was beloved by the Russian working masses. Actually, as his own account of 1924 makes clear, the Poles felt duty-bound to help a fellow Socialist. The Austrian Minister of the Interior was told that Ulyanov and his party were enemies of Tsarism, and very likely to render indirect services to the cause of the Central Powers. After ten days Lenin was freed, and in September he was in Switzerland.[39] From Zurich he sent his thanks to "Highly Esteemed Comrade" Adler. Not for the last time, he had been bailed out by the "opportunists" and "Socialist chauvinists."

Once in neutral territory Lenin turned to an elaboration of his position on the war. "From the point of view of the working class . . . of all the nations of Russia the least evil would be a defeat of the Tsarist monarchy, and its armies which oppress Poland, Ukraine and other nations." [40] And in a letter: "Our slogan must be a civil war." Thus in a catastrophe that befell the European civilization Lenin saw a wonderful opportunity for a Socialist upheaval. The Russian revolutionary became subordinated in him to the planner of world revolution. No longer was he content to fight the other factions of the Russian revolutionary movement. In 1914 he was finally ready to take on the whole international Socialist movement, and three years later the whole capitalist world as well.

There was something preposterously grandiose in Lenin's position during the first months of the war. The majority of the Socialists in the warring countries let themselves be carried away by a patriotic frenzy. After a few ephemeral attempts to oppose the war or to go underground, the German Socialists as well as their Austrian, French, and English colleagues gave the lie to the alleged internationalism of their creed, joined their armies, voted for the war credits, and in some cases accepted ministerial portfolios in the war cabinets. The trial of war has shown how superficial has been the division of the International into "left" and "right," how often a person was a militant Socialist because he was simply militant, and how often a moderate because of humanitarian scruples. The ultraleft French leader Jules Guesde called for a vigorous prosecution of war and was to join the government. The arch-moderate "renegade" Bernstein was

[39] J. Hanecki, "The Arrest of Comrade Lenin in 1914," in *The Collection on Lenin*, Vol. 1, Moscow, 1924, pp. 173–87.
[40] *Works*, Vol. 21, p. 4.

to vote against the war credits in Germany, and to demand peace without annexations and indemnities. The patriotic Socialist always had a political argument to support his nationalistic position. The German was fighting not the Russian people but the Tsarist autocracy. The Frenchman and Englishman were proclaiming their intention to save Europe from German militarism and barbarity. Most important of all, the "masses" responded to and abetted their leaders' national fervor. What was it that Karl Marx wrote: "The workers have no country"? In the summer and fall of 1914 those words of the founder of socialism appeared as a very bad prophecy.

Even among the Russian Socialists the war fever ran high. In the Duma both the Mensheviks and the Bolsheviks opposed the war and voted against the supplementary budget, but the rank-and-file Party members, independently of their factions, were enlisting under the colors. And abroad many of the exiles, some of them veterans of years in the Tsarist jails, joined with patriotic declarations. Their country was fighting on the side of liberty along with France and England against Germany, which was committing unspeakable atrocities in Belgium, and Austria was the traditional enemy of the small Slavic nations. In many a Russian radical there was an inborn hatred of the Germanic type of bureaucracy that since Peter the Great had been imposed upon Russia. The Tsars by descent were of German blood; as early as Bakunin Russian Populism railed against the "German and Tartar autocracy." The very name of the capital, Sankt-Petersburg, symbolized the superimposition upon the Slavic nation and culture of alien and hateful Germanic customs.[41] The war was going to crush not only Germany, the traditional enemy of the Slavs; it was also going to destroy what remained of the alien and despotic in Russia's internal affairs.

Within Russian socialism this patriotic and Germanophobe emotion was best represented by Plekhanov. He had once been a Populist, believer in the Russian people, Marx or no Marx. Now years appear to have vanished and Plekhanov was preaching that the Socialists should fight for the Entente, for Russia, for freedom and civilization. Amazing to relate, this lover of German literature, who interlaced his writings with pages in German, evidently never liked the Germans, whether the Junkers or his condescending Social Democratic colleagues. To a shocked exponent of Lenin's views Plekhanov was quite explicit: "So far as I am concerned, if I were not old and sick I would join the army. To bayonet your German comrades would give me great pleasure." [42] It was astounding how many Socialists, their lives spent in the service of the ideas of the German Master, hated Germany.

The news of Plekhanov's "defensist" ideas reached Lenin. He was al-

---

[41] With the beginning of the war the name was hastily changed to Petrograd.
[42] Samuel H. Baron, *Plekhanov*, Stanford, 1963, p. 324.

ways suspecting the worst, but another part of his nature clung to the hope that his teacher would not commit this, the worst baseness yet. Perhaps it was a passing infatuation with war, Plekhanov having been in his youth a student in the military institute. In October he traveled from Berne to Lausanne to confront Plekhanov at a meeting of the émigrés. The reality exceeded his worst fears and expectations. A Russian general could not have delivered a more patriotic speech. Plekhanov had been in Paris when the war had been declared. Scratch a Russian radical and you would find not only a Germanophobe but an ardent Francophile. And so it was with the father of Russian Marxism. He berated the German Social Democrats as being no better than Wilhelm II (this part of his speech Lenin applauded). But then his pro-French, pro-war enthusiasm broke out. Why did the Social Democrats vote against the war credits in the Duma? At least they should have stipulated that they voted against them because the Tsarist generals were incapable of leading the army to a speedy victory over the Teutonic forces. Lenin was pale and drawn when he made his reply. It was his final breach with his master, with the man "he never ceased to love," but who now along with the majority of the Social Democrats betrayed the working class of Europe.

The very name now became hateful to him. It was time, he wrote, for true Marxists to return to the name "Communist," epitomizing the early and more militant traditions of the Party. The name "Social Democrat" had become soiled and humiliating. For once he criticized even Marx and Engels for the insufficient militancy of their last years. The final traces of awe and respect in which he had held their German heirs now vanished with bitter invective against the "renegade" Kautsky and the other teachers and inspirers of his youth, now revealed as timid collaborators of generals and bureaucrats. The greater the previous veneration the more violent the present attack. As if to resolve some inner doubts, Lenin refuted the charge that to be against the war meant to be devoid of Russian patriotism. In an unusually eloquent article he asserted his pride in being a Russian. To be a true nationalist meant to be against chauvinism. "No nation can be free if it oppresses other nations," he quoted.[43]

He felt himself very much alone in his struggle. Those Socialists who refused to partake of the nationalist mania were for the most part of the pacifist persuasion. This was not enough: "One of the forms of stultifying the working class is pacifism and abstract advocacy of peace." The fact that Martov took an antipatriotic position cheered him up, and, according to Krupskaya, it revived momentarily the affection for the friend of his youth. But one suspects that Krupskaya is trying here to give Stalin's Russia a discreet hint about political tolerance. For in a letter to his agent in Russia Vladimir Ilyich is not very hopeful about Martov. "Though Martov is becoming more radical it is only because he is by himself. . . . Tomor-

---

[43] *Works*, Vol. 21, p. 87.

row he will sink to their level: to stifle the workers' voice (and their mind and conscience) with the help of some rubbery resolution à la Kautsky. . . ."[44] He had passed the point where he sought and welcomed allies. He needed loyal followers.

From Berne and Zurich, where he now was living (away from Plekhanov and the Francophile atmosphere of Geneva), Lenin undertook the now considerably more difficult task of renewing connections with Russia and the remnants of the Bolshevik group. The lines of communication ran through Scandinavia. In Stockholm (from where he clandestinely traveled to Russia) was Lenin's main wartime link with the Bolsheviks at home, Alexander Shlyapnikov. After the Revolution Shlyapnikov was to become one of the main thorns in Lenin's side. His complaints against the Bolshevik bureaucracy, his advocacy of egalitarianism and factional activity, would lead Lenin to demand his ejection from the Party, and the intrepid Bolshevik was to dare to laugh in Lenin's face. But now he was his leader's main confidant, the irreplaceable link with home, and as usual, Lenin knows how to be friendly and solicitous with a man he needs. "If you are mad at me then I am ready with all sorts of apologies, so please don't be angry," he writes seductively after Shlyapnikov had found a request to be unreasonable. And again: "Most cordial greetings and all the best. You will no longer be angry?"

As from his earliest political days, Lenin was accustomed to demand back-breaking work from his subordinates as well as to charge them with impossible tasks. Shlyapnikov was to keep his distance from the Swedish Social Democrats (mostly petty bourgeois) and at the same time to inveigle them to forget their previous loans to the Bolsheviks and to lend them more money. Were he himself to ask them for money, wrote Lenin with his intermittent realism, the chances of a new loan would be very small. The arrest of the Bolshevik Duma deputies for their antiwar agitation (together with Kamenev, who had been delegated to conduct Bolshevik work in Petrograd) filled Lenin with anguish not for the arrested, but for himself: "In any case the work of our Party has become a hundred times more difficult." The accused had followed his instructions in holding an illegal conference and preparing an antigovernment manifesto; it is difficult to see how he could have been surprised either at their arrest or at the severe sentences meted out to them. But there were poignant taunts that he, Lenin, from the haven of a neutral country was exciting his followers to dangerous and foolhardy acts. All of which did not move Lenin in the slightest. He was used, he was to write Inessa, to such vileness. His whole life had been one campaign after another against political stupidity, opportunism, and slander. But he was not going to give up.

The world stage held Lenin's main attention between 1914 and February 1917. In Russia the Bolsheviks' task had to be preservation of their

[44] *The Lenin Collection,* Moscow, Vol. 1, 1924, p. 198.

human resources. The coming revolution was to be international in its scale. His denunciations of the war were interspersed with moments of fear: What if the imperialists concluded a peace before the moment was ripe for turning the war into a world revolution? "The smart exploiters of the leading capitalist country [England] are for peace [in order to strengthen capitalism]. But we should not be confused with the petty bourgeois, sentimental liberals, etc. The era of the bayonet has come. That is a fact and hence we should fight with *the same weapon*," Lenin wrote as early as November 1914. Neither the "clever exploiters" nor the "sentimental liberals" could stop the slaughter and the attempted suicide of European civilization. As the war progressed the initial patriotic exhilaration of the Socialists gave way more and more to second thoughts. But these thoughts turned to the idea of contemptible pacifism, of simply stopping the slaughter. "And objectively who profits by the slogan of peace? Certainly not the revolutionary proletariat. Not the idea of *using* the war to *speed up* the collapse of capitalism." [45] He overlooked the fact that the lives of millions of human beings also could have "profited" by the "slogan of peace."

To prevent the Socialists' gravitation toward pacifism and to rekindle militant Marxism were Lenin's main tasks at the several conferences of the antiwar radicals held in Switzerland at Berne, Zimmerwald (1915), and Kienthal (1916). Though the Socialists who attended these conferences were already in the left wing of their respective national parties the Bolsheviks in their extremism still found themselves practically isolated. Even such future Communists as the German Klara Zetkin and the Russian-born Italian Socialist Angelica Balabanov espoused "simple" pacifism, the demand for a peace with no annexations, and an international reconciliation. Apart from their convictions, there was another reason for the German and French Socialists' unwillingness to adopt the slogan of turning the imperialist war into a civil one. As a German delegate reminded Lenin, *they* were going back to their respective countries. Already in the eyes of their right-wing colleagues, not to mention their governments, they were little better than traitors. There were few non-Bolshevik converts to the views of the Zimmerwald left, as Lenin and his now inseparable lieutenant Zinoviev became known. [46] Altogether they could muster but seven or eight votes at Zimmerwald, out of about forty. But the conference and its

---

[45] *Ibid.*, p. 208.

[46] Among them was Karl Radek, a Galician-born German Socialist "representing" at Zimmerwald the Polish Social Democratic Party. Radek was to become a Bolshevik and a leading figure in the post-Revolution Soviet diplomacy. This picturesquely ugly man was for a long time one of the most effective Communist journalists and propagandists. He was notable and exceptional among the Soviet oligarchs for his sense of humor. Even his recantation (for his pro-Trotsky position) brought down a Party congress. Came the Great Purge of the 1930s and Radek's great wit could no longer save him: in 1938 he was condemned to a long prison sentence, which he did not survive.

sequel at Kienthal were far from being a total loss, despite their pacifist manifestoes. They marked a growing fissure within the European Social Democracy and the preparatory steps toward Lenin's eventual goal of founding a new "pure" Marxist international. What had happened within Russian socialism was now happening on the international scale: moderation stood abashed and guilt-ridden before extremism. Some of Lenin's most resolute opponents at Zimmerwald and Kienthal would become within a few years founders of the Communist parties in their respective countries. Others, though they remained Socialists, would still defend the Soviet Union as a "workers' state." And Martov and Axelrod, who were also there, would continue as they had been under the Tsars, exiles.

In a way the Swiss conferences marked the recovery of Lenin from his isolation. Just as at Stockholm in 1907, though in a minority at those conferences, he was their commanding figure. The Bolsheviks (and the same was to be true of Soviet diplomacy), having always thrived on those conferences and congresses where their opponents tried to argue with them, accounted as a great success and a hopeful sign that these previously unreasonable people were willing to sit down at the same table and talk about unity. Perhaps Lenin was finally seeing the futility and unreasonableness of his position; perhaps, for all the violence and abusiveness of his language, he was "settling down" and would be willing to go along with the majority! He could not lose; the conferences provided him with a European renown among the Socialists quite different from the notoriety he had in 1914 when he was on the brink of being condemned or ejected by the Second International. His temporary moderation ("Why, he is willing to talk!") assured him of the lingering sympathy of his opponents. His fire-breathing extremism, on the other hand, was bound to gain him admirers among the revolutionaries, who were temperamentally unsuited to the fence-sitting tactics of the pacifist Socialists. Whatever personal scores they had to settle with Lenin, they could not but be hypnotized by his singlemindedness and defiance. At Zimmerwald Trotsky began to find himself again under the spell of his old enemy. The more adventurous Mensheviks were growing tired of "buts" and "ifs" of their own leaders. As for Lenin being bound by any resolution that had ceased to serve his purposes, it was simply ridiculous. "Since when do the revolutionaries set their policy depending on whether they are in a majority or minority?" he wrote contemptuously to a French Socialist who begged him to speak more kindly of the Kautskys, Martovs, and others who were seeking in their well-intentioned manner a middle road between the nationalism of their right-wing comrades and the wildness of the Bolsheviks.

Life in Switzerland was also beset with more prosaic problems. For once the Ulyanovs found themselves in financial difficulties. In the beginning of the war Vladimir Ilyich wrote an article on Marx for a Russian encyclopedia, a pedestrian work done to secure some funds. He sought, unsuccessfully, employment as a correspondent for a journal in Russia. By our standards it is still amazing how this notorious revolutionary and instigator of a civil war was allowed to receive money from home. This help did not end with Maria Alexandrovna's death in 1916, one year before she could see her son at the height of his glory, a blow that Vladimir felt deeply. In November of the same year he thanked sister Maria for sending money but hinted at the need for more. He was reduced to working on translations. In February 1917 the man who in nine months would order the nationalization of all the banks in his country wrote exultantly about an unexpected money order from Russia. Where did it come from? It roused Nadezhda Konstantinovna to make a joke (the only one recorded). "You are now getting retirement pay," she told her forty-six-year-old husband, who was greatly amused.

Their quarters reflected the nagging financial worries. When they moved from Berne to Zurich in 1916 (there was a better library in Zurich) they lived first in a shabby boarding house, among whose inmates were a prostitute and a criminal. For all Vladimir Ilyich's alleged fascination with this first-hand acquaintance with the "lower depths" (Krupskaya is not very convincing on this point) they soon moved to more respectable if equally modest accommodations with the family of a shoemaker. Their room faced a yard with a malodorous sausage factory. Krupskaya now had full charge of the domestic arrangements (her mother had died some time before) and she made a startling confession. It was from her landlady that she learned for the first time "how to cook satisfying dinners and suppers with the least expenditure of time and money." They had been married now for nearly twenty years! Still, there were long trips into the country and mountains, and unlike some in his entourage, Lenin did not have to resort to manual labor.

Private cares blended with political. For all his indomitable revolutionary enthusiasm Lenin humanly enough had moments of doubt and depression. The possibility of peace was a constant specter. At times he was very sure, and mistakenly so, as were many also within Russia, that the German and Russian courts were secretly negotiating. It would only be logical, he wrote, and then proceeded to a masochistic vision of Wilhelm II and Nicholas II suddenly announcing an alliance. At least it would be a big laugh on the stupid "Socialist patriots" with their prattle about the fight for freedom and against Prussian militarism. Or another fantasy: the Tsar would *pretend* he was about to conclude a treaty with Germany and would blackmail the French and the British into giving him billions and all sorts of concessions.[47] Need one wonder where Stalin and Khrushchev got their ideas of diplomacy?

Those gloomy apprehensions led Lenin at times to visualize Switzer-

[47] *Works,* Vol. 23, p. 121.

land as his Elba if not indeed Saint Helena. But if so, he would still remain a revolutionary. He was full of advice for the Swiss Socialists. They should shed their own "Socialist patriots," those who proclaimed that they would fight if Switzerland were invaded. His indignation knew no bounds when he wrote of the alleged Socialists who inveighed against the extremists and the foreigners who interfered in their politics. Those hospitable men who appeared to him in 1914 as true proletarian revolutionaries were now revealed as the Swiss copies of Martovs and Kautskys.

Many of the Russian revolutionaries were at the time prepared to go even farther; to leave for the New World. Trotsky went to America in December 1916, convinced that he was seeing Europe for the last time. Bukharin, the rising Marxist theoretician, and some other Bolsheviks were already there. These seeming defections did not depress Lenin unduly. There were obviously *some* revolutionary Socialists in America. One of his closest correspondents during the war, Alexandra Kollontay, was briefed by him as to the Socialist fauna in this continent to which she was traveling: there was a promising group in Boston, the Socialist Propaganda League, with twenty members and "internationalist" in its outlook. Would Kollontay investigate and send him a report? From distant New York Lenin heard (inaccurate) reports of factional struggle among the Russian revolutionaries. Trotsky (still in bad grace) "attempted to seize" control of the *émigré* journal *Novyi Mir* (*The New World*) but thank God was repulsed by Bukharin and other true Bolsheviks.[48] Vladimir Ilyich had for some time been willing to advise the American Socialists how to stir up the revolutionary instincts of the masses. How about the slogan of independence for Hawaii!

The range of his interests is truly impressive. He writes with passion about the squabbles of the Norwegian or Danish Socialists. Everywhere, even in the neutral countries, he detects the noxious "Socialist chauvinists," upbraids the fence-sitting pacifists, and hails the handful of true Marxists lusting for civil war. His letters amusingly reflect his international orientation: they are interspersed with passages in foreign languages. There are several English phrases in his letters to Inessa, and they throw a rather grim light on his alleged mastery of English acquired while translating from English in Siberia and later on in London. Thus references to the "precedent letter" and the concluding greetings, "friendly shake hands" (undoubtedly Lenin believed that he was rendering with the proper Anglo-Saxon reserve the effusive Russian salutation, literally "I firmly clasp your hand"). A lover's playfulness? More likely Lenin is practicing for the correspondence with those twenty Boston Marxists.[49]

[48] *The Lenin Collection*, Vol. 1, p. 282.

[49] Letters to Inessa bear a more personal character than most of Lenin's correspondence at the time, except for those with his family. But this impression is due also to the selective character of the Soviet censorship, which would not allow the printing of the letters testifying to his very close friendship at the time with Zinoviev and his

The culmination of Lenin's internationalism was the treatise on imperialism that he wrote in 1916. Together with *What Is To Be Done?* and with *State and Revolution* it constitutes the triad of his most influential works. Today, this least original of Lenin's important writings is probably best known throughout the world. Such is the irony of history that the collapse of the Western empires and a flagrant refutation of Lenin's thesis has only enhanced interest in his work. And an equal irony, his strictures about imperialism and the inevitable international cataclysm that it must produce, like many Marxian analyses and prophesies, have come to be truer of the world of communism than that of capitalism.

His work is in fact a rephrasing, with a Marxist conclusion, of the work of the English radical J. A. Hobson, *Imperialism*, written in the beginning of the century and inspired by the Boer War. Hobson saw the main cause of imperialism, of territorial expansion, and the competition for colonies in the Western capitalist's drive to secure a profitable market for his investments. Driven from his home market by the falling rate of profit, the English, French, or German financiers invested in areas where low labor costs would guarantee them a huge gain. They then turned to their governments to protect their capital by the flag. Imperialist expansion proceeded in the atmosphere of chauvinist fervor, to the slogans of "the civilizing mission," "spreading of Christianity," but behind lurked the capitalist subjugating his state's power to his own sordid ends.

Hobson could not deny himself the satisfaction of adorning his thesis with the usual Nonconformist reprimands addressed to the upper classes. They obviously derived a great deal of fun out of lording it over the Hindus, Kaffirs, and Chinese coolies. There are seemingly irrelevant observations about foxhunting and horse racing, those guilty pleasures of the rich and well born. And there is the common compulsion of the radical of the left and of the right, a suggestion of the Vast International Plot. Who was naïve enough to think that a war could be started without permission of the House of Rothschild? But his conclusions were those not of a Marxist, but of a radical liberal. An aroused electorate could bring an end to imperialism. The chastened English capitalist could be compelled, rather than to exploit the Hindus, to invest at home (at lower rates of profit, to be sure) and thus to benefit his countrymen. The upper classes rather than enjoying themselves in the tropics could be constrained to do productive work at home.

wife. One letter criticizes Inessa's proposed pamphlet on marriage and free love. Lenin's concern was that Inessa appeared to disregard the class angle of the problem; the real contrast is not between "the loveless kisses of the married couples" and free love, but between the loveless church-sanctioned union of the bourgeois, intellectuals, and peasants, and the ideal of the civil marriage, allegedly held by the working class. *Works*, Vol. 35, p. 140. Other letters, such as those complaining about Gorky's political naïveté ("calflike"), expressing Lenin's hatred of the English for their arrogance, also resemble more the correspondence with a very close friend rather than a mistress.

To the modern reader Hobson comes perilously close to recommending that the non-European areas be allowed to stew in their own juice, or in contemporary terms, underdevelopment. Countless economic historians have also tried to expose the fallacy of his thesis, to point out the unprofitability to the colonial powers of their overseas possessions; the fact is that today's Europe, almost free of colonies, is infinitely more prosperous than the West during its imperial phase. Such arguments make convincing reading to other economic historians. But the Hobson-Lenin thesis, because of its simplicity, because of its psychological appeal, and because of the undoubted depredations and brutalities that accompanied the process of colonization, remains one of the most influential opinions in today's world. Its effect has been similar to that of the theories of Populism in nineteenth century Russia. The "guilt-ridden nobleman" has been succeeded by the guilt-ridden citizen of the West who contemplates the poverty and backwardness of the rest of the world. It is only a heartless conservative who would bring up data and statistics in order to deny the West's responsibility for this state of affairs. As does socialism as a whole, so does the theory of imperialism appeal at once to those discordant emotions of generosity and envy, of guilt, and rage at one's inferior status.

Lenin transformed Hobson's diatribe into a theoretical and tactical weapon of militant Marxism. As a theory it came in handy to stifle the doubts that every Socialist felt about the correctness of Karl Marx's prediction. Since the Master's death capitalism had grown stronger, not weaker, the lot of the worker not more miserable but more prosperous. Now, as in a flash, this seeming inconsistency could be explained away and the Revisionists finally refuted. The English, French, and German workers had been indirect beneficiaries of the exploitation of their Asiatic and African brothers. Western capitalism could afford to throw more crumbs to its own working class, to exploit it less cruelly, since it made up for that by the increased impositions upon the colonial peoples. Marx stood vindicated. It is simply that the fulfillment of his prophecy had been delayed through the emergence of a new factor: imperialism.

In Lenin's scheme, what Hobson had deemed to be a preventable or removable evil became an *inevitable* feature of historical development. By the 1870s Western capitalism had passed its constructive and progressive stage. Free competition gave way to monopolies and trusts, to a hopeless struggle to arrest the falling rate of profit at home. Finally monopolies resorted to investments and the grabbing of cheap raw materials abroad, whether in primitive societies or in such "semicolonial" areas as China and Latin America. Outward annexations and the "spheres of influence" carved by the Great Powers follow. And then rival imperialisms clash in war over the possession of markets and colonies. Hence "imperialism as the highest," that is, the last stage of capitalism.

The tactical implications of the theory are clear. The true Marxists must support liberation and anticolonial movements, no matter what their class character. By striking at the British rule in India one strikes at the very heart of Western capitalism. The people of the colonial countries are the unconscious allies of the proletariat of the West. Their struggle for liberation will bring nearer the day when the British and French workers will be able to dispose of their own capitalists.[50]

The apparent inconsistencies and oversimplifications of Lenin's latest work loomed as insignificant against the testimony offered in its favor by the Great War. It was an *imperialist war*, whatever other causes and reasons had triggered it off. Both sides were stipulating in secret and in open treaties and pronouncements their territorial ambitions and planned annexations. The boast of capitalism had been that it had given Europe a century of (relative) peace and material progress. Now this boast stood exposed. Whatever the pedantic objections to Lenin's theory (and many Marxist scholars were quick to point out that it ran against the facts and the whole logic of Karl Marx's system) it could claim an irrefutable evidence that capitalism bred war, a charge more serious and in 1916 more damning than that of breeding poverty. Militant Marxism, or communism, as it will become, could promise peace, national self-determination, and international friendship. However weak the theoretical structure on which this promise was based, its appeal was enormous. It "made" communism as an international movement. A parochial Russian from the Central Volga region was thus capable of creating a movement and a faith that was to reach every corner of the globe and engage men's emotions on a much vaster scale than the original and intricate doctrine of Karl Marx and Friedrich Engels.

Whatever the position he adopted, Lenin threw himself into it wholeheartedly. Whatever was tactically necessary became for him a matter of conviction. He was now an internationalist cheerfully contemplating the partition of the Russian Empire into its separate nations. Not for him any Marxian scruples about national self-determination. A young Bolshevik, Gregory "Yuri" Pyatakov, aroused his anger by wondering aloud whether some nationalities were ripe for independence. Would you give freedom to the ignorant Byelorussian peasants, to the Egyptian *fellahim*, knowing that they would be led by the nose by their own upper classes, he asks. Yes, replied Lenin, we want independence even if it leads to the rule of the feudal and backward classes. His instinct of the revolutionary tells him that the national and not the class struggle is the most destructive force in the twentieth century. If you want to harness it to your purpose, you cannot afford the "ifs" and "buts" of learned theorists. It is with some effort that one finds the Russian lurking in the internationalist: after the victory

[50] To be sure, there is a logical inconsistency here. If the Lenin thesis were right the Western worker should be a fervent defender of imperialism, since the Western rule over India, Algeria, and similar areas guarantees him a higher standard of living.

of Socialism we shall give independence to Poland, Finland, the Ukraine, other areas, but their separation may not last long.[51] So the Communists will and in most cases the "separation will not last long."

Eight years earlier the flame of the revolution had been extinguished in Russia and his country seemed destined to travel the detestable road to parliamentarism and Western style of democracy. Lenin had responded not by reducing but by enlarging his goal: in the beginning of 1917 he had, he was convinced, the formula for the world revolution. But the possessor of this formula was merely a leader of a small group of exiles and, in Russia, of a few thousand workers who kept up their Bolshevik contacts. This contrast was on his mind when in January he concluded a lecture: "We of the older generation may not see the decisive battles of this coming revolution."

[51] *Works*, Vol. 23, p. 56.

VII

1917

1. A Kind and Considerate Revolution

The Bolsheviks did not seize power in this year of revolutions. They picked it up. First autocracy, then democracy capitulated to the forces of anarchy. Any group of determined men could have done what the Bolsheviks did in Petrograd [1] in October 1917: seize the few key points of the city and proclaim themselves the government. But the government of what? What had once been the Russian Empire was in full dissolution. Part of it lay under enemy occupation; over the rest of it hundreds of little governments sprang up. The Railwaymen's Union was perhaps more important in October than whoever ruled in the capital. It had stopped an attempted army coup some weeks before, it was almost to make the Bolsheviks capitulate to its demands a few days after their seizure of "power." Every city, every regiment felt itself to be autonomous or independent, its compliance with any orders or instructions to be the subject of free decision of its soviet (committee). More than two million deserters wandered throughout the land. Industry was paralyzed and even greater anarchy prevailed in the countryside.

Thus the Bolsheviks' achievement in 1917, great though it was, pales in comparison with the enormous task they accomplished in the next five years in conquering the very anarchy they had helped to create and in building out of the most anarchistic of the revolutions the most authoritarian state in the world. It is not in the maker of the revolution that we can see Lenin's genius in its fullest; far greater is his achievement as its conqueror.

The long-awaited explosion that became known as the February Revolution was compressed in the events of one week. On February 23 ninety thousand workers went on strike in Petrograd. Next day the number reached two hundred thousand. The strikes were partly political in their motivation, but mostly in response to the shortages of food and the ever-growing inflation that had gripped Russia from the beginning of the war. Strikes were followed by street manifestations and disorders. What transformed riots into a revolution was the behavior of the garrison of Petrograd. Called upon to help the police quell the disorders, the soldiers re-

[1] To repeat, this was the name of the capital from the beginning of the war to its rechristening as Leningrad in 1924.

fused, and in some cases fired upon the police. Up to now the script was not too dissimiliar from the events of October 1905. But soon the vital difference appeared: the Tsarist regime disintegrated. The Tsar was at the Supreme Army Headquarters in the Ukrainian town of Mogilev. There was no Witte at the head of his ministry, which was composed of non-entities. Confronted by events it could not control or even understand, it simply stopped functioning. What could take its place? As events were to show, the fall of the Tsarist regime left a vacuum that was to last until October; in the strict sense of the word *Russia* during eight months was to be left without a central government and without a settled form of state organization. What took its place were *several* authorities, which tried to discharge the task of governing the vast country, sometimes working together, sometimes at cross purposes, but increasingly powerless in the face of growing defeat and anarchy and finally conquered by them.

To be sure, an inhabitant of Petrograd on March 1, 1917, could well believe that his country did have a new government, or rather, two governments. Both were the result of overnight improvisations, both were self-proclaimed. One was the creation of the Parliament: the Duma, which disobeyed the Tsar's order to adjourn, selected an executive committee which in turn was to appoint a ministry—the Provisional Government. This was to be, insofar as the letter of the law and the foreign states' recognition were concerned, *the* government of Russia until its demise in October. Having given birth to its child, the Duma itself, the Parliament that had sat since 1912 to all purposes vanished from the scene.

The other improvised government was a throwback to the traditions of 1905, the Petrograd Soviet of the Workers' and (as it soon became) Soldiers' Deputies. On February 27 a group of Socialist leaders of various denominations organized the Provisional Executive Committee of the Workers' Deputies, which then called upon the factories and regiments to select delegates to the Soviet. Though representing but the capital, the Soviet arrogated to itself the authority to speak for the workers and soldiers of all Russia.

Both "governments" issued proclamations indicating their confidence that the old Tsarist regime was a thing of the past.

"The Provisional Committee of the Duma has found itself compelled to take into its own hands the restoration of State and public order."

"The Soviet has set for itself as its main task to organize the popular forces and to fight for the consolidation of political freedom and popular government." [2]

Confronted by those events and refused support by his army commanders, the Tsar abdicated. Attempts to pass the throne first to his son, then to his brother, were thwarted. Russia ceased to be a monarchy with-

---

[2] *Documents of Russian History*, edited by F. A. Golder, New York, 1927, pp. 281 and 287.

out becoming a republic (for its constitution was to be set by the Constituent Assembly, which was not to meet until January 1918). The Tsarist government had collapsed but it was not replaced by any *single* authority possessing clear and unquestioned confidence of the people.

Such are the bare facts of the upheaval. But what did really happen? Here the answers of historians, participants, and eyewitnesses vary according to their ideological viewpoints. To the diehard monarchist and reactionary old Russia was betrayed by the intellectuals and liberals sitting in the Duma and ruling public opinion through their speeches and articles. It was they who took the occasion of some riots and strikes, in themselves not much more significant than many in the previous years, to betray their Emperor, to seize power into their greedy and incompetent hands, and to open the door to anarchy.

Not so, claims the liberal. The old regime collapsed because of its stupidity and corruption, its refusal to heed the pleas of society for a responsible parliamentary government. If anarchy ensued it is "their" fault, the fault of the radicals of the left and the right who frustrated the plans and opportunities to give Russia an enlightened Western type of democracy and parliamentarism.

Then there is the voice of the left, of the non-Bolshevik Socialists. It is they, primarily the Mensheviks and then the Socialist Revolutionaries, who organized the Petrograd Soviet and guided its deliberations until it was on the eve of October torn away from their hands by the Bolsheviks. Their voice is most insistent in pleading for both credit for the events of February and extenuating circumstances for the later course of events. By setting up the Soviet *they* were responding to the will of the masses. *They* represented the people who had had enough of the Tsar, and his bureaucrats, but who were not ready to trust fully the industrialists, lawyers, and professors who composed the Duma government. How were *they* to know that the Bolsheviks were going to abuse the freedoms of newly won democracy, and use the events of February as but the first step in their campaign to cast out not only the Provisional Government, but "revolutionary democracy," the other Socialist parties as well?

The victor's voice is, of course, different. In Trotsky's account of the Russian Revolution it is the forces of history that foreordained the events of February, and the working class was their appointed agent. Even he cannot claim that the Bolsheviks were in any sense the leaders of the uprising, the makers of the Soviet on February 27. They were, as he has to admit, a small minority even within the working class, trailing far behind the Mensheviks and the Socialist Revolutionaries. But he improvises an analysis inspired half by Marxian dialectic and half by a peculiar Bolshevik mystique: though events were chaotic, though the workers superficially seemed to follow other leaders and counsels, they were *in reality* (though unbeknownst to themselves) guided by the Bolsheviks. "To the

question, who led the February Revolution we can answer definitely
enough: Conscious and tempered workers educated for the most part by
the party of Lenin." [3] Not that Trotsky forgot or overlooked the role of
other Socialist parties: they were the villains who dulled the alertness of
the "conscious and tempered proletarians" and persuaded them to surrender power into the hands of the *bourgeoisie,* the Provisional Government. So says Trotsky, who at the moment of uprising was thousands of
miles away in New York, but whose version, of course no longer credited
to its author, remains the official Communist story of the events of the
February Revolution.

And thus myth and propaganda, regrets and excuses for passed-up opportunities, and gloating over the fantastic success scored by the Party,
which in February had perhaps ten thousand members throughout Russia,
all conspire to make even more incomprehensible the most momentous
event in history since the French Revolution. Nobody misjudged it more
than a political exile in Switzerland who in eight months was to become
the heir of the Romanovs. The Revolution, wrote Lenin in the first of his
Letters from Afar, was obviously the work of the English and French embassies, which combined with the liberal and moderate parties and the
generals to overthrow the Tsar and thus to avoid a separate peace with
Germany.[4] He was far from crediting it then to "conscious and tempered
workers educated for the most part by the party of Lenin." One sees in
these words the old Lenin of 1905, incredulous that the long-awaited moment is really at hand, not believing that the workers "by themselves" are
capable of achieving what requires preparation and direction by a political
elite: a "real" revolution.

Yet in this fantastic and pessimistic analysis there was an element of
truth that escapes those who look at the February Revolution through the
prism of the October one. The events of February–March were not caused
simply by an uprising of the workers and a mutiny of the Petrograd garrison. To a much greater extent than anybody in a few weeks would be able
to admit, this was a *patriotic* revolution, bent upon overthrowing a government and regime incapable of pursuing the war to a victorious end.
The populace of the capital revolted under the slogans of "Bread" and
"Down with autocracy," but not yet "Down with the imperialist war." The
rioting and fighting in the streets was decisive but so was the by now firm
hostility of the upper and middle classes, including many of the military
commanders, to the Tsar and the court circles. For more than a year rumor was gaining currency that the German-born Empress was the center
of a clique bent upon concluding a separate treaty with the Central
Powers, leaving Russia's allies to a certain defeat. The repeated and
bloody defeats of the Imperial armies, the scandalous deficiencies in their

[3] *The History of the Russian Revolution,* New York, 1932, Vol. 1, p. 152.
[4] *Works,* Vol. 23, p. 296.

supply and provisionment were blamed as much on the Tsar's personal ineptitude, accentuated when he assumed personally the supreme command, as on actual treason of those close to him. Just as to the revolutionary Ulyanov so to many a general and official it seemed perfectly logical that the Romanovs and the Hohenzollerns, united in their detestation of democracy, should strive to conclude an agreement disregarding Russia's honor, her obligations to her allies, and the millions of casualties expended in the war against Germandom. The news of the overthrow was greeted not only by a democratic but also by a nationalist elation. Now Russia could legitimately take her place in the rank of nations fighting for freedom. The lives of her soldiers would no longer be squandered by treachery and corruption. Free Russia's warriors would match the exploits of the armies of the French Revolution. They would become the scourge of tyrants. Only the extreme revolutionary or the ultrareactionary could detect the unrealism of this combined democratic and nationalist enthusiasm; how could a war-weary, disorganized country, in which the war had reopened the old political and social wounds, be galvanized into new efforts and sacrifices just on the strength of emotion and without a firm and universally acknowledged leadership? It is the contrast between those high expectations and the bleak reality that sets the stage for the tragedy of the Russian Revolution.

In March, as Lenin put it, Russia became the freest country in the world. The Revolution claimed as yet relatively few victims. In Petrograd the total casualties reached fifteen hundred. Elsewhere in this enormous country the overthrow of this century's old regime was almost bloodless. It was only at the naval base of Kronstadt that one could get a preview of future massacres: the sailors, as always the most turbulent and revolutionary element, murdered the commanding admiral and forty other officers. The most detested Tsarist officials were imprisoned but there was as yet little lawlessness, looting, or lynching. Keeping in mind the accumulated hatreds of the decades of repression, the terror and counterterror of 1905–6, one must admit, as the world did, that Russia set an example of a mild and humanitarian revolution. Few had ever thought that a successful *coup d'état* would leave the Tsar alive, but "Nicholas the Bloody," as he was known in revolutionary circles, was merely placed under arrest. The immediate mood of the victorious revolution was one of relief, exaltation, and generosity. Every Russian, whether a grandduke or an anarchist, was to enjoy the new freedom.

The serpent in this paradise was the problem of power, but again in a way unprecedented and ironic. We are told by historians that an overthrow of a regime is followed by a struggle for power among various parties, classes, or individuals. The peculiarity of the Russian situation on the morrow of the February Revolution was the exact opposite of this alleged historic law. Grand Duke Michael refused the throne vacated by his brother. The army generals looked longingly for some sort of central authority to be established to tell them what to do. The Provisional Government set up by the Duma looked with awe at the task ahead of it, desirous to be buttressed now by a figurehead monarch, now by a spokesman for the people—the Petrograd Soviet. And the latter luxuriated in the role of "half government," issuing manifestoes, settling matters of high policy, but resolutely refusing responsibility for such prosaic tasks of everyday governments as the conduct of the war, administration, collecting taxes. The idea of anybody aspiring to fullness of power in revolutionary Russia was so extravagant that when in June Lenin was to declare that the Bolsheviks were quite willing by themselves to assume the government of the country, his declaration aroused not as much indignation as universal amusement. Who indeed would *really* want to cope with a disintegrating army, hunger, rebellious nationalities, and hundreds of other problems that beset Russia?

The very energy of the Revolution appeared epitomized in the Petrograd Soviet of the Workers' and Soldiers' Deputies. Here was a true democracy, a parliament of the common man, very much unlike the Duma elected way back upon a limited franchise, or the Western legislative assemblies filled with the *bourgeoisie* and political connivers. The Soviet was a huge fluctuating body of two to three thousand men, a great majority of them common workers and soldiers subject to recall by their units and factories. The Soviet moved as a matter of course into the building vacated by the Duma, the Tauride Palace, a symbol in itself of the supremacy of the people over bourgeois parliamentarism.

There are many almost lyrical descriptions of the Soviet during the early days of the Revolution. The hustle and bustle of the assembly conveyed the vigor of this militant democracy in action, its stern determination to vest the government of Russia directly in her people. Not the polished sentences of the parliamentarians but the simple heartfelt sentiments of the soldier and the worker were heard in the Tauride Palace. No artificial eloquence, no political bargains marred this picture of democracy in action.

Such, alas, were the appearances. In fact a more penetrating glance would bare the Soviet's weaknesses and its inability to perform even the limited task of governing it set before itself. In the first place it was hardly representative. Though there were many more workers in and around Petrograd than soldiers, the latter constituted a majority of the Soviet. In addition many politicians from the intelligentsia, former political prisoners, and others were either coopted into it or simply joined it on their own. Every meeting was attended by numerous persons "with mandates God knows from whom," notes the chronicler of the Revolution N. N. Sukhanov.

A more basic blemish was its size and unstable character. Hence in its very beginning, and behind the façade of grass-roots democracy, the Soviet's decisions were those of a handful of the intelligentsia and Socialist leaders who set it up. How this huge unwieldy body could be manipulated by a few determined men is well illustrated by an incident that took place at its first meeting. Out of nowhere there appeared a relic of the past, the chairman of the Petersburg soviet of 1905, Khrustalev-Nosar. This man for long had had no ties with revolutionary or Socialist circles. He had been involved in personal scandals and was earning his livelihood by writing for the reactionary press. But now he insisted that as of right the leadership of the new Soviet belonged to him. Such was the reverence for the past and the softness of the initiators of the "revolutionary democracy" that this thoroughly discredited man almost carried his point, and only with great difficulty was persuaded to seek his luck elsewhere.

The official leadership of the Executive Committee of the Soviet was vested in the hands of the Socialists. Menshevik Chheidze, member of the Duma, became chairman; a Socialist Revolutionary, Alexander Kerensky, and another Menshevik, Skobelev, its vice-chairmen. But, as Trotsky observes: "In that first period the inspirer of the executive committee was not its president Chheidze, an honest and limited provincial . . ." (he was a Georgian, which accounts for Trotsky's condescending description). The inspiration of the Soviet came, and here is a repetitive *motif* of Russian revolutionary history, from a handful of radical intellectuals, representing no particular party but a sort of general "leftism." Two of them are worthy of notice; their personalities explain much of what happened to the Soviet and the Revolution.

N. N. Sukhanov wrote a voluminous and garrulous account of 1917.[5] Lenin's judgment of him and his kind was to be not very flattering: "Our petty bourgeois democrats, pedants and cowards." [6] Trotsky's opinion was somewhat more fair: "Semi-Populist, semi-Marxist, a conscientious observer rather than a statesman, a journalist rather than a revolutionary . . . he was capable of standing by a revolutionary conception only up to the time when it was necessary to carry it into action." Yet in a way Sukhanov was an engaging character: during the Revolution he was continually on the run: he gate-crashed Bolshevik meetings, upbraided and pestered Kerensky, seemed to be everywhere during those dramatic first days. By profession a writer on economics, Sukhanov under the old regime pursued a not too untypical career of a radical intellectual: under his real name, Himmer, he worked in the Ministry of Agriculture, under his political one he participated in revolutionary conversations and journalism.

His close colleague and collaborator was Yuri Steklov. A litterateur and essayist, Steklov had for a long time oscillated between the Mensheviks and Bolsheviks. In Soviet Russia, now a Communist, he was to become a leading writer on socioliterary themes. (He wrote valuable biographies of Chernyshevsky, Bakunin, and others.) Like countless others he was to end

[5] N. N. Sukhanov, *Notes About the Revolution* (in Russian), 7 vols., Berlin, 1922.
[6] Lenin jotted this down on January 1923, almost the last thing he ever wrote.

his days in jail, during World War II. The Soviet entrusted Steklov with the then very important job of editing its official paper *Izvestia* (*News*).

Sukhanov, Steklov, and others of their kind, though without any real political support among the workers or soldiers, played an important role in those critical first days because they were "literary people," men who knew how to draft a proclamation, edit a paper, because they had friends and connections among the radical intelligentsia (Sukhanov was then close to Maxim Gorky) and thus could endow the Revolution with eloquence and literary grace. These "rootless intellectuals," to give them a much later Communist description, thus left an important imprint on the policies of the Soviet. They were radical Socialists, nondenominational Marxists, so to speak. There was no organization behind them, their politics reflected vaccillation and doctrinal uncertainty. What should the Revolution, that is, the Soviet, do? The Marxist intellectual's answer was conditioned by two fears. One was of a possible counterrevolution, a restoration of the old regime. Unrealistically, this fear persisted in their minds even in the face of the incredible facility with which the regime had collapsed. There was still the army under its old Tsarist generals and officers. Hence the Revolution, as Sukhanov put it, "had to conquer the army," even at the price of military disorganization and possible defeat in the war.

The other fear had its source in their doctrine. The Revolution had won, the people had overthrown the regime. But could "the people" take over power? Marxism taught that Russia was not ready for socialism, for the people—the proletariat—taking over the government. This was to be the time for "a bourgeois-democratic regime," not yet for socialism. But could this bourgeois regime be trusted with *full* power? Of course not. The bankers, industrialists, and others who would become ministers had to be jealously watched by "the revolutionary democracy," lest they betray the Revolution and the interests of the people. Hence one of the strangest forms of government ever devised was born in the minds of the radical intellectuals and acclaimed by the Socialist Revolutionaries and the Mensheviks: the *bourgeoisie* had to take power and form the Provisional Government. But "revolutionary democracy," that is, the Soviet, would virtuously refuse to participate in this regime of bankers, manufacturers, and professors. It would sternly watch and if need be curb the bourgeois government, and remind it continuously that it ruled only through the magnanimity and self-restraint of the Soviet. This splendid formula had one catch: what, wondered Sukhanov anxiously, if the *bourgeoisie* should refuse to take power? He was deeply relieved when the "capitalists" did agree to form the Provisional Government and spared the Soviet this cruel dilemma.[7]

---

[7] Perhaps it was also personal relief. He records frankly the Soviet chairman's complaint that Sukhanov was interested only in talking about politics and not in doing any work.

The fear of a Tsarist comeback led the Soviet to its perhaps momentous and fateful act. Even before the Soviet was properly organized Steklov and a lawyer, Sokolov, prepared its *Order No. 1,* published on March 1. The order was addressed to *all* Russian military and naval units. It *commanded* them to form soldiers' committees, soviets. Every military unit was from now on subject to the Petrograd Soviet and to its own soldiers' council. All its weapons were to be under the control of the soviets and "under no conditions handed over to the officers even at their demand." The old forms of saluting and address between the soldiers and the officers were abolished. The regimental soviets were to settle any misunderstandings between the rank and file and commanders.

It is very doubtful whether *any* army could have preserved for long its fighting capacity following an order of this kind. After a few days and sober second thoughts, *Order No. 1* was supplemented by instructions pointing out that the authority of the soldiers' committees extended only to political matters. Even the manifesto itself directed that in the discharge of military duties the strictest discipline should prevail. But the harm, of course, could not be undone. The authors rushed through the *Order* not to destroy the army, but in panic lest a "man on a white horse" undo the Revolution. "The Soviet still had to lead a stubborn fight for the army, which it was necessary to snatch from the influence of the *bourgeoisie* in order to safeguard the full victory of the Revolution," writes Sukhanov.[8] But the baby was thrown out with the bathwater. A disciplined apolitical army is one of the main prerequisites of a democracy. *Order No. 1* was bound to make such an army impossible, to transform it into a series of political meetings, to sap its strength and discipline, and thus to make more rather than less probable a military coup from the extreme left or right. Its authors did not intend such consequences; they were simply ignorant of military affairs. And there was not a single Bolshevik among them.

Lenin's followers played in fact a very secondary role in the great events of February and March. The Bolsheviks' following among the politically conscious workers was small compared with that of the Mensheviks and the Socialist Revolutionaries. Their leaders, Shlyapnikov and Molotov, did a creditable job of keeping a small nucleus of their party in being and they were invited, more as a courtesy to fellow Socialists than because of their importance, to sit in the Executive Committee of the Soviet. But neither of them was cast to be an audacious revolutionary leader, ready to improvise in the face of unexpected events. Lenin's previous instructions were obviously obsolete. When the Soviet voted to accept the Provisional Government with its bourgeois composition the Bolsheviks were capable of mustering only nineteen votes against about four hundred. But even so they could not conceive of an alternative. Obviously one could not participate in a bourgeois regime. On the other hand, how could one fight against the will of the proletariat expressed by the Soviet? And the Rus-

[8] Sukhanov, *op. cit.,* Vol. 2, p. 52,

sians were not ready for a Socialist government; even Vladimir Ilyich was saying so a short time before. And so Shlyapnikov and Molotov waited for a word from Switzerland or the arrival of the senior Bolsheviks who had just been released from their Siberian exile. In the meantime they opened shop: *Pravda* began to appear again, and a handsome palace was commandeered for the Party headquarters.[9]

In the first days of March the institutional structure of the Revolution was complete. The Provisional Government, this "half power," had at its head Prince George Lvov, a liberal nobleman, former head of the Union of Zemstvos (Association of Local Governments). This nominally highest official of revolutionary Russia was a man eminently suited to be the president or premier of a *peacetime* constitutional regime. Most historians, after mentioning the formation of Lvov's government, have only one other occasion to mention the Prince's name: when he resigns in July. His government was composed, with one exception, of the Kadets and moderate conservatives. The long-time leader of the Constitutional Democrats, Professor Miliukov, received the portfolio of foreign affairs. A prominent industrialist, former president of the Duma, Guchkov, had the unhappy task of presiding over the Army and Navy Ministry.

The Sukhanovs and Steklovs had dreamed of a perfect harmony and yet separation between the Soviet and the government. But from the beginning this separation was spoiled by one man: Alexander Kerensky, Socialist Revolutionary and vice-president of the Soviet; he accepted the post of the Minister of Justice. Many people were to see in this young lawyer (thirty-five at the time) the future dictator of Russia. He was a leading representative of "the revolutionary democracy," and at the same time a minister of the bourgeois government. The Soviet, which had previously decided that no Socialist dared accept a ministerial portfolio, gave way easily to the emotional appeal of Kerensky: "I speak, comrades, from my soul, from the depths of my heart, and if this is necessary to prove . . . if you do not trust me . . . I am right here . . . just before your eyes . . . ready to die."[10] This was rather typical of his future oratory. The man who loomed so large in March was to be seen in retrospect as a Hamlet of the Russian Revolution. But then the Revolution had many Hamlets and only one serious candidate for dictator.

He was at the time writhing with impatience in Switzerland. Lenin's

[9] The palace belonged to famous ballerina Kshesinskaya, who had been the Tsar's mistress before his marriage, and since then had had to content herself with a succession of grand dukes. On its "requisition" she descended on the Soviet and complained loudly and tearfully. A few months later a despoiled "exploiter," not to mention a lady of Kshesinskaya's background, would have been happy to escape with her life. But such was the mood of those early days that Shlyapnikov was actually embarrassed by her importunities and restored her private belongings, though not the house. The latter, he observes ungraciously, was more suited for the exercise of Kshesinskaya's profession than for transacting Party business: it was full of bathrooms, pools, and such. A. Shlyapnikov, *Year 1917*, Moscow, n.d., Vol. 2, p. 191.

[10] Sukhanov, *op. cit.*, Vol. 1, p. 314.

original analysis of the Revolution—a plot by the French and British embassies to prevent a separate peace—soon gave way to a more realistic recognition of its elemental character. Yet the news, much as it was exhilarating, was also infuriating. Everything was wonderful, but everything seemed to go wrong. It was an automatic reflex for him to exclaim that the Mensheviks and the Socialist Revolutionaries were betraying the proletariat. Yet it was not quite clear what the Bolsheviks themselves were doing. Lenin's original response to events was of necessity chaotic. He wrote in March: we want "peace, bread, and freedom." But so did everybody else. Peace, but with whom and how? As late as the eve of his departure from Switzerland in April [11] Lenin was to fulminate against the possibility of a peace with German *imperialism* and declare that the Bolsheviks would lead a revolutionary war against the German *bourgeoisie*. One of his earliest apprehensions was that complete anarchy might seize Russia. The Socialists, he wrote, needed the state and authority; they were not anarchists.

Gradually, all the pieces began to fall into place. Russia did have a government of a sort; the immediate threat of anarchy that had made him write more tolerantly of the Mensheviks had receded. But now loomed an opposite danger: what if the bourgeois Provisional Government would show its teeth and go about governing and running the war in a business-like way? The exaggerated opinion of the government's strength and capacity is evident in his letter to Kollontay of March 16. He doubted that the Kadets would legalize the Bolshevik Party. (At the time, of course, *every* party had been legalized in Russia.) He added that if, however, they did, "We shall conduct both legal and illegal work." [12] Lenin refused to be impressed by the man who at the time appeared to many as the giant of the Revolution. Kerensky was a "loudmouth," an "idiot," and "objectively" an agent of Russian bourgeois imperialism.[13]

His eagerness to return to Russia turned into a frenzy at the news of what was happening to the Bolshevik organization at home. On March 12 Stalin and Kamenev returned from their Siberian exile. Members of the Central Committee, they were now the senior Party men on the spot. They and another Bolshevik oligarch, Muranov, simply shoved aside their juniors, Shlyapnikov and Molotov, and took over the direction of Party affairs and its press. To Lenin's dismay (even though he himself had not worked out fully an alternative policy) the new arrivals adopted a conciliatory policy toward the Mensheviks, and even, o horror! toward the Provisional Government. Kamenev took a position almost indistinguishable from that of the hateful "Socialist patriots." What was this nonsense mum-

---

[11] It is again important to keep in mind that the dates for events outside of Russia are given according to the Western calendar, thirteen days in advance of the Russian.
[12] *Works*, Vol. 35, p. 239.
[13] *Ibid.*, p. 249.

bled earlier by the Bolsheviks about ending the war *now*, he wrote. "It would be the most stupid policy when an army faces the enemy, to urge it to lay down arms and to go home. That would be a policy not of peace but of serfdom, a policy contemptuously rejected by the free nation." [14] Only an overthrow of imperialism in Germany could lead to a peace. There was nothing in this that could not and had not been said by Kerensky.

Kamenev's words were not motivated, as it was later alleged, by his brother-in-law and enemy, Trotsky, by his natural timidity and un-Bolshevik moderation. They corresponded to the mood of the masses. Even Sukhanov, who proudly declared himself always to have been "defeatist" when it came to the war, gave the following testimony: "During the first weeks the soldiers of Petrograd not only would not listen, but would not permit any talk of peace. They were ready to lift up on their bayonets any uncautious 'traitor' or exponent of 'opening the front to the enemy.'" [15] To an "internationalist," a "Zimmerwaldist," which poor Sukhanov also proudly considered himself to be, this was a deplorable mood. But as Kamenev privately explained, it was one thing for Lenin *in Switzerland* to fulminate against "defensism," it was another for the Bolsheviks in Russia to risk destruction by clashing with as yet prevalent patriotism.

Another item of news likely to raise Lenin's temperature was that the Bolsheviks were evidently contemplating a reunion with the Mensheviks. Just as in 1905, the politically conscious worker could not understand why the Russian Marxists should be divided and quarreling when the Revolution called for a united effort. Before Lenin's eyes there must have arisen the vision of new endless quarrels and debates with the Martovs, Dans, and many others when all possible effort had to be thrown into the making of a new Russian, and through it a European, revolution. He was supremely confident that once in Russia he could redirect his straying cohorts, but he had to get there and fast.

But how? France, England, and Italy were not going to facilitate passage through their territory of a man who believed that the imperialist war should be turned into a civil one. Those Russian revolutionaries who believed in the prosecution of the war, like Plekhanov, were given every encouragement and help to return to Russia. But Lenin and many others were known to be, to put it mildly, not friendly to the Allied cause. Under pressure from the Soviet the Provisional Government helplessly agreed to push for the return of exiles, no matter what their political views. But even so Lenin might well find himself, while crossing France, arrested and interned. There remained one alternative route out of landlocked Switzerland: through the territory of Russia's enemies.

Ever since the beginning of the war the German Imperial Government

[14] Shlyapnikov, *op. cit.*, Vol. 2, p. 183.
[15] Sukhanov, *op. cit.*, Vol. 2, p. 140.

and the General Staff had been conscious of the great help they might derive from the Russian revolutionary movement. Internal subversion of the enemy was already recognized as a legitimate weapon of warfare. And in the case of Russia the opportunities for its use appeared limitless. When it came to the Russian revolutionaries the German government had a most competent expert and adviser. He was Dr. Alexander Helphand, none other than our old friend "Fatty" Parvus, who had authored the theory of "permanent revolution" with Trotsky and who had been a member of the Russian Social Democratic Party. The war had found him in Germany, where he became a "Socialist patriot" but a German one. He grew rich as a war profiteer, helped, no doubt, by informal commissions he deducted from the huge sums the government paid him to sponsor defeatist and subversive propaganda within the Russian Empire.[16]

Helphand knew the Russian Socialists from Axelrod to Zinoviev. It was natural that because of their position the Bolsheviks should become the special object of his interest, but until the February Revolution his efforts to approach them were evidently in vain. Shlyapnikov records that during his Scandinavian stay he rejected Parvus' importunities. The Bolshevik group in Switzerland had certainly suffered extreme financial privation, and it was inconceivable that they should have received any German help prior to February.

But now with the Revolution the situation was drastically changed. The Bolsheviks, and for that matter other antiwar Russian Socialists, needed German help to get back to their country. The German minister in Switzerland sent home a wire saying that he had been told "that leading Russian revolutionaries here wish to return to Russia via Germany, as they are afraid to travel via France because of the danger from submarines." [17] The real reasons, as we have seen, were more involved.

All the Soviet accounts of Lenin's return trip through Germany repeat that the initiative for it belonged to Martov,[18] one of the very rare occasions when the Bolsheviks were willing to credit their enemies with a constructive idea. Furthermore, the tales of Lenin's alternative plans for travel are suspiciously numerous and absurd. He was going to travel through England in a wig. He was going to pass through Germany, but with a Swedish passport, traveling as a deaf and dumb Swede. Hanecki, Lenin's agent in Stockholm, and a very inept liar, gives the most grotesque version: Lenin wrote him in March asking for passports of two Swedes

[16] "Dr. Helphand concluded by saying that about 20 million rubles would be required to get the Russian revolution completely organized." The German Minister in Copenhagen to the Chancellor, quoted in *Germany and the Revolution in Russia. Documents from the Archives of the German Foreign Ministry*, edited by Z. A. B. Zeman, London, 1958, p. 9.

[17] *Ibid.*, p. 25.

[18] Thus in Krupskaya's memoirs: "Martov presented a plan to obtain permits for emigrants to pass through Germany in exchange for German and Austrian prisoners of war. . . ."

who looked like him and Zinoviev. He and his inseparable lieutenant were going to skip through Germany as *two* deaf and dumb Swedes.[19]

All those accounts create a strong presumption, strongly supported by the recently revealed German documents, that at the time Lenin had decided to avail himself not only of German permission to pass through but of German funds as well. Hanecki was also in the employ of Parvus.[20] The negotiations and contacts were evidently handled with extreme caution. Almost all his then and future agents in Sweden, contact men with the German legation, were to be individuals close to him personally and politically, but not as yet officially members of the Bolshevik Party: German Socialist Radek; Hanecki, member of the Polish Social Democratic Party; and Vorovsky, with long-standing Bolshevik connections but also a Pole by birth.

Granted Lenin's premises, his decision to accept German help was perfectly natural. It was not to affect his position an iota: he was working to bring about a new revolution in Russia, but that revolution in turn was to overthrow the German government and bring about the victory of revolutionary socialism in all Europe. The Bolsheviks needed money. Their future prodigious growth in membership and prestige between April and October was to reflect not only the skill of their leaders and the ineptitude of their opponents, but also their superior resources. They were able to spend freely on their newspapers, on full-time agitators and propagandists, and on arms for their Red Guards. These vast sums could not have come from the Party dues (in April they had but 49,000 members) or from the sale of *Pravda*. The revolutionary activities needed money, and just as in 1906 he did not hestitate to obtain it from expropriations so in 1917 Lenin did not scruple to get it from Germany. If he could he would have willingly accepted it from France, England, or the Romanovs.

But there was the matter of appearances. Lenin and his colleagues were under no illusions as to the interpretation that would be put in Russia upon their travel through Germany. It was equally characteristic of him without a moment's hesitation to turn to a political enemy for help. Would the Petrograd Soviet and its chairman Menshevik Chheidze authorize the Bolsheviks' trip so as to prevent future slanders? Needless to say they were willing: it would have been undemocratic to prevent the arrival of the man who was coming with the announced intention of destroying them. But everything the Soviet did, except the issuance of manifestoes, took a long time. Martov and his antiwar Mensheviks would stupidly wait till the official sanction, but Lenin was in a hurry. "He talked with bitterness about the superfluous and unnecessary caution of Martov

[19] J. Hanecki, "The Return of Comrade Lenin," in *The Proletarian Revolution*, No. 1, Jan. 1924.

[20] Further evidence will be considered below in connection with the events of July 1917.

and others. . . . Not a single reasonable man will think that we are going
to Russia on behalf of the Germans. . . . It is simply criminal to sit here
with folded arms when we are so needed by the proletariat in Russia." [21]

A Swiss Socialist, Fritz Platten, finally negotiated an agreement with
the German minister which was intended to refute any future slanders.
The railway car carrying Lenin and his entourage was to enjoy extraterri-
toriality in its passage through Germany (hence the legend of the "sealed
car"). Any dealings with the German authorities were to be through Platten, who went along, and the passage was to be as fast as possible. There
was a much advertised stipulation that "passengers were to be taken re-
gardless of their political opinions and attitudes toward war and peace." [22]
The only obligation the departing Russians incurred was to plead for
the release of an equivalent number of German war prisoners by the Russian government.

Thus on April 9 Lenin, his wife, and more than twenty leading members of his Swiss group, including the Zinovievs and Inessa Armand, set
out for home. After Germany they traveled through Sweden, then Finland. His family on April 2 [23] received a telegram: "We arrive Monday at
eleven at night. Tell *Pravda*." Lenin's mood as he approached his country
was gay but somewhat apprehensive. He wondered aloud whether they
would not be arrested on the Russian frontier. Even in the face of the
news from Russia it was impossible to realize the full impotence of the
Provisional Government and the incredible indecision of the other "half
government," the Petrograd Soviet. At the frontier of what once had been
the Russian Empire Fritz Platten was refused entry. The government that
dared not refuse admittance to the people pledged to work for its overthrow was courageous enough to limit this right to its own citizens. This
undemocratic step was subsequently excoriated before the Soviet and the
ministers by Sukhanov. [24]

The Bolshevik leaders were summoned to board the train some hours
before its arrival in Petrograd. Lenin was eager to orient himself in the
situation. Thus Shlyapnikov, Kamenev, other Party potentates, accompanied by Maria Ulyanov, got on at the frontier post of Beloostrov. They
were immediately besieged by questions: what was the mood of the work-

---

[21] S. Bagocki, *The Meetings with Lenin in Poland and Switzerland*, Moscow, 1958,
p. 50.

[22] The German minister commented in a dispatch to Berlin that Platten had said:
"They believed that they had in this way insured themselves against being compromised
in Russia . . . [he] regards it as quite impracticable to consider the possibility of so-
called Socialist patriots, i.e., opponents of the peace, presenting themselves for the
journey . . ." Zeman, *op. cit.*, p. 36.

[23] We are now back to the Russian calendar.

[24] He told the ministers: "I shall present your refusal to let in Platten in the only
possible way: as a violation of the principle of political freedom. . . ." Sukhanov,
op. cit., Vol. 3, p. 207. It is not impossible that he may have reflected on this incident
during his long imprisonment in Communist Russia, one which lasted, insofar as we
know, till his death.

ers, soldiers, the state of Party affairs? Kamenev was reprimanded by Lenin: "What have you been writing in *Pravda*? I have certainly called you all sorts of names." But this was said good-naturedly and with a smile. Lenin liked Kamenev. More important, with his practical sense he probably realized that Kamenev, through his insubordination and "defensism," unwittingly rendered the Party a service: he saved it from popular indignation during the first and most nationalistic phase of the Revolution. Certainly Kamenev did not seem depressed by the censure of his leader. He ran around the train presenting Petrograd Bolsheviks to his great friend Gregory Zinoviev, with whose career his own was to be mixed so inextricably and tragically.

At 11:10 the night of April 3 the train pulled in at the Finland Station of Petrograd. Vladimir Ilyich was home.

If there was one thing at which the Soviet excelled, it was the organization of welcomes and festive receptions for the returning revolutionary heroes. Thus a few days before, a tumultuous reception had greeted Plekhanov. Special solemn meetings had been held to honor Vera Zasulich and the aged and legendary Populist Katherine Breshko-Breshkovskaya, the "grandmother of the Revolution." [25] The Revolution was still in a holiday and generous mood and their political differences did not prevent the chairman and vice-chairmen of the Soviet, "Menshevik scoundrels" in the parlance of the new arrivals, to hasten to the station to render homage to Comrade Lenin and his party.

To the strains of the "Marseillaise" (the Russian bands had not yet learned the "International" so the "Marseillaise" had to do though it was, alas, not only a revolutionary hymn but the anthem of "French imperialism"), Lenin descended from his car and was engulfed by the greeters. Shlyapnikov, acting, as a witness reports, like a police chief greeting a visiting Tsarist governor, led the way. The guard of honor presented arms, and its commander (military discipline was obviously already going to the dogs) delivered the first short speech, in which he hoped that Citizen Lenin would shortly enter the Provisional Government! A bouquet was thrust into Vladimir Ilyich's hand (nobody noticed whether Krupskaya got flowers; nobody noticed her at all) and he was pushed into the ceremonial waiting room reserved in the old days for the Imperial family.

Here Chheidze on behalf of the Soviet delivered the sacramental greetings: revolutionary democracy has to be defended from domestic and foreign enemies . . . unity is necessary . . . they all hope he will join them in the work for the Revolution. Seemingly ignoring the unfortunate chairman, Lenin addressed "soldiers, sailors, and workers: The dawn of the world-wide Socialist Revolution has risen . . . our Russian Revolution

---

[25] This old lady showed herself, after years of exile and imprisonment, not only full of vigor but also, as Sukhanov sadly notes, of chauvinism. She organized women's battalions to fight the Germans.

marks its beginning and has opened a new era." He was shrewd enough to talk about the approaching revolution in Germany: "Not far away is the hour when at the call of our comrade Karl Liebknecht nations will turn their weapons against the exploiters . . . In Germany everything is boiling." Karl Liebknecht was currently in jail and Lenin had come to Russia through the complicity of the government that had put him there. But such incongruities escaped those who witnessed the historic moment.

After the official welcome Lenin was repossessed by the Bolsheviks. But before leaving the station he had to address the crowd. Standing on an armored car, he repeated the gist of his "reply" to Chheidze. Then in the car, accompanied by armed detachments, banners, and the band, he slowly worked his way to Kshesinskaya's palace. Here there was another speech from the balcony. All Lenin's pronouncements that night contained an uncompromising attack on the continuation of the war: "The [alleged] defense of the Fatherland means the defense of one band of capitalists against another." There was considerable grumbling at those words among the soldiers who were listening, and some suggestions that he should come down and they would show him . . .

The irrepressible Sukhanov pushed his way into Bolshevik headquarters. He was greeted warmly by the great man. Before the war Lenin had deigned to write of some of Sukhanov's economic and journalistic productions: "The impudent lie of Sukhanov; . . . There can be no doubt Mr. Sukhanov is one of the worst windbags. . . ." But bygones were bygones and, as our chronicler notes, whatever epithets the father of Bolshevism had bestowed upon him, it was nothing compared with what he had written about Trotsky. They held a friendly discourse, until the impatient Bolsheviks reclaimed "our Ilyich." Lenin, though he must have been tired, had to speak again to the assembled Party workers. In a two-hour speech he assaulted the Bolsheviks' position prior to his return—their hesitations about the Soviet, the Provisional Government, their actual support of the war. He knew how to shame the fainthearted. It is impossible to believe that he was telling the truth when he declared: "When I was coming here with my comrades I believed that they would take us from the station straight to jail. . . . We do not lose the hope that that will come to pass." Brave words designed to shame the most stalwart "defensists" among the Bolsheviks. Nobody was to remember them a few months later when, finally given an opportunity to go to jail, Lenin fled.

Not until five o'clock in the morning did Lenin leave the palace and his exultant but also confused followers, to repair to his new domicile, sister Anna Elizarova's apartment. The leader of the Revolution did not cease for a moment to be a family man. He took time out in the next few feverishly busy days to visit the cemetery where his mother and sister Olga were buried, and deposited wreaths on their graves.

April 4 marked what was to be until October Lenin's most decisive intervention in the affairs of the Revolution. He held conferences in his sister's apartment in the morning, then in *Pravda's* offices, and in the afternoon he delivered two speeches, which constituted the famous April Theses.[26] The main discourse was at the Tauride Palace, before a joint session of the Bolsheviks, Mensheviks, and nonaligned Socialists. It was to be one of the attempts at a reunion of the Russian Marxists. But after Lenin's speech it was obvious that no such reunion was in the cards. Indeed, the main problem seemed to be whether the Bolsheviks themselves, most of them appalled by the intemperate tone and demands of their leader, would not undergo a split.

What was most jarring was Lenin's rejection of the whole structure of "double power" erected by the Revolution, and now almost a tenet of faith even for such radical Socialists as Steklov and Sukhanov. *All* power should go to the soviets, he asserted. He rejected any idea of support, however conditional, of the Provisional Government. The war was still an imperialist war, and though he by now was careful enough *not* to advocate an immediate peace, he stressed the need for intense antiwar propaganda and for encouraging the front-line soldiers to fraternize with their German and Austrian foes. The land problem was to be solved by immediate confiscation of estates and their transfer to the committees of the poor peasantry. To shut and bolt the door on any reunion Lenin demanded that his Party change its name to "Communist," and that a new militant international be established to exclude not only the "Socialist patriots" but the center (that is, the Kautskys, the Mensheviks, and the like).

To the majority of those present this was a thunderbolt, a repudiation not only of the previous Bolshevik position, but, it appeared, of Marxism itself. "Everybody" knew that this was not the moment for a *Socialist* revolution, but for a bourgeois democratic one. Lenin's theses were a declaration of anarchism, of adventurism unworthy of a Marxist. "But this is nonsense," shouted one Menshevik, "insane nonsense." To others it appeared that surely Lenin was simply out of touch with real conditions in Russia. After he had been around a while he would surely regain his senses. Triumphantly, the Menshevik leaders concluded that this man was obviously politically dead. Just as Plekhanov with his excessive nationalism, so Lenin with his anarchism had obviously read himself out of Russian Marxism.

The very same afternoon Lenin appeared, now a humble petitioner, before the Executive Committee of the Soviet. Would they protect him from the bourgeois slanders about his trip through Germany? The Menshevik-dominated Committee obliged him. That Lenin had to travel through enemy territory was blamed on the Provisional Government,

---

[26] Obviously he could have had scarcely any sleep. One is reminded of a collaborator of his in 1905–6 who wondered, on the basis of his observation of Lenin's daily routine, whether he slept at all.

which obviously was derelict in its duty to facilitate the return of the exiled revolutionaries. This favor to Lenin was the result of the Mensheviks' solidarity with a fellow Socialist who had been slandered, but probably also of their pity for a man who had just utterly discredited himself, very likely forever ending his political career.

Lenin's theses were published in *Pravda* on April 7 and aroused universal indignation. For some days afterward he had to fight to bend the Bolshevik organization to his will. But despite Kamenev's opposition and general protests the Bolsheviks eventually followed their leader. This was to be the pattern for some time to come: an audacious proposal by Lenin would first arouse protests, threats of and actual resignation, but on any major issue he was bound to have his way. This was the legacy of the years of isolation and defiance, 1907–17; he now dominated his Party morally and intellectually. Bolshevism without him was unimaginable.

Then there was an excellent revolutionary logic behind his proposals. "Russia was the freest country in the world," said Lenin. This was not a compliment, but an almost incredulous assertion of the fantastic opportunities for propaganda and agitation. How long could the patriotic prowar mood of the masses last? Russia had had over five million casualties. No military miracle had followed the Revolution. The food situation and inflation were growing worse, the armed forces were already beginning to dissolve into a mass of politicking soviets; national unity, so visible in the first days, was giving way to class suspicions and hostilities. In *What Is To Be Done?* Lenin had written that it was amazing what one determined agitator could do. Soon the Bolsheviks were to have hundreds and thousands of them among the soldiers. Their "line" had the advantage of simplicity compared with the tortuous reasoning of the other Socialists: this is a war for the benefit of the capitalists and imperialists, with no "buts" and "ifs."

"All power to the soviets." This was the key to Lenin's proposals and to their eventual popularity. In 1905 he had made a grave tactical error; he had at first underestimated the popularity and appeal of the soviets. They were an invention of the Mensheviks and reflected the despised "spontaneity" of the masses. Now he saw that the soviets were dear to the heart of the common worker and soldier: they were *his* government, not a distant conniving parliament of the Western type. To plead for them was a masterful psychological stroke. How could anybody accuse the Bolsheviks of lusting after power? They were after all still a small minority within the soviets. Then why are the Mensheviks and the Socialist Revolutionaries afraid of the slogan? Isn't it because they are afraid of responsibility, plotting with the capitalists from the Provisional Government? "It is you gentlemen who have a majority in the [Petrograd] Soviet, not we. Why are you afraid? Why do you lie?" he wrote.

Another dimension of the slogan of which Lenin was not unaware was

that to call for "all power to the soviets" was to call for practical dissolution of political authority, a situation in which a determined minority
could seize power. How could one soberly believe that the Petrograd Soviet, this body of two to three thousand milling members, could in any
effective sense rule Russia? Or its Executive Committee of eighty or
ninety? Or that the Petrograd Soviet could be infused with authority and
determination, that it could dictate to its sister organizations in Moscow,
Irkutsk, or on the Western front? When incredibly enough the Soviet
gathered its resolution and began to act like a government in June and
July Lenin was hastily to abandon his slogan and not to revert to it until
the Bolsheviks secured majorities within the major soviets. It was not conscious Machiavellianism that made him adopt this powerful and perverse
slogan, but the sure instinct of the revolutionary: what remained of central political authority in Russia—the Provisional Government—had to be
destroyed. The Bolsheviks could come to power only as heirs to anarchy.

To the effects of anarchy on his unhappy country Lenin gave but little
thought. He was still a *world* revolutionary. Another installment of revolution in Russia would ignite a flame in Germany which would then spread
to the rest of Europe. Then there would be time enough to restore
authority in Russia and to guide it through an orderly Marxist economic
and social transformation, helped and protected by the comrades from the
more developed countries. But even at this, the most anarchistic phase of
Lenin's career, the scientific Socialist, the Lenin of 1921, occasionally
spoke out. In his theses he was emphatic that Russia was not ripe for an
immediate introduction of socialism. The proletarian government would
only *control*, not yet own, the means of production. While throwing out an
incitement to anarchy and lawlessness in the countryside, "all land to the
peasants" and right away, Lenin incongruously kept repeating that large
estates should be taken over by the state (this "state," which kept vanishing more and more every day) and run as scientific model farms. But this
was the small Marxist print in an otherwise anarchistic manifesto, and
there is no wonder that the worker or the poor peasant could not read it.
To them it was clear that Lenin wanted workers to have factories, and the
poor peasants their own plots.

Confronted by this challenge, the two "half governments" were almost
helpless. A more united, resolute, and unscrupulous authority would
surely have exploited the initial wave of indignation that greeted the public announcement of Lenin's position. Even the sailors of the Baltic fleet,
the most unruly revolutionary element, were outraged. A Bolshevik agitator among them in those April days received an admiral's treatment: he
was thrown overboard. Members of the guard that had greeted Lenin
addressed the following public letter, its tortuous prose a sure sign that it
came from the rank and file: "Having learned that Mister [this probably
hurt him most] Lenin came to us in Russia by permission of His Majesty

the German Emperor and the King of Prussia, we express our deep regret
that we participated in his solemn welcome to Petrograd . . . [had we
known we would have shouted] . . . instead of 'Hurrah,' 'Down with
you, go back to the country through which you came to us.' " [27] On April
17 more than fifty thousand wounded and mutilated veterans passed
through the streets of the capital with signs denouncing the defeatists and
disorganizers of the army. There were shouts demanding Lenin's arrest.

But the "Menshevik scoundrels" from the Soviet interposed themselves
between the wrath of the masses and their enemy. Citizen Lenin was defended before the indignant crowd of the veterans not only by two Mensheviks, but also by that "arch reactionary," president of the almost de-
funct Duma, Rodzianko. The Revolution was not to be soiled by lynchings
and mob violence! The revolutionary democracy, that is, the non-Bolshevik Socialists, persisted in their heroically suicidal course. Thus the Soldiers' Section of the Soviet denounced Lenin and the Bolsheviks' subversive campaign among the front-line troops. But they added that as long as
the Bolsheviks limited themselves just (!) to propaganda, no repression
should be used against them. Lenin quoted this resolution with approval.[28] Yes, his party was in favor of peaceful persuasion. They did not
mean to disorganize the army, they only urged soldiers to fraternize with
the Germans. No, the Bolsheviks did not want a separate peace. This was
a capitalist slander. So who was really threatening violence and undermining the army? Why the Minister of War, capitalist Guchkov! It was he
who was threatening and reprimanding those patriotic military units that
fired their old officers and elected new ones!

Following its overthrow, the Provisional Government did not lack
excellent advice as to what steps it might have taken to preserve democracy in Russia. The usual criticism concerns its failure to make peace and
thus to remove the most persuasive element of the Bolsheviks' propaganda. But to argue this is to misunderstand the situation of Russia right
after the February Revolution. As was natural in a country that had
suffered so many casualties, Russia longed for peace. To an overwhelming
majority of politicians and, as we have seen, to the masses of population
and soldiers as well, the only way to a speedy peace was defeat of Germany. From the perspective of two world wars such resolution looks foolish and suicidal. But to the average Russian of 1917 a separate peace with
Germany and Austria meant only one thing: a victory of the Central
Powers and Europe's domination by Imperial Germany. Russia undoubtedly could have gotten a better peace *then* than subsequently at Brest
Litovsk. But who could conceive of the Western Allies, then barely holding out, being capable of withstanding the assault of *all* Germany's
armies? And in a German-dominated Europe would Russia be allowed to
preserve her territorial integrity, or her newly won republican and demo-

---

[27] Sukhanov, *op. cit.*, Vol. 3, p. 109.
[28] *Works*, Vol. 24, p. 109.

cratic freedoms? Thus it was not only the notions of honor and of loyalty to the allies that made the generals and politicians believe that a victorious prosecution of war was a matter of life and death for Russia, and especially democratic Russia.

But the criticism overlooks an even more basic fact. Had it believed it necessary and beneficial, the Provisional Government and the General Staff still could not have concluded a separate peace. Its severest critics, the "internationalist Mensheviks" and the Bolsheviks, all pleaded for peace, but one to be concluded with the "German workers and soldiers" after they had overthrown their Emperor and generals. Had the Provisional Government at any point shown the slightest inclination to do what the Bolsheviks subsequently did at Brest Litovsk, it immediately would have been denounced for selling out to the Kaiser, for betraying the Revolution and the international proletariat. And Lenin's voice would have been the most insistent in this denunciation.[29]

Equally unrealistic is the argument that the opponents of the Bolsheviks should have beaten them to the punch and introduced *immediately* an agrarian reform giving the peasant what remained of the gentry's land. The peasant masses, the argument runs, would not have been won over or at least neutralized by the Bolsheviks' demagoguery. Any tampering with the ownership of land in wartime, as Lenin's own experience subsequently shows, was bound to make worse the already desperate food situation. And Russia's was a peasant army. How many soldiers would stay with their units if they were told that back in their village the landlord's estate was being partitioned among the peasant households?

Lenin's own slogan, "All power to the soviets," provided ironically the only clue as to the formula through which Russian democracy could break out of the vicious circle. If the soviets, or rather their Menshevik and Socialist Revolutionary leaders, who had behind them the vast majority of the nation, could be persuaded to assume full power, Russia might have had an effective government. But as has been pointed out the soviets were utterly incapable of governing. As to the Socialist Revolutionaries and the Mensheviks, neither party had a Lenin capable of knocking heads together and leading a unified phalanx. The non-Bolshevik Socialists were split into at least three groups. There were those who believed that the war must be prosecuted to a victorious end; the central or "internationalist," group which urged an immediate peace but only with "the German workers and soldiers"; and the left wing, which more and more followed the Bolsheviks in their disruptive tactics.

There were moments when the Soviet appeared *almost* on the point of

[29] The Manifesto of the Soviet of March 14, the work of its left wing, called upon the nations of the world: "Throw out your autocracy, just as the Russian nation has thrown off its Tsar, refuse to serve as the tool of robbery and force in the hands of the kings, landowners, and bankers—with our friendly joint efforts we shall end this terrible war. . . ." But it also said: "The Russian Revolution will not let itself be conquered by force from the outside."

rising to its responsibilities. A certain stiffening in its attitude followed the return from exile of Menshevik Irakli Tseretelli, a great revolutionary orator and one of the few who had no illusions as to where the Bolsheviks would lead Russia. He soon became the leading spirit of the Executive Committee though its nominal chairman remained his indecisive country-man Chheidze. Tseretelli undertook to tell some facts of life to the Soviet: "We should not consider the defense of the country as something which does not concern us, something we don't talk about. It should be for us one of the basic tasks of the Revolution, without which we should not be able to conclude a democratic peace and preserve the achievements of the Revolution." [30] But such frank talk shocked even some of the "defensists." To speak about war, defense, in brief about fighting anybody except the reactionaries was thought to be somewhat indecent for a Socialist. It was up to "them"—the bourgeois Provisional Government. The representatives of the revolutionary democracy, the Soviet, even if they tolerated the de-fense of their country, should confine themselves to the issuance of mani-festoes and stern vigilance over the Revolution.

The majority chafed under this tyranny of revolutionary phraseology. The epithet "Socialist patriot" intimidated the most courageous. Their irri-tation would, however, assume indirect and petty forms. To Tseretelli and the "defensist" majority of the Soviet one of the most loathsome opponents was Steklov. He was the editor of *Izvestia,* the official news organ of the Soviet, the closest approximation revolutionary Russia had to an official ga-zette, and as such was sabotaging the policy of the majority. Yet it would have been "undemocratic," a violation of the minority rights, simply to fire Steklov. Hence his opponents dug out a "scandal." Steklov, whose real name was Nahamkis, had petitioned first the Tsarist and then the Provi-sional Government authorities to have it *legally* changed to his Party pseudonym. This was a shameful, un-Socialist attempt to conceal one's Jewish origin! Steklov was discredited as a revolutionary statesman, but continued editing *Izvestia.* Such were the concerns and issues that agi-tated the Soviet.

In the face of the growing confusion Lenin's tactics were bound to gain him adherents. Some military units in Petrograd which in April had wanted to lift him up on their bayonets were already by May under the Bolshevik influence. In the same month he had to restrain his more impa-tient followers. The masses were not ready yet for a civil war, hence the Bolsheviks should refrain from an overhasty insurrection.[31] "We are now in a minority. The masses as yet don't believe us. We shall know how to wait." He carefully readjusted his propaganda. Attacks upon the Menshe-viks and the Socialist Revolutionaries became less abusive. About Alex-

[30] I. G. Tseretelli, *Reminiscences About the February Revolution* (in Russian), Paris–Hague, 1963, p. 47.
[31] *Works,* Vol. 24, p. 206.

ander Kerensky, still the most popular man in Russia, Lenin kept almost silent. Again hopes were to rise in the camp of his enemies that their erstwhile comrade was becoming reasonable, that perhaps, maybe, unity of socialism in Russia might yet be achieved. Martov, who finally reached Russia (also through Germany) raised his voice on the "internationalist" side, thus partly offsetting the influence of Tseretelli, and rendering the Mensheviks even more divided and impotent as a political force. No wonder the Bolsheviks were gaining in the elections to the soviets. Their members could be elected and recalled practically at any time and Lenin denounced as undemocratic the proposal that the delegates should be elected not more often than once every two or three months.

In May there returned another political exile, Lev Trotsky. He came through the good offices of the Provisional Government, which under pressure of the Soviet had to request from the British his release from Canadian internment. With his arrival the tempo of Bolshevik activity quickened. Officially, of course, Trotsky was not yet a member of Lenin's party. He headed a group of the so-called "interfaction" Socialists. This was a veritable party of revolutionary generals with no soldiers, many of them veterans of the prewar splits from Bolshevism. They had become estranged from Menshevism because of its democratic superstitions, from Bolshevism because of their inability to accept Lenin's dictatorial ways. But now people such as Trotsky, Lunacharsky, Uritsky, and others became almost undistinguishable from Lenin's Bolshevik followers. Many of them were of the revolutionary adventurer type and it was Lenin who promised a new and exciting adventure. From the beginning, Trotsky, his old quarrel with Lenin laid aside, supplied the previously missing element in Bolshevism. He was unmatched as a revolutionary orator and agitator. Lenin, despite the subsequent legend, was as Sukhanov phrased it, somewhat "aristocratic" in his political technique: he disliked giving frequent speeches before the crowds, and was at his best in closed Party gatherings. Most of the old-line Bolsheviks would when it came to addressing crowds simply repeat what their leader had just written; perhaps with the exception of Zinoviev they lacked entirely this fiery individualism and the ability to establish *rapport* with the listeners that shone from every Trotsky speech. For all his previous hostility to the man and despite his temperamental dislike of Trotsky which, being rooted in his own personality, never quite left him, Lenin quickly recognized that he was indispensable for his own task, for the Revolution. What brought Trotsky to the side of the man who had so cruelly abused him in the past, and in whom he had seen, before anybody else, the future dictator? It was partly the recognition of Lenin as the *international* revolutionary, the man who was going to make a world revolution while the others were talking about it. Then there was the realization that Lenin had won the intermittent political struggle in which they had been engaged since 1903: he now loomed as the giant of Russian Marxism, dwarfing the Plekhanovs, Martovs, and Dans. It was better to fight and if need be to fall on the side of a man like this, rather than to resume in the midst of a revolution the existence of a café politician and journalist. Lenin's acceptance of Trotsky was always qualified; after the Revolution and the Civil War he was careful to limit his brilliant partner's political influence. But Trotsky's conquest by Lenin was complete. Until his death at the hands of the assassin in Mexico Trotsky was to retain unbounded admiration and worship for Lenin.

May also brought a ministerial crisis. Some members of the Provisional Government were growing weary of their position of being as it were on public display in a cage labeled "the bourgeois democratic half government," subject to abuse and reprimand by their Siamese twin "half government" of the Soviet. The Foreign Minister Miliukov had just committed an unpardonable sin: he published a note about Russia's foreign policy which emphasized the resolve to continue fighting on the Allies' side and did not have a word about those aims dear to the heart of the "revolutionary democracy": the abjuration of annexations and contributions and the overthrow of the kings and capitalists. It was in especially bad taste since it was published on the International Workers' Solidarity Day.[32] The government's resignation was complicated by a legal difficulty: nobody knew who was empowered to accept it.

Having overcome this obstacle Prince Lvov (he had by now become such a shadowy figure that he was not even mentioned in the usual attacks upon the "capitalist ministers") thought to overcome the fury of the revolutionary democracy by discharging Miliukov and Guchkov (whose health broke down under his impossible job) and including the Socialists in his cabinet. Skobelev became Minister of Labor, Tseretelli Minister of Posts and Telegraphs, Chernov (the head of the Socialist Revolutionary Party, the spokesman for the vast majority of the peasants) became the Minister of Agriculture. And Kerensky, now more clearly than before the key man in the government, became Minister of War.

On paper the new cabinet represented an impressive show of national unity. It should have stilled the shouts of "All power to the soviets." After all, the most prominent members of the Soviet now were in the government. Confronted with this unpalatable fact, the Bolsheviks immediately raised a new slogan: "Down with the ten capitalist ministers." It was explained to the masses that essentially the government still remained that of the plutocracy, and those Socialists by entering it forfeited their claim to represent the people.

If anything, the "betrayal" of the Socialist ministers bewailed by Martov and Sukhanov increased Lenin's good humor and confidence in the future. He attacked the capitalist ministers so violently, largely because he still had a lingering respect for their political and administrative

[32] Which in Russia was celebrated on April 18 to coincide with May 1 in the West.

abilities. For the Mensheviks' and the Socialist Revolutionaries' talents in those spheres he had nothing but contempt. The Menshevik minister, Skobelev, declared that he proposed to tax the "heavy capitalists" one hundred per cent (sic!). Lenin undertook publicly to teach him some common sense and Marxian economics. The Bolsheviks, he wrote, repudiate all such wild and visionary schemes bound to ruin the national economy. They demand for the state just the *control* of industry and commerce. Under the Bolsheviks most of the capitalists would be able to work both profitably and honorably.[33] Though probably few of his readers believed that he was serious he meant every word. It was just like some empty-headed Menshevik phrasemonger to think that the Socialist state could dispense with the vast experience and technical skills represented by the capitalists. Lenin knew better.

The Revolution was turning a corner. A wave of peasant disorders reminiscent of but soon to surpass the events of 1905 had seized Russia. The structure of the state was dissolving. The autonomous movement in the Ukraine was turning toward a demand for independence. There was rapid erosion of all authority. On May 13 the sailors at Kronstadt declared that the only government they recognized was that of the Petrograd Soviet and that the revivified Provisional Government, for all of its six Socialist ministers, was not for them. Though "the Kronstadt republic" was soon persuaded to modify its position, it was a proof that the Bolsheviks' "All power to the soviets" was finding a ready response. Their propaganda among the front-line troops was now bearing fruit. The special organ *Pravda of the Trenches* was freely circulated with its appeals for fraternization, denunciation of the Provisional Government, and hints of a dark intrigue between the capitalists and the generals. Any attempt to reimpose strict military discipline was by now hopeless. The new War Minister Kerensky issued on May 9 a declaration of the rights of the soldiers and sailors, which sanctioned all forms of political propaganda and activity within the army. Every soldier had the right to belong to any political or professional group he chose. When not on actual duty he was given full freedom to participate in politics (it was assumed, of course, that the soldiers could exert this right even in the trenches when not in actual combat); "the right of internal self-government, imposition of penalties and control under the given circumstances" were to belong to the soldiers' elected committees. Thus the declaration sanctified and extended, on behalf of the government this time, the principles of *Order Number 1*. The commanding officers pleaded in vain with the government not to issue or at least to soften the declaration. They were met with the rejoinder, probably realistic, that the declaration merely ratified the *status quo* and that to try to undo it meant risking even greater trouble. A Menshevik minister observed with tragic prescience: "When we are told to bring the Rev-

[33] *Works*, Vol. 24, p. 392.

olution to an end we must answer that a revolution cannot be begun or ended by a decree." [34] Even the "defensist" Mensheviks believed that an army, just like a government, can be run by persuasion. Tseretelli told the generals: "The soldier will trust you if he understands that you are not enemies of democracy. That is the only way by which the Soviet has firmly established its authority." It is superfluous to describe the effect of such pronouncements upon military men. They go very far in explaining why many officers came eventually to hate the democratic Socialists much more than the Bolsheviks.

Though warned by a general that if the Germans attack "the Russian army will tumble like a house of cards," the Provisional Government now announced its intention of launching a *Russian* offensive. With February fighting had practically stopped on the vast front, the Austro-Germans waiting confidently for the inevitable breakup of Russia's armies. The foolhardy decision to attack could with great difficulty be justified on the grounds that inactivity was the greatest enemy of the soldiers' morale, that the Germans were shifting divisions to the Western front to deal a mortal blow to the Allies, and so on. But the major reason was, as with so many policies of the "revolutionary democracy," a fantastic belief in the power of phraseology and badly drawn parallels with the French Revolution. Then the armies of the free people dealt crushing blows to the combined forces of the European despots. Now the "freest army in the world" was going to demonstrate its superiority over the armed slaves of Prussian militarism. The contagion of revolutionary bathos was universal. It would be unfair to forget that the Bolsheviks were also at the moment under its sway. In his blueprint for a Socialist state Lenin envisaged the abolition of the standing army and its replacement by a militia with elective officers.

The embodiment of this revolutionary bathos was Alexander Kerensky. In his order to the army he called on the soldiers "to carry on the points of their bayonets peace, truth, and justice," to go forward in the name of their "boundless love for their country and the Revolution." To the superficial observer he appeared to have worked a miracle in reviving the morale of the army. Everywhere along the front lines his speeches aroused wild enthusiasm of the troops, pledges to die for the Revolution. Sukhanov, whose greatest fear was that a victorious offensive might profit the *bourgeoisie*, pays him this venomous tribute: "At the feet of Kerensky calling on them to go to their death [the soldiers] threw their decorations; women would take their jewels and in the name of Kerensky were offering them for this longed-for (nobody knows why) victory." In his soldier's tunic with an arm in a sling (he suffered from bursitis, but this gave him the appearance of a wounded hero) the Minister of War symbolized the determination of Russian democracy to crush the enemy.

[34] General Anton Denikin, *The Story of Russia's Time of Troubles* (in Russian), Paris, 1921, Vol. 1, Part 2, p. 61.

The danger of a military victory was not absent from Lenin's mind. He had not altered his low opinion of Kerensky's abilities and had a realistic view about the possibilities of a sustained victorious advance. But even a temporary success might arrest or reverse the trend toward Bolshevism among the soldiers and workers. In June, Lenin, who a few weeks before had said "we shall know how to wait," was ready to toy with an insurrection. Both in that month and in July his behavior was close to what he himself described and attacked as "adventurism." He must have been haunted by the memories of 1905. For all the talk about careful preparation and the need to conquer the masses before attempting to seize power, Lenin was aware that there is a moment in every revolution which if not grasped and exploited may never recur.

The chosen time coincided with the All-Russian Congress of the Workers' and Soldiers' Soviets. In that assembly out of 777 delegates with party affiliations the Bolsheviks had over 100 and their allies, the "interfaction" group, about thirty. This was a dazzling accession of strength since February. Still, the Mensheviks and the Socialist Revolutionaries had a substantial majority. Lenin emerged, for the meeting, from the editorial offices of *Pravda* and delivered a more than usually demagogic speech. What created amazement and even some laughter was his statement that there was a party ready to take power by itself: namely, the Bolsheviks. As to his formula for governing, it consisted in the immediate necessity of arresting one hundred of the most substantial capitalists and forcing them to reveal their intrigues that kept the Russian people in war and misery. "Are we Socialists or bullies?" was the rejoinder of Kerensky. The Revolution was still humane and it aroused distaste even among the extreme radicals that a former inmate of the Tsarist jails should call for arbitrary imprisonment. But Lenin was not really talking to his sophisticated audience: his words would be reprinted in thousands of copies of *Pravda;* they would strengthen the suspicions and class bitterness of the proletariat.

On the ninth of June an even more violent proclamation by the Bolsheviks called upon the soldiers and people of Petrograd to take to the streets. The proclamation described the government as a tool of capitalists and landlords. Kerensky's declaration of the soldiers' rights was declared a violation of their civic freedom (!). Immediate peace was demanded, but no separate treaty with Emperor Wilhelm, no secret agreements with the French and English capitalists. It was a call for rebellion and violence barely concealed by the statement that demonstrations should be peaceful: "State your demands calmly and convincingly as behooves the strong." Under prevailing conditions and with passions rising it was unthinkable that violence could be avoided during a demonstration in which thousands of armed soldiers would be participating.

It is equally clear that the Bolsheviks had as yet no concrete plan of seizing power. As the French revolutionary device had it, *On s'engage, puis on voit*—one begins action, then one can see what happens next. The aim was to overthrow the Provisional Government in order to frustrate the decision to launch an offensive, and then . . . Power might come to the Bolsheviks and their allies. They could count on the sympathy of some regiments of the Petrograd garrison where the news of the offensive aroused the natural apprehension that they might be sent to the front. They also had a more reliable force at their disposal in their own armed militia, the Red Guards.

Faced with the danger, the Congress of Soviets unexpectedly rose to the occasion. On the night of June 9 it banned all demonstrations for the next few days. Members of the highest organ of the "revolutionary democracy" were dispatched to the barracks and factories to explain the Bolshevik game to the soldiers and workers. The anti-Bolshevik units of the garrison were put on the alert. Lenin and his lieutenants were put in an unenviable and dangerous situation. The ostensible purpose of the demonstration was to bring power to the soviets. Here the highest organ of the soviets banned this "peaceful" intercession by the people on their behalf. What is more, the military units on the Bolsheviks' side were in a lamentable state of discipline and military readiness. They could be counted on to demonstrate and perhaps to rough up unarmed opponents, but what if it came to actual fighting? Even in October this question was to weigh heavily on the minds of the actual organizers of the Bolshevik military insurrection. The soldiers' willingness to follow the Bolsheviks was directly related to their unwillingness to fight. The statement that the demonstration should be peaceful was not entirely hypocritical; it also contained the assurance that violence should be limited to pushing around some capitalists and "betrayers of the proletariat." On second thought the Bolshevik Central Committee called off the demonstration.

Never backward in making a virtue out of necessity, the Bolsheviks now paraded their exemplary democratic behavior. *They* submitted to the will of the majority, even though that majority had grievously misjudged and slandered their intentions. *They* had to plead with the masses to desist from demonstrating and expressing their wrath with the "capitalist ministers" and the "defensists." And again many non-Bolshevik Socialists found this pleading convincing. Tseretelli's demand before the Congress of the Soviets that measures be taken to prevent the recurrence of the threat of the tenth of June, the calls for disarming of the Bolsheviks' private army —the Red Guards—were met with distaste and opposition by the Martovs and Sukhanovs. How can the Revolution disarm the proletariat? Would it not lead to a bourgeois dictatorship, to a Tsarist restoration? And the Executive Committee of the Congress contented itself with a pious resolution.

Lenin's own reaction to the failure of June 10 was characteristic. He began to wonder aloud whether the slogan "All power to the soviets" still corresponded to the needs of the hour. The soviets, with the Bolsheviks in them still in a minority, appeared suddenly to take this slogan seriously. "Even if the soviets took all power . . . we would not submit to their dictation to narrow down the freedom of our agitation; or to the prohibition of demonstrations in the capital and at the front. . . . We would prefer then to become an illegal officially persecuted party." [35] But his faith in the soviets was soon re-established. They limited themselves to a resolution and were as far as ever from attempting to exert any power, not to speak of "all" power. In three weeks the Bolsheviks were ready to try again.

With June ended the good-natured period of the Revolution. It was born amidst universal democratic and patriotic enthusiasm with the belief that government could be a matter of meetings and resolutions and that peoples and not their rulers should conclude a just and lasting peace. By now the reality was shown to be quite different. From June on, those who hoped for a democratic conclusion and peace had to work with increasing bitterness and despair in their hearts. There was no longer even an appearance of national unity or of "revolutionary democracy." The extreme left was openly committed to the use of force. Among the right there was a growing longing for a military coup that should save Russia from the "Jews and anarchists." The legend of the invincibility of the "most democratic army in the world" was shattered when the June offensive, after some initial success, ended in a disastrous defeat.

The Revolution had run out of its original impetus. There are mirage-like interludes of resolution and authority of the democratic forces. The Congress of the Soviets set up a permanent Executive Committee, thus giving Russia at least nominally a centralized authority. In July this Committee and the Provisional Government would still appear as saviors of democracy. The promise of the "real" Parliament, the Constituent Assembly, would until the last moment keep alive the hope for a democratic conclusion of the Revolution. But no such interludes could change the fact that among the people enthusiasm had been exhausted and patience was drawing to an end. The early Revolution was generous and hopeful. But these sentiments could not survive exasperation with the war, food shortages, and the fumbling and impotent government. It was the setting for a dictatorship.

2. Toward the Great October

"Those who make revolutions by halves are simply digging their own graves." Whatever the truth of this observation of Chateaubriand about the French Revolution, it represented the sentiments of Lenin during the second half of 1917. His impatience reflected not only the worry, excessive

[35] *Works*, Vol. 25, p. 60.

in retrospect, that the pro-Bolshevik trend might be arrested or reversed, but also something else. The Bolsheviks were being carried forward by a wave of anarchy. But this wave could not only carry them to power, it could also swamp them. The masses were being stirred up by demagogic slogans and accusations against the Provisional Government and the non-Bolshevik Socialists. But could their violence be controlled or doled out? Even in June, once the demonstrations had been proclaimed, it became hard to call them off. The mood of the soldiers and the workers was volatile and often uncontrollable. The disciplined serried ranks of the Bolshevik-led Red Guards and soldiers exist very largely in the imagination of the Bolshevik historians. The masses, egged on to violence and "peaceful" demonstrations, expected Lenin and his group to "deliver." If not, they would look elsewhere for guidance. There were, after all, real Anarchists who from the beginning of the Revolution were calling for an overthrow of *all* authority of the Provisional Government, of the soviets, of the Central Committees.

This situation explains why very shortly after the June fiasco the Bolsheviks were ready to engage in another adventure. This time it led them *almost* to a disaster. But there is something providential in the Bolsheviks' failures in June and July. The moment was not ripe. *Had* they seized power in either month they could not have retained it. Even the sluggish, garrulous "revolutionary democracy," the majority in the Soviet and the Central Executive Committee, would have been stirred to an even more drastic action than that which in July came close to bringing an end to Lenin's revolutionary career.

On July 3 Lenin was vacationing in Finland in the villa of his friend Bonch-Bruevich when a messenger brought news that there were riots and demonstrations in Petrograd. Parts of its garrison had been ordered to the front to bolster up the faltering offensive. Apart from the inherent inconvenience of this step to the soldiers who were involved, they had been taught that any attempt to remove them from the capital would be a "counterrevolution." The First Machine Gun Regiment decided to send just some of its units. At a combined political meeting and concert the regiment, after hearing speeches by Trotsky and Lunacharsky, decided, in order to prevent such bothersome requests in the future, to demonstrate in favor of "all power to the soviets." They called on other military units to join. Some of them did; others proclaimed their "neutrality." Soon crowds were milling in front of the Tauride Palace. Thousands of workers from the Putilov Works, a stronghold of Bolshevik influence, joined the demonstrating soldiers. The demonstrators surrounded the Bolshevik headquarters and booed their spokesmen when they urged restraint. Under this pressure from the "masses" the Bolshevik Central Committee decided to join the demonstration again, needless to say, to "assure its peaceful character." And on July 4 Lenin came back to the scene of disorders.

His reaction, as recorded by Zinoviev, was "Maybe we should try it now." But no reliance could be put upon the milling soldiers, now completely out of hand. The Central Committee decided to bring to the capital what was thought to be a more reliable pro-Bolshevik element, the Kronstadt sailors. On the fourth they disembarked in Petrograd, twenty thousand strong, to participate in the "peaceful demonstration."

There is little doubt that this was to be, though very hastily improvised and in a sense forced upon the Bolsheviks, an attempt at a *coup d'état*. In his recollections the sailors' leader, F. Raskolnikov, repeats that any thought of violence, overthrow, or the like was far from their minds. But he does not answer his own question: Why, if it was to be a peaceful demonstration, did the sailors bring their rifles with them? [36] And he finally confesses, the sailor's bluntness breaking through the official Party version: "In the event of the success of the demonstration and its support by the front, the Party always had the possibility of turning an armed demonstration into an armed uprising." The attempt to bring in cruisers to overawe the capital, just as was to be done in October, was stopped by an unusually enterprising deputy minister of the navy. He ordered the mine layers and submarines to sink any larger vessel approaching the capital.[37]

As witnessed from the preceding, the sailors' determination and courage were not on a par with their pro-Bolshevik enthusiasm. Lenin and his staff must have realized with sinking hearts that the sailors were not much of an improvement over the soldiers' rabble that had taken over the streets. The Kronstadt guests marched to Kshesinskaya's palace, from whose balcony they were addressed by Lunacharsky and the Bolsheviks' chief organizer, Jacob Sverdlov. Finally, in answer to shouted demands, Lenin appeared and greeted the sailors as "the pride and beauty of the Russian Revolution." But beyond compliments and an appeal to be vigilant and for "all power to the soviets," he refused to give them any directions.

The "pride and beauty of the Russian Revolution" marched on to the Tauride Palace, but it was obvious that things were going badly with the "peaceful demonstration." An attempt to seize Kerensky misfired; the War Minister had left to summon some regiments for the defense of the capital. The news that front-line units were being called caused a panic. They were still far from following the Bolsheviks. There was a special bitterness among them at this time at the strikes and disorders in their rear with the offensive still going on, and at the Petrograd garrison politicking while

[36] F. Raskolnikov, "The July Days in Kronstadt," in *The Proletarian Revolution*, 1923, No. 5. A famous story has the sailors asking Stalin, who on behalf of the Bolsheviks was summoning them, whether they should bring their rifles with them. Stalin allegedly answered: "Rifles? It is up to you, comrades. We writers always carry our weapons—pencils—with us. As to your weapons, you can judge for yourselves."

[37] The crews of cruisers and battleships were generally pro-Bolshevik or Anarchist, those of the smaller vessels generally "reactionary."

they were fighting. As Lenin said, "The front-line soldiers deceived by the liberals might come and slaughter the workers of Petrograd." As the sailors marched on there were inevitable clashes with the Cossacks, shots from unknown directions, and like disturbances. Instead of a disciplined force at their disposal the Bolshevik leaders soon had on their hands a looting, lynching, panicky armed mob. As Gorky, then an opponent of Lenin, was to describe it: "Trucks filled with people holding rifles and revolvers in their hands which tremble from fear. . . . Those rifles shoot into the shop windows, into people, in all sorts of directions. . . . They shoot because the people holding them want to overcome their fear." Some of the sailors joined the crowds before the building housing those organs which they allegedly were urging to take all power: the Petrograd Soviet and the All-Russian Executive Committee of the Soviets. What next?

The Soviet and its Menshevik and Socialist Revolutionary leaders were clearly at the mercy of the crowd. Prior to this culmination of disorders the Bolshevik minority of the Executive Committee had elected a special group of fifteen, which presumably was to take over its powers, once the "indignant people" had arrested the non-Bolshevik Socialist leaders as well as the "capitalist ministers." Sukhanov in his book relates that Lunacharsky told him that there was a definite plan for a Bolshevik triumvirate of Lenin, Trotsky, and Lunacharsky to take over, and that only Lenin's indecision prevented its being put into effect.[38] But, whatever the previous schemes, the leaders of the demonstration and their Bolshevik managers must have realized right there in front of the Tauride Palace that the game was up. The crowd could be steered to violence against some unarmed politicians, but it was more than doubtful whether the "pride and beauty of the Russian Revolution" could be counted on to defend the Bolsheviks against the front-line units being rushed to the capital.

While the Soviet authorities were deliberating, some of the non-Bolshevik leaders tried to appease the crowd by addressing it with the usual harangues: the need for democracy, to preserve discipline, order, and so on. Such addresses had the normal infuriating effect on the armed multitude, which was chafing under inaction. One of the lecturers, the Socialist Revolutionary Minister Chernov, was seized by some sailors and pushed into a car. This was a moment of great danger to the Bolsheviks. The lynching of Chernov, still an idol to the Russian peasants, would have been blamed on them and could have had incalculably disastrous results. Trotsky and Raskolnikov rushed to the automobile and the former called upon the Kronstadt sailors, "the pride and glory of the Russian Revolution" (there is a striking similarity, if not indeed monotony, in that revolu-

[38] When his book appeared in 1921 Lunacharsky wrote the author denying that he ever imparted such information to him and adding that the only aim of the demonstration was "all power to the soviets." But he adds, "Certainly we did not doubt that if the Menshevik–S.R. Soviet would seize power it would soon pass over to the more left and resolute revolutionary groups." Sukhanov, op. cit., Vol. 4, p. 515. The crux of the matter is, how soon?

tionary oratory) not to soil their cause by hurting "Socialist Chernov." The sailors remained unconvinced, so Trotsky resorted to a democratic way of resolving the issue: "Who is here for violence, raise your hands." It is much easier to indulge in violence than to vote for it. No hands were raised, and the leader of the "revolutionary democracy" was released, shaken but unharmed. Raskolnikov rather naïvely observes that Chernov did not appear to be grateful to him and Trotsky, and would not speak to them. The Bolsheviks were prompt to blame the attempt on *"provocateurs"* (which is most unlikely) or the Anarchists among the sailors, which is more likely, since no disciplined Bolshevik would attempt such kidnaping in public.

After some further harangues and unpleasantness, the sailors desisted from their siege of the Tauride Palace. The Bolsheviks' indecision is reflected in Zinoviev's and Trotsky's order that they should stay in the city. But the same night some regiments abandoned their neutrality and sent detachments to guard the Soviet. They had heard that front-line units were in march on Petrograd, and they did not want to appear to their comrades from the trenches as helping the Bolsheviks, about whom there were now renewed rumors that they had sold out to the Germans. Again Lenin had lost his gamble.

This time the consequences were more serious. The Bolsheviks *did* try to seize power (not even their most fervent defenders among Martov's Mensheviks believed in the story about the "peaceful demonstration") and they *did* lose. The Kronstadt sailors meekly returned to Kronstadt, though some of them wondered, "How can we go back with all power not yet in the hands of the soviets?" But the poor garrulous soviets were for once acting like a unified and determined government. They summoned troops from the front, they ordered strict measures against the Bolsheviks. Suddenly the "revolutionary democracy" appeared to possess teeth and claws.

Overnight from believers in the "revolutionary initiative" of the masses the Bolsheviks became staunch defenders of law and order. Zinoviev, pale and shaking, appeared at the meeting of the Soviet and pleaded that it defend Lenin and himself from slanders and threats of lynching. He was heard in grim silence and upon concluding ran out, not to appear in public until October. Stalin paid a hasty visit to the man who currently dominated the Soviet. Would "Comrade" (first time in months he was called that by the Bolsheviks; he had been "Mr." or at most "Citizen") Tseretelli make sure that the Bolsheviks were protected from mob violence? There were rumors that the Bolshevik headquarters were to be occupied and that would lead to bloodshed. Yes, replied Tseretelli, Kshesinskaya's palace was going to be taken over by government troops, but he did not expect any bloodshed; the Bolsheviks were going to give up the palace. Stalin left without a word.

The military strength behind the Bolsheviks evaporated in the air.

Leaders of the sailors were throwing away their guns, fearful of what might happen should they be arrested carrying weapons. The Bolshevik head-quarters were occupied without a shot being fired. Their presses were smashed. And from the front Kerensky, for once sounding like Danton, wired orders to arrest "the enemies of the people and counterrevolution-aries." The "pride and glory of the Russian Revolution," the Kronstadt gar-rison, threatened with a blockade, surrendered the instigators of the insur-rection. On the face of it the aftermath of the July days looked like an irredeemable catastrophe for the Bolsheviks.

Early in the morning of July 5 Lenin left his apartment. All that day he sought a shelter, moving from one hiding place to another. There was as yet no warrant for his arrest, but in Pokrovsky's words, "He knew how to flee." His hosts were nervous and urged him to move on. They did not relish the possibility of being discovered, warrant or no warrant, sheltering a "German agent." It is all the more remarkable that he found time and composure to compose several brief articles, which appeared next day in a paper the Bolsheviks improvised after *Pravda*'s plant had been smashed. Their titles speak for themselves: "The abominable lies of the reactionary press and Alexinsky"; "calumnies and facts"; and "a new Dreyfus Affair?" On July 6 he finally found a man ready to take him in. He was a Caucasian Bolshevik, S. Aliluyev, the future father-in-law of Stalin.[39] Zinoviev and his wife were already hiding in the same apartment. Zinoviev was at first suffering from fright to the point of incoherence, but Lenin's calm de-meanor restored his spirits.[40] On July 7 an order was issued for the arrest of Lenin and other Bolshevik oligarchs. It was decided that he and the indispensable Zinoviev were to flee. On July 11 Vladimir Ilyich shaved his beard and Zinoviev trimmed his curly hair. Accompanied by Stalin and Aliluyev, they went to a suburban railway station and from there they boarded the train to a small station, Razliv, near which they were to hide until August 8.

For all his outward calm Lenin was close to being convinced that the end, an arrest or worse, might be near. In a note found by the police in his apartment after his flight and addressed to Kamenev he wrote: "Between ourselves, if they bump me off, please publish my sketch on Marxism and the state." (This was his unfinished book, *State and Revolution*, which he was to continue himself in August and September.) It was character-istic of him that even in a state close to panic his first thought was of his literary legacy, the work which, even after he might be gone, would

[39] These facts are based on Aliluyev's article: "How Lenin and Zinoviev Hid During the July Days," in the *Red Chronicle*, Moscow, 1924, No. 9. The chronology and facts are different but undoubtedly more reliable than those given in a much later publication, *Lenin in Petersburg 1890–1920*, Leningrad, 1957, pp. 275–76. The latter would date Lenin's moving in with the Aliluyevs on July 7 and his leaving them on July 9 instead of July 11.

[40] This was written in 1923–24 when Zinoviev was still a great Party figure and an ally of Stalin, so there is no reason to think this account tendentious.

rekindle the flame of the Revolution. But as on many previous occasions, he was to be saved—by his enemies.

The main factor in his ability to avoid arrest was paradoxically the very charge that he had been receiving money from the Germans. This charge was again publicized on July 5, one of its propagators being a former Bolshevik member of the Duma and then a bitter personal enemy of Lenin, Gregory Alexinsky. The charges turned on facts largely familiar to us: Lenin's connections with Hanecki, who in Stockholm was representing the Parvus interests. There were some additional charges of what an escaped Russian prisoner of war allegedly learned while in the Germans' hands, but the crux of the matter clearly turned on the Lenin-Hanecki-Parvus connection.

Today, as mentioned above, there can no longer be any doubt that the substance of the charges, as distinguished from some details, was correct: the Bolsheviks were getting money from the Germans. But what is of interest as we study the July days is the clumsiness of Lenin's attempt to deny the accusation. He was usually much more skillful, and his lying, very transparent even at the time, is a good proof of his alarm. From his hideout he wrote humble letters to Menshevik newspapers which only a short time before he had been denouncing for "philistinism," "near-socialism," and the like. "Dear Comrades," they begin. He, Lenin, had to escape because there was no assurance that if arrested he would be granted the usual guarantees extended "even in the bourgeois countries" to the accused. Hanecki? Why, he, Lenin, barely knew him. He met him only once at the London Congress in 1907 (!!). Insofar as he was aware, Hanecki and the other intermediary, Kozlovsky, were not Bolsheviks but Polish Socialists. Lies and calumnies! And the pregnant warning, so often and successfully used by the Communists: if they arrest us Bolsheviks today, watch out who may be next. It will then be the turn of the left Mensheviks such as Martov, then of the Socialists and all the progressive elements.

At the time Lenin was issuing denials, the Ministry of Justice had copies of his letters to Hanecki and Radek. In one of them, dated April 12, he wrote among other things, "Be accurate and extra cautious in your connections." In another, "Nothing [lately] received from you, neither letters nor money. . . ." In yet another Lenin acknowledged the receipt of a considerable sum from Kozlovsky.[41]

[41] Both the letters and Lenin's denials found their way to the official *Collected Works* of Lenin (to be sure in different volumes). Therein lies a piquant story: In 1923 a Communist archivist working on the files of the old Ministry of Justice found the copies of those letters. Needless to say, he was eager to publish those previously unknown letters of Vladimir Ilyich and he transmitted them to *The Proletarian Revolution*. Its editorial board then turned to Radek and Hanecki to ascertain their authenticity (Lenin was on his deathbed). They returned an amazing answer: yes, they seemed to be authentic, but neither of them recalled receiving them. The money referred to, said Radek and Hanecki, was obviously the money "collected by the foreign committee of the Bolshevik Central Committee." And thus the letters were published in Soviet Russia. *The Proletarian Revolution*, 1923, No. 9, pp. 225 and ff.

But Lenin's warning struck the mark. The Menshevik leaders of the Soviet were already having second thoughts about a too vigorous prosecution of the Bolsheviks. The main threat to the Revolution was after all still from the right, wasn't it? The left wing of the Mensheviks led by Martov thought that even the suppression of the July rebellion went too far. When loyal troops arrived to defend the Soviet from the Bolsheviks Martov shouted, "This is how a counterrevolution always begins." Though numerically weak, Martov's group, largely because of his moral authority, exercised an inhibiting influence on the majority Mensheviks led by Tseretelli and Dan. They reminded Martov how *before the war* he had written that Lenin was not a politician, but the leader of a Mafialike organization within the Social Democracy, bent upon establishing his dictatorship. But in vain. In a manner that was to become traditional with many of the non-Communist leftists, Martov insisted that though the Bolsheviks went too far they were spokesmen for the real grievances of the proletariat. One should not use force against them but one should "tell the workers that their discontent is justified," and adopt the desired reforms. It is only thus that the adventurers could be "morally isolated." [42]

The majority Mensheviks, for their part, while they looked at their enemies more realistically, still could not stomach the accusations that the Bolsheviks were German agents. This charge reflected on all Russian Social Democracy. "If we arrest Lenin we shall be judged by history as criminals," exclaimed Dan. The "defensist" Mensheviks busied themselves denying rumors that the Bolsheviks were in receipt of the German gold. It is easy to see that no serious effort was made to apprehend Lenin. In his hiding place at theAliluyevs' he was visited regularly by his wife and sisters. Later on in his shelter twenty miles from Petrograd he received Bolshevik visitors. It would have been a simple matter to track him down, but such an effort would have embarrassed his captors. A commission was appointed to probe the charges against him and Zinoviev. Gradually its investigation petered out.

More important, the resolution of the "revolutionary democracy" soon faded out insofar as the Bolsheviks as a whole were concerned. Some of their leaders let themselves be arrested: Lunacharsky, Kamenev, and Kollontay. Trotsky with his typical bravado demanded that he be included in their number and his request was satisfied. But no attempt was made to break up the Party. It was, after all, a Socialist and revolutionary party and how could their fellow Socialists soil themselves by such an undemocratic step? The Bolsheviks were taught a lesson; the healthy instinct of the masses would prevent them from following those adventurers again. And the main enemy still remained on the right. The Soviet and the Provisional Government settled down again to their tortuous coexistence: the wrangle about their respective powers and the responsibility for the dismal

[42] Tseretelli, *op. cit.*, Vol. 2, p. 239.

failure of the June-July offensive of the Russian army. Prince Lvov now finally faded out and Kerensky became Prime Minister in name as well as in fact. In retrospect the July crisis was viewed complacently as an additional proof of the strength of Russian democracy. Things were back to their revolutionary normal.

Among the Bolsheviks their ignominious failure led to some soul-searching. The shadow of July was to hang over the beginnings of the October insurrection when many were to believe that it was foolhardy to try to take power by force. Lenin's flight was viewed with mixed feelings. Some Bolsheviks thought that the Party lost thereby a wonderful opportunity for propaganda: Comrades Lenin and Zinoviev should give themselves up and refute in open court the scandalous lies of the *bourgeoisie*. At the Bolshevik Congress late in July there were many voices urging that the hiding heroes should turn themselves in. This attitude was understandable in view of the fact that many Bolsheviks were unaware that the substance of the charges was true. In addition, once the excitement over the insurrection had passed, the reasons given for the flight, the danger to Lenin's life, and so on, could not be taken seriously. The death penalty had been abolished in March. Lynchings, except at the hand of the pro-Bolshevik sailors, were still unheard of. All that threatened Lenin was imprisonment, and it went without saying that he could from his prison as well as from his hideout issue directives for the Party, write articles, and the like. Then why does Comrade Lenin deprive the Party of this wonderful opportunity to expose the bourgeois calumniators? "We should make another Dreyfus case from the trial of Lenin. We should go into the fight with a raised visor. . . . This is demanded by the interests of the Revolution and the prestige of our Party." [43] It was with difficulty that the more realistic of the Party leaders restrained this enthusiasm for the vindication of the Bolshevik honor. The visor remained shut.

Whatever Lenin himself thought about this solicitude to clear his name of the unworthy charges, his attention soon turned to more fundamental problems. The Bolsheviks now clearly had to change their slogans. "All power to the soviets" ceased to be an appropriate device, since the majority of the Mensheviks and the Socialist Revolutionaries had become tools of the counterrevolution. Almost immediately a new device and a new mythology were invented. In July the Bolsheviks tried, so the mythology runs, merely to *persuade* the soviets to take over power from the *bourgeoisie*. Now, it was demonstrated that such attempts were hopeless and that one had to face the "dictatorship of the counterrevolutionary *bourgeoisie*." Hence next time the Bolsheviks should not try any more "peaceful demonstration" of the kind of July 8. "Power can no longer be taken peacefully." The new slogan must be "All power to the revolutionary proletariat." This

[43] D. Manuilsky, *The Sixth Congress of the Russian Socialist Democratic Party (of the Bolsheviks). Protocols,* Moscow, 1958, p. 33.

was a masterful psychological touch for it blamed the failure of an armed uprising on the alleged fact that no such uprising took place. The dispirited could begin to persuade themselves that when the Bolsheviks *really* chose to fight they would win.

The morale of the Party rose. The Sixth Congress claimed a membership of 240,000 members, a dazzling rise from about 50,000 counted in April. The figures of course are a subject of contention, but no one could deny the sensational rise. What was more impressive, almost half the total membership was concentrated in the two capitals: Petrograd with 41,000, Moscow with 50,000. This augured well for the ability of the "revolutionary proletariat" to seize the heart of Russia.[44] Of what countervailing value were the hundreds of thousands of the Socialist Revolutionaries, most of them dispersed throughout the villages of the country, their party, like the Mensheviks, split into several groups and incapable of unified action? In Lenin's absence the day-to-day operations of the Party were supervised by Stalin and Sverdlov. Theirs was a prudent but energetic leadership, which kept the hotheads under control but reassured those who wanted to give up after July. The Sixth Congress demonstrated that Bolshevism could not be checked or destroyed by the arrest of a few leaders. It united two hundred seventy delegates, and its businesslike and well-managed proceedings offer a startling contrast to the chaos, wrangling, and endless oratory that characterized the meetings of every other Russian party. And this was only three weeks after "Bolshevik adventurism" had supposedly been exposed and crushed! [45]

Lenin kept in close touch with the deliberations of the Congress. He lived near Razliv station with the family of Bolshevik N. Emelyanov, who worked in the nearby Sestroretzk arms factory and like many Russian workers also owned a plot of land. The factory was a stronghold of pro-Bolshevik sentiment, its environs presumably one of the most logical places to look for Lenin's hideout. Sharing it with him was Zinoviev. Almost daily, Bolshevik notables would descend on the Emelyanovs to confer with the leaders. The most frequent courier was Felix Dzerzhinsky, the future head of the Communist police, who enjoyed Lenin's complete trust. Occasionally Sverdlov, Stalin, and Molotov would make the twenty-mile trip with their reports and carry back with them instructions and articles. Vladimir Ilyich wrote incessantly.

The Emelyanovs were a typical proletarian family, "rich only in children," of whom they had seven. The oldest boy was an Anarchist, but this did not prevent his preserving secrecy concerning his family's illustrious guest. The accommodations were hardly comfortable: first a hayloft in the barn. Then the host erected for Lenin a tent on the other side of the little

[44] Figures from *The Sixth Congress*, p. 36.

[45] The Congress took place semilegally and in secrecy, allegedly to avoid arrests by the Provisional Government. How in heaven's name could two hundred seventy most prominent Bolsheviks meet for one week in the capital and avoid detection?

lake across which the privileged visitors were rowed. Officially Vladimir Ilyich and Zinoviev were Finnish field hands hired by Emelyanov for the summer. Shaved and in a wig, Lenin could indeed pass for a worker. Those precautions, Emelyanov's account makes clear, were indicated not so much because of the government's pursuit as because of a chance of encountering some patriotically minded army officers who might arrest Lenin on their own.[46]

As in the old days at Alakayevka Lenin wrote in the open, two logs constituting his "green office." Amidst those bucolic surroundings, frequently interrupted by the Bolshevik visitors and occasionally by the approach of a suspicious stranger, the "Finnish farm hand" was composing *State and Revolution.*

The work had been planned and begun in Switzerland. During his passage to Russia Lenin left his notes, including all important quotations from Marx and Engels, in Stockholm. It is characteristic of his thoroughness and also of his readiness to put others to trouble that he insisted that they now be fetched from Stockholm. And so they traveled from Sweden to Petrograd, then to Razliv, then across the lake! The citations had to be precise and in order. A revolution might be hurried or improvised, but not a Marxist treatise!

State and Revolution is an unusual work. The length of its preparation and Lenin's extreme solicitude that the work be completed even if he were to be "bumped off" indicate that this is not a mere propaganda pamphlet addressed to the needs of the hour. At the same time no work could be more *un*-representative of its author's political philosophy and his general frame of mind than this one by Lenin. It was never properly completed: the ostensible reason given by the author was that the October Revolution intervened and that it was more pleasant and profitable to make a revolution than to write about it. But he wrote voluminously after 1918, and yet never chose to complete this work. Within one year of the publication of *State and Revolution* Lenin was to be furious that Bukharin, then head of the left-wing opposition within the Party, was reprinting parts of this work. There is no doubt that after 1918 Lenin, if he could, would have liked to forget and make others forget that he ever wrote *State and Revolution.* But it stays there in his *Collected Works,* a source of bafflement and irritation to his official commentators.

That unfortunate pamphlet is almost a straightforward profession of anarchism. "As long as there is state there is no freedom; when there is freedom there will be no state." [47] The bourgeois state has to be smashed entirely with its bureaucracy, its army, and its classes. There is nothing complicated or involved about running society under socialism. "Within

---

[46] N. Emelyanov, "Ilyich in Razliv," in *The Banner,* Moscow, 1957, No. 2, pp. 132–47. After 1930 no account of Lenin's hideout as much as mentions the fact that he was sharing it with Zinoviev.

[47] *Works,* Vol. 26, p. 140.

twenty-four hours after the overthrow of capitalism" simple workers can control production, the rank-and-file soldiers can run the army, and so on. No need for material incentives; all officials, managers, and similar personnel will be paid the worker's wages. It will be an egalitarian paradise. All citizens will be employees of one vast national syndicate. The art of administration consists of "watching and bookkeeping."

Such is the uncomplicated argument of *State and Revolution* (and one wonders why it took so much labor and research to compose it). Within a few months Lenin would shout that a capitalist who could make a railway run was a million times more valuable than twenty resolutions passed by Communist meetings. To Bukharin's observation that people who make 4,000 rubles a month should be shot he will retort that the Communists should get down on their knees in thanks if they can persuade such people to work for them.[48] The four years granted to him to direct the Communist state would be largely spent in long harangues abusing those who claim that the "simple worker" can run anything, extolling the capitalist's ability to administer and run the economy, calling for material rewards and differentials in pay for the experts, and asserting the need for labor discipline.

Now there is no reason to see the Lenin of 1917 as less "sincere" than the Lenin of 1919 or 1920. Nor even to think, as has often been said, that the practical difficulties of running the state "opened his eyes" to the utopianism of his previous views and recommendations. He was a genuine Marxist. Before 1914 and even during the year of revolution, as we have seen, he often spoke with admiration of the achievements of capitalism, how socialism could grow only from *fully developed* capitalism, how many years, perhaps generations would pass before "half-savage Russia" would be able to afford a fully Socialist structure, not to mention the egalitarianism and the dissolution of the state that occur in the never-never land of communism. But *in* the revolution, in the struggle for power, Marxism subsists and conquers by an appeal to the anarchistic instincts. Such was Lenin's absorption in the doctrine and its psychology that upon coming to power he could pass, as if unconsciously, from a denigration of the state to its staunch defense, from the demand of absolute equality to the insistence on differentials in wages and salaries and functions as the main basis for building the Socialist economy. How indeed could the Bolsheviks come to power if they chose to remind the peasant that Marxism demanded that he forsake his small plot and work as a hired hand on a state-run farm? Or the worker that he must submit to the state-appointed factory director, the soldier that the proletarian dictatorship would not tolerate the lax discipline of the post-February army? It was part of Lenin's greatness that he could argue with conviction and passion for the very thing he was to combat and destroy during his remaining years, rev-

[48] *Works*, Vol. 27, p. 279.

olutionary anarchy. And his conviction was all the stronger because the
Russia of 1917 was for him only the means. An anarchistic revolution in
Russia would touch off the more orderly, more Marxian revolutions in the
economically developed and civilized countries of the West. And with
their help the blessings of socialism would eventually be brought to his
own country.

Anarchy indeed was deepening and by late July little remained of the
elation and the national unity of the first weeks of the Revolution. A wave
of peasant disorders and land seizures was spreading all over Russia. The
government was impotent to arrest this movement and too much divided
to devise a policy that could appease the peasant. The great gamble of the
first democratic phase of the Revolution was the June offensive. But the
attack ended in a disaster. It could not have succeeded, in view of the insufficient equipment and poor conditions of the troops, but in addition the
army, even in the front lines, had been corroded by indiscipline. Whole
regiments refused to participate in the attack or abandoned their positions. And now desertions became as endemic as land seizures.

Whatever the aspect of the anarchy that gripped Russia, the Bolsheviks had a slogan suited to its mood. They urged front-line fraternization
with the enemy. They approved the "revolutionary initiative" of the peasants in seizing the landlords' estates. The trend toward national autonomy
and actual independence from the central authorities that had developed
in many parts of the former Empire, notably the Ukraine and Finland, had
in advance been approved by Lenin's doctrine of complete national self-
determination. The Provisional Government exhorted and threatened but
was increasingly incapable of any action. The Mensheviks and the Socialist Revolutionaries were the prisoners of their ideology and of democratic
scruples. Only the Bolsheviks had ready and uncomplicated (at least on
the surface) solutions.

Historians, with their customary harshness toward the causes and
movements that fail, tend to concentrate on this or that personal or ideological defect of the opponents of the Bolsheviks. They should have concluded peace. They should have distributed land to the peasants. They
spent their time in oratory while the ground was slipping from under
their feet. But by late July no *democratic* solution could have arrested
the trend of events toward a catastrophe. The non-Bolshevik left lived
with the memories of the suppression of the Revolution of 1905 and of
the Tsarist autocracy. Nothing in their experience argued that the Bolshevik threat or rule (and few believed that the Bolsheviks could rule
more than a few days even if they should seize power) could conceivably
be as bad. The Bolsheviks were after all Socialists and democrats, many of
them personal friends of their opponents. Who could imagine mild and
vacillating Kamenev or the esthete and bohemian Lunacharsky in the
role of autocratic officials? Lenin was different, but then Lenin was not yet

the *absolute* ruler of the Bolshevik Party. There were people within it who would be able to restrain him. How long did Robespierre last when he tried to impose his personal dictatorship? And so the only threat was that of a new Bonaparte!

This conviction of the "revolutionary democracy" grew throughout August of 1917, as the hopes and expectations of the right-wing politicians turned increasingly toward the army, the beaten and demoralized Russian army. Among the left, apart from the fear of a rightist *coup,* the only remaining hope still was that the Constituent Assembly (promised from the first day of the Revolution) would be summoned and would perform a miracle in saving both the Russian state and democracy. It is easy in retrospect to see that the Constituent Assembly, though much was hoped from it by the Mensheviks and the Socialist Revolutionaries and much feared by the Bolsheviks, could not have performed any miracles. It would have been then as it was when it assembled in January 1918, dominated by the peasants' party, the Socialist Revolutionaries, a party united only in name, containing Kerensky on one extreme and the people who followed the Bolsheviks on the other, and in between them innumerable groupings and personal followings unable to agree on any single major policy. The eventual fate of the Constituent Assembly was presaged by the enactment of various parliamentary improvisations by the Provisional Government as it sought desperately to bolster its tottering position. There was a State Conference in September in Petrograd, then the so-called preparliament, the Council of the Republic (Russia had finally been proclaimed a republic by Kerensky!), all designed to give some semblance of authority and a popular support to Kerensky's regime. None of them could fill in the vacuum or perform the impossible.

But the dissolution of the existing authority did not as yet mean the certainty of the Bolshevik triumph. Nobody was more aware of that than Lenin, who from August on tried to whip his followers into preparing for a decisive armed action. For all the Bolsheviks' militancy, many of them still had some of their opponents' hesitations and scruples, mainly the complacent belief that the "correctness" of their slogans and their growing popularity would of themselves ensure success. Then, as behooves Marxists, they tended to think in dialectical and institutional terms. That power could be seized and exercised by a man or a group of men was as yet unthinkable: that would be "Bonapartism" or "Blanquism," quite unappropriate for the believers in scientific socialism. "Everybody" knew that political rule could be executed only by a class or an alliance of classes. And how exactly and through what institutions would "the revolutionary proletariat and poorer peasants" rule? Should not the Bolsheviks wait till they secure a majority in the soviets? Or perhaps join with the left Mensheviks à la Martov? Such lingering democratic superstitions infuriated Lenin. Revolution was for him an act of force. Just as the Social Democrat became submerged temporarily in an anarchist, so the believer in historical laws yielded in him to a partisan of action and audacity. In August and September his voice became as strident and insistent as was Tkachev's many years before when he exclaimed, "The revolutionary does not 'prepare' but makes a revolution. So make it! Make it faster! All indecisiveness, every delay, is criminal."

The Bolsheviks' chances of a successful uprising were greatly improved by the events of the last days of August. The threat of Bonapartism appeared to materialize, and then vanished overnight. With it disappeared the last hope that the army could prevent another installment of the Revolution.

In July Kerensky had appointed a new commander-in-chief, General Lavr Kornilov. The new head of the army was a popular hero with legendary war exploits. Futhermore, unlike most of the Tsarist generals (but many more than is usually assumed) he came "from the people," having been the son of a poor Cossack. This combination made Kornilov the man of destiny in the eyes of those conservative and moderate politicians, or, to use the Socialist phraseology, the capitalists and the *bourgeoisie,* who hoped that through him the Revolution might be tamed.

But not only the right pinned its hopes on Kornilov. Kerensky and some in his entourage hoped to use the general to destroy any future Bolshevik threat and to remove or diminish the tutelage of the soviets over the Provisional Government. The new commander-in-chief, a man "with the heart of a lion, brains of a sheep" as a fellow general characterized him, expected the government to restore the army discipline and authority of the officers. Needless to say, such measures proved beyond the feeble powers of the government. Following the disastrous defeats and mass desertions of July the government did indeed reintroduce the death penalty, but Kerensky in his hopeless fashion promised that it would not be applied. To the "'revolutionary democracy" it was unthinkable that a soldier should be executed for cowardice or desertion. Disgruntled, Kornilov began to pay attention to those who whispered that only a military dictatorship could save Russia from traitors and Bolsheviks.

The outlines of the alleged Kornilov plot are blurred by conflicting stories and versions. But evidently what went on was a veritable tragicomedy of errors and self-deception in which the unfortunate commander-in-chief became the unwitting tool and victim of minds subtler than his own. Kerensky ordered him to concentrate an army corps in readiness to march on Petrograd to smash an expected Bolshevik uprising and to overawe the Soviet. The general became convinced that the chief of government wanted him, Kornilov, to become dictator and would be willing to serve under him. Kerensky realized with a start that the commander-in-chief was trying not to help him but to supplant him. Having received evidence, the Prime Minister turned around and ordered Kornilov to lay down his command. The latter, completely befuddled, urged on by his conservative advisers, refused, issuing a proclamation: "I, the Supreme Commander Kornilov, declare to the whole nation that because of my duty as a soldier . . . [and] a citizen of free Russia, and because of my boundless love of the country . . . I refuse to submit to the order of the Provisional Government to resign. . . . Awaken, Russian people, from the foolish blindness and realize . . . the depths to which our country is sinking." [49]

It was the turn of Kerensky to don the armor of the savior of the nation. He publicly denounced the insubordinate general and called upon the soviets and the people of Petrograd to assist in the repulse of the expected military assault. His erstwhile choice was now presented to the nation as the man who would restore Tsarism and take land from the peasants.

From his hideout Lenin wrote his Central Committee that the Bolsheviks should fight Kornilov, but without building up Kerensky. For all his previous public warnings about the threat of Bonapartism, Lenin was obviously taken by surprise. But he was astute enough to realize that the affair would mean not only the end of Kornilov, but the final discrediting of Kerensky's government. "We shall now show everybody the weakness of Kerensky." He urged agitation among the soldiers and killing of pro-Kornilov officers.

And indeed it was the Bolsheviks who were the main beneficiaries of this confused and inept mutiny. Their Red Guards were allowed to rearm (all the "democratic forces" were needed to defend the capital), their imprisoned leaders released. Instead of the expected credit for saving Russian democracy Kerensky confirmed his reputation for ineptness and intrigue. The march on Petrograd disintegrated; Kornilov's forces, uncertain against whom and why they were marching, were easily demoralized by the agitators sent by the Soviet. The unfortunate general and his leading officers were put under a lenient arrest. The Provisional Government began an investigation into the affair, one of its famous investigations that were fated to remain uncompleted.

Thus the government lost whatever remaining credit or influence it had with the army. The officer corps, solidly pro-Kornilov, was by now completely fed up with Kerensky and unlikely to come to the assistance of the regime and the man who, they felt, had tricked their leaders. The soldiers had been taught by the Provisional Government itself that every officer was a would-be plotter to be watched and, if necessary, disarmed and shot. It remains a source of wonder that the Russian army continued to exist after the end of August and that while there were two million deserters, six million soldiers persisted, in a manner of speaking, in holding

[49] Quoted from *The Memoirs of General A. S. Lukomsky* (in Russian), Berlin, 1922, Vol. 1, p. 245.

their positions. Unable to continue the war, unable to end it, the regime staggered on through discussions and investigations to its inevitable end.

So, at least, it must seem today. Yet to contemporaries, even the astute, it was not inconceivable that the deepening anarchy and lack of effective authority could continue for a long time. To politicians faced with unpalatable choices, there remains the consolation that "something will happen" that will save them from the necessity of making them. And nowhere was this consoling thought stronger than in Russia in September 1917. This "something" could be the Constituent Assembly, the elections to which were now "definitely" scheduled. Or the coming meeting of the Allied Powers in Paris. The Russian delegation would press for a declaration demanding a democratic and just peace with no annexations and contributions. The Allies would have to consent; the war would end and everything would be well. That in view of her deplorable situation Russia could hardly dictate to France and Britain, now buoyed up by the accession of the United States, was something the optimists overlooked.

Complacency was not absent among the Bolsheviks. Things were going their way. In September the Petrograd Soviet finally reached a pro-Bolshevik majority and Trotsky, released from jail in the wake of the Kornilov affair, became its chairman. Moscow's soviet soon followed, and the same pattern—a majority for the Bolsheviks and their allies among the Left Socialist Revolutionaries—appeared in the other major industrial cities. It was only a question of time before a new Congress of the Soviets would depose the Central Executive Committee elected by the Menshevik and the Socialist Revolutionary majority in June and enthrone Lenin's party as *the representative* of Russia's workers and soldiers. Then why try to rush things through an armed uprising? The Bolsheviks would be risking a repetition of the July setback.

For Lenin in his current mood, such complacent thoughts bordered on treason. Here was another example of the Russian softness and lackadaisical mood of which he complained many years ago to Anna. An act of force was necessary to separate the Bolsheviks once and for all from the "others"—the Mensheviks and the Socialist Revolutionaries, believers in making revolutions by talking and issuing resolutions. If the Bolsheviks did not burn their bridges behind them, forsake the Social Democratic claptrap about the majorities, the inviolability of this or that, they would clearly be unable to *retain* power even if it should fall in their laps. They would set a melancholy example for the Socialists in Germany and elsewhere. They would disgrace themselves and sink to the level of the followers of Martov and Chernov.

Bolshevik participation in the Democratic Conference and their initial willingness to sit in that other abortive improvisation of the Provisional Government, the Council of the Republic, brought Lenin to a state close to hysteria. There was only one man after his own heart among the Bolsheviks. "Trotsky was for the boycott [of the Council of the Republic]. Bravo Comrade Trotsky." [50] His chief spear-bearers of the years of exile, Kamenev and Zinoviev, now receded to second place. It was his former enemy, Trotsky, a Bolshevik technically of only a few weeks' standing, who rose to the occasion. While Lenin, still hiding, provided the determination behind October, Trotsky would succor him with his tactical skill and passionate oratory. One cannot quarrel with Trotsky's boastful appraisal that without Lenin and himself the Bolsheviks would not have taken the final and decisive step.

The Democratic Conference (September 13) gave rise to an incident among the Bolsheviks that provided another useful reminder of how Lenin's power over the Party, great though it was, was far from absolute. He sent a letter to the Central Committee in which he informed his hardworking lieutenants: "You are nothing but a bunch of traitors and nincompoops unless you surround the Conference and arrest those scoundrels." The Central Committee decided unanimously to burn this letter and pass over this unseemly behavior of Comrade Lenin. To Bukharin, the most tempestuously independent of his followers (that is perhaps not unconnected with the fact that Lenin liked and respected him as a person more than any other Bolshevik oligarch), this was a proof, when he reminisced five years later, that the Central Committee of the Party was sometimes wiser than Lenin. The "cult of personality" in Lenin's time was certainly not like anything under Stalin. [51]

Lenin's fury was increased by the fact that he had to stay away from Petrograd where the Bolsheviks were pursuing their vacillating course. While the others were released, he and Zinoviev were fugitives from justice, the charge of their involvement with the Germans still presumably under investigation. The approach of fall and perhaps rumors of an impending military *coup* had made Lenin in August move still farther from the main scene of political events. On August 21–22 he passed the Finnish frontier posing as a stoker on a railway locomotive. As a refuge Finland was much safer than in the Tsarist times. Finnish Socialists friendly to the Bolsheviks now occupied important positions in the local government. He used a series of rural hideouts where there was always a Finnish Bolshevik who had a wife or mother not interested in politics but overjoyed to shelter Vladimir Ilyich and to cook his favorite dishes for him. He played with children and was in great humor, but he worked very hard! (There is a somewhat suspicious repetition in these accounts.) Finally he moved to the capital, Helsingfors. Here he could not have been safer. His obliging host was a Bolshevik sympathizer who happened to be the city's chief of police.

What comes out even through the carefully manicured accounts of Lenin's stay in Finland is his great impatience and nervousness. He would

[50] *Works,* Vol. 26, p. 37.
[51] *The Proletarian Revolution,* October, 1922. No. 10, p. 319.

argue with the rank-and-file Party workers who sheltered or guided him, proving again and again the necessity for an uprising. He pooh-poohed any practical difficulties and dangers. How would the Bolsheviks run the finances of the state? "Simple . . . ," Lenin is alleged to have replied, "we shall run the printing presses and in a few days will print as much money as is necessary." [52] The lack of qualified personnel to run the administration? Lenin replied in the style of *State and Revolution:* "Nonsense. Any worker could master the affairs of a ministry in a few days . . . it is not necessary to know the technical details, that will be the task of the [former] subordinates, whom we shall compel to work for us."

From Helsingfors on September 17 he moved to Vyborg, closer to Petrograd, ready to rush in whenever the great moment should come. Whether it was genuine worry about his safety or the fear of one of Lenin's terrible verbal dressings-down, his comrades sought to keep him away from Petrograd. The Central Committee appealed to his sense of Party discipline, forbidding a return until it should authorize it. Lenin exploded: "I will not stand for it, I will not stand for it," he shouted.[53]

By the beginning of October Lenin was lashing out at his followers as if they were Mensheviks. In an article, "Will the Bolsheviks Succeed in Keeping Power?" he sought to shame them into action. Here were the liberal Kadet newspapers teasing them and discounting their proletarian valor. One of them wrote that the Bolsheviks were good at disorganizing things, but when it came to action they were cowards. The first day of their power would be their last; they were great ones for making it impossible for others to rule, but they themselves were incapable of constructive work.[54] This attitude, it is true, was gaining among the Bolsheviks' opponents. Let them try to rule and soon they would be cut down to size. But as this moment was approaching many Bolsheviks were also beginning to fear not the possible failure of an uprising but, should it succeed, the responsibilities of governing. How does one really run a ministry? They would have to deliver on their promise to conclude peace but not a "separate peace" with Wilhelm II and his generals. How?

Lenin's answers were not particularly reassuring, for as was typical with him he would write cogently and convincingly for a while, but then passion would overwhelm him and he would break out with abuse. What, it was being asked (reasonably enough in view of future events), if the Bolsheviks once in power fail to conclude a truce or peace; would the soldiers fight better in a "revolutionary war," that is, for themselves, than they were fighting for Kerensky? Answer: "Any moron can ask more questions than ten reasonable people could answer."

His other arguments often partook of a rhetorical flourish. Tsarist Rus-

[52] A. V. Shotman in *Lenin the Leader of October,* Leningrad, 1957, p. 167.
[53] *Ibid.,* p. 166.
[54] *Works,* Vol. 26, p. 67.

sia had been ruled by a handful of landowners and officials. Why shouldn't 240,000 members of the Bolshevik Party be able to take over? The problem of actual administration, which was close to panicking those hardy revolutionaries as they contemplated that the day after tomorrow they might have to run factories, make food distribution, and the like, was approached by him more seriously. "We will make capitalists work for us." The capitalists would have to carry work passports listing their employment, and gradually—and here Lenin is already beginning his transition from revolutionary to administrator—*everybody* would be compelled to work and carry a work passport. Those who loaf or refuse employment would be threatened with being deprived of their food coupons.

It is problematical whether Lenin's urgings, assurances, and threats would have sufficed to galvanize the Bolsheviks into action were he not supported and assisted by Trotsky. The latter was on the scene masterminding the Bolshevik majority of the Petrograd Soviet. In October this Soviet forged the formal weapon of the uprising, the Military Revolutionary Committee. Ostensibly its aim was to defend Petrograd, which as rumor had it Kerensky's government was ready to evacuate and leave to the advancing Germans. The rumor had some substance. Apart from the military threat to the capital many would not have regretted such a decapitation of the Revolution. The Socialist parties rose up against this threat and the government helplessly abandoned any designs it might have had to move to Moscow. It would not have helped anyway; the Moscow soviet was equally under Bolshevik control.

The Military Revolutionary Committee was thus left with the more congenial task of preparing an armed uprising. That it would do exactly that was assured by the refusal of the Mensheviks and the right wing of the Socialist Revolutionary Party to participate in its work. The field was thus left clear to the Bolsheviks and their allies, the Left Socialist Revolutionaries, who were represented by an eighteen-year-old youth who was its first chairman. Trotsky, of course, became its actual leader and as his main subordinates he recruited the commanders of the Bolsheviks' private army, of their own military organization.[55]

The Military Revolutionary Committee politely informed the command of the Petrograd region that it now assumed direct control of the troops. Commissars were dispatched to the separate regiments to counteract possible pernicious interference by their officers. The military authorities (the last word should perhaps be put in quotation marks) were somewhat embarrassed as to their reaction. After all, the Committee officially represented not a single party, but the other "half government," the So-

---

[55] When Trotsky's star began to wane in Soviet Russia this symbiosis was bound to lead to endless historicopolitical quarrels. Did the Soviet's Committee, that is, Trotsky, do most of the work in carrying out the *coup* of October, or was it simply a cover-up for the older, purely Bolshevik, Military Organization? In fact, as suggested below Trotsky's major share in the events cannot be denied.

viet. Could one really resist this usurpation by the "revolutionary democracy"? Prudently, the so-called commander of the Petrograd region chose
a middle course. The Committee's attempt to subvert the soldiers was denounced, but nothing was done in fact to counteract its taking over the
garrison. In any case the question was largely academic: most of the regiments in Petrograd had for some time followed the Bolsheviks rather than
the gentlemen whom it pleased the Minister of War to set over them.

In any other place and time except the fantastic Petrograd of 1917 the
setting up of the Military Revolutionary Committee and its subsequent
countermanding of the government's orders would have been taken as the
beginning of a mutiny. But in fact nobody got unusually excited. The
Council of the Republic went on talking. Its commission on foreign affairs
on October 12 heard a report on the state of the Russian army which was
almost encouraging. The Minister of War reported that "ideological Bolshevism does not exist among the soldiers." True, there were two million
deserters, but six million soldiers still held their posts, thus containing 130
enemy divisions.[56] Kerensky's government continued in its peaceful coma.
There was a discussion as to what instructions were to be issued to the
Russian delegates to the coming Allied Conference in Paris.

Some Mensheviks and Socialist Revolutionaries were, however, curious
as to whether the Bolsheviks really had something up their sleeve. Would
they be so un-Marxist as to attempt to grab power by an armed putsch?
Did they not remember the July days? There was one way to find out: to
ask them.

And indeed on October 14, with all the preparations in full swing, Dan
confronted the Bolshevik majority of the Executive Committee of the Petrograd Soviet with a powerful speech: "We ought specifically to ask our
comrades the Bolsheviks to what purpose they are conducting this policy. . . . I demand that the Bolshevik Party give us a straightforward and
honest answer: yes or no." [57] The major Bolshevik figures were absent;
they were too busy to attend the Soviet. So it fell to a secondary figure,
Ryazanov, as learned in Marxian dialectics as he was useless in action,
to answer that embarrassing question. And indeed Ryazanov in his
reply displayed great dialectical skill: God forbid, the Bolsheviks as good
Marxists cannot conceivably be preparing an uprising. Dan should know
that. But on the other hand, the uprising is preparing itself, or more properly speaking, it is being caused by the policies of the Provisional Government. However, if by any chance the uprising *should* come to pass, the
Bolsheviks could not possibly stay away from the rising masses shouting
for their leadership. The same answer was given four days later by Trotsky himself. The more suspicious among the Bolsheviks' opponents were
not satisfied, much as they admired the Marxian correctness of the formula.

[56] From *The Past*, Moscow, 1918, Book 6, No. 12, p. 33.
[57] Sukhanov, *op. cit.*, Vol. 7, p. 51.

Sukhanov himself had an additional worry: he was very much concerned that the Soviet should hold a solemn meeting celebrating the approaching twenty-fifth anniversary of Maxim Gorky's literary activity. An insurrection would spoil all the plans.

In view of that atmosphere, it becomes more understandable how Lenin was beside himself because of the still prevalent hesitations and doubts about the uprising within the Bolshevik high command. Formally the decision to rise had been made at the famous meeting of the Bolshevik Central Committee on the night of October 10. The circumstances of this meeting partake of the tragicomic atmosphere of the Great October. It was held nowhere else but at the apartment of our friend Sukhanov. He himself was, of course, a Menshevik, a loyal supporter of Martov, an enemy of violence of any kind. But his wife was a Bolshevik. On October 10 she was especially solicitous that her husband should not tire himself by coming home from the other side of Petrograd, where he was working. Why not sleep at the offices of *New Life* (the newspaper published by Gorky with Sukhanov as one of the editors)? Such advice would have disturbed some husbands, but not Sukhanov. To be sure public transportation was in those days like everything else in the city: much of the time it did not function. But through this ideological cuckoldry not only was Sukhanov injured, but history as well; because of the absence of this invaluably indiscreet man we have but a sketchy account of what happened at the momentous meeting that decreed the October Revolution.

The meeting was attended only by twelve out of twenty-two members of the Central Committee. But this fact was of no importance compared with the appearance of Lenin and Zinoviev. On October 3 the Central Committee had finally authorized the return of its leader to Petrograd "in order to have close and continuous contact with him," and since the seventh he was in hiding in an apartment in the Vyborg region of the city. The brief account of his speech does not convey the passion with which it must have been delivered. Once again he went through and refuted the possible objections to an immediate uprising. No point in waiting or talking. Time to begin. The others were skeptical. Uritsky feebly protested that the Bolsheviks were weak: their Red Guards had forty thousand rifles, "but that is nothing." As to the expectation of help from the regiments in Petrograd, do they remember the July days? [58] But finally the will of one man prevailed. By ten to two, with Zinoviev and Kamenev voting against the motion, the Committee called for an armed uprising. Yet the resolution was not as clear-cut and uncompromising as Lenin might have wished: "Having recognized that the armed uprising is inevitable and the moment [for it] ripe, the Central Committee orders all Party organs to be guided by this consideration in connection with the practical problems. . . ." The ques-

[58] *The Protocols of the Central Committee . . . August 1917–February 1918*, Moscow, 1958, p. 85.

tion "when" was obviously not settled. And a further indication that the majority really did not have their hearts in the enterprise was that the Political Bureau of seven elected to guide Party affairs contained the two last-ditch opponents of the gamble, Kamenev and Zinoviev.

The Bureau played no role in the October events; indeed, there is no record at all of its activities. Lenin was not going to work together with two persons whom he currently considered as totally unfit for Party work. Zinoviev and Kamenev compounded their sins by advising various Party organizations of their opposition. "We are deeply convinced that to proclaim an armed uprising now means to gamble not only with the fate of our Party, but also with that of the Russian and the international revolution." At the meeting Zinoviev had given a more personalized version of this pessimism: They will all get shot. Now they pleaded for waiting in terms which were to earn them Lenin's scorn as well as fury: wait for the Constituent Assembly. The Bolsheviks were bound to get at least one third of the seats in that body. To Lenin's horror those tried revolutionaries, for years his closest lieutenants, now revealed themselves as thinking in terms of majorities and political combinations as if they were Sukhanovs or Martovs. Behind their politically sophisticated arguments lurked fear; the fear of responsibility, physical fear for their lives. "The enemy is stronger than he seems." And then discounting all the "workers with rifles," the Bolshevik sailors and regiments, in panic they listed the enemy's resources: "Five thousand military students, *excellently* armed, *organized,* who want to and know how to fight (because of their class characteristics), then the staff, then the shock battalions . . . then the artillery situated around Petrograd. . . ." [59] They begged everybody to remember that *now* the Party was growing in strength and influence. It would soon have a majority in the Congress of Soviets. Why risk everything by "exposing the proletariat to the blows of united counterrevolutionary forces helped by the petty bourgeois democracy"?

It is said that a good front-line officer will make his men more afraid of himself than of the enemy's bullets and this indeed was a characteristic of Lenin in those October days. Kamenev and Zinoviev revealed themselves as less than brave, and indeed the "five thousand military students" argument was going to plague them the rest of their lives. But even the most intrepid of the Bolshevik leaders could not understand Lenin's insistence on an uprising *now*. At a Party meeting on October 16 he had to listen to a pessimistic appraisal of the Bolshevik chances in an open fight: in this region the workers are apathetic, in another they follow the Anarchists, in yet another maybe they will rally around the Bolsheviks. But the majority of the assembled felt almost fatalistically that they *had* to risk everything rather than to repudiate their leader: "If we have no strength now, then we will have even less later on; if we are not capable of shouldering power

[59] *Ibid.,* p. 91. Italics in the original.

now, we certainly will not be able to afterward," said a participant. And thus the previous resolution was confirmed.

Kamenev and Zinoviev were not finished. They demanded convening of the *full* Central Committee. The former resigned his membership in that body. So convinced were they that the Party under Lenin was marching straight into a disaster that they leaked the news of the fateful resolution and of their opposition to Maxim Gorky's *New Life*.

On October 18 Lenin proposed that the two sinners be thrown out of the Party. Their behavior was "a million times more vile" than anything Plekhanov and the Mensheviks ever did. Let Messieurs Kamenev and Zinoviev establish their own party; the Bolsheviks had no further use for them. But he had won his point. There was no time now for settling intra-Party disputes. The quarreling leaders, even the Central Committee, now faded out from the picture. The machinery of insurrection was set. The Military Revolutionary Committee of the Soviet took over. With one exception the main actors in the actual preparation and carrying out of the uprising would be secondary Party figures. Though Kamenev and Zinoviev crept back at the last moment, neither they nor the rest of the Party potentates would distinguish themselves in the events of October 24 and 25.

The man of the hour, with Lenin still hiding, was Trotsky. To an admiring opponent he seemed to be everywhere: issuing orders to the Military Revolutionary Committee, presiding over the Soviet, addressing the soldiers' and workers' meetings. His flamboyance and theatricality, which were to earn so many enemies in sober everyday politics, now served him well when people had to be infused with a sense of daring and the romance of action. One is constrained to think of Churchill in 1940 or, to give the defeated their due, of Kerensky in the *earlier* days of the Revolution.[60] Not as isolated as Lenin was perforce from the current mood of the Petrograd crowds, Trotsky was far from sharing his simple faith in armed action. The enemy had first to be demoralized and disarmed. The pro-Bolshevik elements had to be stirred up to the utmost excitement and the conviction of their opponents' helplessness. The uprising Trotsky saw could not be called out just in the name of one party. It had to have behind it the *mystique* of the "revolutionary democracy," to be initiated on behalf of the Soviet and to coincide with the meeting of the Second All-

[60] The latter comparison is not as fanciful as it might seem at first. Both Trotsky and Kerensky were great orators and wretched politicians. Each had a streak of the Napoleonic pose about him. Against Kerensky's ineffectuality one recalls Trotsky's lethargy in 1924–25 when Stalin was settling his accounts with Zinoviev and Kamenev, when his intervention might have tipped the scale. And finally one remembers Trotsky on the anniversary of the Revolution in 1927, touring Moscow and attempting to address the workers. As for Kerensky and the Mensheviks in 1917, the point where events could be affected by sheer oratory had passed. The parallel with the Mensheviks is evident even to a historian as friendly to Trotsky as Mr. I. Deutscher. See his *Prophet Unarmed, Trotsky 1921–1929*, New York, 1959, pp. 376–77.

Russian Congress of the Soviets where the Bolsheviks were bound to have a majority.

"Those were great days" Trotsky was to say in 1920 when he, the second man in Soviet Russia, had seemingly little reason to be nostalgic about that period of danger and uncertainty. Lenin was impatient, other Bolshevik leaders were frightened or sunk in gloomy introspection and worry as to what Karl Marx would say about the whole business, but Trotsky was clearly enjoying himself. It was fun to titillate the imbecile Provisional Government and the ponderous Mensheviks now with threats of an uprising, and now with pious declarations that the Bolsheviks intended only to defend themselves. The non-Bolshevik Socialists up to the last moment did not lose their faith in Trotsky. It was hopeless to argue with Lenin, but Trotsky and Lunacharsky, it was widely believed, were civilized men, good Marxists who would see the utter hopelessness of an uprising. Sukhanov kept running after the leader of the Soviet, still trusting that he could be persuaded to arrange a great celebration of Gorky's jubilee. Alas, his former friend and fellow editor brushed him off and the diarist of the Revolution finally understood that Trotsky had other arrangements on his mind.

But until October 24 he still kept talking. No subject was too small to escape his attention or to be infused with a revolutionary meaning. The city government chose this time to charge soldiers a fare for riding trolleys and tramways. Of course this was ridiculous; one might as well have ordered them to obey their officers! But Trotsky took this "provocation" as an occasion for an inflammatory speech; the anti-Bolshevik city government proposed to exploit the brave defenders of the country, another proof of how the Socialist Revolutionaries and the Mensheviks held in contempt the common soldier. On the very eve of the rising it was discovered that the Petropavlovsk fortress had 100,000 rifles stored there, and that the delegate of the Military Revolutionary Committee was kicked out by its garrison which was unfriendly to the Bolsheviks. Attack the fortress? But what happens if the garrison shoots? (It was almost axiomatic that if shots were exchanged the pro-Bolshevik soldiers would run.) Trotsky went to the fortress by himself. After his speech the garrison declared itself on the Bolshevik side and delivered up the rifles.

On October 23 the Provisional Government ordered closing down of the Bolshevik newspapers. This took everybody by surprise: no one expected such daring from the dying regime. But suddenly the Bolshevik leaders were brought up with a shock. Their very headquarters, the Smolny Institute (a former girls' school now housing the Soviet and its Military Revolutionary Committee), were completely undefended. The whole staff of the coming revolution could be arrested by a small detachment. Promptly Smolny was fortified with machine guns and cannon. Most of them were in a state of disrepair and could not have been fired, but at least the place assumed a military appearance. The Bolshevik Central Committee assembled in Smolny, and at the motion of Kamenev, now eager to expunge his previous faintheartedness, it was decided that none of its members should leave the building except by its authorization.

The insurrection was to be begun on the night of October 23 by the seizure of the Winter Palace where the Provisional Government had been holding almost continuous sessions. But this plot misfired, evidently because the pro-Bolshevik military units delegated to get hold of the Palace were scared off by the appearance of a squadron of cavalry.[61] This was a bad augury. It underlined what everybody feared: the unreliability of the pro-Bolshevik regiments. Orders had gone out before to bring 1500 sailors from Kronstadt. They and the workers' Red Guards were at least not likely to run off at the first shots.

On October 24 the last dispositions for the uprising were issued. A three-man committee (the habit of doing things by committee was to die but slowly among the Bolsheviks) composed of Antonov-Ovseenko, Chudnovsky, and Podvoisky, was to guide the military operations. Trotsky had to stay in Smolny, for in addition to being the headquarters of the insurrection, this former girls' finishing school was to receive on October 25 the Second Congress of the Soviets, and he was to be the master of ceremonies.

What was the Provisional Government doing all this while? On the very same day, on October 24, Kerensky was boasting before the Council of the Republic that his government *now* had all the needed proofs that the Bolsheviks were up to no good. The regime's wise forbearance to act hastily was presented by the Premier as its special virtue. Nobody could accuse him, Kerensky, of taking decisive measures until and unless the salvation of the state clearly required them. But now the moment had come: "Let the population of Petrograd know that it is dealing with a resolute and determined government." And to underline the democratic instincts of the regime, Kerensky with a fine flourish demanded that the assembly vote formally its support of his determination.[62] The Council of the Republic in its turn was not going to act overhastily; though Kerensky was wildly cheered, a lengthy discussion followed his motion. Martov made a brilliant speech and a felicitous countermotion; it exposed both Kerensky and the Bolsheviks, deprecated any attempted *coup d'état*, but asserted that its cause lay in the policies of the regime. His resolution passed and it embittered Kerensky so much that he, the head of a fast vanishing regime that had but a few hours of life remaining, threatened to resign.

The air of unreality that seemed to envelop the Great October still continued. The same night another meeting took place, that of the Executive

[61] N. Podvoisky, "The Military Organization of the Russian Socialist (Bolshevik) Party and the Military Revolutionary Committee in 1917," in the *Red Chronicle*, Moscow, 1923, No. 8, p. 23.

[62] Sukhanov, *op. cit.*, Vol. 7, p. 133.

Committee of the Soviets elected in June, its last session. This body, dominated by Mensheviks and Socialist Revolutionaries, met nowhere else but
in Smolny, from a different wing of which Bolshevik commanders and detachments were being sent out to their battle stations. The indefatigable
Trotsky reassured his colleagues on the Executive Committee that the rumors of an uprising were greatly exaggerated. Once again Martov deplored the Bolsheviks' methods, but stipulated that his faction of the Mensheviks could not really object to "the people" seizing power from the inept
and reactionary Provisional Government.

By that time Smolny already sheltered the man who within a few
hours would be its master. Impatient of waiting, Lenin in the evening of
October 24 emerged from his hideout and in a wig, with his face band-
aged, sought his way to Bolshevik headquarters. It was far from safe for
him to wend his way through Petrograd. There were still some pro-
government military units desultorily patrolling the city. He might have
been recognized and arrested, thus complicating the task of his subordinates. But he was still not convinced that the more timid among his followers would not call the thing off. He had to be present to cajole and
push them into action even though, in fact, his presence now in Smolny
could influence the course of events but little, and proved to be an embarrassment to the managers of the uprising.

The great day itself, October 25, is subject to the historians' "What
might have happened if only . . ." and, on the other hand, "It could not
have happened otherwise." What might have happened if only there had
been one resolute man in the Provisional Government and a few hundred
troops disciplined enough to give battle. The Bolshevik commanders admit
freely that they had at their disposal but an armed rabble, which except for
some workers' detachments could have been scared off by a greatly inferior
but disciplined body of troops. "The bitter experience of the July days did
not give us a full belief in victory," writes one of them. [63] Except for the
workers at some factories there was no pro-Bolshevik enthusiasm in the
population, only apathy. Not a single Bolshevik could be found among the
3,000 employees at the Central Telephone and Telegraph office.

On the side of "It could not have happened otherwise" there is the undeniable fact that no military force could be roused against the Bolsheviks.
Within a few months the Russian soldiers had been ordered to obey, then
to disobey the Tsar, his officers, Kornilov. There seemed to be no earthly
reason why they should lay down their lives for one type of Socialist,
Kerensky, against another one, Lenin. The non-Bolshevik left appears
most pathetic in its indecision and almost comical with its misplaced democratic and Socialist scruples and vacillations. But the Martovs, Dans, and
Chernovs still lived with the memories of the reaction and punitive expeditions of 1906–7. The true meaning of Bolshevism was hidden to them

[63] *The Proletarian Revolution*, No. 10, October 1922, p. 96.

just as it was hidden to many Bolshevik leaders. After all, in a few days many of the latter were to resign in protest against what they thought was Lenin's high handed and undemocratic behavior. The ineptitude and naïveté of the Mensheviks and the Socialist Revolutionaries was no more striking than that of the Communist leaders in the 1920s as they were picked off one by one by Lenin's successor. As one of the democratic Socialists, losers of October, remarks pointedly, they were the *first ones* to be taken in by the Bolsheviks' slogans and protestations. It is a fair excuse and a commentary on the long army of those who were to be equally deceived.

Before dawn armed detachments began to occupy the strategic points: the power stations, telephone exchanges, bridgeheads. There was no resistance, thus shaming the doubters among the Bolsheviks, and endowing Lenin with the additional prestige of infallibility. The only troops to which the Provisional Government could appeal were the "Junkers," the military students of Kamenev's and Zinoviev's fears,[64] and that dubious improvisation of the revolutionary enthusiasm, the women's battalions. Kerensky escaped early in the morning, going toward the front in order to bring back troops with him to subdue the capital. In July the rumor of this happening sufficed to panic the pro-Bolshevik forces. One of the tragedies of the Bolsheviks' opponents, if one may digress, was their excessive historical memory: at first everybody thought of the French Revolution, then the Mensheviks feared the repetition of 1905–6, the Provisional Government remained foolishly confident remembering the July days. . . . This time the generals showed Kerensky the door, and he was capable of mustering only a few hundred Cossacks.

The headless government assembled in the Winter Palace. By the middle of the day the former Tsar's vast residence was the only island of the lawful regime amidst Bolshevik Petrograd. It was defended by some Junkers and women. The plan called for its early capture. But the triumvirate that directed operations wisely decided that it was too risky to start shooting. The Palace was to be awed into surrender by a cannonade from the cruiser *Aurora* and from the Petropavlovsk fortress. But here again it was thought wiser to use blanks. The sailors had some democratic compunctions about bombarding the city—God only knew what they might hit with their rusty guns. The "storming" of the Winter Palace, which took all day, consisted actually in small groups of the bolder among the Bolshevik soldiers and sailors squeezing into the building, there being disarmed by the Junkers, but in the process haranguing them about the uselessness of defense. There were occasional shots and negotiations with the defenders.

[64] Another peculiarity of the Russian terminology. Just as the Kadets were not cadets but university professors, lawyers, and the like, so the Junkers were not Prussian landowners but cadets, students in the military schools.

Lenin was awaiting the outcome of the operation in Smolny. The delay was embarrassing. The Second Congress of the Soviets was assembling in the same building, and the inability to tell the delegates that the ministers were under lock and key might lead to complications. Or Kerensky might get back with his Cossacks. Though initially the *bourgeoisie,* to quote Shlyapnikov, "from the Guards officers to the prostitutes," had vanished from the streets of Petrograd [65] it was now emerging again, obviously taking heart because the last bastion of reaction was still standing. The City Council decided to march to the square before the Winter Palace and there to interpose their democratic Socialist bodies between the Bolshevik bullets and the seat of the lawful government. This resolution came to nought as a sailors' detachment barred their way and refused either to shoot them or to let them pass. Disconsolate, they went back to pass a resolution.

Lenin was storming and abusing his lieutenants for the delay. He kept interfering in the actual conduct of the operations, even tending to small details such as giving an order for provisions to be issued for the telephone girls (unless they were given bread and tea they would not handle any calls). His interference made one of the triumvirs, Podvoisky, offer his resignation. That led to a rage: this was war, no one had the right to resign; he would have Podvoisky shot. There was some more talk about executions. A few Junkers had been captured. "Some comrades in Smolny" (almost certainly Lenin among them) were for shooting them out of hand to discourage the others. But wisely Trotsky and Podvoisky decided to let the youngsters go, after giving them a lecture. It was much better to work through persuasion and leniency.

In the afternoon Trotsky and Lenin appeared before the Soviet to announce the end of the Provisional Government. But though Lenin ended his speech with "Long live the worldwide Socialist Revolution," there was still no absolute assurance that it had definitely triumphed even in the precincts of Petrograd. Writes Sukhanov: "I was convinced that the Bolshevik rule would be ephemeral and short-lived. Even most of them were convinced of that." Zinoviev was still scared. The Harvard man on the spot reports that some other Bolshevik notables were convinced that the whole thing was insane.[66] The circumstances amply justified Trotsky's insistence that the uprising coincide with the assembly of the Second Congress of the Soviets. Its sanction was to give the Bolsheviks just enough leverage to convince the doubters in their own ranks and to throw confusion among their Socialist opponents who could not see how one could use arms to oppose the will of the legitimate representatives of the working class.

The Congress opened at night and by that time the "siege" of the

---

[65] This class characterization of prostitutes is hardly orthodox; one remembers that in 1905 Lenin urged the formation of revolutionary groups among them.

[66] John Reed, *Ten Days That Shook the World,* New York, 1934, p. 85.

Winter Palace was finally coming to an end. Some of its defenders departed, partly convinced by the agitators, partly confused by the indecision of the ministers. The crowd infiltrating the vast Palace finally became too big for the faithful Junkers to handle. Very late at night the last guard capitulated at the order of the ministers and the "armed people" burst into the Palace. There had been some discussion earlier of the posture in which the Provisional Government of Russia should encounter its oppressors and finally it was decided that the most seemly way was to be at their posts, seated around the cabinet table. The actual scene is famous from many accounts and from Eisenstein's film: Antonov-Ovseenko, looking like a cross between an artist and a secondhand clothing dealer (even though he was once by profession a Tsarist officer), breaking in at the head of the Red Guards. The appropriate formula of surrender had also been prepared: "Members of the Provisional Government submit to force and surrender in order to avoid bloodshed." The soldiers were all for lynching the ministers, but the armed workers kept a decorum appropriate to the historic occasion. One of the ministers, Maliantovich, remembered Antonov: the Bolshevik had been sheltered in his house before the Revolution. Antonov, embarrassed, tried to preserve some revolutionary courtesy. On being escorted from the Palace on their way to prison in the Petropavlovsk fortress some ministers were molested by the soldiers. But the reproach traditionally effective among the class-conscious proletariat stopped the would-be lynchers: "Don't hit them, it is uncultured." Bolshevism triumphed, but the period of terror was still in the future.[67]

The Second Soviet Congress, which received with cheers the news of the fall of the Winter Palace, hardly deserves Trotsky's description as "the most democratic of all parliaments in the history of the world." It was a congress of the workers' and soldiers' deputies, hence totally unrepresentative of the nonsoldier peasants. In addition, inevitably, it had been haphazardly elected. Still, the figure of about 390 Bolsheviks and their affiliates out of 650 members [68] testifies to the Bolsheviks' primacy in the major urban centers. The figures for the Mensheviks of all shades had fallen catastrophically since June, a terrible chastisement for the party that once had led the Russian proletariat and had "invented" the soviets.[69]

The former leaders of the "revolutionary democracy" had the added humiliation of opening the Congress and turning over the Presidium to the

[67] P. N. Maliantovich, "In the Winter Palace October 25–26," in *The Past*, Moscow, 1918, Book 6, No. 12.
[68] That is, in the beginning. By the time the Congress dispersed it had about 900 delegates. Varying figures are given in Trotsky's *History* and in W. H. Chamberlin's *The Russian Revolution*, New York, 1935, Vol. 1, p. 320. Chamberlin's, despite the passage of thirty years, is still the best account of the period.
[69] Perhaps the definitive verdict on the Tseretellis, Dans, Martovs, et al. was delivered not by an expert on politics but one in an equally competitive field: "Nice guys finish last," said Leo Durocher, then manager of the Brooklyn Dodgers.

Bolsheviks. "The president's chair is occupied by Kamenev, one of those phlegmatic types designed by nature itself for the office of chairman," wrote Trotsky venomously of his political enemy and brother-in-law. He himself, far from phlegmatic, kept dashing from the hall of the Congress to the room occupied by the Military Revolutionary Committee, and then to the one where Lenin was resting, lying on some blankets and cushions spread out on the floor. The day—or rather the night—was still Trotsky's. It fell to him to answer the pitiful complaints of the Mensheviks that the Revolution was being violated and disgraced, that the bloodshed had to be stopped, some form of compromise must be devised. "No, a compromise is no good here. To those who have gone out and to all who make such proposals we must say, 'You are pitiful isolated individuals, you are bankrupts; your role is played out. Go where you belong from now on— onto the rubbish heap of history.' " [70] Trotsky's chortling and exultant account, written when the author was himself in exile sharing the bitter fate he had meted out to the Martovs and Dans, makes one uneasy. He could have shown more generosity to the people whose historic defeat was caused by the ideals he had himself at one time shared. But even when an exile from Stalin's Russia, Trotsky would have deemed as "philistine" such compassionate considerations.

His mind relieved by the taking of the Winter Palace, Lenin departed at four o'clock in the morning of October 26 for the apartment of Bonch-Bruevich, where at least he could be assured of a bed. No convoy accompanied the new ruler of Russia, but he left in an automobile "driven by an experienced chauffeur," obviously a rarity in those days. After a brief rest he spent the morning writing the first Bolshevik legislation: the decrees about peace and land. Even if Petrograd were to be snatched away from him in the next twenty-four hours those decrees would be broadcast throughout Russia: the soldiers would know that they could with clean conscience take over the landlords' estates. No counterrevolutionary government would be able to undo those decrees.

Back in Smolny the same night he read the "decree on peace" to the exultant Congress. It was a grandiloquent declaration calling upon the warring peoples and governments to enter into immediate negotiations for a peace without indemnities and annexations. It did not appear important that this appeal was made on behalf of a group of conspirators who had just seized one city and who, at best, could aspire to rule over a disintegrating society and a vanishing army. This was the beginning of a world revolution. After a long applause the Congress broke into the "International." The Bolsheviks' singing and elation aroused Sukhanov's envy. "How I wish I could join in . . . become one in the feeling with the enthusiasm of the crowds and its leaders! But I cannot."

[70] Trotsky, *op. cit.*, Vol. 3, p. 311. The famous simile is variously rendered from the prim "dustbin" to the more picturesque "garbage heap."

Then the "decree on land." [71] This time the enthusiasm was visibly smaller. The "law" had little of Marxism about it: it was purely and simply an attempt to appease the mass of peasants and to reconcile them to the Bolshevik rule. There was an intermission to give the delegates a few minutes to discuss the measure, which changed the whole social system of Russia. Sukhanov utilized the interval to sow new doubts in Kamenev's always apprehensive mind. The new formal head of the Russian state (in his capacity as chairman of the Executive Committee of the Congress of the Soviets) was gulping down tea when our diarist cornered him: "So you have really decided to rule by yourselves. . . . I think this is quite scandalous. I am afraid that when this whole thing fizzles out it will be too late to go back." Kamenev was almost convinced: "Though why should we fizzle out?" the official successor to the Tsars asked uncertainly. But for him as for many Bolsheviks it was easier to try to shoulder the burden of ruling Russia than to face Lenin's terrible wrath.

The land decree duly passed, though this time one delegate voted against the motion. In the first few hours of its rule Lenin's party fulfilled its promise of declaring for "peace and land." But no vote could provide for the other need and aspiration of the tortured country: bread. And even the most uncritical member of the Congress must have realized that it was easy to vote for peace, but more complicated to bring it about, and that the land decree would only deepen the chaos and lawlessness in the countryside. But both these measures—or rather gestures—were the absolute necessities of the moment if the Bolsheviks were to hang on. "The decree on land was . . . also a weapon of the revolution, which had still to conquer the country." [72] Bonch-Bruevich recalls Lenin's pathetic eagerness that the land decree be dispatched immediately to the villages of Russia. With no radio, no other means of broadcasting the news to the peasants (the Bolsheviks could hardly use the Tsarist device of the priests reading it from the pulpit), special emissaries, mostly Bolshevik soldiers and sailors, were to travel with the copies of the precious document. But would not even the most conscientious Bolshevik, in view of the shortage of cigarettes, roll his own with the paper on which the decree was printed? In order to spare the emissaries that temptation (paper was also extremely scarce) it was decided to provide them with used calendars, which they could tear up and roll into cigarette paper to their heart's content.[73] Such were the concerns that had to occupy the new rulers.

There was one more thing to be attended to that day. There had been some discussion earlier as to what should be the name of the new executives of the Russian state. Minister? But that conjured up the image of the Tsarist officials, gentlemen in frock coats or uniforms with epaulettes. Trotsky

[71] It will be discussed below.

[72] Trotsky, *op. cit.*, Vol. 3, p. 334.

[73] V. L. Bonch-Bruevich, "From Recollections about Vladimir Ilyich," from *Lenin in October*, Moscow, 1957.

had a felicitous idea; let them be called People's Commissars. It met with Lenin's immediate approval; the name recalled the days of the French Revolution, and as a matter of fact "commissar" had been the name of envoys attached by the Provisional Government to various armies. Sukhanov records an objection which, though pedantic, had a prophetic ring about it: "minister" etymologically is derived from "servant," "commissar" has other connotations. But "commissar" it was to be until many years later Joseph Stalin decided that the Soviet state had too much in the way of memories of its revolutionary infancy connected with it, and commissars became ministers. Even before this, military ranks, uniforms for the civil servants, and epaulettes had all reappeared; Russia was then a world power and it was thought childish and "uncultured" to cling to the symbols and language of an era long past.

The Council of the People's Commissars was headed by Lenin (though he initially would have preferred to stay out). Insofar as its composition was concerned, he evidently forgot what he wrote a few weeks earlier, that a rank-and-file worker could run any ministry: most of the commissars were from the intelligentsia. Except for Lunacharsky, Commissar of Education, and Trotsky for Foreign Affairs, the names of the new rulers were little known. Such Bolshevik stars as Sverdlov, Kamenev, Zinoviev, and Bukharin were not included. The first three may have been left out because of their Jewish origin. The government had to find acceptance among the masses of peasants and soldiers, among whom anti-Semitism was thought a potent force; hence with the obvious exception of Trotsky no Jews were included.[74] Some attempt was made to find technically qualified personnel. Thus Stalin was the logical choice for the head of the Commissariat of Nationalities and Lunacharsky, writer and dramatist, for Education. But of course there were few among the Bolsheviks with any administrative experience. A ministry was offered to Krasin, but the former terrorist would for the moment have nothing to do with Lenin and the Bolsheviks.

In general the new ministers approached their unfamiliar duties with bewilderment sometimes approaching a panic. They had to be reassured that each commissar was to be but the head of the commission running the given department of state. Shlyapnikov left amusing memoirs of the first moments of his administration of the Commissariat of Labor. He appeared in the ministry and presented his credentials to the janitor, only to be informed that the latter, like all the employees of all the ministries, was on strike. When he tried to recruit some officials he was met with horrified reproaches: "What, you a labor unionist all your life are now recruiting scabs!" Some commissars, tired of sitting in empty buildings, begged to be returned to the more congenial tasks of Party work.

[74] Though it might be pointed out that few peasants would discern Jews behind the Russian names of Zinoviev or Sverdlov, and anyway many anti-Bolsheviks were firmly convinced that Lenin himself was a Jew.

The new rulers' debut as administrators was taking place under conditions of indescribable chaos. Another Bolshevik, S. Pestkovsky, describes his activities as a job seeker. He repaired first to the Commissar of Finances, V. Menzhinsky. The latter's office in Smolny consisted of a sofa over which was the proud inscription: "The People's Commissariat of Finance." Pestkovsky sat on the commissariat and informed the distracted minister that he had studied in the London School of Economics. "In that case we will make you the head of the State Bank," exclaimed Menzhinsky. But the officials of the Bank refused to accept their new director, who had to look for another job. He tried Foreign Affairs. But Trotsky explained that there was no work worth mentioning in that department: "I myself took this job so I would have more time for the Party work. All there is to do is to publish the secret treaties,[75] then I will close the shop." Pestkovsky then offered his services to Stalin. He would set up the ministry for him. And indeed he found a room with a free table, over which he attached a slip of paper reading: "The Commissariat for the Nationalities." "Comrade Stalin, here is your Commissariat," he said proudly to the future dictator. Stalin, writes poor Pestkovsky (to be sure in 1922, but he should have known better) "emitted some nondescript grunt, whether of approval or of dissatisfaction" and began his administrative career. Next Pestkovsky was sent to borrow three thousand rubles from Trotsky for current expenses. "Insofar as I know the Commissariat of Nationalities to this day has not returned that money to Trotsky." He also found a typist for the office, and in general deserves the credit, which he has not received, for having initiated into the secrets of administration one of the most famous practitioners of the art. But working for Stalin, as imprudent Pestkovsky makes too clear, had obvious disadvantages: unlike most of the Bolshevik potentates of those days he was taciturn and gloomy, not a good source of gossip as to the exciting quarrels and other doings in the Central Committtee.[76]

Amidst this madhouse it was only Lenin's authority that kept things moving at all. "Ilyich will be told about it," was usually a sufficient threat to stop the commissars' quarreling with each other, or to bring a delinquent or indolent official back to the path of duty. Gradually the strike of the government's employees was broken, some money secured, and in a manner of speaking the government began to function.

Lenin's insistence also determined that this first government was purely Bolshevik in composition, and not a coalition of the left Socialist parties as many, including his followers, insisted. One can see in this, and rightly so, his lack of democratic principles, but to give him his due, there were good practical reasons for that exclusiveness. As we shall see, for all

[75] Between the Tsarist government and the Allies.

[76] S. Pestkovsky, "About the October Days in Petrograd," in *The Proletarian Revolution*, No. 10, October 1922, pp. 93–103. In 1930 Pestkovsky recorded his recollections again. Need one say that the picture of Stalin is quite different?

the years of tight discipline, for all his enormous authority, it was still hard enough for Lenin to ride herd over the Bolshevik commissars who kept disagreeing and threatening to resign at the slightest provocation. Who could believe that a government with, say, Martov in its ranks would have ever been able to agree on a simple policy, would have ever been able to stop talking? Had Lenin been Thomas Jefferson and John Stuart Mill rolled into one, it still would have been difficult for him to agree to preside over a coalition government. And besides, there were few candidates for ministerial posts from the other parties. Why join this mad adventure of the Bolsheviks, this government that would not last out a week?

But it was to confound the unbelievers. In a few days, though after some really hard fighting in distinction to the almost bloodless takeover in Petrograd, Moscow joined under the Bolshevik rule.[77] Other major cities followed suit.

The feared comeback by Kerensky never materialized. The ex "democratic dictator" was unable to collect any sizable force. He finally began a march on Petrograd with a few hundred Cossacks headed by General Krasnov. Even that meager force created some apprehension in the capital, especially since much larger units sent against it would flee after a few shots. Lenin and Trotsky were constrained to make an appeal to the regular army officers to help them fight off the invasion. Somewhat to their surprise, quite a few officers offered to help. Much as they disliked the Bolsheviks, they hated Kerensky more. In their eyes he was a deceitful windbag who had led on and then betrayed Kornilov, and who had broken his promises to the officer corps. Within sight of Petrograd Krasnov's Cossacks suffered some casualties, which led them to deliberate why in fact they were trying to restore the government they did not care about. Their hesitation increased when Bolshevik agitators arrived in their midst, and began those heated discussions by which most of the political and military issues in those days were decided. One of the arrivals was a colorful figure of the Revolution, Bolshevik sailor Dybenko. He appealed to the Cossacks' sense of humor by proposing that they turn Kerensky over in exchange for Lenin. The former Prime Minister was not going to await the result of this bargaining. He fled in disguise of a sailor. The Cossacks surrendered. Petrograd, where a brief revolt of the Junkers was suppressed at the same time, was safe for the Bolsheviks.

What was in fact this new government erected upon the ruins of the Tsar's and Kerensky's regimes? Neither legally nor in fact can it be characterized by the conventional labels: democracy, dictatorship, oligarchy (though the last one comes closest to describing the actual character of

[77] The Bolsheviks there had to bombard the Kremlin, which brought on the first "ministerial crisis." Lunacharsky in tears declared that he could not remain at his post while the monuments of Russian culture were being destroyed. It turned out that the Kremlin was but little damaged, and the sensitive commissar took back his resignation.

the Bolshevik regime in its first years). Legally it had grown out of the Congress of the Soviets, but if one reads on in the law setting up the Council of the People's Commissars it was to be the provisional government "until the meeting of the Constituent Assembly." Circumstances beyond their control were to make the Bolsheviks summon that assembly though they were certain to be in a minority within it and though they were sure (or at least Lenin was) that they would have to disperse it by force. Having given birth to the new government the Congress of the Soviets was sent home. "It was the shortest Congress in history," Sukhanov notes sadly, oblivious that there had been only one other previously. "The provincial delegates had to hurry home to build the foundations of the proletarian state. And the central authorities had no time or need for further meetings." And indeed this was the first indication of the drastically changed political atmosphere. No more protracted oratorical bouts. No more improvised discussions and conferences in the corridors of the Tauride Palace or Smolny. Government by talk had ended.

Then who ruled Russia? The official collective head of the state was the Executive Committee of the Congress; its chairman, Kamenev, the closest thing Russia had to a president. But in a few days when the incorrigible Kamenev again differed from Lenin, he was unceremoniously dumped from his "presidency" and replaced by Sverdlov. Then was it the Council of the Commissars? But this was a hastily improvised body, which drew its importance mainly from the fact that Lenin and Trotsky were its members. Few people were seriously inclined to think that, say, Teodorovich the Commissar of Provisions or Milyutin of Agriculture were among the real rulers. The Central Committee of the Bolshevik Party? Here we are closer to the actual seat of power, but even that body was often divided and ineffective in coordinating policies. We are thus down to Lenin himself, but his position was still very far from that of a dictator. There was no machinery at his disposal to assure the obedience of the Central Committee or of the Council of the Commissars. A few dissidents in those bodies, and the whole policy of the new government would grind to a halt. No cult of personality as yet. No apparatus of the Party Secretariat that would weed out the disobedient Bolsheviks and assure that all the offices were safely in the hands of "his" men. No secret police yet to terrorize opponents, not to mention fellow Party members.

Lenin's role in the first days of the Soviet government is reminiscent of what Kerensky had been called in derision, because of his addiction to endless oratory: "the persuader in chief." He had to persuade and cajole his colleagues, use the only weapon as yet at his disposal, his moral superiority, to subdue and dispel the almost continuous objections and doubts of the Kamenevs, Bukharins, and others. In *a few months* his authority among the masses would be so great that a Bolshevik regime without him would be utterly unimaginable, but it is not that as yet. In October and

November some Bolsheviks were still capable of considering a coalition
government from which Lenin and Trotsky would be excluded. Thus time
after time Lenin had to sally forth into a new battle and turn the full
power of his logic and invective on the doubters and the fainthearted.

To some extent he enjoyed a battle of wits and a good argument.
Where Stalin would order the arrest of a political opponent Lenin would
write a caustic article or would deliver a harangue before a Party gathering, throwing the opposition into confusion or retreat. He still had something of the revolutionary *intelligent* about him: how delightful to make a
foe admit *freely* that he was wrong, that his position on this or that issue
was un-Marxist or not thought out! His intellectual self-confidence was
very considerable, hence he did not have his successor's sensitivity and
hatred of being contradicted. But this dictatorship by persuasion was very
far from being Lenin's preferred style of ruling. It was the product of
necessity. The Bolsheviks were as yet too small a group, almost like a be-
leaguered garrison, to afford the luxury of purges. Where could one find
an agitator as capable as Zinoviev, or exponents of Marxism to fill the
shoes of Kamenev or Bukharin? And were he to cast them out, others
would be alienated or discouraged.

But this grudging toleration of dissent did not even in the beginning
extend very far. "To tolerate the existence of bourgeois papers means to
cease being a Socialist," he said in November. In his eyes there was no
such thing as political *opposition* to the Bolshevik rule; there could be
only sabotage and betrayal to the class enemy, whether its actual expression was a strike of the ministerial employees or a demand by the Railwaymen's Union for a coalition of Socialist parties. Terror? All that Lenin
was willing to promise on that subject was that the Bolsheviks would not
resort to *unneccessary* terror. "They reproach us that we use terror, but
such terror as practiced by the French revolutionaries who guillotined unarmed people we have not resorted to, and I hope we shall not use." [78]
This statement is often quoted as indicating Lenin's disapproval of terror,
which allegedly gave way only under the necessities of the Civil War. But it
is clear he meant no such thing. In the first place he did not include political arrests under terror (in the same speech he said, "Yes, we are arresting people"), and in the second he clearly intimated that even more drastic
measures would be used if it became necessary.[79] Such apparent acts of
clemency as the release of the Cossack general Krasnov, after exacting
from him a promise not to fight against the Bolsheviks (which he later

[78] *Works*, Vol. 26, p. 261.
[79] Years before a follower asked Lenin: "If the Revolution wins and you will be
in the Provisional Government, will you send Dan to the guillotine?" Lenin replied
laughingly: "No, we shall not guillotine him but it will be necessary to put him in
jail." Vl. Voitinsky, *Years of Victories and Defeat* (in Russian), Berlin, 1923, Vol. 2,
p. 105. This "joke" seriously represents the extent of toleration Lenin was willing to
extend to a fellow Socialist.

violated) were dictated primarily by prudence: it was unwise to provoke
the Cossacks. Also the application of full-scale terror would not have as yet
been tolerated by the majority of the Bolsheviks. It was to take some time,
and the bitterness of the Civil War, to cure them of such Social Democratic
"superstitions."

If Lenin was unique among his Bolshevik colleagues (apart, perhaps,
from Trotsky) in the extent of his political intolerance, then he was far
ahead of them in his readiness to seek collaborators and help among all
the classes, even the hated *bourgeoisie* and capitalists. The Revolution was
hardly one week old, the ink on his *State and Revolution* was hardly dry,
when Lenin chose to remonstrate with the workers that pay differentials
and the privileged position of the specialists were a very necessary thing:
"In order to produce we need the engineers and we greatly value their
work. We shall willingly pay them well. We do not as yet desire to deprive
them of their privileged position." [80] His dislike of the workers' control,
his awe before the capitalists' ability to "run things" were still not as great
as they were to become in a few months' time, but he was already the
practical Lenin, impatient of the dogmatic twaddle about equality, and
about the rank-and-file worker's ability to run a factory. "Our shortcoming
is . . . we have too many meetings." One suspects that in his heart of
hearts Lenin, on the morning after assuming power, would have liked to
undo much of what he had wrought in Russia during the past seven
months: the soldiers should become disciplined again, the workers instead
of constant strikes and meetings should work hard and the bourgeois managers and specialists should remain at the head of their enterprises. He
would have liked, in brief, to have his Bolsheviks run a tidy capitalist
society.

But that of course was out of the question. And besides, despite his
immediate immersion in the problem of governing Russia his horizons and
immediate expectations were still much wider. The flame of revolution in
his own country could not be curbed, for it still had to catch on abroad
and envelop all of Europe. The world revolutionary still holds an upper
hand over the Russian statesman, though the latter is increasingly more
discernible.

Such was the man who stood at the head of the Russian state in the fall
of 1917. This state was still in the process of disintegration and social decomposition. The Bolshevik rule obviously could not last, said reasonable
men everywhere. A German observer stated the most accepted opinion
when he wrote: "For the moment we are dealing with what is simply the
forceful dictatorship of a handful of determined revolutionaries whose
domination is held in complete contempt by the rest of Russia . . . in not
more than a few months when the reason for existence of the new govern-

[80] Speech to the Petrograd Soviet, November 4, 1917, in *Works*, Vol. 26, p. 261.

ment has ceased, and the war against other nations has finally been brought to an end, it will then be swept away by a flood of violent hostility throughout Russia." [81] The character of the new rulers was an enigma to the "well-informed" circles in the West. The Bolsheviks were held either to be wild anarchists or a bunch of German agents (mostly Jews). Harrowing tales were being circulated of their exploits. They were bent upon destroying every semblance of law and order, utterly indifferent to the sufferings of their unhappy nation, and their rule was one orgy of rapine and terror. Those who spread and believed such stories would have been astounded to learn that the leader of this wild anarchic movement was a man of impeccably bourgeois morals and manners, a devoted son of his country, a great admirer of the achievements of Western civilization and capitalism.

[81] Quoted in Zeman, *op. cit.*, p. 90.

VIII

VICTORY

1. *The Statesman*

The imposing title Chairman of the Council of the People's Commissars failed to impress many people in those early days. Lenin's first experiences as a ruler brought him a shocking realization of how lightly governmental authority, any authority, was held in revolutionary Russia. After two days in office, he had occasion to call the headquarters of the Baltic fleet to summon the sailors' help to defend Petrograd. The discussion between the ruler of Russia and the sailor at the other end of the wire speaks volumes: Sailor: "What is new with you in Petrograd . . . ?" Lenin: "There is news that Kerensky's units have taken Gatchina . . . it is necessary to strengthen [the Bolshevik forces in Petrograd] as fast as possible. . . ." Sailor: "What else is new?" Lenin: "Instead of the question 'what else' I expected an immediate announcement that you are ready to come to our help and fight." [1] To the average sailor (or worker or peasant) the idea that there was such a thing as an order to be obeyed unquestioningly, or that another man, whatever his office, was too important to engage in a conversation, was by now almost incomprehensible. The sailors liked Comrade Lenin and they would gladly help him, but they had to be told why he needed their help, and themselves decide whether the reasons were compelling. Thus Lenin (with what feelings one can imagine) had to answer what, under the circumstances, was an idiotic question: "Do you really need reinforcements right away?" Eight months of Bolshevik propaganda had taught the sailors, and the whole country, only too well. It was not entirely in jest that Dybenko offered to swap Lenin for Kerensky. For the moment the sailors greeted the Soviet power and Lenin. But let them only try to start talking about "orders," "discipline," and the like! They would be disabused of such notions the way those Tsarist generals and admirals had been in the past few months.

It was a heart-rending situation for a man so devoted to order and discipline, and so intolerant of "spontaneity." But to meet this anarchy head on was to invite disaster. For a long time the Bolsheviks would continue to pay, and pay dearly, for the success of their pre-October slogans by the destruction of all social cohesion and discipline. But on the very morrow

[1] *Works,* Vol. 26, p. 232.

of October Lenin began, prudently but firmly, the work of reversing the trend. Within a year Russia would have a Red Army and Navy in which death would be the penalty for major infractions of discipline. The Soviet secret police would be created and would infinitely surpass in its severity and efficiency the once dreaded Tsarist Okhrana. If one were to use political terms in their real rather than the conventional and propagandistic sense then one would have to say that October 25, 1917, marks not only the triumph of the Bolshevik Revolution but also the beginning of the counterrevolution carried out by the same party.

But for this task the Party itself had to be reshaped and reformed. It appears fatuous to repeat how in fourteen years of its existence Lenin had tightened the discipline of Bolshevism and disabused his followers of democratic illusions and superstitions. But the idea of one-party government appeared to many Bolshevik veterans not so much undemocratic as fantastic. How could a party of 300,000 members run a country of 150 million people? It was all right to seize power, to demonstrate the rottenness of the Kerensky regime, to proclaim in favor of peace and "all power to the soviets." Certainly those right-wing Mensheviks and Socialist Revolutionaries who had collaborated with Kerensky could not expect any favors. But it was still incredible to many that Lenin and Trotsky while proclaiming for "soviet" would in fact mean Bolshevik power. Would the workers stand for it? As early as the end of October the powerful Railwaymen's Union raised its voice on behalf of a government coalition of all Socialist parties. Its executive reminded Lenin that the railway workers had helped stop Kornilov and Kerensky and they would not hesitate to do the same to the Bolsheviks, should they persist in their undemocratic and unsocialistic attitude.

The incorrigible Zinoviev and Kamenev once again opposed Lenin and insisted on a coalition. But this time they were supported by a number of other Bolshevik bigwigs, including persons as prominent as Rykov, Lenin's future successor as the Chairman of the Council of Commissars, and Shlyapnikov. Victory instead of decreasing had increased dissension in the Bolshevik ranks. And again: if twenty or so people composing the Central Committee could not agree on a policy within a week of their taking over power, how were they going to run Russia?

A lesser man might have capitulated or temporized. But not Lenin. Through the Central Committee's resolution he thundered at his opponents: let them *go* to the Mensheviks, Socialist Revolutionaries, and the rest and join with them, create their own coalition. He, Lenin, and his faithful band would not hesitate to fight them the way they fought Kerensky. The new coalition, wrote Lenin convincingly enough, could bring Russia nothing but "hesitations, impotence, and chaos."

But equally telling and prescient was the voice of his Bolshevik opponents. On November 4 they wrote that without a broad Socialist coalition

Russia faced "further bloodshed and famine." They reminded the rank-and-file Party members that they were laying down their functions in a moment of victory out of the conviction that "the policy of the leading group of the Central Committee leads to the loss by the workers' party of the fruits of this victory, and the crushing of the proletariat." [2] Following this declaration by Zinoviev, Kamenev, and Rykov, a larger group of commissars [3] on resigning their functions delivered even a more prophetic warning: barring a broad coalition the Bolshevik regime could be preserved only "by the means of political terror." In sum five members of the Central Committee out of twenty-two and five major commissars resigned their functions and pledged an intra-Party fight against Lenin. Some veteran Bolsheviks were outspoken. How can a Socialist party insist that any government must be headed by certain people, that is, Lenin and Trotsky, said Ryazanov, slated for long to continue a gadfly at Party gatherings. Was it not a stress on personalities unbefitting a revolutionary party?

Many years later in Stalin's Russia most of the surviving dissenters of 1917 found themselves on the bench of the accused and eventually before the firing squad. Among their crimes their behavior in these days was counted as one of the most heinous: they contradicted and fought against Ilyich, they deserted their posts. But by the rules and spirit of the Bolshevik Party in 1917 there was nothing illegal or immoral in their behavior. It was open to any Party member who disagreed with its decisions to lay down his functions and to state his dissent. "Your demand . . . ," wrote the members of the opposition to Lenin, "that in all our pronouncements we should support the policy of the Central Committee with which we basically disagree represents an unheard-of order to act against our convictions." And so it was even by the then prevailing Bolshevik standards.

But to Lenin the issue transcended whether a few Mensheviks and Socialist Revolutionaries were to be given ministerial posts (in a few days he would agree to the inclusion of some *Left* Socialist Revolutionaries). It was another stage in his struggle for the ideal *Party*, which he began in 1902 with *What Is To Be Done?*. Toleration of dissent, the luxury of individual conscience, were not to be allowed within its ranks. It was not dissent, it was desertion: "The comrades who have resigned are deserters. . . . Remember, comrades, two of those deserters, Kamenev and Zinoviev, even before the insurrection in Petrograd acted as deserters and strikebreakers. . . ." [4] Either they submit or they will be expelled from the Party as a

[2] *Protocols of the Central Committee . . . . August 1917–February 1918*, Moscow, 1958, p. 135.

[3] This word soon came to mean not only ministers of the central government, but upper Soviet officials in general. Thus among the signatories were found a "commissar of the printing shops"; one of the Red Guards; and others.

[4] From the Proclamation of the Central Committee to All the Members of the Party and to All the Toiling Classes of Russia, in *Protocols* (see note 2, above), p. 140.

whole. And submit they did. First Zinoviev came skulking back, covering his submission with grandiloquence: "We prefer to make mistakes together with millions of workers and soldiers and to die together with them rather than to stand apart at this decisive, historic moment."

In itself, the incident was not more significant than the past and future trouncings of the intra-Party opposition by Lenin. Temperamentally the upper ranks of the Bolshevik hierarchy were a willful and unruly lot. Without Lenin's iron hand they would soon have reverted to a discordant chorus à la the Mensheviks. But until his death Lenin's personnel policies, to use this modern term, were to bear an imprint of this experience of October and November. Zinoviev and Kamenev would be readmitted to grace, would still be entrusted with the most important posts. As a Russian revolutionary *intelligent* Lenin would never abandon entirely his predilection for what might be called the old Social Democratic type, epitomized by Kamenev or Bukharin. For all their quarrelsomeness, ideological scruples, and political impracticality they represented to him a part of the Socialist tradition that had to be preserved within Bolshevism. It is a mistake to think that he attacked their temporary apostasy on purely political grounds. It undoubtedly brought him some of the same personal suffering he had experienced over his breach with Martov and Plekhanov many years before. But at the same time he now turned more and more to the people of a coarser moral and intellectual fiber. His main aides for practical affairs now became Stalin and Sverdlov. They were people not given to resignations, displays of emotion and ideological scruples. They were doers and not *raisonneurs* and masters of the phrase. It was the first step in the ascendancy of the administrator over the intellectual in Soviet Russia.

At another level this new proof of the unreliability of the Bolshevik old guard could not but strengthen his complex passion for the "simple man" who unlike Lunacharsky would not burst out crying when a monument was destroyed, or unlike Kamenev or Bukharin would not protest that this was not democratic or Socialist. In the first days of the Bolshevik regime Lenin kept repeating in speeches, "For the first time in Russian history the man with a rifle is not feared," a remark that would be funny if it were not macabre against the background of constant robberies, murders, and exactions by the deserting soldiers and sailors. He himself more than once had been shot at by the trigger-happy Red Guards. But the worker with the rifle becomes in his speeches the symbol at once of proletarian wisdom and of innocence. When the leaders hesitate the "worker with the rifle" knows "instinctively" what the interests of the proletarian state demand. He is implacable, perhaps indiscriminately so, toward the *bourgeoisie,* and at times prone to crime and self-indulgence. But his heart is in the right place, his "class instincts" more reliable than those of the Zinovievs and Kamenevs. . . . And then, as if awakening from a dream, Lenin would shout for the most severe penalties against "men with rifles," unruly workers and soldiers who sowed anarchy and who disgraced the Socialist state.

The strange paradoxes of the first days of the Bolshevik power were reflected in the headquarters and the working style of the Chairman of the Council of the People's Commissars. Like other ministers he continued for a while to live in a private apartment, but soon found it convenient to shift to the seat of the government, still the former girls' school, the Smolny Institute. As his faithful helper of those days describes Vladimir Ilyich's residence it had to fulfill the following requirements: (1) to be close to his office; (2) "to be in accordance with the rules of a conspiratorial residence"; (3) to be comfortable for living; and (4) "for an emergency should have a special exit which could be used only by Lenin" (the last seems redundant in view of No. 2).[5] A formidable list of requirements!

Actually it was a spacious five-room apartment in a separate corridor on the second floor of the building, equipped with electricity and hot and cold running water, adds the aide proudly. A special elevator was reserved for Vladimir Ilyich and the few who had his personally signed pass enabling them to enter his quarters at any time. This modest but, by the Petrograd standards of 1917, considerable comfort was all that the new ruler of Russia required. The precarious nature of his power was underlined by the fact that only he held the keys both to his apartment and to the door opening on the wing (this was presumably one of the conspiratorial requirements). Though there were guards behind the always locked corridor door no stranger could guess that this was not one of the numerous offices but the private residence of the leader. The head of the Soviet state lived as he had lived before October, in hiding.

Another reminder of how fragile and primitive was the structure of the new power was the provisionment of the Council of the People's Commissars. Before their morning session the new ministers were issued tea and a thinly buttered piece of black bread. One dining room served the rulers of Russia, and for their main meals they often had to be content with cabbage soup and bread. In those days it was not a piece of egalitarian ostentation. It was hard to obtain food in Petrograd. Bonch-Bruevich relates a story sentimental but probably truthful. A petitioner soldier appeared in the antechamber of the Council of the People's Commissars. He was probably one of many who came to hear from Lenin himself when the Bolsheviks would, as they had promised, conclude peace and let them go home (there were, amazingly enough, still many who refused simply to desert). His attention was drawn by the lamentations of the serving girl who was to bring Lenin his mid-morning snack: How could she go in with just tea? There was no bread or cheese to be gotten that day. Without hesitation the soldier pulled a piece of bread from his satchel and handed it to the servant.

Party workers and just simple petitioners recalling their visits with

[5] V. L. Bonch-Bruevich, *Recollections about Lenin 1917–1924*, Moscow, 1963, p. 83.

Lenin in those times often mention with gratitude and amazement how he himself would give instructions to have them fed in the dining room of the Council of People's Commissars. Again this was not only an expression of Lenin's undoubted solicitude for the "little people." It was one of the means of governing Russia in those desperate days, of communicating to the masses that amidst all the chaos, anarchy, and destruction the government was striving for something better, that it was *their* government.

There is little doubt that in those early days, the period of its relative impotence, widespread hunger, and chaos, Lenin's government enjoyed more popularity than it was ever to achieve again, except perhaps shortly before his death. The industrial worker was in the main behind it. The peasant, if not converted to Bolshevism, was at least pacified by the land decree. The specter of the Civil War was still not imminent. Far away on the Don the Cossacks under General Kaledin proclaimed their independence. Kornilov and his fellow plotters escaped from their internment following October and were wending their way south to raise the standard of revolt. But in the fall of 1917 and the early months of 1918 Russia's general weakness and exhaustion militated against any major attempt to snatch power from the hands of Lenin and his Party. They could look with some confidence into the future if only . . .

The biggest "ifs" were the questions of bread and peace. They were closely connected. The war had taken millions of peasants from their productive labor. Inflation and the breakdown in communications had aggravated food shortages. They were largely responsible for the riots that helped bring down the Romanovs in February. Continued hunger in the big cities might do the same for the Bolsheviks.

To solve the problem overnight would have required a miracle. The food shortages and accompanying terror, epidemics, and lawlessness were to continue well into 1922. But Lenin's government, while incapable of solving the problem, made it clear that unlike its predecessors it would not remain passive in the face of it.

Its first steps on the food front reveal many of the characteristics of what became known as War Communism: the attempt to govern and run the economy through repression and intimidation, by raising the slogan of the class war, by shifting the blame for shortages and failures to the alleged sabotage of the *bourgeoisie,* and later on of the *kulak,* the well-to-do peasant.

All those elements were visible in Lenin's approach to the problem of feeding Petrograd. On January 18 the local soviet heard a somber report on the situation of the capital. Some military units had not had bread for six days. What little food reached the city failed to be unloaded and distributed. Only forty (!) workers were engaged in unloading the supplies that came to Petrograd by rail.

Lenin's comment was: "All those facts testify as to the amazing inactivity of the Petrograd workers." Let them form special teams to unload the supplies and to search for the speculators who hoard bread. At least one thousand of such detachments should be formed. Those factories and regiments which fail to participate in this work should be deprived of rations for their workers.

But this reproach and threat to the "masses" is accompanied by an appeal to their class feeling. The "well-to-do" part of the population should be stripped of their rations for at least three days. They can always go to the speculator, the black marketeer, and buy bread from him. But this is not going to be easy. For in the *same speech* Lenin demands that the apprehended speculators be shot on the spot.[6] Drastic situation, drastic measures. But presumably among those "well to do" are not only the former princes and Tsarist officials but the engineers, industrial managers, and doctors whom Lenin is so eager to enlist in work for the Socialist state. Are they also to go without bread for "three days," they to whom a few weeks before he had guaranteed a "privileged position"? Thus this paradox of the Soviet rule, which corresponds to Lenin's own deeply ambivalent nature. The same people eagerly sought, courted, and given extra rations and pay become at times the class enemy to be hounded and humiliated by "the man with a rifle." Much of Lenin's future activity, indeed much of the history of the Soviet state, would consist of a vain effort to resolve this tragic paradox.

The main problem before the new government, that of peace, was to prove even less susceptible of a revolutionary solution. Here there could be no "buts" and "ifs," no shifting of the blame to the *bourgeoisie*, the saboteur, *kulak*, or any others. The Bolsheviks had promised peace. If peace were not forthcoming, if the soldier could not go home, no excuses would prevent Lenin from sharing the fate of Nicholas Romanov and Kerensky.

In the very beginning even this problem looked simple. Fortunately for themselves, for otherwise the feeble objections of Kamenev and Zinoviev would have been magnified a hundredfold, the Bolsheviks had been taken in by their own propaganda: they would take over power, issue a worldwide appeal for peace, Russian soldiers would begin fraternization with those in the opposing trenches. Soon the German armies would dissolve into a mass of soviets, kick out their officers, and conclude a people's peace. Very simple.

Censorious historians have never stopped reproaching the Bolsheviks for their simplemindedness in assuming that the German soldier was like his Russian counterpart, or that the blast of the Bolshevik propaganda trumpet would work within the Reichswehr the same wonders it had achieved within the defeated and already demoralized Russian armies. Such judgments are a bit too harsh. In the first place had the average Bol-

[6] *Works,* Vol. 26, p. 455.

shevik before October 25 been able to visualize Brest Litovsk he most likely would have put a bullet through his head or joined the staunchest Menshevik "defensists." To repeat, it was lucky for them that they had been so naïve.

In the second place, was it really so hopelessly naïve in late 1917 to count on the universal detestation of the inconclusive manslaughter that had gripped Europe for more than three years? Mutinies had taken place in the French army, a serious unrest had affected the German fleet, and it was not simple doctrinaire foolishness that dictated to the Bolsheviks their hope.

Did Lenin share fully such expectations? His future conduct would indicate that he had a more realistic understanding of the strength of the German military machine than did most of the Bolsheviks. This essentially provincial Russian had none of the quick enthusiasm of the much more sophisticated and cosmopolitan Trotsky, who believed that in a few weeks the Commissariat of Foreign Affairs could be disbanded and that a prompt revolutionary response in Germany was almost a certainty. Some months later, on February 24, 1918, Lenin talking about Germany's army and its leaders used brutally frank language: "Until now our enemies have been miserable and pathetic . . . an idiot Romanov . . . windbag Kerensky . . . a handful of military students and the *bourgeoisie*. Now we have against us a giant. . . ." [7] Strange language from a doctrinaire Socialist. No mention of classes, of historical laws, and the like. The stress is put on the personal ineptitude of the Bolsheviks' previous foes and on the efficiency of the Germans. Yet another element in Lenin's greatness: his ability to separate himself at decisive moments from any illusions and comforting visions bred by the doctrine.

But at the moment there was no choice. "Soldiers, the making of peace is in your hands. You will not let the counterrevolutionary generals sabotage the great work of peace . . . ," he proclaimed to the Russian soldiers on November 10. Let the front-line regiments elect their own representatives to negotiate with the corresponding German units. They should let the government know about the course of those negotiations.

The same day Lenin still attacked the "lies" of the bourgeois press that the government was seeking a separate peace with Germany. "We propose immediately to begin peace negotiations on a world scale." But in a few days he convinced himself of what he had probably always believed: the Western Allies were not going to recognize this band of anarchists and adventurers as the government of Russia. The illusion or deception that the peace would not be just between Germany and Russia was the first one to collapse.

The next one to go was the idea of the "peace of the trenches." The Bolsheviks understandably enough found it easy to assume control (again

[7] *Works*, Vol. 27, p. 43.

a very imprecise term) of the front-line troops. The new commander-in-chief was Ensign Krylenko, his predecessor who refused to acknowledge the authority of Lenin having been shoved aside, then lynched by the soldiers. But no corresponding developments took place on the German side of the battle line. It was not with any German soldiers' soviet that Krylenko had to reach an agreement on armistice, but with H.R.H. Field Marshal Prince Leopold of Bavaria, the Commander-in-Chief of the Eastern Front. The Bolshevik negotiators would have to sit down to conclude peace with the emissaries not of the workers and soldiers but with those of such potentates as the Emperor of Germany, of Austria, the Sultan of Turkey, and the Tsar of Bulgaria.

Such somber circumstances failed to dampen the Bolsheviks' optimism or their sense of mission. One might think that they, the representatives of a defeated, starving country and of a most precariously situated government, were going to a peace conference as victors. Trotsky perorated that the German and Austrian governments had placed themselves in the prisoners' dock, and that the Russian peace delegation would act as the prosecutor.[8] In negotiating for a truce the Bolshevik delegates stipulated that the Russians should have freedom of propaganda among the German soldiers and that the German command pledge that it would not withdraw any troops from the Eastern front in order to throw them against the Allies in the West. The insolence of such demands on the part of the defeated side made the German negotiators breathless. Eventually the German chief of staff of the Eastern front, General Hoffmann, came out with a formula that preserved German freedom of movement, as well as assuaged the revolutionary pride of the Bolsheviks: no German troops would be shifted during the truce except those already moving, or those for whose shift orders had already been issued.[9] Trotsky proclaimed this face-saving formula as a great victory. It was, he added, also a favor to the Western Allies, notwithstanding their ingratitude in refusing to recognize the Bolsheviks. The listeners (he was addressing the Congress of the Peasants' Soviets) may have been taken in by such boasts, but it is unlikely he believed them himself.

The actual peace negotiations began in Brest Litovsk on December 9 and they were to be concluded with an agreement, if such it can be called, on March 3, 1918.

By nineteenth century standards Brest Litovsk was a harsh treaty. Through its provisions Russia was to lose its Baltic, Polish, and Ukrainian regions. Had not the German collapse and the future course of events nullified the treaty, Russia would have reverted to the status of a second-rate power deprived of its most advanced and fertile provinces, pushed back eastward to where the Empire of the Tsars had been in the middle of

[8] I. Deutscher, *The Prophet Armed, Trotsky 1879–1921*, New York, 1954, p. 352.

[9] As was usual with the German armies nominally headed by royal personages, the chief of staff, in this case Hoffmann, was the actual leader.

the seventeenth century. But by our recent and lamentable international standards, the conditions dictated to the Bolsheviks by Germany (for, of course, the other Central Powers had to follow Germany's lead) do not appear so drastic. Russia had been thoroughly defeated. Germany did not insist upon an unconditional surrender. In the negotiations themselves the victors, as we shall see, displayed an amazing patience and tolerance, at least by comparison with 1940 and 1945. That huge areas were detached from Russia could be claimed by the Germans to be in accordance with the Bolsheviks' oft-proclaimed principle of national self-determination, for these were inhabited predominantly by the Poles, Ukrainians, Lithuanians, Finns, and other non-Russian inhabitants of "the prisonhouse of nationalities," as Lenin had called the Russian Empire. It is amazing how, as if touched by a magic wand, the Bolshevik negotiators at Brest Litovsk turned from "internationalists" into good Russian nationalists. One of them, Pokrovsky, when shown the first (not the eventual and more extreme) set of Germany's territorial demands, broke out in tears: eighteen provinces were to be torn from his country. It was an attitude more befitting a Tsarist or Kadet statesman than an old revolutionary and the leading Marxian historian.

German negotiators put up with what today appears as rather provocative behavior on the part of the representatives of a defeated country. Thus the Russians obviously protracted the negotiations, hoping to the last that they would be interrupted by the news of a revolution in Vienna and Berlin. Some of their demands would strain the patience of the most courteous and affable diplomat. Could the negotiations be delayed so that the chief of the Russian delegation could go to Vienna "to confer with the Austrian workers?" Should not they be shifted from Brest, headquarters of the German command, to a neutral place like Stockholm? The impish Radek, taken along by Trotsky as an alleged expert on Polish affairs, aroused the fury of Hoffmann by presuming to speak on behalf of the Polish soldiers serving in the German army. Thus spoke the Bolsheviks when defeated and desperately in need of peace. How would they behave as victors?

The Germans put up with this behavior of the defeated enemy for several reasons. Their diplomats and generals were still a different species from their successors under Hitler, and at times they were simply astounded by their protagonists' gall. But more important were other considerations. The Bolsheviks' very weakness was their main asset. What if their regime should be overthrown and replaced by one bent upon continuing the war? To be sure that would mean an uninterrupted victorious march of the German armies. But then the vast spaces of Russia would simply eat up the soldiers needed desperately for the Western front. Also, the Central Powers would be denied the food and other provisions they hoped to obtain from a peaceful Ukraine. The Germans still thought, though their doubts were growing rapidly, that the Bolshevik government was their best bet for Russia.

In retrospect, it is doubtful that the Russians' delaying tactics and impudence did them much good. Lenin was almost alone in his conviction that a peace, even a very bad peace, should be signed right away. The hope for an early revolution in Germany was receding rapidly in his mind. At moments this hope returned. On January 21 he heard the rumor that a workers' soviet headed by Liebknecht had been organized in Berlin and he was ready to broadcast the joyful news to all Russia.[10] But the inevitable disillusionments in the wake of such false news would strengthen his determination that illusions and mirages had to be given up. Yes, they were going to sign a shameful peace, and not with the German workers but with the Kaiser.

The diplomatic duel in the grimy Russian provincial town has always fascinated writers who like to depict apocalyptic confrontations. What a contrast between the old world drawing to its inevitable doom and the new one springing into existence; between militarism and aristocracy and the proletarian power; between the elegant foreign ministers— Austrian Count Czernin and German Baron von Kühlmann—and those uncouth Russian Socialists! In fact not one but two dying worlds were at the conference table in Brest Litovsk: the world of privilege and the world of revolution. Both would be destroyed by the twentieth century state. The Kühlmanns and Czernins would lose their offices and privileges, but their Russian opposite numbers, Kamenev, Yoffe, Sokolnikov, Trotsky, and others like them would be destroyed much more literally by the Soviet state. And in a sense these men, highly educated, still partly in the cosmopolitan and humanitarian tradition of nineteenth century Social Democracy, were perhaps closer to the German and Austrian aristocrats than to their successors in Stalin's Russia.[11]

But the drama and personalities of Brest Litovsk could not obscure the main dilemma facing the Soviet state: was it going to accept a harsh peace or not? As the negotiations dragged on, the Germans' price for peace was going to go up. If they were going to be broken off, the Germans would resume military action. The dilemma was most cruel for Lenin, for he could not be comforted by any of the illusions that many of the Bolshevik leaders still held. Some of them had the fantastic notion that they could reject the peace and then alone embark upon a revolutionary war, which soon

---

[10] Works, Vol. 26, p. 464.

[11] For purely ornamental reasons the Russian delegation originally included a Left Socialist Revolutionary, a worker, a soldier, and a peasant. The peasant had been recruited at the last moment. Not until the delegation was on its way to the Petrograd station was it realized that there was no spokesman for the peasant masses among the people's representatives. Hurriedly a typical peasant was picked up from the street and persuaded to go for the ride. John W. Wheeler Bennett, The Forgotten Peace, New York, 1939, p. 86.

would lead to a revolt among the German army. Others groped for a renewal of alliance with the Western Powers and their help in warding off
the Germans. As a prudent statesman Lenin did not fail to investigate any
and all possibilities of getting out of the impasse. He studied closely the
possibility of what remained of the Russian army fighting in the case of a
renewal of hostilities. The old army represented a threat but not to the
enemy. The sooner it was disbanded the better. He and Trotsky talked
with the Western diplomatic representatives, who of course urged Russia
to stay in the war, but what could they offer in the way of help except
promises of money and supplies?

On December 23 Lenin began a six-day vacation in Finland. On his
return his mind was made up: peace had to be made on any conditions.
But he was unable as yet to have his position accepted by the Central
Committee, and this time his opponents had the rank and file of the Party
behind them. How could the Bolsheviks, in view of all their previous
promises and pledges, not only sign a separate treaty, but one that would
abandon to the enemy one third of Russia's population? If Poland, the
Ukraine, and the other areas in question were abandoned, would other
non-Russian areas such as the Caucasus remain in the Bolshevik state?
And how long could the Bolshevik regime hope to survive, after Germany
had her hands free to deal a crushing blow to France and England and
could again turn her attention to the East? In Bolshevik circles and among
their allies, the Left Socialist Revolutionaries, the most popular position
was one in favor of conducting a revolutionary war. It was a cry in effect
for a suicide of the new regime and the country. The Russian army, Lenin
tried to argue, was not even capable of conducting a retreat: there were
not enough horses to pull out the artillery and supplies. Yet the Moscow
Bolsheviks, to take one of the many examples, demanded an immediate
end of the negotiations with the "German bandits." Bukharin assumed the
leadership of the new deviation, the Left Bolsheviks, who cried for a suicidal war. Those who saw the futility of such a step found themselves attracted to the compromise solution of Trotsky: "neither war nor peace."
Russia would refuse to sign a degrading peace, but she would declare that
she also refused to continue fighting. Let the Germans advance if they
dared; their army would soon become demoralized and their soldiers
would join with their Russian brothers. A sober judgment on this position
was delivered by Stalin, who thereby no doubt increased his stature in
Lenin's eyes: "The position of Comrade Trotsky represents no policy at
all. . . . In October we talked about the sacred revolutionary war, because we were promised [12] that one word, 'peace', would bring about a
revolution in the West. But that has not come to pass." [13] Gestures and
slogans were this time unavailing, argued Lenin and those around him;

[12] A typical circumlocution of Stalin: ". . . the Bolsheviks promised that . . ."
[13] The Protocols of the Central Committee August 1917–February 1918, p. 171.

but their logic could not overcome the opposition. At a meeting of the Party dignitaries on January 8 Lenin's position secured 15 votes, the "neither peace nor war" formula of Trotsky 16, and Bukharin's foolhardy proposal received a majority, 32 votes.

Lenin knew how to be unyielding; he also knew when necessary how to compromise and effect a strategic retreat. Let Trotsky go back to Brest Litovsk and try to protract the negotiations. Maybe something *would* happen in Germany and Austria. If everything else failed, he agreed that his brilliant second-in-command should try his "neither war nor peace" formula. Personally, Lenin had no doubt that the only result would be even harsher terms by the Germans, and that they would not be embarrassed in the slightest by this diplomatic improvisation of Trotsky. But he exacted from the latter a promise that should his policy fail he would no longer oppose the conclusion of peace on any terms. Lenin still could smile and joke even in the midst of the terrible decisions and sacrifices he was called upon to make. The additional territorial losses he envisaged as the result of rejecting an immediate peace could be compensated, he said, by the conclusion of a peace with Trotsky. Perhaps Lenin himself would not have made a bad diplomat.

The willingness to temporize on the issue of peace was connected with another grave decision that faced the Bolsheviks: what to do about the Constituent Assembly, which finally was to meet in January?

Finally! From the beginning of the Russian revolutionary movement the summoning of the representatives of the Russian people had been the dream of the liberals and radicals alike; the postulate in the struggle for which countless revolutionaries had gone to the scaffold and into exile. It was to be a freely elected assembly of *all* the Russian people, unlike the Dumas with their limited franchise or the soviets with their special constituency. Democratically elected representatives would meet and decide the fate of Russia.

After their October *coup* the Bolsheviks—who remembers it now?—proclaimed their regime but a "provisional Workers' and Peasants' government until the meeting of the Constituent Assembly." Elections to this sovereign body began to take place during the first days of their power. Because of the vastness of the country and the general chaos elections were protracted over a long period of time. In some districts they never took place. Yet in the end the masses—and this time this word does not need quotation marks—had spoken their mind: more than forty million votes had been cast; of them less than ten million, less than one fourth, were cast for the Bolsheviks.

Only a complete idiot would have supposed that on the appointed day Lenin would solemnly greet the representatives of the people of Russia, ask them for a vote of confidence in the Council of Commissars, and failing that, would turn over power to the Constituent Assembly. But what exactly to do about the Constituent Assembly was a question that taxed Bolshevik ingenuity from the first days of the elections, when it became obvious that they would be in a minority. "Fix" the election? The Bolsheviks were far from having the administrative machinery of a full-blown totalitarian state. In some districts indeed "men with rifles" could terrorize the electors, but in the vast expanses of rural Russia there were hardly any Bolsheviks to put down the "hostile class elements." Occasionally in the villages the Bolsheviks themselves were subject to coercion and chicanery. The Assembly, it was obvious, was going to be dominated by the peasants' party, the Socialist Revolutionaries, who had garnered upward of 16 million votes. Again it was too early to proclaim this Socialist party as "enemies of the people." Not to let the wretched Assembly meet at all? Embarrassing and possibly dangerous.

On November 29 the Bolshevik Central Committee considered the bothersome question. It was decided to delay the meeting of the Assembly and to educate the "masses" as to the dangerous elements within it. Thus the Kadets had got two million votes and might possibly play a dangerous role in stimulating the sluggish Socialist Revolutionaries into a vigorous anti-Bolshevik position. It was coveniently discovered that the Kadets "were a party of the enemies of the people." Their leaders and delegates to the Assembly were ordered arrested. The Bolshevik press began a campaign of intimidation: let the enemies remember the fate of the anti-Bolshevik general Dukhonin (he was lynched).

At the same time the Bolsheviks managed to consummate a split within the ranks of the majority party. The Left Socialist Revolutionaries, long their fellow travelers, concluded a formal alliance sealed by the appointment of some of them to the Council of Commissars. They were to prove most bothersome allies, but for the moment Lenin could claim that the preponderance of the Socialist Revolutionaries in the Assembly was secured under false pretenses: had the class-conscious peasants realized the situation they would have voted for the Left rather than the Right Socialist Revolutionaries.

On January 5 the only (everything considered) freely elected representative assembly in the history of the Russian people met. Its proponents were grimly warned: "Every attempt . . . of any institution to grab . . . functions of the state power will be treated as a counterrevolutionary attempt." More specific was a Bolshevik functionary who was asked what would happen if the partisans of the Assembly were to demonstrate against the Bolsheviks: "First we shall try to dissuade them, then we shall shoot." [14]

Those were not idle words. Petrograd on the day of the Assembly looked like a city under siege. Again specially trustworthy soldiers' and

[14] V. L. Bonch-Bruevich, *op. cit.*, p. 127.

sailors' detachments guarded the strategic points. Bolshevik Uritsky, head of the Petrograd *Cheka* (the Bolshevik secret police) was the master of ceremonies. The Tauride Palace, where the people's representatives were to meet, was in the charge of 200 sailors, headed by the notorious Zheleznyakov. Officially an Anarchist, Zheleznyakov was in fact the head of an armed gang of hooligans who robbed and kidnaped inhabitants of Petrograd. A few weeks later the Bolsheviks themselves had to disarm Zheleznyakov's band and send its leader to a Civil War front, where he died a glorious death (his brother and co-leader of the gang died less gloriously resisting an arrest). But for the moment he was an ideal watchdog over the Assembly. If "incidents" were to occur they could always be blamed on the Anarchists.

Lenin himself deigned to appear at the first and only session. His arrival was accompanied by a characteristic incident. He was greeted by Uritsky, who was in a state of shock. The head of the Petrograd Bolshevik organization had just been dragged by bandits out of his carriage and, in broad daylight, stripped of his fur coat and money. Lenin's reaction was again typical: "He was both pained and amused." Pained that banditry should rule in Petrograd, amused no doubt that the "boys" should perform this act of summary class justice over a notable with a fur coat. Poor Uritsky soon had another reason for worry: "Who is responsible for order in the Tauride Palace?" said Vladimir Ilyich. "I, Uritsky," said our old comrade, hitting himself on the chest. "Permit me to tell you . . . somebody here stole a revolver from my overcoat pocket." [15] Uritsky did not appreciate the humor of the situation. And nobody thought of asking Lenin why he left the gun in the overcoat when he took it off.

The Assembly that met under such promising circumstances turned out as had been expected. When the oldest delegate in the immemorial parliamentary tradition attempted to deliver the appropriate (and undoubtedly long) opening remarks, Sverdlov, the Bolshevik president, pushed him aside. "What business do you have here?" he said to the old man (he was a majority Socialist Revolutionary). As expected, the peasant party's leader, Chernov, was elected president of the Assembly over the Bolshevik and Left Socialist Revolutionary candidates. "Chernov . . . ," the Bolshevik witness continued unfeelingly, "began to talk so lengthily and tearfully that it was obvious there would be no end to his fine oratory." The impatient sailors in the gallery amused themselves by aiming their guns at the orator's head. Lenin dispatched an emissary to remind them that the members of the Constituent Assembly enjoyed immunity! The sailors sullenly promised to behave: "Well, all right. If one can't, one can't. . . . But we are fed up with this Chernov. Is he a 'gentleman' of some sort?" After creating an impossible cacophony during their opponents' speeches the

[15] *Ibid.*, p. 137.

Bolshevik delegates walked out. Brave Zheleznyakov was instructed not to let the Assembly meet again the next day. To forestall such a ruse the remaining delegates decided to stay at their battle posts—not to leave the premises of the Tauride Palace. But at four o'clock in the morning Zheleznyakov banged his fist on the president's table and shouted at Chernov: "We are tired. We cannot protect [!!!] you any longer. Close this meeting." After a hurried proclamation of a new law (the Assembly had been under the illusion that it was legislating for Russia all this time) Chernov complied. The only democratically elected assembly in Russian history dispersed, never to come back.

"How sad . . ." wrote Lenin of his participation in the historic meeting, "to be transposed from a society of living people into a company of corpses, to smell the air of the morgue, to hear again those 'Socialist' mummies . . . Chernov and Tseretelli. . . ." [16] What infuriated Lenin most was the conciliatory tone of those "people from the other world" (the title of the article written the very night of the Constituent Assembly). Chernov had said in soothing tones that the opposition did not plan a civil war, that they would not sabotage the Bolsheviks' work. Confessions of weakness and pleas for conciliation by his opponents usually succeeded in earning Lenin's contempt. The Bolsheviks agreed to have the Assembly meet because, to put it bluntly, they were scared of the consequences of the as yet most open and drastic violation of their democratic professions. They were going to probe the public sentiment, and they found out that their fears had been vain. Apart from a noisy demonstration in the streets of Petrograd no force appeared to support the representatives of the Russian people. The Assembly was "officially" dissolved by the Central Executive Committee of the Congress of Soviets, and nobody but a pedant would ask how the supreme sovereign legislative body of the Russian republic could be dissolved by a more or less extralegal institution. "It is clear . . ." said the dissolving decree in a fine example of the Bolshevik double talk (it was not clear at all) "that the Constituent Assembly . . . could thus be but a cover-up for the struggle of the counterrevolutionaries to overthrow the Soviet power."

It is often pointed out in the obituaries of the Constituent Assembly that the Bolsheviks' argument against it, while completely mendacious from the legal and moral points of view, was a fairly sound one politically. The peasant masses voting in droves for the Socialist Revolutionaries were often unaware of the split within the party. The lack of a violent public reaction to the dissolution of the Assembly shows that the "masses" in general did not care about its fate. The Bolsheviks were strong where it counted: in the big cities, among the sailors and soldiers. But the fate of the Assembly demonstrates among other things the rapid erosion of any

<hr />

[16] *Works,* Vol. 26, p. 392.

lingering democratic feelings among Lenin's followers. There were no prominent Bolsheviks in January, as there had been in October and November, who would argue for a broad Socialist coalition. One-party government (for no one could assume that it was changed by the inclusion of a few Left Socialist Revolutionary fellow travelers) became the accepted and unquestioned norm. And the main justification was the deplorable weakness of the leaders of the majority Socialist Revolutionaries. Were those the same people who for decades had disrupted the Tsar's Empire with their terror? Now with sixteen million votes behind them they meekly disbanded and went home with barely a shot being fired. But the destruction of this democratic Assembly was to have more serious consequences for the Bolsheviks than it seemed at first. It was to feed the flames of the Civil War. And it set a precedent for the disregard of the will of the majority within the Bolshevik Party itself.

The impact of the Bolsheviks' act of force was also bound to be felt at Brest Litovsk, where Trotsky after his "treaty" with Lenin returned at the head of the Russian delegation on January 17. The Bolsheviks' claim to be the legitimate representatives of the peoples of Russia now appeared more fraudulent than ever before. They were ruling through sheer force and this force, adequate to suppress the old dodderers and windbags of the Constituent Assembly, would be like nothing compared to the awesome might of the German army. Also much lustre was stripped from Trotsky's impassioned oratory when he presumed to speak on behalf of the oppressed masses everywhere, of the rights of self-determination, of democracy, and similar matters. It was a fine thing for Trotsky to worry about oppression of the Irish and the Indians. How about the Russians?

If the Bolsheviks thought that they could prolong their discussions and discourses indefinitely they were in for a rude surprise this time. The German negotiators were under strong pressure from home to bring back an agreement or else to terminate the armistice. The most insistent voice on their part was not that of courteous and diplomatic von Kühlmann, the foreign minister, but of General Hoffmann. The latter, as he put it with scant regard for constitutional proprieties, represented the Imperial Army [17] and he was fed up with the elegant and time-consuming diplomatic posturings of his civilian colleagues. Hoffmann came to despise the Bolsheviks and he was eager for an excuse to launch his armies against them. To his military mind all the talk about a peace without annexations and indemnities was so much rubbish. The Bolsheviks were dragging out the negotiations while they were trying to subvert the soldiers. It was time to teach those people a lesson.

The changed atmosphere was immediately evident in the injection of

[17] Trotsky, ever alert and eager for a digression, enquired whether the German army was independent of the government, which led to some embarrassed explanations by von Kühlmann.

the Ukrainian issue: some time earlier the Ukrainian legislature, the *Rada* (Council) proclaimed the independence of the Ukraine and sent its own delegates to Brest Litovsk. At that time (December 28, 1917) Trotsky, much as this secession from Russia must have pained him, read a pious declaration that the Russian delegation "in full agreement with the principle of granting every nationality the right of self-determination, including that of secession, has nothing against the participation of the Ukrainian delegation in the peace negotiations." Since then the Bolsheviks had put their own interpretation upon this right of self-determination: detachments of the Red Guards entered the Ukraine, chased out the nationalist and moderately Socialist Ukrainian government, and were establishing the Ukrainian Soviet Republic.

Trotsky's delegation now included two Bolshevik members of this new allegedly Ukrainian regime. One of them was a Russian and while the other had an undoubtedly Ukrainian name, Shahray, it was, under the circumstances, a most unfortunate one. Translated literally it means scoundrel, rogue, or cheat! Undaunted, Trotsky now proclaimed that the representatives of the *Rada* had really no business at Brest Litovsk. The Ukraine had a new government and it was in a free brotherly agreement with the Russian Bolshevik authorities. Trotsky could not help indulging in his famous sarcasm at the expense of the unfortunate representatives of the *Rada*. The territory they represented was limited to the rooms assigned to them at Brest Litovsk, he said, unmindful that a few German military units could drastically change this picture.

This time the Bolsheviks were paid back in their own coin. A young Ukrainian nationalist, Lubynsky, replied to Trotsky in a language which was as yet new to diplomatic conferences:

> The Bolshevik regime has proclaimed the principle of self-determination only to fight more resolutely against the introduction of this principle into life. The government of the Bolsheviks which is chasing out the Constituent Assembly, this government which is based upon the bayonets of the mercenary soldiers, will never adopt the just principle of self-determination, because it knows that not only regions like the Ukraine, Don, Caucasus and others don't recognize it as the legitimate government . . . but the Russian people as well.[18]

The Bolsheviks, continued the young orator, not only invade with hired mercenaries, they "close down newspapers, break up congresses of the nationalities, arrest and shoot political leaders. . . . Well-known Socialists, veteran revolutionaries are proclaimed by them to be agents of the *bourgeoisie* and counterrevolutionaries." *His* Ukrainian government was the legitimate one as shown by the elections to the Constituent Assembly in which in the Ukrainian districts the Bolshevik list received less than 10

[18] *The Peace Negotiations in Brest Litovsk* (Protocols of the sessions), Moscow, 1920, Vol. 1, p. 152.

per cent of the votes. The Ukrainian Bolshevik regime was a fraud and imposture. What was the principle behind the Bolsheviks' demagoguery? It was as the French proverb has it: "Slander, calumniate, some of it will always stick."

Trotsky, the observers agree, was most uncomfortable during this peroration. Nothing in the feeble and tearful accusations of the Martovs and Chernovs had come up to this standard of violence. Much as he believed in the justice of his cause, he was too intelligent a man not to realize the peculiar interpretation the Bolsheviks were already putting upon the principle of national self-determination. He tried to cover up his discomfiture by ironically thanking the chairman for not interrupting the Ukrainian's unseemly oratory. All the speakers have perfect freedom of speech, said the chairman.

The Ukrainian nationalists were as yet not ready to be cast off on the "rubbish heap of history." The *Rada,* recognized by the Central Powers as the legitimate government, signed a separate peace with them, thus sanctioning the separation from Russia of this vast and fertile country. Soon the German armies would chase out the Bolsheviks who represented themselves as the Ukrainian government and restore the nationalists. The Ukrainian gambit was repeated by Trotsky, but this time without much assurance, in the case of Poland. Again two Bolsheviks claiming to be "the voice of the Polish nation" addressed a series of demands to the Central Powers, demanding an evacuation of Poland by their armies. Time was drawing short for such performances. Nobody even sought to comment on the almost humorously brazen statement of Radek and his Polish colleague: "We announce solemnly on behalf of the Polish proletariat that up to now only revolutionary Russia has guarded the real interests and freedom of the Polish nation and were Poland not occupied she would already enjoy the same freedom as the other nations of Russia." In two years' time the Red Army would try to bring this freedom to Poland.

But the time for such games had passed: either the Bolsheviks were going to sign a debilitating and shameful peace or they had to break off the negotiations. Trotsky may have hurried things a bit: certainly the *civilians* on the German side were prepared to negotiate longer; they had none of the bullheaded Hoffmann's confidence that a renewal of hostilities would be like a parade march for the German army. But Trotsky was eager to produce his secret weapon, the "neither war nor peace" formula.

On January 28 he launched into his famous tirade:

> We no longer desire to participate in this purely imperialist war, where the requirements of the exploiting classes are paid for in human blood. . . . In the expectation . . . of this near moment when the oppressed working classes of all nations will, as it happened in Russia, take power in their own hands, we take our army and nation out of

war. . . . The governments of Germany and Austria want to rule nations and lands by the right of conquest. Let them do it openly.[19]

The Russian government, he announced on its behalf, has concluded the war without signing the peace. It was ordering a full demobilization.

It was a splendid gesture and the Germans were taken aback. It was against all the accepted rules of diplomacy and, again, it is a reminder of how far we are from the spirit of those times, that this declaration which would have brought forth laughter from any of the World War II commanders and negotiators should really have embarrassed the representatives of the German Empire. The Russian delegates warmly congratulated themselves on how they had tricked all those pompous counts, field marshals, and generals. It was a hollow and short-lived triumph. As Stalin had observed, "Trotsky's policy was no policy at all."

With the Russian delegation back in Petrograd the illusion of a great Bolshevik *coup* at Brest Litovsk was allowed to linger but a few days. But on February 16 [20] this exultation was brought to an abrupt end: the Germans were going to terminate the armistice and begin an offensive next day.

Lenin's insistence on the immediate signing of peace now became ferocious. Seldom were his statesmanship and balance shown to better advantage than when he faced the incredibly difficult task of persuading the majority of his colleagues on the Central Committee, on the Executive Committee of the Soviets, and in the Party as a whole to sign this peace, harsh and, as it appeared to everybody but him, fatal for the Soviet power. A lesser man would not have resisted a temptation to say: "I told you so." A weaker man would have gone along with the majority of Bolsheviks, and also this time of the nation, which cried for fighting back the Germans. Sternly and insistently, but without letting personal bitterness intrude into his speeches, Lenin fought to convert the others to his point of view: beg the Germans to renew negotiations, and sign a peace on whatever conditions they submit. He did not choose to ridicule the proponents of the revolutionary war in the manner of Stalin, who said, alas too truthfully, that after five minutes of mass fire the Russians would not have a single soldier left at the front.[21] Lenin worked patiently to beat some realism into the heads of his now quite unbalanced colleagues: "One does not joke with war." If you want a revolutionary war you must stop demobilization (and he knew that they knew that was impossible). Otherwise you sign whatever peace is thrust in front of you.

---

[19] *Ibid.*, pp. 207–8.

[20] On February 1 Western style the Russian calendar jumped thirteen days to conform with the Western usage, a most merciful reform by the Bolshevik regime, and one which, like their simplification of the Russian spelling, even the greatest Western reactionary must applaud.

[21] *Protocols of the Central Committee* . . . , p. 202.

This educational work was proceeding under conditions of extreme danger. The German armies were marching as of February 17 and they were encountering no resistance whatsoever. It was at the height of the famous Russian winter, which had defeated Napoleon and was to help stop Hitler, but this time there was no army to take advantage of the weather. It would have been a simple thing, so it seems, to blow up railways and thus to slow down the German army, which depended on them in those days before mass mechanized transport. But as Lenin had forecast, the Russian soldiers were not even capable of retreating. Whole regiments were being taken prisoner by a handful of German soldiers.

On February 18 he succeeded in getting a Central Committee vote that *could* be interpreted as a mandate to ask the Germans for an immediate conclusion of peace.[22] But even this somewhat contrived authorization appeared at first to come too late. The enemy appeared in no hurry to answer the plea for a renewal of negotiations. The German armies kept on the march.

"Neither peace nor war" now appeared to assume a macabre and unexpected meaning. Defeat and the destruction of the Bolshevik power could be a matter of days. Lenin saw imposed upon him the specter of fighting a "revolutionary war" but without an army. The only weapon left was the weapon of rhetoric. It proved sufficient to stop the demoralized troops of Kornilov and Krasnov, but would it save Petrograd from the disciplined Germans?

On February 21 the Council of the People's Commissars issued a manifesto which in its phraseology already forecasts those appeals to Russian patriotism that Stalin and his regime were to issue in the desperate days of 1941: "The Socialist *Fatherland* is in danger." Not the Revolution, not the Soviet government, but the Fatherland. But the language of class warfare was, unlike 1941, still very much in evidence.

> In order to save our country . . . from new war suffering, . . .we told the Germans about our willingness to sign their conditions for peace . . . but until now there has been no answer . . . The German government . . . evidently wants no peace. . . . Fulfilling the command of the capitalists of all the countries German militarism wants to choke Russian and Ukrainian workers and peasants, return land to the landlords, factories to the bankers, power to the monarchy . . .

The language is one of panic to the point of incoherence("choke the workers . . . return factories to the bankers"). The government is announcing both its desperate willingness to sign peace with the Germans and the conviction that the latter want to overthrow the Bolsheviks. The

[22] Seven voted for his motion, five against. But Dzerzhinsky announced his solidarity with the five and one other member refrained from voting. Thus in fact it was a tie vote. Trotsky voted for the motion only because Lenin reminded him of his pledge in the case his "neither war nor peace" formula would fail.

manifesto calls for national unity, at the same time stipulating that special detachments are to be formed to construct trenches. "In those detachments should be included all the members of the *bourgeoisie* capable of work, men and women. . . . Those who resist are to be shot on the spot." Other parts of the appeal—shoot the German agents, destroy the railway stock and equipment—were bound under the circumstances only to increase chaos and panic. Who were, for instance, the "counterrevolutionary elements"? (Also to be shot on the spot.) Those who argued for peace or those who argued against it? [23] Could Petrograd be saved by digging trenches around it? Weren't the Red Guard units told to guard the bourgeois labor battalions more needed at the front, provided there still was such a thing? The document bespeaks the utter confusion and panic of the Bolshevik regime.

Lenin, as Trotsky was to reminisce, was pleased with the tone of the manifesto (Trotsky claims to have drafted it himself), especially by its appeal to the national sentiment that displeased some doctrinairies: "This shows at once the change of 180 degrees from our defeatism to the defense of the Fatherland." [24] It is, however, unlikely that he was as composed as Trotsky pictures him to have been. Allegedly he considered calmly the possibility of the Bolshevik regime withdrawing as far as the Urals; wondered whether, if he and Trotsky were killed, Bukharin and Sverdlov could take their places, and so on. But even a man of his indomitable will and optimism must have realized that as yet the Bolshevik regime could not survive without its strongholds of Moscow and Petrograd. And this was the moment when his opinion of Bukharin's practical and political abilities was at its lowest.

That he viewed the situation desperately is best seen in his temporary willingness to explore collaboration with the Western Allies. This could have come only out of Lenin's extreme distress, for he viewed the prospect of an Anglo-French victory as a much greater danger to the cause of the Revolution than that of Germany.[25] Now during those frantic few days he at least considered the offers of the Allies' agents to help if Russia stayed in the war.

At the meeting of the Central Committee of February 22 (it was now meeting almost continuously) these proposals were met, however, with a

[23] Quotations (underlined as in the original) from Bonch-Bruevich, *op. cit.*, pp. 140–41.

[24] L. Trotsky, *Lenin*, New York, 1925, p. 137.

[25] This, of course, was not based on any sympathy for Imperial Germany or, to claim which would be the height of absurdity, on any gratitude for the Germans' financial help to the Bolshevik cause. Germany, he believed correctly, was much closer to a Socialist revolution than either France or England, and her Socialist Party much more susceptible to an evolution on the Bolshevik pattern. There was an unspoken, perhaps an unconscious premise in that conviction that the democratic institutions of France and England were more solid and a greater barrier to the spread of communism than those of the Kaiser's Germany.

chorus of indignation and doctrinaire disapproval. How inappropriate the term "cynical" is as yet in describing the mentality of the Bolshevik leaders is best illustrated by the position of Bukharin. At the same time that he was ready to embark upon a sacred revolutionary war with the enemy he resolutely combated seeking any help from France and England. This would mean seeking help from the imperialists, would turn Russia into an Anglo-French colony. Another notable exclaimed perspicaciously but a bit prematurely: "Having seized power we have forgotten about the world revolution." All that while the German armies were marching without meeting any resistance. Lenin in his note to the Committee struck the right tone for soothing the foolish ideological indignation of his comrades: "Please add my vote to those who are in favor of receiving food and weapons from the Anglo-French imperialist robbers." Thus he enunciated the beginning of and the enduring principle of Soviet foreign policy.

The rather foolish Frenchman Jacques Sadoul,[26] who was told the same day by Trotsky that the Bolsheviks had condescended to accept the Allied help, exploded with a premature joy: "A beautiful day. I am glad, overjoyed . . ." he wrote in his diary elegantly composed in the form of letters addressed to his French protector and fellow Socialist, Albert Thomas. "France will never know what she owes me. . . . I have been almost the whole day with Trotsky . . ."[27] Russia would stay in the war. She wanted the French military mission (still cooling its heels in Petrograd) to organize her army. Sadoul concluded idiotically: "In any case if they feel us to be seriously and in good faith on their side the Bolsheviks will regain confidence and will re-enter the struggle." As to the first part of this statement, Lenin's note offers the best commentary. As to the second, M. Sadoul was one of the world's greatest optimists: how could a few Allied military specialists reorganize an army that did not exist? Some months later, when the Bolsheviks had started building the Red Army, the question of their fighting modern and regular troops would at least pass out of the realm of fantasy. For the moment it was out of the question.

This was stated by Lenin on the very next day. The Germans had just sent back their reply: forty-eight hours were given to the Russians to agree, three days only would be allowed for the new negotiations. To that ultimatum Lenin added his own: either the Central Committee agreed to the German conditions or he would leave it and with it the government. "The policy of the revolutionary phrase [demagoguery] has ended." February 23, 1918, was the closest he ever came to being repudiated by his own followers. A member of the Central Committee, his patience at an end, openly challenged him to resign. "We have to take power without Lenin." The invaluable Sverdlov and Stalin were the only

[26] More of him below.
[27] Jacques Sadoul, *Notes on the Bolshevik Revolution* (in French), Paris, 1920, p. 244.

ones firmly on Lenin's side. Stalin as usual put in more brutal and uncompromising words what Lenin meant: "If Petrograd is surrendered it will not be just a surrender but the rotting of the Revolution. Either a breathing spell [by signing the peace] or the destruction of the Revolution. There are no other alternatives." [28] In the voting Lenin's motion barely carried: seven votes for, four votes against, and four abstaining. Again the dissenters led by Bukharin resigned their Party and government offices. This time Lenin was reduced to begging them to stay at their posts. He tried to mollify them by promising that while submitting to the German ultimatum the preparations for a war of defense should continue. But it is clear that he would have accepted any and all of the German conditions short of the Bolsheviks' giving up power in what was left to them of the Russian territory.

He was to beg again next day: no prominent Bolshevik was willing to go to Brest Litovsk to sign his name to the shameful peace. Trotsky offered his resignation as the Commissar of Foreign Affairs. He would not go back to Brest where a short while before he so confidently had teased the Germans. Zinoviev felt he was needed in Petrograd in order to use his oratorical power to explain to the masses why the Bolsheviks had to sign. Sokolnikov argued that he also was needed at home for financial and journalistic work. Petrovsky would go, but only if another prominent Bolshevik would come along as the principal delegate. The committeemen's strained nerves led to squabbles demonstrating how those close associates in victory were beginning to hate each other in defeat. Stalin expressed his opinion that "some comrades" (Trotsky obviously among them) were always threatening to resign, expecting to be begged to stay at their posts. Uritsky shouted that Stalin the day before had wanted to throw the dissenters out of the Party altogether, now he wanted them to keep their positions and thus to sanction a policy of which they disapproved. It fell to Lenin to be the conciliator, to soften the erupting personal antagonism with a joke here and there, and to remind those hardened revolutionaries not to lose their composure. Two successive resolutions proposed by him were needed before Trotsky, his feelings somewhat soothed, decided not to publicize his resignation, at least until the treaty was signed. Many of those present, but not Lenin, were never to forgive Trotsky that at the most critical period of the Soviet state the Central Committee had to spend a considerable time in devising a formula that would least offend his vanity.

Not even his greatest enemy can deny that at this moment Lenin towered like a giant over his Bolshevik colleagues. No other man, unlike Trotsky in October, approached him in stature. Without him the Bolsheviks would have been involved in chaos and irretrievable disaster. Bukharin would lead them to fight the German military might with bare hands. Trotsky would stick to his fatuous formula. Some would be at each other's

[28] *Protocols of the Central Committee* . . . , p. 212.

throats. But in his new role as the conciliator and compromiser Lenin soothed the tension. Sokolnikov would go to sign. Trotsky was mollified. Others promised not to stir up too much agitation against the peace. His comrades' feelings were not so much on Lenin's mind as the imperative necessity of the Bolshevik high command preserving some faint appearance of unity. Without it everything would be lost.

On March 1 the Soviet delegates again reached Brest Litovsk. The delegation, led by Sokolnikov, included G. Chicherin, who had in all but name taken over the duties of the Commissar of Foreign Affairs and who with unusual skill would guide Soviet diplomacy for more than a decade. The delegates were delayed *en route*. The precipitate flight of the Russian troops had disorganized communications. Lenin had another moment of anxiety: were the negotiators on their own again refusing to sign? He wired, "It is intolerable that you should hesitate." Finally they were fetched to Brest to sign the most humiliating peace in Russia's modern history. They begged to be excused the consideration of any details of the treaty. The Russian delegation was not going to lend any assistance to maintaining the fiction that the treaty represented a free agreement. "This peace, I repeat, is dictated to us by sheer force," said Sokolnikov. The negotiators on the other side were very much pained at the Russians' refusal to adhere to the polite hypocrisy of diplomacy. Russia was free to sign the treaty or to continue the war, one of them said courteously. On March 3 the treaty was signed. Russia had lost the Ukraine, Finland, her Polish and Baltic territories. In the Caucasus she had to make territorial concessions to Turkey. The treaty placed the German sphere of occupation close to Petrograd, which on its other side was precariously close to Finland, where the Finnish Bolsheviks were being ejected by the nationalists with German help. Three centuries of Russian territorial expansion were undone. In March 1918 it took a man of unusual vision to believe that the Bolshevik rule could long survive such a treaty. Should it survive a wave of patriotic indignation of their own people, the Bolsheviks would surely be pushed aside by the Germans whenever it would become practical for this to be done. Those circumstances are stressed in the introduction to the *Protocols of the Seventh Congress* of the Bolshevik Party, which assembled on March 6, 1918. The introduction explains that the Protocols could not be published right away (they were not to be issued until 1923) "because at the time of the Brest peace our Party was compelled by the victory of German imperialism to act in its relations to Germans semilegally and even illegally." [29] At the time of the Congress the government was preparing a shift from Petrograd, where it was practically at the Germans' mercy, to

---

[29] *The Seventh Congress of the Communist Party. Protocols,* Moscow, 1923, p. 3. This, of course, was far from being the entire reason. The Protocols testify to a violent disagreement among the Bolshevik hierarchy at the time, and this in itself would have urged postponement.

Moscow. The main, the pressing business of the Congress was, of course, the peace with Germany, signed but not as yet ratified, still an object of a violent and dangerous dispute.

It is all the more astounding that Lenin found time and energy to worry about another issue, at the time seemingly academic. At his insistence the official name of the Bolshevik Party was changed. From March 8, 1918, it bears the name of the Communist Party.[30] It was not without protest that the historic name of the Russian Social Democratic Workers' Party was abandoned. From now on it was to be borne only by the sad remnants of the Mensheviks. But for Lenin the issue was neither unimportant nor unconnected with the emergency. From 1914 on he insisted that the Bolsheviks should abandon the name of Social Democrats, should discard it "like a soiled shirt," and return to the more militant traditions of Marxism expressed in the word "communist." Now it appeared not unlikely that the days of the Bolsheviks were numbered. If they should go down, it was vitally important that the Bolsheviks should leave behind them a new tradition and challenge epitomized in the fresh name. The Bolshevik Revolution might be choked to death by superior power, but it would leave behind it communism, which would be reborn on a world scale.

The composition of the Congress underlined the melancholy turn of events in the Bolsheviks' fortunes. At the previous Congress held in August, when the Bolsheviks were still far from power and their leaders were in hiding, 270 delegates were gathered in Petrograd. Now the ruling party could assemble but 69 delegates, and of 32 of them the Protocols state that their mandates and the right to vote had not been determined. It was indeed a time of great confusion with communications all over Russia in a state of disorganization and with the government obviously preparing to leave Petrograd. Many of the elected delegates clearly could not reach the capital, but it is an open question whether the ingenious Sverdlov, the Party's chief organizer, did not also manipulate things so that Lenin's position would be assured of a majority. There is little doubt that of the Party's 300,000 members the majority was opposed to the ratification of the treaty with the Germans. Bukharin and his Left Communists were continuing their campaign against the peace. In their newly established paper, the *Communist,* they constantly criticized Lenin, reminding him of his previous promises of no separate peace, taxing him with betraying the interests of the international proletariat, and demonstrating that any hope for a breathing spell through the Brest Litovsk Treaty was fallacious. The *Communist,* Lenin was to complain, should really call itself the *Polish*

---

[30] In its various versions: the Russian Communist Party, the All-Union (when the Union of the Soviet Republics was proclaimed) Communist Party; the Communist Party of the Soviet Union. At the last renaming in 1952 the parenthetical addition of "the Bolsheviks" was struck out.

Nobleman (a stock figure of derision in Russian literature because of his hopeless romanticism) for it believes with him that the "war is honorable, peace is shameful." The Left Communists, said Lenin, look at things from the viewpoint of a jingoistic nobleman, he from that of the peasant. He was quite right.

But the Left Communists counted strong and influential figures within the Party. Curiously enough, Lenin's alleged love, Inessa Armand, was one of them. Another female Bolshevik, Alexandra Kollontay, was a most impassioned advocate of the sacred revolutionary war. She pleaded at the Congress for the creation of an international revolutionary army: "Should our Soviet republic perish, others will pick up and raise our flag. Long live the revolutionary war." Outside the Party the Bolsheviks' temperamental allies, the Left Socialist Revolutionaries, were to a man for war. Rumors were rife that they contemplated a *coup*, including the imprisonment of Lenin, and setting up a government pledged to the continuation of war, headed by Bukharin.[31]

What motivated the opposition was not only patriotic indignation but a rising resentment against Lenin. This was surely the lowest point of his popularity within the Party. He was overriding the will of the majority and even those who bowed before his logic resented his methods, chafed under his continuous lectures about political realism, and begrudged him his new role of the statesman. But much of the resentment was really caused by the harsh realities of the moment and the lost illusions. Russia was impotent before German militarism. The German soldiers, among whom the Bolsheviks had sown hundreds of thousands of propaganda pamphlets, appeared unmindful of their obligations to their fellow proletarians. No soviets were springing up in Vienna or Berlin. Some Bolsheviks could still be shocked by the seamy side of governing a defeated and hungry nation. Lenin was urging, along with peace, the most draconic measures for restoring social discipline and preserving the Bolshevik power. In more specific terms, that meant the application of terror. Some Bolsheviks were bold enough to insinuate that the government, unable to stop the Germans, was venting its fury and distracting the popular mind by acts of violence directed against innocent people. Said Ryazanov, who for long was to remain the most outspoken participant in such gatherings: "He who knows what takes place in the name of the Soviet power . . . he who knows this detestable thing which happened two days ago when six entirely innocent people were shot . . . by an order signed by Trotsky . . . he will understand what is being done in the name of the party of the proletariat." Ryazanov was known as an eccentric. "We have often heard his speeches and we are accustomed to pay no attention to them," said Sverdlov. But his eruption testified how in five months some had al-

[31] Twenty years later this story will make a grisly re-appearance during the purge trials of Bukharin and others.

ready grown disillusioned with the Revolution, which had looked so momentous and promising in October.

For those Lenin offered some bitter truths. In October, he said, many had expected one triumphant march after another. They expected a speedy conclusion of the Revolution in Russia, its rapid spread to the West. Yet "Our country is a peasant country disorganized by war . . . placed in an incredibly difficult situation. We have no army and here we have to exist alongside a robber country, armed to its teeth . . . the [world] revolution will not come as speedily as we expected." The country needed a breathing spell. This spell must be used to restore discipline: "Learn to be disciplined, to introduce severe discipline, otherwise you will be under the German heel, just as you are under it now, just as unavoidably you will continue to be until the nation learns to fight, until it will create an army which will not run away, but will be capable of enduring the most extreme hardships."

Lenin mixed his warnings with diplomacy. He praised Trotsky's conduct of the negotiations and did not absolve himself from blame for the disastrous "neither peace nor war." He granted the necessity for preparing for the worst, a renewal of war. Indeed there was no certainty that even after signing the treaty the Germans would not prefer to establish a puppet government in Petrograd. He pleaded pathetically that even the five days gained by the signing of the preliminary agreement represented a great gain: time had been secured for the shift of the government. But his main point was the absolute necessity for peace; he was ready to sign, he said, a peace one hundred times as harsh as that of Brest Litovsk. Did they not remember the Tilsit peace dictated by Napoleon to Prussia? There, in addition to dismembering his enemy, Napoleon compelled the Prussians to give him their own troops to fight his other wars. "Beware that history should not bring you to that extreme form of slavery." The Communist zealots complained that by provisions of the treaty Soviet Russia would be barred from continuing propaganda in Germany and among her soldiers. Were they children or revolutionaries, asked Lenin. Of course Russia would violate such provisions of the treaty: "We have already violated it thirty or forty times."

It was an excellent speech, one of the best and most persuasive he had ever given. And it marked an era, the first and decisive step in the beginning of that transformation of communism from an internationally oriented movement to one of service to the *Russian* Soviet state. It is a situation full of paradox: the Left Communists, driven by anguish over *Russia* losing so much territory, called for a war to the finish against capitalism. We always knew, said Bukharin, that the Russian Revolution "would have to fight international capital. This moment has come." But in his apparent willingness to sacrifice vast provinces and populations Lenin is really more nationalistic than his opponents: the Soviet state, the *Russian* state must

not perish. He would still have moments of enthusiasm and passionate belief in the imminence of the world revolution for which he would be ready
to sacrifice Russian lives and resources. But March 6, 1918, marked the beginning of that policy that would eventually bear the name of socialism in
one country. In time this policy would come to mean the subjugation of
the interests of other Communist parties to that of Russia. And in due
course the whole equation, communism = the interests of the rulers of
Soviet Russia, would be challenged by the rise of Communist China. Such
was the great cycle initiated by Lenin on that day in the city that now
bears his name when he spoke still with the conviction that a world Communist revolution would come, but with the growing determination that
his Communist state had a life of its own.

His position prevailed; first the Party and then in a few days the Congress of the Soviets ratified the treaty. This body was still not purely Bolshevik; apart from the Left Socialist Revolutionaries it contained a handful of the Right Socialist Revolutionaries and Martov's followers. Thus a
substantial opposition was manifested to the ratification, though the issue
had been predetermined by the decision of the Communist Party.[32]

Brest Litovsk marked the end of the age of innocence insofar as the
Bolsheviks' attitude toward foreign affairs was concerned. Not even the
most "left" of the Left Bolsheviks would ever say again that a Communist
state needed no Commissariat of Foreign Affairs and that the world revolution would take care of the whole business of "domestic" vs. "foreign." [33]
Even earlier, the Bolsheviks had entered the primrose path of actual
negotiations with the "imperialist robbers" of the ultracapitalist powers:
Great Britain, France, and the United States. Bukharin had reportedly
cried when the Bolsheviks in the first excitement over the news of the German advance were negotiating with the Western Allies for assistance, but
such foolishness could not last. With the help of Lenin's logic it finally
dawned on the Bolsheviks that, at least for the time being, they were running a state which in the immemorial manner of other states, be they capitalist, imperialist, or what have you, had to deal with other *governments*,
and not with the workers of other countries.

The beginnings of the Soviet-Western diplomatic coexistence bear the
imprint of tragicomedy that has never ceased to be an element in the
strange intercourse of these two worlds. The official representatives of the
West in Russia were of course astounded and repelled by the turn of
events that led to October and to Brest Litovsk. By training, age, and temperament they were entirely unfit to comprehend the drama unfolding
before their eyes, still less to negotiate with those odd creatures who called

[32] The vote was: for the treaty 784; against 261; Bukharin and his Left Communists abstaining.
[33] At the Seventh Congress one delegate objected to the title the *Russian* Communist Party. A Communist, he said, knows no national distinctions.

themselves the new government of Russia. How could Sir George Buchanan, whose whole life had been spent in the dignified atmosphere of the European courts and highest society, be expected to have a diplomatic discourse with Lev Bronstein-Trotsky, whom a few months before His Britannic Majesty's authorities had interned as a dangerous radical? Or Mr. David Francis, the elderly retired American politician, who at least was no greater stranger to communism than to the dignified customs of European diplomacy exemplified by his British and French colleagues? What compounded the difficulty was, on the one hand, the fact that the Allied governments refused to recognize the Soviets and, on the other hand, the Bolsheviks' very unorthodox diplomatic moves: addressing the foreign workers over the heads of their governments, their scant regard for such age-hallowed international customs as the sanctity of foreign property, diplomatic immunity, and the like.

The necessary task of keeping some contact with the new rulers of Russia fell of necessity to the less exalted and less official representatives of the West. There was the French lawyer in uniform, Captain Jacques Sadoul, sent to Russia at the period when the Allied governments thought that their own Socialists would be more likely to find a common language with various Mensheviks, Bolsheviks, and the others than the usual diplomatic species. Sadoul was to become a Communist, but in 1918 he was simply an enthusiastic supporter of Sadoul himself, the only man, he kept repeating to the folks back home, who could sway Bolshevik Russia to the Allied cause. In His Majesty's Service was a young Scot, Bruce Lockhart, whose diplomatic activities were interwoven with a romantic affair of which, in a most un-British fashion, he gives an account in his memoirs. And there was an American, Raymond Robins, officially with the Red Cross mission, the first in the long line of the proverbial hard-headed American men of affairs who, after some initial doubts and revulsions, would decide that, yes, "You can do business with the Russians."

But in a sense all three, and there were others like them, were strangely drawn to the Bolsheviks. Their recollections are a valuable testimony to the undoubted air of romance that surrounded the first period of Soviet power. It was not all a matter of ideological proclamations and dreary sessions of the Congresses and the Central Committees. And the grisly side of the business—terror, the depredations, the savagery of the Civil War—was barely beginning. To the ideologically unsophisticated, the Bolshevik leaders were primarily men of daring and often of very considerable personal charm. They presented a startling contrast to the stereotype of the professional diplomat of the old regime, or to the fatuous lawyer or university professor who briefly succeeded him in Kerensky's period. The more cosmopolitan among them, such as Trotsky and Mme Kollontay, were more than willing to chat with foreigners, to let them in (not always truthfully) on "what was going on," or even to share with them the fascinating stories of their lives.[34] There was mutual titillation in such conversation. The Westerner could feel the thrill of talking with men whose very names aroused panic among the staid *bourgeoisie* at home. The Bolshevik experienced sly pleasure in such a frank discourse with an "imperialist agent" whose real aim was the destruction of the Soviet power.

As to the substantive side of such contacts, it is difficult to reach a conclusive verdict. The West's "man in Petrograd" was bound to feel that his government through blindness, through its hidebound adherence to the rules of the diplomatic game, and through ideological hostility was throwing away the chances of a Bolshevik-Allied collaboration. Robins and Lockhart convinced themselves that had Washington and London grasped the proffered hand of the Bolsheviks and offered help, Lenin would not have ratified the treaty of Brest Litovsk.[35] An American historian is on sounder ground when he holds such opinions "wistfully exaggerated." [36] To repeat, it is difficult to see how anything could have changed Lenin's resolution to sign a peace with the Germans, and those Bolsheviks who like Bukharin were most eager for the continuance of the war were also the most determined opponents of accepting help from the "imperialist brigands."

Why in fact did the Bolshevik leaders continue those discussions with agents of governments which, they were convinced, were bent upon their destruction? For some it was in the way of a relaxation from the cruel tasks of governing and from the maneuverings for personal power that were already beginning within the Bolshevik hierarchy. But certainly not for Lenin. Anything connected with Western political mores, with its hypocritical liberalism and parliamentarism, was for him more hateful and repellent than outright reaction and militarism. The high-sounding principles of President Wilson in which the Allies proclaimed their war aims were a constant irritant and it must have cost Lenin dearly to preserve some outward diplomacy in his discourses with the Westerners. But those contacts and conversations were a reflection of the Bolsheviks' desperate situation during and after the negotiations at Brest. Even with the

---

[34] Sadoul was very solicitous about Mme Kollontay's private life. This charming woman, daughter of a Tsarist general, contracted an incongruous "companionship" with the Bolshevik sailor Dybenko, the unruly hero of the first days of the Revolution. When Mme Kollontay looked aged and exhausted the anxious Frenchman wondered as to the cause: "Is it the burdens of office or her marriage to the ferocious Dybenko which have fatigued her so much" (Sadoul, *op. cit.*, p. 270)—a remark which does little credit to the alleged French sophistication in matters of love. Sadoul had obviously never heard the story of the Russian princess who contracted a similar union with a huge peasant from her estates. Asked by a friend whether she ever regretted her *mésalliance* she replied: "I have regretted it every day, I congratulate myself every night."

[35] Wheeler Bennett, *op. cit.*, p. 303; R. H. Bruce Lockhart, *Memoirs of a British Agent*, New York, 1933, p. 250.

[36] George Kennan, *Russia Leaves the War*, Princeton, 1956, p. 471.

treaty ratified (March 29, 1918, was the day when the ratifications were formally exchanged) there was absolutely no guarantee in the Bolsheviks' eyes that the Germans would not advance further and install a puppet regime in Petrograd or Moscow. This was, it is fair to say, a reflection of their own psychology: certainly *they* would not have hesitated because of a scrap of paper to deliver the final blow to the class enemy.

Behind this nagging worry there was a nightmare that intermittently pestered the Bolshevik potentates. By their lights it would not have been inconceivable—on the contrary, it would have been entirely logical—for the Western capitalists to conclude a peace with the German capitalists and to join in the congenial task of destroying the Bolsheviks, and in partitioning the still remaining vast areas of the Russian Empire. This frenzied fear led Lenin and his lieutenants to tolerate and even seek contacts with the West, to tantalize its agents with the possibility of Russia renewing war with the Germans, and even to hint, at times, that the Allies' intervention and landing in some remote places in the North would not be entirely unwelcome. But there was a counterfear: what if the Allies succeeded in provoking the Germans into an offensive against the Bolsheviks? Thus enticements to the West alternated with insults. When President Wilson sent a message of good will to the people of Russia, the Congress of the Soviets frostily replied ignoring the United States government and addressing the "toiling and exploited classes of the United States of North America" and expressing hope that in the United States just as in other capitalist countries, "the toiling masses . . . will throw off the yoke of capitalism." Thus as Zinoviev said exultantly, "We slapped the President of the United States in the face." [37] No such public slaps were being administered in March 1918 to the august face of Wilhelm II of Germany.

Essentially, Lenin had learned diplomacy in the hard school of Russian internal politics. When things became tough for the Bolsheviks, as in July 1917, "scoundrels Chheidze and Tseretelli" became "dear comrades," whose help was being invoked in the name of Socialist solidarity. Was there a parallel between the Mensheviks so foolishly responsive to such appeals and the Western powers? Much of the history of Soviet diplomacy has consisted in the exploration of that possibility.

The ratification of Brest Litovsk took place in Moscow, which with the arrival there of Lenin and the government on March 10 became the capital of Russia. The move was dictated by the necessities of the hour and was presumably provisional in its nature; but not even after the sounds of foreign and domestic war had died down in 1921 did the Soviet regime return to its birthplace. The departure took place under conditions of secrecy. Lights were not turned on in Vladimir Ilyich's train until it had left the station. At one of the intervening stops the government train encountered another one filled with sailors. It was a moment of real danger. The

[37] Kennan, *op. cit.*, pp. 512–13.

sailors were the same who a few days before, because of their depredations in Petrograd, had been surrounded and disarmed by government
troops. Machine guns appeared on the platforms of the government train,
directed at the wagons filled with the rebellious sailors. After some negotiations the latter agreed to surrender their weapons (their original disarming must not have been very thorough) and "agreed" with the machine guns staring them in the face to let the government train pass on to
Moscow. It was the most vivid commentary yet on Russia's capacity to
prolong war and on the task that faced the Bolshevik government.

2. The Dictator

Few people in Russia in the spring of 1918 had the time and disposition to ponder the significance of the capital being shifted to Moscow.
Two centuries before, Peter the Great left the ancient city that reminded
him of the semi-Asiatic past and customs of the country and transferred
the seat of government to the newly built capital which was to be Russia's
window on Europe, both the symbol and the tangible proof of the new
European ways he tried so despotically to impose on his subjects. Now a
group of revolutionaries was fleeing back to the depths of Russia, to the
old capital of the Grand Dukes and Tsars of Muscovy. Few would have
seen in it an augury of how important Russian communism would become, how this movement conceived in the international spirit would in
due time come to revere the awesome figures who also ruled Russia from
the Kremlin: Ivan the Great and Ivan the Terrible, "the gatherers of the
Russian lands," who would bequeath the task to the son of a Georgian
cobbler. Equally astounded in 1918 would be one told that this movement,
heavily staffed at its highest positions by Jews, Poles, and Latvians, would
become in its personnel and even more in its spirit fiercely nationalistic,
that just as the patriarchs of the Orthodox Church used to thunder against
foreign ways so from Communist Moscow, from the heirs of Marx and
Lenin, would issue edicts and anathemas against the "rootless cosmopo-
lites," the "innovators," the "imitators of the rotten West."

But no historic reflections could be afforded that spring, for the people
had to pay full attention to the needs and miseries of the hour: a catastrophic defeat, the Civil War just beginning in the South, hunger and
disorganization that were bound to grow worse with the loss by Russia
of her most fertile and some of the most industrialized regions. The manner of the transfer of the capital was in itself significant. The government
literally stole away from Petrograd. There had been fears that the Railwaymen's Union, still not fully friendly to the Bolsheviks, would block the
move, or that the Germans by dispatching a few battalions would capture
the fleeing commissars bag and baggage. Only from a nearby station was
the Moscow soviet notified about the imminent arrival of the government

of the Russian Federated Republic headed by Vladimir Ilyich Ulyanov-Lenin.[38] No guard of honor awaited him upon his arrival. As a matter of fact there were no official greeters at all. Another commentary on those times: the arrivals were appalled to discover that the Moscow Bolsheviks had just set up a "government" of their own, the Moscow Council of the People's Commissars, headed by a Left Communist, historian M. Pokrovsky. Lenin was soon to put an end to "that idiocy," as he called it.

The government (the right one) immediately faced the prosaic task of finding offices and living space. After a few days in a hotel the Chairman of the Council of the Commissars moved into the Kremlin. The huge walled enclosure, the ancient seat of the Tsars, was to become a rabbit warren of the Bolsheviks' apartments and agencies. The Kremlin was in a deplorable shape: wartime neglect and the recent fighting in Moscow had left once magnificent living quarters filthy and barely fit for occupation. But there was no alternative: even with the confiscation of the residences of the rich, space was at a premium. As a seat of government and residence of its leaders the Kremlin had another advantage in those tumultuous days: it was, in a manner of speaking, a fortress. Tomorrow, any day, the reaction, the Anarchists, or the Left Socialist Revolutionaries might raise a revolt, and as in the old times the new Tsars would have to fight from behind its walls until help came.

There was as a matter of fact a veritable battle of Moscow waged among various commissariats and agencies for the most desirable residences. Stalin's personal assistant recalls how his boss, dissatisfied with the house assigned for the Commissariat of Nationalities, occupied on his own a building assigned to the State Economic Council. Accompanied by his henchmen, the future dictator tore off the sign the Council had affixed and moved into this former residence of a rich merchant. His assistant hired some Lettish sharpshooters at two rubles a day (they were allegedly the elite guard of the Bolsheviks and one wonders how they reconciled their regular military duties with this "private" employment) to guard his conquest against the economists. But the latter managed to dislodge them, a sign that the Soviet administration was settling down to more conventional ways.[39]

Lenin's own apartment was modest enough. He and Krupskaya occupied five rooms, his one bedroom being in those hard times the legal norm for a state functionary. To the end of his days Lenin would resist the ideas of a more commodious apartment or of extensive repairs to the one he occupied. (They had to be done stealthily, while he was vacationing.) Nor would he accept valuable rugs and furniture from the Kremlin's store-

[38] This is how he now signed official documents. For the circumstances of the flight to Moscow see Bonch-Bruevich, *op. cit.*, pp. 145–55.

[39] S. Pestkovsky, "Work in the Commissariat of Nationalities," in *The Proletarian Revolution*, 1930, No. 6.

room. At a time when some Bolshevik bigwigs were beginning to enjoy the tangible rewards of power Lenin insisted upon the simple unpretentious comfort reminiscent of the conditions under which he had lived in migration. With constant food shortages admirers would insist upon sending him special packages, which he received with embarrassment, often ordering that they be distributed to hospitals or children. Thus the new ruler of Russia lived in the old residence of her Tsars, protected by a guard of Lettish sharpshooters and watched over by the *Cheka*, the Bolshevik political police, headed by a Pole.

With Moscow begins a period of Lenin's life when it is no longer incongruous to call him a dictator. His victory over the Brest Litovsk issue, though it would be fought and disputed in the months to come, carried Bolshevik power through its most perilous moments. The regime gained a few months to sink its roots, and then would be strong enough to resist all the ravages of the Civil War. Within the Party Lenin's position would never again be as violently and fundamentally challenged as in the first three months of 1918. Nobody would dare to argue again in his presence that "we can take power without Lenin." There would be opposition, at times violent, to his policies, votes taken at the Party congresses, but Lenin's word would almost invariably be decisive. Nobody in his lifetime would presume again to appear to aspire to the mantle of leadership, as in a sense Bukharin did in the debate over Brest Litovsk. Trotsky's reputation, though soon enhanced by his performance as the war leader, would never fully recover, at least in the Party circles, from his maneuvers and indecisions when Commissar of Foreign Affairs. Others would wait in the wings and dare to begin their machinations only when the leader was completely disabled. Alone among the Bolsheviks Lenin in his lifetime became a truly national figure, the object of petitions and solicitations from the simple people who somehow were already beginning to differentiate Lenin from "them," the government and its ubiquitous commissars, just as the peasant of old made a sharp distinction between the Tsar and his governors and police officials. This unavoidable cult of personality was thoroughly un-Marxist and its external manifestations, flattery, presents, and the like were strongly resisted by Lenin. But there is no doubt that he welcomed it insofar as his political power was concerned. A most modest and diffident man would have been impressed by his success in two such huge gambles as October and Brest Litovsk. The belief in one's own infallibility that warped the careers of the Napoleons and Hitlers was never Lenin's. But like other dictators he grew increasingly skeptical of the abilities and character of his closest collaborators, more and more impatient of human weaknesses and political ambitions. This characteristic of his certainly did not assume the psychopathic expression it was to find in Stalin, but it finally separated Lenin from one of the mainsprings of the Russian revolutionary tradition: the enthusiasm and camaraderie of the

young radicals' circle. Government became the art of administration and
of issuing orders. Together with disappointment in his comrades came disappointment with the people at large. The "man with a rifle" became
identified as a hooligan, the proletarian masses as consisting largely of
loafers who had to be disciplined or bribed into working for the state. He
never entirely lost his faith in the abiding virtue and innocence of the
"real proletarian" but his doubts on that score made his years of triumph
as ruler perhaps the saddest ones of his life.

The immediate task that faced Lenin, with his government granted an
uncertain reprieve, was to re-establish something Russia had not really
known since February 1917: authority. Socialism could not be built, the
country was defenseless before the foreign and domestic enemies, unless it
were equipped with those two institutions the Socialists had fondly imagined the people's Russia would never need: a standing army and a political
police.

The creation of the Red Army had been begun during the Petrograd
days. Very soon the Bolsheviks realized that their old postulate, a people's
militia instead of a professional armed force, was a dream and a dangerous one at that. Nothing remained of the old army but shattered remnants. It was a relatively good regiment that was reduced through desertions and malingering to only half of its official number of soldiers.[40] Only
the Cossack regiments had, after October, preserved any cohesion and
military discipline at all. But those hereditary warriors did not do it out of
any respect for Bolshevik power. They were eager to get back to their
homes on the Don and the Kuban where a deserter would be pointed out
and shunned by his whole village. In most cases the Bolsheviks prudently
let them go. Among the other units the trouble lay less with those dissolved
in wholesale desertions than those that stayed armed, terrorizing the cities
and countryside, everybody in fact except the enemy. As shown above,
the armed sailors especially were a veritable scourge to their fellow citizens. The Bolshevik officials of Smolny who tried half-heartedly to prevent excesses were told more than once by "the pride and glory of the
Russian Revolution" that if they would not stop bothering them they
would come armed to the seat of the Bolshevik government and "show
them." The government had to resort to forcible disarming of its own soldiers. Special Red Guard units drawn from the workers would suddenly
surround the armed rabble and compel them to turn in their weapons. A
great source of worry were the so-called nationality units: the army regiments and divisions composed exclusively of Poles, Ukrainians, or others.
Except for the famous Letts they were far from friendly to the Bolsheviks.
Lenin himself took a hand in assuring those warriors that they would be

[40] K. Eremeev, "The Beginnings of the Red Army," in *The Proletarian Revolution*,
1928, No. 4, p. 155.

generously provided with food and provisions. They were to be treated tactfully and maneuvered out of the capital and its vicinity.

It finally dawned on the Bolsheviks that they had to begin completely anew. Units were to be created out of volunteers. The Red Army, which began to be formed in December and January, was to rely primarily upon the workers. But where were the officers and noncoms to be found? Even before Trotsky's much publicized mass enlistments of military specialists, the Bolsheviks were issuing appeals to former Tsarist officers to stay on or to rejoin the colors. It was a difficult undertaking. The soldier, especially if he was from the working class, had been taught that the average officer was an enemy and traitor. Now he was once again making a reappearance, to be sure without epaulettes and under a different name (not until late in the Stalinist period was the title "general" to be restored) but still in a position of authority. The famous practice of election of officers by the enlisted men was already in January being discouraged.

The problem of the over-all military command was a ticklish one for the movement that claimed to be the continuation of the French Revolution and hence very mindful of the career made by a certain French revolutionary general. Nobody could mistake the first Soviet commander-in-chief, Ensign Krylenko, for a potential Napoleon, but to be on the safe side commanders of the military units were given commissars to watch over them, as well as over the political morale of the soldiers. The original Soviet concept of command demanded collegiate leadership at the top, again a device of very suspicious and history-minded people. Thus a three-man committee at first presided over the affairs of the Commissariat of the Army and Navy. One of them, our friend sailor Dybenko, gave a fine example of military discipline when in March he had to be imprisoned for flagrant abuse of his official position. Released on parole, Dybenko fled south accompanied by an entourage of sailors. He claimed that he was being persecuted for his political views (like his consort Mme Kollantay, he was a Left Communist) and that he would submit only to the judgment of the people who elected him (presumably other sailors!) and not to that of the envious fellow commissars.[41] Lenin was already growing sick of the collegiate principle, especially in military affairs. In March Trotsky became the new and sole commissar, and with his appointment the story of the Red Army really begins.

No organization epitomized to the revolutionary the inequities of the Tsarist regime as much as the famous Okhrana, the secret police which pursued and infiltrated the radical organizations, and at times achieved the position of a state within a state. Had anyone prophesied that within two months of its creation a Socialist government of Russia would institute its own secret political police and that it would dwarf in its activities and

---

[41] Eventually he came back, was forgiven, resumed the career of a Soviet dignitary and was not shot until Stalin's regime.

significance the Okhrana he would have been called a slanderer and reactionary. Yet not only was such an institution created, but from the beginning it was an object of special solicitude and pride on Lenin's part. Under the old regime even conservative Russians grew to dislike the activities of the Okhrana. Its dignitaries were not exactly welcome in polite society; the ministers spoke of its activities with embarrassment. Public opinion stigmatized its activities. Lenin on the contrary referred to his counterpart of the Okhrana often and with pride: "our excellent Cheka," "our brave Chekists," [42] he was wont to say in public speeches. There was a twofold reason for this praise. First, for quite a while the idea of such an institution was repugnant to many Bolsheviks, with their inherited revolutionary and Social Democratic traditions. It took this constant praise by the leader to accustom them first to the existence of the Cheka, then to the notion that membership in it was one of the most honorable and responsible duties a Communist could aspire to. Then, no doubt, this eulogy of an organization that, even to many a hardened revolutionary, was at first a regrettable necessity, undoubtedly sprang from his own psychology. It ran against all the "nice" ideas of the liberals and the Social Democrats; it embodied and epitomized the stern resolve of the proletariat to deal ruthlessly with its enemies (and with its own unworthy members) in defiance of all the childish notions of the due process of law, of tolerance, of softness, and the whole ballast of liberalism which as a young law student he had learned to hate so much. It was another stage in his never ceasing battle with the traditions of his own class, the intelligentsia, another weapon to astound and terrorize those pompous and hateful professors, lawyers, and journalists who had imagined that the revolution could be performed painlessly and in accordance with the teachings of John Stuart Mill and Tolstoy. He spoke at times as if he envisaged the Cheka and revolutionary terror of which it was the main instrument as a huge joke on the Martovs, Plekhanovs, and their ilk, those windbags of the revolution. As a young Socialist he had condemned individual terror, exemplified in his brother's attempt, seeing it as a form of heroic self-indulgence incapable of changing the course of history. But now he licensed and at times encouraged what was in fact police terror on a mass scale. Was this unaccompanied by any remorse or practical fears as to where this license of lawlessness might lead the Socialist state?

The very history of the Soviet security apparatus throws some light on this question. At first it was assumed that police functions would be handled in a routine fashion by the Commissariat of the Interior. Its collegium in October already contained two men whose names were to acquire ominous fame in the secret police: Dzerzhinsky and Unschlicht. The Commissariat had general supervision over the country's police, rebaptized, of course, into the people's militia. In fact every soviet claimed

[42] Members of the organization.

independent police powers, and like every other Soviet institution the early history of the Commissariat is absorbed in jurisdictional disputes with the local soviets and other ministries. To overcome this bureaucratic morass a special committee was set up to deal with acts of lawlessness and hooliganism in Petrograd. This was the famous "Room No. 75" in Smolny, where sat a special commission presided over by Lenin's friend Bonch-Bruevich, deputized to deal in a summary fashion with all forms of disorder (a fantastic variety to be sure) in Petrograd. On December 7, 1917, the "Extraordinary Commission to Combat Counterrevolution and Sabotage" was organized—its initials read *Cheka*—the first name of the dreaded institution which in its successive embodiments was to play an important part in Russia's history.[43]

The "extraordinary" part of the name was clearly a reassurance and, perhaps, an indication of guilt at recreating an institution running against the grain of revolutionary idealism. Another curious characteristic, even for the early days of Bolshevik power when their leadership was ethnically so varied, the *Cheka* was fairly unique in having a very high proportion of non-Russians among its personnel. Was it perhaps a reflection of what Lenin had said many years earlier to sister Anna: "Our Russians are too soft"?

Its first head was Felix Edmundovich Dzerzhinsky, a man subsequently elevated to the stature of a Communist saint, "a knight without fear or blemish" as almost every Communist writing about him feels compelled to repeat. Born into a family of Polish gentry in the Western provinces, Dzerzhinsky as a boy was hard put to decide whether he should become a Catholic priest or a revolutionary. As the latter most of his adult life was spent in jail and exile. Among the Bolsheviks to whom he came from the Polish Social Democratic Party he had the reputation of a fanatic, a man not excessively endowed with intellect, but of personal probity and great loyalty to Lenin. The latter in turn reciprocated his feelings, and though Dzerzhinsky opposed him at the time of Brest Litovsk, he kept him in the awesome office, despite frequent protestations by other Bolsheviks that he was unbalanced. It is difficult indeed to consider as completely normal a man who like Dzerzhinsky petitioned continuously the Council of the Commissars for the abolition of the death penalty while at the same time presiding over summary shootings of hundreds and thousands of people.

[43] The Communists are compulsive name changers. In the case of the political police, each rebaptism was accompanied by the asssumption (alas, never substantiated) that the successor institution would hew more to the usual legal path. Thus in 1922 the Extraordinary Commission—the *Cheka*—became the mild-sounding State Political Administration but under its initials G.P.U. (or O.G.P.U.) it acquired an even more sinister fame than its predecessor. Nor was "socialist legality" better served by the N.K.V.D. and the M.G.B. We are now in the era of K.G.B., the Committee of State Security, and its chief, while no longer a Beria or Yezhov, is still likely to be a man of great importance.

The *Cheka* began with modest instructions and powers. It was envisaged that one of its most severe sanctions would be to deprive the guilty of their ration cards. But soon Lenin's urgings that the "speculators and counterrevolutionaries be shot on the spot" had their effect. At the time of the armistice with Germany it was expected that the Germans would request the release of the Baltic landowners held by the Bolsheviks and to ward off this eventuality it was decided to shoot them. It was still early in the Bolshevik rule and the Commissar of Justice, a Left Socialist Revolutionary, strongly objected to such a barbarous step.[44] That would have been the first application of "class terror," that is, executing people not for any real or alleged plots but simply because of their class origin.

Dzerzhinsky is much praised by the Communists for allegedly maintaining iron discipline and incorruptibility among his personnel. But the story, as told in the early days by his own subordinates and admirers, casts a lurid light on that assertion. At the time of the transfer of the government to Moscow the *Cheka* had already 120 members. The "Muscovites received the *Cheka* badly" complains its high official Peters.[45] He lists some "minor" incidents that led to such misunderstandings: while refreshing themselves in a tavern some Chekists heard criticisms of Soviet power. They pulled out their guns: seven "hooligans" shot. Not even a place of entertainment was free from the enemies of the people: during a circus performance a popular clown, Bim-Bom, was making fun of the Bolsheviks. Again guns came out (Peters admits that they should have waited to arrest the traitorous clown until after the performance) and several people in the audience were shot. Some detachments of the *Cheka* were made up of people ignorant of the Russian language. All in all, Peters adds sorrowfully, not enough people were shot by the *Cheka* in its first year: "we still were not experienced." The official number of executions given for the first year, certainly an underestimate, is 6300. The crimes for which the penalty was applied are listed with the numbers of those executed for them. Thus for membership in the counterrevolutionary organizations, 1637; insurgency, 2431; incitement to insurgency, 396 (the separation of these three offenses has an eloquence of its own); desertion, 39 (many, many more must have been executed by the military authorities); and so on. Having seemingly exhausted all the capital offenses the *Cheka* leader has another one: "miscellaneous." Under it 1173 offenders were executed in 1918.[46] On November 19, 1917, Lenin had said: "We do not apply terror as did the French revolutionaries who guillotined unarmed people, and I hope we shall not apply it."

[44] M. Latsis, "The Creation of the Commissariat of Internal Affairs," in *The Proletarian Revolution*, 1925, No. 3, p. 166.

[45] Y. Peters, "Work in the Cheka During the First Year of the Revolution," *The Proletarian Revolution*, 1924, No. 10, p. 8.

[46] M. Latsis, *Two Years of War on the Domestic Front: A Popular Review of Two Years' Activity of the Cheka*, Moscow, 1920, p. 75.

That an institution of centrally controlled police was necessary in times of revolution and turmoil can be disputed only by the most passionate idealists. It is equally true, if one thinks of such things in numerical terms, that the number of the victims of the *Cheka* was small in comparison with the prisoners slaughtered on both sides during the Civil War and of the countless civilians killed by both the Red and White forces. But the important thing is the *tone* of the work of the *Cheka*, which left an indelible trace on the Soviet system. Terror from the means of attaining and preserving power had become an *administrative technique* to be used also in cases of inefficiency, red tape, and the like. The seductive and misleading example of how much could be done by coercion, how the *Cheka* was bringing "real" discipline to Russia out of the incredible disorder of the earliest days, carried away Lenin himself. "Shoot," "threaten to shoot," became his recipes for solving even minor administrative problems. A bad telephone connection? In a telegram to Stalin, Lenin advised the way to deal with such problems: "Threaten to shoot the idiot who is in charge of telecommunications and who does not know how to give you a better amplifier and how to have a working telephone connection." [47] A badly printed book without an index led him to recommend that the publisher be given six months in jail. When disorders in Petrograd made the local boss, Zinoviev, curb indiscriminate terror directed against the former middle class, Lenin was displeased. "I protest . . ." he wired Zinoviev, not known for squeamishness, "that we should be meddling with the completely correct revolutionary initiative of the masses." [48]

The rebirth of the institutions of coercion, the army and the police, was bound to deepen the breach between the Bolsheviks and their erstwhile allies, the semianarchistic Left Socialist Revolutionaries and the outright Anarchists. As to the latter, it is impossible to say where a political and philosophical orientation ended and outright banditry began. But the Soviet state could no longer tolerate those people so useful to them in the past few months who, whether the followers of the gentle philosophy of Prince Kropotkin [49] or what we would call today "beatniks," or sheer bandits, stood against everything the Communists were trying to instill in their subjects. In April of 1918 the *Cheka* raids destroyed the Anarchists' centers in Moscow. Privileged foreigners such as Robins and Lockhart were shown the houses where the Anarchists had allegedly indulged in all forms of debauchery until cut down by the fire of the Chekists. But a newspaper critical of the Bolsheviks (some were still

---

[47] *Works,* Vol. 30, p. 338.

[48] *Works,* Vol. 33, p. 275.

[49] The famous veteran revolutionary and preacher of voluntary cooperation as the basis of social organization. Lenin personally esteemed Kropotkin and when the old gentleman was reported to be in need he ordered him to be furnished with special supplies and medical help. He granted him an audience during which the old Anarchist tried to convert him to his philosophy of replacing coercion by cooperation.

being tolerated) made some pointed comments: "Until now the Bolsheviks have made advances to their 'Left' friends. . . . It is exactly on
account of the Bolsheviks' toleration of Anarchists that the latter were in a
postition to seize houses and to take possession of artillery and machine
guns." [50] The Anarchists' organ fulminated and threatened. "You are
Cains. . . . Lenin has built his October throne on our bones . . .
our October is still ahead. . . ." It was an excellent illustration of the
reasons that prompted the Bolsheviks in their action. The Red Army and
the *Cheka* were going to make sure that there would be no further
"Octobers."

The settling of the accounts with the Left Socialist Revolutionaries
was to be a more involved procedure. Nobody could allege that the heirs
of the *Narodnik* tradition were simple bandits or hooligans. And the
drama that unfolded in July and August and which led to the death of
the left wing of the once proud party that had held the loyalty of the
Russian peasantry still retains some elements of mystery.

The Left Socialist Revolutionaries had proved to be impossible allies.
They opposed Lenin vigorously over Brest Litovsk and with the conclusion of peace their representatives, no doubt to his great relief, abandoned the Council of the Commissars. Still a form of tenuous collaboration persisted between the two parties. Most mysteriously, the Left Socialist Revolutionaries were permitted to remain in the *Cheka*, one of
them being a deputy to Dzerzhinsky.

Now in addition to their constant opposition to all and every policy of
the Bolsheviks looking toward strengthening of the state (death penalty,
reintroduction of old specialists into the army and industry, and the like)
the Left Socialist Revolutionaries never ceased their agitation against the
peace with the Germans. The arrival of German ambassador Count Mirbach was greeted by them with insulting suggestions that he was now
going to be, in effect, governor of Russia and that Lenin was taking his
orders from him. The Left Socialist Revolutionaries can infuriate the
historian almost as much as they did the Bolsheviks. They complained
about the Communists curtailing freedom, yet they had joined with them
in chasing out the Constituent Assembly. They wept over the reintroduction of the dealth penalty, yet they kept their men in the *Cheka*. They
were against war but they wanted to provoke a breach with Germany.
The Party's fatuity as a political organization was epitomized by its
leader, thirty-year-old Maria Spiridonova. As a teenage girl she assassinated a Tsarist official and was raped and tortured after the arrest.
Largely on the strength of this lamentable occurrence this hysterical
woman was now laying down policies for her party. In the spring in
some provincial towns the Left Socialist Revolutionaries combined with

[50] *The Bolshevik Revolution 1917–1918, Documents and Materials,* edited by James
Bunyan and H. H. Fisher, Stamford, 1934, p. 584.

others to overthrow the Bolshevik leadership of the local soviets. Their main attack against the Bolsheviks was planned for the meeting of the Fifth All-Russian Congress of the Soviets, due to assemble in July. They were going to be in a minority, the Communists having made sure of their own comfortable margin over the rest. But the Socialist Revolutionaries knew other means of political warfare than those of parliamentary balloting and debates.

It is here that an element of mystery enters the situation. It centers around Count Mirbach, whose assassination allegedly was ordered by the Central Committee of the Socialist Revolutionaries, meeting on June 24.[51] Mirbach after his arrival in Moscow shared at first the official line of his government that the survival of the Bolshevik power was in the interest of Germany, and apparently did not spare funds in their support. Gradually his views shifted. Bolshevism, he wrote in his report of June 25, would soon "fall victim to the process of internal disintegration. . . ." The Germans should seek "to fill the vacuum which will result from its disappearance. . . ." The best candidates for filling this vacuum were in his opinion the right-wing parties and the moderates. He advised that a military attack that would speed up the Bolsheviks' collapse would be greatly in the Germans' interest.[52] That those reports became known to the Bolshevik leaders is verified by what Lenin said to Trotsky following Mirbach's assassination: "Mirbach has continually reported that we are weak and a single blow would suffice." [53] It would not be surprising if somebody within the Communist hierarchy decided to eliminate Mirbach and in such a manner as would persuade the Germans that peace with Russia would be best preserved by a continuance of the Bolshevik regime.

Certainly the circumstances surrounding the assassination are extremely suspicious. On July 4 at the opening of the Congress of Soviets Lenin was subjected to violent attacks by the Left Socialist Revolutionaries (S-Rs). When he mentioned the need for a disciplined army there were shouts, "Just like Kerensky," and "Mirbach will not let you have it." In his turn he went out of his way to be provocative to the S-Rs, talked about Spiridonova's "lies," and asserted that the Bolsheviks made a great sacrifice and mistake when they adopted the Left S-Rs' land program. He made pointed references to his opponents' attempts to destroy peace and to inveigle Russia into war with Germany. The Socialist Revolutionaries then conducted a violent and threatening demonstration against Mirbach, who was listening to the proceedings in his diplomatic box.

It is all the more remarkable that no additional precautions were taken to protect the German ambassador and suspicion must remain that at

---

[51] V. Vladimirova, "The Left S-Rs," in *The Proletarian Revolution*, 1927, No. 4, p. 144.

[52] Quotations from *Germany and the Revolution in Russia. Documents from the Archives of the German Foreign Ministry*, edited by Z. A. B. Zeman, New York, pp. 138–39.

[53] Trotsky, *Lenin*, New York, 1925, p. 156.

least some Communist dignitaries knew of the Socialist Revolutionaries' resolve and that they did nothing about it. On July 6 Jacob Blyumkin and another conspirator, both Left Socialist Revolutionaries and members of the *Cheka*, sought a conference with the ambassador. They were admitted without difficulty: they had passes signed by Dzerzhinsky, and Blyumkin, a nineteen-year-old youth, was the *Cheka* official deputized to guard the foreign representatives (!). Once inside, Blyumkin assassinated Count Mirbach and then made his escape.

Simultaneously with the murder, the Left Socialist Revolutionary members of the *Cheka* staged a revolt and imprisoned their Bolshevik bosses, Dzerzhinsky and Latsis. The revolt was shortly brought under control. Other S-R-inspired revolts broke out in some provincial towns. A Red Army commander of S-R affiliation, Muraviev, on his own declared a war on the Germans and the Bolsheviks. But the government put down this challenge with ease and Muraviev, formerly a great revolutionary hero, ended by shooting himself. In Moscow Spiridonova and the other leading Left S-R lights were arrested. The mutinous members of the *Cheka*, including Dzerzhinsky's deputy Alexandrovich, were shot. Blyumkin vanished to reappear in a year to be forgiven and admitted to the Communist Party. Not until some years later under Stalin (how often this statement has to be appended about figures of this period!) was he to be shot, the first of many Communists to be executed on charges of Trotskyism.

Such are the bare facts of the new "July days" and of the Left S-R plot. They make it at least probable that somebody in the highest Bolshevik circles must have been aware of what the S-Rs were preparing and thought it would be a good opportunity to get rid both of them and of the troublesome German diplomat. Indeed, the finger of suspicion pointed so strongly at Dzerzhinsky that it was thought desirable to suspend him for a time as the head of the *Cheka*. That Lenin himself was deeply involved is doubtful. For all the Germans' desperate need for peace (their offensive in the West had just been brought to a stop) the assassination of their ambassador brought at least some risk of their renewing military operations against Russia. Caution was Lenin's watchword in regard to foreign affairs. It was undoubtedly with mixed feelings that the Chairman of the Council of People's Commissars went to the German Embassy to offer his official condolences.

But he was quick to take advantage of the situation. With the ready and outrageous perversion of political facts and labels that was to become characteristic of the Communists, Lenin accused the Left Socialist Revolutionaries of acting in the interests of monarchists and of the Anglo-French capitalists. Those misguided and confused people, in fact to the left of the Bolsheviks, were pictured by him as "petty bourgeois" adventurers. It was thought wise to show clemency toward their leaders, so the unfortunate Spiridonova and others were soon pardoned. But the back of the Left S-R Party was broken. It could never again compete with the Bolsheviks. Its dangerous and popularity-gaining slogan, "Down with the dictator-commissars," was now hopelessly obscured by the foolish assassination and a half-baked attempt to seize power. And, as before in the history of Russian Populism, individual terrorism stood helpless before mass repression.

The latter was now applied in full force. Numerous executions followed the Bolsheviks' recapture of various cities seized momentarily in the July rebellions. Though the rebellions were the work of the Left S-Rs (and in one case, in the city of Yaroslav, of the right-wing S-Rs) the most severe terror was applied in fact against the former exploiting classes and the intelligentsia, who seldom could be connected with those attempts.

Discarding for a moment what the Communist would call the philistine, humanitarian objection to terror, one might still question whether it was accomplishing its purpose, that is, consolidating the Bolshevik rule. The heightening of the Civil War in the summer of 1918 is usually given as the reason for terror by the Red government, but it is arguable that insurgency and bitterness against the Communist rule grew in fact in the wake of executions and other inhumanities perpetrated by the *Cheka* and other authorities, and that many elements, at first friendly or lukewarm in their opposition to the Bolshevik power, became its fanatical enemies because of terror. One does not have to consult White propaganda to reach that conclusion. The most famous novel of the Civil War written by a Communist eyewitness, Mikhail Sholokhov's *And Quiet Flows the Don*, presents an instructive tale of how it was mostly through Bolshevik atrocities that the rank-and file apolitical Don Cossack, like the hero of the novel, Gregory Melekhov, was turned into an anti-Bolshevik fighter. Far from being a regrettable necessity, the extent of the Bolshevik terror was one of the factors that made their victory in the Civil War more difficult.

The complex psychological reasons for terror and the equally involved rationalizations given for it are well illustrated in the story of the assassination of the former Tsar and his family on July 16, 1918, in the city of Ekaterinburg in the Urals. He had been under arrest since March 1917. What to do with Nicholas II was one of the problems to which the revolutionary authorities, whether under Kerensky or under Lenin, could not, in view of their other preoccupations, give much time. The revolutionary etiquette would have required a great trial-demonstration, in which after a recital of the Emperor's iniquities the Russian people would duly send him to the scaffold. Trotsky in his recollections relates that he proposed such a trial to Lenin and that he, Trotsky, fancied himself as the public prosecutor.[54] Lenin refused, pleading shortage of time. But no doubt he would

---

[54] "I proposed that we hold an open court trial which would reveal a picture of the whole reign with its peasant policy, labor policy, national minority and cultural policies, its two wars, etc. The proceedings of the trial would be broadcast throughout the country by radio . . ." (Here Trotsky himself put a question mark in his

have refused in any case: there was other business to be attended to in this summer of 1918 and Trotsky's proposal smacked of theatricality, which was entirely alien to his nature. Most of all, he must have realized (and how strange that Trotsky did not) that from the Communist point of view Nicholas II would have made a very poor prisoner in the dock: his very lack of intelligence combined with his dignity and Christian resignation would have made him an object of pity rather than of popular indignation. Indeed, the former Emperor, an abject failure while on the throne, displayed while prisoner the kind of fortitude and equanimity that moved even his jailers.

The issue was determined by the threat that Ekaterinburg would fall in the hands of the anti-Bolshevik forces then operating in the Urals. Though the decision to kill the Tsar (the first communiqué concealed the execution of the rest of the family) was announced to have been made by the local soviet, Trotsky's narrative makes it clear that it came from Lenin himself. Sverdlov told Trotsky when he returned from a front late in July: "We decided it here. Ilyich believed that we should not leave the Whites a live banner to rally around, especially under the present difficult circumstances." Later on Trotsky comments that Lenin realized that it would have been difficult "under judicial procedures" to execute the Tsar's family and yet it was necessary to do so because of the problem of succession. This casts some doubt on the accuracy of Trotsky's recollections: Lenin, a lawyer by training, must have been perfectly aware that none of the Emperor's four daughters would have been eligible to succeed to the throne. Nor, it must be added, would the Emperor's doctor and personal servants, who were shot at the same time.

As to the real motivation behind Lenin's decision one must refer to his curious historical sense. Even before the Bolsheviks took over he had complained petulantly that the English and French revolutions executed their monarchs, and that the Russian one was being terribly backward in that respect. The same note was struck by Lenin after the executions: "In England and France they executed their Tsars some centuries ago but we were late with ours," he said in an appropriately homely language, speaking to the Congress of the Committees of Poor Peasants.[55] Yet another symptom of Russia's cultural backwardness.

That he was genuinely worried about any political influence the ex-Emperor might exert if freed, is extremely unlikely. The rationalization given by Trotsky simply does not fit the facts of Russia in 1918. He writes: "The execution of the Tsar's family was needed not only to frighten, horrify and dishearten the enemy, but also in order to shake up our own ranks

Diary; it was clearly a fantastic delusion: radios in the Russian villages in 1918!) "Accounts of the proceedings would be read and commented upon every day." Trotsky's Diary in Exile 1935, Cambridge, Mass., 1958, p. 80.

[55] Works, Vol. 28, p. 153.

to show them that there was no turning back, that ahead lay either complete victory or ruin. . . . The masses of workers and soldiers had not a minute's doubt. They would not have understood and would not have accepted any other decision. This Lenin sensed well." [56] Yet to Lenin the Tsar was "idiot Romanov," a person politically of no consequence. With his practical sense he must have realized that the former Emperor was unpopular even among the monarchists, who were casting off other members of the Romanov family. Not even the most reactionary White movement during the Civil War made an effort to appeal to the monarchist sentiment. If anything, the physical presence of the ex-Emperor in the Whites' camp would have been an embarrassment to them and a political asset to the Bolsheviks. Why then did Lenin sanction the execution? Partly it was his historic sense of which we spoke above, and partly (here Trotsky's account is closer to the mark) for the effect it would have upon his own followers. Lenin was forever complaining to Trotsky, "Russians are too kind . . . lazybones, softies." Even the old terrorist tradition had elements of the "softness"; an assassin would often go to great lengths and run additional danger to avoid harming women and children, who found themselves in the vicinity of his intended victim. The murder of the Tsar and his family was probably thought to be a good lesson "that one does not enter the realm of revolution with white gloves and on a polished floor."

Such reminders soon became superfluous. Terror struck at the Bolshevik leaders. On the morning of August 30 M. Uritsky, chief of the Petrograd *Cheka*, was struck down by an assassin. When the news reached Moscow, Lenin, who was scheduled to address two public meetings the same day, was implored by his sister Maria, Bukharin, and others to postpone his appearances. But he refused. The first speech passed without an incident. He then went to the Michelson factory and addressed the workers. His chauffeur waited outside with the limousine. He reported later on that he was accosted by a woman who asked him whether it was Comrade Lenin's car. After finishing his speech Vladimir Ilyich paused outside the factory to answer some questions from his listeners. He then turned to enter his car. Here the woman who had been so inquisitive fired three times from her revolver. Two bullets hit Lenin.

What happened immediately afterward is, apart from the drama of the moment, highly illustrative of the conditions of those days. Few among the crowd paid any attention to the wounded leader. The militiamen present set in pursuit of the terrorist. Others dispersed in panic. It fell to the chauffeur to tend to Lenin. He did not lose consciousness and

---

[56] Trotsky's *Diary, op. cit.*, p. 81. The very same day in 1935 Trotsky records anxiety about his son still in Russia within Stalin's vengeful reach: "No news about Seryozha, and perhaps there won't be any for a long time." His son met the fate of other members of Trotsky's family who had remained.

when his driver proposed to take him home he assented. Why not the hospital? The chauffeur gives his version: "Somebody . . . insisted I take Vladimir Ilyich to the nearest hospital—I replied decisively 'I am not taking him to any hospital, I am taking him home.' " [57] This was Moscow, 1918. Who could vouch that in a hospital Lenin would not fall into the hands of a doctor with Kadet or S-R sympathies? No one even thought of summoning a doctor to be present when Vladimir Ilyich got back to his apartment in the Kremlin. The wounded man was supported-pushed to his fourth-floor residence (he refused to be carried). There he continued to lie unattended, for his sister Maria and a woman employee of his secretariat were close to hysteria and unable to help (Krupskaya was away). It was only the arrival of the secretary of the Council of Commissars, Lenin's old friend, Bonch-Bruevich, that brought some order. It fell to him to administer first aid to the wounded man. But even Bonch-Bruevich would not dream of calling a hospital directly. He telephoned his wife, who happened to be a doctor, and *then the Moscow soviet* to ask for the names of reliable doctors. All this time Lenin was writhing in pain, convinced that he had been shot near the heart. Finally after a long delay (no automobiles could be found to fetch them) Mme Bonch-Bruevich and other doctors began to arrive. Lenin by that time mercifully had lost consciousness. Had the bullets hit a major artery he would in all probability have been dead.

Apart from the Communist distrust in the average doctor's professional probity, the theme to be repeated in the history of the Soviet state,[58] there is another, usually overlooked, sidelight of this attempt on Lenin's life. As even Bonch-Bruevich's account makes clear, his and other Bolsheviks' primary concern was lest the attempted assassination were part of a major plot to wrest power from the Bolsheviks. Thus *before* hastening to the side of his stricken leader and friend, who was lying virtually unattended, Bonch-Bruevich spent some time issuing instructions to the Commander of the Kremlin to double the guard and to put the Red Army units on the alert. Other Bolshevik leaders dispersed to their ministries and command posts, and only after making sure that there was in fact no uprising repaired to the Kremlin to hear the news about Lenin's condition. This was in line with the Bolshevik unsentimental attitude in such matters and perhaps it would have been approved by Lenin himself, but it hardly

[57] Quoted in Bonch-Bruevich *Memories of V. I. Lenin 1917–1924*, Moscow, 1963, p. 288.
[58] Two doctors from the Kremlin medical staff were among the accused in the purge trial of 1938. They confessed to a fantastic variety of medical murders, including that of Maxim Gorky, done allegedly at the instigation of Henryk Yagoda, a successor of Dzerzhinsky. Then there is an equally weird and still unexplained story of the "Doctors' Plot" of nine eminent Soviet physicians, most of them of Jewish origin, whose arrest was announced in January 1953 and who were released and rehabilitated after Stalin's death.

bears out the tales of "the boundless love" that his closest collaborators were said to have felt toward him. During Lenin's convalescence, when Sverdlov took charge of affairs, Bonch-Bruevich was surprised to hear from him: "You see, Vladimir Dimitrievich, we can manage even without Lenin." He appends his own interpretation: obviously Sverdlov must have meant that indispensable though Lenin was, the cause of communism transcends any man—but one wonders.

It would take a doctor to appraise the conflicting reports of the extent of Lenin's wounds, though even a layman may be skeptical about one account that a massive hemorrhage pushed his heart slightly to the right side.[59] Soon he was on the mend. The bullets stayed in his body [60] but there does not seem any evidence that his health was permanently affected by the shooting. He was an impatient invalid and by the third week in September he was back at work. In the meantime the attempted assassination by an insane woman cost thousands of innocent people their lives.

That the would-be assassin, Fanny Kaplan, was insane is testified by the earliest Soviet sources and the records of her interrogation by the *Cheka.* Arrested near the scene of the crime, she was asked, "Why did you shoot Comrade Lenin?" and replied, "Why do you have to know?" [61] Interrogation brought out the fact that she had been a terrorist under the old regime, had been sentenced to hard labor, and freed only by the February Revolution. In the Tsarist prison she suffered from continuous headaches, and would for no apparent physical reason lose sight for long periods. She did not tell who gave her a revolver or who if anybody were her accomplices. She shot Lenin because he "sold out the Revolution and his further existence would undermine the faith in socialism." She had been an Anarchist, she declared, and she would not tell what was her present political affiliation, though she admitted sympathy for the Constituent Assembly and Chernov.

The Soviet authorities never succeeded in tying up Kaplan's attempt to any organization whether of the Left or the Right S-Rs, the "reaction," or foreign agents. That was probably why the poor demented woman was shot without a trial. But her deed was taken as the pretext for a wholesale terror that now swept the country. A circular from the Commissar of the Interior urged the soviets to deal mercilessly with the *bourgeoisie.* "A considerable number of hostages must be taken from among the *bourgeoisie* and the officers." Not to be outdone, the *Cheka* cleared the jails of the Tsarist officials and capitalists, even those who had been there for a long time and who could not in the most remote sense be connected with

[59] Dr. V. N. Rozanov in *Recollections About V. I. Lenin,* Vol. 2, Moscow, 1957, p. 336.

[60] One was removed in 1922 just before the beginning of his final disease.

[61] "The History of the Attempt on Lenin," in *The Proletarian Revolution,* 1923, No. 6–7, p. 280.

resistance to the Bolsheviks. "Not more than six hundred people were shot by the Moscow *Cheka* alone," says its chief.[62] Finally the "masses' " initiative was also applied when it came to executions, one workers' meeting deciding to shoot on their own "ten capitalists." That the would-be murderer was insane, and if connected with any party at all then with one of the left, appeared to be totally irrelevant in selecting victims.

The long hand of the British secret service was also discerned in the plot. The Allies had just begun their intervention in the North; their agents, such as Lockhart, were undoubtedly dabbling in the dangerous game of making contact with the anti-Bolshevik elements, hence it was thought to be of educational value to have them linked to the attempted assassination. A British officer was killed in Petrograd while resisting arrest in the old embassy building, and in Moscow Lockhart, until shortly before a privileged foreigner with personal access to Trotsky, had a very narrow escape. Lockhart foolishly had listened to some persons, evidently *agents provocateurs*, who proposed bribing the Lettish regiments in order to turn them against the Bolsheviks. He now spent a harrowing month in prison, being interviewed by another Latvian, the *Cheka* chief, Peters. As the recollections of both gentlemen testify, their intercourse, considering the circumstances, was fairly amiable. Peters, who considered himself a man of the world, yielded to Lockhart's entreaties and freed his Russian girl friend. It pains him, Peters writes in 1924, to reveal something he had refrained from mentioning previously for fear of hurting Lockhart's career in England, namely that the Englishman's beloved had all along been a German agent.[63] Eventually Lockhart and other French and British officials were released and expelled from Russia. The British reciprocated by releasing the Communist agent in London, Maxim Litvinov, the future Commissar of Foreign Affairs.

The summer of 1918 marked the full development of those two related threats to Soviet power: foreign intervention and the Civil War. On April 4 the Japanese had landed in Vladivostok. Now troops of other Allies, Britain, France, and the United States, would land in Archangel and Murmansk in Northern Russia, Odessa in the South, Vladivostok in the far East: Allied money and supplies would be furnished to the anti-Bolshevik forces. But even within the interior of Russia the Czechoslovak Army, stretched along the vast areas from the Volga through Siberia, would play a vital role in the domestic struggle.[64] As the Germans, weakening before

---

[62] Peters, *op. cit.*, p. 31.

[63] Peters, "Work in the Cheka During the First Year of the Revolution," in *The Proletarian Revolution*, 1924, No. 10, p. 29. He felt absolved from his discretion because of Lockhart's ungallant attacks upon the Soviets after his return to England.

[64] The Czech units were organized in the Tsar's army from the beginning of the war, the liberation of fellow Slavs from the Austro-Hungarian yoke being one of the professed aims of Russian policy. Those units grew with the enlistment of the Czech and Slovak war prisoners eager to serve in the crusade against their Hapsburg rulers.

their approaching defeat, ceased being a threat to the Bolshevik rule, the Allies, "the Western capitalist bandits" would present both directly and indirectly from the late spring of 1918 a new challenge to Lenin and his associates.

The Civil War did not need a foreign impetus. As early as the preceding winter the so-called Volunteer Army had been fighting the Bolsheviks in the South. Led by the former Tsarist commanders Alexeyev and Denikin (after the death in battle of General Kornilov) it became the nucleus of the South Russian White Army, which in 1919 was to come closest of all the anti-Bolshevik forces to delivering a decisive blow to the Red Army. It was inevitable that sooner or later the Bolsheviks would clash with the groups and movements seeking independence or autonomy not only from the Soviet rule but from Russia in general such as the Ukrainians (once German protection was withdrawn from them), the Georgians and Armenians in the Caucasus, the Don and Kuban Cossacks, and others. But the violent flare-up of the Civil War was provoked by the fact that the repressive policies of the new regime were now being felt. Peasants were being alienated by the extortion of food; the non-Russian nationalities occasionally woke up to the double meaning of the Communist doctrine of national self-determination. In places even the workers arose against the government they had greeted so warmly in November and December. Bolshevik rule found acquiescence at first because Lenin and his associates had promised every group and every nationality a full satisfaction of its postulates. Now the Bolsheviks stood revealed as Indian givers. In the army Trotsky was trying to establish a discipline the likes of which no Tsarist Minister of War would have dreamed of introducing. Lenin's efforts to revive industrial production prompted a workers' delegation to tell him, as he repeated sadly to Trotsky: "One sees that you too, Comrade Lenin, take the side of capitalists." [65]

But most important of all, the people now woke up to the fact that it was *Bolshevik* or Communist rule they were under. The workers, soldiers, and sailors who fought for Lenin and his party in November were not fighting for any Marxian or even Socialist philosophy or state. They fought for *Soviet* rule. This word was not thought to be synonymous with the rule

On the Bolsheviks' assumption of power a series of involved negotiations led to the agreement to have the Czechoslovak Corps with its arms evacuated through Vladivostok to the Western front, where it would fight under French command. Inevitable clashes developed during this protracted process of evacuating an alien army over 6,000 miles, with the transportation facilities being in a state of unimaginable chaos. In May the Bolshevik authorities decided to disarm the Czech troops strewn along the Trans-Siberian Railway. The Czechs refused to submit, seized vast stretches of the railway, and extended their armed support to various anti-Bolshevik movements, ripening into uprisings in the Volga region and Siberia. Thus this foreign force of less than 40,000 soldiers dispersed over vast areas triggered off the intensive period of the Civil War.

[65] Lev Trotsky, *Lenin*, New York, 1925, p. 152.

by one party or a coalition of parties. Indeed, the magic efficacy of this word would last through the Civil War and be one of the main reasons for the Bolshevik victory. To the masses it meant originally *self-rule,* the right of every regiment, factory, city, to elect its council, which would control its own destiny and have but a loose connection with the authorities in Petrograd or Moscow. The jarring reality of the spring and summer of 1918 showed the emptiness of such expectations: local and professional soviets were increasingly being dissolved or chased out and in their place a Communist emissary, a commissar, took over. To us who have grown accustomed to consider the words "Bolshevik," "Soviet," and "Communist" as practically synonymous, it is startling to find as a frequent slogan of mutinies and rebellions of 1918–21, "Long live the soviets; down with the commissars" (or the "Bolsheviks"). In the popular mind there grew the legend of the golden period of Bolshevik rule, the period of the soviets. It was a time of intoxicating freedom and equality, when every village and every town ran its own affairs. And then a "commissar" came down from Moscow or the provincial capital and told them that their elected representative were *kulaks* and the petty bourgeois, and must be replaced by a truly proletarian, that is, Bolshevik, soviet. And very frequently the *Cheka* moved in with him.

This cycle of anarchy, repression, and then an anti-Bolshevik revolt is well illustrated in the tale of Samara in 1918. The provincial soviet in this Volga metropolis had a majority composed of Anarchists and extreme Left S-Rs. For all practical purposes the Samara region was in the spring an independent republic paying little heed to events in Moscow. To fish in these troubled waters there came in April the celebrated Dybenko, currently under investigation and in disgrace with the Bolshevik government. The redoubtable sailor was accompanied by a gang of his personal followers and he evidently thought of organizing his own little state from which he could conduct a vendetta against the ungrateful Communist authorities. It was with great difficulty that the local Communists, headed by V. Kuibyshev, whose name the city now bears, succeeded in expelling Dybenko. His example now led to a flare-up of a revolt against the Communists, which was helped by such incidents as the cabmen having their horses "mobilized" for the Red Army. With such slogans as "Let us be done with the Jewish commissars" the population rose up and for some time complete anarchy prevailed in Samara. The Bolsheviks with the help of military units finally managed to put down the revolt. The Anarcho-Left S-R soviet was dissolved and other repressions followed.[66]

But the ground was laid for the next and more serious anti-Bolshevik revolt. In June some Socialist Revolutionaries persuaded the Czech troops to help them seize Samara. The province was then proclaimed to be the

---

[66] G. Lelevich, "The Anarchist Revolution in Samara," in *The Proletarian Revolution,* 1922, No. 7.

seat of the legitimate Russian government, based upon the members of the
Constituent Assembly (mostly Right S-Rs) who collected in Samara. This
government soon expanded its territory, seizing Lenin's native town, Simbirsk, and in August another major town associated with the history of the
Ulyanov family, Kazan.

This was the period of which Trotsky was to write:

> One unconsciously asked the question whether the life forces of
> the exhausted, shattered, despairing land would last until the new
> regime was in the saddle. Provisions were not at hand. There was no
> army. The state apparatus was being put together. Conspiracies were
> festering everywhere. The Czechoslovak army stood on our soil as an
> independent power. We could offer almost no opposition to them.[67]

Over the vast territory of Russia by the end of the summer *eighteen*
insurgent governments competed with the Bolshevik one of Moscow.[68]
On the face of it the situation of the Communist regime looked hopeless.
Its central and north Russian territory was literally surrounded by the rival "governments." In the West, German troops still stood on its frontiers,
at the same time that the Allies' intervention was already beginning. The
collapse of the German power would bring an intensification of the Allied threat: France and England would presumably have no compunction about dislodging a government so openly hostile to them, which had
concluded peace with Germany, repudiated its debts to the West, and
annihilated their citizens' property and investments in Russia.

All the more remarkable was the equanimity and the quiet confidence
Lenin displayed even during the darkest periods of the Civil War. This
confidence was based partly on the feeling that the Bolshevik government
had already survived much longer than anybody before October had
thought it could survive by its own exertions. It was based upon the still
present expectation of a world revolution, the hope that would momentarily resume its original intensity with the German revolution in November 1918 and with the briefly lived Soviet-type regimes in Bavaria and
Hungary in 1919.[69]

But most important, Lenin's confidence was based on a sober appraisal
of the weaknesses, material and psychological, of the enemies of communism. Foreign intervention would have to be massive in numbers of sol-

[67] Trotsky, *Lenin*, p. 152.

[68] This is not counting five "independent" governments existing under the German
occupation, e.g. the Ukraine and Lithuania, nor the states formerly within the Russian Empire but which now declared themselves independent, such as Finland and
Georgia. James Bunyan, *Intervention, Civil War and Communism in Russia April–
December 1918*, Baltimore, 1936, p. 277.

[69] In the summer of 1919 Lenin was again to speak in terms implying that a Communist revolution would sweep the West within a year. See E. H. Carr, *The Bolshevik
Revolution 1917–1923*, New York, 1953, Vol. 3, p. 129. But it is problematical whether
his and other Bolshevik leaders' utterances in this vein were entirely sincere. This
was the low point in the Communists' fortunes in the Civil War and such official
optimism was needed for a morale-building purpose.

diers to decide the issue in Russia. But after four years of the bloodiest of wars, how could the democratic governments of the West recruit large armies to fight in a distant land and for a cause that was alien and confusing to a vast majority of their citizens? *Military* intervention of the Allies was bound to be a small-scale and piecemeal business, more likely to compromise the anti-Bolshevik forces that sought Western help than to affect the Civil War decisively.

In addition, because of their mutual rivalry and divided councils the Allies were never able to devise a unified and cohesive policy on Russia and Bolshevism. The United States was following warily the Japanese designs on Siberia, and indeed a desire to check them was one of the main reasons for American intervention in that region. A basic difference of outlook separated the two principal interventionist powers: France longed for a reunited Russia under a "respectable" regime that in due time would resume the role of her Eastern ally; Great Britain, at times, looked with favor at the separatist tendencies of the Caucasian and Central Asiatic nationalities. Some Allied politicians longed simply for the "dust to settle down" in the whole area of the former Russian Empire, so that trade relations could be renewed with this vast potential market. Some, such as Mr. Churchill, saw Bolshevism as a major threat to Western civilization and influence, which unless checked in its infancy would bring ruin to the rest of Europe. Others considered communism a lesser evil bound to perpetuate anarchy in Russia when contrasted with a restoration of a nationalist regime that would resume the expansionist march of the old Empire.

Those differences of outlook and rivalries of the "imperialist bandits" were already being exploited by Bolshevik diplomacy. That the Soviet state like any other state must play a diplomatic game and that there could be no more nonsense about "abolishing" foreign relations was recognized by Lenin as early as Brest Litovsk. Now the world revolution was seen as something in the far future. In March 1919 he said: "We live not only in a state but in a system of states, and the existence of the Soviet republic together with imperialist states is in the long run unthinkable." But the important words here were "in the long run." In the meantime he initiated the technique of Soviet diplomacy, skillful intermixture of promises, threats, and cajolery, well calculated to confuse and tantalize both the politicians and electorates of the West.

This technique was adjusted to what the Bolsheviks conceived to be the main foibles and weaknesses of the ruling classes of the major capitalist countries. In the case of France it was assumed to be the greed of the French *rentier*. In the summer of 1919 when things were going badly for the Communists, Lenin held out the alluring prospect of repaying the foreign debts of which the French held a major share. If "we get a real peace" he said in an interview, the Russian government was ready to repay *all* the debts to France.[70]

[70] *Works*, Vol. 29, p. 487.

In the case of the United States, the Bolsheviks recognized very early the American proneness to "fall" for democratic phraseology and soothing reassurances. In December 1918 Deputy Commissar of Foreign Affairs Litvinov addressed a note to President Wilson, "the old hypocrite Wilson," as Lenin called him in his less diplomatic moments, which not so much as breathed a word about the world revolution but contained a handsome tribute to the President's "sense of justice and impartiality." In an interview with the *Chicago Daily News* Lenin himself avowed that the Soviet regime "guarantees" nonintervention in the affairs of foreign countries.[71] The next entry in his *Collected Works* contains messages to the Italian, French, and German Communist parties. He was eager to collect and display favorable comments about the Bolshevik regime from the foreign press. Red Terror? Why, even an American bourgeois journalist, Stuart Chase, had written in the *New Republic* that the Bolsheviks were much less repressive than the regime of Baron Mannerheim in Finland.[72] (When in the midst of all his occupations in that fearful year of 1919 and before the days of specially prepared press digests did Lenin find time to read the *New Republic?*)

For the British ruling class Lenin had more respect; he esteemed them shrewd and relentless in their hostility to communism. But he was aware of the growing stature of labor in British politics and of its inhibiting role in the machinations of the capitalists and politicians such as Churchill. For the British Labour Party as such Lenin had unbounded contempt; in fact for decades the British worker had been the despair of the Marxists: with his lack of "theoretical sense" he had refused to countenance class war and worked merely for better living conditions and democracy. Still, it was even more irritating to have the small bunch of the British Communists fail to realize that they would be of more use to Soviet Russia and the world revolution if they joined the Labour Party and worked within it rather than to have a noisy and doctrinaire group of their own. When it came to dealing with the British Socialists of all varieties Lenin's nerves became frayed. They asked such stupid questions, and had to have everything explained to them. A delegation of the Labourites that visited him in 1920 asked such questions as: Is it more important to have a British Communist Party or to work for peace with Russia? [73] Lenin ill-humoredly comments it would only hurt the cause of the proletariat to have such people as Communists. Or another query: Why is there terror in Russia, persecution of the Mensheviks, lack of the freedom of press and assembly, and all such? Here Lenin simply lost his patience (all this in a letter to the English Socialist and Liberal papers): "I have so often explained the reasons for it, that it was not very pleasant for me to repeat them." Still the

---

[71] *Works*, Vol. 30, p. 32.
[72] *Ibid.*, p. 11.
[73] *Works*, Vol. 31, p. 119.

play for the sympathies of the British labor class had to be made and it brought some results: it was largely the pressure of the trade unions that was responsible for curtailing and then ending intervention. But the obtuseness of the English working class and the English Communists was to cause Lenin further irritations.

Without a massive foreign intervention, the Civil War in Russia could have ended in a Bolshevik defeat only if the opposite side had produced a leader of unusual appeal and organizing ability, or if the Whites, the name under which all the anti-Communist forces are somewhat confusingly lumped together, could have produced a political organization possessing the cohesion and sense of mission of the Communist Party. Neither of those conditions was forthcoming, and the Whites' success even at the highest point of their military advance, as in the summer of 1919 or in the fall of the same year when Petrograd almost fell to the armies of General Yudenich, had a somewhat ephemeral appearance.

Militarily the reasons usually adduced for the Bolsheviks' victory stress their domination of the center of the country, with relatively short interior lines while their enemies were on the outside, disunited, with vast distances to travel before they could come to grips with the main Red forces. The Whites' offensives were not so much defeated as they were spent in long marches through partisan-infested territory, the long communication lines, lack of supplies, and disease (especially typhus) taking toll of their armies even before they faced the enemy. Their troops were almost always inferior numerically to the Bolsheviks', since there was no practical coordination, and really in the nature of things there could not be any, between the major White centers in Siberia, in the south of Russia, and on the Baltic. The military aspect of the Civil War seldom alarmed Lenin. He was never to experience the near panic that he had felt in February 1918, when it looked as if the Germans would be in Petrograd within a few days. When in the fall of 1919 Yudenich was before the old capital, he very calmly contemplated the abandonment of the birthplace of the Revolution. The Whites, Lenin considered, grew only weaker the more territory they occupied. The German war machine had been a "giant," the White forces were merely an armed rabble, perhaps not much different in this respect from the Bolshevik troops, but lacking the political organization and the sure political instincts that characterized the Communist Party.

The political weakness of the Whites has been variously ascribed to the reactionary character of their regimes, their inability to "sell" themselves to the peasants in whose eyes they represented the returning landlords and capitalists, and to "corruption," a historian's convenient catch-all explanation for the failure of movements and governments. All such characterizations, though they contain a kernel of truth, fail to account for the fatal ineptitude of the anti-Bolshevik movements, and some of them could with equal justice be applied to the Communists. Certainly, the mass of the peasants by the middle of the Civil War had been weaned from their acquiescence in the Red rule. Corruption, hooliganism, and all forms of excesses were as rife among the lower ranks of the Bolsheviks' hierarchy as among the Whites.

The real reasons for the failure of anti-Bolshevik movements are much more comprehensive. They lie in the same complex of causes that brought down the democratic regime of pre-October Russia. In every White territory there was enacted a variant of the tragedy of Russia as a whole between February and October 1917: the military regime working at cross purposes with the civilian authorities, the conservatives coming to hate the moderates, the latter unable to coexist with the anti-Bolshevik left. There was in almost every case an attempt to build upon a broad democratic front, usually anchored to the local Socialist Revolutionary organization of one hue or another. Then this ramshackle structure would break down because of the incompatibility of the military with this unhappy party, in which they still saw one of the main causes of Russia's tragedy. A "dictatorship" would be set up like that of Admiral Kolchak in Siberia, but the term would soon become a mockery, for the regime with no political support, with the contending leftist and conservative factions, would soon disintegrate even before a military defeat. Some regimes, like the one in Northern Russia, were headed for a while by such venerable names of the Russian revolutionary chronicle as N. Chaikovsky, who in the 1870s was one of the initiators of the famous Pilgrimage to the People, but famous names meant little in a starving and convulsed country. The Bolshevik Revolution did not cause the anti-Bolshevik Socialist parties to learn or forget anything: they remained addicted to oratory, suspicious of the military, and intensely distrustful of each other. The average professional officer in turn saw little difference between those people and the Bolsheviks, and came to hate all the politicians for their ill-timed democratic and humanitarian scruples and vacillations. The fact that so many professional officers of the Tsar were ultimately enlisted in the Red Army cannot be ascribed solely to compulsion or the need for employment and livelihood. There was also the attraction for the military mind of Trotsky's "New Model": an army where professional competence and discipline were to be the ruling considerations.

Another and perhaps decisive advantage of the Bolsheviks lay in their flexible and skillful nationality policy. By 1919 and 1920 much lustre had indeed rubbed off the famous doctrine of "national self-determination." To the more perceptive it came to mean paper independence or autonomy superimposed upon the old-style centralization. But there was still an enormous propaganda appeal and some reality in the Soviet declaration that every nationality within Russia should enjoy autonomous or if it so wished independent political and cultural existence. Lenin himself must deserve a lion's share of credit for this policy and its success. With infinite patience he would correct or put down his colleagues' premature or excessive manifestations of Russian nationalism or centralizing passion. His eye was firmly on the main goals: first the consolidation of Soviet rule and ultimately a wider revolution. He could wait. When necessary Lenin shrugged off the loss of Finland, the Baltic states, or Poland. After Kolchak's regime collapsed in Siberia in the winter of 1919–20 Lenin warned the local Communists about a premature sovietization. It was wiser to have an "independent" Siberian republic which, once the Great Powers turned away from Russian affairs, would quietly and unobtrusively rejoin Soviet Russia. He had none of the compulsive jingoist's impatience when it came to territorial questions.

Here the contrast between the Bolsheviks and their opponents was very vivid. It can be best illustrated by considering General Anton Denikin, the most effective of the anti-Bolshevik leaders thrown up by the Civil War. Few people appeared to be as well qualified to lead in the destruction of communism and in the regeneration of Russia. By origin Denikin could claim that he came from the people in a much truer sense than a great majority of the Bolshevik leaders: his father had been born a serf, his mother had been a domestic servant. Half Polish and brought up in Poland, he could be assumed to have a special feeling for the involved nationality problem of Russia. He distinguished himself in the war, both as a front-line and staff officer and, qualities rather unusual in a general, he was an eloquent speaker and a man of fairly advanced social views.

But despite such qualifications and undeniably high motivations, Denikin was unable to forge an effective anti-Bolshevik movement. Part of his failure lay in inability to control his subordinates. As he himself admits, some of his commanders indulged, despite his prohibition, in the shooting of prisoners, anti-Jewish pogroms, and depredations over the peasants in the territories they recovered from the Reds. But the greatest weakness of his regime was inability to cope with the nationality problem. His base of operations, Southern Russia and the Northern Caucasus, was a mosaic of nationalities, each after the Revolution aspiring to independence and distrustful of the White regime, which never concealed its Great Russian orientation. Denikin himself, as happens not infrequently with people of mixed national origin, was a more fervent nationalist than most pure-blooded Russians. He even hesitated to admit, despite the fact that by 1919 it was a *fait accompli*, the separation of Poland and Finland, holding, perhaps correctly from the legal point of view but politically foolishly, that only the future free assembly of Russia had the right to sanction the secession of former parts of the Empire. It was this fact that was perhaps decisive in the decision of the Poles to preserve neutrality when his own offensive was pushing the Bolsheviks back in 1919, and when a blow from the West could well have meant the difference.

Within his own domain the general had to deal with the aspirations to independence coming from such claimants as the Ukrainians, the Don and Kuban Cossacks, and the Moslems of the Crimea and Northern Caucasus. His relations with the British, the Allies, and suppliers of the southern Russian Whites were poisoned by the fears, not always unfounded, that they looked with favor upon the claims of Georgia and other Caucasian nations to full independence. A more subtle and Machiavellian politician would have refrained from such frequent declarations in favor of "Russia, great and undivided," at least until the main business at hand, the defeat of the Bolsheviks, had been accomplished. But Denikin reflected the simple nationalistic mentality of the average Russian officer. Thus he alienated even his most natural allies, the Kuban and Don Cossacks, who furnished a large number of his troops and who had most to lose by a victory of Bolshevism. In many cases, as with the Cossacks who could hardly be considered a separate nationality, the claim for independence was raised to secure a guarantee that the future Russian state would be a federation, and no longer ruled centralistically from Moscow or Petrograd. But the Whites were not capable of offsetting the dazzling promises made by Bolshevik Moscow. The rigidity of their Great Russian nationalism cost them dearly both at home and abroad. As Denikin himself writes: "From Paris we often heard: The help from the Allies is not more extensive because the struggle of the South and East [74] is not popular among the European democracies; in order to gain their sympathies it is necessary to say two words: 'Republic and Federation'—those promises we never made." [75] And Denikin stubbornly repeats that those demands represented foreign interference in Russian internal affairs, and that the future Russian constitution could only be determined after the country had been liberated, and by its own freely elected representatives. The limitations of the military mind are best expressed in his verdict on the Civil War: "It is not declarations and formulas which could change the course of history." But what, if not declarations and formulas, were "All power to the soviets," "All land to the peasants," "The right of every nationality to choose its own form of government," which certainly helped sway the course of the Russian Revolution and the Civil War?

The war was not only a duel of armies and policies, it was also a test of endurance and morale of the two contending parties. The White camp was the scene of almost continuous intrigues, personal rivalries, and political dissonances. The end of the two most prominent White leaders is symptomatic in itself of those depressing conditions. With his regime and army in total collapse, Admiral Alexander Kolchak scorned the chance to escape and turned himself in to the Czechoslovaks. The latter, by then tired of the Russian politics and eager to go home, surrendered Kolchak

[74] I.e., of the White regimes of Denikin and Kolchak respectively.
[75] A. Denikin, *The History of Russia's Time of Troubles*, Berlin, 1925, Vol. 4, p. 245.

into the hands of the pro-Bolshevik authorities in Irkutsk, who proceeded to have the former "Supreme Ruler" executed in February 1920. Not long afterward Denikin, his authority undermined by his officers who blamed him for the military and moral collapse of the White armies of the South, turned over the command of their remnants to Wrangel and left Russia on a British ship. With the Whites now confined to the Crimea, their final defeat could no longer be avoided and it came within a few months.

Personal rivalries and intrigues were also rife in the Bolshevik camp but there was a glaring difference insofar as the leadership was concerned. There was an indisputable authority at the top, that of Lenin.

His role in the Civil War might well appear to be drab and undramatic compared to that of Trotsky, or indeed some other Party leaders who often rushed down to the most exposed parts of the front, exhorting the Red Army by their own example. It is curious to find Lenin at the most crucial moments devoting his time to tasks and concerns that normally would escape the attention of a busy politician, even under the most peaceful and stable conditions. In September and October of 1918 he was continually agitated about busts and statues. Foreign intervention was gathering force, the White armies were threatening, but the Chairman of the Council of Commissars was engaged in a peevish correspondence with the Commissariat of Culture and the Moscow City soviet about the deplorable condition of the statues in the city's streets and parks. The unfortunate city official was told that he should be jailed for a week (Lenin's precision in such matters is another example of his meticulousness). Lunacharsky, at the head of Soviet cultural affairs, was asked who were the "saboteurs" responsible for the shocking fact that not a single bust of Marx was to be seen.[76] A strange preoccupation for those times!

The impression of Lenin's remoteness from the actual conduct of the Civil War is also conveyed by Trotsky in his memoirs. In most cases Lenin was content to let the management of military affairs rest in his, Trotsky's, hands; he confirmed his every decision, loyally defended him against the intrigues of Stalin and others. Despite his great and genuine admiration for Lenin, Trotsky could not avoid stressing the fact that on those rare occasions when Lenin intruded his military judgment he was proved to have been wrong, and Trotsky right. At times Trotsky's unconscious vanity led him to make assertions which are hard to believe. Thus Lenin supposedly did not know of the extent of the employment of the former Tsarist officers in the Red Army, and in the spring of 1919 he was ready, until "straightened out" by Trotsky, to have all the former officers fired.[77] But we know that Lenin was extremely scrupulous in acquainting himself with all the aspects of administration, civil and military, and his respect for professional competence was at least as strong as Trotsky's.

[76] *Works*, Vol. 35, p. 303.
[77] Lev Trotsky, *My Life*, New York, 1930, p. 447.

In fact Lenin's contribution to the conduct of the Civil War is one of the most persuasive illustrations of his greatness. No dictator and few even among democratic wartime leaders have resisted the temptation to play the role of the supreme military strategist. Lenin's good sense made him eschew that pose. He scorned the gesture of visiting the front lines or army headquarters. Only rarely did Lenin interfere in purely military matters. He realized that in Trotsky he had a war minister of supreme ability and in most cases he was ready to follow his advice and judgment. Yet that did not mean that he stood apart from military matters or was content to be merely a rubber stamp for his brilliant War Commissar.

Without Lenin's tactful support Trotsky's position would soon have become untenable. Without his occasional overruling of the War Commissar many other Communist bigwigs would have become alienated and lost for the effective prosecution of the struggle. He thus acted as the court of last resort, never losing sight, as others did occasionally, of the political side of the problem. There was perhaps an element of selfish calculation in this role. Trotsky often had to take the responsibility for measures and policies that were intensely unpopular among the Communists. But on the surface, at least, Lenin was ungrudging in his praise for the man who had for so long been his political enemy, and against whom in his exile days he had directed the most bitter invective. When in July 1919 Trotsky created a scene and threatened a resignation from his office (he had just been overruled on the choice of the commander-in-chief) Lenin did not choose to remind him, as he had told a Bolshevik commander in October 1917, that one does not resign in the middle of a war, and that he ought to be shot for threatening it. He went to great lengths in assuaging Trotsky's feelings and persuading him to stay on.

At about the same time he gave Trotsky a document that the latter proudly reproduced in his memoirs: a blank followed by the text: "Comrades, knowing the strict character of Comrade Trotsky's orders, I am so convinced, so absolutely convinced, of the correctness, expediency, and necessity for the success of the cause of the order issued by Comrade Trotsky that I unreservedly endorse this order." Signed V. Ulyanov-Lenin.[78] "I will give you," added Lenin, "as many forms like this as you want." A strange document conferring, as Trotsky exultantly exclaims, the power of life and death. But neither he nor Lenin appeared to have reflected that with a few stylistic changes the document might have issued from the chancery of Ivan the Terrible or Peter the Great rather than from the office of the Chairman of the Council of the People's Commissars.

The partnership of the two men forms a fascinating story, though our information about it is far from complete. Trotsky's version is biased and, apart from its subjectivity, he is not always accurate with his facts.[79] As

[78] *Ibid.*, p. 469.
[79] In his *Diary* there are several references to meetings of the Politburo, before this institution was in fact in existence. See for example p. 80.

for Soviet historiography, it has of course long been under compulsion to expunge all materials and references favorable to Trotsky and even de-Stalinization has not basically affected this blatant falsification of his role.

The famous partnership had its moments of tension. Trotsky's mind was more rigid than Lenin's. As he writes: "I elbowed away those who interfered with military success, or in the haste of the work trod on the toes of the unheeding and was too busy even to apologize." The creation of the Red Army was seen by him to be mainly a technical problem requiring the restoration of discipline and military professionalism. One of his first visits to the front made him realize the shocking state of affairs. The Volga armored steamship Trotsky boarded was immobilized. "It is always that way," said its commander good-naturedly. "When we have to withdraw the engine works perfectly, but when we have to attack the engine goes on strike." [80] Desertion was rife among the Red Army troops. Trotsky's immediate answer was to have the local military Commissar and 26 others shot for desertion. It was August 1918 and the idea of having Communists shot (as against threatening to do so as Lenin often did) was novel. The memory of the "executed Communists of Svyazhsk" was to be held against Trotsky for a long time. But Svyazhsk was saved and the Red Army had it first victory.

Now the pattern was established: in his famous armored train Trotsky would appear at the most exposed sections of the front, curb defections and lassitude, and restore discipline by the most drastic measures. It is very likely that their severity was often excessive. As we have seen as early as March 1918, Trotsky, then Commissar of Foreign Affairs, was accused by Ryazanov, a Communist known for his integrity, of having ordered the execution of six innocent people.

The War Commissar's disciplinary instincts often made him clash with those private cliques that were forming within the Communist hierarchy. In Petrograd Zinoviev was already establishing his little political kingdom from which he would not be dislodged by Stalin until 1925. The latter in turn was creating his own entourage. In Tsaritsin,[81] where Stalin was the political Commissar, he and the army commander Voroshilov formed an alliance based on their mutual dislike of Trotsky and his high-handed ways. It is clear that if he could have prevailed, Trotsky would have had Voroshilov shot for disobeying orders. The relative merits of his and the Stalin-Voroshilov positions are very hard to assess. But it is obvious that had he been convinced of the absolute correctness of Trotsky's policy (as he probably was), Lenin still could not have approved having one veteran Bolshevik shot and another one disgraced. Old Bolsheviks were not as yet expendable. It tells much about his diplomacy that all three persons were retained in high positions. What would have been the consequences of a

[80] Trotsky, How the Revolution Armed, Moscow, 1923, Vol. 1, p. 237.
[81] Later on Stalingrad, recently Volgograd.

prominent Bolshevik's going over to the other side in the midst of the Civil War?

Lenin's restraint upon Trotsky was based, however, not only upon political considerations. There was also the question of differing temperaments. The guilty passion for the unruly, anarchistic, even partly criminal "man of the people" never quite left Lenin, but it was entirely absent in Trotsky's make-up. In the latter's view the conduct of the war required a regular army staffed by professional officers. He looked with distaste upon partisan activities and the undisciplined private detachments that were a notable feature of the Civil War.

The war had spawned many private bands and armies, neither Red nor White in their political complexion. Sometimes they were led by Anarchists and sometimes by soldiers of fortune, but in practically every case there was a strong admixture of the outright criminal element. The most famous of those armies was led in the Ukraine by Nestor Makhno. A half-illiterate Ukrainian peasant, self-professed Anarchist, Makhno appeared in the spring of 1918 in Moscow where he had an interview with Lenin, who received him graciously and facilitated his return to the Ukraine, still under Austro-German occupation. Once on his home ground Makhno organized a guerrilla band, which intermittently fought every armed force that passed through the unfortunate land: the Germans, Ukrainian nationalists, Denikin's, and other partisan bands. At times he would collaborate with the Red Army in its fight against the Whites, at other times he would turn against them. Captured Communists, especially if they were connected with the *Cheka,* were often executed by his forces. Still, at the most critical period of the Civil War the Bolshevik policy was to establish some form of collaboration with Makhno. In April 1919 no less a dignitary than L. Kamenev was dispatched to negotiate with Makhno. It must have been an incongruous conference: one of the most scholarly of the Communists conferring with this barely literate and usually intoxicated Anarchist chieftain. "Father Makhno," as he was known to his followers, assured Kamenev that he was a friend of the Soviet power and showed him the tree where with his own hands he had just hanged a White colonel. He denied the charges of banditry and anti-Semitism, and his visitor, evidently satisfied, told Makhno that his forces were included in the Red Army and addressed him as "Comrade." [82]

Though Makhno compared favorably with other partisan leaders insofar as he discouraged, not always successfully, pillaging and Jewish pogroms, Trotsky's reaction to this alliance was one of anger and humiliation. His comments on Makhno's partisans even when they were fighting alongside the Reds against Denikin are characteristic of his military philosophy: "There is no regard for order and discipline in that 'army.' No

[82] V. S., "The Expedition of L. Kamenev to the Ukraine, in April 1919," in *The Proletarian Revolution,* 1925, No. 6.

sources of supply. . . . In that 'army' officers were elected. . . . Dark deluded . . . armed masses become a blind instrument in the hands of adventurers. . . . High time to end this half kulak, half anarchist dissipation. . . ." [83] But Makhno continued his uneasy collaboration with the Red Army long after Trotsky had written those words. Only in 1921, when his help was no longer needed, was his band liquidated and he himself forced to flee from the country.

Except for being headed by an avowed Anarchist, Makhno's forces were not really too different from many an early Soviet army or partisan detachment. Trotsky worked ceaselessly to have them transformed into regular disciplined units. He was an early and enthusiastic proponent of the employment of the former Tsarist officers. That the latter contributed decisively to the Red Army's victory is one thing on which both the Bolshevik and White sources are unanimously agreed. The employment of those people was bound to encounter strong opposition. If we discount the story of Lenin's hesitation on this count, it is still a fact that many old-line Communists found this step unpalatable, and for some of them who had assumed command or were commissars this represented a direct threat. As is well known, Trotsky accompanied his policy with the famous circular warning that his ministry would keep a register of the professional officers' families and that they would be held responsible for their desertion or disloyalty. But he was an enthusiastic defender of the professional officer, whom he praised frequently and protected from attacks by the doctrinaires. In Party circles his defense of the "gentlemen" was being caustically compared with his readiness to punish Communists. Another of his famous orders stipulated that in the case of a unit's desertion its commissar would be shot first and *then* the commanding officer. He had none of Lenin's occasional toleration of hooliganism when produced by an excess of proletarian zeal. Severe penalities awaited the Red Army soldiers caught looting and Trotsky's sense of orderliness went so far as to make him protest against exactions and humiliation inflicted upon the *bourgeoisie* in the recaptured territory.

Ironically enough, it was Lenin who can be said to have been the main political beneficiary of his War Commissar's severity and authoritarianism. Himself a stern disciplinarian under whose hand many Bolsheviks had chafed in the first months of the Revolution, Lenin now appeared as almost a semianarchist when compared with Trotsky. This would be a recurrent pattern throughout Lenin's leadership of Soviet Russia: a lieutenant of his would propose a policy that would outrage many by its excessive authoritarianism; Lenin, while accepting the substance of the proposals, would couch them in a more moderate, acceptable language. He would thus gain credit for moderation and soothe or rather cover up the growing personal antagonisms among the ambitious Communist hier-

[83] Trotsky, *How the Revolution Armed,* Vol. 2, Part 1, p. 191.

archs. This technique solidified his hold on the Party and avoided his identification with this or that faction. But at the same time it laid the ground for the violent struggle for power that erupted into the open once Lenin's hand was no longer at the helm.

It still fell to Lenin to intervene directly in some of the most important military decisions. Over Trotsky's objections he sanctioned the replacement of the Commander-in-Chief of the Red Army J. Vatsetis by another former Tsarist colonel, S. S. Kamenev.[84] The new commander reported in his recollections that he saw Lenin but seldom. On one occasion he sketched to him a proposed military operation, and could not help pointing out the beauty of the maneuver. Lenin retorted drily that his job was to beat the enemy, and whether it was done in a beautiful manner or not was immaterial.

Lenin's caution in military matters abandoned him only when he could sense the possibility of a Communist revolution in the West. The fall of the German Empire in 1918 made him envisage a Berlin version of October 1917. The new Socialist government of Germany was offered supplies, even though the shortage of food in Russia was much worse. Lenin called for the expansion of the Red Army to three million "to help the German nation" in its expected struggle against "the Franco-English imperialists."[85] It was a brief rebirth of the Lenin before October 1917: Russia was starving and in the throes of the Civil War, the Red Army was barely beyond the first stage of its organization and plagued by wholesale desertions, and yet it was supposed to fight on *foreign soil* the combined forces of the victorious Allies and of the regular German army. Certainly the defeat of German communism in January 1919 when the Spartakus revolt was crushed and its leaders, Karl Liebknecht and Rosa Luxemburg, killed might well have been providential in saving Russian communism from a fatal adventure.[86]

The mirage of an ideological expansion to the West flickered on and off during the next two years. In the cases of the short-lived Soviet regimes in Hungary and Bavaria Lenin could do little but offer some good advice.[87]

[84] This is one of the rare occasions when we have the record of Lenin mentioning a high state matter to his wife. He writes "dear Nadya," on July 9, 1919, that he expects much from the replacement of Vatsetis by Kamenev. A less modest husband would not have resisted the temptation to say "I have decided to appoint . . ."

[85] *Works*, Vol. 28, p. 83.

[86] If one indulges in historical conjectures one might also speculate that *Russian* communism was fortunate in the failure of Liebknecht and Luxemburg to seize power in Germany. Luxemburg, "pompous Rosa" as Lenin used to call her before 1914, was an old antagonist of his. Her last work was a severe indictment of the Bolshevik dictatorship, and it is probable that under her leadership German communism would soon have clashed with Lenin's. And, finally, in 1964 we could see what happens when communism triumphs in another major nation.

[87] He wired the Bavarian Communists in April 1919 asking them whether they had taken "hostages from the *bourgeoisie*," tripled the pay of the poor peasants, and so on. *Works*, Vol. 29, p. 298.

But in 1920 he was once again to throw prudence to the wind, for a chance to carry communism to the heart of Europe.

To be sure the circumstances were much more promising than in 1918–19. The Red Army was now a formidable force. Except for Wrangel's army, holed up in the Crimea, the major White forces had been crushed. The Poles, who in the spring had advanced into the Ukraine and reached Kiev, had overextended their lines and in the next few weeks the Red Army pushed them back into Poland. The foreign danger and then the defeat of the traditional enemy gave rise to the first instance of outright Russian nationalism being summoned to bolster up the ideological appeal. The chauvinistic note sounded by some Communist publications went so far that Trotsky felt compelled to reprimand the military journal that contrasted "the perfidious Jesuitism of the Poles" with the "open and honest" nature of the Russians.[88]

In Lenin, however, the military successes of the Red Army revived an old dream: the Red Army reaching the frontiers of Germany and bringing an encouragement to the strong Communist movement in that country. In March he claimed that the Communists had become more realistic since the early days of their power. "We made a lot of silly mistakes at the time of Smolny . . . when chaos and enthusiasm ruled." [89] But in July he was again carried away by enthusiasm for the idea of the Russian Revolution linking arms with the still seething German proletariat. With the ejection of the Poles from the Ukraine and Byelorussia, Russia could have secured a very comfortable peace. But the Bolsheviks, and in this case it was Lenin who was most insistent, pressed for an advance to Warsaw. The Soviet conditions offered to Poland, now apparently defeated, would have turned the country into a Russian satellite. More eloquent than the conditions was the creation of the Polish Revolutionary Committee, which was obviously to become the first Polish Bolshevik government. Its chairman was Julian Marchlewski, among its members Dzerzhinsky and his colleague on the *Cheka*, I. Unschlicht. None of its members had had for years the slightest connection with the Polish working class. The very names of the members of this intended government were enough to make the most radically minded Polish worker join in the defense of his country.

In his very untypical impatience and insistence upon the speediest possible march upon Warsaw Lenin was disregarding the warnings of both his Polish and military experts. The former pointed out that it was illusory to count on the possibility of proletarian uprisings in Warsaw or any other major cities, and that the link with Russia compromised Polish communism in the eyes of the Polish workers and peasants. The military claimed that haste could be purchased only by stretching the Red Army's communication and supply lines to the breaking point. Trotsky was

[88] Trotsky, *How the Revolution Armed*, Vol. 2, Part 2, p. 153.
[89] *Works*, Vol. 30, p. 428.

among the doubters. But his and others' objections were swept away by Lenin's insistence.

In August the Poles counterattacked and the Red Army suffered the most severe defeat of its three years' existence. The analyses of the defeat have always been inextricably linked with political controversy. It was Stalin, claims Trotsky, who as the political commissar of the Southern front refused to authorize his armies to render assistance to the main Red force marching on Warsaw. The latter's commander, Tukhachevsky, a twenty-seven-year-old former Tsarist lieutenant, had himself been accused of sheltering political ambitions that made him imprudently search for quick success. Finally, Lenin's own insistence that the Red Army reach the frontiers of Germany as fast as possible was in itself a cause of the dispersion of the Russian forces and their crushing defeat.[90]

Whatever the explanation, it is hard to believe that Soviet Russia was as yet strong enough to conquer and rule a nation of 25 million or, still more fantastic, that an attempt to sovietize Germany by force could have been successful. It is just as likely that the seizure of Warsaw could have had, in the long run, fatal consequences for communism in Russia.

Lenin afterward was to admit freely his overoptimism in the Polish campaign and his share of blame in the defeat. Still his dream, Soviet Russia joining hands with a revolution in Germany, died hard. Even following the armistice with Poland, which led to the territorial settlement that prevailed until 1939, he still spoke nostalgically of the missed chance: "If Poland had become Soviet, if the Warsaw workers received the help from Soviet Russia that they expected . . . the Versailles Treaty would have collapsed." [91] An untypically wistful statement for Lenin. He was not wont to cry over lost causes or to delude himself over the facts (the Polish workers *expecting* Soviet help). But it was the final sigh over the dream of the world revolution that now had to be laid aside, and, as he probably realized, that he would not see fulfilled in his lifetime. The major episodes of armed struggle were now behind, and he had to turn to the task of rebuilding a society in a country shattered and brutalized by six years of war and revolution.

[90] This is implied in the Polish commander's work on the campaign: J. Pilsudski, *Year 1920* (in Polish), London, 1941, p. 129.
[91] *Works*, Vol. 31, p. 281.

IX

THE WORLDS
OF COMMUNISM

1. The Old Economic Policy

Though the Civil War ended officially in 1920 with the capture of the Crimea by the Red Army, peasant uprisings and insurrections in the non-Russian parts of the now-Communist empire went on into the middle twenties. But the most catastrophic and heroic period of the struggle for power was over; Lenin's Party was the master of the vast multinational area, most of the Tsar's former domains.

Yet was the Civil War ever in fact concluded? What was Stalin's collectivization campaign of 1929–33 but an almost military operation directed against a large part of Russia's population, a campaign, to be sure, against people who had no means of armed resistance, but who by their very mode of existence blocked the road to Communist objectives? Somewhere between 1917 and 1921 the Communist struggle ceased to be merely a struggle against the Whites and foreign intervention and became also a fight against the way of life, habits, and ideas of a vast majority of the Russian people and not merely those of the *bourgeoisie* and the *kulaks*. And in some ways this struggle still goes on.

It fell to one who had always been close to communism but never quite within it to express this heritage of the Civil War in terms that most Bolsheviks could not or would not admit even to themselves. Following the attempted assassination of Lenin, Maxim Gorky renewed his friendship with the man whom in 1917 he had denounced as a fanatic and destroyer of the Social Democratic tradition. Lenin, for his part, eagerly welcomed him back. Even the most modest dictator welcomes a prominent man of letters in his entourage, but in addition Lenin, for all his past irritations with Gorky's politics and philosophy, was genuinely fond of him. Personal likes and dislikes with Lenin could never be entirely apolitical. He once wrote to Inessa Armand that Gorky was "calflike" in his political naïveté. And yet there was something in the great writer's political thinking, in his vision of the future, that was close to his own.

What Gorky wrote at the conclusion of the Civil War as his own reflections about it has, then, a more general interest. Because of its savage tone, because of its total disregard for the official Communist mythology, the little book has never been reprinted in Soviet Russia. But as one follows Lenin's utterances or the official Bolshevik policies during his remaining years, one will find in them, as it were, echoes of Gorky's bitter thoughts about Russia and the Russians.[1]

The Civil War was for Gorky not a struggle between good and evil, between progress and reaction, but one mostly against the inherent anarchy and inertness of the Russian people. He has no sympathy for the complaints of the anti-Communists: "Let me remind you that the most evil and shameless lies are those spread by the defeated and the humiliated." Not that he absolves the Bolsheviks from atrocities and baseness: "The politicians of all kinds are the most sinful of the sinners. . . . Whatever the ideas by which men pretend to be guided, in practice they all behave like animals. . . ." But the main target of Gorky is the common man, the object of idolization and hope of the generations of the revolutionaries: the Russian peasant. He has never seen in him, he writes, a noble savage, a man naturally kind, hospitable, and with a primitive yet real wisdom. The actual man of the people is narrow-minded, cunning, tight-fisted, and indolent. From the Civil War Gorky picks out the harrowing tales of how the peasants, whether in the Red, White or their own detachments, behaved with a cruelty often surpassing that of the most sadistic *Cheka* or White officials.

Most of all Gorky, himself of proletarian origin, has none of the intellectual's inhibitions when it comes to pointing out the stupidity and primitive malice of the "man of the people." There is his story of the peasant who confessed to a city gentleman that he was greatly worried: he has killed a native Bashkir and stolen his cow; will he be prosecuted for his theft? Asked whether he did not fear punishment for the murder the peasant replied: "That is nothing, people now come cheaply." The same lack of inhibitions makes the writer brush aside the official myth of the Revolution as having been accomplished by the "masses." The Revolution, he says, was the work of a "numerically tiny group of the intelligentsia leading a few thousand workers who have been indoctrinated by it. . . ."

What of the future? There is hope, writes Gorky, that "like the Jews, led out by Moses from Egyptian bondage, so the half-savage, stupid and heavy people of the Russian villages and countryside will die out." The men who will replace them will not be terribly attractive. The Russian of the future will not "eagerly think of Einstein's theory or understand the significance of Shakespeare or Leonardo da Vinci . . ." but he will learn "the meaning of electrification, the value of a scientific agronomist, the use of the tractor, and the necessity of having in every village a qualified doctor and a paved road." Perhaps not a bad description of the Russian

[1] Maxim Gorky, *The Russian Peasant* (in Russian), Berlin, 1922, 45 pp.

peasant in this year of 1965, or, for that matter, of the American farmer.

Gorky's gloomy reflections represent, of course, only one side of the picture, that of an embittered townsman and *intelligent*. Even though his pamphlet was published in Berlin, Gorky could not, even if he wanted to, have pointed out the other side of the picture: how much the peasant was sinned against both by the Reds and the Whites. The Bolshevik requisitioning expeditions in their search for grain for the starving cities tortured and executed countless peasants. Trotsky's order required burning of every dwelling where a Red Army deserter had been given shelter. Since the total number of deserters from the Red Army reached over two and a half million (in practice, on being apprehended they were usually given an opportunity to re-enlist and "only" incorrigible deserters were shot) it would have meant a wholesale burning of the villages had the order been followed literally.

But in this new and equally one-sided stereotype of the Russian peasant Gorky touched on something deeper: the Civil War tended to produce even in the most idealistic Communist a feeling of disillusionment with the old slogans and postulates under which the Party had seized power. It was not only the "poor peasant" who was now seen in a different light (the "middle peasant" was always suspicious, and the *kulak* an out-and-out bourgeois) but so were the other clichés and stereotypes of the doctrine. The industrial worker, the traditional backbone of the Party, turned out upon many occasions to be hostile to the Bolsheviks. Lenin had a hard time explaining why the most class-conscious and best-organized segments of the working class had an annoying tendency to relapse under the Menshevik and S-R influence. The printers, he argued, were for the Mensheviks because they obviously were bribed by the *bourgeoisie*, that is, they made money by printing Menshevik and other bourgeois publications. But even this bizarre logic could hardly be applied to the railwaymen, whose union was for long a thorn in the side of the Bolshevik Party.

Most of all, the Communists' disillusionment was growing in regard to their own party and its rule. It had always been organized upon an elitist basis, but it had preserved something of the old Social Democratic tradition of comradely equality and freedom of discussion. During the war Trotsky did not hesitate to imprison and execute veteran Communists. His fellow commissars would keep Party workers and petitioners cooling their heels in the antechambers of their ministries. Even at its earliest period, communism in power already displayed alarming symptoms of its congenital disease, bureaucratism. Within a year the same people who in October 1917 begged off ministerial duties were surrounded by secretaries, personal entourages, were quarreling with each other about their respective spheres of power, busily complaining in the Central Committee or with Lenin himself about their colleagues' intrigues and inattention to duties. In August 1918 the number of state and Party officials in Moscow alone reached the number of 231,000. Even to the most realistic Communist this luxuriant growth of bureaucracy, with its attendant phenomena of official privileges, of red tape, and of the haughty attitude toward the average citizen had about it something of the unexpected and monstrous. To the last, Lenin never became reconciled to the melancholy fact that no modern dictator or statesman could hope to control fully his own administrative machinery or to impose upon it his own sense of urgency. He would become furious at examples of red tape or of official highhandedness brought to his attention. A heated letter to a Commissariat or a soviet would follow, demanding the guilty official's removal, his imprisonment for a week, a year. But those occasional forays could affect, of course, but a minuscule number of cases. And bureaucracy and bureaucratic manners grew on and on.

It was not within Lenin's power to conquer bureaucratism, for the only means of restraining this monster, a government of laws, was to him equally hateful as a bourgeois and philistine concept. Always sensitive to official brutality, rudeness, or red tape, he could not quite admit that there was one way of combating them: legal procedures. On May 17, 1922, when the Civil War was already over, the candidate of laws, former member of the bars of Samara and St. Petersburg, Vladimir Ulyanov-Lenin wrote to his Commissar of Justice: "Courts cannot dispense with terror, to promise that would be a self-deception or lie." [2] One cannot see sadism in that or a delight in terror for terror's sake, but again his recurrent irritation at anything reminiscent of the ideology of the vanished world of the liberal intelligentsia, at the "philistine" notions of impartial justice and independent judiciary that had been the aspirations of the Russia of his youth.

Thus Lenin's struggle against bureaucratic ossification of the Party and the state was to continue to his very end. On his deathbed he still turned over in his mind various schemes by which Soviet institutions could recoup their original contact with the feelings and aspirations of the masses. And practically his last communication to the Party was a complaint against official rudeness, this time directed against his own family: Stalin, his creature and trusted lieutenant, had threatened and insulted his wife, Krupskaya.

The complex job of dealing with the disillusionments and contradictions that power brought to the Bolsheviks was faced as early as March 1919 when the Eighth Congress of the Russian Communist Party assembled. The Congress in itself provided a paradox. The heaviest trials of the Civil War were still ahead but the assembly discussed the new Party program and its over-all policies with quiet confidence, as if its rule for generations ahead was already assured and the Denikins, Kolchaks, and Yudeniches presented no threat at all. A vast difference from the spirit of

[2] *Works*, Vol. 33, p. 321.

the Seventh Congress one year before, when a handful of delegates deliberated in secrecy, unsure whether a new German advance would cut short not only the Congress but Soviet power as well. Lenin was then attacked and reviled when he argued desperately for the necessity of ratifying a humiliating treaty that to some spelled the end of communism in Russia. Now he was the unquestioned leader of the victorious though still struggling Party, and his appearance brought four hundred delegates to their feet in an ovation.

But behind this self-assurance and the air of self-congratulation there was the Communists' growing disillusionment with the masses and with themselves, the puzzled uncertainty as to where the Party was moving in the economy, the nationality question, a hundred other problems where actuality clashed both with the doctrine of Marx and their own early ideals and hopes.

To those doubts and questionings Lenin sought to give answers. "How can you start on the greatest of all revolutions, knowing in advance how you will complete it?" he asked himself, preparing the assembly for the dazzling paradoxes he proceeded to unfold. Each departure from earlier idealism and from prerevolutionary promises was shown to be the result of harsh practical experiences. "We often have to change our policies in a way that a superficial observer might deem strange and incomprehensible. 'How is it,'—he would say—'yesterday you made promises to the petty *bourgeoisie* but today Dzerzhinsky says that the Mensheviks and the Left S-Rs will be stood up against the wall and shot. What a contradiction.'"[3] What a contradiction indeed, and the "superficial observer" would undoubtedly call his explanation a piece of casuistry: the Bolsheviks fight the *bourgeoisie,* not the S-Rs and the Mensheviks, but if the latter turn against them, then, alas, the wall. One or two years earlier, the majority of those present would have risen in protest against this cynicism masquerading as dialectic in defense of one-party rule, but by now the lesson of political intolerance had been learned by the Communists; no one objected to the brazen characterization of the other Socialist parties as "petty bourgeois," nobody mentioned that the remnants of Martov's party were preserving exemplary loyalty to the Soviet regime, despite persecutions, closing down of their newspapers, and the like.

It was not cynicism that Lenin sought to impose upon the minds of his followers but this strange ambivalence of his own mind. The Bolsheviks should *not* preach what they practiced. A purely tactical cynical approach to a political problem aroused his ire. Everybody knew by now—and Lenin could not delude himself that it was otherwise—that the Bolsheviks practiced the strictest political centralization and that the independ-

[3] *Protocols of the Eighth Congress of the Russian Communist Party,* Moscow, 1933, p. 18.

ence, say, of the Ukrainian Communist Party was, even in 1919, a polite fiction. Yet stating this fact bluntly would lead to an explosion on his part. Pyatakov, a young rising Bolshevik, had the gall to suggest that a spade should be called a spade and that the Party program should state openly that all the national Communist parties (the Ukrainian, the Central Asian, all the others) were under the (Russian) Central Committee. Any Communist who would put such a statement in the program ought to shoot himself, said Lenin. On the broader national question a similar bluntness of Bukharin led to one of Lenin's most memorable epigrams. "Scratch a Russian Communist and you will find a Russian chauvinist." [4] All that poor Bukharin had said was that the Bolshevik postulate for national self-determination should be interpreted on paper as it was in practice, that is, the right of the given working class (or to beat Bukharin at his bluntness, the right of the local Bolsheviks) to rule the given country. He, Bukharin, did not care whether the Polish *bourgeoisie* wanted independence of Poland, he was going to respect only the desires of the Polish workers. Sinking even deeper in the morass of political realism, Bukharin said that the postulate of independence for *every* nationality was obviously a tactical gambit. The Communists could not seriously believe that "the Hottentots and Bushmen" should become independent; they put it in their program to embarrass and weaken the British imperialists. Such frankness brought Lenin's strongest reprimand. Years later on his deathbed he might have had this episode in mind when he wrote that Bukharin, who among all the Bolshevik leaders was his special favorite, "has never understood the dialectic." It was not easy.

The national problem is perhaps the best illustration of the strange workings of Lenin's mind. He was perfectly sincere in his detestation of gross Russian chauvinism, loved to repeat that the Poles and Finns are more cultured nations than the Russians. The heavily oppressive national policies of Tsarist times had aroused his contempt and loathing. Intermittently, as we shall see, his fury was aroused by those of his lieutenants who would apply the same policies to the Ukrainians, Georgians, or Bashkirs. Yet he saw no inconsistency in the fact that the head of the Ukrainian Communist Party and government was a Bulgarian by birth, that most of its high officials were Russians who did not even speak Ukrainian, and that any gesture of independence by one of the national or regional divisions of the Communist Party would bring a quick reprisal by Moscow. There was undoubtedly an element of cunning in his nationality policy. Even though practice clashed with the fine principle of "self-determination" for everybody, the Polish *bourgeoisie* and the Hottentots included, the principle was attractive enough to help the Bolsheviks win the Civil War and to gain them followers and admirers throughout the whole colonial world.

[4] *Ibid.*, p. 107.

But beyond that the impression must remain that Lenin believed himself to be entirely consistent. He was the possessor of the secret "dialectic," which enabled him to steer the Party clear between the dangers of doctrinaire idealism and cynical enjoyment of power for power's sake.

One may quarrel with this conclusion and see in all his maneuvers and formulas nothing but Machiavellianism designed to maintain his and the Party's power, and to delude the masses into believing that the Soviet rule was something else than just oppression and government by force. Some time later we find him making a statement more worthy of Bismarck than of a faithful disciple of Marx and Engels: "Great problems in the life of nations are decided only by force." [5] But in any case one cannot deny him an enormous pedagogical success. His own tortuous thinking became that of the whole Party. Politics does not consist in looking up the solution of this or that problem in Karl Marx, nor is it *simply* the question of using force. There is the "dialectic." . . .

This lesson was also propagated by Lenin in regard to the peasant. Many of the delegates to the Congress had been participants in the food detachments sent to the countryside to requisition grain from the peasants. The worthlessness of money and the lack of manufactured goods made the peasant unwilling to part with surplus grain. But this unwillingness and huge black market were not, as the Communists or as the townsmen in general believed, the product of the peasant's greed and depravity. They reflected also his misery, the fact that grain requisitioned as surplus was often needed for his own consumption or for his cattle, and finally the brutal and terroristic methods of exacting supplies. Yet in Lenin's version the whole terror campaign of the Bolsheviks in the countryside was directed against the small class of rich peasants, the *kulaks*. For the poor and middle peasant the intentions and methods of the Bolsheviks, Lenin declared, were friendly: "We do not allow any measure of force in regard to the middle peasant." Even the *kulak*, he intimated, is not really terrorized, though the Bolsheviks have to suppress his "counterrevolutionary endeavors." Practically everybody at the Congress knew from his own experience executions, beatings, and confiscations of property that accompanied the exaction of food. That the stereotype division of the peasantry broke down in practice was admitted by the speaker. The peasant would ask the invading food detachment: "I have two horses and one cow. Am I a middle peasant?" It finally taxes one's belief in Lenin's sincerity to hear him preach that the Communists should learn "the whole history of the peasant's household and his attitude toward the poor and rich" in order to explain to the *moujik* his class status. Such sociological studies were beyond the province of the food detachments, which operated in a hurry and with rifles, not statistical tables.

Insofar as the peasant was concerned, no dialectic, no contradiction

[5] *Works,* Vol. 31, p. 319.

within Lenin's own thinking could obscure or explain away the essentially repressive and hypocritical policy of the Bolsheviks. The basic reason for this attitude was included in the original dilemma of the Russian Marxists: they could conquer power only by promising the peasant something they did not believe in, the untouchability of his property. The frenzy of the Civil War turned this ideological dislike into hatred. The peasant appeared to the Communist as "half savage, stupid and heavy" in his struggle to survive. He withheld grain from the worker and the soldier. To the famished city worker the countryman was now much more hateful than the bourgeois: the latter had been stripped of his property, the former allegedly had plenty to eat and made money on the black market.

Repugnant as the peasant was to the regime, the policy of *sheer* oppression and exaction could not be successfully applied to 80 per cent of Russia's population. In their attempt to find some base of support in the countryside the Communist authorities varied their policies, or at times pursued several differing approaches at once. "We often take with one hand what we give with the other," admitted Lenin and in no sphere of Soviet policy was this characterization truer than in agriculture.

There was an attempt to split the peasants, to raise the banner of the class war in the villages. In the summer of 1918, once the regime felt some firm ground under its feet it proceeded to ordain the creation of the Committees of Poor Peasants. Who was the poor peasant? According to the Communist semantics he was a man who had little or no land and who in order to survive had to hire himself to the landowner (in the old times) or the *kulak*. The village poor, however, soon proved themselves to be a double-edged instrument when dealing with the rural problem. They naturally enough oppressed their more affluent neighbors, helped the food detachments in unmasking black marketeers and hoarders of grain, but by the same token they could hardly help in assuring a steady production of food. Faced by oppression by the state, exposed to indignities at the hands of the shiftless, often criminal, elements in his village, the peasant would refuse to sow or would slaughter his cattle. At the end of 1918 the Committees of the Poor Peasants were disbanded, and the Party turned to its new hope in the countryside, "the middle peasant."

"We have not yet learned to regulate our relations with the millions of the middle peasants, we haven't yet learned how to win their confidence," said Lenin in an obvious understatement at the Eighth Congress.[6] It was one of those dazzling tactical shifts that were to become a regular feature of Soviet policies: an abused, persecuted social element was suddenly summoned to trust and support the Soviet power. Their previous sufferings were declared to have been the result of misunderstandings, of abuse of authority, and a regrettable excess of zeal by the local officials, of their inability to show the peasant the consideration and understanding which

---

[6] *Protocols of the Eighth Party Congress*, p. 353.

he, Lenin, and the central Party authorities had always preached. Conveniently for this purpose, Jacob Sverdlov, Chairman of the Executive Committee of the Congress of Soviets and thus officially the head of the Bolshevik state, had just died. Sverdlov was of Jewish origin, something the Bolsheviks in the first flush of their victory considered as quite irrelevant to a man's fitness for this or that post.[7] But now, with the Civil War in full swing, with all the cries about the "Jewish commissars," it was an excellent opportunity to entrust this figurehead post to a "real" Russian. Michael Kalinin, who was elevated to this office and who, wonder of wonders, was to survive Stalin's purges in it, was described by Lenin as "a middle peasant from the Tver province, which he visits every year." [8] It was not entirely a lie, since like a vast majority of Russians Kalinin was of peasant ancestry. But he was an industrial worker by profession, an old Bolshevik who had spent all his adult life in Party work in major urban centers. To be sure, Kalinin fell in with his role, and to the end he was to play a simple *moujik* befuddled by the grandeur of his presidency.

Such gestures had their propaganda value: the head of the Soviet state was a "simple peasant" while the White regimes were led by generals and admirals whom the peasant identified with the former landlords. But the essence of the agricultural problem could not be affected by the appointment of even a hundred "middle peasants" to responsible Soviet positions. The war period witnessed other experimentation in agriculture: there was a bow to Marxian orthodoxy, an attempt to form large-scale farms out of the landowners' estates. There were the first primitive efforts at collectivization; the communes, formed usually on the poorest land, and by the most inefficient cultivators. To the average peasant those experiments were hardly less odious than the activity of the food detachments. He had accepted the Bolshevik rule, because the Bolsheviks promised to respect his *own* plot of land, and he did not want to become a hired hand, or to join the local riffraff in their commune. And besides, large-scale cultivation of land, so dear to the heart of the Marxist, was under wartime conditions barely more efficient than that of the family plot. Where were the machines, where was the trained personnel, which alone make it worthwhile?

In Lenin's thinking, the disappointment with the people, the disillusionment with the "revolutionary initiative of the masses," whether those of the poor peasants or the workers, tended to increase his already strong faith in technology. Economic problems would be overcome, human foibles and apathy conquered, through an industrial breakthrough or a technological miracle. The village would be conquered for socialism overnight if the Communists could give the peasants "one hundred thousand

[7] Trotsky claims that in October he refused Lenin's offer of the Commissariat of the Interior on grounds that its head should not be a Jew. But it is very likely that he simply was not interested in the job.

[8] *Works*, Vol. 29, p. 240.

good tractors, gas . . . trained mechanics. . . ." In the Russia of 1919 this was sheer fantasy. But perhaps it was fortunate for him that he did not live to see Russia furnished with tractors and mechanics beyond his fondest expectations, but he saw only the peasant still disgruntled, still far from having been won for communism.

Faith in the machine, in techniques, in organization: Those characteristics had always been present in Lenin. Now with the experience of power, the *other* side of his nature became more and more subdued. The semianarchist of *State and Revolution* was laid to rest within a few weeks after the October Revolution. His earlier oratory was increasingly referred to by Lenin as "that foolishness of the Smolny period," "the time of enthusiasm and chaos." His constant refrain now: order, discipline, and organization. And imperceptibly the very instrument of power, the Communist Party, was being turned into a machine.

It is most unlikely that this process could have been fully consummated while Lenin was alive. The puppetlike unanimity of the Party's congresses in Stalin's era, the effusive tributes to the Leader and his henchmen of the moment, complete domination of the entire structure by a bureaucratic clique, all these phenomena would have revolted Lenin. The Party was for him not a discussion club, but by the same token it should not be a collection of automatons. He enjoyed some secondary characteristics of the Party gatherings: their informality, comradely joshings. Within limits, he even liked dissension and being criticized, provided that eventually he had his own way. At times Lenin delighted in intra-Party machinations and intrigues: to side with Zinoviev in order to confound Trotsky, to draw a Congress' attention to the perennial foolhardiness of Bukharin's proposals, meant perhaps to revert to his younger and happier days of impassioned duels with Martov and Plekhanov. Before his final incapacitating stroke Lenin, Trotsky tells us, planned to join him "in a bloc against bureaucracy in general and against the Organizational Bureau in particular" (in fact against Stalin). He had grown to distrust Stalin, but also, with his life ebbing away, Lenin must have felt like having one more good fight and victory at a Party congress. The debater and the journalist in his make-up interfered somewhat with the dictator.

It is equally true that the longer he continued in power the greater grew his irritation at being contradicted or opposed within the Party circles. His irritation took many expressions: at times he would protest at the Party's being infiltrated by the former Mensheviks and S-Rs or by the careerists. At other times, and more violently, he would rant at the Anarchist and Social Democratic tendencies still afflicting many old Bolsheviks. We noted that as early as the time of Brest Litovsk he grew disenchanted with the conspirator-orator type of Bolshevik and turned more toward those who "could do things," the species that flowered under Stalin as the *apparatchik*, the man of the inner apparatus of the Party. Lenin's growing absorption in administrative work, coupled perhaps with his waning strength, made him more short-tempered. In his last two years he grew tired of explaining things to the comrades, of presenting instructive paradoxes and long historical lessons. He began to demand strict obedience and sanctions against those Bolsheviks, even the most respected and deserving, who had dared to cross him on a basic issue.

The portents of change are clearly seen at the Eighth Congress. It heard the first elaborate complaints of bureaucratism and of arbitrary decisions made by the individual commissars. It still did not dawn on the Communists that the dictatorship of the proletariat was increasingly becoming that of one man and a bureaucracy. To many, Lenin appeared as a brake upon the authoritarian tendencies of the commissars and the petty Lenins who were springing up all over Russia. One of the speakers naïvely described the change that had taken place in the year and a half of Soviet government. At first "all the important decisions were made by elective bodies which were close to their electors and received their powers from them"; now "another practice has grown up and taken hold: all powers are concentrated in the hands of small cliques of administrators or even those of individuals." The speaker, V. V. Osinsky, was unrealistic enough to believe that he was describing conditions in the state organs only and not those of the Party. That the former were rapidly becoming a mere window dressing for the rule of the Party was still not clear to many Communists, a demonstration of how people can come to believe their own slogans. But even Osinsky [9] referred to the fact that some of the most important decisions on Party and state matters were made by Lenin alone or in conjunction with the late Sverdlov or some other collaborators.

It was a very mild complaint, but to Lenin clearly a danger signal: the Congress should not become a parliament; his own energies could not be wasted in constant reassurances to the disgruntled Bolsheviks that the Party was keeping its original faith. Hence the Party structure was overhauled. Within the Central Committee two smaller bodies were created, the Politburo of five full members, and the Organizational Bureau. The office of the Party Secretary had in fact been filled by Sverdlov, a man with infinite capacity for detail, excellent memory, and complete submission to Lenin. With his death it became necessary to set up an official secretariat, headed at first by a secondary Party figure, N. Krestinsky, but in three years it was to have a more enterprising and famous occupant. The Politburo, theoretically subordinate to the Central Committee, could not but grow to become its master, in view of the caliber of its members: Lenin, Kamenev, Trotsky, Stalin.

Sixteen years earlier, an apparently silly quarrel as to whether the Party journal should have six or, as Lenin wanted, three editors led to the fateful

---

[9] One of the few qualified economists in the Bolshevik ranks, and probably the only one born a prince; his real name was Obolensky.

split of the Russian Social Democracy and the birth of Bolshevism. Now another administrative reshuffling was to have equally grave consequences. On the surface, the overhaul of the Party machinery was long overdue. It was ridiculous that the ruling Party should have no formal secretarial branch. Until 1919 its administrative staff consisted practically of one man, Sverdlov, "who carried the Party files in his head," and one woman, old Bolshevik Elena Stasova, with her famous locker containing the Central Committee minutes and various secret documents. These two had a few part-time helpers. The Central Committee itself was still not too large a body, around twenty or so, but the emergencies of the Civil War obviously called for a directory of a few persons who could make decisions on the spot.

In fact, the reorganization was bound to change the whole character and spirit of the Party. Its original concept envisaged no such thing as Party administration or gradations of its members. A Social Democratic party was a party of equals; the only administration it needed was that of a recording secretary and treasurer. Now the Secretariat and the Organizational Bureau were not to be confined to such humble functions. They were to take care that the Party organization in Kursk should not speak differently from that in Tambov. The next logical step was to make sure that the officials in both Kursk and Tambov should enjoy the confidence of Moscow; the next, that they should in effect be nominated by Moscow. The further series of "logical steps" was to make the official bearing the humble title of Secretary of the Central Committee, the General or, as now, First Secretary, a potentate with powers undreamed of by emperors and kings of old.

Almost equally far-reaching were the implications of the creation of the Politburo. In the days of their illegal existence the Bolsheviks could not afford the luxury of intra-Party democracy. Democratic centralism meant in practice the selection of their executive committees by appointment and cooptation. But power brought with it the threat of intra-Party democracy. Lenin, though he himself often had to defend his policies and did not escape criticisms, obviously occupied a special place in the esteem of the rank and file. After the Brest Litovsk debate no one could say, "We can take power without Lenin." His subordinates often chafed under his command; his debility, as after the assassination attempt or in 1922, would be met with mixed emotions. He was still to the average Communist *the* leader of the Party and the state. But as to the other leaders, their standing in the Party depended on their popularity and following. It did not occur to anybody to consider Zinoviev or Trotsky to be by virtue of his office a being of a different order from any other Bolshevik. The creation of the small inner circle was a major step toward the crystallization of the Bolshevik hierarchy under Stalin: the divinity, the Secretary-General, is in turn surrounded by semidivinities, his "companions at arms," each within his own sphere to be blindly obeyed and worshiped. It would not occur even to a Central Committee member that any of the oligarchs, as long as he retained the Leader's favor, could be approached on a basis of equality, still less criticized.

It was not Lenin's intention to create specially privileged groups within the Party, but both the logic of the situation and his own temperament were driving him inexorably in that direction. It was becoming increasingly onerous and distasteful to him to deal with disagreements, to overcome an opponent through an argument or speech. In the Central Committee there was always a Shlyapnikov, Kollontay, or Osinsky ready to challenge him on a matter of principle, recalling to him and others Lenin's previous and quite different views on this or that question. It seemed preferable to work with a smaller group of men who could be counted upon to agree with him and who would settle the given issue promptly and without unnecessary oratory. In the Politburo, Trotsky or Bukharin would occasionally object, but the majority were now thoroughly cowed. Zinoviev and Kamenev, Stalin and others would take the Leader's word as law. The submission of those willful and ambitious men was not secured by Lenin for nothing; he had to close his eyes to their weaknesses and to tolerate the creation of their own semi-independent spheres of authority and personal cliques. Thus oligarchy fastened upon dictatorship. And with it favoritism, servility, and corruption crept into the Party.

"We don't believe in 'absolutes.' We laugh at 'pure democracy,'" wrote Lenin in 1921 to an old Bolshevik who had complained to him of the moral decomposition of the ruling Party.[10] The writer dared to suggest that the only remedy was freedom of the press "from the monarchist journals to anarchist ones." Such a suggestion in Stalin's time would have earned its author a bullet or a trip to a concentration camp, and today in a more tolerant era, probably a mental examination. But it was still an understanding dictator who chose to write a long reply to this eccentric comrade and to reassure him as if he were speaking to a sick child. "You have seen so many sordid and painful things that you have fallen into despair. . . . My advice is, don't give way to despair and panic." Hard work was the best cure for Myasnikov's ailing nerves.[11] As to his specific complaints, the Organizational Bureau would appoint a commission to consider them. . . .

That there were a lot of painful and sordid things about the Party he had created and led, Lenin did not and could not deny. His later years, as we shall see again and again, were filled with grasping at straws, in trying to remedy this situation into which his own personality and philosophy had inevitably led the Communist Party and the Soviet state. In the very

[10] *Works*, Vol. 32, p. 479.
[11] G. Myasnikov, the writer of the letter, earned the reputation of a ferocious terrorist during the Civil War and it is eloquent in itself that a man like that should have become an advocate of freedom of the press.

same letter he came up with one of those miragelike solutions: let us "revive" the soviets (obviously in the third year of the Soviet state they were already dead as real organs of power), let the non-Party people check the activity of the Party organs: an idea which, if put forth seriously, was another sign that Lenin was not free of self-delusion.

For the Party had choked every other political organization and force in Russia. It was the Party that had to be the foundation of that brave new world Lenin proposed to construct. Socialist Russia, of which Chernyshevsky and Herzen had dreamed, for which countless revolutionaries had laid down their lives, could be constructed only if the individual Communist kept up the sense of mission and enthusiasm that had brought his party power. But what was the reality?

"Comrade Lenin, let me ask you a question . . . ," said a prominent Communist to his face: "Do you think the salvation of the Revolution lies in the mechanical obedience [of the Party members]?" It had been only one year since administrative changes had been decreed at the Eighth Congress, but bureaucracy was already getting a stranglehold on the Party.

> Why then talk about the dictatorship of the proletariat, about self-initiative of the workers? There is no such initiative. You are turning the Party member into a record player . . . [Party members] have no right to elect their own committees. Let me now ask of the Comrade Lenin: who will [eventually] appoint the Central Committee? After all there you also have one-man leadership . . . and if we finally reach that stage [when the Central Committee is appointed] the Revolution will be lost.[12]

The speaker's agitation was so great that his speech was almost incoherent.

What lay behind this agitation was a seemingly banal administrative problem. The collegiate leadership of the Party and state institutions was being rapidly discarded in favor of one man's direction. That this was the only sensible arrangement when it came to industry and state administration was evident to Lenin as early as October. But in this as in many other things, he had to bow to the anarchic feeling he had himself engendered. Committees ran factories as well as ministries. After all, a loose translation of "Soviet power" is government by councils or committees. As time went by the necessities of war were increasingly invoked to dispense with collegiality. Its inconvenience became a favorite topic with Lenin, in fact an obsession of his. Was not the War Ministry run better now that Trotsky was in sole charge than in the old days "of enthusiasm and chaos" when its three commissars continuously quarreled with each other? How could a committee of workers efficiently direct a factory? It was obviously the job

[12] Speech by T. V. Sapronov, *Protocols of the Ninth Congress of the Communist Party* (March–April 1920), pp. 57–58.

for an expert. He laughed indulgently over his past superstitions and mistakes in this respect. Why could not some other comrades also see the light?

As a polemicist Lenin was a master at confusing issues, and thus he managed to bamboozle the opposition on this count. To many, both within the Party and among the historians, his opponents appeared as fanatical opponents of technical competence and of one-man management in industry. That there were such there is no doubt. But the main burden of the complaints was that the Party was being run dictatorially and by bureaucratic methods. In 1920 it could still be said openly: "One should say once and for all that the Central Committee is responsible to the Party, and it is not an autocratic power," [13] which shows how Lenin was usually one jump ahead of his critics. To talk about the Central Committee when there was an already much tighter oligarchy at the top, the Politburo!

Lenin might have reflected that his position was growing into something like that of the Tsar of old. It was becoming taboo to criticize him personally. *Somebody* was corrupting the spirit of the Party, leading it along the dictatorial and bureaucratic path, but who that somebody was the critics did not quite say. It was partly reverence for the Leader. A speaker at a Party congress could say that the applause which greeted a statement of Lenin's indicated not that the delegates approved the ideas that he expressed but that they were simply applauding Vladimir Ilyich. It was also a reflection of his political skill, of the ability to attribute to the subordinates or simply to "them" the ills besetting the country and the Party. After all he dealt with people who in the main had been under his spell for years, whom he had successively guided through being terrorists, anarchists, and now servants of state capitalism, while persuading them at each phase that they were acting in an orthodox Marxist way. If Lenin was at the head of the Party how could it really be all those horrible things that people were alleging? Why, said one product of this long-term brain washing, the critics are trying to persuade us that "we have at the very top government by an oligarchy, a small clique of rulers which has seized power over the Party and decides everything"! How could one say such things about the famous Communist Party, which had conquered Russia and was now building socialism?

Whatever personal complaints were being brought against Lenin at Party gatherings, they were usually accompanied by the premise that Vladimir Ilyich did not know what was being done in his name, or did not fully realize the dangerous implications of his ideas. Thus one speaker would cite a gross violation of the Soviet constitution: the Executive Committee of the Soviets (by the letter of the law the highest organ of the state except for its parent body, the huge unwieldy Congress of the Sovi-

[13] *Ibid.*, p. 52.

ets, but almost equally unimportant in fact) passed a law. Within a week this law was completely contravened by an edict of the Council of the Commissars "that was a gross violation of the ruling of the All Russian Central Committee by the Council of the Commissars." As the most unsophisticated Bolshevik must have realized, Lenin was in effect the Council of the Commissars. He, a very busy man, probably felt that he could not be bothered to summon the "Parliament" and browbeat it into changing the inconvenient law. But for the speaker it was not Vladimir Ilyich but the Council of Commissars that had sinned.

The same circumlocution was obligatory when it came to protests about the chicaneries applied to those Communists who opposed Lenin or simply got on his nerves. The method of the purge was as yet humane and considerate. An intractable Communist would, especially before an important Party gathering, be sent on a lengthy diplomatic mission. Or the talents of Comrade X would be suddenly required in some place far away from Moscow: the Urals or Central Asia. "The Ukraine . . ." said one, "has been turned into a regular place of exile." This custom again has had a long tradition in Russia. A tactless reference to Alexander II's mistress earned his chief of police promotion to the embassy in London. Imperial displeasure was often expressed in the command that the offending minister retire to his estates or at least refrain from visiting the capital. Compared with the practice under Stalin, Lenin's way of dealing with the opposition was restrained. But in his last two years he was to demand expulsion and arrest as the way to deal with the most obstreperous comrades.

That his hand was behind the punitive measures was incontrovertible. Furthermore, occasionally he was caught lying on this count. Shlyapnikov, he told the Ninth Party Congress, had left on a diplomatic mission on his own (!) without the slightest pressure being put upon him by the Party authorities. Here an indiscreet listener, K. Yurenev, interrupted, "But he told me himself about being pressured." Wonder of wonders, it was soon discovered that Yurenev himself had an amazing aptitude for diplomacy. In 1922 he began his long foreign service, which was to take him all over the world.

It might be thought that the splendor of diplomatic life would be considered, especially in those days of hunger and discomfort in Moscow, to be a reward rather than a punishment. Also, that a Bolshevik would welcome the opportunity to be a big boss in Ufa or Kharkov rather than a subordinate in the capital. But as in all absolutist systems—and in itself it was a good symptom that the Soviet state had become one of them —the attraction of being at the center of things outweighed everything else. The French nobleman of the time of Louis XIV treasured his cubicle at Versailles over and above his castles and estates. The same passion accounted for the Bolshevik dignitary's frantic desire to be in Moscow, near the center of power and gossip.[14] But even the indignity of a diplomatic or other exile was seldom attributed to Lenin personally. It was the Central Committee that delegated Comrade X to Oslo, transferred Comrade Y to Ufa, and so on.

The question must then be posed: To what extent did the Communists and Lenin himself realize that Russia was under the dictatorship not of the proletariat, not of the Party, but of one man? The most fervent opponent of his within the Party would have called such an allegation a vile slander. And of course there were appearances that seemed to confirm that judgment. It was a strange dictator who pleaded with his Party, acknowledged his mistakes, and (to be sure, very rarely and with increasingly bad humor) allowed himself to be outvoted in the Politburo and the Central Committee. When the modern historian says "dictator" he has in mind Hitler or Stalin; it seems grotesque to range Lenin alongside. But the essence of dictatorial power was certainly his: as long as he was well no process short of a revolution could wrest the rule of Russia and communism from his hands. Theoretically the Soviet Parliament—the Executive Committee of the Soviets—could fire him as the Chairman of the Council of Commissars; the Party congress might not re-elect him to the Central Committee. But in fact such eventualities were as unthinkable as that Stalin in the 1930s should not be reappointed Secretary-General of the Party. Lenin did not want to consider himself a dictator. But he also did not want to be restrained by "bourgeois legality," did not like to waste time in convincing obstreperous comrades, and did not allow anybody else the right to decide what was or was not the correct Marxist policy for the moment. What could be the practical effect of the sum of those dislikes?

"We have done, thank God, with purely theoretical debates, quarrels about general issues, endless resolutions about principles. That is a stage we have passed, that task was settled yesterday and before. Now we have to go forward, we have to understand that before us lie practical tasks. . . ." Those words of Lenin's of 1920 [15] well illustrate the perversity of his mind with which the average Party member was unable to cope. What were the general issues settled yesterday? From October on the Communist Party had fought one emergency after another. Every ideological objection was dispatched by Lenin with the argument, "This is not the time." Kerensky, the Germans, Denikin, the Poles, were beating at the gates. One had to be practical, forget *for the moment* what Marx wrote to

[14] This factor was one of the many that enabled Stalin to secure such a grip on the provincial Party organizations and through them on the Party as a whole. None of the prominent Bolsheviks was willing to go into the provinces, and those positions fell into the hands of the gray men of the "apparatus." Zinoviev was the head of the Petrograd (Leningrad) organization, and it held out longest against Stalin. But even Zinoviev was in fact an absentee provincial boss, spending much of his time in the new capital.

[15] *Protocols of the Ninth Congress*, p. 90.

Engels in 1858, what he himself had written in *State and Revolution.* Now, seemingly, was the time for "resolutions about principles," for discarding those features of Soviet society that were justified on the basis that they were short-term passing phenomena demanded by an emergency: political terror, suppression of the independent press, intolerance and persecution of opposition within the Party, deciding in which direction and how the Soviet state should move to achieve socialism. Yet for Lenin the emergency was never to end. Famine on the Volga, a typhus epidemic, the uprising in Kronstadt, were successively invoked as the reason why the Party could not afford to tolerate political opposition or dissension within its own ranks. How can one allow the luxury of free political discussion, he would ask, when there are two million Russian refugees abroad? Or when the capitalists have not desisted from their plans to overthrow the Soviets?

Many, many years before, Martov had accused his old friend of having introduced a "state of siege" in the Russian social democracy. He meant that by his continuous search for enemies, his constant "unmasking" of people and of serving ultimatums, Lenin made normal political life of a party impossible. In those days Lenin could rejoin that for a conspiratorial party normal political life was indeed impossible. If only the Russian Socialists were in the happy position of their French or German colleagues! "How long before we can have meetings like that in Russia?" he said longingly in London in 1907 after listening to political oratory at Hyde Park Corner. But his own mentality made sure that it would be a very long time indeed.

The psychology of the state of siege now was imposed upon the Communist Party and then on Soviet society as a whole. If one studies the behavior of the Soviet government under Lenin carefully (and this characteristic has persisted down to our own days) one will come up with a startling conclusion: *it is in times of crisis, of real emergency, that it has allowed most freedom and tolerated dissent;* "normal" peaceful conditions have brought with them the maximum of political oppression. As long as the Civil War lasted the remnants of loyal Mensheviks à la Martov and the S-Rs were semitolerated; some of them even found their way into the representative organs, the soviets. With the end of the wars this niggardly toleration became a dangerous luxury for the Communists: the worker would claim that they should now redeem their promises, and in his disillusionment he might vote for the Mensheviks in his union and in soviet elections. And so the last leaders of the Mensheviks went to jail or into exile. With the great famine of 1921 the government set up a special All Russian Committee to fight the famine, which included not only non-Party people, but also former Mensheviks and even Kadets. It was to enlist the support of what might be called Russian public opinion, and help from abroad. Its mission accomplished and the extreme emergency alleviated, largely through the help of Hoover's American Relief mission, the non-Party committee was dissolved in August 1921 and "its leading bourgeois members arrested." [16] Absence of an emergency was for Lenin's regime in itself a political emergency. And this was the situation that faced the Communists at the end of the Civil War. "The practical tasks" with which Lenin and his associates wanted to get on were the tasks of ruling, administration, reviving the country's shattered economy and power. The Bolsheviks then proposed to put together what they had helped to smash to bits in 1917. But where was socialism, where were the pledges of October? As to the first, Lenin made a startling discovery that, properly speaking, there was no such thing as a Socialist economic system. As to the pledges to the workers, his own ideas in October, they were the product of the "chaos and enthusiasm" of those rapturous days, which now had to yield to the sober reality of economics.

"Socialism . . . ," he once wrote, "is nothing else but a monopoly of state capitalism, instituted for the benefit of the whole nation, and by virtue of that ceasing to be a capitalist monopoly." But the concrete part of this intricate formula was that socialism was simply capitalism when exercised not by a multitude of capitalists, but by one, the state. The Socialist Party became at his urging Communist, but at the same time he looked longingly to the future when War Communism could be replaced by capitalism. "State capitalism would be a step forward for us. It would mean victory if we could introduce state capitalism in a short time in Russia," he said with a sigh in 1918.[17] The word "state" was not enough of a fig leaf to conceal the shameful truth: at the same time that he was instituting the workers' control of the factories, the peasant communes, and other experiments which go under the name of War Communism, the leader of communism dreamed of a return to money economy, labor discipline, one-man management and those other things which are called capitalism. Truly he said, "We take with one hand what we give with another." For War Communism was very largely his own creation, the product of those feverish sessions of the commissars in Smolny when one after another industrial and commercial undertaking would be decreed nationalized, when workers' control would be ordered for the whole industry. He then rode roughshod over orthodox Marxian objections to such steps: the workers had to be won over to Bolshevism. They had to be convinced that this was *their* state. The workers in turn could be excused for believing that the words "workers' control" meant just that, that they would now run the factories and not merely elect a committee to look on while their bourgeois manager, rechristened "specialist" and made a Soviet official, would order them around as before. In a short time the Bolsheviks managed to erect an elaborate industrial bureaucracy, ranging from the Su-

---

[16] E. H. Carr, *The Bolshevik Revolution 1917–1923*, Vol. 1, 1951, p. 179.
[17] *Works*, Vol. 26, p. 261.

preme Economic Council through ministries and state trusts down to the individual industrial undertakings. But this vast army of officials presided over a disintegrating economy. The loss of expert management and the disappearance of labor discipline contributed as much as the war to the utter collapse of industrial production and commerce.

Until now it had not been possible to make a frontal attack upon this state of affairs. The Bolsheviks had not been able to give the worker enough bread or peace, but they gave him the satisfaction of being the boss, of seeing the former boss deposed and humiliated, and of having the peasant stripped of his surplus (and often more) in order to feed this allegedly new ruling class. Now the time had come for the Communist Party to kill War Communism.

"Can any worker administer the state? Practical people know that that is fantasy. . . . After they [the workers] spend years in learning, they will know how, but this takes time." It was thus that Lenin in 1921 before a labor union meeting urged the Russian worker to accept a new image of himself: no longer the master, he was to be an apprentice. The running of the state, the management of industry, was up to the specialist. The very term grated on the workers' mind, as *burzhuy* had in the days of old. And the Soviet state had for the worker the same message as the old regime of Russia: be patient. In due time, through learning and obedience to orders, the individual worker might expect to advance himself in the world, to become a specialist, to get a specialist's extra rations and higher pay.

The reader by now must be sick of being reminded, as was Lenin, of how drastically those ideas clashed with what he himself had said in *State and Revolution*, what he had kept saying throughout 1917. All that he now classified as "syndicalist nonsense . . . to be thrown into a waste-basket." The workers were told that in due time they would indeed be running things by themselves. When? Perhaps in twenty years' time when all Russia would be electrified. Why hadn't the Revolution been postponed till then? Didn't they believe him? "Everybody believes the Bolsheviks' word [because] they have gone through twenty years of Party work," said Lenin with his peculiar logic.[18]

The struggle between Lenin and his old anarchist ghost occupied the last active years of his life. This struggle is often described as the campaign by the Party against its two "deviations": the Workers' Opposition and the group that called themselves Democratic Centralists. The latter may well be cited as the classical case of the befuddlement in which Communists find themselves when after years of obedience they discover that something is wrong with the policy of the Party. The Democratic Centralists objected to bureaucratism, but what the remedy was for this evil was beyond them. Their very incoherence provided a convenient foil for Lenin

[18] *Works*, Vol. 32, p. 41.

and his associates. What was it that Osinsky and his colleagues wanted with their mumblings about the need to delimit the spheres of competence of various state and Party institutions? A code of administrative law, the way they have it in the rotten plutocracies of the West? A fine way for the workers' state to operate, through administrative handbooks and bourgeois legality! And the unfortunate Democratic Centralist would retreat in confusion and amidst the comrades' derision.[19]

The Workers' Opposition was on the other hand a much more serious matter. There is a great temptation to describe its defeat as the turning point in the history of communism, the definite passage from earlier idealism to acquiescence in the role of the ruling class. But this is the temptation that confronts the historian more than once, in writing about 1903, 1912, October, the chasing out of the Constituent Assembly, and so on. The crisis of 1921 was one further step that Lenin's party, as long as it was his, had to take.

Behind the Opposition lay the rising discontent of the working class. With it was combined the disgruntlement of many veteran Communists at being shoved aside, at being replaced by the people who "just joined the Party" or the non-Party people in state and managerial posts. Among the leaders of the Workers' Opposition was the incongruous pair Shlyapnikov and Mme Kollontay. In dark days, 1914–16, they were among the handful who remained faithful to Lenin. Kollontay, indefatigable in working for him, traveling through Scandinavia and the United States to collect funds and supporters for the lonely exile in Switzerland; Shlyapnikov preserving Bolshevism in Russia, performing invaluable services in the first days after the February Revolution. Now the two of them were united in politics as well as in romance. Mme Kollontay wrote a pamphlet depicting the sufferings of the worker in the "workers' state." His position was shameful and materially unbearable. At the labor-union meetings Shlyapnikov fulminated at the Party being filled with bourgeois newcomers and careerists who were pushing aside the deserving Bolsheviks. The argument against the new ruling class and its privileges was thus combined with more personal grievances of a segment of the old Bolsheviks.

The practical postulates of the Opposition were equality of pay and of status, and that the economy should be run by the labor unions. "All appointments to administrative economic positions shall be made with the consent of the union. All candidates nominated by the union are now removable . . . all the cardinal questions of Party activity and Soviet policy are to be submitted to the consideration of the rank and file and only

[19] An interesting prerogative of the dictator in Soviet Russia, whether it be Lenin or Khrushchev, is that he is the sole person allowed to hold something done in the West as an example to be emulated. The usual crushing retort to a criticism is that what the speaker proposes is being done in the non-Communist world: "Comrades, do we want to do things the way they do it in England [France or America] . . . ?" Here the delegates will invariably indicate their indignation or amusement.

after that are to be supervised by the leaders." [20] This was hardly a call for democracy; for the vast nonworker majority of the population Mme Kollontay evidenced scant regard. It was a call to return to what Lenin had promised in *State and Revolution.*

Though by this time Lenin had been thoroughly disgusted with having proletarian equality crammed down his throat, though both Kollontay and Shlyapnikov were by now personally odious to him,[21] his conduct in the crisis was restrained and is another example of his marvelous political skill and of his knowledge of the psychology of the people he had to deal with.

At first he played the role of a moderator between two factions of the Party. Trotsky, whose impatience with the worker was as great as his own but whose political ability and tact were considerably inferior, proposed a much more open attack against the "syndicalist nonsense." His wartime experience inspired Trotsky with respect for professional expertise, military discipline, and a distrust of the "initiative of the masses." Now he believed that the trade unions should be made strictly subordinate to the state agencies, that not only should their claims to run economic life be vigorously repulsed but that they should be put in their place, which ought to be that of militarylike subagencies of the state and Party bureaucracy. With his sure political instincts Lenin spent as much time denouncing Trotsky's "theses," which were close to his own thinking, as he did those of Kollontay and Shlyapnikov, which he abhorred. Within the Party, Trotsky now became a sort of lightning rod attracting to himself the charges of authoritarianism and military thinking and allowing Lenin to play the role of a broad-minded conciliator. Abolish the trade unions, as Trotsky in effect proposed? Never. They should continue to play the role of the "school of Communism," a flattering but hardly meaningful formula. "It should be said that Comrade Trotsky's theses are completely incorrect and ought to be rejected."

With all such maneuvers the fact remained that the sentiments expressed by the Workers' Opposition probably still had the support of a majority of the Party members. But it was an unequal contest, the discontent of the majority against the iron determination of one man, Vladimir Ilyich. It was now not so much affection as a superstitious fear of what could happen without him that kept the majority of the Communists behind Lenin and made it unthinkable that a vote at a Party congress could go against him. *He,* as against practically everybody else, was right at the time of Brest Litovsk. *He* never lost his confidence during the most harrowing moments of the Civil War. *He* protected the Party against the ambitious designs of Zinoviev, Trotsky, and others. A few of the Opposition-

[20] A. Kollontay, *The Workers Opposition in Russia,* Chicago, 1921, pp. 33, 40.
[21] Kollontay because she not only practiced but preached free love; Shlyapnikov because he behaved toward him with what in 1917 used to be described as comradely frankness but in 1921 became insolence toward the leader of the Party and the state.

ists could be disrespectful. Shlyapnikov and Kollontay charged that he was terrorizing the dissenters. One man was to characterize Lenin at the Tenth Party Congress as the "chief bureaucrat." Such was his power and prestige, however, that without winning him over no opposition could hope to change the course of the Party.

But Lenin's design was not merely to repulse the Opposition. He was eager to drive into the ground the last remnants of democracy and anarchism that stuck to Bolshevism, and to have the Party ready "to get on with practical tasks." Those tasks included a decent burial for War Communism, laying down the basis for socialism in Russia or, to eschew euphemisms, a return to the practices of capitalism.

The impudent young Ukrainian delegate at Brest Litovsk who charged that the Bolsheviks' device was "slander, calumniate, something will always stick," hit upon a psychological weapon of Lenin's that seldom failed him. This was a persistent mislabeling of his opponents to which he held with dogged tenacity until they were forced to retreat in confusion and panic. The Mensheviks were not simply the people who disagreed with him, they were Liquidators. During the Revolution his epithet "petty bourgeois," with which he prefaced almost every reference to the Socialist Revolutionaries and Mensheviks, also hit the target. The Martovs, Dans, and Chernovs were bound to wonder; perhaps in their fight against Bolshevism they were fighting the truly proletarian party; perhaps they were revealing unconsciously their own middle-class roots. Now in the fight against the Workers' Opposition the same purpose was served for Lenin by one word, "syndicalism" (sometimes varied to "anarchosyndicalism"). In vain did his opponents decry the psychological terror to which they were subjected through Lenin's consistent charge that they were acting not as Marxists but as . . . syndicalists. Their psychological counteroffensive, the cry "bureaucratism," was repulsed by Lenin with bland self-assurance. He was the first to admit, he said, that there were a lot of undesirable bureaucracy and bureaucratic practices within the Party. Why, then, didn't his opponents return the compliment and admit that they were syndicalists? Poor Shlyapnikov cried that through this word Lenin was attempting to terrorize him. How could he ever do such a thing, Lenin would ask workers, with the indignation of a slandered man: he and Shlyapnikov had been through so much together, the underground, the Revolution. Would he try to terrorize his old comrade? Why did not Shlyapnikov then admit that he was a syndicalist?

At a Party congress a more than usually perceptive and courageous Communist talked bluntly about Lenin's psychological chicanery:

> Comrade Lenin, one can say, has categorically, as if by administrative decree and without the slightest proof, pasted the label of syndicalism on the Workers' Opposition. Psychologically, it is not difficult to understand. Comrade Lenin is the Chairman of the Council of the

Commissars. He rules our Soviet policies. Evidently, every movement, from whatever direction, which interferes with this rule is labeled as petty bourgeois (in its character) and extremely harmful.[22]

This characterization was greeted with laughter by the majority of delegates. One may warrant the supposition that the laughter was nervous: this was the closest anyone got to saying (and still how indirectly) that Comrade Lenin liked power, proposed to keep it, and woe to those who disagreed with him!

Nobody who knew the man could think that he would be abashed by such psychological insights. He could outlast and "outlabel" the staunchest opponent. "I maintain that there is a connection between the ideas and slogans of the petty-bourgeois, anarchic counterrevolution and the slogans of the Workers' Opposition," [23] said Lenin in his summing up. Who could have had the temerity and patience to unravel the fantastic confusion of terms and slander contained in this short sentence? The Workers' Opposition counted in its ranks the oldest and the most loyal of the Bolsheviks. Now they were accused of having a "connection" with those who had risen against the Communist rule and were fighting it in an insurrection. The latter, the sailors of Kronstadt, were in turn slandered in the same breath as being petty bourgeois, anarchists, and counterrevolutionaries (that is, presumably the proponents of bringing back the Imperial regime!).

The Kronstadt rebellion, which coincided with the Tenth Congress, gave Lenin another occasion for a political gambit. On the surface it might appear that this rebellion by the sailors, "the pride and beauty of the Russian Revolution," as Lenin had called them not long ago, would have proved the most drastic illustration as yet of the mismanagement of the country by the Bolshevik oligarchy. The sailors rose to demand the fulfillment of the pledges of October. They demanded real elections to the soviets, and not their nomination by the Communists; political freedom, *not* for the "bourgeois and the landlords," but only for other Socialist parties and Anarchists, and the end of terror. Reflecting their peasant and worker origins, the sailors demanded also the end of oppression of the peasant, and a greater equality of reward in industry.

At first the regime tried to persuade the sailors out of their demands. Kalinin was dispatched to plead with them and to perform his act: how could things be so bad for the common people in Russia if he, a country yokel, "the middle peasant from Tver province," occupied the highest position in the state? But the sailors would not listen to him and the other "commissars." The regime then initiated armed action against the Kronstadt base (the sailors had refused to be the first to attack) and after several repulses the special *Cheka* and Red Army troops stormed across

[22] Y. Milanov at the Tenth Party Congress. *The Tenth Congress of the Russian Communist Party, March 1921, Stenographic Report,* Moscow, 1963, p. 83.
[23] *Ibid.,* p. 113.

the ice, and took the fortress. In their last proclamations the mutineers inveighed against the ruling bureaucracy. But once again Lenin was not the object of a direct attack. It was "the bloody field marshal Trotsky" and Zinoviev, the boss of neighboring Petrograd, where he had just suppressed a workers' strike, who were the particular targets of the sailors' hatred. In 1917 these two had been the special favorites of the men of Kronstadt and the Baltic fleet.

The Kronstadt rebellion is alleged to have prompted Lenin to change decisively the course of economic policy. But as we have seen, the change in the economic course and the abandonment of chaos that went under the name of War Communism had long been implicit in his thinking. That he had expected uprisings à la Kronstadt is suggested by a speech of the preceding January when he prophesied in his typical "everything is connected with everything else" way: "The capitalists of the West will try to exploit the sickness of our Party to organize a new invasion and Socialist Revolutionaries will try new plots and uprisings. But we are not scared of them. . . ." Now, according to this predetermined scenario, the Kronstadt rebellion, a truly grass-roots, confused movement of protest against hunger and oppression, was pictured by Lenin as a vast plot involving the Western powers, the Kadets, and God knows whom else. He had definite proof, he said, that the White generals were directing the uprising, its aims being the restoration of the landlords, bankers, and the like. Far from being an embarrassment, Kronstadt was used as another club with which to beat the Workers' Opposition. "Why is not Shlyapnikov being turned over to a court for such statements? Are we in an organized Party, do we talk seriously about unity and discipline?" The central Party organs now received the right to exclude a disobedient Communist from the Central Committee, or even from the Party itself, by a vote of two thirds. This was a weapon that the majority of the Central Committee could use at will to deal with any opposition. That such would ever be the case Lenin fervently denied. This provision was included in the Party rules only to stress the gravity of the crisis through which it had just passed. God forbid that it should ever be applied in practice! As a matter of fact the new rule should not be published. It would not do to tell the rank-and-file member that a man elected by the Congress to the Central Committee could be fired by any body other than the Party congress itself. Anyway, he kept repeating that the new rule would probably never be used. Within a few months he was to call for its application in regard to several old Bolsheviks, including Shlyapnikov.

Thus the Workers' Opposition and its shadowy allies, the Democratic Centralists, began their march to the "rubbish heap of history," there to await the arrival of the future Communist deviationists: the Left and Right Oppositions, the Trotskyites, and recently the Stalinists. Perhaps more truly than their successors in the path of deviations, the followers of

Kollontay and Shlyapnikov had retained scraps of original Bolshevik ideal-ism and that revolutionary intrepidity which made them an anachronism in a bureaucratic and police state. But under the Soviet regime "deviation" has usually meant a repudiation by the ruling group of the moment of its own past policies and mistakes, and the *deviationist* has served the role of a sacrificial goat. And to a large extent this was true with the Workers' Op-position. Lenin wisely refrained from making its leaders the objects of an *immediate* purge and risking turning them into martyrs. Shlyapnikov was retained on the Central Committee. Mme Kollontay soon began a long and honorable diplomatic career.

It was obviously part of a prearranged design that half-baked, semisyndicalist ideas (to give Lenin his due, there was a kernel of truth in his characterization) and the general sense of uneasiness about bureauc-racy and growing inequality should have been made the target of a long denunciatory campaign. The Opposition had been lured to come out into the open and to suffer a crushing defeat at the Party Congress.[24] Better to have it that way than to suffer continuous grumblings and revolts in the local Party and labor-union organizations. Lenin's sense of drama made him conclude the Tenth Congress on a note of urgency and the need for unity. He read to the assembled the absurd stories being spread abroad about the internal situation in Russia: the Kronstadt mutineers had cap-tured Petrograd; Lenin and Trotsky had fled to the Crimea; Trotsky had had Lenin shot, and vice versa. The average delegate must have returned home with his head spinning under the impact of confusing impressions: Trotsky wanting to turn the unions into military units, Shlyapnikov pro-claiming anarchy; Martov and Denikin from abroad jointly exciting the Kronstadt sailors to turn their guns against the Soviet state; and all those things somehow connected. It was good to have Ilyich diagnose and ward off all those dangers so brilliantly and rapidly. Lenin's talent as a parlia-mentarian has never been properly appreciated and perhaps it was largely wasted: he was dealing with people who were ready to follow him any-way. Occasionally, and only to himself, he must have reflected that it was a pity that there was no Plekhanov or Martov to argue with: the others were like schoolboys. But his maneuvers and chicaneries were to have an ominous influence on the future of the Communist Party: for the average unsophisticated Communist free criticism, opposition *within* the Party, and counterrevolutionary activity became hopelessly entangled with each other. The words "Party unity" were forever on Lenin's lips. But he did not appear to notice that his policies were such that the only effective basis of unity was the leader. He himself grew into that position and did not need terror to retain it, but anybody who tried to achieve his stature once he was gone (and somebody had to because otherwise the Party would

---

[24] In the voting Lenin's resolution on the labor unions had 336 votes, Trotsky's 50, and that of the Workers' Opposition only 18.

break down into a chorus of discordant factions) would have to use more violent means. Who then was the real father of the cult of personality?

Lenin's pyrotechnics at the Tenth Congress were so effective that it slipped by most delegates that they had just witnessed a very fundamantal turn in economic policy, the burial of War Communism and the birth of *Nep* (the New Economic Policy). Under ordinary circumstances this would have provoked a lively discussion, charges of betraying socialism, and of appeasing the peasant. But now only a very brief debate followed Lenin's announcement that the requisitioning of grain surplus would be ended, and instead the peasant would pay a tax in kind; a *scheduled* part of his crop would be required from him by the state. He would be able to sow and reap in confidence, knowing exactly what percentage of the crop would be taken from him. No food detachment would descend upon the village to ransack the barns and to confiscate at will.

That this sensible policy had to be, so to speak, smuggled in by Lenin illustrates the other side of his domination of the Party. Only he could undo his own mistakes, disabuse the Communists' minds of the mistaken notions and mirages he had implanted in them before. Such a mirage was the basic notion of War Communism: that somehow through enthusiasm and compulsion you could change the economic system of a country overnight, that in primitive, starving Russia you could introduce socialism and change the mentality of the peasant. "It was a fantastic idea for a Communist to dream that in three years you could drastically change the economic structure of our country . . . and let us confess our sins: there were many such fantasy-makers in our midst. But how can you begin a Socialist revolution in our country without fantasy-makers?" [25]

"But Comrade Lenin," somebody might have objected, "weren't you the fantasy-maker-in-chief, did you not have to convince most of the Bolsheviks that socialism in Russia was not a wild, fantastic dream, that those like the Mensheviks who were saying exactly that were fainthearted betrayers of the working class?" No such voice was raised. Having allowed that the responsibility for past errors and fantasies was collective, Lenin proceeded to pile it on. The food detachments, once hailed by him as a measure of class justice and a legitimate instrument of the class war, were pictured now as brutal marauding expeditions that terrorized the countryside and destroyed the peasant's incentive to produce food. "They would come and take two and three times over from the peasant, leaving him in an unbearable position; the most efficient producers suffered worst; any possibility of stable economic conditions was destroyed." It was a faint preview of Stalin's tactics when, having ordered forcible collectivization, he paused in the middle of famine and the ruin of Russia's agriculture to call for moderation and persuasion instead of

[25] *Tenth Congress*, p. 193.

force, blaming the excesses on brutal subordinates or those "dizzy with success."

Lenin's fury was directed not only against "our" mistakes in agriculture. "We have sinned . . . in going too far in nationalizing trade and industry, in closing down local commerce. Was this a mistake? Undoubtedly." Reassurance to the peasant. The encouragement of his (including, horrible to say, the *kulak's*) private initiative. Toleration of private trade. Leasing by the state of nationalized factories to individual entrepreneurs. All those measures were a desperate necessity in the country where industrial production was but a fraction of what it had been before the war, where the worker was receiving less than half the wages he had gotten while in "bondage to capitalism," and where trade had degenerated into the most primitive system of barter. Yet it was only Lenin who could have worked this (counter) revolution. The fantastic dream he had imposed upon his followers was so strong that these sensible measures coming from anyone else would have been greeted by charges of betrayal of the Revolution, of selling out to the peasant, and so on. The hostility instilled in the worker's mind against the peasant was especially great. It was paradoxical, for in Russia the separating line between the two classes could not be very clear. During and immediately after the Civil War many workers abandoned their ruined or nonfunctioning factories and returned to the countryside from which they had come. Famines, such as the great one of 1921, would strike the villages even more cruelly than the cities. But the worker had been taught by Bolshevism to regard the peasant as a "petty bourgeois." No matter how miserable he appeared he was sure to have some food hidden somewhere. This prejudice was too strong for even Lenin to overcome fully. And he had his own: the peasant was a petty producer, the creature who, according to Marxism, forms the biggest obstacle to rapid economic development. Lenin could not rest content to present the new policy as a common-sense measure, an act of justice to the sorely tried peasant. No, it was also and paradoxically an act of great generosity by the workers toward the peasants. Even during the Civil War "the peasants were the beneficiaries of more economic advantages than the working class." [26] Now this new unheard-of concession: the state would stop what he had just described as robbing the peasants, but let them realize: "We shall make you comrade peasants a great many concessions, but only within certain limits and up to a point, and of course, we shall judge up to what point."

The Bolshevik attitude toward the peasant has always been tinged by what can only be described as paranoia, and on this count Lenin was not different from most of his followers. His practicality made him laugh off the charges of inconsistency or ideological betrayal on any other count. Yes, in the workers' state there is a great disparity of pay and living conditions, and it is perfectly all right. The old piteous complaints of the Men-

[26] *Works*, Vol. 32, p. 396.

sheviks and the S-Rs now coming from Paris or Berlin were often cited good-naturedly by him in his speeches. Yes, those gentlemen were perfectly correct when they talked about the lack of political freedom, and terror. The very fact that *they* complained showed that the Communists were on the right path. But the charge of softness to the peasant touched a raw spot. The comments of the exiles on conditions in Russia were hardly more perceptive than their analyses when they were still tolerated within the country. The *Nep* was maliciously acclaimed by them as a confession of the Bolsheviks' failure and a "victory for the peasant." Why should they begrudge and the Bolsheviks be ashamed of this alleged victory for the great majority of the Russian people? One remembers Gorky's words about "the half-savage, stupid and heavy people of the Russian villages."

The *Nep*, Lenin declared, was conceived by the Party seriously and as a *long-run* policy. After three and a half years in power the Bolsheviks' record for having any long-run policy except that of clinging to power was not very strong. They had given the peasant land, then they tried to communize him by force, then they wooed the middle peasant. Now the hand was extended to the peasantry as a whole. Were the Communists going to leave the peasant in peace and tolerate private enterprise in commerce and industry? Apart from any reasons of policy and ideology, Lenin's terrible restlessness, which he had communicated to the Communist Party as a whole, would not have allowed him to stand still. The wisdom of the *Nep* was soon evident: the economic and social wounds were healing. At the end of the *Nep* in 1927–28 the average Russian was probably better off than at any time since the beginning of the World War, and he was not again to enjoy the same standard of living until after Stalin's death. But the very success of the *Nep*, the return to some "normalcy" in economic life, was for Lenin a threat and a challenge. Within a year after the launching of the New Economic Policy he was to announce that the "retreat" had ended. Had he not been stricken in 1922 it is not improbable that the *Nep* would have ended sooner than it did. His successor needed time to consolidate his position before launching a new offensive: the forced collectivization and rapid industrializiation and the mass terror that followed in their wake were to subject the Russian people to a decade of suffering equal to or surpassing the ravages of the Civil War.

One can be of two minds as to whether Lenin would have countenanced such suffering for the sake of a vast social experiment. Certainly his belief in the power or necessity of *sheer* compulsion was not equal to that of Stalin. But as with the cult of personality, so with mass terror and compulsion, his own psychology made inevitable the future and more brutal development under his successor. That the Communist should consider the human cost of social engineering was for Lenin almost unthinkable. Before a Comintern meeting he denounced a foreign Communist for asserting that the workers should not be made to suffer in a "workers' state."

For Lenin this was not only naïveté but treason. "Revolution," he says, "should be undertaken only if it does not injure too much the situation of the workers. I ask, is it allowable in the Communist Party to speak in such a way? That is a counterrevolutionary way of speaking . . . when we established the dictatorship the workers became more hungry, and their standard of living went down. The victory of the workers is impossible without sacrifices, without a temporary worsening of their situation." [27] The word "temporary" saves Lenin's statement from being *completely* a modern phrasing of "mortification of the flesh is good for the soul." The foreign Communists were not as yet as indoctrinated as the Russian comrades. None was found, however, to protest that neither by normal nor by Marxist logic did his statement make any sense: Why should the workers strive and sacrifice only to find their condition worse than before? Who would risk being labeled not only a counterrevolutionary, but also, which is probably worse since it implies being ridiculous as well as harmful, a philistine?

John Dewey once observed that those who do not believe that happiness should be the aim of human existence live up to their principle by making others unhappy. A Marxist is bound to believe that he is working for the happiness of mankind in the most concrete sense of the word: freeing the world from misery and social injustice and replacing the realm of necessity by the realm of freedom. It was not, however, so much that distant goal as the sense of struggle that constituted for Lenin the salt of life. He accepted cheerfully many a "temporary worsening" of his own situation, and tended to assume that his own psychology in this respect should be that of the workers. Vladimir Ilyich Ulyanov forsook the quiet and probably brilliant career of a lawyer in favor of privations, arrest, and exile. Why then should a "heroic proletarian" be unwilling to suffer privations for the sake of the future? In a rare moment of self-pity Lenin wrote to Inessa Armand in 1916: "Since 1893 on, one struggle after another, against political stupidity, vileness, and so on." He did not reflect that most of those struggles were of his own making and that he enjoyed them. Once in power, struggles continued. Even the end of the Civil War did not put a stop to them. On the contrary, the most routine tasks of government now became struggles. When he got rid of his ailing tooth, Lenin wrote to Stalin, he would begin a struggle to death against "Russian chauvinism." The struggle or campaign against bureaucracy. Against capitalism in the countryside. The struggle to electrify Russia. Those who have written their recollections of Lenin have often fallen into the same terminology. "Ilyich had to struggle hard against his love for Martov but his sense of Party duty prevailed." [28] In brief, there was very little in his private or public life that was not an aspect of the struggle. Good health and exercise were not mere

[27] *Works*, Vol. 31, p. 233.
[28] Party duty is as close as one can get to the rather untranslatable *partiynost*.

matters of private concern; a revolutionary had to keep in good physical shape.

It was, then, almost natural to suggest that for the people at large the Revolution and the Civil War were accompanied by only minor inconveniences when weighed against the glory and excitement of participating in the heroic struggle. Said Lenin about the alliance of the workers and peasants: "The three-year Civil War has brought great difficulties in this respect but it has also facilitated our task. This may appear to sound strange but it is a fact. The war was nothing new to the peasant: he understands the struggle against exploiters, against great landowners." [29] It does sound strange. The human cost of the Civil War is dismissed as "great difficulties," which can be charged against the facilitation of "our task." The peasant in Lenin's version appears to have welcomed the war: its burnings, massacres, and requisitions were after all something to which he was accustomed, and in this case they made him understand the necessity of an alliance with the worker.

When he did remember the human cost of the Revolution Lenin, following the example of Marx and Engels, was fond of the image of birth pains. Will a real human being, he exclaimed, refrain from love and having children because giving birth turns woman "into a tortured, lacerated, pain-crazed half-dead lump of flesh?" His knowledge of such matters, confessed Lenin, scrupulous in his references, came from Emile Zola's literary descriptions and from "A Doctor's Notebook," by one Veresaev.[30] That the metaphor had lost much of its strength through the progress in anesthesia and in medical science in general since the days of Marx and Zola did not occur to Lenin, who returned to it again and again.

What was the nature of the new society born in the Revolution amidst such suffering? When it came to naming it Lenin experienced Marxist scruples: it could not be called socialism; witness the small producer in agriculture, witness the toleration of private enterprise under the *Nep*. Such names as "transition" or "state capitalism" were hardly appropriate. And so it became and has remained Soviet society. Today the name no longer jars, as it must have at first, because of the meaninglessness of the literal translation: council society, society of councils.

The name had to be invented and unique for it described a unique and paradoxical society: a Socialist party, which called itself Communist, was valiantly striving to introduce (state) capitalism into a country which as the result of the Civil War could be now called, with much greater justice than before 1914, primitive, barbarous, and semi-Asiatic. The Party ruled in the name of the working class, but this class had just been told that any attempt by it to interfere with the rule of the economy of Russia was syndicalism and would not be tolerated. The other class, the peasantry, was

[29] *Works*, Vol. 32, p. 461.
[30] *Works*, Vol. 27, p. 459.

officially an ally of the working class, but it was also told in unmistakable language that they were not to be the masters of their destiny. "We shall judge up to what point" the peasant is to be left in peace. To add to the contradictions, the only group in this new society exempted from the general rule of equality that the Party imposed upon itself and required, up to a point, from the population at large, were the former (and perhaps also the present, it was not quite clear) class enemies, the bourgeois "specialists." A member of the ruling elite, a commissar, would be confined to 500 rubles per member of his family, and as long as Lenin was active this self-denying ordinance was enforced fairly strictly.[31] A valuable class enemy, industrial manager or engineer, would on the other hand be entitled to receive thousands or, more important in the earliest postwar days, special extra rations and living accommodations. After 1921 the same indulgence was extended to the type who in the official nomenclature was not only the class enemy but the "social parasite" as well, the *Nep* man, the private entrepreneur.

Apart from his continuous struggles, Lenin surveyed the whole bizarre structure with some satisfaction. Had he been personally conceited he might have reflected that probably no other man had been able to mold a society so much in his own image. Its very paradoxes often reflected those of his own mind. At one of his sudden improvisations or changes of course, the Party, in whose name he claimed to do everything, would be left gasping at his audacity in retreating or advancing or going in both directions at once; after his explanation and some judicious chicanery, most of the people would conclude that once again Ilyich had torn off the blindfold from their eyes; yes, this was the only course that Marxism and the urgency of the situation required.

The common lot of dictators is to suffer disenchantment with their own work and to become disillusioned with the people over whom they have condescended to assume the power of life and death. Here Lenin was more fortunate than most. His growing irritability in the last years did not make him lose faith. He lacked personal vanity. He was a humble servant of the forces of history and for all the imperfection of the human material he had to work with, for all the disappointments of the last years, the struggle to build a new society, a new world, would go on after he was gone.

What was to be the nature of this new world? Here a pupil of Marx had to think of the eventual classless society, of material abundance, of international brotherhood, and the world state. But that was far, far away. For the nearer future Lenin's thoughts turned increasingly to the possibility of great breakthroughs in science and technology to bring his country out of its ruined condition and to overcome the inertness of the human material. Chernyshevsky would have been disappointed to find his pupil

---

[31] In a much publicized incident Lenin severely reprimanded the secretary of the Council of Commissars for increasing its chairman's salary to 800 rubles.

dreaming not of transforming Russia into one vast flowering garden but rather of covering it with a network of industrial cities and power stations. "Communism is Soviet power plus the electrification of the whole country." [32] In the Russia of the future, he promised, there would be less and less talk about politics. Engineers and agronomists would replace the politicians and administrators at public meetings. Thus he contemplated cheerfully, but oh how prematurely, the demise of his own kind, the politician, and his replacement by something we call today a technocrat.

With those sentiments we get close to the real Lenin of his last years. Many years earlier, he grew tired of the famous Russian propensity to talk, talk, talk, so prevalent among the intelligentsia, his own kind of people. He founded a party devoted to action, whose "talk" itself was to be a form of action: agitation and propaganda. Now he had grown weary of those propagandists and agitators who constituted the bulk of the old-time Bolsheviks. Experts, scientists, managers, those would be the people to run Russia. It would be the final doom of his own class, the intelligentsia, the people "who knew about everything and could not do anything."

It was a dream as paradoxical as the rest. For the intelligentsia was composed not only of the garrulous and pompous lawyers, professors, and journalists, but also of the people he now wanted to draw into his privileged circle, engineers, doctors, and other "specialists." And were anybody else to suggest that the country should be run by apolitical specialists, unable to quote the chapter and verse of Marx but competent to build power stations and run factories, he would be immediately denounced as a counterrevolutionary trying to turn Russia back to the capitalists.

In his dream of science being the magic key to the future Lenin was both a faithful disciple of Marx and at one with that sizable portion of the Russian intelligentsia who with Gorky, having despaired finally of purely political solutions, saw in technology the most hopeful way of civilizing "the half-savage, stupid and heavy" common man. He was also son of a man who received his training in mathematics and brother of a promising biologist. By the same token his expectation of science as a molder of society had inevitably something excessive and dilettantish about it. Would the electrification of the country with or without "Soviet power" make one hundred eighty million Russians into Communists? When Russia was finally electrified in twenty years as he promised, would the workers be really able to "run things," or would they be in fact farther than ever from that goal? The words "after the electrification of Russia" now assume in Lenin's mouth the same role that the words "after the Revolution" played prior to October. Everything will be different.

Both in science and in economics Lenin recognized his own limitations. He was the product of classical and legal education and his enthusiasm for

[32] *Works*, Vol. 31, p. 484.

science and technology was not matched by any practical knowledge. Once or twice he made lamentable attempts to discuss such topics as the theory of relativity (but largely in connection with philosophical theories he combated), but for the most part he wisely eschewed passing as a scientific authority. The Soviet hagiographers' stories of his unusual knowledge of technical subjects are sufficiently disproved by his published correspondence. To his old friend Krzhizhanovsky, an engineer and now the head of the Soviet Commissariat for Electrification, he wrote letters which testify that he was a typical cultured Russian gentleman of his generation: he knew the world-shaking importance of electricity, but probably could not change a fuse. The same applies to many aspects of the practical utilization of science. As early as his exile in Siberia he was an eager reader of books about mechanical inventions, the calculating machines, and the like. His interest in the Taylor speed-up system was also of long standing. With all that he would not dream, and wisely so, of going into the intricacies of industrial techniques. Every Russian Socialist felt that he was an expert on agriculture. In his time Lenin wrote, and voluminously, on the American or Prussian system of land tenure, on the advantages of cooperative vs. individual landholding, and the like. But he would not and probably could not have discoursed, as Khrushchev often did, on crop rotation, methods of sowing, or the most useful types of fertilizer.

This lack of practical knowledge accounts both for Lenin's intermittent optimism that with a little training the worker could run the most complex machinery and his much more lasting and characteristic awe of the specialist. We must guard the specialists as the apple of one's eye, he urged.[33] The remnants of the *bourgeoisie* became for him a precious human fund to be guarded and coddled like an exotic species.

The "specialist" soon came to include not only the technical expert but, embarrassing to say, the capitalist as well. Again, this development was not completely sudden. A careful reader of Lenin's speeches before the Revolution will come across some startling passages such as the one which promised the capitalists that in the Socialist state they would be able to work "honorably and profitably." But the bulk of his utterances was of course devoted to the characterization of the capitalist as a bloodsucking parasite, and all sorts of other unpleasant things. The experience of War Communism caused Lenin to make a belated discovery: the capitalist was not only a valuable specialist; he was also the possessor of some magic gift that the "heroic proletarian" completely lacked and that could not be learned by reading Marx and Engels. Lenin's praise not only of capitalism, which is normal for a Marxist, but of the *capitalist* now became so extravagant that it would sound embarrassingly excessive in the mouth

[33] A figure of speech of great popularity among the Communists: something (unity of the Party, the armed strength of Soviet Russia) is always guarded like the apple of one's eye.

of a president of an American Chamber of Commerce. "The capitalists knew how to provide goods and you don't know how," he told the last Communist Party Congress he attended in 1922.[34] He bewailed the extinction of the breed in Russia. It needed little for Vladimir Ilyich to assert that the extirpation of the Russian capitalists or their migration abroad was part of a counterrevolutionary plot by the Mensheviks and the Socialist Revolutionaries. Who would now provide for the lost skills to produce and trade? Even the father of socialism was not spared in his reproaches. Karl Marx wrote about everything else, he bewailed, but there is not a word in his writings about how "state capitalism can coexist with communism." Not long previously he had acclaimed the closing down of the Sukharev market in Moscow. The market, he said in December 1920, was the symbol of the mentality of capitalism. "As long as the Sukharev market [mentality] exists the capitalists can return to Russia and become stronger than we." [35] Now he was frantic to revive the traditional fairs and markets. Where to turn, whom to find to replace those invaluable capitalist bloodsuckers?

For some time Lenin's thoughts on the subject had taken a turn at once childish and Machiavellian. The capitalist was, as it were, the possessor of a secret to make the economy bloom. This secret he would not divulge gratis. But one could count on his greed. Why not invite *foreign* capitalists to Russia, promise and give them enormous profits? "Our people" would observe the foreign capitalists, learn their secrets and employ them to make Russia catch up with the West. It was difficult even for Lenin to force his colleagues to accept this policy. Before the war not only the Marxists but many conservatives had resented the penetration of Russia by foreign capital. It was being alleged that Russia was being turned into a semicolonial country. The foreign industrialist exploited the worker much more cruelly than his domestic counterpart. Many an Orthodox clergyman while preaching to the workers the need for obedience to the constituted authority (that is, the impermissibility of strikes) would add that it was not a sin, however, to strike if the enterprise was owned by a Frenchman or Englishman who abused the Russian people in his employ. Now Lenin proposed a policy of concessions to foreign capitalists on a scale so vast that any Tsarist minister who would have dared to suggest them would have been instantly dismissed. The Council of the Commissars, much as many of them bridled against them, accepted Lenin's proposals in principle as early as February 1919. Its subsequent enactments expanded the scope of proposed concessions.

Had Lenin's hopes been realized, vast tracts of Russia, her precious minerals, forests, many factories would have been leased out to foreign concessionaires, and again, under conditions that even the most corrupt

[34] *Works*, Vol. 33, p. 244.
[35] *Works*, Vol. 31, p. 483.

old regime minister would have refused to accept. "We would not begrudge the foreign capitalist even a 2000 per cent profit, because we must improve the conditions of the workers and peasants, and that must be done come what may," said Lenin piteously.[36] The foreign capitalist would be allowed unheard-of privileges, he would be exempted from any interference by the unions, he could establish the company shop where his workers *would have to* buy everything they needed. The Soviet regime, it was clear from Lenin's words, was ready to do for the foreign capitalist what no bourgeois regime was nowadays willing to do for its own, to protect him from strikes. Any Communist, he warned, who would inject his ideological scruples into negotiations about concessions belonged in a madhouse.

That the proposed policy was felt to be shameful can be judged from the comments that Lenin himself has quoted: "Why chase out our capitalists only to invite the foreign ones?" said a Communist. Protest was heard from the "semi-savage, stupid . . . people of the Russian countryside," as epitomized in a peasant saying: "We can put up with famine for another year but don't sell any part of Mother Russia." But such ideological and sentimental objections could not stop Lenin in his determination to pay any price in order to learn capitalist techniques and to lift the country from economic ruin. Such was his eagerness to lure the foreign capitalist to Russia that in the pursuit of this idea he became (and this is the only time when this adjective can be applied to him) ridiculous. How else can one describe his role in the Vanderlip affair?

Washington B. Vanderlip, Jr., who reached Soviet Russia in the fall of 1920, was of the species by now all too familiar. They appear in this century in such places as Indonesia and the Congo, congratulating the new rulers on the overthrow of despotism, offering them their American "know how" (for a price), and intimating a considerable influence in the official circles in Washington. In 1920 the type was still a novelty, and one can forgive Lenin for thinking that Vanderlip was an answer to his prayers. The American entrepreneur who, to Lenin's amazement, knew some Russian (he had been in Russia previously) was willing to "rent" Kamchatka. This was really too good to be true. As Lenin enthusiastically explained to the Eighth All Russian Congress of Soviets, in December 1920, renting Kamchatka to the American would kill two birds with one stone: it would bring those clever capitalists to Russian soil where they could be observed and their methods learned, and in the second place it would pit the Americans against the Japanese, who had their own designs on the Far Eastern peninsula. He was ready to give the U.S.A. a naval base on Kamchatka, and in the manner of the Shakespearean villain's loud aside to the audience, he let them in on a secret: Kamchatka "in fact is not ours at all, because there are Japanese troops there. To fight Japan now is beyond our re-

[36] *Works,* Vol. 32, p. 294.

sources . . . we drag American imperialism into a fight against the Japanese." [37] Let the imperialists knife each other.

One gnawing doubt remained: was Mr. Vanderlip really a "billionaire" and did he really have the Republican Party in his pocket? President-elect Harding had just announced that he did not know any Vanderlip. But, said Lenin, cunningly attributing to poor Harding some of his own guile in politics, obviously the President had to say that during the elections: to reveal that he was a fervent believer in a rapprochement with Soviet Russia would have meant losing "several hundred thousands of votes." Still, the doubt remains: "inasmuch as the counterintelligence of the *Cheka*, excellent as it is, has not yet penetrated the U.S. we have not checked on those Vanderlips." Yet Lenin could not refrain from a note of triumph: there was something to Vanderlip after all. *After* the elections he published articles in the American press wherein he compared Lenin to Washington. Here a certain snobbery enters into Lenin's discourse: see who is defending us in the U.S., not only "some journalists" (obviously an ungracious reference to John Reed and other American enthusiasts of communism), but "the worst type of exploiters."

The mirage of Mr. Vanderlip renting Kamchatka and huge tracts of land and paying the Russian workers in scrip, which they could then reclaim in the company stores, stayed with Lenin for a long time. So did his touching belief in Warren Harding as a strenuous proponent of Soviet-American understanding. One of the charges he threw againt the Workers' Opposition in 1921 was exactly that they were undermining this understanding (!). The Republicans were just installed in power in the United States, they were dying to give Russia billions of dollars and technical help, but obviously they shied away, seeing the Kronstadt uprising and all the mischief that Shlyapnikov and Kollontay were up to.

Gradually, Mr. Vanderlip and that unwitting hero of Soviet-American friendship, Warren Gamaliel Harding, faded away. Sad to say, Vanderlip was not a "billionaire," only a namesake of one (wasn't there a single *Who's Who* in Moscow?), America did not "rent" Kamchatka, nor go to war with Japan.[38]

There were people in the Soviet hierarchy who must have realized the childish nature of such fantasies. His old friend and rival Leonid Krasin, who now rejoined the regime and was intermittently Commissar of Trade and diplomatic representative abroad, was a man of great technical expertise and knowledge of foreign conditions. In view of what was going on in Russia, in view of the cancellation of foreign debts and confiscation

---

[37] *Works*, Vol. 31, p. 437.

[38] There was some shock expressed at Lenin's glee at the prospect of war between the U.S. and Japan. One comrade wrote to him pointing out that though the war would involve two imperialist countries, it would still be the American and Japanese "peasants and workers" who would fight and spill their blood. It took Lenin some time to get out of that one. But he did.

of foreign property no capitalists, it was pointed out, would risk large-scale investments. It was also urged that any large-scale foreign concessions, should they by some miracle materialize, would put the regime in an almost impossible position: workers in foreign-run enterprises would surely enjoy higher wages and better conditions of work than those run by the state or the *Nep* entrepreneurs. Krasin, who is the unsung hero of the revival of trade in Soviet Russia, worked hard to separate what was practical from what was fanciful in Lenin's dreams; to obtain Western agreement for a revival of trade with Russia to enable her to import machinery and hire technical experts.

With all its exaggerations and ridiculous sides, Lenin's rediscovery of the usefulness of the specialist and the entrepreneur played a decisive role in the recovery of the Russian economy. Just as the professional officer inherited from the Tsar's army won the Civil War for the Bolsheviks, so the bourgeois specialist and the ex-industrialist, despised and persecuted for so long, enabled the country to begin its progression toward becoming one of the greatest industrial powers in the world. This progress would perhaps have been more rapid, certainly its human cost smaller, had Lenin been able to overcome not only the Communists' ideological scruples but also the perverse side of his own temperament.

It was a noble and eminently reasonable ambition of his: to pull the country out of its backwardness and torpor, to cure human misery through the application of science and planning. *Intellectually* he realized that this ambition required discarding the brawlers, fanatics, and intriguers with whom he had won power and installing technically competent and businesslike people in positions of honor and responsibility. But *emotionally* he could not quite stomach the idea of the hated intelligentsia reappearing in the guise of the civil servants and technicians of the Socialist state. In his search for the magic secret of the capitalist he would not admit to himself that its major component was one word: security. This security Lenin and communism would not grant to any class or to any profession. Thus the clinging to terror, after the emergency that allegedly had justified it had passed; thus his outbursts (in the midst of the very campaign he conducted against lawlessness) against the idea that laws, courts, and other rotten bourgeois concepts and institutions could ever fully replace terror and the "revolutionary initiative of the masses."

This side of Lenin's character, which he himself acknowledged when he said, "We give with one hand and we take away with another," is nowhere better illustrated than in a recollection of him that appeared in *The Red Chronicle* in February 1925. Its author, a certain Gordienko, recalls an incident in 1918 which brought him face to face with Vladimir Ilyich:

"Our regional *Cheka* fell upon hard times. . . . It had practically nothing to do." Reasons for this deplorable situation, the author explains, were in the nature of his district: the Vyborg borough of Petrograd was inhabited almost exclusively by workers. Try as you might, you would find no counterrevolutionaries, no bourgeois to rough up. Suddenly a ray of hope entered the lives of the unemployed terrorists: " 'To hell with it. We are not going to sit with our arms folded,' said the president of our *Cheka* when he received the news from somebody." It turned out that a promising capitalist was uncovered in a neighboring region. Despite some doubts about the propriety of transgressing its territorial jurisdiction, the Vyborg Chekists raided the exploiter, a member of the millionaire Ryabuchinsky family, and by means which can be imagined persuaded him to part with thirty thousand rubles in cash and several million in shares. This expedition was not viewed with favor by the competent authorities. "You have no right to attack the capitalists of our region." "We have none of our own," replied the brave Vyborg boys. They generously turned over the millions in shares (which of course were not worth the paper they were printed on), but refused to part with the cash. The jurisdictional dispute was about to be settled by the city boss, Zinoviev, when the Vyborg people decided to cut through official channels and to appeal their case to Vladimir Ilyich himself.

The emissary, the writer of this charming recollection, confronted Lenin with some trepidation. It must have penetrated even through his thick skull that the Vyborg exploit was hooliganism, for the likes of which people were occasionally being shot. But he was encouraged to notice, as he told his tale, that Ilyich could not resist a smile. "Well, the thing is in the bag, I thought, he will call me a few names and that will be all." But suddenly "Ilyich" became Vladimir Ulyanov, Counselor-at-Law: "Where is the protocol?" Gordienko could only say "What?" and stand gaping when Lenin explained that he assumed that the Vyborg Chekists had made an official protocol noting that Rybuchinsky's money was being confiscated by the state. At his explanation that in the excitement of the moment no one had thought to make any protocols, Lenin exploded: "So that is how you do things. Took the money, spent it, and you have no document. He will sue you." Here the proletarian's shrewdness came to our worthy's help: They would make a protocol *now* and would antedate it. "I cannot describe Comrade Lenin's reaction. He changed completely. . . . After a long good-natured burst of laughter he patted me on the head and said: 'You boys are smart, very smart. . . .' I understood immediately that the matter was closed, and that the thirty thousand rubles were ours." Off he went to dictate the protocol and the final note: "What I felt in my heart as I dictated is hard to express; but how much new strength and energy I felt after this meeting with Ilyich!" [39]

To be sure, that was in 1918. In 1920 or 1921 Dzerzhinsky for similar exploits would put his men against the wall, protocol or no protocol, and the appearance of this memoir must have been due to a slip-up on the

[39] *The Red Chronicle*, Leningrad, No. 2, 1925, pp. 154–55.

editor's part. But the incident well portrays Lenin's helplessness to combat his own emotions. He realized that an orderly economic development was impossible without teaching people to respect hard work, competence, and property, and that that respect obviously could not coexist with the spirit epitomized by the Vyborg boys. Yet the latter were such splendid human material, so free from the stuffy bourgeois notions about law and conventions, so full of the instinctive class spirit. One could not really be too harsh with them! This guilty passion stayed with Lenin to the end of his life and it was to cost him and Russian society dearly.

The burden of having been by heredity and upbringing an *intelligent* was for Lenin a severe handicap in trying to enlist the best brains for the construction of the new society. The loathing for his own class would break through every attempt to extend a hand to the people without whose help Russia could not advance.

In 1921 the government, facing a complete chaos in transportation, decided to appoint Felix Dzerzhinsky as Commissar of Transport. The name of the dreaded head of the secret police, it was thought, could not fail to help trains run on schedule, make the still bothersome railway workers heed the government pleas, and in general bring a great improvement in this crucial field. But Dzerzhinsky, finding himself in an unfamiliar job, asked Lenin to give him a qualified engineer as a deputy. He had a ready candidate from the *Cheka* files, one Borisov, whose apartment, because of his "reactionary views," had been searched three times and who for the same reason was now on the verge of starvation, his wife dying of typhus, unattended. Lenin approved and on the spot Dzerzhinsky called his underlings at the *Cheka:* "Go to Borisov and in a *most delicate way* invite him to come with you to the Kremlin . . . Yes, yes. And say that he is going to the Kremlin to Vladimir Ilyich. He has a sick wife. Do not scare her." [40]

The scene that now follows has something of the *Arabian Nights* about it: the class enemy is suddenly transformed into a valued "specialist," a bulwark of Soviet administration. In the office of the Chairman of the Council of Commissars he sets his conditions to Lenin. The Kremlin medical service dispatches a doctor and nurses to Borisov's wife and a sailor to clean up his apartment. Dzerzhinsky becomes a humble supplicant of the man whom he had come so close to having arrested or worse. The engineer's condition for becoming a deputy commissar: "I request the authority to fire the unqualified officials and to replace them by new ones. Especially to return to their previous employment the former signal men, warehouse watchmen, and workers who have been promoted to positions for which they are not qualified by ability or experience, that is, station directors, traffic directors, masters of repair shops. . . ." "To return to their previous employment . . . ," thoughtfully repeated the author of *State*

[40] V. L. Bonch-Bruevich, *op. cit.,* p. 201.

and Revolution. "Well said," and Lenin empowered Dzerzhinsky to employ the means at his disposal to persuade the former signal men and janitors to abandon their executive splendor and to return to the honorable calling of the rank-and-file worker. Borisov demanded several of his professional colleagues for the main railway administrators. They also turned out to be well known to the *Cheka*, whose agents began to round them up (undoubtedly in "the most delicate way") to bring them to the Kremlin for consultation. And thus it was that Felix Edmundovich Dzerzhinsky, the scourge of the *bourgeoisie*, restored the bourgeois specialists on the Russian railways and sent their erstwhile proletarian administrators back to their brooms and mops.

There are many such tales of Lenin's transforming a starving, despised *intelligent* into a high Soviet official. Their tellers never fail to draw the moral: how understanding and generous was Vladimir Ilyich, how he would overlook a man's class origins and even his political views to give him a chance to work honestly for the Soviet state. Unlike Trotsky, however, whose acceptance of the specialist was wholehearted and unaccompanied by any inner revulsions at seeing a former "exploiter" in a position of power, Lenin could never accept wholeheartedly what he knew must be done for the sake of efficiency.

The ambivalence of the Communist position, really Lenin's, on the intelligentsia is illuminated in a letter from an agronomy professor that Lenin reprinted together with his reply in *Pravda*. The letter excoriated the Soviet government for wooing the specialists on the one hand, while submitting them to all sorts of persecutions and humiliations on the other. The professional men, wrote the professor in a rage, do not need extra pay and rations as special inducements to attract them to serve their country to the best of their abilities. They are patriotic Russians who claim no special privileges for doing their duty to society. But they cannot be expected not to resent the suspicion with which they are surrounded and the hooliganism at the hand of the authorities to which those who have been spared execution or prison are daily exposed. To cite his own example: a Red Army detachment was billeted in his house and its young commander requisitioned his bed, thus compelling the good professor to share his wife's!

Lenin replied soothingly, pointing out that hooliganism toward loyal citizens was regrettable and should be punished. He welcomed the professor's declaration of his willingness to work for the state. But he could not refrain from reading him a lesson. He should not forget that many a worker's family did not have more than one bed. He should not begrudge the military commander a good night's sleep. And so on. The answer is all Lenin. Any intelligent reader must have concluded that it was not simply the case of a Red Army man requisitioning politely a spare bed that led to the professor's outburst. He and his wife were probably subjected to indignities that he could not bring himself to describe. But Lenin, while gravely stressing the need for legality, the desirability of the technical intelligentsia's loyally supporting the Soviets, could not deny himself the pleasure of putting the whole thing in a ridiculous light. We have compelled the bourgeois to sleep in the same bed with his wife. How the proletarian readers of *Pravda* must have chuckled! [41]

The society he forged inherited Lenin's own ambivalence in respect to the intellectual. He taught, "We should value every representative of bourgeois culture, of bourgeois science, of bourgeois technology. Without them we shall not be able to build communism." But he also taught by his own example that those valuable people should be surrounded by suspicion and vigilance. In the post-Lenin era the specialist, especially the technical one, would be loaded with all sorts of honors and rewards, to make even his already privileged position in 1921–22 appear austere by comparison. But he would not be trusted. The engineer, doctor, the scientist could overnight be transformed from a pampered favorite into a "saboteur." The period of the first five-year plan, 1928–33, would witness blood-curdling stories of engineers and technicians sabotaging production and food distribution. Famous trials, as in 1928 and 1930, would attempt to divert attention from the unparalleled sufferings of forced collectivization by having distinguished scientists and engineers plead guilty to the most absurd charges of espionage for Germany, France, and England, or forming an "industrial party" to overthrow the Communist regime. And then the wheel would turn again. A Stalinist official would declare: "We are not accustomed to value the human being sufficiently. To withdraw men from important posts in industry and civil service by arresting and sentencing them without adequate justification has caused the state tremendous loss." [42] The "spies" and "saboteurs" who were still alive would be released, restored to their former positions, often promoted and awarded honors. This rehabilitation would be accompanied by the Party's congratulating itself on its ability to face and correct its own mistakes, marveling at its generosity, and expecting the victims and the whole world to stand astounded in gratitude. This would all be subsequently ascribed to Stalinism, the "cult of personality." But the origins of it all go back to such episodes as the one just described. It was only when engineer I. N. Borisov appeared in Lenin's study that he ceased to be an abstract category, a "class enemy," and materialized as a human being with valuable qualifications, in need of help. But to treat the Borisovs differently, to overlook their class affiliations, even when they were not desperately needed by the state? That, Vladimir Ilyich would have said, would be petty bourgeois, philistine sentimentality unworthy of a revolutionary.

Sentimentality, both in his own make-up and in the field of human re-

[41] *Works*, Vol. 29, p. 207.
[42] Quoted in M. Fainsod, *How Russia Is Ruled*, Cambridge, Mass. 1963, p. 431.

lations in general, was one of the things he always struggled against. He became nervous listening to music: it made one soft, incapable of that brutal decisiveness the revolutionary hero should possess. In his personal relationships this fear of appearing soft and sentimental made him ruthless toward his old friends and associates who had strayed away. After the October Revolution Plekhanov, then very sick, was subjected to all forms of indignity; on one occasion a band of sailors broke into his house and came close to lynching the father of Russian Marxism. He was finally removed by his wife to Finland where he died in May 1918, completely ignored by the Party of which he had been the founder. It would have pleased many Bolsheviks to have some courtesy or help extended to the man Lenin had always acknowledged as his teacher. But no such gesture was made. Streets and institutes were named after Plekhanov in Soviet Russia, but for the dying veteran Lenin's Party had no further use. Martov, whom Lenin is also asserted to have "loved," exhibited scrupulous loyalty toward the Bolshevik regime during the Civil War. Even Trotsky found a generous word to say about Martov's attitude during the Russo-Polish War. But Lenin's references to his old friend were invariably opprobrious: "cretin," "Milyukov's lackey" are some of the epithets he used in public speeches. Old friendships or former services to the cause counted nothing when weighed against present insubordination. He was not personally vindictive, but was afraid to teach his followers tolerance. The Bolsheviks won because they were hard-boiled, because they overcame that Russian softness and the easy-going ways of which he always complained. Now the Party must not relax, for though power is theirs, they are still a tiny minority in Russia's population. How can they keep power if Martovs, Plekhanovs, and others of their ilk reappeared among them with their scruples and sensitivities and transformed the Party into a babel of talk and argumentation?

The maker of new Russia could hardly profess any nostalgia for the old one. Yet if one follows through his articles and correspondence one finds occasionally something that looks suspiciously like a twinge of regret for the good old bad times. He reads a story by Ivan Bunin. The great writer now in exile uses the refrain: "What have they done to our Russia?" Lenin in his comments is properly derisive. One feels, however, that the cultured gentleman in Lenin cannot quite repress his own very private sigh. There was an element of charm about the old world, and no one, Lenin included, would dream of applying this term to his creation. During his last illness he was to read avidly through Sukhanov's *Notes on the Russian Revolution*. Again, his observations were scathing but the book obviously fascinated him. It recalled the feverish atmosphere of pre-October politics, of interminable discussions, manifestoes, and the like. A doomed world, justifiably discarded on the famous rubbish heap, but in retrospect strangely attractive. Who after a long and close association with the

Stalins and Dzerzhinskys could help being a bit nostalgic about Martov or Potresov?

The end of the Civil War, the *Nep* . . . The old revolutionary becomes more and more harnessed to the task of everyday administration of the vast state, of curbing the various deviations that sprout up in the Party, of arbitrating quarrels among his powerful lieutenants. It is only infrequently that he can turn to his avocation, that of journalist. Even during the war he would occasionally dash off a short article in *Pravda* reminiscent in tone of the days when the pen was his only weapon and when the "excellent *Cheka*" and the Red Army, three million strong, were not yet available to subdue the opposition. Thus in November 1918 a learned professor had announced his intention of forsaking politics and his old party (the S-Rs) and of devoting himself to scholarly activity. Hardly a reason for notice by the head of an embattled state. But to Lenin it was an occasion such as in the old days: an ideological opponent confessing his mistakes and laying down his arms. Bravo, Professor, wrote Lenin. It was a "valuable admission of Pitirim Sorokin." What a good example to the intelligentsia to stop yapping about politics, principles, and so on, and to confine themselves to their laboratories and libraries. But a year or two passed and Lenin's suspicious gaze would follow them there. What is Sorokin doing, writing about marriage and other problems that belong to the sphere of competence of the Party? And eventually the distinguished sociologist, former member of the Constituent Assembly, had to remove to the less censorious atmosphere of the United States where his theories would irritate or enthuse only his academic colleagues.

With 1920–21 such amusements became rarer. Possibly because of his worsening health but also because much of the original zest of the struggle and facing danger had passed, Lenin became more irritable and more prone to fatigue. The word "resignation" could not hitherto be applied to him. He fought and strove against the current. But now that he had to spare and dole out his time and energy, there were major aspects of Soviet life that he watched with almost helpless disapproval and resignation. Such was the whole trend of cultural development under the Soviets which, as we shall see, caused him much bitterness. But absorbed in state and Party work he could not spare time for intervention in that field. A younger and more vigorous Lenin would not have been content merely to rule Russia from Moscow. But now such was the pressure of business and his conviction that in his absence things would begin to disintegrate that he was loath to leave the Kremlin for long. Even his badly needed vacations were taken in the vicinity of the capital, much as his health and disposition would have profited from the better climate of, say, the Crimea, where his successors would have luxurious residences. Writing to him from Switzerland, where he was convalescing, Gorky alluded to Lenin's obsession to sit in Moscow and mind the store: "Why, you could come here for a month to rest from conducting the Old Economic Policy [that is how Gorky referred irreverently but appropriately to the *Nep*]. I am joking. I know you will not travel anywhere." [43]

2. The World of the Comintern

The weariness of Lenin in his last years and his constant absorption in practical work at hand accounts for much of the character of his other historic creation, the Third International. To lay the foundations of the international Communist movement appeared to him at one time as being of much greater consequence than to conquer *just* Russia for the Revolution. The new International would break away from the fatal tradition of the Second. It would bring true revolutionary socialism to the leading industrial countries in the world. It would light the flame of revolution in the backward colonial areas, thus dealing an indirect but eventually fatal blow to the hateful capitalists of France and England. It would really be the beginning of a new world of which the Communist experiment in Russia, with all its imperfections resulting from the backwardness of the country and the lack of culture among its masses, would be but the first and by no means the most exciting development.

Yet inevitably the problems and cares of Russian politics began to monopolize Lenin's attention. Furthermore, though he would not have admitted it himself, that intense internationalism that had characterized him between 1914 and 1918 really began to recede. It was a meaningful metaphor that he employed at the time of Brest Litovsk: the Revolution in Russia was already a healthy infant, while in the West its birth was still to come. After repeated miscarriages in Hungary, Bavaria, Germany as a whole, it was only natural that his thoughts would turn increasingly to the growing child. When the Third International was created in 1919 it was logical that Lenin could not become its official head. Gregory Zinoviev was named Chairman of the Executive Committee of the Comintern. But after 1920–21 one would have expected Lenin to lend the incomparable prestige of his name to the leadership of the International. He did not. That he was its real leader and inspirer there could be no doubt, but his actual utterances on international communism become more sporadic and more and more grounded in the needs and echoes of Russian policy. They lacked the freshness and the avid interest he displayed during the World War. Then minute affairs of the Norwegian or Swiss Socialist Party, the activity of "20 Marxists" in Boston, Massachusetts, would draw his impassioned comments. Now such worries were left to Zinoviev and Radek. How characteristic that his last writings during his illness contain not a word about international communism: they reflect his frantic worry about the conflicts within the Central Committee of the *Russian* Communist

[43] *V. I. Lenin and A. M. Gorky,* Moscow, 1961, p. 186.

Party, his dissatisfaction with the *Soviet* administration, his fears about the nationality policy in the *U.S.S.R.* About the Comintern, about the direction of the world Communist movement, its founder was to leave us no last instructions or reflections.[44]

The Comintern was born in an atmosphere of haste and certain neglect. It was a strange and slightly fraudulent assembly that gathered in Moscow in March 1919. Apart from the Russians most of the other delegates had very dubious credentials or "represented" various Communist and Socialist parties that existed only on paper or for the moment in Moscow. The French Communist Party, still to be born, was represented by and consisted of our old friend, Jacques Sadoul. The former French representative whose ecstatic letters about the Revolution had received a chilly response in Paris decided to stay in Moscow rather than to go back to his law practice and small-time provincial politics. A gentleman named Reinstein, who had been a resident of Russia for some years, spoke for the American Socialist Workers' Party. Christian Rakovsky was currently the Bolshevik boss in the Ukraine, but because he was born a Bulgarian and Rumanian citizen he was the logical choice for the plenipotentiary of something called the Balkan Revolutionary Federation. In the case of Poland insult was added to the fraud: the most important Pole in the Soviet hierarchy, Dzerzhinsky, was too busy to tend to such matters, and so the Polish Communists had to be content with being represented by his subordinate in the *Cheka*, Unschlicht.

Such inauspicious beginnings did not unduly perturb Lenin and his associates. After all, whom did the nine people who had assembled in Minsk in 1898 represent except themselves? Yet they had established the Party that now ruled in Moscow. The German delegate's pedantic objections, which represented the feelings of the pro-Communists in his country, that the moment was not quite ripe for the establishment of a new International or for a definite break with the other Socialist movements, were brushed aside. For all the fraudulent circumstances the meeting still took place in a spirit of some exhilaration. Bolshevism was facing the most dangerous and glorious year of the Civil War. Communism in the West was, from the organizational point of view, almost nonexistent, but the revolutionary sentiments among the workers were undoubtedly strong. Thus it would have been churlish to await clarification of the situation, verification of mandates, other routines. International communism was born. The name "Social Democracy" was discarded as Lenin had said it would be during the war, like a "child's soiled shirt."

To many it was clear that such a step would irreparably split the Socialists in every country, that it would weaken the political influence of the working class, and make it less capable of coping with movements, already

[44] Except for his reflections on how changes within the Russian Communist Party were likely to affect communism elsewhere.

discernible, that in a few years would make the names of Mussolini and Hitler as well known as Lenin's. But what was the point of having an international movement if it was, like the prewar Second International, to house within it "renegades" and "opportunists" as well as genuine revolutionaries?

For Lenin the erection of the Third International was not only the fulfillment of the vow he had made in the summer of 1914 when he heard about the betrayal of the French and German Socialists. It was also in a way the settling of long-standing accounts with those elders of the Second International who for many years had been so infuriatingly patronizing toward the Russian Socialists. How many times did he himself have to wait upon German or Austrian comrades to ask them for help with funds, identification papers, or protection from the police? How many times did he have to listen to fatherly sermons about the Bolsheviks being too excitable, about the need to work together with the other Socialist and progressive forces in his country, to the taunts as to why the Russians could not settle their disputes in a civilized manner? In his pamphlet *The Proletarian Revolution and the Renegade Kautsky,* written in November 1918, Lenin had paid the chief of those protector-tormentors in full. Kautsky thought the Bolshevik regime uncivilized. The Russian's fury at this epithet (only the Russians themselves had the right to call their country uncultured) erupted in a violent diatribe: "Oh, the civilized custom to crawl on one's belly before the capitalists and to lick their shoes." This is the same Kautsky who for years was for him the shining light of Marxism, the true heir of the Master, the conqueror of Revisionism. In Siberia, young Ulyanov practically memorized word for word his treatise on agriculture. Now the aged theoretician was an "idiot" and "Judas." How pleasant to read him out of the revolutionary movement! Let Kautsky and his like stick to their own "yellow" International.

Lenin's theses at the first meeting of the Comintern reflected his accumulated bitterness at the humanitarian, cosmopolitan tradition of the Second International. The false Socialists, he instructed in them, can be spotted immediately by such slogans as "pure democracy," by their hypocritical solicitude for such various freedoms as that of assembly and press. True socialism rejects such freedoms and parliamentarism. It demands the establishment of soviets as the only form of state power. "The conquest of the majority in the soviets constitutes [our] main task in the countries where Soviet power has not as yet conquered." [45] To the vast majority of workers in other countries the sentence was hardly comprehensible. Where except in Germany and Hungary had there been soviets at all? The literal translation of the word was "council." Council power? What could it mean in Lyons or Birmingham?

Thus from the beginning the Russian pattern was held out as a model

[45] *The First Congress of the Communist International,* Petrograd, 1921, p. 123.

for the Communists of other countries. To be sure the atmosphere at the earliest meetings of the Comintern still partook of cosmopolitanism. The language of deliberation was that of Karl Marx and Friedrich Engels. This accounts for the lack of intervention in those early debates by such home-grown products as Stalin (how it must have gratified Trotsky and Zinoviev: imagine a Marxist not knowing German!). It also could not but irritate the Anglo-Saxons who were present and who failed to learn this indispensable tool of scientific socialism. And with the Frenchman's linguistic arrogance —Sadoul simply declared that he knew neither German nor Russian.

Apart from such outward characteristics the Russian domination of the Comintern was fairly obvious from the first moment of its existence. For one thing, it was grounded in the character of the foreigners who were at-tracted to Russian communism. With few exceptions (mostly among the Germans) they were possessed by a sense of inferiority and an awe of their Russian colleagues. Here were those people who a few years before were just insignificant journalists and agitators in a backward country. Now they were rulers. The cult of personality was born in foreign com-munism long before it took roots in Soviet Russia. Certainly no Russian Communist would refer to Lenin in his lifetime in such fulsome terms as did the foreign comrades. And for them Trotsky approached if not indeed equaled Lenin in stature. He appeared at the first two Congresses in his military tunic, fresh from the front. Some of his listeners must have re-flected that the victory of communism in their countries would enable them also to play at field marshals. Sadoul referred to him as a genius, a remark which must have haunted him during his subsequent long career as a Stalinist. For all his long stay abroad and linguistic proficiency, Lenin was as Russian as they come. And in those early days a foreign Communist could not but feel closer to such persons as Trotsky and Bukharin, so much more cosmopolitan in their outlook.

The above suggests, which is true, that communism for all the mag-netism it exerted upon the Western working class in the immediate post-war years of depression and chaos, failed to attract foreign Socialists of major stature. The murder of Rosa Luxemburg in 1919 deprived foreign communism of one person who could have stood up to Lenin, and pre-vented the transformation of the Comintern into an obedient tool of So-viet policy. It is doubtful that "pompous Rosa" and Lenin could have coex-isted in the same organization for long. In her last months she was a severe critic of the Soviet regime.[46] Lenin in turn always referred pointedly to

---

[46] There was a fear in the Communist circles that her critical work on the Russian Revolution would be published (as it eventually was in 1922). Lenin wrote to Zi-noviev in 1921 that that old German Communist war horse, Klara Zetkin, "is afraid that one of Levi's friends might come up with the idea to publish Luxemburg's man-uscript against the Bolsheviks. If so, she [Klara] would announce in the press that she believes such an action disloyal. She had known Rosa better than anybody else and is convinced that Rosa later on acknowledged her views as mistaken. . . ." *Lenin Collection*, Vol. 36, Moscow, 1959, p. 295.

Liebknecht as *the* leader of the German proletariat. Her death gained German communism a martyr, and probably spared Lenin the necessity of assigning her to the same camp with Bernstein and Kautsky. A full life's span is not a good way to reach the Communist Hall of Fame.

When the Second Congress of the Comintern assembled in July 1920 the Bolsheviks had emerged triumphantly from the Civil War and their armies were pushing the Poles back toward Warsaw. The Congress felt its most urgent duty was to do its bit for the Russian armies which, it was thought, would soon reach the frontiers of Germany carrying the revolution into the heart of Europe. Hence the Comintern issued a flamboyant declaration to the proletarians of all countries, urging them to sabotage the attempts of their government to help the "landlords' Poland." The mover of the resolution, the German Paul Levi, was so carried away by the occasion that he paraphrased the famous signal of Nelson at Trafalgar. "Russia expects everybody to do his duty," he exclaimed in English, unmindful that most of his listeners did not understand the language and probably would not have known about the reactionary English admiral anyway. But poor Levi (shortly afterward he parted ways with German communism) unwittingly provided the Comintern with a very realistic device: "Russia expects everybody to do his duty" would have been a much more fitting motto to emblazon on its banner than "Proletarians of all countries unite." [47]

What this duty was it fell to Lenin to explain to the foreign comrades, who had not been through the hard school of Bolshevism, and who consequently could not as yet repress their amazement at the sudden shifts and reversals of position in which they were supposed to acquiesce. What attracted many to communism at its birth was its uncompromising revolutionary posture, its extremism, its proud rejection of any compromise with the rotten and doomed capitalist state. Lo and behold, a few months pass and the Russian comrades urge them not to spurn too hastily the bourgeois institutions and even, oh horror, to take it easy in denouncing the opportunists and reformers of the regular Socialist parties. Such was the gist of Comrade Lenin's pamphlet, *Left Communism—Childish Disease of Communism.* The argument was that the foreign Communists should not be doctrinaire but flexible. They should not spurn the opportunities that the capitalist state affords through its rotten freedoms. Thus the Communists ought not to reject the chance to use parliaments, and to work through the trade unions; if an occasion warrants they should join in a bloc or even enter the opportunist Socialist parties.

Such flexibility or, if one prefers, cynicism, was quite beyond the idealism and innocence of many neophytes. They had been told to view their Socialist countrymen, the MacDonalds, Hilferdings, and all, as traitors to

[47] *The Second Congress of the Communist International, Stenographic Report,* Moscow, 1920, p. 48.

the cause. Now the oracle of world communism was upbraiding them for naïveté and urging them to join ranks with the traitors. The examples given by Lenin of the Bolsheviks' past tactics could mean but little to the foreigners: how the Bolsheviks, despite their mortal hostility to the Mensheviks, had coexisted with them in the same party, how, though they loathed parliamentarism, they had participated in the Duma elections, and so on. It was all very confusing.

A less preoccupied Lenin would have been able to offer more convincing guidance and to develop more feeling for foreign conditions and moods. But he was impatient and the contentiousness of the foreign Communists only aroused his irritation. When it was argued that a given Communist Party should decide its own policy he exploded: "What would become of the International if every small faction came and said: Some of us are for this and others are for that, let us decide it ourselves." [48] The Comintern had to decide.

That somehow those decisions of the supreme court of world communism would always reflect the interests of the Russian state was something that Lenin would not have admitted. Yet his thinking on the desirable tactics of the given Communist Party always fitted in with the Soviet policy of the moment. In England there was at the time among the workers a great sympathy for Soviet Russia, yet organized communism was a negligible quantity. The English "Mensheviks," that is, the Labour Party, were performing a valiant service for the Bolsheviks by threatening the Lloyd George government with a general strike should it help Poland or the remnants of the Whites. The moral was quite clear: the British Communists should enter the Labour Party and do their good work within it rather than remain a small and negligible sect. To the British Communists this was bewildering. Compared with the official leadership of labor, a person such as Kautsky was a flaming revolutionary. Comrade Lenin could not really mean that they should associate with such disgusting moderates as Ernest Bevin and Ramsay MacDonald?

The British Communists were a particular cross to Vladimir Ilyich and he must often have recalled what a disappointment the English worker had been to Karl Marx. But then it was due to the vulgar practicality of the English and their inability to understand the sublime theoretical beauty of scientific socialism. Now in revenge the British Communists appeared as raving doctrinaires breathing extremism and violence, and unable to understand that they were a contemptible little sect that should bide its time. *Everything* had to be explained to the British comrades. No, he did not want them to lose their identity when they entered the Labour Party. They should preserve their freedom of agitation and propaganda. They could denounce MacDonald et al. to their heart's content. To assuage

[48] *Works*, Vol. 31, p. 212.

their feelings he resorted in his *Childish Disease* to a felicitous analogy: they should support the official Labour Party leadership the way a rope supports a hanging man. He, Lenin, could tell them that the Labour Party was not really a party, but a confederation of parties; hence they could enter it without losing their precious Communist honor. Couldn't they see, he practically said, that the important thing was not to parade their idiotic doctrinairism but to help the Labour Patry defeat people such as Churchill, who were uncompromising enemies of Soviet Russia and who would, if they could, renew intervention and on a much vaster scale?

A shiver of horror must have run down Lenin's spine when he contemplated some of the foreign comrades. For all their admiration of himself and Soviet Russia, their behavior appeared reminiscent of the first undisciplined days of organized socialism in Russia. What could one make of Comrade Sylvia Pankhurst? This redoubtable veteran of the suffragette movement in England saw only one meaning in communism: an uncompromising fight. Not any more just against men, but against all the powers that be. "I shall answer the observation of Comrade Lenin that one should not give oneself up to 'leftism.' I find on the contrary that it is necessary to become more 'left' than we have been until now. In England especially there are not enough brave people. Though I am a Socialist I participated a long time in the struggle of the suffragettes, and I could see the importance of radicalism and personal bravery in the defense of our ideas." [49] Comrade Pankhurst lusted for the old days when the female warriors smashed windows, horsewhipped cabinet ministers, and showed those cowardly English males that women would not be downtrodden. Try to persuade the enraged spinster that she should obediently join the Labour Party!

Pankhurst's complaints were echoed by other English and American delegates. Communism for them meant at this point an opportunity to stage their own ten days that would shake the world. And what were they being told: Be good boys, join the Labour Party and the American Federation of Labor and work from within them. In addition to their militancy, the Anglo-American delegates to the Comintern Congress were sensitive about their delegates' rights. They were forever on their feet protesting about their speeches being cut out of the official proceedings, their objections being disregarded, not being provided with translations of other delegates' speeches, and so on. They could not understand that this was not a debating society and that compared, say, with the Germans they were unimportant and could not be fussed over. They were made to feel guilty because their countries were the richest, their workers most satisfied with their bondage, and their Communist parties most insignificant.

That feeling of guilt perhaps accounts for the fact that for all their ob-

---

[49] *The Second Congress of the Communist International*, p. 520.

jections the English and American Communists chose to hew to the line indicated for them by the Comintern. For years the British Communist Party would present itself at the annual Labour Conference and declare in a small voice that they were just another group of Socialist persuasion, say like the Fabian Society, and won't the Labour Party please take them in? The need persisted for the Russian comrades to guide the English by hand like children. On August 13, 1921, we find Lenin writing to Comrade Thomas Bell about a journal to be published in South Wales. The contents of the letter would warm the heart of Mr. J. Edgar Hoover: "You should be [at first] very careful. In the beginning the newspaper should *not be too revolutionary.* If you have three editors, then at least one should *not be a Communist.* At least two should be real workers." [50] Lenin also finds it necessary to explain that the English capitalists support free food distribution "*in order* to distract the attention [of the workers] from *political aims.*" The capitalists, he warns, are "clever, wily, and cunning." And the English Communists?

This indulging in loud stage whispers might be thought naïve. But Lenin's insight, the product of his lifetime experience in *Russian* politics, told him that very often you weaken your enemy's resolve if you tell him ahead what to expect. Nor do you necessarily increase his hostility. The Bolsheviks poured abuse on the Kadets. Yet well-meaning Kadet lawyers defended Bolsheviks in the Tsarist courts. They openly schemed and intrigued against the Mensheviks, yet the latter for long pleaded for Socialist unity and up to the very eve of October defended Lenin's Party from suppression. The ringing declarations of the Comintern, its open stirring up of sedition in India and elsewhere in the colonial world, did not prevent many English and French capitalists from looking with favor upon the prospects of renewing trade with the country bent upon their destruction. In the *Manifesto* Karl Marx wrote that the Communists scorned concealing their aims. Then it was but an empty boast; who in the capitalist world of the mid-nineteenth century even heard of the young German radical and his few associates? But in the post-World War I West the situation was different. True, some politicians felt about their Communists the way the St. Petersburg police chief did about Lenin's Marxist circle in 1896: "Such a small group, something might come out of it in fifty years." But to many intellectuals the dynamism and brazenness of communism presented something very attractive and alluring. And for all the Comintern's mistakes, it was never to lack faithful followers among the working masses of the depression-ridden world.

The challenge flung into the face not only of the capitalist world but also that of non-Communist socialism was thus only partly naïve and partly a piece of sound psychological insight; the denounced enemy for all his superior strength would become unsure of himself, apologetic, and

[50] *Works*, Vol. 32, p. 485.

would try in vain to appease and mollify this frightening new force. The
fearful incantations of communism would be met by their opponents'
pleas that they were not really so vicious. Their original and extravagant
violence would make every subsequent concession or softened epithet appear to the non-Communists as a world won, the beginning of a new era.
But this technique could not remain in the sole possession of Moscow. It
was to be used by Hitler. And today, the heirs of Lenin are the targets of a
similar campaign, forced to defend themselves from the same epithets and
charges of faintheartedness that their predecessor had hurled at the Kautskys, MacDonalds, and Turatis, and which they hear daily from the Chinese. To be sure they are showing a more spirited response than those Social
Democratic renegades.

Certainly the famous twenty-one conditions of acceptance of foreign
parties into the Communist International voted by the Second Congress
bore Lenin's imprint not only in their content but also in their style. He
began his career as a revolutionary journalist, and so Article One is about
the Communist press, which is to brand "systematically and ruthlessly not
only the *bourgeoisie* but its helpers, the reformists of all shades." He struggled through both legal and illegal means and so the American or Swedish
Communist, though he lives in a society so different from the Russia of
1895, is told that his Party *must* have an illegal as well as a legal apparatus. Lenin prided himself on teaching the Russian Marxists the importance
of propaganda in the countryside. Article-condition 5 solemnly obligates
the Communists everywhere to "conduct this work through *worker*-rev-
olutionaries who have their ties with the villages." No other item illustrates as well the senseless transposition of the conditions of Russia of
Lenin's youth to other societies. It conjures up the vision of the Communist
worker from New York or London beating on the door of a peasant's hut
in Iowa or Norfolk and stirring him up against the local landlord and
government official. And the stern admonition, "the refusal to undertake
this task or turning it over to undependable half-reformist elements is
equivalent to a betrayal of the proletarian revolution." No alliance with
the English or American Socialist-Revolutionaries!

The 21 Conditions [51] do not represent Lenin at his best and most sophisticated. They bear the trademark of his impassioned repetition as if
every point had been inserted only after a most violent debate and opposition (which was hardly the case) and had literally to be hammered into
the thick skulls of the foreign Communists. Thus the need for an illegal
Communist work within the armed forces of the given country. Something
that should go without saying. But again Lenin cannot forbear threatening: "The refusal to do such work is equivalent to a betrayal of the Revolution. . . ." Those English and American Communists cannot get away
with just making revolutionary speeches!

[51] Actually Lenin's authorship is acknowledged as to the first 20. See *Works*, Vol.
31, pp. 181–88.

If the Anglo-Saxons are obtuse, then the Italians are notoriously soft-hearted and sentimental over old friendships. An Italian Lenin would to the end sneak out for a glass of wine with an Italian Martov. To break the Italian Communists of this disgusting habit Lenin accords the Italian renegades the honor not granted even to Kautsky: their opprobrious names appear in the 21 Conditions: "The Communist International cannot tolerate that the notorious reformists Turati, Modigliani, and others should have the right to consider themselves as members of the Third International. . . ." Indeed, reading the document one cannot determine whether the main task of the Communists is to fight capitalism or their former Socialist comrades. The devil (that is, the Socialist) appears in many guises; sometimes he is a "Socialist patriot," sometimes a "hypocritical Socialist pacifist." Whatever form he assumes he is to be unmasked, be he but a "hesitating centrist." But even in the midst of the Communist parties there will inevitably be found undesirable elements. Hence Condition 14 imposes the duty of periodic purges of every party to cleanse it of petty bourgeois elements.[52]

Such were some of the conditions of membership in the new club. They were bound to alienate many sincere admirers of Soviet Russia and many militant Socialists who yet could not stomach the humiliating submission to Moscow that they implied. That submission was far from being then what it was to become in the succeeding years (an almost invariable refrain in comparing any policy of Lenin's with Stalin's), but even one year of the Comintern's existence witnessed a considerable movement in that direction. In the beginning it was assumed that the seat of the Comintern would eventually be in one of the major centers of Western Europe, perhaps Paris or Berlin. Now it was decided that the Executive Committee should stay in Moscow. A rather bothersome Dutch delegate objected: "One should not pretend that we have a really international Executive Committee." [53] Why not say that they have in fact a Russian-dominated apparatus of world communism? And he urged that whenever possible the seat of the executive organ should be shifted to another country. Otherwise the foreign Communists who sat on the Executive Committee would lose touch with their countrymen. The workers would say: "There [in Moscow] sits our leader. . . . They accepted his view . . . which does not agree with the real situation in the European or American countries." This somewhat incoherent warning that if the central authority of the Comintern stayed in Moscow it was bound to reflect the Russian viewpoint on all issues was answered very tactfully by the Soviet delegation: with all the modern means of transportation and communication how

[52] That international communism was in its infancy is best illustrated by the fact that after the word "purge" it was thought necessary to add an explanatory note: "revising the register of names."

[53] *The Second Congress of the Communist International,* p. 477.

could it be claimed that a French or German Communist resident in Moscow would lose touch with the masses in his own country?

To repeat, it is impossible to believe that the original structure of the Comintern would have been so clumsy, its character as a tool of the Soviet policy so transparent, had Lenin been able to devote more time to its affairs, had he had the health and time to study the peculiarities of the political and social situation of the major European countries. But the actual leadership of the organization was in the hands of such persons as Zinoviev and Radek. Foreign Communists revered Lenin and admired Trotsky, but they had not as yet been trained to take the word of any Soviet dignitary as law. Willie Gallagher, afterward a long-time Communist member of the House of Commons, said at the Second Congress that when Lenin criticized him he accepted it like a son taking his father's reprimand. He'd be damned, the Scottish miner implied, if he was going to show the same respect for Comrade Radek. The latter, Secretary of the Comintern, was indeed a poor candidate for the father figure. Voluble and impudent, he screamed insults like "madman" and "stockbroker" at foreign Communists who contradicted him, and tried to make up by insolence what he lacked in authority. Both Zinoviev and Radek loved to order the foreign comrades around and to make them feel inferior in view of the revolutionary backwardness of their countries. Lenin would not dream of treating a rank-and-file *Russian* Communist in the contemptuous fashion in which his proconsuls in the Comintern dealt with the veterans of the international Socialist movement. The atmosphere of personal intrigue and favoritism, which was muffled within the Russian party as long as Lenin was well, took root almost from the beginning in the International. There were to be "Zinoviev's men" and "Bukharin's men"; a Communist's standing with the "masses" at home soon became secondary to his connections in Moscow. Delegations traveled to the Communist Mecca to complain noisily about Comrade X's leftism or Comrade Y's opportunism and to plead with the Russian comrades to render judgment.

To be sure in those early days there was an atmosphere of excitement about the Comintern. The fiction of its supranational character was still strong enough in 1922 to make 22 Russian Communists appeal to it against their own Party. Of course it was a fatuous gesture; the Commission of the Comintern gravely investigated the charges and then rejected them. The Communists were not invulnerable to illusions of their own making. The work in the Comintern had its compensations. To those Russian Communists who felt out of place in the prosaic tasks of government now required of them in their own country, it gave a scope for continuing their revolutionary activity, for directing the strategy of the "masses" in Poland or Germany, for indulging in inflamatory oratory, increasingly unfashionable in purely Russian gatherings. Running a ministry, state trust, or a branch of the Party Secretariat, was beginning to be the avenue of advancement within Russia. In the Comintern the propagandist and the theoretician still held sway. Occasional forays to foreign countries combined the pleasure of travel and the thrill of clandestine revolutionary activity, all this while being protected by the Soviet passport. Even if one was arrested, as was Radek in 1919 in Germany, the chances were that the imprisonment would be of brief duration and not too uncomfortable. While the Eighth Party Congress and the Comintern were passing resolutions extolling Radek's martydom ("he is bound with heavy iron chains, confined to a damp, cold, underground vault," melodramatically said a German delegate to the Comintern Congress), this victim of political persecution was granting audiences to the German radical Socialists and instructing them on their tactics. Released from prison, he was sheltered by a former general in whose apartment he continued receiving, this time, major German industrialists and Reichswehr officers.

The atmosphere of the Comintern could not but breed cynicism in its Russian personnel. Its formative years were the period when many of the most idealistic Party members found themselves in opposition to the official policy. Many of them, for instance Kollontay, would have been ideally suited for work with the foreign Communists. But they were kept at an arm's length from the Comintern for fear of infecting it with their own heresies. The same was true of the former Mensheviks who had joined the Bolsheviks and who were being widely utilized in administrative and diplomatic positions of secondary importance. The foreign Communists drawn into the central machinery of the Comintern were selected largely on the basis of their docility and their knowledge of Russian (the latter accounts for the high proportion of Bulgarians and Finns). They tended to become rapidly russified. The vision of their assuming power in their own countries growing more distant, many of those people developed an unfailing instinct for the shifts in the power structure of the Russian Party and the ability to trim their sails according to the way the wind was blowing. The Finn Otto Kuusinen was, for instance, able to satisfy such successive and dissimilar bosses as Zinoviev, Bukharin, and Stalin, and was to die in ripe old age as a member of the Presidium of the Communist Party of the Soviet Union in the era of Nikita Khrushchev.[54]

One of the 21 Conditions stated explicitly that the duty of every Communist party was to lend every assistance to Soviet Russia. At the Third Congress of the Comintern Lenin went into further detail. "It would be extremely instructive, and I think the foreign comrades will do it, to follow systematically the more important developments, tactical moves, and currents of the Russian counterrevolutionaries. The counterrevolutionaries work mostly abroad and it would not be particularly difficult for foreign comrades to follow their activities." [55] There is just a barely perceptible

---

[54] Few were to be so fortunate. For all their political adaptability the foreign Communists in the Comintern were decimated during the Great Purge, 1934–39.

[55] *Works*, Vol. 32, p. 459.

hint of embarrassment in this request. Lenin asks the foreign Communists to spy on the Russian political exiles. The Comintern is to perform the service for the Soviet state that the late Okhrana performed for Tsarist Russia. Often a victim of *agents provocateurs,* Lenin could not quite bring himself to say in so many words that the foreign comrades should do good work as spies and infiltrators, hence the shameful suggestion is veiled in pedagogic terms: "These counterrevolutionary exiles are very smart, excellently organized, good strategists . . ." (Lenin is much too flattering to the poor *émigrés*) "and I think that a systematic comparison and study of how they are organized and how they use this or that means may have a strong influence on the working class from the point of view of propaganda." Could the knowledge as to how the Paris Mensheviks were organized help the French Communists propagandize their own workers?

Again, it would not have occured to Lenin in 1921 that the "excellent *Cheka*" should infiltrate the Workers' Opposition and learn how they use "this or that means." That he is willing to make such demands of foreign Communists cannot but indicate his opinion of their moral—and intellectual—worth. At the Congress of the International he was brazen enough to say: "We see how the 'free' Russian press abroad, beginning with the Socialist Revolutionaries and the Mensheviks and ending with the most reactionary monarchists, defends large landed property." [56] And by the same token, since the Russian comrades read those words as well, the implication was clear that they accepted with equanimity this talking down to the foreigners.

Those passages indicate how the internationalist in Lenin became submerged in the ruler of Russia. His oft-repeated refrain throughout the speech was the danger of "a million and a half or two million" Russian *émigrés* abroad and the "fifty newspapers" that they were publishing. By now the foreign comrades had stopped asking bothersome questions about terror in Russia. Nobody would be naïve enough to wonder aloud why capitalist oppression in the West had nowhere produced such a mass political migration as in Russia, or why two million Russians abroad should with one voice demand the return of a handful of landlords to their large estates. To Lenin those *émigrés*, for the most part destitute and split into a hundred factions, as of old fighting each other much more vigorously than the Bolsheviks, were still a great danger. As a matter of fact his paradoxical mind conjured up a threat greater than that of 1917 or 1918. "At the time when we took power with one push, the Russian *bourgeoisie* was unorganized and politically undeveloped. Now it has reached the Western European level of development." Most of his foreign listeners must have witnessed this "Western European level of development"; people with their shattered lives trying to eke out a living in Paris or Brussels. Soviet Russia, having triumphed in the Civil War, was now in mortal danger from those people: "We should take that into consideration,

[56] *Ibid.,* p. 459.

we should improve our own organizations and methods, and we should work for that with all our strength." And the foreign Communists, also, must help.

These words provide a clue as to why Lenin found it so difficult to concentrate on the problems of foreign communism, and why no matter whether he starts speaking about the Italians or Germans he wanders and returns to Russia and Russian problems. In retrospect, the victory of Bolshevism in Russia seems to have been so easy—"one push"—and hence so incredible. It *must* be that the real danger, the real test, is yet to come. Lenin is a sober statesman; this is 1921. The threat of intervention is over, the main capitalist powers are much too preoccupied with their political problems and with the postwar economic depression to try an intervention in Russia. And, anyway, he declares, the Soviet system is unconquerable and has passed through its most difficult period. But next moment the worry returns: it has really been too easy. The enemy must be lurking someplace: perhaps in the foreign capitalist, the Russian peasant, or those *émigrés* who have now learned to organize and still plot. And so he anticipates the coming struggle, compared with which the Bolshevik conquest and the Civil War "have been relatively easy."

In the context of that continuing suspicion and gnawing worry which at times takes on a morbid character,[57] the problem of the world revolution takes a very secondary place. The misshapen form of the Comintern, the result of its parent's neglect and impatience, was most noticeable in its activities in Western Europe. Here, as pointed out above, the Soviet experiment was greeted with much sympathy among the working class and the intellectuals. The postwar depression and the disillusionment with liberalism and moderate Socialist leadership offered an opportunity to translate this initial fund of good will into organized Communist strength. Even in England the moment seemed propitious for building up a sizable Communist party.

But all those chances were squandered or tossed away. The Comintern was to serve the interests of the Russian state and it was to wreak vengeance on the foreign renegades and opportunists, but by its very nature it could not attract the loyalty of organized labor in the more advanced countries. The 21 Conditions are notable for one omission: amidst various duties imposed upon the participating parties not a word is said about the continuous struggle for the improvement of the material conditions of the

[57] There are indications, such as in his main speech before the Comintern, July 5, 1921, that he was not an entirely well man. Though he presumably had a written summary of the speech in his hand, he was at times incoherent. Thus the full sentence from which an excerpt has been quoted ran: "It was easy for us, and I think it will be easy for other revolutions to deal with those *two* classes of exploiters." *Ibid.*, p. 460. Yet he had spoken only of *one* exploiting class, the *bourgeoisie*. *Subsequently* he talked of two classes but not exploiters: the peasants and workers. This lack of clarity, natural enough in somebody else tossing around the Marxian categories, is very uncharacteristic of Lenin.

working class. Instructions on trade unions are limited to two rather inconsistent orders: every Communist party must infiltrate and attempt to capture the already existing trade unions. Also, it must propagandize for a breach of its national unions with the International of Trade Unions, which united all the major professional organizations of workers, in favor of the projected Red International of Unions. As a young Marxist Lenin readily accepted the point of view that political agitation among the workers was fruitless unless it was combined with the struggle for higher pay and better working conditions. But now this lesson was neglected: foreign Communists should not play at reformism. All their energies were to be expended in the pursuit of power, help of Russia, and the reviling of the Socialists. We have seen how enraged Lenin was at the suggestion that revolutionary activity should not lead to the lowering of the workers' standard of living. In Russia the victory "of the workers" led to a catastrophic decline of their living conditions. Why should the foreign workers be less self-sacrificing? The foreign comrades could only mumble that he was not making their task easier.

Equally embarrassing for many a Western Communist must have been the Comintern's brusque rejection of the whole parliamentary nonsense. The machinery of democratic elections was to be utilized by the Communists, but they were not to be bound by any democratic or parliamentary scruples. Their deputies were to be under the strictest discipline of the Central Committee; they must not dare to act independently or try to represent their electors. Parliamentary immunity? A wonderful cover for subversive work. "In those countries where the Communist-deputy enjoys some parliamentary immunity, he should use it in order to help the Party organization in its illegal work. . . ." [58] In general the Communist representative should act like a bull in a china shop, his whole behavior designed to discredit the parliamentary institutions. Even the ridiculously militant English Communists could not forbear pointing out that such behavior, in a country where the parliamentary superstition was still strong among the workers, would serve to discredit not Parliament but the Communists. Lenin's thought was not on the House of Commons, but on the distant days of the Duma and how the handful of Bolshevik deputies disrupted proceedings and embarrassed the stuffy lawyers and professors who thought that they could impose parliamentarism on Russia! [59]

In fact, in contemplating the artificial mold imposed upon Western

[58] *The Second Congress of the Communist International*, p. 593.

[59] His own experience is amusingly reflected in the Comintern's set of instructions on parliamentarism. Thus they warn against sending lawyers to parliamentary institutions, perhaps an echo of Lenin's hatred of his own profession. Also, the Communist deputies are to *read* their speeches. Vladimir Ilyich undoubtedly remembered how he used to write speeches to be delivered word for word by the Bolsheviks in the Duma, and how it exasperated its authorities because of the rule common to many legislatures that speeches should not be delivered from a written text.

communism it is difficult to determine where Machiavellianism ends and a childish perversity begins. The self-indulgence of Lenin in reviling and making ridiculous the liberal and parliamentary institutions was translated into a code of behavior for world communism. Some Western comrades proved to be apt pupils. The minutes of the German Reichstag in the twenties abound in Communist-inspired incidents designed to destroy the prestige of that institution. Leather-lunged deputies shouted at ministers: "Swine," "Executioner," and at their Socialist colleagues: "Renegade," "How much did they pay you?" thus loyally fulfilling the directive of the Comintern: "Communist deputies should use the parliamentary tribune not only to unmask the *bourgeoisie* and its open followers, but also the Socialist-patriots, reformists, the neither-here-nor-there centrists, and other enemies of communism. . . ." And to be sure, in Italy and in Germany the Communists did help to destroy the masses' illusions about rotten parliamentarism.

For all his other preoccupations and the sporadic character of his intervention in the affairs of the Comintern, Lenin was loath to make it appear that foreign communism was to him of secondary interest. It was represented more than once that, for the sake of appearances at least, he should not be formally affiliated with the Executive Committee of the Comintern. The Foreign Commissar, Chicherin, was gravely explaining to the enraged Western governments that the Comintern was a private institution, which happened to be located in Moscow, but for the activities of which the Soviet government, God forbid, bore no responsibility. It would help him, he more than once urged Lenin, if the head of the government preserved a suitable distance from this organization of international revolutionaries. But Lenin, who ordinarily could have been expected to applaud such deception, refused. "There can be no question of me and Trotsky leaving the Executive Committee," he wrote Chicherin.[60] Such steps, he argued, would only create the impression in the West of Soviet weakness.

Also, he hated to admit even to himself that he was beginning to lack the time and energy for any meaningful direction of world communism. Months of neglect would be followed by a hurried reading of the French or German press and a directive to Zinoviev or a letter to the foreign comrades. The sporadic and necessarily dilettantish character of such interventions can be judged from a letter of July 13, 1921, to M. Borodin, then an expert on American affairs. He asks about an American third party, "the Worker Peasant or the Worker Farmer Alliance" (actually the Farmer Labor Party) which allegedly is "in power" in North Dakota. "I would like to have *a few*, but *the most important* documents about this party and its activity in North Dakota . . . and a short note from you about this whole question." [61] On receiving Borodin's reply Lenin jotted

[60] *The Lenin Collection*, Vol. 36, Moscow, 1959, p. 338.
[61] *Ibid.*, p. 287. My italics.

down on it for his secretary: "Please bring it to my attention within a week." Borodin was subsequently charged with analyzing the Farmer Labor materials for the Comintern journal, but he was ordered to omit from his article their anti-Communist polemics.

"Front to the masses," "united front from below," "the campaign against centrism," such were some of the jerky, shifting postures through which the Western Communists had to go in those early days. In fact their story is like a replaying of the drama of the history of Bolshevism in Russia, but this time, if one disregards the awesome consequences in Italy and Germany, as a comedy.

But this comedy encompassed many a personal tragedy. Their idealism drained out of them, their craving for adventure dulled by the need of obeying the Moscow bureaucracy, many an early Communist turned into an obedient puppet, or with bitterness and rancor left the Party of his dreams to bear to the end of his life the stigmata of disillusionment.

Lenin's instincts served him better in the case of the revolution in the East. For one thing, in the Orient his political realism could operate unencumbered by his terrible passion. Western problems could be discussed rationally until such words as "Kautsky," "parliamentarism," "lawyers," would appear and then Vladimir Ilyich would react like a man possessed, and sensible policies would become buried under a mountain of invectives. But in the colonial and dependent world those disgusting phenomena of Western civilization were not in evidence, or if they were, they appeared in a much more favorable light. The sleek pashas, the rapacious landowners, even the Oriental despots were the enemies of Communist Russia's enemies, and hence potential revolutionaries. The toiling masses of India or China did not have to be weaned away from their trade unions or pro-parliamentary prejudices. Even the newly born Asiatic intelligentsia, the word that Lenin like Nicholas II could not pronounce without a shudder, provided a favorable soil for revolutionary propaganda. In brief it was natural for the author of *Imperialism* to harness the course of revolution in the colonial world to nationalism. The colonial problem was for Lenin the jugular vein of British and French capitalism. The movement for independence in those vast areas would directly threaten Western imperialism, and indirectly promote the cause of revolution in England and France. The unfortunately high standard of living of the Western worker, this standing reproach to Karl Marx's wisdom and prophecies, would be destroyed by the loss of India and other Western possessions and spheres of influence.

The Bolshevik Revolution was thus bound to prove a magnet to many elements in the East. To a pedantic Marxist the idea of propagating communism in Asia, not to mention Africa, was a heresy, compared with which the Communist seizure of power in "semiwild, primitive, Asiatic Russia" was the height of orthodoxy. Why, capitalism was still many a light year away in Persia or in China, and you prepare to introduce socialism there! But Lenin brushed away such scruples. When Bukharin exclaimed in 1919 in a burst of his typical and unfortunate frankness that he was for a revolutionary propaganda among the "Bushmen and the Hottentots" because it vexed the British, but not because there was any earthly chance of their having a modern state, let alone socialism, he was gravely reproved by Lenin. What would have happened to Marxism in Russia had the Russian Marxists agreed to sit with folded arms for fifty or so years until capitalism ran out its course and gave birth to socialism? Now you could not tell those eager Indian and Korean comrades, young though they were, that they also should wait to become the local Lenins and Trotskys until the ponderous forces of history and economics worked themselves out. This vision should be presented to the Eastern comrades: "With the help of the proletariat of the most advanced countries the backward nations can reach the Soviet system and pass through the respective stages of development to communism, having skipped the capitalist stage." [62] Without that promise the task of recruiting the Communist parties of China, India, Korea would have been hopeless. To work for the future generations is a noble ambition, but most politicians believe that they can fulfill this lofty aim by achieving power in the present one. Where did Menshevism get by its leaders being eternally in a quandary as to whether the "moment was ripe" for a Socialist revolution, for taking power, and the like? "The idea of Soviet organization . . . ," said Lenin alluringly and with deliberate imprecision, "is simple and can be used not only in relation to proletarian but also to peasant, feudal, and semifeudal relations."

We are quite accustomed today to having seen Khrushchev clasp, say, Nasser to his bosom as a friend of the Soviet Union at the very same time that the latter is unfeelingly keeping the Eyptian Communists under lock and key. The roots of this policy go back to Lenin's time. The Soviet state had friendly relations with Kemal at the same time that the father of modern Turkey was imprisoning Communists or having them drowned in the Bosporus. The necessity of stirring up anti-British feelings in their sphere of interest made for cordial relations with such potentates as Amanullah of Afghanistan and Riza Shah of Persia. Insofar as all those gentlemen were persecuting Communists, they were on appropriate occasions and before appropriate audiences discreetly denounced. But their value as opponents of that fortress of capitalism, Great Britain, their undoubted role as leaders of what in today's parlance would be called the liberation movements, made them be treated gently and at times helped by the Soviet government. In 1920 the Comintern staged in Baku the Congress of the Peoples of the East. There the irrepressible Zinoviev and Radek appeared in yet new roles as leaders of the downtrodden masses of the East, calling them to a holy war against the British. Radek (born a Jew in Austrian Poland) had

[62] *The Second Congress of the Communist International,* p. 120.

played a German Socialist, leader of Polish socialism, advocate of an alliance between German nationalism and Bolshevism. Now he was in a new incarnation: he was leading the Moslem toiling masses in their fight against the Unbelievers.

It might be remarked that in devising this policy Lenin was hardly more original or Machiavellian than in egging on the British Communists against parliamentarism and the trade unions at the same time that he was urging them to infiltrate the Labour Party and the unions. But by the Marxist standards of 1919 the policy of an unabashed alliance with nationalism, and at times conservative nationalism at that, was still a breathtaking innovation. It came easily to a man who in his distant Geneva days considered seriously the possibility of young Marxism seeking revolutionary allies among the Russian sectarians, that is, among the most backward and superstition-ridden segments of the Russian peasantry.

The Comintern tactics in the East were equally if not more cynical, and equally designed in the *Russian* interest, like those in the West. But there is this vital difference. In the West the tactics were not only mendacious, they were also inept, based on the alleged and fictitious love of the Western worker for the Soviet institutions and his equally nonexistent hatred of the "reformists and opportunists." In the East the policy ultimately designed by Lenin (though such theatricalities as the Baku Congress were staged by subordinates) throve on real human aspirations and real social evils. The rising intelligentsia of the East saw in Bolshevism an ally in their fight against imperialism, and in Soviet Russia an example of a society trying to overcome its backwardness and poverty.

Lenin's genius as a politician lay in his ability to spot and profit by the self-destructive elements and delusions in his opponent's make-up. With the liberals it was their humanitarian and legalistic scruples, with the Mensheviks it was their dream of "the working-class solidarity." His opponents within the Party would be rendered impotent by his appeal that "Now there is no time for . . ." the luxury of intra-Party dissension, the ending of the terror, the observance of Marxist orthodoxy. In striking at imperialism he was attacking the most vulnerable sector of the Western state system and world order. The European intelligentsia's (after World War I this term can perhaps be applied in the West) doubts and guilt feelings about their countries' imperial role, the democratic electorates' growing disinterest in such hallowed categories as "national prestige . . . honor . . . power" all conspired to make the emancipation of colonies inevitable, even if the final stage of the process had to await World War II. The weakened grip of the West, the appearance on the world stage of new states obviously incapable of achieving political and social stability, were going to be grist for the mill of Soviet diplomacy and world communism. Faced by economic trouble at home, their hands increasingly tied by colonial unrest, the Western powers would be incapable of attempting intervention in Russia, or even of presenting a solid front against communism.

In the old days of Geneva and Paris the Russian exiles waited longingly for the news of a political or economic disaster at home. Now Lenin applied the old revolutionary device, "The worse it is, the better," to international politics. Anything promoting international stability, a reconciliation of the Great Powers, was viewed as a major danger. His hostility to "the old hypocrite Wilson" sprang largely from the fear that the League of Nations might prove to be a viable institution, the source of a new world order. He seized eagerly upon John M. Keynes's criticism of the Versailles system and crudely exaggerated the English economist's skepticism about the American president. "Wilson was the idol of the *bourgeoisie* and pacifists à la Keynes and the bunch of heroes of the Second International . . . who prayed for '14 Points' and wrote 'scholarly' books about the bases of Wilson's policy because they hoped that Wilson would save 'social peace,' would reconcile the exploiters with the exploited, would realize social reforms . . . Keynes unmasked Wilson . . . as a little fool. . . ." [63] No Midwestern isolationist greeted Harding's election with greater joy than did Lenin. As we have seen, he looked longingly for an armed clash of the American and Japanese "bandits." Those "clever and cunning" Western capitalists managed to cheat Marx by raising the standard of living of their workers. But they would not be able to avoid bloody revolutions in their empires, and most of all, their greed would draw them into wars with each other. This vision could still provoke some uneasiness among the Communists, as we saw in the incident of the disingenuous listener who asked Comrade Lenin whether if Japan and American clashed it would not be the American and Japanese "peasants and workers" who would die and suffer. But such objections were picayune as against Lenin's cataclysmic vision of history.

One must not therefore judge Lenin's Eastern policy as a failure because in his lifetime and for a long time afterward communism failed to conquer in any Oriental country. Granting his premises, he showed prescience and tactical skill. He turned the attention of communism to the area where the masses indeed had "nothing to lose but their chains." That the first beneficiaries of this policy were not the local Communists but such nationalist leaders as Kemal, Riza Shah, and Chiang Kai-shek was not a total loss: the victory of nationalism in Asia was bound to undermine the Western Powers' influence, prestige, and self-assurance. And the Communist hour in Asia would come. The nationalist leaders would be no more capable of dealing with the problems of their shattered societies, of counteracting the impact of the new economic forces and aspirations, of displaying the necessary combination of ruthlessness and flexibility than had been the Kolchaks and Denikins. And if the West intervened it would

[63] *Works,* Vol. 31, p. 199.

be in the same insufficient, fumbling, hesitant way in which various European powers tried to affect the fortunes of the Civil War. As Lenin explained after the fact of the failure of the intervention: "Weak, torn apart, downtrodden Russia . . . turned out victorious . . ." against "the rich mighty countries which rule the world . . . Why? . . . because among these powers was not a shadow of unity, because all of them worked at cross purposes. . . ." [64]

As he contemplated the receding prospects of the world revolution, Lenin must have remembered his words of May 1917: "We [Bolsheviks] will know how to wait." The experience of those days was put before the foreign Communists: he recalled how universally condemned was his defeatist position when he had returned to Russia in April. But then the mood changed. And so the foreign comrades should also learn to wait. A bold foreigner might have pointed out that it was all right for Comrade Lenin to be philosophical. *He* was in power, they were a loathed minority. And was he always so patient? How about October 1917? But there was an element of wisdom in his patience: the destructive forces pitted against Western civilization were too strong to be repelled or long delayed by a League of Nations or any other device. Communist reverses were bound to be temporary, a good training for the future successes. "One who has been whipped is worth two who have not" was his favorite proverb.

The fact of Russian domination of the foreign Communist parties was based not only on the prestige of the only Communist state in the world, and the financial help extended to the foreign comrades, even in those days when the starving country could ill afford the expenditure. It was also grounded in the peculiarity of Communist tactics and in their strange rationale. Who abroad could juggle the Marxian categories and historical parallels as dexterously, extract the essence of the political situation of the moment as cleverly as Comrade Lenin and his subordinates? It was better to leave to them those brilliant analyses and breath-taking paradoxes, beyond the power of comprehension of a Scottish unionist from Clydeside or an American radical from the East Side. We have notes for a speech by Lenin that he delivered to a group of foreign Communists at the Third Congress of the Comintern. It is a typically meticulous, paradoxical performance of his: points, subpoints, subsubpoints (the last indicated by Greek letters): apposite sayings in French and German. It is a *tour de force* which in its polished form must have dazzled all his listeners, except perhaps the Germans, accustomed to similar ideological calisthenics from their native masters of Marxism.

> 1) The more "opportunistically" the faster you will gather . . . around yourselves the masses . . . 3) Comparisons with Russia of April 4, 1917, and April 21, 1917 . . . 4) Do not fear to say that we have all returned from Moscow [after the Third Congress of the Com-

[64] *Second Congress of the Communist International*, p. 29.

intern] more prudent, smarter, wiser, more to the right. That is strategically correct . . . 5) The more to the right now, the more correct tomorrow. One should draw back to jump better [in French; a favorite proverb of Lenin's]. Overnight possible, but within 2–3 years also possible [in German; obviously he means the revolution]. Don't become nervous and impatient . . . 7) All together unanimously. Start approaching the workers *as if from the beginning.* More carefully . . . the more solid the preparation the more assured the victory.[65]

Who would dare to inquire: "But Comrade Lenin, why are we to be opportunistic even in quotation marks? Isn't that what is wrong with Kautsky?" Or to point out that the "masses" would be confused if the very same people who the year before had returned from Moscow screaming the most radical and violent slogans now came back patient and relaxed, saying "Now, now, let us start from the beginning." Some early Communists parted ways with the doctrine because they found the Comintern too much to the left, or too much to the right, or because its officials favored the Milan faction over the Turin one, or Comrade X over Comrade Y. But no one, to the author's knowledge, ever got up and said: "Comrade Lenin, this is subtle and Machiavellian to the point of being ridiculous." The intellectual tradition of the nineteenth century that encompassed the Social Democracy was that of light and reason, of calling a spade a spade. In the Second International ideological terms had their common-sense meaning: a leftist was a man who believed in revolution, a right-wing Socialist one who envisioned the achievement of his aim through evolution and nonviolent means. Now this whole orderly world of concepts was fatally undermined: a Communist, supposedly the most radical type of Socialist, would at times display a moderation surpassing that of the most constitutionally minded Socialist. At other times he would grasp the hand of a professed Fascist. And there would be moments when he would urge the masses to the barricades—"the creative paradoxes of communism," as Stalin was to call them. Within the context of the Russian revolutionary tradition much of this juggling of concepts, of the sudden changes of the ideological front, made sense. But abroad these shifts, the condemnations of the former allies, the extolling of the erstwhile enemies—they all had to be taken on faith. Among the leading foreign Communists, not bereft of critical judgment, it was probably the fear of ridicule that kept them from exclaiming that the Emperor had no clothes. Later on it was the disinclination to sever long-time associations, to part with the movement which, for all its perversities, was so dynamic and filled a purpose in life that kept them within the fold. Or it was cynicism.

[65] *The Lenin Collection,* Vol. 36, p. 280.

X

THE LAST STRUGGLES

1. Medicine and Administration

After the spring of 1921, when he smashed intra-Party opposition and introduced the new economic course, only one year of active work was left to Lenin. He was to suffer a stroke in May 1922, return to work for a few weeks in the fall, and the second stroke in December was to make him an invalid until his death.

Next to a great man's love life, his health is the most enticing subject of curiosity and rumors. In Lenin's case, while there is very insufficient information about the former, a great deal is known concerning his medical history. He had a veritable obsession about health and fitness, both his own and those close to him. As early as his Siberian exile he took an extraordinary interest in medical matters and was profuse with his advice in this field. Is brother Dimitri getting enough exercise in his prison? Why doesn't Maria Ilinichna take a trip abroad to shake her out of her depression? The cult of physical exercise, somewhat unusual in a Russian *intelligent* of his generation, was always connected in Lenin's mind with the need of keeping fit. He would drag out his fellow exiles from their lairs in Geneva and Paris cafés for mountain-climbing expeditions, bicycle tours, and other healthy diversions. When during his Cracow period a fellow Bolshevik became mentally disturbed, Lenin attended him personally and then dispatched him to Switzerland with instructions where and under what doctors he should pursue his cure.

On the surface, all that was a sensible and humane concern about well-being, both his own and of those close to him. But one can also discern in it an apprehension, whether grounded in some incident in the family's history or his own, that the strains and stresses of a revolutionary's existence lead, unless counteracted by a strict regimen and exercise, to a mental and physical breakdown. One recalls his mother's letter about Vladimir Ilyich when a teen-ager, in which she implored for his readmission to the university and argued that forced inactivity made her son contemplate suicide. He himself anxiously inquired about brother Alexander's last months in a way indicating doubt as to his stability. The stereotypes of the nervous vacillating *intelligent* and of the staunch nerveless proletarian that played such

515

a great role in Lenin's political and personal attitudes were again based partly on his peculiar medical philosophy.

This philosophy stayed with him through the period of power. And like many other personal characteristics of Lenin it was to have an important influence on the development and nature of the Soviet regime.

In the first place it affected seriously, and in one case it was to affect fatally, his judgments as to the personalities of the leading Bolsheviks. A man who objected to some unsavory aspect of the Bolshevik rule was almost invariably classified as suffering from nerves, in need of long rest or, contrariwise, hard work (Lenin was not more consistent than most amateur psychoanalysts) to cure him of his depression, and by the same token usually judged unfit for responsible political work. We have seen how Lenin indulged his medical penchant in the case of Myasnikov, who wrote to him arguing that only the restoration of some political freedom could save the regime from corruption. He was advised to take care of his nerves, and to work harder. Within a year he was thrown out of the Party, and later on instead of a sanitarium he was sent to jail. A member of the Workers' Opposition was sent for a cure to Berlin. From there he addressed a bitter letter to Lenin complaining about the persecution of his fellow oppositionists. Lenin's answer was typical: "I expected that in Berlin having rested somewhat, improved in your health, and having looked at the situation from a distance . . . you would come to clear and correct conclusions." [1] He carefully and tolerantly goes through his opponent's complaints point by point and tries to refute them. But at the end Lenin reverts to his class-medical philosophy: "A decadent petty bourgeois intellectual when he sees an untoward incident or injustice whimpers, cries, loses his head, his self-control, gossips and puffs himself up to talk nonsense about the 'system.' . . . The proletarian . . . seeing something wrong goes about correcting it in a businesslike way . . . he carries it through firmly to the end. . . ." And his poor correspondent gets this final advice: "I shall say because of our old friendship: you should cure your nerves."

The same fatherly advice was addressed by Lenin to Adolf Yoffe. In this case the point was perhaps well taken. The distinguished Soviet diplomat had suffered from intermittent nervous troubles.[2] But his letter was a reasonable complaint about being shifted from post to post, and about being ignored in the selection to the central legislative body. In his anguish Yoffe incautiously identified Lenin as dictator. "You are the Central Committee," he wrote. This stung Lenin to the quick: "How can you give way to your nerves to the point of using this *absolutely impermissible,*

---

[1] *The Lenin Collection,* Vol. 36, p. 246.
[2] He was probably the first prominent Bolshevik to undergo psychoanalysis. Later on, Yoffe was to commit suicide in despair over his friend Trotsky's deportation to Central Asia.

utterly impermissible phrase that I am the Central Committee." [3] And again: "You have to take a serious rest. . . . Think, would it not be better to go abroad to a sanitarium?" The friendly, solicitous tone of the letter cannot conceal the fact that, for Lenin, Yoffe was now in the category of those intellectuals who "whimper and cry." And he does not refrain from citing the example of a "proletarian" who bore uncomplainingly this being shifted from one job to another that so disturbed Yoffe. His name was Stalin.

At times Lenin wrote and acted as if he were himself the head of a sanitarium. Solicitude for the health of his subordinates, so humane and reasonable at first glance, was to have another fateful effect on Soviet politics. It was through Lenin's insistence that the principle was established that a man's health, if he was a Soviet official, was of concern not only to him, his family, and his doctors, but, and primarily, to the Party. The latter could on its own order an official to undertake a cure, prescribe its terms, compel him to submit to an operation, and the like. The following letter of Lenin's speaks for itself: "To the Organizational Bureau of the Communist Party. I ask that the chairman of the Planning Commission, Comrade Krzhizhanovsky, be *compelled* to go with Krasin to Riga, there to spend in a sanitarium or in a private apartment *one month* of cure and rest. . . . I have become convinced the chairman of the Planning Commission has almost broken down. His repair [*sic!*] is necessary, and not to be delayed." [4] There was no reference to a medical authority and what was almost morbid was that Lenin took upon himself to prescribe the exact length of the cure. Incidentally Vladimir Ilyich was unduly worried. His old friend survived him and, what is more remarkable, Stalin, and lived hale and hearty into his late eighties. How striking the impression of Lenin's medical solicitude must have been can be judged from the fact that when Lenin (long after his death) appeared to Trotsky in a dream he addressed him precisely on this matter rather than, as one might have supposed, about Stalin's villainies: "[Lenin] was questioning me anxiously about my illness: 'You seem to have accumulated nervous fatigue, you must rest . . . Then you should *seriously* . . . consult the doctors.' . . ." [5]

Many an American business executive must have experienced mixed feelings on hearing from his boss, "You look tired, why don't you take a rest or see a doctor?" Within the context of a totalitarian society such words can sound equally ominous. Will the job still be there when the recipient of this solicitude returns from his vacation? Won't his temporary replacement uncover "irregularities" or the fact that the convalescent had staffed his agency with the ex-Mensheviks or other enemies of the people? Lenin's unlicensed medical advice at times reached absurd propor-

[3] Italics by Lenin.
[4] *Ibid.*, p. 313.
[5] L. Trotsky, *Diary in Exile, 1935,* p. 145.

tions. One official on appearing in the Kremlin was told that he looked ill and must be immediately off to the Caucasus. He was not even allowed to go home: an automobile whisked him off to the railway station. When the German doctors examined Lenin, he decided that it was an excellent opportunity to have the health of his subordinates checked. Several high officials including Dzerzhinsky were rounded up and told to strip for an examination. But there was nothing comical in some of the consequences of this benevolent medical despotism. During his own last illness it was the Politburo, over and above his doctors, that regulated his treatment and regimen. The patient and his family could but helplessly witness how political rather than medical considerations were applied in ordering his complete isolation from the outside world. It was then that the words, "If I were only a free man," were to escape from Lenin. But he himself had set the pattern.[6]

A prudent concern for his own health clashed in Lenin with his inability to endure idleness, and, when in power, with apprehension as to what "they" were doing in his absence. Still, he would go on vacations regularly. Even in January 1918, when the whole Bolshevik regime hung by a thin thread, he disappeared for a few days' rest in Finland. After a move to Moscow, a *dacha* (villa) was found for him in the nearby village of Gorki and this became his favorite spot for vacations, He still, even at the most critical times of the Civil War, liked to take hunting trips and forays into the countryside. One of them almost cost him his life. In January 1919 he was driving to visit his ailing wife, then in a children's sanatorium near the capital. His car was stopped by bandits who forced him and the other passengers out at gun's point and then disappeared with the automobile. Incidents of violence and hooliganism *that he personally experienced* always strongly affected Lenin. Eyewitnesses mention only that he regretted the loss of the car and was indignant that his chauffeur and bodyguard did not offer resistance. But more than a year later in his *Childish Disease of Left Communism* there is a passage that undoubtedly recalls the unpleasant experience and fright. Writing about the situation of the Soviet government at the time of Brest Litovsk, he tells his readers: "Put yourselves in the position of [passengers in] an automobile that was stopped by armed bandits. . . . You give them your money, passport, revolver [as he did]. [In return] you are saved from the pleasant company of the bandits . . . so one can escape with one's whole skin." [7] But for all the dangers inherent in venturing into the countryside in those unsettled times the trips continued. With 1921 and his health beginning to fail, Lenin spent more and more time in Gorki. Hunting trips now gave way to

---

[6] In 1925 Mikhail Frunze, Trotsky's successor as Commissar of War, died on the operating table; it was widely rumored that Frunze had been compelled by the Politburo to submit to the operation.

[7] *Works,* Vol. 31, p. 20.

the more sedate forms of exercise such as walks and collecting mushrooms. The latter was the distinguishing mark and the typical avocation of a country man and Lenin pursued it proudly and confidently. Anyone brought up as a child in the Russian countryside could tell poisonous from edible mushrooms.

It was not only bad health that contributed to the impatient, irritable mood of his last years. After unparalleled struggles and sufferings during the four years since October Russia was at peace and supposedly in the promised land of Socialist construction. Upon a closer examination both the peace and socialism were shown to be illusory. Widespread bandit activities and peasant unrest persisted through 1921 and 1922. At times their suppression required the use of regular army units. After Kronstadt the specter of another mutiny weighed heavily on Lenin's mind. He inquired discreetly of Trotsky whether it would not make sense to "shut down" the navy for at least a year. There was no conceivable use for it in the immediate future, and the coal and food expended in maintaining it were badly needed elsewhere.[8] But there was also the unspoken fear that the turbulent sailors, the erstwhile "pride and beauty of the Revolution," were still a threat to the Bolshevik power.

And socialism. To talk about it in Russia of 1921 seemed a mockery. Where was it? Lenin's dialectical skill could convince many that socialism meant state capitalism, or that communism was Soviet power plus electricity; but to the rank-and-file worker such formulas sounded increasingly hollow. His own material position was infinitely worse than in Tsarist times. During the period of War Communism there had been at least the compensating factor of the workers being their own bosses. This too had proved an optical illusion. The bourgeois specialists were now running the factories. Now that the intra-Party opposition had been censored, Lenin abandoned his reticence to put the unions in their place. "Any direct interference by the trade unions with the management of the [state] enterprises . . . should be considered harmful and inadmissible," he said firmly in January 1922.[9] He added that the unions should collaborate closely and permanently with the state. To the older workers this must have sounded strangely familiar. Was it not the police chief, Zubatov, who under the Tsar had advocated a similar theory of unionism? The workers should look upon the state as their friend and protector and not listen to the agitators (then the Social Democrats, now the Workers' Opposition).

Upon a closer examination the whole Socialist verbiage looked like a huge hoax. The *Nep* revived private trade and speculation. The peasant was reassured as to his property and given the right to dispose freely of his surpluses. Lenin's often proclaimed motto that we have "the commanding heights" of the economy, that is, that the state held heavy industry, bank-

[8] *The Trotsky Archive* T 654.
[9] *Works*, Vol. 33, p. 164.

ing, and transportation in its hands, was one of those circumlocutions which in 1921–22 could fool only the foreign Communists and commentators. Who in postwar Russia did not realize that "we" were the Party and state bureaucrats, a group which already was assuming the characteristics and manners of a ruling class?

It was a society not yet sufficiently totalitarian for popular discontent not to express itself, and for groups and individuals not to raise their voices in protest against what they considered a debasement of the Revolution, and the broken promises. At the same time, since all the other avenues of protest and criticism in Russia had been blocked, it was within the Communist Party that this current of dissatisfaction and turbulence was felt most strongly. The last paradox in Lenin's life was perhaps the most striking. In the country at large his regime achieved perhaps the greatest popularity since the very earliest days when he had promised peace, bread, and land. By the time of his death the *Nep* had produced a marked economic amelioration. The peasant and the "specialist" felt that it was Lenin who almost singlehandedly saved them from the ravages and the persecutions of War Communism. They felt, perhaps overoptimistically, that as long as he was at the helm they would be protected from the doctrinaires and new outbursts of lawlessness. But within the Party at large the same period was one of his declining popularity. The more ideologically-minded felt that the *Nep,* which he had authorized, had delivered the country to the *petite bourgeoisie* and put new chains on the proletariat. The opponents of oligarchy and favoritism in the Party, who even in 1921 felt that if "Ilyich only knew the facts" he would be with them, were no longer so sure of that a year or two afterward. To some of them *he* now appeared as the supreme conniver, the main enemy of the intra-Party democracy, the man who would expel or imprison those who dared to contradict him. For his closest lieutenants and would-be successors Lenin had for long ceased to be the fatherly leader and dispassionate arbiter among factions. They had all suffered at his hand (and being ambitious, willful people they would scarcely balance that against the favors they received and the fact that he made them what they were), experiencing the growing irritability and arbitrariness of his last years. Some of the inner group must have realized that as long as he lived he protected them from each other, and that his legend veiled the Party from a closer look into its corruption and intrigues. This legend they would try to preserve and enhance after his death. But for the man himself in his last illness they showed very little consideration. The real feelings of many high and intermediate Party officials on the death of the man who had raised them from insignificant agitators to undreamed-of heights were perhaps to be best expressed in the verdict of one Medvedev, a former member of the Workers' Opposition: Comrade Lenin's death, he wrote, was "a major and depressing event. But in this world everything is relative." [10]

[10] *The Trotsky Archive* T 804.

The drama of Lenin's last years was compounded by his undoubted realization of the growing distrust of communism and of himself in particular. Had he been capable of complete cynicism, there would have been no reason to grow concerned over the ideological impasse in which communism found itself at the end of the Civil War. The Communist Party was in power, the *Nep* was a sensible policy bound to restore Russia's economy. Why worry about the old pledges, about the campaign oratory of October, and the heroic period of the Revolution? And perhaps such complacency would have induced a healthier atmosphere in the Party than the search for the never-never land of socialism. It would have settled down much sooner to what it essentially is now, an agglomeration of hard-working and earnest bureaucrats, managers, and successful people from every level of society, most of them happily free from any ideological twinges or doubts. But had that been Vladimir Ilyich's mentality there would have been no reason for him to abandon a provincial law practice.

To his very end he continued the search for the magic formula. Lenin had been masterful in analyzing the weaknesses of and in destroying the old order. But what were to be the guiding lines for the new one? Marx, as he had confessed, was not of much help. The Master had written convincingly and voluminously about the inherent contradictions and self-destructive tendencies of capitalism. But this was Russia of 1921 and where does one begin?

The New Economic Policy was proclaimed as being intended "seriously and for a long time." Within a few months, in October 1921, the *Nep* was presented as a "temporary retreat." A few more months and Lenin had another formula: we have stopped our retreat. The same perversity intruded into his views about the future of the Party. It was, he had promised, to be staffed and led increasingly by men of practical sense and competence. The old-time agitator and phrase maker, he suggested, had outlived his usefulness. Not long after this startling and, to many comrades undoubtedly painful prospective, Lenin laid down the criteria for the forthcoming Party purge ordered by the Tenth Congress. He wanted a specially rigorous scrutiny to be applied to the following categories: "those occupying the duties connected with special privileges," that is, the very same specialists and professional people whom Lenin had so recently been eager to draw into the Party; the state officials whose service predated 1917; and other managers and officials.[11] In brief, the Party members who represented experience and administrative ability were to be treated especially harshly; the old-time "agitator and phrase maker" with indulgence. Many of the former Mensheviks had by 1921 joined the Communist Party, where they had been warmly welcomed. Many of them were economists and professional people badly needed by the regime. They behaved for the most part with exemplary loyalty, staying away from the intra-Party factions and intrigues. Here is what Lenin had to say of them

[11] *The Lenin Collection,* Vol. 36, p. 263.

in September 1921: "In my view among the Mensheviks who entered our Party after the beginning of 1918 not more than one in a hundred should be reconfirmed as a member and even that one should be checked three or four times." [12] He had laughed publicly at those who asserted that his, Lenin's, rancor against the Mensheviks was based on their old quarrels. But now in the article on the purge he went far to confirm his inability to forget and forgive. As early as 1903, he wrote, the Mensheviks had shown what first-rate intriguers and Machiavellians they were!

"We give with one hand, we take away with another." This is one enduring principle that Lenin imprinted on Bolshevism. His own restless temperament became characteristic of the whole movement. How many times in our own days have the Soviets, say, decentralized economic administration, only to centralize it again after a passage of time, with loud anathemas and penalties applied to those unfortunate administrators and economists who had believed the previous policy to be intended "seriously and for a long time"? How many times did foreign experts celebrate a shift in Soviet foreign or agricultural policy as a decisive and permanent turning point and expend their learning on proving how logical and inevitable it was, only to have the latest pronouncement by Stalin or Khrushchev make them snatch away their manuscripts from the printer? [13]

We noted previously how this restless tossing to and fro, the search for a magical formula for socialism was accompanied in Lenin's mind by a very Marxist belief that some form of technological breakthrough would provide an answer. Things would be different when . . . Russia is fully electrified in twenty years . . . , foreign capitalists teach the Russians to run their economy or (another variant on the same theme) the Communists in a more advanced country seize power and lay material help and their expertise at the service of the Soviet comrades.[14] But for a practical politician such formulas could not provide a fully reassuring answer. Would the Soviet system endure until Russia is fully electrified or until the German comrades are ready to help? In the Marxist's mind the confidence that the forces of history are working out in his favor is intermittently disturbed by the horrible suspicion that it is not so, or that they might take an unexpected and circuitous road to get where they are going. Thus Lenin's growing apprehension that there were forces at large in Soviet Russia which if unchecked would interfere with this "inevitable" march toward socialism. Take the peasant. The *Nep* restored to him some eco-

[12] *Works,* Vol. 33, p. 19.

[13] "Now, *here,* you see it takes all the running *you* can do to keep in the same place," L. Carroll, *Through the Looking Glass.*

[14] The theme, "things will be different when . . ." (and here you fill in industrial statistics or a technological breakthrough) has also been repeated in Soviet history. Communism will be fully achieved, wrote Stalin, when *every* worker has reached the level of very high technological and even scientific training. By 1980 when the U.S.S.R. would produce 200 million tons of steel, Khrushchev promised in 1961, she will have entered the stage of communism.

nomic freedom, gave him incentives to produce more. On the face of it, on every ground a sensible policy. The economy would gain and the peasant through his material progress would raise himself from the "semisavage, Asiatic" condition in which he had lingered for so long. But at the same time that Lenin was approaching the formulation of this policy, he was already possessed by a corresponding fear: "Petty production gives birth to capitalism and the *bourgeoisie,* continuously, every day, every hour, spontaneously, and on a mass scale." [15] Even from a Marxian point of view it could not be argued that that was such a bad prospect. On the contrary, the primitive inefficient peasant would eventually be replaced by a skilled farmer. Vladimir Ulyanov in his first major work on the development of capitalism in Russia had written approvingly about the appearance of capitalism in the countryside: the peasant was living "more cleanly," he was becoming a more efficient producer. Why should Vladimir Ulyanov-Lenin now, after the passage of twenty-five years, view the whole prospect as catastrophic?

Or take the cooperative movement. Obviously postwar Soviet Russia should have welcomed the growth of cooperatives of all forms. The cooperative movement favored the development of skills and incentives so very badly needed by the economy. If you license private trade and speculation then (especially if you are a Socialist), you should cherish and encourage the growth of cooperation. What other form of economic organization is as free from the vices of capitalism, as useful as a school for socialism? Wasn't the heroine of *What Is To Be Done?* demonstrating her Socialist principles by organizing a seamstresses' cooperative? Alas, in retrospect Vera Pavlovna is now seen as an ideological forerunner of the Martovs and Chernovs rather than a true revolutionary. Lenin's verdict was that cooperation works well economically, but in politics "as if by chemistry" it gives birth to the Socialist Revolutionaries and the Mensheviks!

Every rational sensible policy is accompanied by nightmarish possibilities. In every useful element in society there lurks a potential enemy: in the contented peasant a future capitalist, in the cooperator a Menshevik, in a conscientious trade union official an "anarchosyndicalist," in a hardworking Soviet administrator a bureaucrat. Even that salt of the earth in Lenin's opinion, the "brave proletarian," turns upon occasion into a hooligan.

Such are the frantic worries and apprehensions that trouble Lenin's last period. If one adds to them his failing health and his growing disillusionment with his closest collaborators one might receive the impression of a great personal drama and of a man disenchanted and despairing of his life's work. But nothing could be further from the truth than a lachrymose picture of Lenin repenting or despairing as his strength ebbed away

[15] *Works,* Vol. 31, p. 8.

and his collaborators' unlovely characteristics become only too obvious. He was to the last a fighter ready to struggle against bad health and false friends, contemplating with delight how he would rise from his sickbed and confound those members of the Politburo who had kept him a virtual prisoner. Nor is there a sign of despondency about the Revolution: everything seems to have failed but maybe the simple and honest rank-and-file workers can cure the Party of its corruptions and divisions and return it, and with it the whole Soviet state, to the right path.

From 1921 on he ruled Russia in an increasingly authoritarian way. He was perplexed and shocked when it was suggested that he was the Central Committee, but in fact opposition and contradiction would throw him into a rage. None of his main coadjutors was now personally close to him. At one time or another each of them had been censored and put down a peg. Zinoviev and Kamenev had been discredited during the October. Trotsky, whose star at one time seemed as bright as his own, was put down in his place during the trade-union controversy; Bukharin by his past as a "Left Communist" and his behavior during the Brest Litovsk negotiations. Some close political companions of the past have fallen completely from the inner group: Shlyapnikov, Kollontay, Lunacharsky have shown themselves unfit for political leadership, left sulking in the opposition or in jobs of no political importance. Then there were others such as Stalin and Rykov whose roles appeared to be those of faithful executors of Lenin's orders. To talk of his having a rival would have been ridiculous.

His lonely stature was emphasized by his growing personal isolation from even the most important Party and state figures. None of the Soviet oligarchs could now boast of personal intimacy with Vladimir Ilyich. Those very close friends of the pre-1917 period, the Olminskys, Bonch-Brueviches, Lepeshinskys, and the others were for the most part in very secondary positions or confined to such out-of-the-way institutions as the Institute of Party History. Lenin was solicitous about his old acquaintances: he wrote to get Adoratsky a better apartment and a position as an archivist. But an old and intimate friendship with him was usually a barrier to a high position rather than vice versa. Gleb Krzhizhanovsky had been the closest friend of his Siberian exile, one of the few he ever addressed as "thou." Now, because of his professional competence Krzhizhanovsky headed the Electrification, then the Planning Commission, but was addressed as Comrade Krzhizhanovsky and played no political role. "Dear Gregory" became Comrade Zinoviev, and though one of the most important men in the regime, his personal intimacy with Lenin had ended. In the whole history of the Bolshevik Party there had been only one man who had competed with Lenin for its leadership, Leonid Krasin. He returned to the Party after the Revolution and occupied important diplomatic and managerial positions. Lenin had, and justifiably so, a high opinion of Krasin's integrity and capacity. But again, he was not allowed to play an important political role.

This self-imposed distance from even his most important associates was in Lenin's eyes probably a necessary element in his technique of governing. During the period under discussion he had to avoid the appearance of favoring this or that of his lieutenants, who were already embroiled in their fateful struggles. But in addition he required rest and relaxation from politics and these could not be obtained if the Party dignitaries could be allowed to intrude on his private life. Trotsky in his autobiography goes to great lengths to imply his personal intimacy with Lenin. Their apartments in the Kremlin shared a dining room. Vladimir Ilyich used to like to play with Trotsky's boys, and so on. But despite such proximity their personal intercourse appears to have been rather limited. They were both passionate hunters but, Trotsky admits wistfully, "Lenin and I never had a chance to go hunting together. . . ." He preferred to vacation with people who could be counted on not to discuss politics.

For relaxation Lenin retreated within his family circle. Krupskaya worked assiduously in the Commissariat of Education. There are hints in her memoirs that the new style of living, with its official grandeur, was not quite to her liking. It meant the severance of old associations and friendships. Insofar as material amenities were concerned, their life in the Kremlin was really not very much different from that in Geneva or Paris. But the informality and conviviality of those times were gone. Nadezhda Konstantinovna had been a close collaborator and her husband's only secretary. Now she was a rather minor Soviet official. For all the formal emancipation of women the atmosphere of Soviet politics was severely masculine. In the revolutionary world women often had played a leading role. Now the female veterans of Bolshevism were for the most part consigned to special women's organizations, the ministry of education, journalism, and the like. One could not readily imagine a woman Party official ordering the execution of the kulaks (though there were a few who did), breaking down the "sabotage" of the railwaymen, or working in the Cheka with Dzerzhinsky.

Among other members of his family sister Maria was now the one closest to him, a constant companion in the Kremlin and Gorki. Anna, one feels from her first recollections after her brother's death (later on they fall in with the general Stalinist pattern of such writings) was, like her sister-in-law, somewhat out of tune with the official Soviet atmosphere and the beginnings of the Lenin cult. Her husband, Elizarov, had been the first Soviet Commissar of Communications. He did not satisfy his brother-in-law's expectations, but who could in those days and in that job? [16] All the Ulyanovs, as a matter of fact, had state jobs: Anna in the Commissariat of Education, Maria with the editorial board of Pravda. Even Dimitri, the most shadowy figure among them, worked in the state medical administration. At one time he had seemed slated for more important things: he

[16] Mark Elizarov died in 1919.

headed the Bolshevik organization in the Crimea, but whether this aroused his brother's displeasure or whether Dimitri simply was not cut out for politics, he was soon returned to the occupation for which he was professionally qualified.[17]

One can hardly accuse Lenin of nepotism. His relatives' jobs were minor, and in view of their revolutionary past and their professional qualifications the Ulyanovs perhaps would have reached them even without their powerful connection. That Lenin's family could count on official favors beyond the reach of an ordinary citizen is, however, documented by at least one piece of evidence. On April 9, 1921, Lenin wrote to the Deputy Commissar of War informing him that Maria, accompanied by Bukharin and his wife and some other friends, was traveling to the Crimea in a special railway carriage, and asked that the car be attached to a military train so it would be sure to get there faster.[18]

Beyond the family circle Lenin found a relaxation in his renewed friendship with Gorky. There was, as we have seen, a great deal in common between the two men. For Lenin this relationship represented a link with the old world of the intelligentsia, which he hated so much and yet strangely missed in the new Russia. Gorky commendably exploited this friendship to beg favors for those men of the vanished world. Thus a characteristic telegram of Lenin's to a provincial authority: "Writer Ivan Volny has been arrested. Gorky, his friend, asks that the investigation be very careful and impartial. Couldn't he be released and just watched? Wire." And the inevitable sequence, Lenin to Gorky: "The chairman of the Orlov investigation commission . . . has wired that Ivan Volny temporarily released pending an investigation." [19] But Gorky's attempts to soften Vladimir Ilyich's wrath toward his own class and to make him treat those pariahs of Soviet society more humanely ran into his friend's uncompromising aversion. "One cannot refrain from arresting *all* of this Kadet and its like crowd in order to forestall conspiracies. . . ." he wrote Gorky's mistress, "They are all capable of helping the conspirators. It would be criminal [*sic!*] not to arrest them. Better that . . . hundreds of the intelligentsia spend a few short [!] days and weeks in jail rather than 10,000 should be slaughtered, [20] so help me, much better."

It was the closest Lenin came to rationalizing and apologizing for his

---

[17] Alone among the Ulyanovs, Dimitri had progeny. The Elizarovs adopted a son.

[18] *The Trotsky Archive* T 668. Trotsky kept this far from world-shaking item among his papers, which has perhaps an eloquence of its own. In his *Diary in Exile 1935* he reminisces uncharitably about Maria Ulyanova: "An old maid reserved and persistent. . . . In taking care of Vladimir Ilyich she vied with N. K. Krupskaya . . . was closely connected with Bukharin. . . . Ulyanova's jealousy was strengthened by her narrowness and fanaticism and also by her rivalry with Krupskaya." In brief, Trotsky saw in Maria an accomplice of Stalin and Bukharin, p. 33.

[19] *V. I. Lenin and A. M. Gorky*, Moscow, 1961, pp. 125–26.

[20] It is not clear whether Lenin means 10,000 people in general or that 10,000 of the intelligentsia would be lynched after uncovering a "plot."

terrible hatred, for dealing with those broken people in a way that the most tyrannous police chief under the Tsars would not have dreamed of. But at other times he mocked his friend's softness. Those are the very same people being arrested, cried Gorky once, who had helped him, Lenin, and his comrades, had hidden them and served the cause of the Revolution. "Yes . . . ," said Vladimir Ilyich, "excellent people, kind-hearted people and that is why we search and investigate them . . . because they are excellent people and kind hearted. They sympathize with the downtrodden, they don't like persecutions. And what do they see now? The persecutor, it is our *Cheka,* the persecuted the Kadets and the S-Rs, who run away from it. . . . And we have to catch the counterrevolutionaries and render them harmless. Hence the moral is clear." Here, records Lunacharsky who heard the conversation, Lenin laughed "with his laughter in which there was not a trace of malice." [21] Great humorist, Lunacharsky.

Still, through Gorky's intercession individual writers and scientists were being retrieved from the tentacles of the *Cheka.* In his curious way Lenin even conspired with his friend to subsidize the publication *abroad* of the *émigrés'* books, including such anti-Bolshevik works as Martov's and Chernov's memoirs. It is a commentary on Soviet conditions and on the alleged democratic instincts of the Workers' Opposition that some of its members viewed Gorky's influence with dark suspicion. He was softening Ilyich's heart toward the *bourgeoisie* and the "specialists." He was causing good Soviet money to be spent on the publication of Menshevik trash. He and Krasin were two evil spirits trying to protect the remnants of the former exploiting class from a just retribution. When one proletarian hero wrote in this vein to Lenin, he exploded: it was a "bare-faced lie," he wrote, to allege that some of his decisions were influenced not by state considerations but by a "desire to appease Gorky." It is hard to feel sorry for Lenin's correspondent, or for that matter, for many of those fighters for "intra-Party democracy."

The paradoxical strain in his friend's make-up was appreciated by Gorky. "Watch yourself . . ." he warned Lenin, "remember a Russian is capable of the most unexpected outbursts—he will do some swinishness and then will wonder: what the devil made me do that?" [22] Did he mean that Lenin should be on guard against others, against assassination, or perhaps the writer also had in mind Lenin's own fearsome temper?

On Lenin's part the friendship was not without a practical aspect. Gorky was one of the few Soviet cultural figures with an international reputation. When the great famine of 1921 began, Gorky was very instrumental in mobilizing foreign help for its victims. Would he contact Bernard Shaw and H. G. Wells for this purpose, wrote Lenin. And indeed

[21] *Ibid.,* p. 341.
[22] *Ibid.,* p. 186.

Gorky was helpful in creating an atmosphere of good will toward Soviet Russia among the international intellectual community. He was also one of the very few who, without any political design or motivation on their part, would bring to Lenin's attention the instances of official abuse and red tape. Their correspondence is a pathetic commentary on the contrast between the dream and reality of Soviet conditions. Both men saw the Communist experiment as the means of raising Russia to new cultural and scientific heights; they envisioned learned institutes and technological marvels spreading all over the land. Yet, to actually make the bureaucracy show the slightest consideration for such lofty aims was like pulling teeth. The Council of Commissars allotted funds to send Russian savants abroad, but, complained Gorky, Litvinov in the Commissariat of Foreign Affairs saw no reason to issue them passports. A professor was delegated to do important chemical research in France, but the *Cheka* refused to give him clearance. Won't Lenin write to Litvinov and the *Cheka?* Nothing else would do.

In fact the infant Soviet state was already smothering in red tape. Just as in his struggles against intra-Party intrigues, so in his fight against bureaucratism Lenin was fatally handicapped by his unwillingness to admit that he was a dictator. Unlike his successors, he had no elaborate private secretariat at his disposal, no special "apparatus" apart from that of the state, and the Party. A secretary of his was exactly that: a woman to take dictation, to deliver messages and orders. No grey eminence such as Stalin's Malenkov or Poskrebyshev hovered at his side to relieve him from constant watchfulness both for major intrigues and for inconsequential trifles. In addition to everything else, Lenin undertook the job of being the All-Russian complaint bureau. Peasants in some village complain of being unjustly persecuted as *kulaks* by the local boss. Lenin dashes off a note to the local *Cheka* or executive committee to investigate: "Please send me a line or two after you find out." It was a hopeless struggle. Or, how to avoid the suspicion that his subordinates were cheating him? To the Commissar of Foreign Affairs: "I have grounds to suspect that the Commissariat is in *fact ignoring* the decision of the Council of Commissars. I warn you. I request a most detailed reply . . ." [23] Or his subordinates inveigle him into their intrigues and never-ending quarrels. Litvinov in the Foreign Affairs Commissariat had used derogatory language about a possible rival, a fellow Soviet diplomat. He in turn wrote an insulting letter to Litvinov, which the latter hastened to convey to Lenin. Follows a Solomon's judgment, which is in favor of the wily Deputy Commissar of Foreign Affairs: Litvinov used some strong language but his opponent's retort was shamefully and inexcusably insulting. A sharp reprimand is to be entered in his record.[24] A Party official complains that "they" don't like his pamphlet

[23] *The Lenin Collection*, Vol. 36, p. 205.
[24] *Ibid.*, p. 335.

about the agricultural tax and don't want to have it published. Thus the leader of the Soviet state and world communism has to write to the state publishing house that he likes the pamphlet and thinks it ought to be published. If "they" think otherwise let them complain to the Central Committee.

Or the hurt feelings of his old comrades: when the All-Russian Famine Committee was set up some old Mensheviks were dragged into it to facilitate the flow of money from abroad. The Commissar of Health, Semashko, objected to such by-passing of his ministry. That his old fellow conspirator should think seriously that he planned to use the ex-Mensheviks for anything but show put Lenin in a very joking mood. "My beloved Semashko, don't sulk, my dear little soul." His official authority is not being curtailed, the Mensheviks and their like are put on the Committee to impress the foreign "Quakers." He, Semashko, will remain in charge.[25]

The many facets of the new bureaucracy must occasionally have reminded Lenin of the old Tsarist times. To be sure, on the surface the change was tremendous. The new officials did not wear uniforms, orders, and epaulettes. Instead of the old elaborate names of the state institutions, all the Soviet Commissariats and Commissars were known by their abbreviations. Possibly it saved paper, though one wonders if what was saved in paper was not more than lost in time in trying to decipher the meaning of such hieroglyphics as *KomVnuTorg* (Commissariat for Internal Trade, to the initiated). The old ways of the Tsarist bureaucracy, leisurely and decadently polite at the top, brutal and servile at the bottom, were supposedly replaced by the consistently polite, brisk, and alert manner of the Soviet officials. "To His High Excellency . . . My Gracious Lord, Most Highly Regarded . . ." First name and patronymic follow, and so on until he has used a whole page before getting to the matter at hand. So would write a Tsarist dignitary to a colleague. "Comrade Zinoviev" was all the preface that Lenin needed before plunging into the latest Party affair. No effusive politeness at the end, again a brisk "I shake your hand."

Alas, behind this brave veneer was a labyrinth of circumlocution, red tape, and subterranean intrigues that would have astounded the most inveterate *chinovnik* of old. It was practically with tears of rage that Lenin confessed that an inquiry by the Politburo had uncovered 120 subcommissions of the Council of Commissars where at most 16 were necessary.[26] The perennial Soviet complaint, you don't get any decision until you get to the very top, that is, to the Politburo, was already voiced by Lenin. *Every* trifle had to be referred for decision to the Politburo or to him personally. Nothing could be settled without the concurrence of at least two high officials. A shipment of canned goods fully paid for is lying in a foreign port.

[25] *Ibid.*, p. 287.
[26] *Works,* Vol. 33, p. 275.

It cannot be brought to Moscow until Trade Commissar Krasin gets together with Politburo representative Kamenev and issues instructions to the Commissariat of Transport, which in turn . . . Foaming at the mouth, Lenin exclaims that *everybody* concerned should be put in jail. Hopeless; you cannot arrest the personnel of a whole Commissariat and to all his inquiries Vladimir Ilyich would receive a standard reply: "The guilty party has not been identified."

In addition to the personal rivalries already depicted, professional jealousy and prejudices split the ranks of the bureaucracy. Thus Lenin recounted at a Party gathering how two state economic agencies in the Ukraine, the *K.I.M.* and the *C.P.K.P.* (too long to recount what the initials stand for; his listeners undoubtedly did not care either) engaged in a violent quarrel. He, Lenin, inquired what it was all about. Nobody knew. "Evidently there was some intrigue and an appalling mess, which the Institute of Party History could not get to the bottom of even if it were to spend ten years on it." The personnel of the Commissariat of Foreign Affairs looked on the people in the Comintern as wastrels and trouble makers. Other state agencies in turn surprisingly viewed the diplomats in the same light in which they were considered in the rotten bourgeois countries: parasites, "cookie pushers," etc. The Moscow city authorities would engage in such games as "drafting" officials of the Commissariat of Foreign Affairs for Party work. Again, Chicherin had to beg Lenin: Will Vladimir Ilyich write to the Moscow Party secretary to cease such practices? He cannot run his ministry without personnel. The automatic hostility that existed between the local Party secretary and the corresponding *Cheka* official was already proverbial.

Thus the fine old Russian art of writing *"donosy"* or clever denunciations of one's rivals and superiors was already at its prerevolutionary level of excellence. An old-time official would delicately note his colleague's corruption, or what was worse, his liberal views, and his suspicious contacts abroad, or goad him into an unseemly outburst. With luck the intelligence would reach His Majesty's desk and be annotated: "Let this swine be dismissed within 24 hours," as Alexander III wrote about a bulwark of his administration. Now a Litvinov would play a variant of the same game: a fellow diplomat would be provoked into using outrageous language, and the proof would be conveyed triumphantly to Vladimir Ilyich. Or at a higher level, Trotsky would in anguish acquaint Lenin with the bad preparations for a Comintern meeting in Petrograd. Evidently no thought had been given to procuring decent accommodations for foreign delegates, not enough rooms and beds, poor food. What would the foreign comrades think? What an evidence of the "lack of culture" in Russia (always a sensitive point with Lenin). Would it not hurt the cause of the Revolution? Who was the boss both of the Comintern and Petrograd? Out of delicacy Trotsky does not name him, but it was Zinoviev.

The parallel with old Russia must have struck Lenin even more forcibly in his wanderings in the countryside. After being robbed and stripped of their automobile by the bandits in 1919 Lenin and his companions reached the nearest government office on foot. Here they were confronted by the eternal Russian constable who would not let the "strangers" in and whom no news of crime would disturb out of his slumber and equanimity.[27] Having finally penetrated the interior of the local soviet, the party was confronted by an equally intrepid telephone operator. His visitor could be Vladimir I. Lenin, he possibly could have been robbed, but all that he the operator knew was that the telephone could not be used without the authorization of the chairman of the soviet, who, of course, was away. Under less dramatic circumstances Lenin would also encounter the torpor of local officialdom. Sometimes during a hunting trip the word would get around to the local peasants that the "chief Bolshevik" was in the vicinity. The *moujiks* would surround him and pour out their complaints about official wrongdoing. A chance trip in a freight train provided another insight into how things were being done. The train was supposed to bring in a valuable cargo and was under a special escort. Its commander sought Vladimir Ilyich's intercession: at various stations cars were detached because "the locomotive was tired." When they reached Moscow *he* was going to be held responsible by the *Cheka* for the loss of precious supplies.

At times Lenin tried to laugh at his predicament with his bureaucracy. He told the comrades of his experiences with giving legal advice to neighboring peasants while in exile in Siberia. His "practice" suffered both from the peasant's inability to get to the bottom of things and from the worship of the "official papers" without which nothing could be done. A woman would come in and start talking incoherently about her relatives and the white cow which "they" took away from her. "Where are the documents, Mother?" Counselor Ulyanov would interrupt. And she would go away mumbling "and without a document he would not even listen about my white cow." Now, after twenty-five years, and the Revolution, the same incoherence and the same worship of the "documents," under piles and mounds of which the whole Soviet system was being buried.

It would be mistaken to consider Lenin's struggle with the bureaucratic red tape as something secondary or incidental to his main work. During his last phase it absorbed more and more of his energy and filled him with increasing anguish. Other shortcomings of the Soviet system might be rationalized away or blamed on the fact that the Bolsheviks were just learning to rule. But the administrative rut, the lack of an efficient, cultured, and humane attitude of the official toward the citizen was an

---

[27] When the Tsarist Minister of the Interior, Plehve, "the great scoundrel," was blown up by an assassin the police cordoned off the area. A bystander asked the policeman who was killed and received this classical answer, which unfortunately loses much in translation: "It is nothing to you. He whose business it was got killed."

ominous sign. The Revolution and socialism had obviously failed to work that change in human hearts and minds that all Russian reformers and radicals from the Decembrists on had hoped and prayed that they would. At times Lenin blamed this on the old officials inherited from the Tsar's times or the ex-Mensheviks infiltrating the Soviet institutions. At other times he appraised the situation more truthfully. Ninety-nine per cent of the officials lack culture, he declared, good Communists though they are. The word stood for humaneness and feeling in dealing with people. But at precisely what point did those qualities degenerate into the squeamishness and softness unworthy of a Communist?

Lenin tried to demonstrate by his own example. His letters abound in such good advice as "show him consideration," "do it delicately," and the like. He was, as we have seen, a solicitous boss. Apart from his concern for the health of his subordinates he would interest himself in their living conditions. Is Stalin's apartment in the Kremlin comfortable enough? Another commissar has a large family and Lenin orders that his salary be increased beyond the legal maximum. A son of his old comrade wants to be released from the army so he can pursue his studies: can something be done? Nadezhda Alliluyeva, daughter of the man who had sheltered him, and incidentally Stalin's wife, has been suspended from the Party; Lenin successfully intercedes on her behalf. Yet there was a whole range of problems in which Lenin's contradictory requirements could hardly be met. Could one annex a country such as Georgia and introduce there the Soviet system while displaying "delicacy" and "understanding"? And when he himself became ill was he to be treated in accordance with the strict code of communism in such matters, as a man who because of his incapacity should not be allowed to meddle with the business of government, or with special indulgence because he was Lenin, and sick?

For all his readiness to tackle the evils of bureaucracy singlehanded, Lenin realized the necessity of institutional checks and controls. The day had not yet come when the secret police could openly interfere with a *Communist* official. The mere suspicion of such control would raise a storm at a Party gathering. Dzerzhinsky and his strong-arm lads were all right when dealing with the counterrevolutionaries, but the very idea of those people sniffing around a Party man . . . The Party Secretariat, until Stalin was installed there, was a weak reed, though the situation then was to change rapidly. Hence a recourse to the creation of special control organs within both the Party and the state.

The history of those organs is a melancholy illustration of an authoritarian regime's inability to cope with its own abuses. The state organ, renamed in 1920 the Commissariat of the Workers' and Peasants' Inspection (the *Rabkrin* or the *R.K.I.* in abbreviation), had been since its original inception in 1919 under the guidance of Stalin. It was to be a "special" commissariat watching over the activity of other ministries and state commissions, combating abuses and bureaucratism. Its officials were to be nominated with the concurrence of some professional bodies such as the trade unions. In theory it was to be an organ of the people's control over their administrators, a stern and watchful censor of the official morals and practices.

In fact it was of course a fantastic delusion to believe that this could cure the bureaucratic evil, or that the other Soviet oligarchs would meekly accept the right of one of them, Stalin, to investigate and censor the activities of their commissariats. From its beginning the *Rabkrin* became one of the most bureaucracy-ridden agencies in the whole government. Its officials, who had nothing else to do but to snoop around, complain, and censor the work of others, came to be considered the dregs of the Soviet administrative corps. Instead of relieving Lenin of his administrative worries the *Rabkrin* added to them. He had to defend Stalin's ministry from the complaints of other Party bigwigs, especially of Trotsky, who spared no occasion to note its shortcomings and assault its policies. Lenin's comments on the *Rabkrin* show this inevitable tendency of every Soviet institution, no matter what its original concept, to become encrusted with the barnacles of bureaucratism and red tape. His Commissariat, he wrote Stalin, had already 12,000 officials and worked badly. Would it not be better to cut down their number? To separate the good ones from the bad, he wrote helplessly, to select those who are "unconditionally honest and capable"? [28] He could not understand that *nothing* in the Soviet system could remain apolitical. To others the Commissariat represented not control by the workers and peasants, but by Stalin. Had any other Soviet notable been put in charge, the situation would have been essentially the same. Had a self-effacing, second-rank Communist become the commissar then nobody would pay any attention to his agency.

The dream of a magic wand with which to cure the ills of bureaucratism stayed with Lenin. In 1920 he sanctioned the institution of a network of Control Commissions *within the Party*. Here special care was taken that they should not degenerate into tools of personal intrigue. Thus the Central Control Commission was to be elected by the Party Congress, and its members could not simultaneously sit on the Central Committee. Local Control Commissions were to be elected by the corresponding Party organizations, their members likewise barred from sitting on the corresponding executive and legislative organs. Here, it appeared, was finally an infallible check on corruption, inefficiency, and favoritism in high and low places. The Control Commissions were divorced from politics; they were decentralized, a genuine organ of the rank-and-file honest Party member who would call his superiors to account. In addition to their fight against bureaucratism, the new organs were to keep a check on the morals and behavior of the Party members. A Communist's private life was not

[28] *Works,* Vol. 33, p. 317.

exclusively his own concern. Were he a debauchee, drunkard, a speculator for private gain, he would be reprimanded by his comrades, and in case he did not mend his ways, stripped of the honorable name of Communist.

Alas! The reality was soon to show how puerile such expectations had been. At the very high level the Party control organs abetted rather than diminished bureaucratism. It was not to be expected that Comrade A. Soltz, who in view of his position as Chairman of the Central Control Commission was the chief censor of the Party's morals, would show much enthusiasm in investigating the abuses and derelictions of the members of the Politburo, that he would scold Comrade Lenin for chicaneries against those who opposed him, or that he would remonstrate with Comrade Rykov because of the latter's fondness for vodka. On the contrary, human nature and Soviet Russia being what they are, the Central Control Commission soon conceived its duty as being that of an additional arm of repression by the ruling Party regime rather than of a restraint upon it. One of the central duties of the control organs became to put down any and every opposition to the Party "line" laid down by the Central Committee, that is, by Lenin. With loving care they would go through the *curricula vitae* and current behavior of former members of the Workers' Opposition, would note their "disloyal" utterances, spy on their private meetings. When Stalin became the General Party Secretary in 1922, the Central Control Commission became one of his chief instruments in achieving absolute power and in terrorizing his opponents.

At the local level the Control Commissions became a veritable scourge to the Party members. An average Communist's past often, to put it mildly, did not bear too close an examination. Some had been Mensheviks, others had concealed their class origin, still others showed an excess of proletarian zeal during the Civil War. If the same people displayed any sign of independence or opposition to the leadership, the discreditable facts would come out in the open. One of the most widely practiced and easily detectable frauds concerned the length of one's service in the Party. To have been a Bolshevik before 1917 was a sign of distinction and a sure title to preferment. To have joined the Party before 1905 was equivalent to having had one's ancestors come on the *Mayflower*. At the same time it was virtually hopeless to determine what constituted membership in the Party before 1917. Attendance at some meetings? Jail sentence? Where could one in those days draw a clear-cut line between the Mensheviks and Bolsheviks? The example of doctoring one's Party seniority came from the very highest circles. Lenin listed himself as having joined in 1895; yet the Russian Social Democratic Party had not existed prior to 1898 and was not really organized until 1903, and he simply projected his membership in a Socialist discussion and agitation group in St. Petersburg. Who was there to testify whether Stalin really did join the Party in 1898?

But when the "undependable" Bolsheviks indulged in such practices

the Control Commission raised a fuss and alleged falsification of records. Mme Kollontay claimed membership since 1898. What a fraud, said
the redoubtable Soltz at the Party Congress. Why, everybody knew that
the woman had been a Menshevik at least until 1917. So-and-so claimed to
have been born a poor peasant's son. The wretch was unmasked as having
been born in a *kulak's* family. The work of scrutinizing one's fellows' private affairs does not always attract the highest type of people. Within a
year of their institution the controllers of the Party's conscience achieved
the reputation of meddlesome snoopers, if not blackmailers or worse. At the
Eleventh Party Congress in 1922 voices were heard for the abolition of the
Control Commissions. Worthy Soltz related with anguish how one intrepid Communist told him off: "We do not trust you. . . . I have not
elected you," and he complained: "For Comrade Medvedev the decisions
of the Party Congress do not exist; he is above everything." [29] The
snooper-in-chief then related how some other people who criticized the
Party falsified their date of joining. One such person "came to the Party
recently and already wants to improve it, instead of working on his self-
improvement." Soon the Control Commission would offer their services in
improving the recalcitrant comrades. For that purpose they would enter
into a close collaboration with the *OGPU* and before the end of the decade this Party organ, designed to promote intra-Party democracy and curb
favoritism, would not only be a bastion of bureaucratism itself, but for all
practical purposes an auxiliary branch of the secret police.

Everywhere one looked, every institution one set up to fight the evil
was almost immediately affected by the dry rot of bureaucratism and red
tape. That this was an inevitable result of the system was something that
Lenin would not admit even to himself, and every suggestion to this effect
would throw him into a rage. Yet even the most astute domestic and foreign critics of Soviet Russia failed to point out that the greatest trouble
with the system was its hopeless lack of clarity. Fiction was piled upon
fiction, paradox upon paradox. A grass-roots democracy was supposed to
coexist with dictatorship, socialism with capitalism, intra-Party democracy
with an oligarchical rule. At what point did honest criticism, expected of
every Communist, degenerate into a deviation or anarchism? Where was
the separating line between the decisiveness and ruthless devotion to the
cause that every official was to demonstrate and bullying and "the lack of
feeling for the people"? Only one man knew the answers to all those questions. No wonder that his collaborators suffered from "nerves" in trying to
meet his impossible and contradictory requirements, and in trying to keep
afloat in this wonderland of bureaucracy and personal intrigue that was
Soviet Russia.

Lenin must have realized that this whole bizarre structure was held

[29] *The Eleventh Congress of the Russian Communist Party,* March–April 1922,
Moscow, 1961, p. 176.

together only by his own person. A suspicion must have flashed occasionally through his mind that, once he was gone, the whole system would either disintegrate through a war of factions and his would-be successors, or could be held together only through a more overt use of terror and administrative despotism. But if so, he was simply incapable of devising an institutional framework to ward off those two extremes. Nor was he capable of delegating power or grooming a successor. Just as his strength began to give way during the last period so he became more unwilling to delegate responsibility and attempted to lay down the rules for the most trifling administrative matter. A typical document in this respect is his set of instructions for his two deputies in the Council of Commissars: Rykov and Tsyurupa. It was written in April 1922, when his health no longer allowed him a regular attendance in the Council and he had to envisage the possibility of someone else taking the chair.

The work in the Council was his life and it is clear that he neglected or much more willingly delegated authority in the Party in favor of tending to administrative details. *This* was business. He would sit with a watch in his hand, allowing at most ten minutes for an argument. The meetings had to be held punctually. No one was allowed to smoke, and those suffering from the addiction had to have recourse to schoolboys' tricks such as excusing themselves to attend to an urgent need, or ducking behind the big stove, which concealed the smoke. Lenin loved this work of briskly running a committee meeting, of eschewing boisterous oratory of the Party gatherings, of settling things in a "cultured," businesslike manner. That he could no longer attend regularly to this little authoritarian world of his was a source of deep anguish. But even if occasionally absent, he was going to regulate the affairs of the Council *down to the last detail*, hence this amazing document.

The two deputy chairmen of the Council, Lenin wrote with his customary and naïve precision, should spend "nine tenths of their time on affairs of the economic ministries, one tenth on the rest." [30] Each of them is to have two stenographers. If really needed, two good dictaphones are to be ordered from abroad. Neither of his deputies is to lord it over the other. If he, Lenin, is absent then Tsyurupa is to preside over the meeting for the first two hours, then Rykov takes over. But whoever is presiding, the other one *has* to be present. If the two of them quarrel then the Politburo is to decide the issue in his, Lenin's, absence. Short of specifying the time that Comrades Tsyurupa and Rykov are allowed to devote to their natural needs, nothing is left to the discretion of the two deputies. Painfully enumerated are the Commissariats under the surveillance of each. The two dignitaries are to read regularly *Economic Life* and watch out for the tendency of its editors to run it as "a half-independent, intelligentsia-

[30] *Works*, Vol. 33, p. 300.

bourgeois journal of opinion" rather than as the organ of the state.[31]

It is incumbent upon his deputies (one has guessed it) to struggle against "bureaucratism, red tape, nonfulfillment, lack of accuracy, and the like." The means for this struggle: to fire the guilty person, turning him over to the court and "arranging through the Commissariat of Justice for colorful [sic!] show trials."

Poor Lenin. The document in question was of course a perfect blueprint for bureaucratic confusion. The two deputies were tied down hand and foot as to procedure and policy. The natural result of this schoolmasterish instruction could only be that Tsyurupa and Rykov would watch each other like hawks, making sure that neither would get a jump on the other. The startling lack of the sense of political reality from which Lenin was beginning to suffer is demonstrated in this instruction: "The deputies should free themselves as much as possible from personal interviews with the individual commissars . . . which consume a lot of time . . ." How could Tsyurupa, who for all his state position was a rather minor Party figure, deny an interview to Stalin or Trotsky, mere "individual commissars" though they were? Or how could he in fact exercise any authority over them at all? About the same time Trotsky was to refuse the offer to become yet another Deputy Chairman of the Council of Commissars. Politically, it was an extremely foolish step, but the reason given by him was cogent enough: all those deputies had nothing to do except watch each other. In Lenin's absence the Council of Commissars became politically impotent and all the important decisions were made by the Politburo or the Organizational Bureau.[32]

Much of Lenin's trouble stemmed from his obvious dislike of "politics," which is apparent in his last phase. Master politician that he had been, Lenin became fascinated with administration and economic problems, disenchanted and weary of the endless squabbles of the Party Congresses and the Central Committee. His proposed solutions for all sorts of problems became platitudinous homilies: "get some good people," "recruit one hundred outstanding workers," "reorganize the State Planning Commission so that it has some real authority." Yet everything was now pervaded with politics, and that he ignored this was a sure sign of his isolation and growing bad health. Apart from finding "good men" to staff the administration one had to decide whether they were going to be "Zinoviev's men" or "Trotsky's men." Very often the official in charge of a commissariat would be a retainer of one of the Party's potentates, his deputy a retainer of another. Lenin's sure touch in sensing and maneuvering his

---

[31] The sick man's frantic attention to a trifling detail is evident in this passage about the journal: "To turn *Economic Life* into a real organ of state economic administration, into a real organ of Socialist construction, will take years of struggle, but this struggle, relentless and systematic, is necessary." *Ibid.*, p. 302. Why not simply change the editors?

[32] *The Trotsky Archive* T 773.

lieutenants' conflicts and in warding off their violent confrontations was less in evidence. He simply had no strength to keep count of the personal intrigues that surrounded him, no patience to probe into his lieutenants' satrapies and circles of retainers. Thus his eagerness to regulate everything involved him in trifles while the basic issues remained unattended to.

There were many things in new Soviet society that Lenin disliked but about which he could do little. The Revolution and the Civil War contributed to the loosening of the family ties and the kind of libertinism he abhorred. Mme Kollontay, in addition to her other sins, was a vigorous advocate of the rejection of bourgeois morality and the desirability of free love. The sexual act, she wrote, should be deemed of no greater importance than drinking a glass of water. "But who wants to drink from a soiled glass," the maker of the Soviet world is reputed to have exclaimed. But it was still too early in the Revolution for the state to play the role of the enforcer of bourgeois morality, or for a pupil of Chernyshevsky to appear as a defender of the sanctity of the marriage tie. He was already being accused of talking like an old-fashioned capitalist and he was not going to incur the charge of preaching like a bishop.

The same mixture of amusement, incomprehension, and distaste characterized his attitude toward the new artistic trends. For a man who had the philistine notion that a novel should have a plot, poetry should rhyme, and paintings and statues look like what they are supposed to represent, the situation in Soviet art was a sore trial. Occasionally his patience would run out: he would grab Lunacharsky and ask him what was this peculiar slab of marble. On being told that it was a statue of Kropotkin, Lenin would explode: he knew the old Anarchist personally and could vouch for the fact that he had a head and two eyes. His Commissar of Culture was a man of easy enthusiasms. Just as Lunacharsky had fallen in the old days for "God seeking," so he now horrified Lenin by his tolerance and encouragement of cubism, futurism, other isms. The collective name for the new horrors was Proletarian Culture, or, since everything was being abbreviated, *Proletkult*. Its partisans professed mortal enmity and contempt for the old bourgeois culture. As one of the proponents of the *Proletkult* sang: "We have been seized by a rebellious, passionate intoxication. Let them shout about us 'You are destroyers of beauty.' In the name of our Tomorrow we shall burn Raphael, demolish museums, melt down the masterpieces of art."

Lenin in his encounters with Young Communists could only preach that such "squares" as Pushkin or Nekrasov should not be neglected, that before they rejected the old they should learn what it was all about. As to the new idols, he was quite cool. He was not an admirer of Mayakovsky's poetry, he said, though he enjoyed his satires about Soviet bureaucracy and the Communist propensity to hold endless meetings.[33] But he did not feel competent really to interfere in such matters. It was still another childish disease of communism, and let Lunacharsky deal with the intrigues and denunciations which, analogous with politics, were already flourishing in the literary and artistic world. He could not attend to everything.

But in the spring of 1922 Lenin had to face another Party crisis. The sum of all the disappointments and tensions in Soviet society was now focused in this overwhelming threat: the Communist Party was in danger of disintegration.

The reasons for this situation were complex. We have seen how Lenin's absorption in administration and economics drew him away from other matters, how the Party had resolved itself into personal cliques, and so on. The Workers' Opposition, trounced in 1921, once again raised its voice and lamented the workers' predicament in the alleged workers' state.

But beyond those phenomena one encountered a general dissatisfaction among the Communists, not only with how things were run in Russia, but also, this time, with their status and obligations as Party members. Earlier, the average Communist could think of himself as a member of the ruling Party, and in a way of a privileged class (however he would have abhorred using that phrase) in society. He had special obligations, but also special rights and privileges. Now a Party member of the highest seniority might be shoved aside from his job in the government and industry, his position going to a former Menshevik or bourgeois specialist, a man who very likely had been on the opposite side in the Civil War.

But even more important than material considerations was the wounded pride that many a Communist must have felt at his new and humiliating position. Some of that independent and turbulent spirit that made people join the Bolsheviks when their cause looked hopeless still existed in their ranks. Many of the people who rankled under the discipline and bureaucracy were, of course, hooligans and uneasy spirits who in any case would have found it impossible to adjust to peacetime and normal occupations. But there was many a Communist who felt it disgraceful that he, a veteran of this or that, should be treated like an unruly child, told what to do and say, and how to behave.

That they were treated that way is reflected in the universal complaints against the Control Commissions, which in a brief existence had become a universal scourge and pest. Some Communists in their exasperation petitioned the Central Control Commission to issue a special book of etiquette specifying how the Communist is supposed to behave. An official of that body pretended great indignation at this derisive request. Why! Do they expect Communist morals to be codified like those of the *bourgeoisie*, to

[33] *Works,* Vol. 33, p. 197.

be told how many glasses of vodka one may drink, what kind of presents one may receive? But, exactly, the average Communist did not know at what point conviviality became debauchery, and receiving a present became graft. It all depended on the local Mrs. Grundy of either sex, who sat on the detestable Commission and watched *him*, a famous revolutionary veteran.

Equally disturbing was the new phenomenon of the growing disparity of status within the Party and at all levels. In the old days (not so old, actually) the local Party secretary was a comrade in every sense of the word. If he gave himself airs he would soon be replaced and told off. Now the most insignificant local boss aped the imperious manners of Zinoviev or Trotsky. In many cases he was imposed upon the local organization and a man who proposed that Comrade X should be removed was in for all sorts of unpleasant investigations. Again, there were inescapable parallels with the Tsarist times. Then a local official who was venal and a drunk was viewed as a tolerable evil. Much worse, it was thought, was the other stereotype, that of a fanatic for efficiency and order. He would build roads and improve schools, but at the slightest provocation would order the peasants flogged and the local Jews imprisoned, interfering with everything and everybody. Now the same pattern was being repeated. The greatest scourge in a province or a county was the Party secretary with a passion for improvement. The Eleventh Congress was convulsed by the story of one such satrap who would browbeat "his" Communists into continuous sessions devoted to self-improvement. Every evening the comrades had to assemble and listen to lectures on the Paris Commune, Russian Populism in the 1880s, American capitalism, and the like. Woe to one who failed to show, or fell asleep.

At another level it was still a novelty for a rank-and-file Communist to be told to shut up, that a criticism of the *Nep* or the Central Committee was not up to him. Something unimaginable one year before was now happening: the secret police were taking active interest in the activities of those Communists who were too loud. In their complaints, the former Workers' Oppositionists asserted that some of them had been visited by an agent of the *Cheka* masquerading as one of them. Would not Kollontay and Shlyapnikov be interested in establishing a Fourth International? [34] The *agent provocateur* had been used before in connection with the Mensheviks and the S-Rs, but to have him tempt distinguished Party members was an unheard-of outrage. So were the police searches of the apartments of those members of the Central Committee who were in opposition. Shlyapnikov's mail was regularly intercepted. We are at the threshold of Stalinism.

But those practices which would within a few years be accepted as a normal state of affairs still were recent enough to arouse indignation.

[34] *The Eleventh Congress of the Russian Communist Party*, Moscow, 1961, p. 753.

Many a veteran Bolshevik in 1921–22 tore up his Party card. In some major centers Communist discussion groups were set up, by-passing the Party hierarchy. Here the bolder members would read papers on such subjects as the causes of the corruption of the regime and the possible remedies. At least at one such gathering it was proposed that the only possible solution was to legalize not only opposition within the Party but other Socialist parties as well.

If the whole trend were unchecked the Communist Party might soon resemble the Russian Social Democratic Party before 1914, a conglomeration of groups and factions. What was the point of abolishing and persecuting the Mensheviks and the Socialist Revolutionaries if their unhappy quarrels and indignant accusations were to be reborn within the bosom of communism? To some this might appear not such a horrendous thing. Why not allow freedom of criticism, an open clash of opinions within the Party, *real* intra-Party democracy rather than the phony one masquerading under the name of democratic centralism? It would be better than having cliques maneuvering and intriguing for power. But to Lenin and to most of the Party oligarchs such a prospect was inadmissible. Even had they wished to do so, they had entirely lost the ability to deal with anything resembling democracy. The Soviet potentates who sat on the Politburo took for granted each other's intrigues, but the idea of their being criticized by a rank-and-file Party member was almost unbearable to all of them. Thus with one exception they were fashioning their own nooses.

Another consideration must have weighed heavily with Lenin. The alternative to the dictatorship by and *within* the Party could no longer be an orderly democracy, but anarchy. The Bolshevik regime had passed the point of no return; it could either disintegrate or grow more totalitarian. It could not reform itself. It is quite natural for non-Soviet historians to view with sympathy many of the oppositionists of 1921–22. Yet few of them were blessed with a genuine democratic spirit. Most of them accused the regime of being *too tolerant*, of leaving the peasant in peace, of giving jobs to the former Mensheviks and to the bourgeois specialists. They decried the salutary policies of the *Nep*, longed for a return to the "enthusiasm and chaos" of the heroic days. To many of them the main villain on the scene was not one of the Party oligarchs who ruled Russia but the humane and sensible Leonid Krasin. This ex-terrorist fought intrepidly for jobs to go to people on the basis of competence rather than Party seniority, derided empty revolutionary phrasemongering, and hobnobbed with the foreign capitalists (which was, of course, his job in trying to procure loans and foreign trade for Russia). There were undoubtedly persons of sincerity and conviction, such as Ryazanov and Osinsky, among the opponents of the Party policy, but there were also brawlers and adventurers who missed the excitement of the old days. It was late in the day, anyway, to rethink the whole philosophy that had been with Lenin since 1903. Wearily, he sanctioned a policy of repression within the Party.

This time the policy of repression was not going to be accompanied by any gestures of appeasement. As early as August 1921 Lenin had wanted Shlyapnikov to be expelled from the Party, despite his promise of a few weeks before that such a course in regard to a distinguished Party leader was to be but an extreme, almost unthinkable, punishment. At that time the Central Committee bridled at this step [35] and he did not press it. But in February 1922 G. Myasnikov was expelled despite his excellent past record in the Civil War as a partisan leader and ferocious terrorist, the same Myasnikov who had tried to persuade Lenin that the only remedy for the evils of the system was full freedom of the press from monarchist to anarchist! Lenin got tired of corresponding with Myasnikov and arguing with him in a fatherly way about how mistaken he was. This strange man was never to return to the Party. He soon left Russia and returned only after World War II. At least he was fully consistent, which cannot be said about the other opponents of the ruling Party faction.

A group of them in February 1922 took a step as fatuous as it was scandalous. Twenty-two of them, headed by Kollontay, not yet embarked on her diplomatic travels, and Shlyapnikov, petitioned the Comintern about the repression within the Russian Communist Party. The gist of their complaints was mentioned earlier. In addition the wretches gossiped about the regime with the embarrassed foreign Communists: in the workers' state the army was being used to break up strikes; they (the foreign Communists) were being shown parades and spectacles whereas the workers were starving and being forbidden to strike.[36] That they had every right to do so was admitted and repeated monotonously by their accusers. Communism was an international movement, the Russian Communist Party just one of its branches. But, it was immediately added, how scandalous their behavior, how really counterrevolutionary to wash dirty linen in public before the foreigners. How idiotic, one can add. The Executive of the Comintern was composed of the pensioners of the Soviet government. They issued an embarrassed condemnation of the twenty-two: "The position of the complaining comrades . . . did not help the Russian Party in its struggle against the abnormalities which have arisen objectively [!] . . . but on the contrary it weakened the Party, and at the same time has given a weapon to the enemies of communism and of the proletarian dictatorship. . . ." But the matter could not be left there. The Eleventh Party Congress, which was to meet in March, was supposed to expel the main culprits and deal energetically with all the trouble makers and dissidents.

Lenin was already ill and incapable of participating either in the prep-

[35] The motion lacked three votes of the necessary two thirds.
[36] *The Eleventh Congress*, p. 754.

aration of the Congress or in most of its deliberations. Shortly before it he wrote that he must be freed either from attendance at the Central Committee meeting or from the main report at the Congress: he was not equal to both. If he should be able to speak at the Congress he needed a co-reporter: "I am not quite sure I can do that [deliver the main report], but also for months I have been unable to keep up with the current work of the Politburo." [37] Not yet fifty-two, he was a terribly tired and mortally ill man. He sketched what he proposed to say to the Congress, if it was given to him to deliver the speech: "Our main deficiencies: lack of culture and that we really do not know how to rule."

He did appear before the Eleventh Congress, his last, to deliver the main report. This exertion and the irritation he experienced were probably instrumental in speeding the progress of his illness. But to those who had followed him closely over the years it must already have been obvious that he was not the old Lenin. Hardly a trace of that enjoyment he used to take in confounding the opposition, of that careful attention to the proceedings, and of that deceptive humor in which he had veiled threats against his opponents. There was now only unremitting anger at being contradicted; anger mixed with humiliation at the administrative and economic mess in Soviet Russia, anger at his own inability to keep fully abreast of what was going on and at having to rely on inept or scheming subordinates (he kept repeating "I have been told," "they tell me," and the like). His few attempts at humor were cruder than usual. Thus about his deputy Rykov, of whom he currently had great hopes as an administrator: he went to Germany for a cure and a German surgeon "has cut off a bad part of Rykov . . . and has sent the good part completely cleansed back to us." If one could only do that with other Communists! But one would perhaps have to "purge" a part of their anatomy other than the appendix. Perhaps Rykov would be able to straighten out the administrative mess which, Lenin confessed, was now beyond his powers.

When it came to Party matters he broke into almost incoherent threats against the opposition. As Osinsky protested: "Comrade Lenin struck a false note . . . he said one should beat, shoot, squeeze, etc." [38] Lenin's anger was turned against those who dared to talk back to him. In regard to them he speaks in a way soon to be made familiar by Stalin: "If Comrade Osinsky will not in a comradely way pay attention to those counsels which the Central Committee has to give him all the time . . . then he will inevitably and completely sink in the mud." Shlyapnikov dared to joke about similar friendly advice given to him by the oligarchy. He had often been judged, he declared, by the Central Committee, more than once threatened. "Vladimir Ilyich has said that we are spreading panic and with such people one should deal with machine guns. . . ." Look at the ma-

[37] *Works*, Vol. 23, p. 225.
[38] *The Eleventh Congress*, p. 89.

chine gunners, exclaimed Shlyapnikov pointing at the Presidium of the Congress, with Lenin among them. The man who had led the Party during the February Revolution was not going to be intimidated and the delegates responded sympathetically to his defiance and barbs. Lenin, at the end of his endurance, declared that such jokes were inadmissible. Shlyapnikov, he cried, "will not scare anybody or arouse pity for himself. Poor Shlyapnikov. Lenin sets his machine guns against him." [39] But even his most docile followers asked him to moderate his language and not to scandalize the Party by violent threats against one of the most deserving and popular members of the old guard.

Not since Brest Litovsk was Lenin treated with such scant respect and subjected to so many personal attacks as at the Eleventh Congress. His speech contained nothing new, one brazen delegate declared; it had all the old stuff that Vladimir Ilyich had been saying for some time, no real answers to criticisms, no recognition of the evils afflicting the Party. In some ways the assembled must have sensed that the old leader was weakening, and that the very violence of his language concealed an inability to rule with an iron hand as before. His rage often appeared senseless. He resented that the Mensheviks were gloating over the *Nep* as a fulfillment of their prophecy that Russia was not ready for socialism and were saying to their conquerors, "Allow us to repeat it once more." He heard it too often and he replied, "Allow us to put you against the wall. Either you will keep your mouths shut or . . . When you want to go on advocating your political opinions . . . we will deal with you the way we have with the worst and most harmful reactionaries." [40] This was strong medicine: to shoot people for repeating what he himself had said more than once. And anyway, those who taunted "I told you so" were in Berlin or Paris, out of the reach of the *Cheka*. In his final remarks before the Congress Lenin came as close as he ever did to apologizing for the violence of his language.

The Congress and the Party were getting out of hand. The ruling group, the Politburo, was, outwardly at least, solidly behind their leader. But the rank and file were growing unruly and impudent. Their sympathy lay with those persecuted by the oligarchy. In addition to the sympathetic reception given to Shlyapnikov, the most symptomatic development was the response of the Congress to Ryazanov. This veteran Bolshevik had for years exasperated the Party leaders. Of great personal integrity, fearless in his criticism, he seemed a throwback to the early Social Democratic type and what kept him in the Bolshevik ranks is indeed a mystery. That "Ryazanov is not to be taken seriously" had been a standing joke at the Party gatherings. By the same token he was treated with affection, as one man who said what no one else would dare. Nobody could accuse him of a "deviation" or plotting: he was too much of an eccentric.

[39] *Ibid.*, p. 141.
[40] *Ibid.*, p. 25.

By some unfortunate slip-up in the Party apparatus Ryazanov had been delegated to work in the union movement. He was hardly the man to carry out the Party line and persuade the workers that everything was perfect in the workers' state. The unions with which he became connected were soon a beehive of impassioned oratory and criticism of the authorities. As a Party bureaucrat said: "Ryazanov behaved the way he always behaves, and unexpectedly for himself he received a majority . . ." for a resolution attacking the Central Committee. Summoned to explain himself, the old revolutionary said: "You know, comrades, that I am temperamental." He was banned from further professional activity and speaking, and sent back to editing the classics of Marxism.

Now he recounted his indignities to the Congress: he, who had joined the Socialist movement before Lenin, was forbidden to speak at Party and union gatherings, mistreated by some dull bureaucrat who was not even born when he, Ryazanov . . . He coined one of the most memorable witticisms in the history of the Communist movement. They say that the English Parliament can do anything except turn a man into a woman: "Our Central Committee is incomparably stronger; it has turned more than one revolutionary into an old woman, and the number of such cases is multiplying in a most astounding way." [41] Everybody knew who were his main targets. The chief Communist organizer in the union movement was M. Tomsky. He had aroused Lenin's wrath for his softness and had been transferred to Party work in Turkestan. A few months in the desert convinced Tomsky of the essential correctness of the Party line and the groundlessness of the workers' complaints. He was recalled, and as a reward for his conversion was given a seat on the Politburo. Politically he hardly qualified for the inner circle, but Tomsky was a man with enormous popularity and influence among the industrial workers, and this was of overwhelming importance when the proletariat was practically in open revolt against its alleged vanguard, the Communist Party. The fact that his old companion at arms had sold out was the subject of Ryazanov's taunts and attacks, and he did not spare other "old women." In vain did the oligarchs try to mollify the enraged veteran. Ryazanov, said Trotsky, had written an excellent book on the *Communist Manifesto,* such as no one else could write. Why doesn't he stick to books and leave the trade-union movement to others? Here Ryazanov interrupted from his seat: why does not the War Commissar stick to *his* job and leave the economic problems to others? Well, said Trotsky, soothingly, maybe the day will come when *he* will be spanked for writing and talking of things not within his competence. [42]

There was no stopping Ryazanov. He was forever on his feet offering motion after motion, ridiculing the pompous Party bureaucrats to the obvious delight of the assembled. In reading the reports of the Congress

[41] *Ibid.,* p. 79.
[42] *Ibid.,* p. 275.

Lenin (he could not attend most sessions) must have felt like pinching himself: was this a Communist congress in Soviet Russia, or was it one of the congresses of the prewar Russian Social Democratic Party?

But there was a more serious side to the whole business than just impudent oratory. On the most important issues the Party managers barely succeeded in getting the Congress' approval for the official policy. On one measure they had to compromise. It had been proposed to exclude from the Party the main trouble makers: Shlyapnikov, Kollontay, and others. But the Congress would not approve; only some marginal and less well known oppositionists were expelled. The main culprits stayed in. On a yet more important matter the Central Committee got its way only by falsifying the results of a vote. Some wild spirits proposed to abolish the hated Control Commission. *Officially* this motion was rejected by a vote of 223 to 89. But at a subsequent Party congress a high official of the Central Control Commission confessed good-naturedly that this vote had been falsified and that one of the regime's most essential instruments of repression was almost abolished.[43]

It was clear that if further decomposition of the Party was to be prevented some exceptional measures had to be taken. Lenin himself had neither the strength nor the inclination to tend to the needed reforms and repression. What energy was left to him he proposed to employ in the work of his beloved Council of Commissars, in administration and economy rather than chasing after a Communist discussion club in Saratov or the Metalworkers' Union. The work of holding the Party together and avoiding such scandals as those at the Eleventh Party Congress should have been performed in the Secretariat. Ever since 1919, however, it had been impossible to find a really satisfactory man to head this institution. There were currently three Party secretaries, the principal one being V. M. Molotov. Among the more turbulent Party members the idea of Molotov exercising any real authority was considered a joke. He was one of those men who seem to have been born in a pince-nez and a double-breasted suit. Though an old Bolshevik, he had no personal following. At the Congress where he delivered a co-report with Lenin his bureaucratic manner was the subject of many ironic remarks. He was not the man to command respect and restore discipline in the Party. Many dissenters were already congratulating themselves on their future victory. Wait till the next Congress. Lenin, if he is still around, will have to admit the justice of their cause, stop coddling the peasants and bourgeois specialists, turn again toward the workers and restore the intra-Party democracy (it was not ex-

[43] Matvei Shkiryatov declared that the Eleventh Congress "had almost abolished the Commissions. The protocols, it seems, say that there were only 89 votes [for the abolition], *but it was not so.*" *The Twelfth Party Congress, Stenographic Report,* Moscow, 1923, p. 224. Shkiryatov was subsequently one of the gray eminences of the Stalin era.

actly clear what these last two phrases were supposed to mean). The hated bureaucrats would be thrown out. But one day after the Congress closed, the Central Committee elected Joseph Vissarionovich Stalin as Secretary General.

That he was Lenin's personal nominee there can be no doubt. When at the Eleventh Congress one delegate complained that Stalin in addition to his Party offices held two commissariats [44] Lenin spoke of him in a tone that implied limitless trust in and admiration of Stalin's ability to work and command respect. Where do you find a man, he asked, "whom the representative of any nationality can visit and tell in detail his troubles?" No other candidate but Stalin. Or for the work in the state control: "In order to deal with control you need at the head of the ministry a man with authority, otherwise we would sink, we would drown in petty intrigues." [45] Patient, persevering, selfless Stalin! One may shake one's head over Lenin's famous perspicacity or conclude that he was already very ill. But in fact Stalin was the logical man for the job. His record had been one of absolute loyalty to Lenin. He bore uncomplainingly the heavy administrative duties imposed upon him. No other Politburo member thirsted after the job with the prosaic title of "secretary," with its mass of paper work, of constant interviews with the provincial dignitaries, and the like. None of them had the patience for administrative work. Even Trotsky during his great tenure in the War Ministry left the day-to-day administrative drudgery to his assistants while he formulated the policies and dashed to the front. In April of 1922 the choice of Stalin was one to excite least jealousy. He aroused less antagonism than any other of the Party oligarchs and while they already looked upon him with a certain suspicion it was mainly on account of his favor with Lenin. By himself Stalin was thought incapable of reaching any great political heights. Why, how could one even imagine as the leader of Marxism a man who did not know any civilized languages? [46] One could not give him a really important job, such as running the Comintern or editing Pravda (Bukharin's main occupation). Buried in the Secretariat, his energies absorbed in the hopeless task of coercing the choleric Communist yokels in Tambov or Kazan, Stalin would soon become as insignificant a figure as Molotov.

The beginnings of this literally world-shaking tenure of office were placid enough. An announcement in Pravda gave the days and hours when the new Secretary General and his two assistants (one of them Molotov, finally to find his life's fulfillment as the second-in-command)

[44] Of the Nationalities and the Workers' and Peasants' Inspection. The latter one he surrendered on becoming General Secretary.

[45] The Eleventh Congress, p. 143.

[46] "His ignorance of foreign languages compels him to follow the political life of other countries at second hand. His mind is stubbornly empirical and devoid of creative imagination . . . he always seemed a man destined to play second or third fiddle." Trotsky, My Life, p. 506.

would receive visitors on Party business. Stalin's simple manner must have contrasted favorably with the airs the other leaders of the proletariat had begun to give themselves. Up to now he had spoken infrequently at Party gatherings and congresses. We have noted that he enjoyed a reputation for taciturnity, again an exception among the rather gossipy Communist types of that era. His personal following lay mostly within the intermediate level of the Soviet officialdom; many of those people resented the airs and the intellectual pretensions of Zinoviev, Trotsky, and Bukharin and felt closer to this simple, uncomplicated Georgian. It is characteristic that he secured the complete loyalty and subordination of Molotov, whom he pushed from a leading position for the second time.[47] That he was capable of being ruthless was well-known: there had been complaints during the Civil War of his ordering the execution of innocent men. But which Communist was free of such accusations? He had two gifts of supreme importance to a politician: the ability to learn and a sense of timing. The protocols of the Central Committee from the days of the Revolution show Stalin acidulous and boorish toward his colleagues. After the war Stalin cultivated successfully the reputation for (one should not laugh) broadmindedness and tolerance. It is a gross oversimplification to see in Stalin a Machiavellian politician with no convictions save a drive for power. He was a typical product of Leninism, but without those internal contradictions and vestiges of Western Socialist traditions that never left Lenin. Of all his pupils Stalin can be most accurately described as a fanatic, a man who once the need for political dissimulation has passed cannot restrain his terrible wrath against the people who are "wrong" and who will not admit it. "The best lack all conviction, while the worst are full of passionate intensity." [48]

With the Party machinery in Stalin's hands, Lenin turned back to his favorite occupation of drawing up tables of organization for Soviet administration. The constant reorganization tended to induce in the Soviet administrators either a blissful complacency, like that of the president of the State Bank to whom Lenin wrote, "Your words that the Bank is now a mighty institution made me laugh," or nervous strain. Faithful Tsyurupa broke down. He, like Rykov, had been sent to Germany for a cure, but as Lenin lamented, the doctors had tended only to his heart ailment and not to his nerves, which needed a cure. Kamenev was made an additional chairman of the Council of Commissars, charged with doing "political" work while the other two deputies were to tend to administrative matters. This unfortunately only served to increase the confusion. For some time Trotsky, now that the War Commissariat could no longer fully occupy his

---

[47] After the February Revolution Stalin and Kamenev, returning to Petrograd, shoved aside Shlyapnikov and Molotov, until then the leaders of the Bolshevik faction.

[48] W. B. Yeats, "The Second Coming," in The Collected Poems, New York, 1951, p. 185.

energies, kept bombarding the Politburo with memoranda on economic and administrative questions. It was to him that Lenin turned for help. Would Trotsky become yet another deputy chairman? As we have seen, Trotsky rejected this offer and was to persist in his refusal over Lenin's repeated bids. Objectively, his reasons were convincing, but politically they could not but cast a new reflection on Trotsky. Ready to criticize everything and everybody, he was yet unwilling to lend his hand to correct the abuses. What a contrast with Stalin's readiness to accept an ungrateful and back-breaking job!

To cure his own health Lenin toyed with an idea of taking a vacation in a distant spot. He was not sure whether the headaches, insomnia, and inability to work that afflicted him with an increasing frequency were due to an organic ailment or a nervous strain. On April 7 he wrote to Ordzhonikidze, currently in charge in Transcaucasia, to inquire about a possible vacation spot in the South. He wanted a secluded place not too high up in the mountains (Nadezhda Konstantinovna had a heart condition). But in the same letter he confessed his inability to envisage a really long journey for a rest. Even when vacationing near Moscow "stories" would occur which would make him rush back to the capital. Would there not be "stories" (it is not quite clear what Lenin means: being dragged into local squabbles, importuned?) if he went to the Caucasus? And how inconvenient to pack up at a minute's notice and rush back all the way from Tiflis.[49] He continued to build up imaginary difficulties in the way of a long trip: an old Bolshevik (this was Kamo, the famous "expropriator") asked to come along. Would it embarrass Ordzhonikidze (why, one wonders): if so, please telephone him, Lenin. He must have known all along that he would not be able to tear himself away, far from Moscow, far away from the business of government.

His inability or unwillingness to travel stripped him of the opportunity to head the Soviet delegation to the Genoa Conference. In January he had been designated to head in person this first appearance of the Soviets at a major international conference. But in April, when it began, his place had to be taken by the suave and diplomatic George Chicherin. His Commissar of Foreign Affairs was a man after Lenin's heart: he stayed away from politics and worked like a slave. In 1922 those qualities came, in Lenin's eyes, close to representing perfection. But even so he could not quite believe that anybody but himself was capable of handling those wily Western capitalists. Won't Chicherin be seduced into promising to pay Russia's prewar debts and compensation for the foreign capitalists' property? He was so apolitical! He bombarded Chicherin with instructions warning him to be on guard, especially against the deceitful British. Eventually, the Genoa Conference, which was called to revive international trade and to normalize Europe's economic life, came to nothing. But a little

[49] *The Lenin Collection*, Vol. 35, p. 344.

spa near Genoa, Rapallo, became the scene of the first great success of Soviet diplomacy. It was here that the two outcasts among the European powers, Germany and Russia, signed a treaty.

The Rapallo Treaty, which established normal diplomatic relations between the two countries and led to their economic and clandestine military collaboration, was very much after Lenin's heart. A few months earlier he had underlined a passage in Gorky's letter where the writer urged the necessity of a Russo-German alliance. Finally, an advanced Western country was going to help Russia with her industrial and commercial problems! There had been some usual disapproving clucking over a treaty with a bourgeois country, indeed over the whole idea of going to Genoa and sitting down with the "imperialist bandits." But Lenin, his hopes in Harding and Vanderlip abandoned, was overjoyed. Faith in German efficiency had survived his faith in the German Marxists. The incongruous alliance between the capitalists and the Reichswehr and the Communists was to last into the Hitler era. It was a decisive breach in Soviet Russia's diplomatic isolation. Increasingly "respectable" countries were establishing diplomatic missions in Moscow and entering into commercial relations, even though the old-fashioned statesmen and the holders of the Imperial Russian bonds sighed. No other branch of Soviet administration, with the possible exception of the *Cheka-OGPU*, gave Lenin as much satisfaction as his foreign service. To be sure, it was seeded with ex-Mensheviks (among them Chicherin himself) and those in political eclipse in the Party, but it performed admirably in breaking down the prejudice of the foreign governments against the new Russia. It was difficult to see in an impeccably attired and cosmopolitan Krasin or Chicherin a representative of the "bandits and anarchists." Experience in Russian politics was a good training for diplomacy. One who could keep his head above water in the Communist world would not be easily outfoxed by the wiliest foreigner.

But on one occasion, in April, Lenin was to feel that the Communists were "taken in." He wrote, "The *bourgeoisie* have turned out more skillful than the representatives of the Communist International." His complaint was hardly justified. The issue concerned was as complex as it was sordid. Some time before, the Soviet government had decided to mount a great show trial of 47 Socialist Revolutionaries, many of them having been for years in the hands of the *Cheka*. There was no doubt as to the reasons for the trial: it was a classical case of an attempt to distract public opinion from the economic distress and the intra-Party friction by parading out those people and reviving the now irrelevant story of the S-R's old sins and villainies.

Unfortunately, at the same time Soviet Russia and the Comintern were in the phase of the "united front," trying to secure good will and collaboration on some matters on the part of the European Socialists. At a meeting of three Internationals (the third, second, and the so-called two-and-one-half, representing those groups which were neither with the Communists nor with the old-line Socialists) the Soviet representatives, Bukharin and Radek, were finally persuaded to promise that none of the accused would be sentenced to death, and that foreign defenders and observers would be allowed at the trial. This was the news that aroused Lenin's fury.

His article in *Pravda* of April 11, 1922, was entitled "We Paid Too Dearly." [50] He was offended both as a lawyer and as an enemy of bourgeois legalism. Legally, it was an intolerable interference with Soviet Russia's internal affairs. But beyond this indisputable point his anguish was caused by the fact that the Soviets had tied their hands. And what did they get in return except for some feeble promises from the Socialists? How can one *not* send the S-Rs to death? They will continue their revolutionary, oops, counterrevolutionary activity, terrorism against the Soviet power. But Lenin regretfully concluded that once made, the agreement should be kept for the sake of the united front. If only Bukharin and Radek had not been such bad diplomats!

When the trial was being performed Lenin was ill. But the authorities must have taken his criticisms to heart. There was not a shadow of bourgeois legality about the proceedings. The foreign defenders, led by the Belgian Socialist, Emil Vandervelde, were appalled by their reception. They had been under few illusions as to what to expect. Still, it was a shock to be met at various stations leading to Moscow by crowds which denounced not only the accused but also their counsel. Vandervelde was reminded by placards and shouts that he had been a minister in a bourgeois government. The German Socialist Theodor Liebknecht was reproached for coming to plead for the same kind of people as those who had killed his brother in Germany. (Karl Liebknecht, of course, had been killed by the German reactionaries.) Their amazement knew no bounds when, at the Moscow station where the main "spontaneous" demonstration was taking place, they recognized amidst the hooting, jeering crowd none else than Nikolai Bukharin. The brilliant Marxist theoretician, reputed to be one of the most civilized and humane Soviet leaders, was not to be outdone by the masses.

There were further surprises in the courtroom. The number of accused had been reduced to 34. They were clearly divided into two groups. Twenty-two were being "really" tried while the rest were *agents provocateurs* and ex-S-Rs now in the hands of the secret police, their main function to confess and to accuse the genuine S-Rs. The "guilty" ones were being defended by the foreigners, while the "innocent" ones were defended by a galaxy of Bolsheviks, including the playful Bukharin. Among the prosecutors were such luminaries of Soviet culture as Lunacharsky, the leading Communist historian, Pokrovsky, and for good measure (there were foreign defenders; why shouldn't there be foreign prosecutors?) the

[50] *Works*, Vol. 33, pp. 294–98.

German Communist Klara Zetkin. Gravely presiding as the judge was the up-and-coming young Communist Gregory Pyatakov. Needless to say, legal training was not a prerequisite for being judge, defender, or prosecutor. Further evidence of a complete divorce from the criteria of bourgeois legality were the frequent manifestations in the courtroom by the workers, demanding death to the traitors.

In one detail the trial fell short of the future pattern of such performances. The main figures among the accused did not confess. They admitted to such crimes as defending the Constituent Assembly and opposing the Bolsheviks politically, but rejected the imputations that the Central Committee of the S-R Party had been involved in the attempt on Lenin's life, in collaboration with Denikin and others. Despite the agreement, the twelve leading S-Rs were condemned to death. There was some hesitation among the Bolshevik hierarchy as to whether the sentence should be confirmed. Lenin, after all, had urged that the agreement should be kept. Trotsky, Stalin, and Bukharin demanded that the sentence should be put into effect, unless the convicted leaders repudiated their anti-Communist stand, in which case they should be sent for hard labor in the "Northern Provinces." (There was still some squeamishness in saying "Siberia"— too reminiscent.) Others pleaded for an exile from Russia. Finally a compromise was arrived at through Kamenev's motion. The sentence was confirmed but its execution was indefinitely postponed; should the S-Rs engage in some further sabotage and terror against Soviet Russia, the twelve would be executed. The foreign Socialists fussed, collected petitions, and talked about a "moral blockade" of Soviet Russia, but such protests had their usual results. Some of the Communist actors in the grotesque proceedings were unknowingly rehearsing their own trials under Stalin, notably Bukharin and Pyatakov. But they were to confess, and for them there was to be no reprieve.

The trial of the Socialist Revolutionaries, which coincides with the time when rule is finally snatched out of Lenin's hands by illness, is in many ways a very characteristic conclusion of the Leninist period in Soviet history. Its disorderly character and contempt for legal norms reflected his own scorn for such amenities. Stalin's trials would have lawyers as judges, prosecutors, and defenders, and on their surface would adhere to the punctilio of the law, much as their spirit would be its obscene perversion. The accused would confess and help the prosecution. Apart from their political content, Stalin's trials would bear the imprint of the dictator's personal vengeance against the people who for so long had blocked or interfered with his plans, an attempt to obliterate them not only physically but morally and from the pages of Soviet history. Lenin's attitude was thoroughly businesslike: the S-Rs were a danger to the Soviet regime; they should be shot unless the Communists got "something in return" for clemency. The trial in some ways demonstrated the same thing as the Eleventh Congress of the Communist Party: the impossibility of preserving this *semi*totalitarian structure that Lenin erected and to which he clung so tenaciously. If you have a show trial, its effect is spoiled if the accused do not confess but reaffirm their principles. How efficiently can one run a dictatorial system if freedom of criticism is still admitted within the ruling party? It was perhaps fortunate for Lenin that it fell to someone else to resolve those dilemmas.

2. Intrigue and Death

Lenin's stroke on May 26 culminated a long period of ill health. Its causes have previously been attributed to exhaustion, "nerves," other physical complications. A few weeks before the stroke one of the foreign consultants recommended the removal of bullets lodged in his body since Kaplan's attempt in 1918 on the grounds that they "might be poisoning the system." This diagnosis was thought ridiculous by other doctors. That it was given and that one bullet was removed by surgery might indicate that the physicians were at their wits' end, because of Lenin's demands that they cure him and restore his capacity for work. A minor operation might produce a psychological uplift in the patient. Now the stroke led to a partial paralysis of the right side and loss of speech. Though he soon began to improve, the attending physicians saw the writing on the wall. "The disease might linger for weeks, days, years, but the future prospects were far from being cheerful." [51]

The official communiques breathed optimism but Lenin's collaborators must have realized that it was unlikely that he would be spared for many more years, and almost out of the question that, even if he recovered, he could ever exercise control in the manner in which he had prior to the end of 1921. Neither of the possibilities seemed very reassuring: he might die, and then with the Party still in disarray and the country still in the throes of acute distress, would the regime be able to maintain itself without the man who so miraculously succeeded in pulling it out of all the previous defeats and difficulties? Or he might return, but as an invalid. That eventuality must have appeared even more frightening to the oligarchs. Even in good health Lenin had been, from their point of view, irritable and capricious. What ideas might enter the head of a semiparalyzed dictator? To change completely the top leadership of the Party? To legalize the Mensheviks? None of those possibilities could be excluded when dealing with a man who while well had driven the Party against its hesitations and fears to pull the October *coup* and adopt the New Economic Policy.

It was, therefore, quite natural that following the May stroke the other leaders should have drawn together to contemplate a joint front

[51] Prof. V. N. Rozanov in *Recollections About Lenin*, Vol. 2, p. 344.

both against the outsiders and, if this should prove necessary, against Vladimir Ilyich himself. This conclusion is almost inescapable in view of the events that were to unroll during the second crisis in Lenin's illness from December 1922 on. Nor, granting the premises of Soviet politics, was there anything unusual in this conspiracy. The Communist Party could not be allowed to dissolve into warring factions, with the "tried" leaders of the Politburo being outshouted by the Ryazanovs and Osinskys. Nor should Lenin, if he would prove unbalanced or unfit, be allowed to disrupt his own life's work.

With Lenin's stroke is usually associated the beginning of that struggle for succession that was to occupy the center of the political stage for the next six years and lead to the establishment of Stalin's primacy in 1924 and his absolute dictatorship by 1928–29. The first phase of this struggle, the formation of the triumvirate Zinoviev-Kamenev-Stalin, goes back undoubtedly to the summer of 1922, when Lenin lay convalescing and the Party potentates were uncertain whether and in what shape he would be able to return to work. Still, it must be stressed that the conspiracy, for such it was, was not limited to those three. To a lesser or greater extent *all* the members of the top leadership shared mixed feelings and fears as to Lenin's future role and *all* decided to present a united front.

This interpretation clashes with the usual assumption that upon Lenin's incapacitation all the would-be pretenders to the mantle of leadership fell out among themselves. Trotsky in his highly subjective and *varying* accounts of the period emphasizes Stalin's role as the chief plotter, and the other leaders' reluctant acquiescence in the intrigue, the result allegedly of their fear and envy of him, Trotsky, as the logical successor of Lenin. But as the course of events shows, the leaders' first concern was for their *collective* position, and that of the Party as a whole. It is only somewhat later that one of them, Trotsky, began halfheartedly to break this united front of the Politburo against all others, including Vladimir Ilyich.

The reasons for this precarious unity are not difficult to see. There were violent hatreds among the individual members of the Politburo, most notably between Trotsky and Stalin. (On Trotsky's part at least this hatred was grounded in a clash of temperaments rather than in rivalry for the highest position. As late as 1926 he would cling to the illusion that Stalin was being led and used by someone smarter than himself: first by Zinoviev, then by Bukharin.) But much as they hated and feared each other, the ten or so members of the Politburo and their alternates considered themselves as beings of an order different from just "plain" members of the Central Committee. The latter in turn exhibited the same feeling toward the rest of the Communist hierarchy, and so on along the Soviet official pyramid. No matter what their personal ambitions and feelings, the members of the Politburo shared in the frantic desire not to let power slip from their hands into those of the wider body. The rest of the Central Committee members, however envious of their seniors, must have realized that an open rebellion on their part would bring to the surface all the tensions and dissatisfactions within the Party at large. If the high command were to appear openly divided at the next Congress they *all* might lose their jobs.

This complicated skein of motivations and fears led to the "Party unity" in view of Lenin's illness, and to collective leadership. Its nucleus was the triumvirate; Zinoviev was its natural leader because of his long association with Lenin, his leadership of international communism, and the base of power in Petrograd. Kamenev was the chairman of the Politburo in Lenin's absence, head of the Moscow government and, as far as such things went, most respected by the other oligarchs. Stalin was the Party's chief organizer and work horse. Other leaders accepted this working arrangement. Standing somewhat to the side but not in open breach with the trio was Trotsky.

The crystallization of the pattern was interrupted by Lenin's partial recovery. On July 12 he wrote exultantly to his secretary that he was on the mend and that the best proof was that his handwriting was now fairly legible ("my handwriting *begins* to look human"). Would she start preparing books for him? He was allowed scientific works and novels, and soon expected to be permitted to read about politics.[52] Party potentates began to descend upon Gorki. Among them was Stalin, who sketched his impressions in an article in *Pravda*. His first visit in July found Lenin "fresh and reinvigorated" though with traces of exhaustion, impatient to get back to politics. "We laugh over the doctors who cannot understand that professional politicians cannot refrain from talking about politics when they meet." One month later, Stalin continued, Lenin was fully recovered and surrounded by political materials. His "calmness and resolution have fully returned. Our old Lenin. . . ." They had a good laugh together, this time over the stories in the *émigré* press that Lenin was dying. He smiled and said: "Let them lie and rejoice. One should not deprive the dying of their last consolation." [53]

On October 2 Lenin returned to Moscow. He was far from being "fresh and reinvigorated," but he would not pay any heed to the pleas to prolong his convalescence. Though he agreed to limit his activity he was in fact back at a schedule that would tax the resources of a well man. His secretary notes that between the second of October and December 16, 1922, Lenin wrote 224 letters and memoranda, received 171 official visitors, and presided over 32 meetings of government bodies and commissions.[54] He delivered three major public speeches, including a lengthy one at the Fourth Congress of the Comintern on November 13.

This frantic activity had its source not only in Lenin's sense of duty

[52] *The Lenin Collection*, Vol. 35, p. 351.
[53] *Memories of Lenin*, Vol. 2, Moscow, 1957, p. 659.
[54] L. A. Fotyeva in *Problems of the History of the Communist Party*, Moscow, 1957, No. 4, p. 149.

and his inability to live without politics. He must have sensed the desire of his collaborators to limit his control of the vast state-Party apparatus and to cut him off from any extraneous sources of information concerning their own doings. Thus Lenin bridled at the suggestion of Rykov that he be allowed to see official visitors only after they have been seen and "cleared" by one of the three deputy chairmen of the Council of Commissars or a Party secretary. It was alleged, and possibly true, that the reason for this demand was solicitude for Vladimir Ilyich's health. Why should he concern himself with trivial things which might be handled by his deputies? But it could equally be imagined, especially by a man in bad health, that there was an effort afoot to turn him into a rubber stamp, a figurehead who was to be kept away from any independent sources of information. The same pathetic fear is visible in Lenin's unwillingness to take a few days' break in Gorki. On December 7 he had to be coerced to go there for five days, but no sooner was he in his villa than he was on the telephone to the secretaries. He was furious that the Politburo had made two decisions in his absence (they were voted on after he had left its meeting to travel to Gorki). On December 8 he dictated the draft of a regulation that would prevent the Politburo's reaching decisions behind his back: it was to meet on Thursdays at eleven, its meetings were never to last more than three hours (this obviously tailored to his own endurance). The agenda were to be distributed one day in advance. Additional material could be presented to the meeting only in the case of extreme emergency, only in written form, only if no member of the Politburo objected.[55] After the worsening of his condition on December 16 he would not even hear about being transported to Gorki. He alleged reasons that were obviously fabricated: going by sleigh was too tiring, and by automobile too difficult, because the snow made the roads impassable (a division of the Red Army could be mobilized to sweep the roads in a few hours!). He was not going to be incarcerated and kept in the dark as to what was going on.

In this frame of mind it was only natural that Lenin would take a new look at his lieutenants. He had advanced Stalin because he had seen in him one man who would not stoop to an intrigue and because, perhaps unconsciously, he also could not envisage him as a candidate for the succession. As late as April, when he half thought of going to the Caucasus, he asked that arrangements be made for him to have coded communications with the Central Committee *and Stalin*. Whatever the personal ambitions of others, Stalin was fully loyal to him and to the Party. Now Stalin was siding with "them." There appeared to be no breach in the suspiciously solicitous united front of the Politburo members who importuned Vladimir Ilyich to take care of himself, not to attend to trifles, and to take long rests. Quite apart from anything else, the sick man's resentment and envy must have been aroused by the realization of how much

[55] *The Lenin Collection,* Vol. 35, pp. 359–60.

power and influence Stalin had accumulated. Almost every major business of the Party and the government touched on Stalin: the new constitution being prepared for the Union of Soviet Republics, the troubles in Georgia, foreign trade, and so on. It was Stalin who had in his hand the threads of information about everything. Quite apart from power, that already made Stalin the pivot of the whole government. "Ask Svidersky what Tsyurupa wrote; if he does not know then ask Stalin," writes Lenin in one of his typical frantic attempts to find out what was going on. Had the two men been most intimate and selfless friends, the new relationship still must have produced visible suspicion on the part of the older and suppressed bitterness in the younger.

One recalls the mysterious events surrounding Stalin's last months. With his time running out the old despot enlarged the Politburo, introducing into it completely new men (some of whom have not been heard of since his death). And a few weeks before *his* stroke the senior doctors in the Kremlin medical service were arrested and charged with fantastic crimes. Also, if we are to believe Khrushchev, Stalin contemplated the purge of such old collaborators as Molotov and Mikoyan. Did he have in mind Vladimir Ilyich's last illness, and was he afraid that in the case of *his* debility he would also become an almost helpless prisoner of the Politburo, with the doctors obeying them rather than him and his family?

Lenin's behavior during his partial recovery went far to justify his colleagues' apprehensions. His temper was brittle, he would fuss over issues to which in the old days he would hardly have paid any attention. An ex-Menshevik professor was allowed by the Politburo to reside in the capital. Lenin, then absent in Gorki, telephoned to express his indignation, demanded that the matter be brought up before the full Central Committee. The Politburo members must have shaken their heads: to appease Vladimir Ilyich the professor was exiled to a provincial town.

On more important matters Lenin's interventions bore a somewhat hysterical character. There was the problem whether the monopoly of foreign trade should be modified or not. It was a technical matter; once Lenin would have demanded a summary of arguments *pro* and *con*. Now it became an obsession with him that a full monopoly of foreign trade must be preserved and that no hesitation on that account should be allowed. Again, memoranda to Stalin and Trotsky: Lenin will not hear about a reconsideration of the decision being postponed until he can attend in person. He wants the Central Committee in his absence to bow to his will and restore the state monopoly of foreign trade. His reasons are cogent enough but the strain of pleading and anxiety reflects his illness and the fear that things are slipping out of his grip. He worries that some of the business transacted in his absence may escape his attention, at the same time that he is less and less capable of following a lengthy memorandum. To his chief secretaries he orders that all the papers sent to him by the Central Committee are to be registered in a special book, their content to be summarized in a telegraphic style in less than three lines. His secretaries are to indicate about the petitions, "what they want, how much they demand, what they are complaining about, what they are striving for." They will be held personally responsible for any inaccuracy of the summary.[56]

To break up the solicitous conspiracy of the Politburo Lenin probed for its weak link. It had to be Trotsky.

In his autobiography Trotsky relates the conversations he had with Lenin a few weeks prior to his relapse. Lenin proposed the formation of a bloc to fight the bureaucracy and the Organizational Bureau of the Central Committee in particular. At the next Party Congress the two of them were to make a joint attack and propose structural changes that would sap the strength of the Party's apparatus, Stalin's special preserve. This story is credible, but Trotsky's deduction that at that time Lenin intended to destroy Stalin is not. It is also dubious, for reasons that will be given later, that Lenin intended Trotsky to be his successor in the post of the Chairman of the Council of Commissars, Trotsky writes modestly, but Trotsky obviously hoped for more than that.[57] As to the political (the time had not yet come for a more thorough blow) "destruction" of Stalin, nothing until January 1923 indicates that Lenin had anything else in mind but to take Stalin down a peg, the way he had done in the past with Zinoviev and Kamenev, and with Trotsky himself. They all had been the subject of his vitriolic criticism; in the case of the first two he had once proposed to throw them out of the Party, and yet they had come back to resume their places in the inner circle. It was probable that Lenin looked forward with zest to trimming the sails of yet another lieutenant of his. The prospect of a struggle at a Party congress where he would outmaneuver the dumfounded oligarchs and show them who was the boss recalled earlier and happier times.

With Stalin he had already had some clashes. The "wonderful Georgian" was still in charge of the nationality policy and as such was drafting the Constitution for the proposed union of Russia and other "independent" Soviet republics such as the Ukraine and Georgia. His proposal was unduly centralistic and emphasized the dominance of the Russian component of the future federation. One might well ask of what importance were various constitutional niceties, when the important fact was the domination by the Communist Party with its Central Committee in Moscow. But those constitutional fictions were then thought of, and actually were, of some symbolic importance. Lenin had always been sensitive on the point of "Russian chauvinism" and in his current mood was prone to be overly critical. He expressed to Stalin his very basic objections to the draft. Stalin's reply was amazingly bold and impatient in tone. On September 27

[56] *The Lenin Collection*, Vol. 35, p. 359.
[57] Trotsky, *My Life*, p. 479.

he addressed a memorandum to the Politburo which stressed that some of Lenin's objections were purely stylistic and did not make any difference. His more basic criticisms were attributed to what Stalin disapprovingly called Lenin's "liberalism" on the national question.[58]

With Lenin then on the mend this might be thought to have been extremely bad politics on Stalin's part. But in fact it shows his amazing acumen. Nothing was bound to increase the sick man's suspicion more than that Stalin should immediately and completely reverse his previous position after encountering Lenin's criticism. Stalin's note was ill-mannered, but Lenin's belief that brusqueness and lack of ceremony indicated proletarian forthrightness had not been fully undermined.[59] Had Lenin contemplated a "destruction" of Stalin he certainly would not have continued employing as one of his confidential secretaries Stalin's wife, Nadezhda Alliluyeva.

It is very difficult to guess how events would have developed had Lenin's recovery lasted, say, a year rather than about two months. It is clear, however, from his subsequent writings when he saw that his days were numbered, that he experienced no basic regrets for the past actions, and contemplated no basic changes. An enlargement of the central Party bodies, some new bureaucratic devices to curb the curse of bureaucracy —those were the remedies he contemplated. That he would have enthroned Trotsky as his successor, as the latter argues, is more than doubtful.

In any case, he was not going to have an opportunity. In December his health deteriorated again. On the thirteenth he had, it appears, two minor strokes, and on the sixteenth a major one. The paralysis of the right side returned. He took to bed, but his colleagues must have been appalled to learn that on December 21 he was recovered enough to start dictating memoranda. Warned by the doctors, Vladimir Ilyich threatened that unless he were allowed some political activity he would refuse to be treated. On the twenty-fourth of December a committee of the Politburo composed of Stalin, Kamenev, and Bukharin held a conference with the doctors. It was decided that "Vladimir Ilyich has the right to dictate every day for 5 to 10 minutes, but this cannot have the character of correspondence and Vladimir Ilyich may not expect to receive any answers. It is forbidden for him to receive any [political] visitors. Neither friends nor those around him are allowed to tell Vladimir Ilyich any political news. . . ."[60]

Without encroaching upon the medical sphere it is still hard to see how

---

[58] *The Trotsky Archive* T 755. There is an excellent discussion of the whole issue in R. Pipes, *The Formation of the Soviet Union*, Cambridge, Mass. 1964, pp. 272–74.

[59] On Lenin's return to active work in October his views on the nature of the federal union prevailed and were incorporated in what was to become the Constitution of the U.S.S.R.

[60] "The Record Book of the Secretaries Attending V. I. Lenin," in *Problems of the History of the Communist Party of the Soviet Union*, Moscow, 1963, No. 2, p. 68.

this regimen could be rationalized purely in terms of a solicitude for the stricken leader's health and the desire to spare him excitement. One might think, for instance, that an occasional visit from a collaborator might have a soothing effect rather than vice versa. Knowing Vladimir Ilyich's temperament, his colleagues must have realized that this complete isolation and the ban on all news would only serve to increase the excitement and discomfort of the sick man. Such was in fact the case. Repeated prohibitions would throw him into tantrums. As his secretary notes, "Vladimir Ilyich became convinced that it is not the doctors who give guidance to the Central Committee, but the Central Committee which has instructed the doctors." [61] He was a prisoner of his own Politburo.[62] Under the veneer of solicitude for his health they took steps to prevent his interference with their rule and to keep any single politician from gaining Lenin's ear.

He was caught in a net of his own making. It was Lenin who had established the principle that a leader's health was not his own business, but that of the Party. A Communist could not live nor was he allowed to die according to his own wishes. It was up to the Central Committee and really up to the smaller body. His wife and sister Maria, who were constantly by his side, were put in an impossible position. He was still perfectly lucid, his speech had not left him, and he begged them for news, and to run political errands for him. But, again by the standards he himself had established, they were just rank-and-file members of the Party and as such prohibited from interfering with the treatment of their husband and brother. The Politburo delegated Stalin to be their liaison with the doctors, in fact to supervise Lenin's treatment. That he accepted this job must have been taken by his colleagues as another sign of Stalin's simple-mindedness: should Lenin have another spell of recovery, Stalin would be held responsible for all the restrictions on his freedom, the unavoidable clashes with Krupskaya, all difficulties.

It is under those conditions that there unfolds the last and most heroic conspiracy of Lenin's life. The sick man struggled to outwit his colleagues and the doctors as well as his failing health. He had before been able to turn small concessions by an enemy into weapons for victory. Now with equal cunning he would stretch the few minutes allowed him to dictate every day his "diary" and would address lengthy memoranda on state and Party matters, and thunder, even from his deathbed, at his subordinates and jailers.

His last act of subversion concerned the secretaries on duty with him. Step by step the old master of conspiracy had involved the girls in his own intrigue. From the "five to ten minutes" they were allowed to take dictation

[61] *Ibid.*, p. 84.

[62] Its members at the time, in addition to Lenin: Kamenev, Stalin, Trotsky, Zinoviev, Rykov, Tomsky, and alternate members Bukharin, Molotov, Kalinin, and Kuibyshev.

the period grew into an hour. Wouldn't they just once make a "secret" telephone call on his behalf? Try to find out what the Politburo is up to? He played upon their sympathy, showed himself chivalrous and solicitous. "Why are you so pale?" he would ask one of them. (Well she might be. Stalin kept calling and asking, undoubtedly in his usual polite manner, who was telling news to Vladimir Ilyich.) Were they getting enough rest? He was sorry to monopolize all their time. "If I were only free . . ." and then catching himself he repeated it, but smiling, "I would not be importuning you so much." [63] He tricked them into revealing the news they were not supposed to communicate to him. But frightened though they must have been, the women found it difficult not to violate the strict regulations imposed by the doctors and/or the Politburo. It must have been a pathetic spectacle: Lenin semiparalyzed, with a compress on his head (he still suffered intermittent headaches), begging them to stretch the rules, dictating frantically, sometimes losing the thread of his thought. The all-powerful dictator, whose reaction to inefficiency or inattention used to be "threaten to shoot" or "imprison for six months," would now complain mildly and wistfully: "As to our 'conspiracy,' I know you are just deceiving [appeasing] me." When the heartbroken woman tried to deny it he persisted: "I will stick to my own opinion about it."

Among the six secretaries who took turns in waiting on Lenin, there was Nadezhda Alliluyeva, Stalin's wife, then in her early twenties. But after December 18 her somewhat ungrammatical and naïve notes [64] in the secretaries' log cease. Whether in view of her connection it was thought improper for her to attend Lenin or whether he himself insisted on her transfer is not known. The principal secretary was Lydia Fotyeva, an old personal friend of Lenin and Maria Ilinichna. The lines of medical, political, and family authority hopelessly crisscrossed. "Nadezhda Konstantinovna letting me in said that he [Lenin] has illegally [sic!] spent too much time in proofreading the article and that the nurse on duty did not want to let me in," notes a secretary. Lenin conceived an understandable rancor against his doctors, who unlike his wife and secretaries would not fall in with the "conspiracy." After a while he would not allow one of them, Professor Otfried Foerster, in his room, and the distinguished German neurologist had to make his diagnoses secondhand, on the basis of the examinations by other doctors.

Amidst this turmoil Lenin somehow found the energy to concentrate on the main object of his "conspiracy": the writing of a directive to the Congress of the Communist Party, the document that was to become famous as "Lenin's Testament." The Congress was to take place in March (actually it met in April) of 1923. At the time of the writing (it was com-

[63] *Ibid.*, p. 80.
[64] A sample: "Maria Ilinichna communicated Vladimir Ilyich wants to dictate at 5:45, and at 6 talk with Rykov, he has come and is sitting at home."

posed in several installments between December 23 and 26) Lenin clearly envisaged the possibility of dying before the Congress met. The document was typed in several copies, sealed in envelopes marked "absolutely secret," and "not to be opened except by V. I. Lenin and after his death by Nadezhda Krupskaya." [65] Some copies were placed in his wife's care, some in his own safe, and one was sent to the offices of *Pravda*.

Most of the interpretations of the *Letter to the Congress* see it as a directive on who should be Lenin's successor and/or an indictment of Stalin. It is neither of these things.

Presumably the *Testament* expressed the policies that Lenin himself would have urged were he able to attend the next Party gathering. It begins: "I would strongly advise that this Congress should adopt several changes in our political system." What were those changes to be? In fact, except for some technical generalities for the reorganization of the Planning Commission, Lenin had only one concrete proposal: to increase the number of members of the Central Committee to 50 or 100 (the current Central Committee had 27 members and 19 alternates). The additional members were to be preferably rank-and-file workers and not those who have had long government experience, because the latter "have already formed well-known habits and biases exactly against which we must resolutely struggle." [66] Why this increase? The reason given by Lenin was that the current Central Committee was deeply divided within itself and that the Party itself was in danger of a split. "I think that those workers, being present at all meetings of the Central Committee, at *all meetings of the Politburo*, reading all the documents of the Central Committee . . . can add stability to the Committee and work . . . to renew and improve the [Party] apparatus." [67]

The greatest threat to the solidarity of the Central Committee, Lenin continued, lay in the (bad) relations between Trotsky and Stalin. Here he lapsed into his celebrated characterization of the several Soviet oligarchs. "Comrade Stalin having become the General Secretary, has accumulated enormous power in his hands, and I am not quite sure whether he will always be able to use this power carefully enough." Trotsky? "As shown by his fight against the Central Committee in connection with the Commissariat of Communication he is characterized not only by eminent abilities. Personally, he is to be sure the most capable man in the current Central Committee, but is too much possessed by self-confidence and given too much to the administrative side of things." Kamenev and Zinoviev: "I shall only recall that the October [1917] behavior of Zinoviev and Kamenev was not accidental, but it should not be held against them personally any more than Trotsky's separation from Bolshevism" (that is until

---

[65] The secretary skipped the words "after his death."

[66] *Works*, Vol. 36, p. 547.

[67] My own italics.

the summer of 1917). As to the others, Lenin mentioned only Bukharin and Pyatakov. Bukharin was not only the Party's most valuable theoretician, but also a universal favorite among the Communists. Unfortunately, for all his theoretical eminence he had not mastered dialectic.[68] Pyatakov, again, was a man of outstanding abilities but (like Trotsky) too much taken with the administrative side of things to be relied upon in serious political things.[69]

To a casual reader, just as to the average Communist, if he had the chance to read it at the time, the document breathes fatherly solicitude about the Party. Its personal characterizations are full of insight and yet humane and tolerant. But the private reaction of the members of the Central Committee when they were acquainted with the document by Krupskaya before the Thirteenth Congress in 1924 and when they decided *not* to release it to the delegates in contravention of the dead leader's wishes must have been "What a trickster! Up to his old tricks even on his very deathbed." For the *Letter*, or *Testament*, was to them an apparent attempt to undercut the collective leadership of the Politburo in the first place, and of the (then) Central Committee in the second. For far from being a plea for unity, it was in fact an attempt to sow dissension among the top leaders, an attempt to break up their solidarity that Lenin encountered, at least as against himself, during his last months. If he was not going to be there himself to confound their plans, he still wanted to make sure that none of them would be allowed to grasp the succession. Hence the sly listing of their characteristics, with each of the principal candidates found wanting in some vital respect to occupy his, Lenin's, place. Why mention Zinoviev's and Kamenev's unheroic behavior in October, if it is not to be held against them? Why draw attention to Stalin's enormous influence (few among the Communists at the time had realized its full extent)? Why increase the already prevalent envy of Trotsky's intellectual gifts and the resentment of his authoritarian manner? (For the administrative penchant of Trotsky is a euphemism for that.) Bukharin's lack of seriousness as a political leader is cleverly insinuated. As to Pyatakov, being younger and "just" a member of the Central Committee, he was hardly in the same class with the others. Why Lenin included him is not clear. The other leaders, notably two full members of the Politburo, Rykov and Tomsky, were not mentioned at all, something they could perhaps be counted upon not to forgive their six colleagues on whose gifts and defects Vladimir Ilyich dwelt so lovingly. In brief, a document well calculated to sow suspicion and envy among the top leaders and to curtail their excessive claims and domination insofar as the Party as a whole was concerned.

As to the Central Committee, Lenin saw it as being under the thumb

---

[68] What Lenin tried to express by this apparently self-contradictory judgment is referred to above in discussing the Eighth Congress, p. 454.

[69] *Ibid.*, pp. 544–45.

of the Politburo. Its enlargement through the usual process, that is, by elevating to it the officials next in line, would not mend this state of affairs: they were bound to be "Zinoviev's men," "Stalin's men," and so on. Hence the proposed recruitment of simple workers unpolluted by politics, not in debt to the oligarchs. Were he to remain alive, the new members would take his word as law and would enable him to break out of this encirclement by his lieutenants. After his death and fortified by his warnings, these new virtuous recruits to the Central Committee would keep a watch on the intrigues of the oligarchs and cut them down to size. He was not Stalin during his last phase: he did not propose to destroy his old "trusted" friends, or even to remove them from power. The Party needed their abilities. But if alive he was going to fight their humiliating tutelage of himself, if dead his *Testament* was going to prevent their lording over Russia and communism either collectively or singly.

From this general outburst against his closest subordinates (though the word by now became almost inappropriate) Lenin soon passed into a rage against one of them: Stalin. The reasons were both political and personal.

Politically they touched on the involved business of Georgia. This Caucasian country became independent in the wake of the Bolshevik Revolution. Having always been, even under the Tsars, the stronghold of the Menshevik influence, Georgia found itself with a Social Democratic government. Bolshevik Russia and Menshevik Georgia signed a treaty in 1920 in which the former recognized the latter's full independence. The fires of the Civil War were still burning and at the time the Red Army had its hands full with the Poles. Once those emergencies passed the days of independent Georgia were numbered. The rest of Transcaucasia was in Bolshevik hands. For a few months the tiny Menshevik republic was the toast of the Western Socialists. Their delegations visited Georgia and reported glowingly on the virtues of the native socialism, which eschewed Bolshevik terror and repression. (True to the Menshevik tradition, the Georgian government released imprisoned Communists, who began immediately to prepare for an uprising.)

When in 1921 the uprising did materialize and the Red Army stood ready to help the Georgian Communists, Lenin experienced some last-minute doubts. Soviet Russia's sitution was still precarious; the great famine was just on the horizon. He had burnt his fingers on the Polish adventure. Would Russia's "image" in the West, now when she was trying to get financial help from abroad, be damaged by this rape of a small country? Finally he authorized the venture. Georgia was invaded and taken. Even now Lenin urged caution and delicacy in dealing with the country where native communism was weak and the Menshevik tradition strong. Violence and forcible russification would produce a bad impression in the Orient, where the Bolsheviks were posing as champions of nationalism. To his viceroy in the Caucasus, Ordzhonikidze, Lenin kept telegraphing instructions urging that he "deal with special consideration with the sovereign organs of Georgia and the Georgian people." [70] But foreign criticisms of the conquest aroused his typical reaction. He suggested to Chicherin that he should inspire articles in the Soviet press drawing attention to the fact that while the British were shedding tears over Georgia they were torturing millions of Hindus, Irishmen, and others. The feeble protests by the Labour Party aroused his particular anger. He detested ineffectual appeals to world public opinion in which the British left specialized.

The next phase of the Georgian problem found Georgian *Communists* creating trouble. It was a mild case of premature Titoism. Moscow's overlord in the Caucasus, Ordzhonikidze, though himself a Georgian, was considered by the local Communists russified, and most of all he ruled with an iron hand, paying little attention to their objections. Behind him at the center was another Georgian, Stalin, likewise little disposed to pay heed to his countrymen's claims to preserve a more distinct autonomy and separateness from Moscow. Russian Communists were imported wholesale into Georgia. Even the local *Cheka,* one Georgian Communist was to say plaintively, was pushed aside by the officers of its central organization. The crowning blow was the Stalin-Ordzhonikidze plan to merge Georgia with other Caucasian countries (Armenia and Azerbaidzhan) and only this federation was to become in turn one of the units of the future U.S.S.R. The local Communists, their nationalism suddenly aroused, saw themselves being swamped by the Russians, Armenians, and others. The unkindest cut of all was to be treated this way by two of their russified countrymen.

The local Communist leaders, Budu Mdivani and Philip Makharadze, kept appealing to Lenin. In October 1922 he reprimanded them for fussing and told them to follow Stalin's directives.[71] But then the second phase of his illness intervened, and as on some other things Lenin's attitude toward the complaints of the Georgians underwent a change.

A commission of the Politburo headed by Dzerzhinsky went to Tiflis in November to investigate the Georgian mess. Now increasingly suspicious, Dzerzhinsky tended to follow Stalin; Lenin also sent Rykov to check on the situation. A few days before his turn for the worse on December 9 and 12 Lenin had interviews with the investigators. What they reported deeply depressed him and preyed on his mind throughout his illness. Ordzhonikidze evidently behaved brutally, with none of the "delicacy" that Lenin had recommended. At a session with a local leader Ordzhonikidze, provoked by some Georgian insult or curse, slugged his interlocutor.

The last incident, one might think, should hardly have excited Lenin. He had said more than once that the Communist Party was not like a

[70] *The Trotsky Archives* T 646.
[71] R. Pipes, *op. cit.,* p. 274–75.

girls' finishing school, admired the proletarian forthrightness. But equally strong was his detestation of *khamstvo*, the gross bullying boorishness he always associated with the manners of Russian officialdom. His illness and the unfeeling treatment he himself experienced made him more sensitive to tales of brutality. In the enemy of bourgeois manners and polite usages there was suddenly reborn Vladimir Ulyanov, hereditary nobleman and member of the intelligentsia, who suffered physical revulsion when he heard that an official had struck his inferior. Behind Ordzhonikidze he saw Dzerzhinsky trying to whitewash him, and behind both of them, the Secretary General.

At the end of December the sick man began to dictate another memorandum, this time on the nationality problem.[72] He boils with rage at Ordzhonikidze: "If things have come to such a pass that Ordzhonikidze could lose control of himself and use physical force . . . then one can imagine in what kind of mud we have sunk." He wants an "exemplary punishment" to be meted out to him, probably ejection from the Party. But the real culprits are Stalin with his "hastiness and administrative penchant" [73] and Dzerzhinsky, who have tried to protect the bully. The fact that neither of them was an ethnic Russian made the situation even worse. Lenin must have remembered how even under the Tsars renegade Poles and Ukrainians were thought to be the worst russifiers and chauvinists.

His anguish was undoubtedly real. He accompanied it by insistence that in the future Soviet federation national equality should be genuine and central organs of the government should be confined to a minimum. But here again he was caught in his own trap; of what good could be the most thorough *administrative* decentralization if the Communist Party had to be, as he had always insisted, centralized and run from the center? His colleagues when they read his notes on the national problem (unlike his *Testament*, they became known to the select group by the time of the Twelfth Congress in April 1923) must have again shaken their heads: what did the old man want? Would he, in the fullness of his powers, have tolerated the slightest defiance by the Ukrainian Communist Party, or any other national subdivision?

But his anger was now channeled directly against Stalin and the national problem was just one of the many reasons. Sometime before, Stalin, in the exercise of his unenviable job as Lenin's chief jailer, called Krupskaya and harangued her about allowing her husband to write about politics and about personally taking his dictation on a forbidden matter. If she was not going to mend her ways he was going to take it up with the Control Commission (meaning she might be expelled from the Party). The poor woman, hopelessly divided between her duties as a wife and as a

[72] This is to be distinguished from his *Testament*.
[73] Compare the use of this term in connection with Trotsky and Pyatakov.

Party member, appealed for help to her husband's and her own old friends Kamenev and Zinoviev. "Dear Lev Borisovich," she pleaded with the former, "what one can and what one cannot discuss with Ilyich—I know better than any doctor, because I know what makes him nervous and what does not, in any case I know better than Stalin. . . . I beg you to protect me from rude interference with my private life and from vile invectives and threats." [74] She did not, it appears, get much support from her old friends, one of whom, Zinoviev, had been especially close to her during the long years of exile. Stalin was acting on their behalf.

Lenin must have heard of or sensed his wife's distress, and that in addition to his accumulated political distrust of Stalin prompted him to strike directly without his usual caution and circumlocution. On January 4 he dictated a postscript to his *Testament*. He did not waste words: "Stalin is too rude, and this defect, which is tolerable in the intercourse between us Communists, is intolerable in the person of a General Secretary." Hence he recommends "finding a way" to transfer Stalin and replace him with a man who is different in only one quality, namely, "more tolerant, more loyal, kinder, more thoughtful toward the comrades, less capricious, etc." There is just a hint of embarrassment in this personal attack, and that he should deem manners of such great importance. Hence a rather lame excuse, that this is of political importance in view of the split between Stalin and Trotsky, which he had mentioned. All this may be a trifle, writes Lenin, paradoxical to the end, "but a trifle which may assume a decisive importance." [75]

By a curious irony, everything Lenin did against him helped prepare the road to Stalin's advancement. When the *Testament* became known, the other leaders must have rubbed their hands and dismissed the fear of Stalin from their minds; with such an incriminating document in their dossier the General Secretary could be brought down at a moment's notice; it was wiser to concentrate on the other rivals. The document was locked in with the others parts of his *Testament* and along with them read to the select members of the Party in May 1924 before the Thirteenth Congress.

One may wonder, to digress, what would have happened had the whole document then been made public and read to the Congress as Lenin had intended and as the Central Committee had refused to allow. One may risk the conclusion that despite all its guile the *Testament* would not have achieved its objective of weakening the grip of the oligarchy and removing Stalin from his position. He could have made the case that for all its insights and solicitude the *Testament* was the work of a sick man easily upset and incapable of distinguishing facts from suspicions. Take

[74] This letter was made public by Khrushchev in his speech to the Twentieth Party Congress in 1956. Bertram D. Wolfe, *Khrushchev and Stalin's Ghost*, New York, 1957, p. 98.

[75] *Works*, Vol. 36, pp. 545–46.

the passage about Bukharin: how can a man be the most valuable Marxian theorist and yet not understand the dialectic? Or Lenin's proposed method of enlarging the Central Committee: can you take fifty people straight from the work bench, put them in the highest Party organs, and expect anything but chaos and confusion? As to the accusations against himself, Stalin had an unbreakable alibi: the Politburo *as a whole* charged him with supervising the care of Vladimir Ilyich, and he selflessly accepted the job, which was bound to involve him in conflicts with the sick man and his wife. On at least one occasion Stalin sought to resign the invidious charge and was prevailed upon by the Politburo to continue as the supervisor of Lenin's treatment. Had Trotsky or anyone else ever protested this decision or demanded that another man be charged with this impossible and ungrateful task? There is no doubt that there would have been a great deal of disenchantment within the Party at the revelations. It would have been more difficult to build up the legend of Stalin as Lenin's faithful pupil and intended successor. But it is most doubtful that the course of events would have been drastically different.

Some of the same conclusions must have been reached by Lenin after he had dictated his impulsive postscript about Stalin. For throughout January and until the middle of February his written or rather dictated attacks on Stalin become more circuitous and indirect. For another thing, during this month and a half there were moments of considerable improvement in his condition and the sick man began to hope that he might recover enough to address the next Party Congress in person. At times he would delude himself that his debility was due to "nerves" and that physiologically he was sound.[76] If so, there was no reason to attack Stalin and his other lieutenants in such a startling, and to the Communist public unduly scandalous, manner. With the urgency removed he would be able to attend to the business in a slower and more cautious way.

The new indirect line of attack took the form of Lenin's written reflections about the Soviet administration and especially about its organs of control. He was mentioning no names, but the fact that he was concentrating on the Commissariat of Inspection (the *Rabkrin*) would make everyone aware that he was aiming his criticisms at Stalin, until recently its head, and whose influence there still lingered on. The gist of his proposals was hardly new or startling: he urged the combination of the Party and state control organs, again drawing into the work the rank-and-file workers and peasants who would somehow assure greater efficiency and less red tape. But in the second installment of his apparently innocent musings on administration entitled *Better Less But Better* his tone about the *past* and current work of the commissariat becomes sharper. "Let us speak frankly.

[76] He said that "his illness is nervous and such that at times he is fully well, that is his head is perfectly clear. . . ." Diary of the Secretaries . . . in *op. cit.*, p. 84.

The Commissariat of Inspection has not a shadow of authority. Everybody knows that there are no institutions which function more poorly than those of the *Rabkrin.* . . ." [77] Again Lenin's remedies are those he has always clung to in his hopeless struggle with the monster of bureaucracy: learn, get good people, send experts to Germany and England to find out how they do things, and so on. All this advice reflected undoubtedly his genuine and objective solicitude about the future of Soviet administration. But smuggled into the text and unmistakable were references to the man who allowed this bureaucratic mess to occur, *Rabkrin*'s former head, Stalin. "The new *Rabkrin*, let us hope, will leave behind it the quality which . . . we can call ridiculous affectation, or ridiculous self-importance . . ." and which can be found not only in the state but also in the Party bureaucracy. "Let us say, by the way, bureaucratism is found not only in the state institutions but in the Party ones as well." This line of attack was obviously sounder and more dignified than personal references, and this embarrassing business of bad manners disqualifying a man as Secretary General. This way the Party members were bound to ask themselves: is the man who made a mess of the *Rabkrin* the proper man to run the Party machine?

Lenin's articles had one intended result. They led to a tentative breach in the solidarity of the Politburo. He wanted to have them printed in *Pravda*. Needless to say, Stalin was not enchanted by this prospect. One version has it that Kuibyshev proposed that in order to appease the sick man a dummy copy of *Pravda* should be made up with Lenin's article in it. But Trotsky and Kamenev insisted on publication. Besides, Lenin through his secretary managed to circulate it to some other Party leaders. There was nothing scandalous about the piece and the criticism of Stalin was oblique enough to enable the others to argue for publication without encountering the charge of an open violation of the united front. And so on March 4 *Better Less But Better* was printed in *Pravda*. To cover up for the delay, the date when the article had been finished was given as March 2. In fact the article had been ready for the press three weeks before.

But before Lenin's article appeared he decided again upon a change of tactics, and a more direct blow against Stalin. This was probably connected with his reassessment of the possibility of appearing at the next Congress, scheduled for March (but which did not take place until April). By a relentless pressure through his secretaries he coerced his colleagues into letting him see the protocols of the Politburo meetings on the Georgian issue. He decided that another attempt was being made to whitewash the brutalities committed in Georgia. On February 14 he dictated notes, presumably for a future and lengthier written conclusion: "1) One should not brawl. 2) One should make concessions. 3) One cannot equate the

[77] *Works*, Vol. 33, p. 448.

behavior of a large country with that of a tiny one.[78] Did Stalin know? [79]
Why did he not react? To blame people for deviation toward chauvinism
and Menshevism [may well] show the existence of this very deviation in
the accuser who is on the side of centralization." [80] But he never had the
chance to develop these themes in writing.[81] Between February 14 and
March 4 there are no entries in the secretaries' log, which indicates (though
with Soviet historical materials one can never be sure) that Lenin's condition did not allow him further dictation. Then on March 5 two thunderbolts!

On March 5, 1923, for the first time in more than thirty years Vladimir
Ilyich Ulyanov forgot that he was primarily a Party member and a politician. He was a man who had been insulted both personally and through
rudeness to his wife. Whether he learned for the first time the full details
of Stalin's pressures on Krupskaya or whether he sensed his coming complete disability, he abandoned any restraint, any veiling of his sentiments
in political phraseology. Summoning his secretary at 12 noon, he asked
her to take two letters, one for Trotsky and one for Stalin. He felt very
ill.[82]

He wrote to the man whom he elevated to be the Party's chief officer,
in whom he had put full trust, toward whom he had displayed fatherly
solicitude extending to such details as finding a larger apartment for his
family, insisting on Stalin's taking a full rest, and so on:

> Dear Comrade Stalin: You permitted yourself a rude summons of
> my wife to the telephone and a rude reprimand of her. Despite the
> fact that she told you that she agreed to forget what was said, never-
> theless Zinoviev and Kamenev heard about it from her. I have no in-
> tention to forget so easily that which is being done against me and I
> need not stress here that I consider as directed against me that which
> is being done against my wife. I ask therefore that you weigh care-
> fully whether you are agreeable to retracting your words and apologiz-
> ing, or whether you prefer the severance of relations between us.[83]

The letter was not sent the same day. He reread it on March 6 and
then Krupskaya begged him not to send it. She then asked the secretary
not to deliver it. But the latter, on March 7, felt that she could not disobey
Lenin's implicit instructions. She waited on Stalin with the letter, informing him that she must have his answer immediately. He dictated an apology, the text of which we do not know. Copies of Lenin's ultimatum went
to Zinoviev and Kamenev. Stalin's apology could not be delivered to Lenin

[78] I. e., one should take into account the Georgians' national sensitivity.

[79] Presumably that Ordzhonikidze beat up an opponent.

[80] Stalin and his group accused Mdivani and his Georgians exactly of those
deviations.

[81] They are from the Diary of the Secretaries in *op. cit.*, p. 91.

[82] *Ibid.*, p. 85.

[83] First revealed in Khrushchev's 1956 speech. Bertram Wolfe, *op. cit.*, pp. 98–99.

the same day, as his condition took a turn for the worse. When and how he received the apology, the guardians of the Party archives have not seen fit to inform us.

This letter was an act of desperation and self-indulgence on the part of the sick man. He must have known that Stalin would apologize and would remain the Politburo's chief watchman over him. Zinoviev and Kamenev did not help Krupskaya when she first told them of her mistreatment; why should they help now? The reader might well ask why the dictator, to be sure a crippled dictator, was so helpless. Why not dispatch a letter to all the Politburo, all the Central Committee members, revealing his demand that Stalin be dismissed, asking that he himself be allowed to live and die as he pleased, and not in an incarceration? To repeat, Lenin was caught in his own trap. He had always acted or pretended to act in the name of the Party, of the Central Committee, always said "we," "on behalf of." Any other behavior would be taken as a sign that he was deranged. If the events surrounding Lenin's illness and death deeply affected Stalin's future behavior, as we must believe they did then we can understand the fantastic extent of the "cult of personality" that Stalin erected. Apart from his vanity, he did not ever want to find himself in the position of his predecessor. He wanted to be so much above everyone else that, even if debilitated, at his orders a militiaman on duty in the Kremlin would shoot the most powerful of his lieutenants.

The letter to Trotsky was written with the same haste, and it was to be telephoned to him before being delivered, the answer to be communicated "as soon as possible." In it Lenin once again was trying to break the iron ring surrounding him. Will Trotsky take upon himself the defense of the Georgian case? "The matter is now being prosecuted by Stalin and Dzerzhinsky, on whose objectivity I cannot rely. Quite the contrary." He enclosed his December memorandum on the nationality question with its devastating criticism of Stalin et al. If Trotsky does not agree to plead the case of the Georgian dissidents will he return the materials to him? Trotsky's telephone answer must have been pusillanimous. Now in utmost despair, trying to force the issue into the open, Lenin threw all caution and the Party regulations to the wind. He wrote on March 6 to the Georgian dissidents, with copies to Trotsky and Kamenev: "I follow your case with all my heart. I am appalled by the coarseness of Ordzhonikidze and the connivance of Stalin and Dzerzhinsky. I am preparing for you notes and a speech."

Trotsky's behavior in the matter was unheroic. What is more, it displayed fantastic political blundering. Since Trotsky's own version of the story departs from the facts [84] as they can be gleaned from the documents

---

[84] Written when Trotsky was in exile in 1929, in *My Life*, pp. 482–88, repeated with some but not all and not completely reproduced documents of the case in his *Stalin*, New York, 1946, pp. 362–64.

that he himself had retained and are now in his *Archive,* it is well to go into some detail.

Lenin's letter spoke for itself. Trotsky was to retain the nationality memorandum *if* he was going to defend the Georgians (in the Central Committee and presumably elsewhere). Return of the memorandum would signify that he refused to take up the case. He did return Lenin's typescript (for some reason only one copy was typed) which meant his refusal, *but* he made a copy of it for his own future use, something Lenin had not authorized him to do if he was not going to take the case. The contents of Lenin's devastating attack were not communicated by him to anybody else. In his memoirs Trotsky claims lamely that Lenin did not want him to acquaint anybody, not even Kamenev, with the contents of the nationality memorandum. This is palpably absurd: how could Lenin want Trotsky to defend the Georgian case before the Central Committee and lend him for that purpose the only copy of his document if the gist of his criticisms was to remain secret? And as we have seen, the very next day, March 6, hoping to shame Trotsky into action, he sent Trotsky and Kamenev a copy of his wire to two Georgians who were not even members of the Central Committee, in which he made abundantly clear his attack on Stalin and that he was preparing notes and a speech on this subject.

To anticipate our story, Trotsky must have felt some shame at his behavior. For later on in March, when Lenin was already hopelessly paralyzed, he made some feeble moves in the Politburo on the Georgian issue. He proposed a recall of Ordzhonikidze from Transcaucasia and defended, but not very strongly, the Georgian oppositionists. He enclosed a copy of his motions in the Politburo for Lenin's secretary, the very same one who had handed him the explosive memorandum and then had to take it back.[85] But not a word in Trotsky's motions about Stalin and Dzerzhinsky or about an exemplary punishment for Ordzhonikidze. There the matter might have rested, buried with Lenin's nationality memorandum and with nobody but Trotsky knowing its full contents, but for the courageous action of the chief secretary of the paralyzed leader, Fotyeva.[86] The Party Congress was about to meet, and yet not a word about Vladimir Ilyich's memorandum, which she knew he wanted to become widely known. On April 16 she wrote to Kamenev as chairman of the Politburo, giving the full story of the incident.[87] The fat was in the fire. Trotsky was caught on two counts. First, he had kept secret from the Politburo the fact that he received a communication from Lenin. In the second place he had let Vladimir Ilyich down; he did not make the fight

---

[85] *The Trotsky Archive* T 792, dated March 28, 1923.
[86] One wonders how she managed to survive the Stalin era.
[87] *The Trotsky Archive* T 793.

that Lenin had begged him to make. He had shown himself both devious and fainthearted.

It was now possible for Stalin to assume the pose of injured innocence. He wrote to members of the Central Committee: "I am greatly surprised that those articles of Com. Lenin which, without a doubt, are of a distinct basic significance, and which Com. Trotsky received as early as 5 March of this year—he has considered admissible to keep his own secret for over a month without making their content known to the Political Bureau or to the C.C. plenum, until one day before the opening of the Twelfth Congress of the party." [88]

Trotsky attempted an explanation, which he circulated to the Central Committee the very same day. It speaks for itself. Yes, he did receive a memorandum from Lenin on March 5. "I made a copy of it as a basis of my corrections to Comrade Stalin's theses on nationality (which were accepted by Comrade Stalin) and also of my article in *Pravda*. . . ." Lenin's memorandum had a great importance but "on the other hand it includes a severe judgment on three members of the Central Committee." *Now* Trotsky says that he sees no alternative but to acquaint the members of the Central Committee with Lenin's piece (it was going to be distributed among them anyway), but he promises to let it go no further. "If no member of the Central Committee, due to intra-Party considerations, will bring the memorandum in one form or another to the knowledge of the Party or the Party Congress then I for my part will consider it as a silent authorization relieving me from personal responsibility in the matter in connection with the Party Congress." [89] The reaction of the Party oligarchs to this explanation, which would not have fooled a schoolboy, can well be imagined. Next day Trotsky addressed another more detailed letter in which he gets even more entangled. He, Trotsky, had no idea as to what Lenin planned to do with his piece on the nationality problem. He repeats that he copied it *only* to make some corrections in Comrade Stalin's theses on the national problem. Won't the Central Committee state that he acted absolutely correctly? As to whether Lenin's memorandum ought to be published: "The problem should be decided according to the political desirability of such a step. I could not take the responsibility alone for such a decision and hence turned [the document] over to the Central Committee." [90]

In his panic Trotsky passed to threats. He wrote to Stalin on April 18 that the latter had assured him that he acted correctly in the matter and that he would write to the members of the Central Committee in this vein.

[88] Quoted in Bertram D. Wolfe, *Khrushchev and Stalin's Ghost*, New York, 1957, p. 278.
[89] *The Trotsky Archive* T 794.
[90] *Ibid.*, T 795.

Why hasn't Stalin written this letter yet? (Their conversation took place only the day before.) If he does not write it immediately he, Trotsky, will demand that a special commission investigate the matter and the insinuations made about him. "You better than anyone else can estimate that if I haven't done it up to now it was not because such a step might hurt me." [91] Stalin must have smiled as he complied with this request and wrote to the Committee members that Comrade Trotsky's behavior in connection with Lenin's memorandum was perfectly understandable and correct.

Few are the cases of brilliant and clever men being caught so red-handed and piling up one fatal political error upon another. Trotsky's explanation of his behavior written when he was already in exile from Stalin's Russia is pathetic in its half-truths and attempts to gloss over the facts, which are clearly spelled out in the papers he himself kept and which are now in his *Archive.* He tried to shift the blame to Kamenev, invented conversations with Lenin's secretary that obviously could not have taken place, and the like.[92] He ends up by crediting himself with having acted with great magnanimity toward Stalin, whom he could have crushed then and there if he had chosen to do so.

What were in fact the reasons for his behavior? Here one must admit that upon receiving Lenin's letter and the enclosed memorandum on March 5, Trotsky was put in a very difficult position. He was bound to reveal the fact that he received the communication, if not indeed its contents, to the other members of the Politburo. Then, had he pledged to pursue the matter further, he would have had to attack Stalin, Dzerzhinsky, and Ordzhonikidze at the meeting of the Central Committee, where most likely he would have been opposed by all his colleagues from the Politburo and defeated, even though he could have invoked Lenin's authority. This course at least would have had the virtue of forthrightness. By refusing to take up the Georgian case and clandestinely copying Lenin's memorandum for his future use Trotsky thought he was taking the safest course. Lenin might recover and tend to the business himself. If not, he would produce the bomb against Stalin in his own good time, while in the meantime nobody could accuse him of breaking the solidarity of the Politburo and intriguing with the sick man. He could not have foreseen that on April 16 Fotyeva would take it upon herself to reveal the whole story to his colleagues.

In addition there might have been another element of calculation in Trotsky's conduct. Suppose that he had carried the struggle to the Central Committee and managed, against considerable odds, to impugn Stalin's

[91] *Ibid.,* T 796.

[92] A careful reading of his account in *My Life* will show that he intentionally confuses the dates when the various letters were dispatched by Lenin, and completely omits the fact that on March 5 he was asked point blank over the phone whether he was going to undertake the defense of the Georgian case. Pp. 483–86.

position. Who would have been the beneficiary? In his *Memoirs* written in 1929 Stalin, of course, is made the villain and the enemy. But in 1923, much as he hated Stalin, Trotsky saw Zinoviev as his chief rival for Lenin's mantle. Any discrediting of Stalin, much as it would have pleased Trotsky, would have redounded to the advantage of the Zinoviev-Kamenev faction. They held a majority on the Central Committee, in all likelihood they would have nominated the next Secretary General of the Party. In the country and to the world Trotsky was clearly the second man in Russia. But within the Party, both among its oligarchy and among the membership at large, the situation was quite different. "Comrade Trotsky has no idea about the local Party organizations, he is a military man," said Anastas Mikoyan, then a young delegate at the Eleventh Party Congress.[93] He had warm admirers and fervent partisans, but to the oligarchs he was a relative newcomer to Bolshevism, and to the rank and file a specialist on military and economic problems. If he was going to succeed to the leadership it would not be through the Party organization. Hence it was perhaps safer to leave it in the "neutral" hands of Stalin rather than to add it to the already preponderant mass of assets held by Zinoviev and Kamenev.

Such calculations took place against the now virtual certainty that Lenin would not return to the helm. On March 7 his condition deteriorated still further. On March 9 he suffered yet another major stroke. This time he was completely incapacitated. Full paralysis of the right side was joined with aphasia. He could speak only with difficulty and but a few words. No more dictation. No more conspiracies. Amazingly enough, his indomitable will still persisted. He tried to communicate by signs, would fly into a rage at being misunderstood. At times he would chase out the doctors and nurses, and could be appeased only by his wife or sister. He could no longer resist when in May he was taken from the Kremlin, where he had lain all this time, to Gorki.

In his absence the event took place that he had so fervently hoped to attend, the Twelfth Congress of the Communist Party, the first one since 1903 in which he could not participate.[94] Kamenev, who opened the proceedings, gave reassuring news about Lenin's health. He was getting better, the danger had passed, they could hope for "a full recovery of Vladimir Ilyich." [95] Those with any inkling of medical knowledge or just with common sense could wonder how a man who had been in failing health for some time and who had had three major cerebral strokes within a few months could ever be expected to achieve a "full recovery," or to resume even a small part of his previous duties. Equally honest was

---

[93] *The Eleventh Congress*, p. 430.

[94] If we except the Sixth Congress in 1917, when he was hiding but with which he was in communication.

[95] *The Twelfth Party Congress*, April 17–23, 1923, *Stenographic Report*, Moscow, 1923, p. 1.

Kamenev's other assurance: the Congress was being run according to Vladimir Ilyich's wishes.

The Politburo faced the Congress with the appearance of iron solidarity; behind the scenes there were already the first signs of the future struggle for the succession. During an earlier discussion on who should deliver the central report, usually given by Lenin, there had been a veritable Gaston and Alphonse act with the oligarchs seeking to avoid this invidious and envy-attracting honor. Finally Zinoviev accepted the charge. Within the Party and the country at large there was a considerable confusion as to what was going on in Lenin's absence, who was going up, who down, the particulars. This confusion was reflected in the traditional greetings to the Congress from factories, youth organizations, and the like. Some of them hailed as "our leaders" Lenin and Zinoviev, some coupled Trotsky with the sick man in their greetings. The more prudent saluted "Lenin, Zinoviev, Kamenev, and Trotsky," or still more wisely omitted any name but Lenin's. In at least one organization the faith in internationalism still burned brightly: they hailed Lenin, then Klara Zetkin, the old war horse of the German Communist Party, and only then the fraternal trio of Kamenev, Zinoviev, and Trotsky. But no one thought of paying a special tribute to the modest, self-effacing man who was the General Secretary of the Party.

The outward unity of the top leadership was dictated by imperative reasons. Again there was turbulence both within the rank and file and outside the Party ranks. Various workers' groups had sprung up that continued propagating the slogans of the old Workers' Opposition which reflected dissatisfaction with the *Nep* and the appalling living conditions among the city proletariat. At the Congress there were open complaints against the dictatorship by the Politburo, which, as one delegate put it, had become "an infallible pope." [96] Few could sense the direction in which political events were moving; thus the individual among the oligarchy who attracted most criticism and obviously aroused most fear was Zinoviev. The perennial malcontent, Osinsky, praised two members of the directing triumvirate, Stalin and Kamenev, but implied that he would like to see Zinoviev with his "general's" manners out of there. Zinoviev (and one has to realize that at the time he was credited with much of the same guile and skill that has since then become associated with Stalin's name) sought to disarm his critic. What was all this talk about power, about him and other members of the Politburo being power-oriented? "Please lay off, Comrade Osinsky," he begged. They all already had more power than they knew what to do with. Their only thought was for the good of the Party. "Nobody worries about power."

Stalin's performance was masterful. If he was embarrassed by the knowledge that many in the hall had read Lenin's strictures about him he

[96] *Ibid.*, p. 105.

did not betray it. He warded off criticisms with a joke or irrelevancy. Somebody had complained about the lack of freedom of speech at this Congress. How could he have said that, wondered Stalin: this Congress had been better prepared by the Central Committee than any previous one. Osinsky was warned not to try to stir up any trouble among the ruling group. Stalin breathed tolerance and open-mindedness. How encouraging to see the former S-Rs and Mensheviks seeking entrance into the Communist Party! The Party needed new blood; its leadership was getting old and worn out—look at Comrade Lenin. Hence he urged the expansion of the Central Committee by adding to it "men with independent minds." He could not have known of Lenin's *Testament*, but Stalin's proposed additions were obviously not to be "simple workmen," but the trusted functionaries from his apparatus who would help him reduce Zinoviev's preponderance on the Central Committee. The Politburo had been accused of doing some things in secret. Well, said Stalin, you cannot reveal *everything*; the enemy is listening. The Party is altogether in a splendid shape. How tragic that Comrade Lenin is not here, how proud he would be to see what is going on!

The few critics who somehow felt differently groped for a way to stir up some conflict among the higher ups, which in turn would encourage the intimidated delegates to loosen their tongues. After a discussion on a sensitive issue had been hastily adjourned, there were shouts in the hall: "Why does not Rykov speak? Let Rakovsky talk about it." But all in vain. "Our Party is healthier than ever," said even Bukharin, the most outspoken and temperamental among the oligarchs.[97]

Strangely enough, the one individual who was attacked most frequently at the Congress was Leonid Krasin. The chief Soviet commercial negotiator delivered what was under the circumstances a very unpolitic speech. He asked the Congress whether they thought that the Party could be run the way it had been ten years earlier, by "agitators and journalists." They were now in power; they needed professional competence and less politics. "What do you think, you can lead a successful policy by interfering with the recovery of production?"[98] It must have crossed the oligarchs' minds that here was the man whom Vladimir Ilyich, were he in good health, might well have advanced to a high position. But now Krasin could be attacked with impunity; he had no following. Radek ridiculed Krasin as a self-proclaimed candidate for the vacant leadership, and with his typical impudence implied that the veteran Bolshevik had sold out to Lloyd George! Others poured out their pent-up resentment against this protector of bourgeois specialists. Soon Krasin was to be permanently exiled to a diplomatic post.

And the nationality issue? The Georgian malcontents Mdivani and

<hr>

[97] *Ibid.*, p. 172.
[98] *Ibid.*, p. 113.

Makharadze were at the Congress to raise their voices in protest, though they referred but gingerly to Lenin's letter to them and to the memorandum. The latter had been shown to some select delegates with the explanation that it would be unseemly and irreverent to Vladimir Ilyich to have it published. The two Georgians had some harsh words to say about Orzhonikidze and his brutal behavior in their country, but they were answered by Stalin's other Georgian lieutenant, Enukidze. To the majority of the delegates this was undoubtedly an obscure business having its roots in some tribal hostilities among the Georgians. As to Lenin's intervention, Enukidze gave plausible explanations: he was "a victim of incorrect information." If someone comes to a sick man and stirs him up with tales of people being beaten, humiliated, and the like, it is no wonder that he reacts in a hysterical fashion and unwittingly slanders the people in whom, when well, he had put his full trust. The dissident Georgians' case was valiantly seconded by Rakovsky, the chief commissar in the Ukraine, who attacked the whole concept of Stalin's federalism as leading to Russian domination. Laws and treaties were being signed in the name of the Ukraine, Rakovsky said, without its prime minister's knowledge. But here again the delegates must have wondered what suddenly made the Bulgarian-Rumanian Rakovsky such a defender of Ukrainian nationalism. The Politburo preserved its united front on the national issue. True, Bukharin kept interrupting when an attempt was made to distort Lenin's attitude on the subject. And he did say: "If Lenin were here he would wash the heads of the Russian chauvinists." [99] But his remarks were in a teasing rather than serious tone. Not a peep was heard from Trotsky on the Georgian business. He absented himself from the sessions of the Congress on the nationality problem, allegedly on the grounds that he was preparing a speech on economics. Stalin promised to make some mechanical adjustments in his scheme for the federation of the Soviet republics. The Congress approved his proposals and passed over the issue. Vladimir Ilyich's last conspiracy had failed.

He himself was now in the final stage of his inexorable disease. The autopsy was to reveal that he had suffered all along from an advanced cerebral arteriosclerosis.[100] To the last the organism struggled against the inevitable end. In August, with Krupskaya's help, he started to relearn to speak. In September he could walk with a cane. On October 19, amazingly enough, he insisted on being driven to Moscow to the Kremlin and for the last time looked at his office, where so much history had been made. The stories of those days refer occasionally to Lenin hunting for mushrooms in Gorki, or talking with some visitors, but evidently his hunting consisted in being wheeled outside the villa, and his speech never fully returned.

[99] *Ibid.*, p. 564. As he had washed his, Bukharin's, for precisely the same reason at the Eighth Party Congress.

[100] N. Semashko and others, *What Was the Disease From Which Lenin Died?* Leningrad, 1924, p. 35.

The government kept publishing optimistic bulletins and superficially there was enough improvement to warrant guarded optimism about his life, but hardly the talk about full recovery, still less of his return to his duties. He tried to learn to write with his left hand and we do not know whether even in this last phase he did not attempt to leave a political communication. His wife recalls reading to him about the companions of bygone days: Martov and Axelrod. Lenin was saddened to hear about Martov's illness: his thoughts must have gone to the old times in Munich and London when this lovable and exasperating man would drop in for a chat and stay for five or six hours, while Lenin tried to work. Old Axelrod was also ill, also in exile. In 1898 in Siberia Vladimir Ilyich was thrown into a rapture on receiving a letter from this already venerable co-founder of Russian Marxism, in which Axelrod praised the initiate's pamphlet on the labor question. He also listened to and liked an article by Trotsky in which he compared Lenin with Marx. For all of Trotsky's sins of omission and commission, both Vladimir Ilyich and his wife sensed in him personal attachment and chivalry sadly lacking in the old Bolsheviks. After the death, Nadezhda Konstantinovna wrote Trotsky a heartfelt letter which is no less moving for the fact that it glosses over the ancient and bitter quarrels and recent disappointments: "The feelings which Vladimir Ilyich showed you when you came to us in London from Siberia did not change up to his death. I embrace you, Lev Davidovich." It was another happy memory: of young Trotsky in 1902 banging on the Ulyanovs' door at an ungodly hour in the morning, waking up the whole house and rushing in to ask Lenin about *Iskra*. To Gorky, Krupskaya was to write, "To his very death he was himself, a man of massive will, self-control, prone to laughter and jokes to the very end. . . ."

On the night of January 20 Lenin pointed at his eyes. It was thought advisable to summon an oculist, Professor M. Auerbach. He had previously examined Lenin and found that he was nearsighted in one eye. Now he could discover nothing untoward about the patient's sight. He reported this to the doctors in attendance, and was ready to return to Moscow when Vladimir Ilyich unexpectedly entered from his room. He indicated, mostly in sign language, one would think, that he was worried about Professor Auerbach returning at such a late hour and that he should spend the night in Gorki. The doctor, touched by this solicitude of the sick man, could only explain that he had to be back in his clinic the next day. He persuaded Lenin to go back to his room, which he did after satisfying himself that the professor was being taken care of. In the morning Lenin suffered his last stroke. The end came in the evening of January 21, 1924.

The next day members of the Central Committee present in Moscow (Trotsky was on a sick leave in the Caucasus) repaired to Gorki to render homage to their dead leader. There began a series of elaborate mourning rites, which would not have pleased the man who with all his other qualities believed in simplicity.

INDEX

583

DATE DUE
